LEADERSHIP

Theory, Application, Skill Development

Third Edition

LEADERSHIP
Theory, Application, Skill Development

Robert N. Lussier, Ph.D.
Springfield College

Christopher F. Achua, D.B.A.
University of Virginia College at Wise

SOUTH-WESTERN
CENGAGE Learning™

Australia • Brazil • Japan • Korea • Mexico • Singapore • Spain • United Kingdom • United States

SOUTH-WESTERN
CENGAGE Learning™

Leadership: Theory, Application, Skill Development, 3e
Robert N. Lussier and Christopher F. Achua

VP/Editorial Director:
Jack W. Calhoun

VP/Editor-in-Chief:
Dave Shaut

Executive Editor:
John Szilagyi

Developmental Editor:
Leslie Kauffman, LEAP, Inc.

Senior Marketing Manager:
Kimberly Kanakes

Production Editor:
Juli A. Cook

Manager of Technology, Editorial:
Vicky True

Technology Project Editor:
Kristen Meere

Web Coordinator:
Karen Schaffer

Manufacturing Coordinator:
Doug Wilke

Production House:
Interactive Composition Corporation

Printer:
Transcontinental
Louiseville, Quebec

Art Director:
Tippy McIntosh

Internal Designer:
Christy Carr
Christy Carr Design

Cover Designer:
Christy Carr
Christy Carr Design

Cover Images:
© Getty Images

Library of Congress Control Number:
2005937625

For more information about our products, contact us at:

Cengage Learning
Customer & Sales Support
1-800-354-9706

South-Western Cengage Learning
5191 Natorp Boulevard
Mason, Ohio 45040
USA

Dedication

To my wife Marie and our six children:
Jesse, Justin, Danielle, Nicole, Brian, and Renee
Robert N. Lussier

To my family, especially my wife Pauline, my mother
Theresia Sirri Achua, and our children: Justin, Brooke,
Jordan, Cullen, and our new arrival Gregory
Christopher F. Achua

Brief Contents

Contents

PART 2 Team Leadership

CHAPTER 8
TEAM LEADERSHIP AND SELF-MANAGED TEAMS   292

PART 3 Organizational Leadership

CHAPTER 9
CHARISMATIC AND TRANSFORMATIONAL LEADERSHIP   356

Preface

Target Market

This book is intended for leadership courses offered at the undergraduate and graduate level in schools of business, public administration, health care, education, psychology, and sociology. No prior coursework in business or management is required. The textbook can also be used in management development courses that emphasize the leadership function, and can supplement management or organizational behavior courses that emphasize leadership, especially with an applications/skill development focus.

Goals and Overview of Competitive Advantages

In his book *Power Tools,* John Nirenberg asks: "Why are so many well-intended students learning so much and yet able to apply so little in their personal and professional lives?" Is it surprising that students cannot apply what they read and cannot develop skills, when most textbooks continue to focus on theoretical concepts? Textbooks need to take the next step, and develop students' ability to apply what they read and to build skills using the concepts. I (Lussier) started writing management textbooks in 1988—prior to the calls by the Association to Advance Collegiate Schools of Business (AACSB) and Secretary's Commission on Achieving Necessary Skills (SCANS) for skill development and outcomes assessment—to help professors teach their students how to apply concepts and develop management skills. Pfeffer and Sutton concluded that the most important insight from their research is that knowledge that is actually implemented is much more likely to be acquired from learning by doing, than from learning by reading, listening, or thinking.[1] We designed this book to give students the opportunity to learn by doing.

The overarching goal of this book is reflected in its subtitle: theory, application, skill development. We developed the total package to teach leadership theory and concepts, to improve ability to apply the theory through critical thinking, and to develop leadership skills. Following are our related goals in writing this book:

- To be the only traditional leadership textbook to incorporate the three-pronged approach. We make a clear distinction between coverage of theory concepts, their application, and the development of skills based on the concepts. The test bank includes questions under each of the three approaches.

- To make this the most "how-to" leadership book on the market. We offer behavior models with step-by-step guidelines for handling various leadership functions (such as how to set objectives, give praise and instructions, coach followers, resolve conflicts, and negotiate).
- To offer the best coverage of traditional leadership theories, by presenting the theories and research findings without getting bogged down in too much detail.
- To create a variety of high-quality application material, using the concepts to develop critical-thinking skills.
- To create a variety of high-quality skill-development exercises, which build leadership skills that can be used in students' personal and professional lives.
- To offer behavior-modeling leadership skills training.
- To make available a video package, including 7 Behavior Model Videos and 11 Video Cases.
- To suggest self-assessment materials that are well integrated and illustrate the important concepts discussed in the text. Students begin by determining their personality profile in Chapter 2, and then assess how their personality affects their leadership potential in the remaining chapters.
- To provide a flexible teaching package, so that professors can design the course to best meet the leadership needs of their students. The total package includes more material than can be covered in one course. Supplemental material is included, thus only one book is needed—making it a low-cost alternative for the student.

Flexibility Example

The textbook, with 11 chapters, allows time for other materials to be used in the leadership course. The textbook includes all the traditional topics in enough detail, however, to use only the textbook for the course. It offers so much application and skill-development material that it cannot all be covered in class during one semester. Instructors have the flexibility to select only the content and features that best meet their needs.

Specific Competitive Advantage— Pedagogical Features

Three-Pronged Approach

We created course materials that truly develop students into leaders. As the title of this book implies, we provide a balanced, three-pronged approach to the curriculum:

- a clear understanding of the traditional **theories** and concepts of leadership, as well as of the most recently developed leadership philosophies
- **application** of leadership concepts through critical thinking
- development of leadership **skills**

The three-pronged approach is clear in the textbook and is carried throughout the Instructor's Manual and Test Bank.

Theory

Leadership Theories, Research and References, and Writing Style. This book has been written to provide the best coverage of the traditional leadership theories, presenting the theories and research findings clearly without being bogged down in too much detail. The book is very heavily referenced with classic and current citations. Unlike the textbooks of some competitors, this book does not use in-text citations, to avoid distracting the reader and adding unnecessary length to the text chapters. Readers can refer to the notes at the end of the book for complete citations of all sources. Thus, the book includes all the traditional leadership topics, yet we believe it is written in a livelier, more conversational manner than those of our competitors.

The following features are provided to support the first step in the three-pronged approach—theory.

Step-by-Step Behavior Models. In addition to traditional theories of leadership, the text includes behavior models: how-to steps for handling day-to-day leadership functions, such as how to set objectives, give praise, coach, resolve conflicts, delegate, and negotiate.

`step 1.`

Learning Outcomes. Each chapter begins with learning outcomes. At the end of the chapter, the learning outcomes are integrated into the chapter summary.

Key Terms. A list of key terms appears at the beginning and end of each chapter. Clear definitions are given in the text for approximately 15 of the most important concepts from the chapter (with the key term in bold and the definition in italic).

Chapter Summary. The summary lists the learning outcomes from the beginning of the chapter and gives the answers. For each chapter, the last learning outcome requires students to define the key terms of the chapter by writing the correct key term in the blank provided for each definition.

Review and Discussion Questions. These questions require recall of information generally not covered in the learning outcomes. They are designed to get students thinking about and discussing the concepts presented in the text.

Product Support Web Site. The product support Web site, **academic. cengage.com/management/lussier,** has information for both professors and students. Students can take interactive quizzes, quiz themselves on key terms, and view the videos.

Test Bank (Assessment of Understanding of Theory/Concepts) and Instructor's Manual. The Test Bank includes traditional assessment of student knowledge. It also includes the Learning Outcomes and Review and Discussion Questions for each chapter. The Instructor's Manual includes the answers to all Review and Discussion Questions.

Application

The second prong of our textbook is to have students apply the leadership theories and concepts so that they can develop critical-thinking skills. Students develop their application skills through the following features.

Opening Case

At the beginning of each chapter, information about an actual manager and organization is presented. The case is followed by four to ten questions to get students involved. Throughout the chapter, the answers to the questions are given to illustrate how the manager/organization actually uses the text concepts to create opportunities and solve problems through decision making. An icon appears in the margin (as here) when the opening case is applied in the text.

InfoTrac. New to this edition is the integration of InfoTrac into the opening cases. Students can use InfoTrac's fast and easy search tools to find relevant news and analytical information from more than 15 million articles in the database—updated daily and going back as far as 20 years—all at a single Web site. Sample article numbers are given to get students started with their search.

Work Applications. Open-ended questions, called Work Applications, require students to explain how the text concepts apply to their own work experience; there are over 100 of these scattered throughout the text. Student experience can be present, past, summer, full-time, or part-time employment. The questions help the students to bridge the gap between theory and their real world. The Work Applications are also included in the Test Bank, to assess students' ability to apply the concepts.

Applying the Concept. Every chapter contains a series of two to seven Applying the Concept boxes that require students to determine the leadership

WorkApplication1

Recall a specific task that your manager assigned to you. Identify which steps the manager did and did not use in the oral message-sending process.

_____

_____

_____

_____

_____

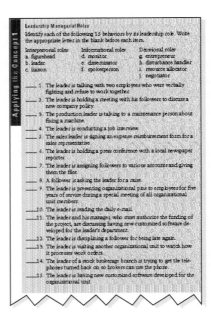

concept being illustrated in a specific, short example. All the recommended answers appear in the Instructor's Manual with a brief explanation. In addition, the Test Bank has similar questions, clearly labeled, to assess students' ability to apply the concepts.

Ethical Dilemma. New to this edition are 22 ethical dilemma boxed items. The boxes present issues of ethics for class discussion, with many presenting actual situations faced by real companies. Each dilemma contains two to four questions for class discussion.

Ethical Dilemma 2

Executive Compensation

As discussed, executive management skill has a direct impact on the success of the firm. Top executives should be paid well; after all, if it weren't for effective CEOs, some companies would not be making the millions of dollars of profits they make each year. They deserve a piece of the pie they help create. The *Business Week* 2000 compensation survey reported that the average yearly total pay for CEOs of the 362 largest U.S. public companies was $12.4 million.

Chapter Cases. Following the review questions, students are presented with another actual manager and organization. The students learn how the manager/organization applies the leadership concepts from that chapter. Each case is followed by questions for the student to answer. The InfoTrac Web site address is provided, allowing students to do further research on the organization.

Chapters 2 through 11 also include cumulative case questions. Cumulative questions relate case material from prior chapters. Thus, students continually review and integrate concepts from previous chapters. Answers to the case questions are included in the Instructor's Manual.

Video Cases. All chapters include one video case. Seeing actual leaders tackling real management problems and opportunities enhances student application of the concepts. The 11 Video Cases have supporting print material for

Video Case

LE MERIDIEN HOTEL: COMMUNICATING IN ORGANIZATIONS

Le Meridien is a luxury hotel chain famous for offering a unique European experience with a French flair to its more than 100,000 visitors each year. The hotel group operates over 130 hotels in 56 countries around the globe, and its reputation for service has made it one of the leading hotel brands in the world.

View the Video (11 minutes)

View the video on Le Meridien Hotel in class or at **academic. cengage.com/management/lussier.**

Read the Case

For Assistant General Manager Bob van den Oord, communication plays a crucial role in managing Le Meridien's world-class operations. His job involves communicating with department heads, staff, guests, suppliers, and senior management, through both formal and informal channels. The assistant general manager is personable and has become known for his "management by walkabout" style—a daily routine of monitoring operations and staff by conducting a walk-through inspection of the entire hotel.

In addition to his daily walkabout encounters with employees, van den Oord creates a variety of meetings where

managers can discuss their duties and schedules while receiving important feedback. Between meetings, employees utilize various communications technologies to coordinate efforts and report back to the assistant general manager. Although van den Oord concedes that technology-based communications like e-mail and text messaging are convenient and have a place in hotel operations, he prefers the channel richness of face-to-face communication and tells his workers that digital communications should never be a substitute for personal interaction.

Bob Van den Oord believes that good communication is the key to good business at Le Meridien. The ability to communicate consistently and clearly is essential for developing a happy staff and serving customers properly. And, as van den Oord notes with a smile, "A happy staff equals happy guests."

Answer the Questions

1. Explain how Bob van den Oord uses the oral message-sending process.
2. How important is nonverbal communication at Le Meridien Hotel? On what types of nonverbal communication does Bob van den Oord rely?
3. How does van den Oord foster effective communication at Le Meridien Hotel?

both instructors and students, including a brief description and critical-thinking questions. Answers to the video case questions are included in the Instructor's Manual.

Test Bank (Assessment of Application Ability) and Instructor's Manual. The Test Bank includes Work Applications and Applying the Concept questions. The Instructor's Manual contains detailed answers for all of the application features.

Skill Development

The difference between learning about leadership and learning to be a leader is the acquisition of skills, our third prong. This text focuses on skill development so students can use the leadership theories and concepts they learn to improve their personal and professional lives.

Self-Assessments. Scattered throughout the text are 33 Self-Assessments. Students complete these exercises to gain personal knowledge. All information for completing and scoring the assessments is contained within the text. Students determine their personality profile in Chapter 2, and then assess how their personality affects their leadership in the remaining chapters. Self-knowledge leads students to an understanding of how they can and will operate as leaders in the real world. Although Self-Assessments do not develop a specific skill, they serve as a foundation for skill development.

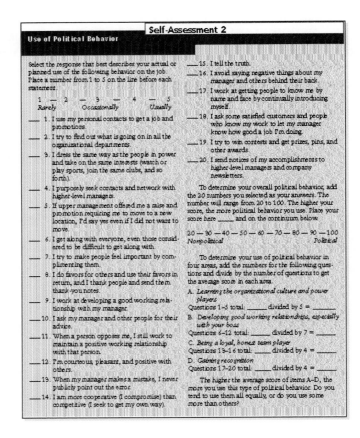

Case Role-Play Exercise. Following each case are instructions to prepare students to conduct an in-class role-play, based on a situation presented in the case. Through role-playing, students develop their skills at handling leadership situations. For example, students are asked to conduct a motivational speech to influence followers to change, and to present a brief business plan to open a new business venture of their choice.

Behavior Model Videos. There are seven Behavior Model Videos that reinforce the development of skills. The videos demonstrate leaders successfully handling common leadership functions, using the step-by-step behavior models discussed earlier in the Theory section. Students learn from watching the videos and/or using them in conjunction with the Skill-Development Exercises. Material in the text integrates the videos into the chapters. Ideas for using all videos are detailed in the Instructor's Manual.

Behavior Model Video 4

MEDIATING CONFLICT RESOLUTION

Objective
To view the process of mediating a conflict resolution between employees.

Video (6½ minutes) Overview
This is a follow-up to the advertising agency conflict (Video 3). The two employees end up in conflict again. Their manager,

Peter, brings them together to resolve the conflict by following the steps in "Mediating Conflict Resolution" on page 317–318 (Model 6-5 in text).

Note: There is no skill-development exercise.

Behavior Model Skills Training. Six of the Skill-Development Exercises may be used as part of behavior modeling by using the step-by-step models in the text and the Behavior Model Videos. Meta-analysis research has concluded that behavior-modeling skills training is effective at developing leadership skills. For example, students read the conflict resolution model in the text, watch the video in class, and then complete a Skill-Development Exercise (role-play) to resolve a conflict, using the model and feedback from others.

Behavior Model Skills Training

In this behavior model skills training session, you will perform three activities:
1. Read the section, "Delegation," in this chapter (to learn how to use Model 7-1, page 284).
2. Watch Behavior Model Video 1, "Delegating."
3. Complete Skill-Development Exercise 2 (to develop your delegating skills).

For further practice, use the delegation model in your personal and professional life.

Skill-Development Exercises. There are between one and four Skill-Development Exercises at the end of each chapter. We use the term *skill-development exercise* only in referring to an exercise that will develop a skill that can be used in the students' personal or professional lives at work. Full support of 27 activities can be found in the Instructor's Manual, including detailed information, timing, answers, and so on. There are three primary types of exercises:

Individual Focus. Students make individual decisions about exercise questions before or during class. Students can share their answers in class discussions, or the instructor may elect to go over recommended answers.

Group/Team Focus. Students discuss the material presented and may select group answers and report to the class.

Role-Play Focus. Students are presented with a model and given the opportunity to use the model to apply their knowledge of leadership theories through role-playing exercises.

Test Bank (Assessment of Skill Development) and Instructor's Manual. The Test Bank includes skill-development questions. The Instructor's Manual contains detailed answers for all of the skills featured in the text, including timing, information, answers, logistics, and so on. It also explains how to test on the specific Skill-Development Exercises, and provides information that can be shared with students to help them prepare for exams.

Ancillary Support

Instructor's Manual with Test Bank (0-324-36183-1)

(Prepared by Robert N. Lussier, Christopher F. Achua, and Ross Mecham, Virginia Polytechnic Institute and State University)
The Instructor's Manual and Test Bank are organized to complement the three-pronged approach of the text—theory, application, and skill development.

The Instructor's Manual contains the following for each chapter of the book: a detailed outline for lecture enhancement, Work Application student sample answers, Review and Discussion Question answers, Applying the Concept answers, Case and Video Case Question answers, instructions on use of videos, and Skill-Development Exercise ideas (including set-up and timing). The Instructor's Manual also contains an introduction that discusses possible approaches to the course, and provides an overview of possible uses for various features and how to test and grade them. It explains the use of permanent groups to develop team leadership skills, and provides guidance in the development of a course outline/syllabus.

The Test Bank offers over 800 true/false, multiple choice, and fill-in-the-blank questions from which to choose. In addition, the authors provide distinct questions to test each of the three components of the text—theory, application, and skill development.

ExamView® (0-324-36184-X)

All questions from the printed Test Bank are available in ExamView®, an easy-to-use test-creation program compatible with both Windows and Macintosh operating systems, on the Instructor's Resource CD.

PowerPoint™ (0-324-36181-5)

(Prepared by George Crawford, Clayton College & State University)
PowerPoint slides are available on the Instructor's Resource CD and the product support Web site for a more flexible and professional presentation in the classroom.

Behavior Model Videos (VHS 0-324-36180-7, DVD 0-324-36179-3)

To reinforce the development of skills for students, seven Behavior Model Videos are provided. The videos teach students, step-by-step, how to handle common leadership functions such as giving praise, communicating, coaching, resolving conflict, delegating, and decision making. Students learn from watching the videos and/or using them in conjunction with the Skill-Development Exercises. Material in the text integrates the videos into the chapters. Ideas for using all videos are detailed in the Instructor's Manual.

Video Cases (VHS 0-324-36180-7, DVD 0-324-36179-3)

Accompanying and integrated within the text are 11 Video Cases. These videos show real businesses dealing with issues that are discussed in the text. These video cases add variety in the classroom presentation and stimulate students to learn about organizations, teams, and leadership.

Instructor's Resource CD-ROM (0-324-36182-3)

Get quick access to the Instructor's Manual with Test Bank, ExamView, and PowerPoint slides from your desktop via one CD-ROM.

Product Support Web Site

The dedicated *Leadership* Web site, **academic.cengage.com/management/lussier**, offers broad online support. Log on for downloadable ancillaries and more.

InfoTrac College Edition

With InfoTrac College Edition, students receive online access to a database of full-text articles from thousands of popular and scholarly periodicals, such as *Newsweek, Fortune, Entrepreneur, Journal of Management,* and *Nation's Business,* among others. InfoTrac is a great way to expose students to online research techniques, with the security that the content is academically based and reliable. An InfoTrac College Edition subscription card is included with copies of the *Leadership,* 3e, text. For more information, visit **academic. cengage.com/infotrac.**

The Business & Company Resource Center

Put a complete business library at your fingertips with The **Business & Company Resource Center.** The **BCRC** is a premier online business research tool that allows you to seamlessly search thousands of periodicals, journals, references, financial information, industry reports, company histories, and much more.

- The **BCRC** is conveniently accessible from anywhere with an Internet connection, allowing students to access information at school, at home, or on the go.
- The **BCRC** is a powerful and time-saving research tool for students—whether they are completing a case analysis, preparing for a presentation or discussion, creating a business plan, or writing a reaction paper.

- Instructors can use the **BCRC** as an online coursepack, assigning readings and research-based homework without the inconvenience of library reserves, permissions, and printed materials.

The **Business & Company Resource Center** is available as an optional package item with *Leadership,* 3e. To learn more about the **BCRC,** contact your local Thomson representative and visit **academic.cengage.com/bcrc.**

Summary of Key Innovations

Our goal is to make both students and instructors successful in the classroom by providing learning features that not only teach about leadership but also help students become leaders. Here are the special ways in which this is done:

- three-pronged approach (theory, application, skill development) in the textbook, and corresponding assessment of the three areas in the Test Bank
- unique skill-development materials that build leadership skills for use in students' personal and professional lives
- unique application material to develop critical-thinking skills
- unsurpassed video package, with 11 Video Cases and 7 Behavior Model Videos
- flexibility—use any or all of the features that work for you!

Changes to the Third Edition

The third edition has been thoroughly revised:

- Although we have maintained the *individual, team, organizational* parts framework, we have reorganized some of the chapters in Parts 2 and 3. Chapters 8 and 9 in Part 2 have been combined and re-titled "Team Leadership and Self-Managed Teams," which brings the number of chapters down to 11. Chapter 11 in Part 3, "Strategic Leadership and Managing Crises and Change," has been moved to be the last chapter of the text.
- The number of references has increased from slightly over 900 to over 1,100, to reflect current theory and concepts.
- Over half of the chapter opening and end-of-chapter cases are new, and most of the remaining cases have been updated. The opening cases now include questions, which are answered throughout the chapter. The end-of-chapter cases for Chapters 2–11 include cumulative case questions, which are questions related to prior chapters that review and integrate multiple concepts.
- A new InfoTrac feature has been added to the opening case in each chapter.
- Each chapter now includes two new Ethical Dilemma boxed features, with two to four questions each for class discussion, to get students thinking about ethics and how they will react when confronted with ethical challenges.
- Three new Self-Assessments (called Self-Assessment Exercises in the previous edition) have been added.
- Eleven new Video Cases have been added.
- One new Skill-Development Exercise has been added.
- All chapters have new and updated Test Bank questions and PowerPoint slides.

Chapter 1

The "Why Leadership Is Important" subsection has been updated. The discussion of peer leadership and coleadership in the "Defining Leadership" subsection has been deleted. Exercise 1-1 from the previous edition is now Skill-Development Exercise 1.

Chapter 2

The "Emotional Intelligence" subsection has been rewritten and expanded to include a more in-depth discussion of the four components of EQ. Four new key terms—relationship management, self-awareness, self-management, and social awareness—have been added. The "Ethical Leadership" section has been expanded and now includes an updated Self-Assessment 6, an explanation of the Sarbanes-Oxley Act of 2002, and a new subsection—"Being an Ethical Leader."

Chapter 3

The discussion of contributions of behavioral leadership theory in the "Leadership Grid and High-High Leader Research and Contributions" subsection has been reduced in length. The "Motivational Process" subsection now includes a brief discussion of organizational citizenship.

Chapter 4

The "Research on Power" subsection has been deleted. The "Acquiring and Losing Power" subsection has been reduced in length. There are new Self-Assessments on networking and negotiating. There is a new Skill-Development Exercise 1—Influencing Tactics.

Chapter 5

There is a new Self-Assessment 2—Your Personality and Contingency Leadership Theories—to help students understand how their personality affects their use of contingency leadership styles.

Chapter 6

References have been heavily updated throughout the entire chapter.

Chapter 7

The name of the chapter has been changed to "Leader/Follower Relations" to emphasize its focus on leader-follower relations and their impact on organizational performance. Due to this change, some of the sections and subsections have been renamed. The "Vertical Dyadic Linkage (VDL) Theory," "Leader-Member Exchange (LMX) Theory," and "Systems and Networks" subsections have been heavily edited. The "Followership" section has also been heavily edited. Learning Outcome 5 has been changed. Followership and leader-member exchange (LMX) have been added as new key terms, while the Pygmalion effect and leader-member exchange (LMX) theory have been deleted as key terms.

Chapter 8

Chapter 8 combines Chapters 8 and 9 from the last edition. The name of the chapter has been changed to "Team Leadership and Self-Managed Teams" to reflect this change.

Chapter 8, 2e. The "Use of Teams in Organizations" section has been heavily edited and now contains the "Characteristics of Effective Teams" section from the last edition as a subsection. The "Team Creativity" section and its subsections from the last edition have been heavily edited and moved to the "Characteristics of Effective Teams" subsection, and "creativity driven" has been added as one of the characteristics of effective teams. The "Determinants of Effective Team Decisions" subsection has been deleted. The "Leader's Role in Group Decisions" subsection has been renamed "Leader-Centered versus Group-Centered Approach." The discussion of the traditional approach in this subsection now refers to the leader-centered approach. The "Meeting Leadership Skills" section has been renamed "Leadership Skills for Effective Team Meetings." There is a new definition for team effectiveness. Functional fixedness has been deleted as a key term.

Chapter 9, 2e. The "Understanding Self-Management" section has been renamed "Self-Managed Teams." The "Success Factors of Effective Self-Managed Teams" subsection has been renamed "Self-Managed Team Effectiveness." The "Team Growth Stages and Leadership" section has been deleted. Stages of group development, team forming stage, team norming stage, team performing stage, and team adjoining stage have been deleted as key terms.

Chapter 9

Chapter 9 was the previous edition's Chapter 10. The "Personal Meaning" subsection under the "Charisma" section is now a separate section and has been moved to the very beginning of the chapter. A "Factors that Influence Personal Meaning" subsection has been added to the "Personal Meaning" section. The "Transformational versus Transactional Leadership" subsection has been heavily edited, with an added discussion of the research of James McGregor Burns and Bernard Bass. The rest of the material in the chapter has received light revision and editing.

Chapter 10

Chapter 10 was Chapter 12 in the previous edition. This change is in response to reviewer feedback, which recommended that the order of Chapters 11 and 12 in the previous edition be switched. Information on Ouchi's Theory Z has been added to the "Characteristics of High-Performance Culture" subsection. New examples have been added to the discussions of Realigning Rewards/Incentives and Resource Allocation in the "Leaders as Culture Creators" subsection. The rest of the material in the chapter has received light revision and editing. Demographic diversity and organizational knowledge have been added as new key terms.

Chapter 11

Chapter 11 now becomes the capstone for the text. The "Strategic Leadership" section has been heavily edited. An introductory paragraph to the "Crisis

Leadership" section has been added at the end of the "Strategy Evaluation" subsection. The "Crisis Leadership" section has been heavily edited, with recent examples of real-life crises and an added discussion of effective management plans/models. The rest of the material in the chapter has received light revision and editing.

Acknowledgments

I dedicate my first acknowledgment for this book to Judi Neal, University of New Haven, because of her influence on my work and this on text. Judi indirectly influenced my use of the three-pronged approach by making me aware of an article in the *Journal of Management Education*[2] comparing my *Human Relations in Organizations: Applications and Skill Building*[3] to other skills books. Author John Bigelow gave it a top rating for a general Organizational Behavior (OB) course in "Managerial Skills Texts: How Do They Stack Up?" I got the three-pronged idea by reading John's suggestions for improving skills training books (thanks, John). I have used the three-pronged approach successfully in the new sixth edition of *Human Relations in Organizations*, and in *Management Fundamentals: Concepts, Applications, and Skill Development* (third edition), also published by South-Western Cengage Learning. The "three levels of analysis" framework for this book was Judi's idea. I'm deeply honored that Judi wrote the Appendix, "Leadership and Spirituality in the Workplace."

I also want to thank my mentor and coauthor of many publications, Joel Corman, for his advice and encouragement during and after my graduate education at Suffolk University.

I hope everyone who uses this text enjoys teaching from these materials as I do.

Robert N. Lussier
Springfield College

Coauthoring this book with Bob is the culmination of a friendship and mentoring relationship that started quite accidentally. I met Bob at my very first Small Business Institute (SBI) conference. He offered his assistance in helping me through the publication minefield and I took it. Over the years, we have published and presented papers together at various conferences. I was honored and appreciative when he asked me to coauthor this text, now going into its third edition. It has been a wonderful journey so far, and I look forward to many more years of sharing his talents and friendship. I would also like to thank all my professors, who helped mold me into what I am today through their nurturing and effective teaching. I have not forgotten you, even if we have not been in touch regularly. To the friends who found it in their hearts to make me a part of their families, I say, "Thank you, and God bless you for all your kindness." And, finally, I give recognition and thanks to my colleagues, friends, and administrators at the University of Virginia's College at Wise who have supported me morally and materially in this endeavor.

Christopher F. Achua
The University of Virginia's College at Wise

Finally, we both would like to acknowledge the superb assistance we received from our editorial team. The guidance, support, and professionalism of John Szilagyi (executive editor), Kimberly Kanakes (marketing manager), Juli Cook (production project manager), Erin Donohoe (ancillary coordinator), Tippy McIntosh (art director), Kathy Shaut (permissions editor), Kristen Meere (technology project manager), and Karen Schaffer (Web coordinator) were invaluable to the completion of this project. Special thanks to Leslie Kauffman (developmental editor) for all her help in updating and upgrading this new third edition. We sincerely acknowledge the reviewers and survey respondents who provided feedback that greatly improved the quality of this book in many areas.

Reviewers

Chris Adalikwu
Concordia College—Selma, Alabama

Kathy Bohley
University of Indianapolis

John Bonosoro
Webster University

Brian W. Bridgeforth
Herzing College

Carl R. Broadhurst
Campbell University

Jon Burch
Trevecca Nazarene University

Debi Cartwright
Truman State University

Don Cassiday
North Park University

Ken Chapman
Webster University

Felipe Chia
Harrisburg Area Community College

Valerie Collins
Sheridan College

George W. Crawford
Clayton College & State University

Joseph Daly
Appalachian State University

Frederick T. Dehner
Rivier College

Melinda Drake
Limestone College

Rex Dumdum
Marywood University

Ray Eldridge
Freed-Hardeman University

Debi Carter-Ford
Wilmington College

Gerald A. Garrity
Anna Maria College

Thomas Garsombke
Northland College

Ronald Gayhart
Lakeshore Tech College

Michele Geiger
College of Mount St. Joseph

James Gelatt
University of Maryland University College

Don R. Gibson
Houston Baptist University

Eunice M. Glover
Clayton College & State University

Garry Grau
Northeast State Community College

Ray Grubbs
Millsaps College

Deborah Hanson
University of Great Falls

Mary Ann Hazen
University of Detroit Mercy

Linda Hefferin
Elgin Community College

Marilyn M. Helms
Dalton State College

Mary Hogue
*Kent State University, Stark
Campus*

Stewart Husted
Virginia Military Institute

Gale A. Jaeger
Marywood University

Lori Happel-Jarratt
The College of St. Scholastica

Thomas O. Jones, Jr.
Greensboro College

Paul N. Keaton
University of Wisconsin-La Crosse

Gary Kleemann
Arizona State University East

Bill Leban
DeVry University

Chet Legenza
DeVry University

Sondra Lucht
Mountain State University

James Maddox
Friends University

Kathleen B. Magee
Anna Maria College

Charles Mambula
Suffolk University

Gary May
Clayton College & State University

Lee E. Meadows
Walsh College

Ken Miller
Mountain State University

Steve Morreale
Worcester State College

Jamie Myrtle
MidAmerica Nazarene University

Patricia Parker
Maryville University

Jeff Pepper
Chippewa Valley Tech College

Nicholas Peppes
St. Louis Community College

Melinda Phillabaum
Indiana University

Laura Poppo
Virginia Tech

William Price
North County Community College

Gordon Rands
Western Illinois University

Kira K. Reed
Syracuse University

Marlys Rizzi
Simpson College

Mary Sacavage
Alvernia College Schuylkill Center

Khaled Sartawi
Fort Valley State University

Christopher Sieverdes
Clemson University

H. D. Sinopoli
Waynesburg College

Thomas G. Smith
Fort Valley State University

Emeric Solymossy
*Western Illinois University—Quad
Cities*

Shane Spiller
Morehead State University

Bill Tracey
Central Connecticut State University

Robin Turner
Rowan-Cabarrus Community College

John Waltman
Eastern Michigan University

Kerr F. Watson
Mount Olive College

Kristopher Weatherly
Campbellsville University

Amy Wojciechowski
West Shore Community College

Mike Woodson
Northeast Iowa Community College

Benjamin R. Wygal
Southern Adventist University

Kimberly S. Young
St. Bonaventure University

Joseph E. Zuro
Troy State University

About the Authors

Robert N. Lussier

Robert N. Lussier is a professor of management at Springfield College and has taught management for more than 25 years. He has developed innovative and widely copied methods for applying concepts and developing skills that can be used in one's personal and professional life. He was the director of Israel Programs and taught there. Other international experiences include Namibia and South Africa.

Dr. Lussier is a prolific writer, with over 275 publications to his credit. His articles have been published in the *Academy of Entrepreneurship Journal, Business Horizons, Business Journal, Entrepreneurial Executive, Entrepreneurship Theory and Practice, Journal of Business & Entrepreneurship, Journal of Business Strategies, Journal of Management Education, Journal of Small Business Management, Journal of Small Business Strategy, SAM Advanced Management Journal,* and others.

When not writing, he consults to a wide array of commercial and nonprofit organizations. In fact, some of the material in the book was developed for such clients as Baystate Medical Center, Coca-Cola, Friendly Ice Cream, Institute of Financial Education, Mead, Monsanto, Smith & Wesson, the Social Security Administration, the Visiting Nurses Association, and the YMCA.

Dr. Lussier holds a bachelor of science in business administration from Salem State College, two master's degrees in business and education from Suffolk University, and a doctorate in management from the University of New Haven.

Christopher F. Achua

Christopher F. Achua is a Full Professor in the Department of Business and Economics at the University of Virginia's College at Wise. He is a professor of strategy who has been teaching leadership and other management courses for over 14 years. Dr. Achua's interest in engaging students in real-life learning opportunities led him to create and direct programs such as the Center for Entrepreneurship, Leadership, and Service (a program funded by the Appalachian Regional Commission) and the Small Business Institute (an SBA program) at his university. These programs focused on developing students' leadership and entrepreneurial skills through applied theory in real-world situations.

Dr. Achua has actively presented scholarly papers at regional and national conferences. His papers have been published in many refereed proceedings and the *Journal of Small Business Strategy*. He has also consulted to a variety of public and not-for-profit organizations. When not involved in academic pursuits, he lends his expertise to community development programs and initiatives. He has served on several boards of organizations in the local community, and was chair of the Mountain Empire Regional Business Incubator Board of Directors.

Chris received his undergraduate degree in business administration and accounting from the University of Sioux Falls, South Dakota; his MBA from the University of South Dakota; and his doctorate from the United States International University (now Alliant International University) in San Diego, California.

PART 1

Individuals as Leaders

Who Is a Leader?

1

LEARNING OUTCOMES

After studying this chapter, you should be able to:

1. Briefly describe the five key elements of leadership. p. 5
2. List the 10 managerial roles based on their three categories. p. 10
3. Explain the interrelationships among the levels of leadership analysis. p. 16
4. Describe the major similarity and difference between the trait and behavioral leadership theories. p. 17
5. Discuss the interrelationships between trait and behavioral leadership theories and contingency theories. p. 18
6. Define the following **key terms** (in order of appearance in the chapter):

leadership
influencing
managerial role categories
interpersonal leadership roles
informational leadership roles
decisional leadership roles
levels of analysis of leadership theory

leadership theory
leadership theory classifications
leadership paradigm
leadership trait theories
behavioral leadership theories
contingency leadership theories
integrative leadership theories

Opening Case Application

General Electric (GE) is the world's largest public company,[1] and *Fortune Magazine, Financial Times, Forbes,* and *Business Week* consistently rank GE among the most admired companies. You are either a customer of GE or have indirectly been exposed to its products and services without realizing it.

GE is a conglomerate with multiple lines of business under the following business directory: GE Advanced Materials, GE Commercial Finance, GE Finance, GE Consumer & Industrial, GE Energy, GE Equipment Services, GE Healthcare, GE Infrastructure, GE Insurance Solutions, GE Transportation, and NBC Universal.

John (Jack) Welch was Chief Executive Officer (CEO) of GE from 1981 to 2001. Jack Welch's peers consistently rated him as the most respected CEO. Jeffery (Jeff) Immelt replaced Jack as CEO, and the *Financial Times* named Jeff Immelt as 2003 Man of the Year.[2] Under Immelt's leadership, GE has remained the world's largest company, with record earnings as he remakes GE to face the challenges of the twenty-first century by changing strategies to focus on growth from developing countries.[3]

Opening Case Questions:

1. Why is GE so successful?
2. Does GE use our definition of leadership ("the influencing process of leaders and followers to achieve organizational objectives through change")?
3. Can leadership skills be developed, and can you develop your leadership skills through this course?
4. What leadership managerial roles does CEO Jeff Immelt perform at GE?

You'll find answers to these questions about General Electric and its leadership throughout the chapter.

To learn more about General Electric, visit the company's Web site at **http://www.ge.com** or log on to InfoTrac® College Edition at **academic.cengage.com/infotrac**, where you can research and read articles on General Electric and CEO Jeff Immelt. It's worth taking a glance at InfoTrac now, if you haven't done so already, just to get a sense of what you'll find on the site and how its search functions work. To get started, take a look at a recent article discussing the cultural transformation at GE that is being pushed by CEO Jeff Immelt. Use the advanced search option to key in record number A130787602 to access the article. Related articles on GE and Immelt can be found at the bottom of the article page.

Jack Welch and Jeff Immelt are just two examples among thousands of great leaders who understand the importance of leadership development. The focus of this chapter is on helping you understand what leadership is and what this book is all about. We begin by defining leadership and the ten roles that leaders perform. Then we explain the three levels of leadership analysis, which provides the framework for the book. After explaining the four major leadership paradigms that have developed over the years, we end this chapter by stating the objectives of the book and presenting its organization.

Leadership Is Everyone's Business

In this section, we begin with a discussion of the importance of leadership, followed by our definition of leadership that is used throughout this book. We end by answering the question: Are leaders made or born?

Why Leadership Is Important

Here are just a few reasons why leadership is so important.

- The well-known management guru Peter Drucker, who has been a consultant to GE and other organizations around the globe,[4] says that, above all, the performance of the managerial leadership determines the success or failure of the organization.[5] Well-publicized corporate failures (Enron and WorldCom) have brought home the critical role that leadership plays in the success or failure of almost every aspect of the profit and not-for-profit environment.[6] Poor leadership leads to failure,[7] and good leadership to success. Domino's Pizza chain CEO David Brandon states that the success of each store is based on the leadership provided by the manager.[8]
- In the United States, 60 percent of employees believe that their organizations are not well managed,[9] and 77 percent are not happy with their jobs.[10] The number one reason that employees stay or leave is how they are treated by their leaders.[11] Thus, it is hard to overstate the importance of leadership.[12]

As the examples illustrate, there is a great need for better leaders.[13] If you want to be successful, you must develop your leadership skills.[14] To this end, the focus of this book is to help you develop your leadership skills, so that you can become a successful leader in your personal and professional life.

1. Why Is GE So Successful?

GE is known as the company that develops leaders. More executives from GE have developed leadership skills and then gone on to become CEOs of other major firms than from any other company—more than a dozen, with hundreds more who have gone on to hold senior corporate positions.[15]

A major reason that Jack Welch is admired by others is his commitment to developing leaders, and his ability to do so. He is acknowledged around the world for his innovative management ideas and hands-on management style.[16] As he has said, "We have made leadership development the most important element in our work. We focus on some aspect of it every day. My most important job is to choose and develop business leaders."[17] One of the reasons Jack Welch left GE was to work about half as many hours; he wanted to cut down to around 40 hours a week. As a consultant, Jack Welch is still building leaders as a confidant to CEOs and corporate coach, as well as becoming an author.[18]

Ethical Dilemma 1

Is Leadership Really Important?

Scott Adams is the creator of the cartoon character Dilbert. Adams makes fun of managers in part because he distrusts top-level managers, saying that leadership is really a crock. Leadership is about manipulating people to get them to do something they don't want to do, and there may not be anything in it for them. CEOs basically run the same scam as fortune-tellers, who make up a bunch of guesses and when by chance one is correct, they hope you forget the other errors. First, CEOs blame their predecessors for anything that is bad, then they shuffle everything around, start a new strategic program, and wait. When things go well, despite the CEO, the CEO takes the credit and moves on to the next job. Adams says we may be hung up on leadership as part of our DNA. It seems we have always sought to put somebody above everybody else.[19]

1. Do you agree with Scott Adams that leadership is a crock?
2. Do we really need to have someone in the leadership role?

Learning Outcome 1

Briefly describe the five key elements of leadership.

Defining Leadership

The topic of leadership has generated excitement and interest since ancient times. When people think about leadership, images come to mind of powerful dynamic individuals who command victorious armies, shape the events of nations, develop religions, or direct corporate empires. How did certain leaders build such great armies, countries, religions, and companies? Why do certain leaders have dedicated followers while others do not? How did Adolf Hitler rise to a position of great power? It wasn't until the twentieth century that researchers attempted to scientifically answer such questions, using many different definitions. Today, we understand better the answers to some of these research questions; but much of the research generates more questions, and many questions surrounding the mystery of leadership remain unanswered. In this book, you will learn the major leadership theories and research findings regarding leadership effectiveness.

There is no universal definition of leadership because leadership is complex, and because leadership is studied in different ways that require different definitions. As in leadership research studies, we will use a single definition that meets our purpose in writing this book. Before you read our definition of leadership, complete Self-Assessment 1 to get a better idea of your leadership potential. In the following section, we will discuss each question as it relates to the elements of our leadership definition and to your leadership potential.

Leadership Potential

As with all the self-assessment exercises in this book, there are no right or wrong answers, so don't try to pick what you think is the right answer. Be honest in answering the questions, so that you can better understand yourself and your behavior as it relates to leadership.

For each pair of statements distribute 5 points, based on how characteristic each statement is of you. If the first statement is totally like you and the second is not like you at all, give 5 points to the first and 0 to the second. If it is the opposite, use 0 and 5. If the statement is usually like you, then the distribution can be 4 and 1, or 1 and 4. If both statements tend to be like you, the distribution should be 3 and 2, or 2 and 3. Again, the combined score for each pair of statements must equal 5.

Here are the scoring distributions for each pair of statements:

0–5 or 5–0	One of the statements is totally like you, the other not like you at all.
1–4 or 4–1	One statement is usually like you, the other not.
2–3 or 3–2	Both statements are like you, although one is slightly more like you.

1. ____ I'm interested in and willing to take charge of a group of people.

____ I want someone else to be in charge of the group.

2. ____ When I'm not in charge, I'm willing to give input to the leader to improve performance.

____ When I'm not in charge, I do things the leader's way, rather than offer my suggestions.

3. ____ I'm interested in and willing to get people to listen to my suggestions and to implement them.

____ I'm not interested in influencing other people.

4. ____ When I'm in charge, I want to share the management responsibilities with group members.

____ When I'm in charge, I want to perform the management functions for the group.

5. ____ I want to have clear goals and to develop and implement plans to achieve them.

____ I like to have very general goals and take things as they come.

6. ____ I like to change the way my job is done and to learn and do new things.

____ I like stability, or to do my job the same way; I don't like learning and doing new things.

7. ____ I enjoy working with people and helping them succeed.

____ I don't really like working with people and helping them succeed.

To determine your leadership potential score, add up the numbers (0–5) for the first statement in each pair; don't bother adding the numbers for the second statement. The total should be between 0 and 35. Place your score on the continuum at the end of this assessment. Generally, the higher your score, the greater your potential to be an effective leader. However, the key to success is not simply potential, but persistence and hard work. You can develop your leadership ability through this course by applying the principles and theories to your personal and professional lives.

0——5——10——15——20——25——30——35
Low leadership potential   *High leadership potential*

Leadership *is the influencing process of leaders and followers to achieve organizational objectives through change.* Let's discuss the five key elements of our definition; see Exhibit 1-1 for a list.

Leaders–Followers

Question 1 of Self-Assessment 1 is meant to get you thinking about whether you want to be a leader or follower. If you are not interested and not willing to

Exhibit 1-1 *Leadership definition key elements.*

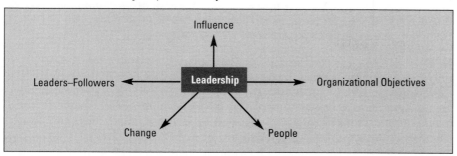

be in charge, you are better suited to be a follower. However, as you will learn in this section, good followers also perform leadership roles when needed.[20] And followers influence leaders. Thus in our definition of leadership the influencing process is *between* leaders and followers, not just a leader influencing followers; it's a two-way street. Knowing how to lead and developing leadership skills will make you a better leader and follower.[21] So whether you want to be a leader or follower, you will benefit from this book.

Throughout this book, leadership is referred to in the context of formal organizational settings in business corporations (GE, IBM), government agencies (Department of Motor Vehicles, the Police Department), and nonprofit organizations (Red Cross, Springfield College). Organizations have two major classifications of employees: managers, who have subordinates and formal authority to tell them what to do; and employees, who do not. All managers perform four major functions: planning, organizing, leading, and controlling. Leadership is thus a part of the manager's job. However, there are managers—you may know some—who are not effective leaders. There are also nonmanagers who have great influence on managers and peers. Thus, in this book we do not use the terms *manager* and *leader* interchangeably. When we use the word *manager,* we mean a person who has a formal title and authority. When we use the term *leader,* we mean a person who may be either a manager or a nonmanager. A leader always has the ability to influence others; a manager may not. Thus, a leader is not necessarily a person who holds some formal position such as manager.

A *follower* is a person who is being influenced by a leader.[22] A follower can be a manager or a nonmanager. Good followers are not "yes people" who simply follow the leader without giving input that influences the leader.[23] In short, effective leaders influence followers, and their followers influence them. The qualities needed for effective leadership are the same as those needed to be an effective follower. Throughout this book, we use the term *behavior* when referring to the activities of people or the things they do and say as they are influenced. You will learn more about followership in Chapter 7.

As implied in question 2 of Self-Assessment 1, good followers give input and influence leaders. If you want to be an effective follower, you need to share your ideas.[24] Also, as a leader you need to listen to others and implement their ideas to be effective.[25]

WorkApplication1

Recall a present or past job. Were you both a leader and a follower? Explain.

_____

_____

_____

_____

_____

Influence

Influencing *is the process of a leader communicating ideas, gaining acceptance of them, and motivating followers to support and implement the ideas through change.* Influence is the essence of leadership. Question 3 of Self-Assessment 1 asked if you were interested in and willing to influence others, as a leader or follower. When you have a management position, you have more power to influence others. But, effective followers also influence others. Your ability to influence others (to get what you want) can be developed. Influencing includes power, politics, and negotiating; you will learn more about these concepts in Chapter 4.

Influencing is also about the relationship between leaders and followers.[26] Managers may coerce subordinates to influence their behavior, but leaders do not. Leaders gain the commitment and enthusiasm of followers who are willing to be influenced. Most of the leadership research is concerned with the relationship between leaders and followers.[27] Effective leaders know when to lead and when to follow. Thus leaders and followers often change roles through the influencing process. Question 4 of Self-Assessment 1 asked if you want to share management responsibility as a leader.

Organizational Objectives

Effective leaders influence followers to think not only of their own interests but the interest of the organization. Leadership occurs when followers are influenced to do what is ethical and beneficial for the organization and themselves. Taking advantage of followers for personal gain is not part of leadership. Members of the organization need to work together toward an outcome that the leader and followers both want, a desired future or shared purpose that motivates them toward this more preferable outcome.[28] Leaders need to provide direction; with the input of followers, they set challenging objectives and lead the charge ahead to achieve them. Setting specific, difficult objectives leads to higher levels of performance.[29] As implied in Question 5 of Self-Assessment 1, effective leaders set clear goals. You will learn how to set objectives in Chapter 3.

Change

Influencing and setting objectives is about change. Organizations need to continually change, in adapting to the rapidly changing global environment.[30] At its website, GE says it's the only company listed in the Dow Jones Industrial Index today that was also included in the original index in 1896. The other companies may have become too comfortable with doing business the same old way,[31] perhaps causing these former business stars to fade. Effective leaders realize the need for continual change to improve performance. Jack Welch continually reshaped GE, as does Jeff Immelt.

Statements like these are not in a successful leader's vocabulary: *we've always done it this way; we've never done it that way before; it can't be done; no one else has done it;* and *it's not in the budget.* Leadership involves influencing followers to bring about change toward a desired future for the organization. Jack Welch asked his managers for every idea they had to improve the performance of their work unit. For ideas that he liked, Welch asked, "What resources do you need to make it happen?" And he gave them the resources.

WorkApplication2

Briefly explain the influencing relationship between the leader and followers where you work(ed).

_____

_____

_____

_____

_____

WorkApplication3

State one or more objectives from an organization where you work(ed).

_____

_____

_____

_____

_____

As implied in question 6 of Self-Assessment 1, and the information in this section, to be an effective leader and follower you must be open to change.[32] The people who advance in organizations are those who are willing to take a risk and try new things.[33] When was the last time you did something new and different? You will learn more about leading change in Chapter 11.

People

Although the term *people* is not specifically mentioned in our definition of leadership, after reading about the other elements, you should realize that leadership is about leading people.[34] As implied in question 7 of Self-Assessment 1, to be effective at almost every job today, you must be able to get along with people.[35] Effective leaders and followers enjoy working with people and helping them succeed.[36] You will learn how to develop your people skills throughout this book.

Research, experience, and common sense all point to a direct relationship between a company's financial success and its commitment to leadership practices that treat people as assets.[37] There is little evidence that being a mean, tough manager is associated with leadership success.[38] It is the collective efforts of people that make things happen.

OPENING CASE APPLICATION

2. Does GE Use Our Definition of Leadership ("The Influencing Process of Leaders and Followers to Achieve Organizational Objectives Through Change")?

Jeff Immelt is clearly the leader at GE, as Jack Welch was. However, both of them clearly believe in giving power to their business unit presidents, and they are influenced by these executives. Jack Welch was well known for his objective that GE should be number 1 or 2 in any business, or get out of it. GE consistently changed under Jack Welch. He was a deal-maker who oversaw the acquisition of 993 businesses while selling 408 businesses. He developed a reputation as a "pushy hothead who rubbed some the wrong way but prodded his team to new heights,"[39] and as a "competitive hard-charger always seeking a new challenge or crusade."[40] He was impatient with things that did not move quickly and broke down much of the bureaucracy at GE. When given credit for GE's success, Jack Welch was quick to say that GE is not a one-man show—it is the team effort of GE people that makes it successful.

Are Leaders Born or Made?

You may think this is a trick question, because the answer is neither and both. Effective leaders are not simply born or made, they are born with some leadership ability and develop it.[41] So natural ability may offer advantages or disadvantages to a leader.[42] You will learn more about leadership traits in Chapter 2.

Legendary football coach Vince Lombardi once said, "Contrary to the opinion of many people, leaders are not born, leaders are made, and they are made by effort and hard work." We are all leaders, and all people have potential leadership skills.[43] Whatever your natural leadership ability is now, you

---

WorkApplication4

Are the managers where you work(ed) effective at influencing their employees to bring about change? Explain.

_____

_____

_____

_____

_____

WorkApplication5

Do managers where you work(ed) treat their employees as valuable assets? Explain.

_____

_____

_____

_____

WorkApplication6

Do you believe that you are a born leader? Do you believe that you can develop your leadership skills to improve job performance?

_____

_____

_____

_____

can invest in developing your leadership skills, or you can allow them to remain as they are now. You may never become the CEO of a large business like GE, but you can improve your leadership ability through this course. We'll talk more about this in the last section of this chapter.

3. Can Leadership Skills Be Developed, and Can You Develop Your Leadership Skills Through This Course?

If top-level managers did not believe that leadership skills could be developed, they would not spend millions of dollars annually to do so. The primary place where GE executives receive leadership development is the John Welch Leadership Center. So the answer is yes,[44] leadership skills can be developed, and as Vince Lombardi would say, you can develop your leadership skills through this course if you put in the effort and work hard at it.

--- Learning Outcome 2 ---

List the 10 managerial roles based on their three categories.

Leadership Managerial Roles

In this section, we discuss what leaders do on the job—the leadership managerial roles.[45] Henry Mintzberg identified ten managerial roles that leaders perform to accomplish organizational objectives.[46] The roles represent the dominant classes of behavioral activities that managers or their followers perform.[47] Mintzberg defined a *role* as a set of expectations of how a person will behave to perform a job. He grouped these roles into three categories. *The* **managerial role categories** *are interpersonal, informational, and decisional.* Mintzberg's management role theory has been supported by research studies.[48] Exhibit 1-2 shows the 10 managerial roles, based on the three categories.

Interpersonal Roles

The **interpersonal leadership roles** *include figurehead, leader, and liaison.*

Exhibit 1-2 *Managerial roles.*

Interpersonal Roles	Informational Roles	Decisional Roles
Figurehead	Monitor	Entrepreneur
Leader	Disseminator	Disturbance handler
Liaison	Spokesperson	Resource allocator
		Negotiator

Figurehead Role

Leaders perform the *figurehead role* when they represent the organization or department in legal, social, ceremonial, and symbolic activities. Top-level managers are usually viewed as figureheads for their organization. However, leaders throughout the organization perform the following behavior, as well as other related activities:

- Signing official documents (expense authorization, checks, vouchers, contracts, and so on)
- Entertaining clients or customers as official representatives and receiving/escorting official visitors
- Informally talking to people and attending outside meetings as an organizational representative
- Presiding at meetings and ceremonial events (awards ceremonies, retirement dinners, and so on)

Leader Role

According to Mintzberg, the *leader role* is that of performing the management functions to effectively operate the managers' organization unit. Therefore, the leader role pervades all managerial behavior. In other words, the leader role influences how the leader performs other roles.[49] You will learn more about the leadership role throughout this book. Here are some of the many leader behaviors that can be performed by managers or followers:

- Hiring and training
- Giving instructions and coaching
- Evaluating performance

Liaison Role

Leaders perform the *liaison role* when they interact with people outside their organizational unit. Liaison behavior includes networking to develop relationships and gain information and favors. Organizational politics is an important part of the liaison role, and you will learn more about how to conduct politics in Chapter 4. Here are a few of the liaison role behaviors:

- Serving on committees with members from outside the organizational unit
- Attending professional/trade association meetings
- Calling and meeting with people to keep in touch

Informational Roles

The **informational leadership roles** *include monitor, disseminator, and spokesperson.* You will learn more about informational roles in Chapter 6.

Monitor Role

Leaders perform the *monitor role* when they gather information. Most of the information is analyzed to discover problems and opportunities, and to understand events outside the organizational unit. Some of the information is passed on to other people in the organizational unit (disseminator role), or to people

WorkApplication7

Give one job example of the specific behavior you or some other leader displayed when performing the figurehead, leader, and liaison roles. For each of the three roles, be sure to identify the leader as you or another, the role by its name, and the specific behavior.

_____
_____
_____
_____
_____

outside the unit (spokesperson role). Information is gathered by behavior, including:

- Reading memos, reports, professional/trade publications, newspapers, and so forth
- Talking to others, attending meetings inside and outside the organization, and so forth
- Observing (visiting a competitor's store to compare products, prices, and business processes)

Disseminator Role

Leaders perform the *disseminator role* when they send information to others in the organizational unit. Managers have access to information that is not available to employees. Some of the information that comes from higher levels of management must be passed on to employees, either in its original form or paraphrased. Information is passed on in one or both forms:

- Orally through voice mail, one-on-one discussions, and group meetings. You will learn how to conduct meetings in Chapter 8.
- Written through e-mail and snail mail (U.S. mail)

Spokesperson Role

Leaders perform the *spokesperson role* when they provide information to people outside the organizational unit. People must report information to their boss (board of directors, owner, managers) and people outside the organizational unit (other departments, customers, suppliers). Leaders lobby and serve as public relations representatives for their organizational unit. Here are some examples of when the spokesperson role is performed:

- Meeting with the boss to discuss performance and with the budget officer to discuss the unit budget
- Answering letters
- Reporting information to the government (the IRS, OSHA)

Decisional Roles

The **decisional leadership roles** *include entrepreneur, disturbance handler, resource allocator, and negotiator.*

Entrepreneur Role

Leaders perform the *entrepreneur role* when they innovate and initiate improvements.[50] Leaders often get ideas for improvements through the monitor role. Here are some examples of entrepreneur behavior:

- Developing new or improved products and services
- Developing new ways to process products and services
- Purchasing new equipment

Disturbance-Handler Role

Leaders perform the *disturbance-handler role* when they take corrective action during crisis or conflict situations. You will learn more about how to handle conflicts in Chapter 6. Unlike the planned action of the entrepreneur role to take advantage of an opportunity, the disturbance is a reaction to an unexpected

WorkApplication8

Give one job example of the specific behavior you or some other leader conducted when performing the monitor, disseminator, and spokesperson roles. For each of the three roles, be sure to identify the leader as you or another, the role by its name, and the specific behavior.

_____
_____
_____
_____
_____

event that creates a problem. Leaders typically give this role priority over all other roles. Here are some examples of emergencies leaders may have to resolve:

- A union strike
- The breakdown of important machines/equipment
- Needed material arriving late
- Has to meet a tight schedule

Resource-Allocator Role

Leaders perform the *resource-allocator role* when they schedule, request authorization, and perform budgeting activities. Here are some examples of resource allocation:

- Deciding what is done now, done later, and not done (time management; priorities)
- Determining who gets overtime or a merit raise (budgeting)
- Scheduling when employees will use material and equipment

Negotiator Role

Leaders perform the *negotiator role* when they represent their organizational unit during routine and nonroutine transactions that do not include set boundaries (such as only one price and term of a sale/purchase for a product/service, or pay of an employee). When there are no set prices or pay and conditions, leaders can try to negotiate a good deal to get the resources they need. You will learn how to negotiate in Chapter 4. Here are some examples of negotiations:

- Pay and benefits package for a new professional employee or manager
- Labor union contract
- Contract with a customer (sale) or supplier (purchase)

Although managers are responsible for all 10 roles, which roles are more important—and which roles the manager performs and which are performed by other leaders—will vary based on the manager's job. The relative emphasis placed on these roles will vary as a function of organizational technology, the day-to-day problems faced by leaders, and the task environment of their organizations.[51] After answering Work Applications 7 through 9, you should realize that you and others perform the leadership roles.

WorkApplication 9

Give one job example of the specific behavior you or some other leader performed when fulfilling the entrepreneur, disturbance-handler, resource-allocator, and negotiator roles. For each of the four roles, be sure to identify the leader as you or another, the role by its name, and the specific behavior.

_____

_____

_____

_____

_____

4. What Leadership Managerial Roles Does CEO Jeff Immelt Perform At GE?

Like all managers who are good leaders, Jeff Immelt plays all 10 roles, and he delegates these roles to his followers. Immelt's interpersonal roles include signing documents, entertaining customers, running and attending meetings; leadership development and evaluation of followers; and serving on committees and boards. His informational roles include extensive communications. Immelt's decisional roles include developing new products and processes to keep ahead of the competition, dealing with crises, deciding which business units to give resources to and which to drain, as well as which to buy and to sell.

OPENING CASE APPLICATION

Leadership Managerial Roles

Identify each of the following 15 behaviors by its leadership role. Write the appropriate letter in the blank before each item.

Interpersonal roles	Informational roles	Decisional roles
a. figurehead	d. monitor	g. entrepreneur
b. leader	e. disseminator	h. disturbance handler
c. liaison	f. spokesperson	i. resource allocator
		j. negotiator

_____ 1. The leader is talking with two employees who were verbally fighting and refuse to work together.

_____ 2. The leader is holding a meeting with his followers to discuss a new company policy.

_____ 3. The production leader is talking to a maintenance person about fixing a machine.

_____ 4. The leader is conducting a job interview.

_____ 5. The sales leader is signing an expense reimbursement form for a sales representative.

_____ 6. The leader is holding a press conference with a local newspaper reporter.

_____ 7. The leader is assigning followers to various accounts and giving them the files.

_____ 8. A follower is asking the leader for a raise.

_____ 9. The leader is presenting organizational pins to employees for five years of service during a special meeting of all organizational unit members.

_____10. The leader is reading the daily e-mail.

_____11. The leader and his manager, who must authorize the funding of the project, are discussing having new customized software developed for the leader's department.

_____12. The leader is disciplining a follower for being late again.

_____13. The leader is visiting another organizational unit to watch how it processes work orders.

_____14. The leader of a stock brokerage branch is trying to get the telephones turned back on so brokers can use the phone.

_____15. The leader is having new customized software developed for the organizational unit.

Levels of Analysis of Leadership Theory

One useful way to classify leadership theory and research is by the levels of analysis. *The three* **levels of analysis of leadership theory** *are individual, group, and organizational.* Most leadership theories are formulated in terms of processes at only one of these three levels.[52] You will briefly learn about each level in this section, and the details of each in Parts I through III of this book.

Individual Level of Analysis

The individual level of analysis of leadership theory focuses on the individual leader and the relationship with individual followers.[53] The individual level can also be called the *dyadic process*. As discussed in our definition of leadership, dyadic theories view leadership as a reciprocal influencing process between the leader and the follower.[54] There is an implicit assumption that leadership effectiveness cannot be understood without examining how a leader and follower influence each other over time. Recall that influencing is also about the relationships between leaders and followers. As a leader and as a follower, you will influence other individuals and they will influence your behavior at work. You will also have multiple dyadic relationships at work. In Part I, "Individuals as Leaders" (Chapters 1–5), the focus is on the individual level of analysis.

Group Level of Analysis

The second level of analysis of leadership theory focuses on the relationship between the leader and the collective group of followers. This level is also called *group process*. Group process theories focus on how a leader contributes to group effectiveness. Extensive research on small groups has identified important determinants of group effectiveness, which you will learn about in Part II, "Team Leadership" (Chapters 6–8). An important part of group process is meetings. In Chapter 8, you will learn how to conduct productive meetings.

Organizational Level of Analysis

The third level of analysis of leadership theory focuses on the organization. This level is also called *organizational process*. Organizational performance in the long run depends on effectively adapting to the environment and acquiring the necessary resources to survive, and on whether the organization uses an effective transformation process to produce its products and services.

Much of the current research at the organizational level focuses on how top-level managers can influence organizational performance. Successful leaders, like Jack Welch of GE, have had a positive impact on organizational performance. You will learn more about determinants of organizational performance in Part III, "Organizational Leadership" (Chapters 9–11).

Ethical Dilemma 2

Executive Compensation

As discussed, executive management skill has a direct impact on the success of the firm. Top executives should be paid well; after all, if it weren't for effective CEOs, some companies would not be making the millions of dollars of profits they make each year. They deserve a piece of the pie they help create. The *Business Week* 2000 compensation survey reported that the average yearly total pay for CEOs of the 362 largest U.S. public companies was $12.4 million.

(Continued)

Ethical Dilemma 2

(*Continued*)

Executive compensation is based on multiple factors. Valuable managerial skill seems to be the most important factor in how much executives make. Firm size and performance also affect compensation, as does the power of the executive to influence pay.[55] A pay-for-performance exception is the CEO at Tyco, who received a 12 percent decrease in total compensation, based on stock value, when the company stock fell 71 percent in 2002; he still made $82 million, and was the second highest paid executive.[56]

Top executives have been criticized for getting richer as employees get poorer. For example, while the company was about to go bankrupt, top executives at American Airlines negotiated special pension protection worth $41 million for themselves, while pilots, mechanics, and flight attendants were asked to agree to pay and benefit cuts averaging around 23 percent. In 1989, CEOs were paid 56 times as much as the average worker; in 2002, they were paid 200 times as much.[57]

1. Do executives deserve to make 200 times as much as the average worker?
2. Is it ethical for managers to take large pay increases while laying off employees?
3. Are companies being socially responsible when paying executives premium compensation?

Learning Outcome 3

Explain the interrelationships among the levels of leadership analysis.

Interrelationships among the Levels of Analysis

Exhibit 1-3 illustrates the interrelationships among the levels of analysis of leadership theory. Note that the individual is placed at the bottom of the triangle, because group and organizational performance are based on individual

---

Exhibit 1-3 *Interrelationships among the levels of analysis of leadership theory.*

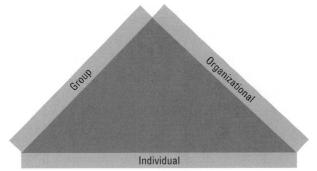

performance. It has been said that an organization is the sum of all of its individual transactions. Depending on the size of the group and organization you work for, your individual performance may influence the performance of the group and organization positively or negatively. If individual performance is low throughout the organization, the triangle will fall because it will not have a firm foundation, or performance will be low.

The group-level approach provides a better understanding of leadership effectiveness than the individual, but groups function in a larger social system, and group effectiveness cannot be understood if the focus of research is limited to a group's internal process level of analysis. Thus, the group part of the triangle supports the organizational side. If the groups are not effective, the triangle will fall or organizational performance will be low.

Both group and organizational performance also affect the performance of the individual. If both the group members and the group are highly motivated and productive (or not productive), chances are the individual will be productive (or not) as well. Success tends to be contagious. Working for a winning organization tends to motivate individuals to perform at their best to stay on top. However, an organization and its performance are more than the simple sum of its individuals and groups.

Leadership Theory Paradigms

The first thing we need to do is define the important concepts of this section. *A* **leadership theory** *is an explanation of some aspect of leadership; theories have practical value because they are used to better understand, predict, and control successful leadership.* It has been said that there is nothing as practical as a good theory.[58] There are four major classifications of leadership theory,[59] also called *research approaches*, used to explain leadership. **Leadership theory classifications** *include trait, behavioral, contingency, and integrative.* In this section, we discuss each classification and indicate where it is covered in more detail later in this book.

A **leadership paradigm** *is a shared mindset that represents a fundamental way of thinking about, perceiving, studying, researching, and understanding leadership.* The leadership paradigm has changed in the 60 years during which it has been studied. The four major classifications of leadership theory all represent a change in leadership paradigm. You will also learn about the change in paradigm from management to leadership in this section.

—————————— Learning Outcome 4 ——————————

Describe the major similarity and difference between the trait and behavioral leadership theories.

The Trait Theory Paradigm

Early leadership studies were based on the assumption that leaders are born, not made. Researchers wanted to identify a set of characteristics or traits that distinguished leaders from followers, or effective from ineffective leaders. **Leadership trait theories** *attempt to explain distinctive characteristics accounting for leadership effectiveness.* Researchers analyzed physical and psychological traits, or qualities, such as high energy level, appearance, aggressiveness, self-reliance, persuasiveness, and dominance in an effort to identify a set of traits that all successful leaders possessed.

The list of traits was to be used as a prerequisite for promoting candidates to leadership positions. Only candidates possessing all the identified traits would be given leadership positions. Hundreds of trait studies were conducted during the 1930s and 1940s to discover a list of qualities. However, no one has come up with a universal list of traits that all successful leaders possess, or traits that will guarantee leadership success. On the positive side, although there is no list of traits that guarantees leadership success, traits that are related to leadership success have been identified.[60] You will learn more about trait theory in the next chapter.

The Behavioral Leadership Theory Paradigm

By the 1950s, most of the leadership research had changed its paradigm, going from trait theory to focusing on what the leader actually did on the job (behavior). In the continuing quest to find the one best leadership style in all situations, researchers attempted to identify differences in the behavior of effective leaders versus ineffective leaders. Another subcategory of behavioral leadership focuses on the nature of management work.[61] Thus, **behavioral leadership theories** *attempt to explain distinctive styles used by effective leaders, or to define the nature of their work*. Mintzberg's 10 managerial roles are an example of behavioral leadership theory. Behavioral research focuses on finding ways to classify behavior that will facilitate our understanding of leadership. Hundreds of studies examined the relationship between leadership behavior and measures of leadership effectiveness. However, there was no agreement on one best leadership style for all management situations. On the positive side, Mintzberg's leadership theory is widely used to train leaders. And other researchers did identify two generic dimensions of leader behavior: task- and people-oriented leadership, which have importance in accounting for leadership effectiveness.[62] You will learn about some of the most popular behavioral leadership theories in Chapter 3 and about applications in Chapter 4.

──────────── Learning Outcome 5 ────────────

Discuss the interrelationships between trait and behavioral leadership theories and contingency theories.

The Contingency Leadership Theory Paradigm

Both the trait and behavioral leadership theories were attempts to find the one best leadership style in all situations; thus they are called *universal theories*. In the 1960s, it became apparent that there is no one best leadership style in all situations. Thus, the leadership paradigm shifted to contingency theory. **Contingency leadership theories** *attempt to explain the appropriate leadership style based on the leader, followers, and situation*. In other words, which traits and/or behaviors will result in leadership success given the situational variables? The contingency theory paradigm emphasizes the importance of situational factors, including the nature of the work performed, the external environment, and the characteristics of followers. One aspect of this research is to discover the extent to which managerial work is the same or different across different types of organizations, levels of management, and cultures. You will learn about the major contingency leadership theories in Chapter 5.

The Integrative Leadership Theory Paradigm

In the mid-to-late 1970s, the paradigm began to shift to the integrative, to tie the theories together,[63] or neo-charismatic theory.[64] As the name implies, **integrative leadership theories** *attempt to combine the trait, behavioral, and contingency theories to explain successful, influencing leader–follower relationships.* Researchers try to explain why the followers of some leaders are willing to work so hard and make personal sacrifices to achieve the group and organizational objectives, or how effective leaders influence the behavior of their followers.[65] Theories identify behaviors and traits that facilitate the leader's effectiveness, and explore why the same behavior by the leader may have a different effect on followers depending on the situation. The integrative leadership theory paradigm is emphasized in our definition of leadership and thus influences this entire book, especially Chapters 6 through 11.

From the Management to the Leadership Theory Paradigm

There are differences between managers and leaders.[66] In the first section we talked about some of the differences between a manager and a leader, because the overarching paradigm has shifted from management to leadership. Today's managers have an evolving role: Successful managers use a truly democratic form of leadership as they share the responsibility of management with employees.[67] Today, managers must be able to lead as well as manage. Thus, they must continue to manage and focus on leading to be successful. [68] In general, women make good leaders because they focus on people and relationships. [69]

Under the old management paradigm, managers were primarily autocratic, making all the decisions, and maintained tight controls over employees. Under the new leadership paradigm, managers are primarily participative, and focus on leadership by sharing the management functions. Leaders and followers have a good working relationship, as people are the most important asset. They set objectives together, and influence each other to bring about change to continually improve the organization.

Although we have made a comparison between managers and leaders, you should realize that successful leaders are also good at managing, and successful managers are good leaders. There is overlap between the two paradigms. To simplistically stereotype people as either managers or leaders does little to advance our understanding of leadership.[70] Also, because the term *manager* is an occupational title, to foster an inaccurate, negative stereotype of managers is not our intent.

Objectives of the Book

The overarching objectives of this book are reflected in its subtitle: *Theory, Application, and Skill Development.* We call it a three-pronged approach, with these objectives:

- To teach you the theory and concepts of leadership
- To develop your ability to apply leadership theory through critical thinking
- To develop your leadership skills in your personal and professional life

WorkApplication11

Does your present or past manager focus more on management or leadership? Explain, using examples.

_____

_____

_____

_____

_____

Applying the Concept 2

Leadership Theories

Identify each research approach by its leadership theory paradigm. Write the appropriate letter in the blank before each item.

a. trait
b. behavioral
c. contingency

d. integrative
e. management to leadership

_____ 16. The researcher is investigating the specific company, work environment, and followers to determine which leadership style is most appropriate.

_____ 17. The organization's human resources director is training its managers to be more effective in their interpersonal relationships with their followers, so that managers can better influence their followers to work to accomplish the organization's vision.

_____ 18. The researcher is observing managers to determine how much time they spend giving employees praise for doing a good job and criticism for poor performance.

_____ 19. The researcher is attempting to understand how leaders who are charismatic influence followers to achieve high levels of performance.

_____ 20. The researcher is attempting to determine if there is a relationship between how a manager dresses and leadership effectiveness.

This book offers some unique features relating to each of the three objectives (see Exhibit 1-4). So that you can get the most from this book, we encourage you to turn back to the preface and read (1) our goals in writing this book, and (2) descriptions of the features.

Leadership Theory

Throughout this book, you will learn about several leadership theories and the concepts they are based on. You will learn about the relationship between leadership and organizational success, as well as the difficulties and challenges leaders face. Your knowledge of leadership theory may be part of your grade;

Exhibit 1-4 *The three-pronged approach: Features of the book.*

Theory	Application	Skill Development
Research	Opening cases—Internet	Self-assessment exercises
References	Work applications	Case role-playing exercises
Step-by-step behavior models	Applying the concepts	Behavior model videos
Learning outcomes	Cases—Internet	Skill-development exercises
Key terms	Video cases	Behavior modeling training
Summary	Ethical Dilemmas	
Review and discussion questions		

you may be tested. As shown in Exhibit 1-4, this book offers seven features to help you learn leadership theory.

Application of Leadership Theory

Understanding the theory and concepts is essential to going on to the next level of applying the theory. If you don't understand the theory and concepts, how can you apply them to develop critical thinking skills?[71] As Goethe said, "Knowing is not enough; we must apply." However, research indicates that students are weak in applying theory,[72] that leadership education needs to close the gap between theory and practical application,[73] and that students need to be given the opportunity to practice using theory.[74] In other words, reading and lectures are not enough to lead; you need to learn by doing, through applying the theory.[75] To this end, this book offers you six features (Exhibit 1-4) to practice applying the concepts and theory. The ability to apply leadership theory may be part of your grade; you may be tested.

Leadership Skill Development

The third and highest-level objective is to develop leadership skills that can be used in your personal and professional life as a leader and follower. Organizations are investing substantial amounts to develop the leadership skills of their employees,[76] because there are bottom line implications.[77] As a cost savings, they are hiring people that have leadership skills.[78] As discussed, you can develop your leadership skills through this course.[79] Peter Drucker says that you need to develop leadership skills by doing.[80] To this end, this book offers you five features (Exhibit 1-4) to help you develop your leadership skills. Skill development may be part of your grade; you may be tested. We discuss behavior modeling in more detail here.

Models versus Exhibits

All of the behavioral "models" in this book provide specific, step-by-step instructions, and they are labeled as models. They are "prescriptive models." When we offer general advice without a specific instruction, we label the guidelines "exhibits." However, the purpose of both models and exhibits is to help you improve your performance.

Behavior Modeling Leadership Skills Training

Behavior modeling is the only multiple leadership skills training that has been empirically validated by rigorous procedures.[81] In some of the chapters, the features listed in Exhibit 1-4 are combined in behavior modeling skills training. For these exercises you may do a self-assessment. In any case, follow this procedure: (1) read the step-by-step models, (2) watch a behavior modeling video, and (3) practice the skill (which may include role-playing) through a skill-development exercise. The last step in this training is using the skill in your personal and/or professional life for further development of the leadership skill.

Practice

A major concern in organizational leadership training is the transfer of training to on-the-job application. As with just about everything in life, you cannot become skilled by simply reading or trying something once. Recall that Vince Lombardi said that leaders are made by effort and hard work. If you want to develop your leadership skill, you need to learn the leadership concepts, do the exercise preparation, and do the skill-development exercises. But most important, to be successful, you need to practice using your leadership skills in your personal and professional life.[82]

Flexibility

This book has so many features that they most likely cannot all be covered in class during a one-semester course. Your instructor will select the features to be covered during class that best meet the course objectives and the amount of class time available. You may do some or all of the features not covered in class on your own, or do some exercises with the assistance of others outside of class.

Organization of the Book

This book is organized by level of leadership analysis and leadership theory paradigm. See Exhibit 1-5 for an illustration of the organization of this book.

Go to the Internet (academic.cengage.com/management/lussier) where you will find a broad array of resources to help maximize your learning.

- Review the vocabulary
- Try a quiz
- View chapter videos

Exhibit 1-5 *Organization of the book, including level of analysis and leadership paradigm.*

PART I. INDIVIDUALS AS LEADERS (individual-level analysis of leadership theory—Trait, Behavioral, and Contingency Leadership Theories)

    1. Who Is a Leader?
    2. Leadership Traits and Ethics
    3. Leadership Behavior and Motivation
    4. Influencing: Power, Politics, Networking, and Negotiation
    5. Contingency Leadership Theories

PART II. TEAM LEADERSHIP (group-level analysis of leadership theory—Integrative Leadership Theory Applications)

    6. Communication, Coaching, and Conflict Skills
    7. Leader/Follower Relations
    8. Team Leadership and Self-Managed Teams

PART III. ORGANIZATIONAL LEADERSHIP (organizational-level analysis—Integrative Leadership Theory Applications)

    9. Charismatic and Transformational Leadership
    10. Leadership of Culture and Diversity, and the Learning Organization
    11. Strategic Leadership and Managing Crises and Change

Chapter Summary

The chapter summary is organized to answer the six learning outcomes for Chapter 1.

1. Briefly describe the five key elements of leadership.
Leader–Follower—leaders influence the behavior of followers, and vice versa. *Influencing*—the relationship between leaders and followers, who change roles. *Organizational objectives*—outcomes that leaders and followers want to accomplish. *Change*—needed to achieve objectives. *People*—leadership is about leading people.

2. List the 10 managerial roles based on their three categories.
Leaders perform the interpersonal role when they act as figurehead, leader, and liaison. Leaders perform the informational role when they act as monitor, disseminator, and spokesperson. Leaders perform the decisional role when they act as entrepreneur, disturbance handler, resource allocator, and negotiator.

3. Explain the interrelationships among the levels of leadership analysis.
The three levels of leadership analysis are individual, group, and organizational. The individual performance affects the group and organizational performance. The group performance affects the organizational performance. And both the group and organization affect the performance of the individual.

4. Describe the major similarity and difference between the trait and behavioral leadership theories.
The similarity between the trait and behavioral leadership theories is that they are both universal theories, or they are seeking one best leadership style for all situations. The difference is the approach to determining leadership effectiveness. Trait theory attempts to explain personal characteristics of effective leaders, whereas behavioral theory attempts to explain what leaders actually do on the job.

5. Discuss the interrelationships between trait and behavioral leadership theories and contingency theories.
The contingency theory is interrelated with the trait and behavioral leadership theories because it uses these two theories as the foundation for determining which leadership style is most appropriate—based on the leader, followers, and situation.

6. Define the following key terms (in order of appearance in the chapter).
Select one or more methods: (1) fill in the missing key terms from memory; (2) match the key terms from the following list with their definitions below; (3) copy the key terms in order from the list at the beginning of the chapter.

_____ is the process of influencing leaders and followers to achieve organizational objectives through change.

_____ is the process of a leader communicating ideas, gaining acceptance of them, and motivating followers to support and implement the ideas through change.

_____ are interpersonal, informational, and decisional.

_____ include figurehead, leader, and liaison.

_____ include monitor, disseminator, and spokesperson.

_____ include entrepreneur, disturbance handler, resource allocator, and negotiator.

_____ are individual, group, and organizational.

_____ is an explanation of some aspect of leadership; theories have practical value because they are used to better understand, predict, and control successful leadership.

_____ include trait, behavioral, contingency, and integrative.

_____ is a shared mindset that represents a fundamental way of thinking about, perceiving, studying, researching, and understanding leadership.

_____ attempt to explain distinctive characteristics accounting for leadership effectiveness.

_____ attempt to explain distinctive styles used by effective leaders or to define the nature of their work.

_____ attempt to explain the appropriate leadership style based on the leader, followers, and situation.

_____ attempt to combine the trait, behavioral, and contingency theories to explain successful, influencing leader–follower relationships.

Key Terms

behavioral leadership theories, 18
contingency leadership theories, 18
decisional leadership roles, 12
influencing, 8
informational leadership roles, 11

integrative leadership theories, 19
interpersonal leadership roles, 10
leadership, 6
leadership paradigm, 17
leadership theory, 17

leadership theory classifications, 17
leadership trait theories, 17
levels of analysis of leadership theory, 14
managerial role categories, 10

Review and Discussion Questions

1. Do you agree that, in general, mean or tough bosses are not successful leaders?
2. Are leaders born or made?
3. Why does the leadership role pervade all management behavior?
4. How is the monitor role related to the disseminator and spokesperson roles?
5. What is the key difference between the entrepreneur and disturbance-handler roles?

6. Do you agree with the interrelationships, and triangle analogy, of the levels of leadership analysis?
7. How can the shift in paradigm from management to leadership possibly help—and hurt—the management profession?
8. Can a person develop critical-thinking skills for applying leadership theory, and develop leadership skills, without first understanding the leadership theory?

Case

SCOTT LIVENGOOD—KRISPY KREME

Krispy Kreme's mission is to strive to provide the highest quality product and the best service to customers. Vernon Rudolph, the founder of Krispy Kreme, always believed in top quality and top service, as well as focusing on people, both customers and employees. These values have helped Krispy Kreme grow from a small donut shop founded in 1937 in Winston-Salem, North Carolina, to a national phenomenon in the 1990s.

Scott Livengood started at Krispy Kreme as a personnel trainee and became CEO in 1998. Livengood transformed Krispy Kreme Doughnuts from a sleepy regional company to a highflying and hungry national phenomenon. Krispy Kreme had less than 100 stores in 1996, when it opened its first store in Manhattan. This move gave Krispy Kreme doughnuts cult status, leading to explosive growth. In early 2005, it operated 435 stores in 45 states and 4 other countries. Krispy Kreme also sells doughnuts in some 20,000 supermarkets, convenience stores, truck stops, and other outside locations.

However, Krispy Kreme ran into problems—as its doughnuts became more widely available, their popularity dropped. With sales dropping, problems in relations with frachisees, and facing accounting probes from the Securities and Exchange Commission, Krispy Kreme had to restate fiscal year 2004 earnings due to accounting errors. Krispy Kreme went public in 2000 with its stock price of $5.25, and soared to a high near $50, only to fall to less than $9 a share in January 2005. Livengood claimed that the low-carbohydrate diet trend was a major cause of the decline.

As a result of these problems, the board pressed Scott Livengood to resign as CEO to take on an advisory/consultant role to Krispy Kreme. The high-profile turnaround expert Stephen Cooper replaced Livengood as CEO, part-time, as he continued as CEO of Enron. Cooper planned to develop a turnaround strategy within 90 days, or by mid-April 2005; he expected to close some company-owned stores and scale back plans to open new ones. Cooper's first order of business was to meet with Krispy Kreme bankers to extend its credit line.[83]

GO TO THE INTERNET: To learn more about Krispy Kreme, log on to InfoTrac® College Edition at **academic. cengage.com/infotrac** and use the advanced search function.

Support your answers to the following questions with specific information from the case and text or with information you get from the Web or another source.

1. Explain how each of the five elements of our definition of leadership applies to Scott Livengood leading Krispy Kreme's growth from 1996 to 2005 (see Exhibit 1-1).
2. Identify leadership roles played by Scott Livengood as CEO. Which role was the most important?
3. Which level of analysis is the primary focus of this case?
4. Explain how each of the leadership theory classifications applies to this case, and which one is most relevant.
5. Is the low-carbohydrate diet a major reason for Krispy Kreme's performance problems? Explain.
6. Was there a leadership problem at Krispy Kreme, and do you agree with the board's decision to replace Scott Livengood as CEO? Why or why not?

Case Exercise and Role-Play

Preparation: Assume that you are the chairman of the board of Krispy Kreme. You were involved in promoting Scott Livengood to CEO and have worked with him for over six years. The board has agreed that Scott must be replaced, and you have to tell him the bad news, which you know he will not want to hear. How would you handle the meeting with Scott—what would you do, and what would you say to him?

Your instructor may elect to let you break into small groups to share ideas and develop a plan for your meeting with Scott. If you develop a group plan, select one leader to present the meeting with Scott.

Role-Play: One person (representing themselves or their group) conducts the meeting with Scott Livengood to notify him of his removal as CEO, before the entire class. Or, multiple role-plays may take place in small groups of 5–6; however, role-players can't conduct the meeting before the team that developed the meeting plan. The people role-playing Scott should put themselves in his place; he doesn't want to lose his job as CEO.

Video Case

CVS Corporation: Foundations of Behavior in Organizations

The CVS Corporation is a drugstore chain of over 4,000 stores that sell prescription drugs and a variety of general merchandise, including over-the-counter drugs, greeting cards, photo finishing services, beauty products, and convenience foods.

View the Video (14 minutes)
View the video on CVS Corporation in class or at **academic.cengage.com/management/lussier.**

Read the Case
When CVS recently began a rapid expansion of its retail operations, management decided the company needed to quickly develop new talent for local, district, and regional management positions. To achieve this objective, CVS created a new initiative called Emerging Leaders, a program that provides skills and training for future leadership within the organization.

The program begins by identifying and recruiting employees with traits deemed necessary to become leaders in the company. CVS assigns mentors to these potential leaders, and offers continuous learning opportunities so they can develop skills for moving up in the organization. The video case offers an example: Regional Manager Jeff Raymond is assigned to be a mentor for new Emerging Leader Todd Peloquin, a district manager at the company. In turn, Mr. Peloquin educates individual subordinate store managers about Emerging Leaders, and encourages them to take the opportunity to enter the program as a stepping-stone to career growth. This process motivates CVS employees by providing a clearly structured path of advancement, and enables them to gain a broad perspective of the company and its goals that they would not be able to obtain on their own.

By identifying potential leaders with the right personality traits and equipping them with the essential tools needed to handle any situation, the CVS Corporation's Emerging Leaders program ensures the firm's continued growth and success.

Answer the Questions
1. What key personality traits does CVS management look for when trying to identify a good potential leader?
2. What do managers at CVS consider to be a pitfall that prevents employees from pursuing leadership opportunities at the company?
3. How does CVS teach complex problem-solving skills to employees in the Emerging Leaders program?

Skill-Development Exercise 1

GETTING TO KNOW YOU BY NAME

Preparing for Skill-Development Exercise 1

Complete Self-Assessment 2 on page 27, and read the accompanying information before class.

Objectives
1. To get acquainted with some of your classmates.
2. To get to know your instructor.

Skill Objective
To develop your skill at remembering and calling people by their name.

In this chapter you learned about the importance of leader–follower relationships. An important part of leadership relations is making people feel important. It has been said that the sweetest sound people can hear is their own name. Have you ever had a person whom you don't know (or hardly know) call you by name? Have you ever had a person whom you believe should be able to call you by name, not be able to—or call you by the wrong name? How did these two situations make you feel? Being able to call people by name will improve your leadership effectiveness.

Tips for Remembering People's Names

- The first thing you need to do is make a conscious effort to improve your skill at calling people by name. If you say you are no good at remembering names, you won't be. If you say "I can be good at it, and work at it," you can.

- When you are introduced to a person, consciously greet them by name. For example, say, "Hi, Juan, glad to meet you." Then, during your conversation, say the name a few more times until it sticks with you. Use the person's name when you ask and answer questions.

- When you meet a person whom you will see again, without being introduced by someone else, introduce yourself by name—and get the other person to say their name. Then, as before, call them by name during your conversation. For example, if you get to class early and want to talk, introduce yourself to someone rather than just talking without learning the person's name. If someone you don't know just starts talking to you, introduce yourself.

- When you are in a small group being introduced to people, don't just say hi and ignore the names. Depending on the number of people, you can say hello and repeat each name as you look at the person. If you don't remember a name, ask ("I'm sorry, I didn't get your name"). You may also want to mentally repeat the person's name several times. As you talk to the people in the group, use their names. If you forget a name, listen for others to say it as the discussion continues.

- If you have been introduced to a person and forget their name the next time you meet them, you have two choices. You can apologetically ask them their name. Or, before talking to the person, you can ask someone else for the person's name, then greet them by name. Again, use the person's name during the conversation.

- Use association to help you remember. For example, if you meet John Higby you could picture him hugging a bee. If the person's name is Ted, picture him with the body of a teddy bear. If you know the person likes something, say tennis, picture them with a tennis ball on their head. Think of other people you know who have the same name and make an association.

- Ask for a business card, or ask for the person's telephone number so you can write it down, to help remember the name. In business, it's a good idea to carry a pen and some small pieces of paper, such as your own business cards or a few 3 × 5 cards for taking notes.

- Write down the person's name and some information about them after you meet them. Sales representatives use this technique very effectively to recall personal information they may forget. If you are on a committee with people you don't know and don't see very often, use the membership list of names (or write them yourself). Then write an association for each person, so that you can identify all members (this may be done during the meeting without drawing attention). Your notes might include personal characteristics (tall, thin, dark hair) or something about their work (marketing, engineer). Then, before the next meeting, review the list of

names and characteristics so you can make the association and greet each person by name.

Doing Skill-Development Exercise 1 in Class

Procedure 1 (5–8 minutes)
Break into groups of five or six, preferably with people you do not know. In the group, have each member give his or her name and two or three significant things about himself or herself. After all the members have finished, ask each other questions to get to know each other better.

Procedure 2 (2–4 minutes)
Can anyone in the group call the others by name? If so, he or she should do so. If not, have each member repeat his or her name. Follow with each member calling all members by name. Be sure that each person has a turn to call everyone by name.

Procedure 3 (5–8 minutes)
Select a person to play the spokesperson role for your group. Remember, this is a leadership course. The spokesperson writes down questions in the following two areas:

- *Course:* Is there anything more that you want to know about the course, such as any expectations or concerns that you have?
- *Instructor:* Make a list of questions for the instructor in order to get to know him or her better.

Procedure 4 (10–20 minutes)
Each spokesperson asks the instructor one question at a time, until all questions are asked. If time permits, people who are not the spokesperson may ask questions.

Conclusion
The instructor may make concluding remarks.

Apply It (2–4 minutes)
What did I learn from this experience? How will I use this knowledge in the future? Specifically state which tip for remembering names you will use in the future. Identify precisely when you will practice this skill. (For example, on *x* day/date when I go to class—or to work, or to a party—I will introduce myself to someone I don't know.)

_____

_____

_____

Sharing

In the group, or to the entire class, volunteers may give their answers to the "Apply It" questions.

Self-Assessment 2

Names

On the line before each statement, write Y for yes, or N for no.

_____ 1. I enjoy meeting new people.

_____ 2. I'm good at remembering people's names.

_____ 3. When I meet new people, I learn their names and call them by name.

_____ 4. I'm interested in and willing to improve my ability to remember and use names.

If you answered yes to questions 1–3, you have developed some skill in this area. Your answer to question 4 indicates whether you intend to further develop your skill. The choice is yours.

Skill-Development Exercise 2

Identifying Leadership Traits and Behaviors

Objective
To gain a better understanding of leadership traits and behavior.

Preparing for Skill-Development Exercise 2

Read and understand the trait and behavioral leadership theories. On the following lines, list specific traits and behaviors that you believe effective leaders have or should have. Your answers may or may not be based on your observation of successful leaders.

Traits: _____

Behaviors: _____

Doing Skill-Development Exercise 2 in Class

Option 1 (5–15 minutes)
Students give their answers to the instructor, who writes them on the board under the heading of _traits_ or _behaviors_. During or after answers are listed, the class may discuss them.

Option 2 (10–20 minutes)
Break into groups of five or six, and select a leader to perform the spokesperson role (remember this is a leadership class). The spokesperson records the answers of the group, then writes them on the board (5–10 minutes). The instructor leads a class discussion (5–10 minutes).

Leadership Traits and Ethics

2

LEARNING OUTCOMES

After studying this chapter, you should be able to:

1. List the benefits of classifying personality traits. p.31
2. Describe the Big Five personality dimensions. p.32
3. Explain the universality of traits of effective leaders. p.35
4. Discuss why the trait of dominance is so important for managers to have. p.36
5. State how the Achievement Motivation Theory and the Leader Profile are related and different. p.42
6. Identify similarities and differences among Theory X and Theory Y, the Pygmalion effect, and self-concept. p.48
7. Describe how attitudes are used to develop four leadership styles. p.53
8. Compare the three levels of moral development. p.56
9. Explain the stakeholder approach to ethics. p.61
10. Define the following **key terms** (in order of appearance in the chapter):

traits
personality
Big Five Model of Personality
surgency personality dimension
agreeableness personality
  dimension
adjustment personality dimension
conscientiousness personality
  dimension
openness-to-experience
  personality dimension
personality profiles
self-awareness
social awareness
self-management
relationship management
Achievement Motivation Theory

Leader Motive Profile Theory
Leader Motive Profile (LMP)
attitudes
Theory X and Theory Y
Pygmalion effect
self-concept
ethics
moral justification
displacement of responsibility
diffusion of responsibility
advantageous comparison
disregard or distortion of
  consequences
attribution of blame
euphemistic labeling
stakeholder approach
  to ethics

Opening Case Application

Lorraine Monroe was the principal of Harlem's Frederick Douglass Academy from 1991 to 1997. When Monroe started the new high school, the goal was to create a special college preparatory high school. The prior school was well known for its violence, its poor attendance, and its persistently low level of academic achievement. Within five years, student test scores ranked among New York City's best, and 96 percent of the school's graduates went on to college. How did she turn an inner city school around? Through great leadership. Monroe restored order and discipline primarily through her "Twelve Non-Negotiable Rules," which are based on respect for oneself, for one's associates, and for property.

In order to develop school administrators' leadership skills, she founded the School Leadership Academy at the Center for Educational Innovation in 1997. She went on to found the Lorraine Monroe Leadership Institute (LMLI) in July 2001. She is its director and continues to consult to develop leaders. Monroe is the author of *Nothing's Impossible: Leadership Lessons from Inside and Outside the Classroom* and *The Monroe Doctrine: An ABC Guide to What Great Bosses Do*.

The Lorraine Monroe success story was told on TV (*60 Minutes, Tony Brown's Journal, The McCreary Report*), in magazines (*Ebony, Reader's Digest, Fast Company*) and in several newspapers (including the *New York Times* and the national Sunday supplement *Parade*).[1]

Opening Case Questions:

1. What Big Five personality traits does Lorraine Monroe possess?
2. Which traits of effective leaders does Lorraine Monroe possess?
3. Does Lorraine Monroe have the personality profile of an effective leader? And what does she say in response to businesspeople who continually ask her, "What makes a good leader"?
4. How did "attitude" help change the performance of Frederick Douglass Academy?
5. How did Lorraine Monroe's self-concept affect her leadership?
6. What role did ethics play in changing the performance of Frederick Douglass Academy?

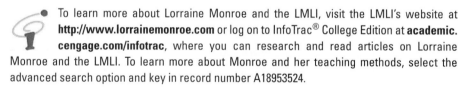 To learn more about Lorraine Monroe and the LMLI, visit the LMLI's website at **http://www.lorrainemonroe.com** or log on to InfoTrac® College Edition at **academic. cengage.com/infotrac**, where you can research and read articles on Lorraine Monroe and the LMLI. To learn more about Monroe and her teaching methods, select the advanced search option and key in record number A18953524.

L orraine Monroe is a strong, entrepreneurial leader. The focus of this chapter is on leadership traits, which includes ethics. We begin by learning about personality traits of leaders and the personality profile of effective leaders. Next we learn how attitudes affect leadership. We end with a discussion of ethics in leadership.

Personality Traits and Leadership

Recall that trait theory of leadership was the foundation for the field of leadership studies.[2] Trait theory is still being studied.[3] The original study of trait theory was called the *Great Man (Person) Approach*, which sought to identify the traits effective leaders possessed. Trait researchers examined personality, physical abilities, and social- and work-related characteristics.[4] Substantial progress in the development of personality theory and traits has been made since the early 1980s.[5] In this section we discuss traits and personality, the Big Five Model of Personality, reasons why executives fail, and the traits of effective leaders.

Before you learn about personality traits, complete Self-Assessment 1 to determine your personality profile. Throughout this chapter, you will gain a better understanding of your personality traits, which help explain why people do the things they do (behavior).

Self-Assessment 1

Personality Profile

There are no right or wrong answers, so be honest and you will really increase your self-awareness. We suggest doing this exercise in pencil or making a copy before you write on it. We will explain why later.

Using the scale below, rate each of the 25 statements according to how accurately it describes you. Place a number from 1 to 7 on the line before each statement.

Like me		Somewhat like me			Not like me	
7	6	5	4	3	2	1

____ 1. I step forward and take charge in leaderless situations.

____ 2. I am concerned about getting along well with others.

____ 3. I have good self-control; I don't get emotional, angry, or yell.

____ 4. I'm dependable; when I say I will do something, it's done well and on time.

____ 5. I try to do things differently to improve my performance.

____ 6. I enjoy competing and winning; losing bothers me.

____ 7. I enjoy having lots of friends and going to parties.

____ 8. I perform well under pressure.

____ 9. I work hard to be successful.

____ 10. I go to new places and enjoy traveling.

____ 11. I am outgoing and willing to confront people when in conflict.

____ 12. I try to see things from other people's points of view.

____ 13. I am an optimistic person who sees the positive side of situations (the cup is half full).

____ 14. I am a well-organized person.

____ 15. When I go to a new restaurant, I order foods I haven't tried.

____ 16. I want to climb the corporate ladder to as high a level of management as I can.

_____ 17. I want other people to like me and to view me as very friendly.

_____ 18. I give people lots of praise and encouragement; I don't put people down and criticize.

_____ 19. I conform by following the rules of an organization.

_____ 20. I volunteer to be the first to learn and do new tasks at work.

_____ 21. I try to influence other people to get my way.

_____ 22. I enjoy working with others more than working alone.

_____ 23. I view myself as being relaxed and secure, rather than nervous and insecure.

_____ 24. I am considered to be credible because I do a good job and come through for people.

_____ 25. When people suggest doing things differently, I support them and help bring it about; I don't make statements like these: it won't work, we never did it before, no one else ever did it, or we can't do it.

To determine your personality profile: (1) In the blanks, place the number from 1 to 7 that represents your score for each statement. (2) Add up each column—your total should be a number from 5 to 35. (3) On the number scale, circle the number that is closest to your total score. Each column in the chart represents a specific personality dimension.

Surgency			Agreeableness			Adjustment			Conscientiousness			Openness to Experience		
		35			35			35			35			35
		30			30			30			30			30
_____	1.	25	_____	2.	25	_____	3.	25	_____	4.	25	_____	5.	25
_____	6.	20	_____	7.	20	_____	8.	20	_____	9.	20	_____	10.	20
_____	11.	15	_____	12.	15	_____	13.	15	_____	14.	15	_____	15.	15
_____	16.	10	_____	17.	10	_____	18.	10	_____	19.	10	_____	20.	10
_____	21.	5	_____	22.	5	_____	23.	5	_____	24.	5	_____	25.	5
_____	Total	Bar	_____	Total	Bar	_____	Total	Bar	_____	Total	Bar	_____	Total	Bar

The higher the total number, the stronger is the personality dimension that describes your personality. What is your strongest and weakest dimension?

Continue reading the chapter for specifics about your personality in each of the five dimensions.

You may visit **http://ipip.ori.org** to complete a 50- or 100-item Big 5 personality assessment.

Learning Outcome 1

List the benefits of classifying personality traits.

Personality and Traits

Why are some people outgoing and others shy, loud and quiet, warm and cold, aggressive and passive? This list of behaviors is made up of individual traits.[6] **Traits** _are distinguishing personal characteristics._ **Personality** _is a combination of traits that classifies an individual's behavior._ Understanding people's personalities is important because personality affects behavior as well as perceptions and attitudes.[7] Knowing personalities helps you to explain and predict others' behavior and job performance.[8] For a simple example, if you know a person is very shy, you can better understand why they are quiet when meeting new people. You can also predict that the person will be quiet when they go places and meet new people. You can also better understand why the person would not seek a job as a salesperson; and if he or she did, you could predict that the person might not be very successful.

Personality is developed based on genetics and environmental factors. The genes you received before you were born influence your personality traits.[9] Your family, friends, school, and work also influence your personality. There are many personality classification methods. However, the Big Five Model of Personality traits is the most widely accepted way to classify personalities, because of its strong research support.[10]

Learning Outcome 2

Describe the Big Five personality dimensions.

The Big Five Model of Personality

The purpose of the Big Five is to reliably categorize, into one of five dimensions, most if not all of the traits you would use to describe someone else.[11] Thus, each dimension includes multiple traits.[12] *The* **Big Five Model of Personality** *categorizes traits into the dimensions of surgency, agreeableness, adjustment, conscientiousness, and openness to experience.* The dimensions are listed in Exhibit 2-1 and described below. As noted in descriptions, however, some researchers have slightly different names for the five dimensions.[13]

Exhibit 2-1 *Big Five dimensions of traits.*

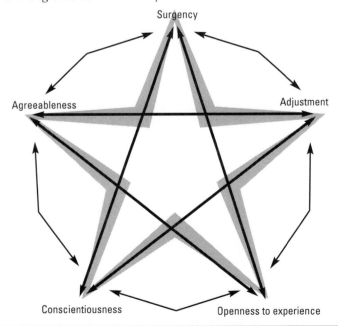

Source: Adapted from T. A. Judge, D. Heller, and M. K. Mount. "Five-Factor Model of Personality and Job Satisfaction: A Meta-Analysis." *Journal of Applied Psychology* 87 (June 2002). 530(12).

Surgency

The **surgency personality dimension** *includes leadership and extraversion traits.* (1) People strong in surgency—more commonly called *dominance*—personality traits want to be in charge. Their dominant behavior ranges from interest in getting ahead and leading through competing and influencing. People weak in surgency want to be followers, and don't want to compete or influence. (2) Extraversion is on a continuum between extravert and introvert. Extraverts are outgoing, like to meet new people, and are willing to confront others, whereas introverts are shy. Review Self-Assessment 1 statements 1, 6, 11, 16, and 21 for examples of surgency traits. How strong is your desire to be a leader?

Agreeableness

Unlike surgency behavior to get ahead of others, the **agreeableness personality dimension** *includes traits related to getting along with people.* Agreeable personality behavior is strong when a person is called warm, easygoing, compassionate, friendly, and sociable; it is weak when a person is called cold, difficult, uncompassionate, unfriendly, and unsociable. Strongly agreeable personality types are sociable, spend most of their time with people, and have lots of friends. Review Self-Assessment 1 statements 2, 7, 12, 17, and 22 for examples of agreeableness traits. How important is having good relationships to you?

Adjustment

The **adjustment personality dimension** *includes traits related to emotional stability.* Adjustment is on a continuum between being emotionally stable and unstable. *Stable* refers to self-control, being calm—good under pressure, relaxed, secure, and positive—praising others; *unstable* is out of control—poor under pressure, nervous, insecure, and negative—criticizing others. Review Self-Assessment 1 statements 3, 8, 13, 18, and 23 for examples of adjustment traits. How emotionally stable are you?

Conscientiousness

The **conscientiousness personality dimension** *includes traits related to achievement.* Conscientiousness is also on a continuum between responsible/dependable to irresponsible/undependable. Other traits of high conscientiousness include credibility, conformity, and organization. People with this trait are characterized as willing to work hard and put in extra time and effort to accomplish goals to achieve success.[14] Review Self-Assessment 1 statements 4, 9, 14, 19, and 24 for examples of conscientiousness. How strong is your desire to be successful?

Openness to Experience

The **openness-to-experience personality dimension** *includes traits related to being willing to change and try new things.* People strong in openness to experience seek change and trying new things, while those with a weak openness dimension avoid change and new things. Review Self-Assessment 1 statements

5, 10, 15, 20, and 25 for examples of openness-to-experience traits. How willing are you to change and try new things?

Personality Profiles

Personality profiles *identify individual stronger and weaker traits.* Students completing Self-Assessment 1 tend to have a range of scores for the five dimensions. Review your personality profile. Do you have higher scores (stronger traits) on some dimensions and lower scores (weaker traits) on others?

Personality profiles are used to categorize people as a means of predicting job success.[15] Many organizations (such as the National Football League teams, including the Giants, 49ers, and Dolphins) give personality tests to ensure a proper match between the worker and the job. For example, a study revealed that personality profiles of engineers and accountants tended to be lower in the trait of surgency but higher in the trait of dependability. Marketing and salespeople were lower in dependability but higher in surgency.[16] Forty percent of organizations give personality tests to determine if a person has the personality profile that can predict job success.[17]

The Big Five model has universal application across cultures. Studies have shown that people from Asian, Western European, Middle Eastern, Eastern European, and North and South American cultures seem to use the same five personality dimensions. However, some cultures do place varying importance on different personality dimensions. Overall, the best predictor of job success on a global basis is the conscientiousness dimension.[18]

WorkApplication1

Select a present or past manager, and describe his or her personality profile using each of the Big Five dimensions. After rating each dimension as strong, moderate, or weak, give an example of traits and typical behavior of the manager for each dimension. Which dimensions are strongest and weakest?

_____

_____

_____

_____

_____

Applying the Concept 1

Personality Dimensions
Identify each of these seven traits/behaviors by its personality dimension. Write the appropriate letter in the blank before each item.

a. surgency
b. agreeableness
c. adjustment
d. conscientiousness
e. openness to experience

_____ 1. The manager is influencing the follower to do the job the way the leader wants it done.

_____ 2. The sales representative submitted the monthly expense report on time as usual.

_____ 3. The leader is saying a warm, friendly good morning to followers as they arrive at work.

_____ 4. The leader is seeking ideas from followers on how to speed up the flow of work.

_____ 5. As a follower is yelling a complaint, the leader calmly explains what went wrong.

_____ 6. The leader is being very quiet when meeting some unexpected visitors in the work unit.

_____ 7. The leader is giving in to a follower to avoid a conflict.

OPENING CASE APPLICATION

1. What Big Five Personality Traits Does Lorraine Monroe Possess?

To a large extent, Lorraine Monroe was a successful founder and leader because of her strong personality in the Big Five: She has a strong need for surgency while being agreeable and well adjusted, yet she is conscientious and open to new experience.

Derailed Leadership Traits

Before we go on to the next section and discuss the traits of effective leaders, let's identify traits that led to leadership failure. A study was conducted that compared 21 derailed executives with 20 executives who had successfully climbed the corporate ladder to the top.[19] The derailed executives had prior success and were expected to go far, but they were passed over for promotion again, were fired, or were forced to retire early. See Exhibit 2-2 for a list of the six major reasons for derailment.

None of the derailed executives had all six weaknesses. Overall, their problem was poor human relations skills; they did not treat people as valuable assets. Derailed executives failed to make the paradigm shift from management to leadership. Destructive narcissistic (adjustment trait) managers cause significant damage to an organization.[20] Greed and resistance to change also lead to failed leadership.[21]

Successful leaders have a range of stronger and weaker dimensions in the Big Five. However, as our definition of leadership indicates, they are relatively strong on all five dimensions and avoid derailment.[22]

You'll learn about the more specific personality profile of successful leaders in the "Leader Motive Profile Theory" section of this chapter. But first, let's identify specific traits of effective leaders.

WorkApplication2

Select a present or past manager, and state whether he or she has any of the six traits of derailment. Give specific examples of weaknesses.

_____

_____

_____

_____

_____

--- **Learning** Outcome 3 ---

Explain the universality of traits of effective leaders.

Exhibit 2-2 _Why executives are derailed._

- They used a bullying style viewed as intimidating, insensitive, and abrasive.
- They were viewed as being cold, aloof, and arrogant.
- They betrayed personal trust.
- They were self-centered and viewed as overly ambitious and thinking of the next job.
- They had specific performance problems with the business.
- They overmanaged and were unable to delegate or build a team.

Traits of Effective Leaders

Researchers who were not concerned with personality or a system of categorizing traits wanted to identify a list of traits that effective leaders have. There appear to be some traits that consistently differentiate leaders from others, so trait theory does have some claim to universality.[23] For the theory to be truly universal, all leaders would have to have all the same traits. However, again you should realize that there is no one list of traits accepted by all researchers, and that not all effective leaders have all these traits. In this section, you will learn which traits have strong research support. So if you are not strong on every one, it doesn't mean that you can't be a successful leader. Furthermore, you can develop these traits with some effort.

See Exhibit 2-3 for a list of the nine traits. In the following paragraphs, we will categorize each trait using the Big Five.

Learning Outcome 4

Discuss why the trait of dominance is so important for managers to have.

Dominance

Dominance, which we called leadership, is one of the two major traits of the *surgency* Big Five section. Successful leaders want to be managers and to take charge.[24] However, they are not overly bossy, nor do they use a bullying style. If a person does not want to be a leader, chances are they will not be an effective manager. Thus, the dominance trait affects all the other traits related to effective leaders. For example, if you push people into management positions, there is a high probability that they will lack self-confidence and not have much energy for the job. Due to the pressure of the job they don't want, they may also not be stable in the position or sensitive to others, and the trait of intelligence may be questioned. To reach full leadership potential, you've got to want to be a leader, work to develop your skills, and enjoy it.[25]

High Energy

Leaders have drive and work hard to achieve goals.[26] They have stamina and tolerate stress well. Leaders have enthusiasm and don't give up. They deal with

---

Exhibit 2-3 *Traits of effective leaders.*

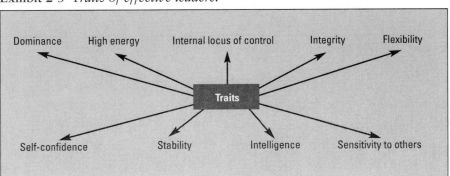

but don't accept setbacks.[27] However, they are not viewed as pushy and obnoxious. They have a high tolerance for frustration as they strive to overcome obstacles through preparation. Leaders take initiative to bring about improvements rather than ask permission; they don't have to be told what to do.[28] High energy is best categorized as the *conscientiousness* dimension of the Big Five. Do you have a high energy level?

Self-Confidence

Self-confidence, on a continuum from strong to weak, indicates whether you are self-assured in your judgments, decision making, ideas, and capabilities. Leaders display self-assurance about their abilities and foster confidence among followers.[29] As leaders gain their followers' respect, they also influence them.

Self-confidence influences individual goals, efforts, and task persistence. Without strong self-confidence, leaders are less likely to attempt to influence followers, to take on difficult tasks, and to set challenging objectives for themselves and followers.[30] Self-confidence is positively related to effectiveness and is a predictor of advancement to higher levels of management.[31]

Leaders are, however, realistically self-confident;[32] they are not viewed as arrogant "know it alls" who alienate people. Self-confidence is best categorized as the *conscientiousness* Big Five dimension, because people who are dependable often have high self-confidence and high energy. Even though most people with a high surgency dimension have self-confidence, not all people with self-confidence want to be managers. People with strong self-confidence also often, but not always, have strong *adjustment* traits. Are you self-confident?

Locus of Control

Locus of control is on a continuum between external and internal belief in control over one's destiny. Externalizers believe that they have no control over their fate and that their behavior has little to do with their performance. They generally have lower levels of performance. Internalizers (leaders) believe that they control their fate and that their behavior directly affects their performance.[33] Leaders take responsibility for who they are, for their behavior and performance, and for the performance of their organizational unit. Internalizers tend to be future oriented, setting objectives and developing plans to accomplish them. They are usually self-confident and learn from their mistakes, rather than blaming others or just bad luck.[34] The Big Five category is the *openness-to-experience* dimension. Externalizers (followers) are generally reluctant to change. Are you more of an internalizer or an externalizer?

Stability

Stability, the *adjustment* Big Five dimension, is associated with managerial effectiveness and advancement. Stable leaders are emotionally in control of themselves, secure, and positive.[35] Unfortunately, there are some unstable leaders[36]—such as Adolph Hitler—who misuse power. It has also been shown that effective leaders have a good understanding of their own strengths and weaknesses, and they are oriented toward self-improvement rather than being defensive.[37] This

WorkApplication3

Select a present or past manager. For that person, decide which of the following traits is or was strongest and weakest: dominance, high energy, self-confidence, internal locus of control, and stability. Explain your answers.

_____

_____

_____

_____

_____

relates to effective leaders knowing when to lead and when to follow; they compensate for weaknesses by letting others with the strength lead in those areas. If you are an internalizer, you will tend to believe this; and if you are conscientious, you will work to improve yourself and advance.

Integrity

Integrity refers to behavior that is honest and ethical, making a person trustworthy.[38] Ethics will be discussed later in this chapter. Honesty refers to truthfulness rather than deception.[39] Honesty is nearly always the best policy; many believe that integrity is the most important asset you can possess.[40] Trustworthiness is an important part of business success; trusting relationships are at the heart of profit making and sustainability in the global knowledge-based economy.[41] Honesty and trust are so important at CompUSA that any employee caught telling a lie is fired immediately; according to the CEO, "We all trust each other."[42]

The ability to influence is based on integrity. Followers must trust the leader. Unless you are perceived to be trustworthy, it is difficult to retain the loyalty of followers or to obtain cooperation and support from peers and superiors.[43] To be viewed as trustworthy, leaders need to be honest, support their followers, and keep confidences.[44] If followers find out their leader has lied or in some way manipulated them for personal gain, changed his or her mind after making a decision, blamed others for a poor decision, taken credit for followers' work or given blame that is unjust, or betrayed confidences, then the leader will lose the followers' trust. Recall that these negative types of behaviors lead to executive derailment. Integrity is so important at GE that it is its core value. Former CEO Jack Welch told employees to do everything with integrity. Integrity is categorized as the Big Five dimension of *conscientiousness*. Do you have integrity?

Ethical Dilemma 1

Downsizing and Part-Time Workers

As firms struggle to compete in the global economy, many have downsized.[45] *Downsizing* is the process of cutting resources to get more done with less to increase productivity. The primary area of cutting is human resources, and many laid-off factory workers find their jobs drying up for good.[46] With downsizing, many firms are using new structures that have fewer levels of management.[47] In some firms, downsized full-time employees are replaced with part-time workers.

Another method of keeping costs down is to use part-time employees that do not receive benefits (i.e., health care), rather than full-time employees with benefits. Wal-Mart is known for having a very heavy ratio of part- to full-time employees to keep costs down. Wal-Mart is expanding its sales of grocery items, competing directly with supermarket chains. One of the reasons Wal-Mart has lower prices is because it uses mostly part-time workers at minimum wage, or close, without benefits. Most supermarket chain employees are

(Continued)

Ethical Dilemma 1

(*Continued*)

unionized and get higher wages and more benefits. In 2003 into 2004, supermarket workers were on strike in California to keep higher wages and benefits. The supermarket chain stated that it can't afford wage and benefits increases, as it must compete with Wal-Mart.

1. Do you view Wal-Mart as a company with integrity?
2. Is downsizing ethical and socially responsible?
3. Is using part-time employees, rather than full-time, ethical and socially responsible?

Intelligence

Leaders generally have above-average intelligence. *Intelligence* refers to cognitive ability to think critically, to solve problems, and to make decisions. Organizations are investing heavily in developing their intellectual capital, as they train people to think critically and creatively.[48]

Contemporary research on intelligence offers renewed potential for leadership trait research. The notion of multiple intelligence has implications for managerial roles, meaning that differences in cognitive abilities between leaders and nonleaders may well go beyond conventional intelligence quotient (IQ) measures.[49] Simply, multiple intelligence means that people are better at some things than others. Intelligence has been categorized with the Big Five *openness-to-experience* dimension. Being in college implies that you most likely have above-average intelligence. This is one reason why most college graduates get better jobs and are paid more than those who do not go to (or finish) college.

Emotional Intelligence

An offshoot of IQ is EQ (emotional quotient or intelligence—EI), which is clearly related to the Big Five personality dimension of *adjustment*. EQ is the ability to work well with people. People's emotions both on and off the job affect human relations at work. September 11, 2001 brought out emotions in the workplace. EQ is a hot management topic today because emotions affect job performance.[50] Many organizations, including Intel, Sun Microsystems, Netscape, Advanced Micro Devices, and Lucent Technologies, have their employees attend EQ training programs to build better relationships.

Jeff Taylor, founder of Monster.com, and Matt Goldman, cofounder of Blue Man Group, recommend developing your people skills, or your EQ.[51] It has been said, "IQ gets you the job, EQ gets you promoted."[52] There are four components of EQ:[53]

- **Self-awareness** *relates to being conscious of your emotions and how they affect your personal and professional life.* Using your "gut feelings" can help you make decisions. Some believe that self-awareness is the greatest predictor of success in everything we do.[54] Use your self-awareness to accurately assess your strengths and limitations, which leads to higher self-confidence.

- **Social awareness** *relates to the ability to understand others.* Steve Case, cofounder of America Online, recommends developing your empathy skills.[55] Empathy is the ability to put yourself in other people's situations, sense their emotions, and understand things from their perspective. Successful leaders can deal with a diversity of people with different points of view and feelings, including personalities that are not emotionally stable.[56] Social awareness also includes the ability to develop networks and play organizational politics, which we discuss in Chapter 4.
- **Self-management** *relates to the ability to control disruptive emotions.* Successful leaders don't let negative emotions (worry, anxiety, fear, anger) interfere with getting things done effectively.[57] Characteristics of self-management include: self-motivation, integrity/trustworthiness, conscientiousness, adaptability, and optimism. You need to be optimistic despite obstacles, setbacks, and failure. Optimism can be learned,[58] so think and be positive.
- **Relationship management** *relates to their ability to work well with others,* which is dependent on the other three EQ components. Successful leaders build effective relationships by communicating, responding to emotions, handling conflict, and influencing others. Most of this book focuses on developing relationship management skills.

These four components of EQ explain the way we manage emotions. How high is your EQ?

Flexibility

Flexibility refers to the ability to adjust to different situations. Recall that leaders who set objectives and possess the ability to influence others bring about change. Leaders need to stay ahead of the immense changes in the world, and the pace of change will continue to increase. Without flexibility, leaders would be successful only in the limited situations that fit their style of leadership. Thus effective leaders are flexible and adapt to the situation. Cynthia Danaher, general manager of the Hewlett-Packard Medical Products Group, says, "Change is painful, and someone may have to be the bad guy. You need to charge ahead, accepting that not everyone will follow and that some won't survive."[59] Flexibility is categorized with the Big Five *openness-to-experience* dimension. Are you flexible?

Sensitivity to Others

Sensitivity to others refers to understanding group members as individuals, what their positions on issues are, and how best to communicate with and influence them. To be sensitive to others requires empathy. In today's global economy, companies need people-centered leaders, because financial success is increasingly being based on the commitment to management practices that treat people as valuable assets.[60]

Lack of sensitivity is part of the reason for executive derailment. You need to have and convey an interest in other people. Sensitivity means not focusing on putting yourself first and remembering that often the more you give away, the more you have. Sensitivity is critical when playing the negotiator leadership role. If you are concerned only about yourself and don't understand what the

WorkApplication4

Select a present or past manager. For that person, decide which of the following traits is or was strongest and weakest: integrity, intelligence, flexibility, and sensitivity to others. Explain your answers.

_____

_____

_____

_____

_____

other party wants, you probably will not be very successful. You will learn how to negotiate in Chapter 4. Sensitivity to others is categorized as the Big Five dimension of *agreeableness*. Are you sensitive to others?

Personality Traits of Effective Leaders

Identify each of the following eight behaviors by its trait. The leader may be behaving effectively, or the behavior may be the opposite of the effective trait behavior. Write the appropriate letter in the blank before each item.

a. dominance
b. high energy
c. self-confidence

d. internal locus of control
e. stability
f. integrity

g. intelligence
h. flexibility
i. sensitivity to others

_____ 8. The leader is engaged in getting the production line working.

_____ 9. The leader is acting very nervously while she is disciplining an employee.

_____ 10. The leader tells a follower that he can have Tuesday off next week. But the next day, the leader tells the follower that he has changed his mind.

_____ 11. The leader very attentively listens to the follower complain, then paraphrases the complaint back to the follower.

_____ 12. The leader in situation 1 is still working to solve the problem; it's her fifth attempt.

_____ 13. The leader is telling her manager that her unit's poor performance is not her fault; she says that the employees are lazy and there's nothing she can do to improve performance.

_____ 14. The leader is telling his manager that his department is right on schedule to meet the deadline, hoping that he can catch up before the boss finds out.

_____ 15. The leader assigns a task to one follower, giving him very specific instructions. Then the leader gives another assignment to a different follower, telling her to complete the task any way she wants to.

Applying the Concept 2

2. What Traits of Effective Leaders Does Lorraine Monroe Possess?

She has dominance, high energy, and self-confidence, and she founded and led two leadership institutes and was a high school principal. Monroe is an internalizer (locus of control); she believed she could turn a poorly performing high school into a top performer. The key to Monroe's leadership success in high school was her stability and integrity, and the teachers trusted and followed her to success. She is intelligent, holding a doctorate degree, but she also has emotional intelligence to motivate others to achieve her vision. Monroe is also flexible as shown in her doctrine where she suggests breaking the rules to meet your mission. Her sensitivity to students and faculty was critical to the successful turnaround of Frederick Douglass Academy.

OPENING CASE APPLICATION

The Personality Profile of Effective Leaders

Effective leaders have specific personality traits.[61] McClelland's trait theories of Achievement Motivation Theory and Leader Motive Profile Theory have strong research support and a great deal of relevance to the practice of leadership.[62] Achievement Motivation Theory identifies three major traits, which McClelland calls *needs*. Leader Motive Profile Theory identifies the personality profile of effective leaders. You will learn about both of these theories in this section.

―――――――――――――― Learning Outcome 5 ――――――――――――――

State how the Achievement Motivation Theory and the Leader Motive Profile are related and different.

Achievement Motivation Theory

Achievement Motivation Theory *attempts to explain and predict behavior and performance based on a person's need for achievement, power, and affiliation.* David McClelland originally developed Achievement Motivation Theory in the 1940s.[63] He believes that we have needs and that our needs motivate us to satisfy them. Our behavior is thus motivated by our needs. However, McClelland says this is an unconscious process. He further states that needs are based on personality and are developed as we interact with the environment. All people possess the need for achievement, power, and affiliation, but to varying degrees. One of the three needs tends to be dominant in each one of us and motivates our behavior.

The Need for Achievement (n Ach)

The *need for achievement* is the unconscious concern for excellence in accomplishments through individual efforts. People with strong n Ach tend to have an internal locus of control, self-confidence, and high energy traits. High n Ach is categorized as the Big Five dimension of *conscientiousness*. People with high n Ach tend to be characterized as wanting to take personal responsibility for solving problems. They are goal oriented and set moderate, realistic, attainable goals. They seek challenge, excellence, and individuality; take calculated, moderate risk; desire concrete feedback on their performance, and work hard.[64] People with high n Ach think about ways to do a better job, how to accomplish something unusual or important, and career progression. They perform well in nonroutine, challenging, and competitive situations, while people low in n Ach do not.

McClelland's research showed that only about 10 percent of the U.S. population has a "strong" dominant need for achievement. There is evidence of a correlation between high achievement need and high performance in the general population.[65] People with high n Ach tend to enjoy entrepreneurial-type positions.[66]

The Need for Power (n Pow)

The *need for power* is the unconscious concern for influencing others and seeking positions of authority. People with strong n Pow have the dominance trait and tend to be self-confident with high energy. High n Pow is categorized as the

Big Five dimension of *surgency*. People with a high need for power tend to be characterized as wanting to control the situation, wanting influence or control over others, enjoying competition in which they can win (they don't like to lose), being willing to confront others, and seeking positions of authority and status. People with high n Pow tend to be ambitious and have a lower need for affiliation. They are more concerned about getting their own way (influencing others) than about what others think of them. They are attuned to power and politics as essential for successful leadership.

The Need for Affiliation (n Aff)

The *need for affiliation* is the unconscious concern for developing, maintaining, and restoring close personal relationships. People with strong n Aff have the trait of sensitivity to others. High n Aff is categorized as the Big Five dimension of *agreeableness*. People with high n Aff tend to be characterized as seeking close relationships with others, wanting to be liked by others, enjoying lots of social activities, and seeking to belong; so they join groups and organizations. People with high n Aff think about friends and relationships. They tend to enjoy developing, helping, and teaching others. They seek jobs as teachers, in human resource management, and in other helping professions. People with high n Aff are more concerned about what others think of them than about getting their own way (influencing others). They tend to have a low n Pow; they tend to avoid management because they like to be one of the group rather than its leader.

Your Motive Profile

Note that McClelland does not have a classification for the *adjustment* and *openness-to-experience* Big Five personality dimensions; they are not needs. A person can have a high or low need for achievement, power, and affiliation and be either well adjusted or not, and either open or closed to new experiences. So these two dimensions of personality are ignored in determining the Achievement Motivation Theory personality profile. Complete Self-Assessment 2 to determine your motive profile now.

Knowing a motive profile is useful, because it can explain and predict behavior and performance. For example, if you know people have a high need for affiliation, you can understand why they tend to have friends and get along well with people. You can predict that if they are assigned a job as a mentor, they will enjoy the tasks and display helpful, supportive behavior toward the mentoree and will do a good job. Complete Work Application 5, then read on to determine if you have the motive profile of an effective leader.

Leader Motive Profile Theory

Leader Motive Profile Theory *attempts to explain and predict leadership success based on a person's need for achievement, power, and affiliation motive profile.* McClelland found that effective leaders consistently have the same motive profile, and that Leader Motive Profile (LMP) has been found to be a reliable predictor of leader effectiveness.[67] Let's first define the profile of effective leaders and then discuss why it results in success. *The* **Leader Motive Profile** *includes a high need for power, which is socialized; that is, greater than the need for affiliation and with a moderate need for achievement.* The achievement

WorkApplication5

Explain how your need for achievement, power, and/or affiliation has affected your behavior and performance, or that of someone you work with or have worked with. Give an example of the behavior and performance, and list your predicted motive need.

————————————————

————————————————

————————————————

————————————————

————————————————

Motive Profile

Return to Self-Assessment 1 and place the scores from your Big Five personality profile in the following blanks, next to their corresponding needs. On the number scale, circle your total score for each need.

Need for Achievement (conscientiousness)	Need for Power (surgency)	Need for Affiliation (agreeableness)
35	35	35
30	30	30
25	25	25
20	20	20
15	15	15
10	10	10
5	5	5
Total Score _____	Total Score _____	Total Score _____

There is no right or wrong score for this profile. To interpret your score, check to see if there is much difference between the three need scores. If all three are about the same, one need is not stronger than the others are. If scores vary, one need is higher than the others and is called the stronger or dominant need, and the lower score is the weaker need. You can also have other combinations, such as two stronger and one weaker, or vice versa. Do you have stronger and weaker needs?

score is usually somewhere between the power and affiliation score, and the reason is described below.

Power

Power is essential to leaders because it is a means of influencing followers. Without power, there is no leadership. To be successful, leaders need to want to be in charge and enjoy the leadership role. You will need power to influence your followers, peers, and higher-level managers. You will learn more about how to gain power and be successful in organizational politics in Chapter 4.

Socialized Power

McClelland further identified power as neither good nor bad. It can be used for personal gain at the expense of others (personalized power), or it can be used to help oneself and others (socialized power).[68] Social power is discussed later, with ethics. Effective leaders use socialized power, which includes the traits of sensitivity to others and stability, and is the Big Five *adjustment* dimension. Thus a person with a low need for affiliation can have a high sensitivity to others. McClelland's research supports the reasons for executive derailment, because these negative traits are personalized power. Socialized power is not included in the motive profile, so complete Self-Assessment 3 to determine your motive profile with socialized power.

Achievement Motivation Theory

Identify each of the five behaviors below by its need, writing the appropriate letter in the blank before each item. The person may be behaving based on a strong need, or the behavior may be the opposite, indicating a weak need. Also state how the behavior meets the need and predict the performance.

a. achievement   b. power   c. affiliation

_____ 16. The person is refusing to be the spokesperson for the group.

_____ 17. The person is going to talk to a fellow employee, with whom she had a disagreement earlier in the day, to peacefully resolve the conflict.

_____ 18. The person is working hard to meet a difficult deadline.

_____ 19. An accounting major has volunteered to calculate the financial analysis for the group's case and to make the presentation to the class.

_____ 20. The fellow employee in situation 2 has made up his mind that he will not be the first one to make a move to resolve the conflict with the other person; but when the other party comes to him, he will be receptive.

Applying the Concept 3

Self-Assessment 3

Motive Profile with Socialized Power

Return to Self-Assessment 1 and place the scores from Self-Assessment 2 (your motive profile) in the following blanks. On the number scale, circle your total score.

Need for Achievement (conscientiousness)	Need for Power (surgency)	Socialized Power (adjustment)	Need for Affiliation (agreeableness)
35	35	35	35
30	30	30	30
25	25	25	25
20	20	20	20
15	15	15	15
10	10	10	10
5	5	5	5
Total Score _____	Total Score _____	Total Score _____	Total Score _____

Again, there is no right or wrong score. The adjustment score will give you an idea if your power is more social or personal. Also realize that the questions in Self-Assessment 1 (3, 8, 13, 18, and 23) are not totally focused on social power. Thus, if you believe you have higher sensitivity to others, your score on McClelland's LMP could be higher.

Achievement

To be effective, leaders generally need to have a moderate need for achievement. They have high energy, self-confidence, and openness-to-experience traits, and they are *conscientious* (Big Five dimension). The reason for a moderate rather than high need for achievement, which would include a lower need for power, is the danger of personalized power. People with a high need for achievement tend to seek individual achievement, and when they are not interested in being a leader, there is the chance for personalized power and derailment.

Affiliation

Effective leaders have a lower need for affiliation than power, so that relationships don't get in the way of influencing followers. If the achievement score is lower than that for affiliation, the probability of the following problems occurring may be increased. Leaders with high n Aff tend to have a lower need for power and are thus reluctant to play the bad-guy role, such as when disciplining and influencing followers to do things they would rather not do—like change. They have been found to show favoritism behavior toward their friends. However, recall that effective leaders do have concern for followers—socialized power.

The Leader Motive Profile is included in the definition of leadership. Our definition of leadership includes the five key elements of leadership (Exhibit 1-1) in the LMP. Our definition of leadership includes *influencing* and *leaders-followers* (power) and getting along with *people* (social power). It also includes *organizational objectives* (which achievers set and accomplish well) and *change* (which achievers are open to).

WorkApplication6

Make an intelligent guess about your present or past manager's motive profile. Is it an LMP? Explain.

_____

_____

_____

_____

_____

OPENING CASE APPLICATION

3. Does Lorraine Monroe Have the Personality Profile of an Effective Leader? And What Does She Say in Response to Businesspeople Who Continually Ask Her, "What Makes a Good Leader?"

Lorraine Monroe has an LMP. Her need for power is illustrated through being a school principal and founding tow leadership institutes to train leaders. Monroe has a socialized need for power as she shows concern for students, teachers, and administrators. Her need for achievement leads to continued success. She also has a lower need for affiliation as she set standards for discipline in school, and she consistently observed teachers (although they complained at first), improving their performance.

Businesspeople continually ask Monroe, "What makes a good leader?" Part of her answer is that the leader is the person who keeps a vision in front of people and reminds them of their mission. Leaders need to give employees a sense of purpose beyond a paycheck, the feeling that they can make a difference, and something to be proud of. Leaders have high expectations and demand continuous measurable improvement through creativity. Employees have latent productivity; it is the leader's job to bring it out. Leaders demonstrate their ability. They walk around and watch people do their work and talk to them about improving as they give praise. Leaders treat people well, listen to what they have to say, do nice things for them, and get them together to talk so they feel connected.

Do you have an LMP? Complete Self-Assessment 4 now.

Before we go on and discuss leadership attitudes, let's review what we've covered so far in Exhibit 2-4 by putting together the Big Five Model of Personality, the nine traits of effective leaders, and Achievement Motivation Theory and LMP.

Leadership Attitudes

Attitudes *are positive or negative feelings about people, things, and issues.* There has been considerable interest in how attitudes affect performance, and companies are recruiting workers with positive attitudes.[69] We all have

Self-Assessment 4

Leadership Interest

Select the option that best describes your interest in leadership now.

_____ 1. I am, or want to become, a manager and leader.

_____ 2. I am, or want to become, a leader without being a manager.

_____ 3. I am not interested in being a leader; I want to be a follower.

If you want to be a leader, recall that research has shown that you can develop your leadership skills.

If you selected option 1, do you have an LMP? If you answered yes, it does not guarantee that you will climb the corporate ladder. However, having an LMP does increase your chances, because it is a predictor of leadership success. On the other hand, an LMP is not enough; you need leadership skills to be successful. If your Self-Assessment 3 score doesn't indicate that you have an LMP, go back to Self-Assessment 1 and review questions 1, 6, 11, 16, and 21. Did you score them accurately? The most important question is 16. If you believe you have an LMP, be aware that your profile could be different using McClelland's LMP questionnaire. Also recall that not all successful leaders have an LMP, so you can still be successful.

Developing your leadership skills, through effort, will increase your chances of leadership success.

If you selected option 2, don't be concerned about your LMP. Focus on developing your leadership skills. However, your personality profile can help you to better understand your strengths and weaknesses to identify areas to improve on. This also holds true for people who selected option 1.

If you selected option 3, that's fine. Most people in the general population probably would select this option. Many professionals who have great jobs and incomes are followers, and they have no interest in becoming managers. However, recall that research has shown that leaders and followers need the same skills, that organizations are looking for employees with leadership skills, and that organizations conduct skills training with employees at all levels. To increase your chances of having a successful and satisfying career, you may want to develop your leadership skills. You may someday change your mind about becoming a leader and manager.

Your need for power and LMP can change over time, along with your interest in leadership and management and your skill level, regardless of which option you selected.

Exhibit 2-4 *Combined traits and needs.*

The Big Five Model of Personality	Nine Traits of Effective Leaders	Achievement Motivation Theory and LMP
Surgency	Dominance	Need for power
Agreeableness	Sensitivity to others	Need for affliation
Adjustment	Stability	Socialized power (LMP)
Conscientiousness	High energy Self-confidence Integrity	Need for achievement
Openness to experience	Internal locus of control Intelligence Flexibility	No separate need; included within other needs

favorable or positive attitudes, and unfavorable or negative attitudes about life, leadership, work, school, and everything else.[70]

Optimism is a good predictor of job performance.[71] W. Marriott, Jr., president of Marriott Corporation, stated that the company's success depends more upon employee attitudes than any other single factor. Larry King, host of CNN's *Larry King Live,* says that the right attitude is basic to success. Legendary football coach Lou Holtz says that attitude is the most important thing in this world and that we each choose the attitude we have. So being a positive or negative person is your choice.[72] People with positive, optimistic attitudes generally have a well-adjusted personality profile, and successful leaders have positive, optimistic attitudes. So follow Jack Welch's advice and have a positive attitude to advance.[73]

Like personality traits, attitudes have an important influence on behavior and performance.[74] For example, attitude toward a class or job can be positive or negative. Generally, if you like a class or job, you will attend more often and work harder; but not necessarily. Even if you have a negative attitude toward a class or job, you may still attend and work hard due to other factors, such as your personality traits and motives. If you have a high need for affiliation, and you like the instructor and/or students, you may try hard. If you have a high need for achievement, you may work hard to succeed even with a negative attitude toward the class or job.

In this section, we'll discuss how leadership attitudes relate to Theory X and Theory Y, and how the Pygmalion effect influences followers' behavior and performance. Then we will discuss self-concept and how it affects the leader's behavior and performance. Lastly, we will consider how the leader's attitudes about followers, and about his or her self-concept, affect the leadership style of the leader.

Learning Outcome 6

Identify similarities and differences among Theory X and Theory Y, the Pygmalion effect, and self-concept.

Theory X and Theory Y

Today, **Theory X and Theory Y** *attempt to explain and predict leadership behavior and performance based on the leader's attitude about followers.* Before you read about Theory X and Y, complete Self-Assessment 5.

Douglas McGregor classified attitudes or belief systems, which he called assumptions, as *Theory X* and *Theory Y*.[75] People with Theory X attitudes hold that employees dislike work and must be closely supervised in order to do their work. Theory Y attitudes hold that employees like to work and do not need to be closely supervised in order to do their work. In each of the eight pairs of

Self-Assessment 5

Theory X and Theory Y Attitudes

For each pair of statements distribute 5 points, based on how characteristic each statement is of your attitude or belief system. If the first statement totally reflects your attitude and the second does not, give 5 points to the first and 0 to the second. If it's the opposite, use 0 and 5. If the statement is usually your attitude, then distribution can be 4 and 1, or 1 and 4. If both statements reflect your attitude, the distribution should be 3 and 2, or 2 and 3. Again, the combined score for each pair of statements must equal 5.

Here are the scoring distributions for each pair of statements:

0–5 or 5–0   One of the statements is totally like you, the other not like you at all.
1–4 or 4–1   One statement is usually like you, the other not.
2–3 or 3–2   Both statements are like you, although one is slightly more like you.

____ 1. People enjoy working.

____ People do not like to work.

____ 2. Employees don't have to be closely supervised to do their job well.

____ Employees will not do a good job unless you closely supervise them.

____ 3. Employees will do a task well for you if you ask them to.

____ If you want something done right, you need to do it yourself.

____ 4. Employees want to be involved in making decisions.

____ Employees want the managers to make the decisions.

____ 5. Employees will do their best work if you allow them to do the job their own way.

____ Employees will do their best work if they are taught how to do it the one best way.

____ 6. Managers should let employees have full access to information that is not confidential.

____ Managers should give employees only the information they need to know to do their job.

____ 7. If the manager is not around, the employees will work just as hard.

____ If the manager is not around, the employees will take it easier than when being watched.

____ 8. Managers should share the management responsibilities with group members.

____ Managers should perform the management functions for the group.

To determine your attitude or belief system about people at work, add up the numbers (0–5) for the first statement in each pair; don't bother adding the numbers for the second statements. The total should be between 0 and 40. Place your score on the continuum below.

Theory X 0—5—10—15—20—25—30—35—40 *Theory Y*

Generally, the higher your score, the greater are your Theory Y beliefs, and the lower the score, the greater your Theory X beliefs.

statements in Self-Assessment 5, the first lines are Theory Y attitudes and the second lines are Theory X attitudes.

Managers with Theory X attitudes tend to have a negative, pessimistic view of employees and display more coercive, autocratic leadership styles using external means of controls, such as threats and punishment. Managers with Theory Y attitudes tend to have a positive, optimistic view of employees and display more participative leadership styles using internal motivation and rewards. In 1966 when McGregor published his Theory X and Theory Y, most managers had Theory X attitudes, and he was calling for a change to Theory Y attitudes. More recently, the paradigm shift from management to leadership also reflects this change in attitudes, as more managers use participative leadership styles.[76]

Managers should acknowledge the influence of attitudes on behavior and performance.[77] A study of over 12,000 managers explored the relationship between managerial achievement and attitudes toward subordinates.[78] The managers with Theory Y attitudes were better at accomplishing organizational objectives and better at tapping the potential of subordinates. The managers with strong Theory X attitudes were far more likely to be in the low-achieving group. Your attitudes are important, because your leadership style will spring from your core attitudes about your followers. If you scored higher in Theory X for Self-Assessment 5, it does not mean that you cannot be an effective leader. As with personality traits, you can change your attitudes, with effort.[79] You don't have to be an autocratic leader.

The Pygmalion Effect

The **Pygmalion effect** *proposes that leaders' attitudes toward and expectations of followers, and their treatment of them, explain and predict followers' behavior and performance.* Research by J. Sterling Livingston popularized this theory, and others have supported it as discussed here.[80] We have already talked about attitudes and how they affect behavior (how to treat others) and performance, so let's add expectations. In business, expectations are stated as objectives and standards. Effective leaders set clear standards and expect the best from their followers.[81]

In a study of welding students, the foreman who was training the group was given the names of students who were quite intelligent and would do well. Actually, the students were selected at random. The only difference was the foreman's expectations. The so-called intelligent students did significantly outperform the other group members. Why this happened is what this theory is all about: The foreman's expectations influenced the behavior and performance of the followers.[82]

Lou Holtz advises setting a higher standard; the worst disservice you can do as a coach, teacher, parent, or leader is to say to your followers, "I don't think you are capable of doing very much—so I'm going to lower the standard," or just to do it without saying anything. Lou says there are two kinds of leaders: those who are optimists and lift others up, and those who pull everybody down. If you are in a leadership role, don't worry about being popular (need for affiliation); worry about raising the self-image and productivity of your followers. Having two different teams win the national college football championship within a couple of years after he took the job as head coach shows Lou's ability to set a higher standard.

WorkApplication7

Give an example of when a person (parent, friend, teacher, coach, manager) really expected you either to perform well or to fail, and treated you like you would, which resulted in your success or failure.

_____

_____

_____

_____

_____

4. How Did "Attitude" Help Change the Performance of Frederick Douglass Academy?

A major factor in Lorraine Monroe's turning Harlem's Frederick Douglass Academy from a poor performer into a high performer, with 96 percent of inner-city graduates going on to college, was through her Theory Y attitude and use of the Pygmalion effect. Monroe encouraged her faculty to be creative and try new things. She set higher standards and treated students and teachers like capable winners—which they became.

Self-Concept

So far, we have discussed the leaders' attitudes about followers. Now we will examine leaders' attitudes about themselves. **Self-concept** *refers to the positive or negative attitudes people have about themselves.* If you have a positive view of yourself as being a capable person, you will tend to have the positive self-confidence trait.[83] A related concept, *self-efficacy*, is the belief in your own capability to perform in a specific situation. Self-efficacy is based on self-concept and is closely related to the self-confidence trait, because if you believe you can be successful, you will often have self-confidence.[84]

There is a lot of truth in the saying, "if you think you can you can, if you think you can't you can't." Recall times when you had positive self-efficacy and were successful or negative self-efficacy and failed. Think of sports: sinking a basket, getting a goal or a hit, running a certain distance or time, or lifting a weight. Think of school: passing a test, getting a good grade on an assignment, or getting a certain final grade. Think of work: completing a task, meeting a deadline, making a sale, or solving a problem. Successful leaders have positive attitudes with strong self-concepts, are optimistic, and believe they can make a positive difference.[85] If you don't believe you can be a successful leader, you probably won't be.

5. How Did Lorraine Monroe's Self-Concept Affect Her Leadership?

Lorraine Monroe grew up in Harlem and went to its public schools. Her parents did not go to college, but they did teach her to never doubt that she could do whatever she applied herself to accomplish. If she did not believe she could successfully turn the academy around, things would not have changed. Monroe began her leadership training in school. For example, she served as class president in high school. As stated in her doctrine, "Becoming a leader is an act of self-invention. Imagine yourself as a leader: Act as if you are a leader until you actually become one."

Developing a More Positive Attitude and Self-Concept

Your behavior and performance will be consistent with the way you see your-self.[86] You cannot be an effective leader, or follower, if you don't have a positive self-concept. The environment around us influences our attitudes. Usually we cannot control our environment, but we can control our attitudes.[87] Think and act like a winner, and you may become one. Following are some ideas to help you change your attitudes and develop a more positive self-concept:

1. *Consciously try to have and maintain a positive, optimistic attitude.* If you don't have a positive attitude, it may be caused by your unconscious thoughts and behavior. Only with conscious effort can you improve your self-concept.

2. *Realize that there are few, if any, benefits to negative, pessimistic attitudes about others and yourself.* Do holding a grudge, worrying, and being afraid of failure help you to succeed?

3. *Cultivate optimistic thoughts.* Scientific evidence suggests that your thoughts affect every cell in your body. Every time you think positive thoughts, your body, mind, and spirit respond. You will likely feel more motivated and energetic. Use positive self-talk—I will do a good job; it will be done on time; etc. Also use mental imagery—picture yourself achieving your goal.

4. *If you catch yourself complaining or being negative in any way, stop and change to a positive attitude.* With time, you will catch yourself less often as you become more positive about yourself.[88]

5. *Avoid negative people, especially any that make you feel negative about yourself.* Associate with people who have a positive self-concept, and use their positive behavior.

6. *Set and achieve goals.* Set short-term goals (daily, weekly, monthly) that you can achieve. Achieving specific goals will improve your self-concept, helping you to view yourself as successful.

7. *Focus on your success; don't dwell on failure.* If you achieve five of six goals, dwell on the five and forget the one you missed. We are all going to make mistakes and experience failure. Winston Churchill defined success as the ability to go from failure to failure without losing your enthusiasm. The difference between effective leaders and less-effective leaders is that the successful ones learn from their mistakes.[89] They bounce back from disappointment and don't let it affect them negatively in the future. Lou Holtz says happiness is nothing more than a poor memory for the bad things that happen to you.

8. *Accept compliments.* When someone compliments you, say thank you; it builds self-concept. Don't say things like it was nothing, or anyone could have done it, because you lose the opportunity for a buildup.

9. *Don't belittle accomplishments or compare yourself to others.* If you meet a goal and say it was easy anyway, you are being negative. If you compare yourself to someone else and say they are better, you are being negative. No matter how good you are, there is almost always someone better. So focus on being the best that you can be, rather than putting yourself down for not being the best.

10. *Think for yourself.* Develop your own attitudes based on others' input; don't simply copy others' attitudes.

11. *Be a positive role model.* If the leader has a positive attitude, the followers usually do too.[90]

We can choose to be optimistic or pessimistic—and we usually find what we are looking for. If you look for the positive, you are likely to be happier and get more out of life; why look for the negative and be unhappy? Even when the worst in life happens to you, you have the choice of being positive or negative. Christopher Reeve was a successful film star, best known as Superman, until he fell off a horse and was paralyzed. Rather than being bitter and negative toward life, and sitting at home feeling sorry for himself, Reeve started a foundation (The Christopher Reeve Foundation) to raise money to develop a cure for spinal cord injuries. Reeve raised millions of dollars by getting out and asking for donations. He also starred in a TV movie and was a director. During an interview, he said, "I'm actually busier now than I was before the accident. I find work more fulfilling than ever." When asked how he maintained a positive attitude that kept him going, he said, "I believe you have two choices in life. One is to look forward and the other is to look backwards. To look backwards gets you nowhere. Backwards thinking leads to a place of negativity. That's not where I want to dwell."[91] Hopefully, your disappointments in life will not be so dramatic. But we all have disappointments in life, and we have the choice of going on with a positive or negative attitude. Here's one final tip:

12. *When things go wrong and you're feeling down, do something to help someone who is worse off than you.* You will realize that you don't have it so bad, and you will realize that the more you give, the more you get. Volunteering at a jail, hospital, soup kitchen, or homeless shelter can help change your attitude.

WorkApplication8

Recall a present or past manager. Using Exhibit 2-5, which combinations of attitudes best describe your manager's leadership style? Give examples of the manager's behavior that illustrate his or her attitudes.

_____

_____

_____

_____

_____

――――――――― Learning Outcome 7 ―――――――――

Describe how attitudes are used to develop four leadership styles.

How Attitudes Develop Leadership Styles

We now put together the leader's attitudes toward others, using Theory X and Theory Y, and the leader's attitude toward self, using self-concept, to illustrate how these two sets of attitudes develop into four leadership styles. Combining attitudes with the Leader Motive Profile (LMP), an effective leader tends to have Theory Y attitudes with a positive self-concept. See Exhibit 2-5 to understand how attitudes toward self and others affect leadership styles.

Ethical Leadership

Before we discuss ethical behavior, complete Self-Assessment 6 to find out how ethical your behavior is.

Ethics is an especially hot topic, because it is a major concern to both managers and employees.[92] It is so important that some large organizations have ethics officers who are responsible for developing and implementing ethics codes. Business ethics, and ethics codes, should provide assistance in making

Exhibit 2-5 *Leadership styles based on attitudes.*

	Theory Y Attitudes	Theory X Attitudes
Positive self-concept	The leader typically gives and accepts positive feedback, expects others to succeed, and lets others do the job their way.	The leader typically is bossy, pushy, and impatient, does much criticizing with little praising, and is very autocratic.
Negative self-concept	The leader typically is afraid to make decisions, is unassertive, and self-blaming when things go wrong.	The leader typically blames others when things go wrong, is pessimistic about resolving personal or organizational problems, and promotes a feeling of hopelessness among followers.

Self-Assessment 6

How Ethical Is Your Behavior

For this exercise, you will be using the same set of statements twice. The first time you answer them, focus on your own behavior and the frequency with which you use it for each question. On the line before the question number, place the number 1–4 that represents how often you "did do" the behavior in the past, if you "do the behavior now," or if you "would do" the behavior if you had the chance. These numbers will allow you to determine your level of ethics. You can be honest without fear of having to tell others your score in class. *Sharing ethics scores is not part of the exercise.*

$$\text{Frequently} \qquad \text{Never}$$
$$1 \qquad 2 \qquad 3 \qquad 4$$

The second time you use the same statements, focus on other people in an organization that you work/worked for. Place an "O" on the line after the number if you observed someone doing this behavior. Also place an "R" on the line if you reported (whistleblowing) this behavior within the organization or externally.

O—observed   R—reported

1–4O–R

College

____ 1. ___ Cheating on homework assignments.

____ 2. ___ Cheating on exams.

____ 3. ___ Passing in papers that were completed by someone else, as your own work.

Workplace

____ 4. ___ Lying to others to get what you want or stay out of trouble.

____ 5. ___ Coming to work late, leaving work early, taking long breaks/lunches and getting paid for it.

____ 6. ___ Socializing, goofing off, or doing personal work rather than doing the work that should be done and getting paid for it.

____ 7. ___ Calling in sick to get a day off, when not sick.

____ 8. ___ Using the organization's phone, computer, Internet, copier, mail, car, and so on for personal use.

____ 9. ___ Taking home company tools/equipment without permission for personal use and returning it.

____ 10. ___ Taking home organizational supplies or merchandise and keeping it.

____ 11. ___ Giving company supplies or merchandise to friends or allowing them to take them without saying anything.

____ 12. ___ Putting in for reimbursement for meals and travel or other expenses that weren't actually eaten or taken.

____ 13. ___ Taking spouse/friends out to eat or on business trips and charging it to the organizational expense account.

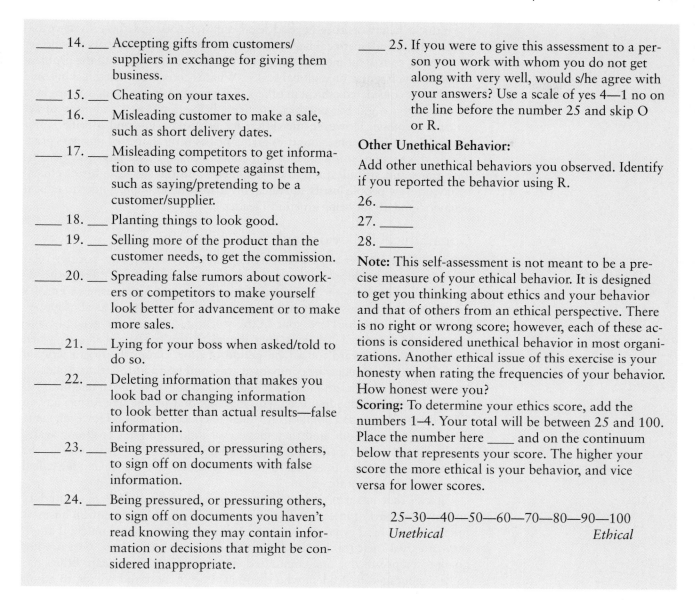

_____ 14. ___ Accepting gifts from customers/ suppliers in exchange for giving them business.

_____ 15. ___ Cheating on your taxes.

_____ 16. ___ Misleading customer to make a sale, such as short delivery dates.

_____ 17. ___ Misleading competitors to get information to use to compete against them, such as saying/pretending to be a customer/supplier.

_____ 18. ___ Planting things to look good.

_____ 19. ___ Selling more of the product than the customer needs, to get the commission.

_____ 20. ___ Spreading false rumors about coworkers or competitors to make yourself look better for advancement or to make more sales.

_____ 21. ___ Lying for your boss when asked/told to do so.

_____ 22. ___ Deleting information that makes you look bad or changing information to look better than actual results—false information.

_____ 23. ___ Being pressured, or pressuring others, to sign off on documents with false information.

_____ 24. ___ Being pressured, or pressuring others, to sign off on documents you haven't read knowing they may contain information or decisions that might be considered inappropriate.

_____ 25. If you were to give this assessment to a person you work with whom you do not get along with very well, would s/he agree with your answers? Use a scale of yes 4—1 no on the line before the number 25 and skip O or R.

Other Unethical Behavior:

Add other unethical behaviors you observed. Identify if you reported the behavior using R.

26. _____

27. _____

28. _____

Note: This self-assessment is not meant to be a precise measure of your ethical behavior. It is designed to get you thinking about ethics and your behavior and that of others from an ethical perspective. There is no right or wrong score; however, each of these actions is considered unethical behavior in most organizations. Another ethical issue of this exercise is your honesty when rating the frequencies of your behavior. How honest were you?

Scoring: To determine your ethics score, add the numbers 1–4. Your total will be between 25 and 100. Place the number here _____ and on the continuum below that represents your score. The higher your score the more ethical is your behavior, and vice versa for lower scores.

25–30—40—50—60—70—80—90—100
Unethical   _Ethical_

ethical decisions.[93] However, you cannot go too many days without hearing or reading, in the mass media, some scandal related to unethical and/or unlawful behavior. **Ethics** _are the standards of right and wrong that influence behavior._ Right behavior is considered ethical, and wrong behavior is considered unethical.

Government laws and regulations are designed to help keep business honest. After the unethical and illegal business practices of WorldCom, Enron, and Arthur Andersen, Congress passed the Sarbanes-Oxley Act of 2002 to help ensure that complaints about financial irregularities would surface and be swiftly acted upon, without retaliation against the person who exposed the unethical behavior ("whistle-blower").[94] However, we can't depend on the government to make people ethical.[95]

Ethical behavior goes beyond legal requirements and the difference between ethical and unethical behavior is not always clear because there is no set of rational, consistent moral principles within one country,[96] and the problem becomes much worse on a global scale.[97]What is considered unethical in some countries is considered ethical in others. For example, in the United States, it is ethical to give a gift but unethical to give a bribe (a gift as a condition of acquiring business). However, the difference between a gift and a bribe is not always clear-cut. In some countries giving bribes is the standard business practice. In this section, you will learn that ethical behavior does pay; how personality traits and attitudes, moral development, and the situation affect ethical behavior; how people justify unethical behavior; some simple guides to ethical behavior, and about being an ethical leader.

Does Ethical Behavior Pay?

Generally, the answer is yes. Research studies have reported a positive relationship between ethical behavior and leadership effectiveness.[98] From the societal level of analysis, the public has a negative image of big business. Enron's unethical behavior cost many organizations and people a great deal of money directly, but it also hurt everyone in the stock market, and the general economy, as the unethical behavior contributed to the bear market (i.e., when stocks trend downward for a long period of time). From the organizational level, Enron is no longer the company it was, and its auditor Arthur Andersen lost many of its clients and had to sell most of its business due to unethical behavior. From the individual level, you may say that people like former Enron CEO Kenneth Lay made millions for their unethical behavior. However, some could end up in prison, and they may never hold high-level positions again. With all the negative media coverage, unethical leaders' lives will never be the same. Unfortunately, greed has destroyed leaders. Mahatma Gandhi called business without morality a sin.

Recall that integrity is an important trait of effective leaders, and ethics and trust are part of integrity. The Enron scandal and other unethical business practices have bred cynicism as many employees question how much, if at all, they can trust their top bosses. Employees who don't trust their boss are not going to be productive and committed employees.[99] Talk is cheap. Ethics has to be encouraged by leaders who themselves are honest and willing to admit their mistakes. Effective managers lead by example and reward integrity in others.[100]

Learning Outcome 8

Compare the three levels of moral development.

How Personality Traits and Attitudes, Moral Development, and the Situation Affect Ethical Behavior

Personality Traits and Attitudes

Our ethical behavior is related to our individual needs and personality traits.[101] Leaders with surgency (dominance) personality traits have two choices: to use power for personal benefit or to use socialized power. To gain power and to be conscientious with high achievement, some people will use unethical behavior;[102] also, irresponsible people often do not perform to standard by cutting corners and other behavior which may be considered unethical. An agreeableness personality sensitive to others can lead to following the crowd in either ethical or unethical behavior; having a high self-concept tends to lead to doing what the person believes is right and not following the crowd's unethical behavior. Emotionally unstable people and those with external locus of control (they do not take personal responsibility for their behavior—it is not their fault) are more likely to use unethical behavior. Being ethical is part of integrity. People open to new experiences are often ethical. People with positive attitudes about ethics tend to be more ethical than those with negative or weak attitudes about ethics.

Moral Development

A second factor affecting ethical behavior is *moral development*, which refers to understanding right from wrong and choosing to do the right thing. Our ability to make ethical choices is related to our level of moral development. There are three levels of personal moral development, as discussed in Exhibit 2-6. At the first level, preconventional, you choose right and wrong behavior based on your

Exhibit 2-6 *Levels of moral development.*

---

3. Postconventional

Behavior is motivated by universal principles of right and wrong, regardless of the expectations of the leader or group. One seeks to balance the concerns for self with those of others and the common good. Will follow ethical principles even if they violate the law at the risk of social rejection, economic loss, and physical punishment (Martin Luther King, Jr., broke what he considered unjust laws and spent time in jail seeking universal dignity and justice).

"I don't lie to customers because it is wrong."

The common leadership style is visionary and committed to serving others and a higher cause while empowering followers to reach this level.

---

2. Conventional

Living up to expectations of acceptable behavior defined by others motivates behavior to fulfill duties and obligations. It is common for followers to copy the behavior of the leaders and group. If the group (can be society/organization/department) accepts lying, cheating, stealing, etc., when dealing with customers/ suppliers/government/competitors, so will the individual. On the other hand, if these behaviors are not accepted, the individual will not do them either. Peer pressure is used to enforce group norms.

"I lie to customers because the other sales reps do it too."

It is common for lower-level managers to use a similar leadership style of the higher-level managers.

---

1. Preconventional

Self-interest motivates behavior to meet ones' own needs to gain rewards while following rules and being obedient to authority to avoid punishment.

"I lie to customers to sell more products and get higher commission checks."

The common leadership style is autocratic towards others while using one's position for personal advantage.

| **WorkApplication9** |

Give an organizational example of behavior at each of the three levels of moral development.

_____

_____

_____

_____

_____

Source: Adapted from Lawrence Kohlberg, "Moral Stages and Moralization: The Cognitive-Development Approach." In Thomas Likona (ed.), *Moral Development and Behavior: Theory, Research, and Social Issues* (Austin, TX: Holt, Rinehart and Winston, 1976), 31–53.

self-interest and the consequences (reward and punishment). With ethical reasoning at the second level, conventional, you seek to maintain expected standards and live up to the expectations of others. At the third level, postconventional, you make an effort to define moral principles regardless of leader or group ethics. Although most of us have the ability to reach the third level of moral development, postconventional, only about 20 percent of people reach this level. Most people behave at the second level, conventional, while some have not advanced beyond the first level, preconventional. How do you handle peer pressure? What level of moral development are you on? What can you do to further develop your ethical behavior? We will discuss how to be an ethical leader.

The Situation

Our third factor affecting ethical behavior is the situation. Highly competitive and unsupervised situations increase the odds of unethical behavior. Unethical behavior occurs more often when there is no formal ethics policy or code of ethics, and when unethical behavior is not punished, and it is especially prevalent when it is rewarded. People are also less likely to report unethical behavior (blow the whistle) when they perceive the violation as not being serious and when the offenders are their friends.[103]

To tie the three factors affecting ethical behavior together, we need to realize that personality traits and attitudes and moral development interact with the situation to determine if a person will use ethical or unethical behavior.[104] In this chapter we use the individual level of analysis, meaning: Am I ethical, and how can I improve my ethical behavior? At the organizational level, many firms offer training programs and develop codes of ethics to help employees behave ethically. The organizational level of analysis is examined in Part III of this book; therefore, ethics and whistle-blowing will be further discussed in Chapter 10.

OPENING CASE APPLICATION

6. What Role Did Ethics Play in Changing the Performance of Frederick Douglass Academy?

As discussed thus far, Lorraine Monroe possesses the traits and attitudes of effective leaders; therefore we can assume that she uses ethical behavior. Monroe is on the postconventional level of moral development. During her consulting, ethics is an important issue. As a school principal, in her "Twelve Non-Negotiable Rules," Monroe made it clear what ethical behavior was and rewarded it, and what unethical behavior was and punished it. Ethics played a role in transforming Frederick Douglass Academy.

How People Justify Unethical Behavior

Most people understand right and wrong behavior and have a conscience. So why do good people do bad things? When most people use unethical behavior, it is not due to some type of character flaw or being born a bad person. Few people see themselves as unethical. We all want to view ourselves in a positive manner. Therefore, when we do use unethical behavior, we often justify the behavior to protect our self-concept so that we don't have a guilty conscience or feel remorse. Let's discuss several thinking processes used to justify unethical behavior.[105]

Moral justification *is the process of reinterpreting immoral behavior in terms of a higher purpose.* The terrorists of 9/11 killed innocent people, as do suicide bombers, yet they believe their killing is for the good and that they will go to heaven for their actions. People state that they have conducted unethical behavior (lie about a competitor to hurt its reputation, fix prices, steal confidential information, etc.) for the good of the organization or employees.[106]

People at the postconventional level of moral development may seek higher purpose (Martin Luther King, Jr.), as well as those at lower levels. However, people at the preconventional and conventional levels of moral development more commonly use the following justifications.

- **Displacement of responsibility** *is the process of blaming one's unethical behavior on others.* "I was only following orders, my boss told me to inflate the figures."
- **Diffusion of responsibility** *is the process of the group using the unethical behavior with no one person being held responsible.* "We all take bribes/kickbacks; it's the way we do business," or "we all take merchandise home (steal)." As related to conventional morality, peer pressure is used to enforce group norms.[107]
- **Advantageous comparison** *is the process of comparing oneself to others who are worse.* "I call in sick when I'm not sick only a few times a year; Tom and Ellen do it all the time." "We pollute less than our competitors do."
- **Disregard or distortion of consequences** *is the process of minimizing the harm caused by the unethical behavior.* "If I inflate the figures, no one will be hurt and I will not get caught. And if I do, I'll just get a slap on the wrist anyway." Was this the case at Enron?
- **Attribution of blame** *is the process of claiming the unethical behavior was caused by someone else's behavior.* "It's my co-worker's fault that I repeatedly hit him and put him in the hospital. He called me/did xxx, so I had to hit him."
- **Euphemistic labeling** *is the process of using "cosmetic" words to make the behavior sound acceptable.* Terrorist group *sounds bad but* freedom fighter *sounds justifiable.* Misleading *or* covering up *sounds better than* lying *to others.*

Which justification processes have you used? How can you improve your ethical behavior by not using justification?

WorkApplication10

Give at least two organizational examples of unethical behavior and the process of justification.

—————————————

—————————————

—————————————

—————————————

—————————————

Ethical Dilemma 2

Sex and Violence

Over the years, various social activist groups, including the Parents Television Council, National Viewers and Listeners Association, and the National Coalition Against Censorship, have taken a stance for and against censorship of sex and violence on TV and in the movies. People call for more censorship to protect children from seeing sex and violence (many children watch as many as five hours of TV per day), while others don't want censorship, stating it violates free speech laws.

The Federal Communications Commission (FCC) has the power to regulate television. Based on societal pressures, the FCC was considering imposing a more severe form of regulation and the possible termination of specific television programs containing explicit sex and violence.[108]

Advocates for less regulation state that TV shows like *CSI: Crime Scene Investigation* are shown late at night while children should not be watching. However, advocates of regulation state the fact than many daytime soap operas are sexual and that cable stations show reruns of major network shows in the day and early evening when children are watching. For example, many of the former Seinfeld shows were based on sexual themes, and the show was not aired until 9:00, but now it is shown on cable stations at all hours.

1. Does the media (TV, movies, and music) influence societal values?
2. Does the media, with sex and violence, reflect current religious and societal values?
3. Should the FCC regulate the media, and if yes, how far should it go? Should it require toning down the sex and violence, or take shows like *Sex and the City* off the air?
4. Is it ethical and socially responsible to show sex and violence against women, and to portray women as sex objects?
5. Which of the six justifications of unethical behavior does the media use to defend sex and violence?

Simple Guides to Ethical Behavior

Every day in your personal and professional life, you face situations in which you can make ethical or unethical choices. As discussed, you make these choices based on your personality traits and attitudes, level of moral development, and the situation. Never misrepresent yourself.[109]

Following are some guides that can help you make the right decisions.

Golden Rule

Following the golden rule will help you to use ethical behavior. The golden rule is:

"Do unto others as you want them to do unto you." Or, put other ways,

"Don't do anything to other people that you would not want them to do to you."

"Lead others as you want to be led."

Four-Way Test

Rotary International developed the four-way test of the things we think and do to guide business transactions. The four questions are (1) Is it the truth? (2) Is it fair to all concerned? (3) Will it build goodwill and better friendship? (4) Will it be beneficial to all concerned? When making your decision, if you can answer yes to these four questions, it is probably ethical.

──────────── Learning Outcome 9 ────────────

Explain the stakeholder approach to ethics.

Stakeholder Approach to Ethics

Under the **stakeholder approach to ethics,** *one creates a win-win situation for relevant parties affected by the decision.* A win-win situation meets the needs of the organization and employees as well as those of other stakeholders, so that everyone benefits from the decision. The effective leader uses the moral exercise of power—socialized power, rather than personalized. Stakeholders include everyone affected by the decision, which may include followers, governments, customers, suppliers, society, stockholders, and so on. The higher up in management you go, the more stakeholders you have to deal with. You can ask yourself one simple question to help you determine if your decision is ethical from a stakeholder approach:

"Am I proud to tell relevant stakeholders my decision?"

If you are proud to tell relevant stakeholders your decision, it is probably ethical. If you are not proud to tell others your decision, or you keep justifying it, the decision may not be ethical. Justifying by saying everybody else does it is usually a cop-out. Everybody does *not* do it, and even if many other employees do it, that doesn't make it right. If you are not sure whether a decision is ethical, talk to your manager, higher-level managers, ethics committee members, and other people with high ethical standards. If you are reluctant to talk to others for advice on an ethical decision because you think you may not like their answers, the decision may not be ethical.

Being an Ethical Leader

It is sad that a recent survey found that over two-thirds (71 percent) of Americans rated corporations low for operating in a fair and honest manner.[110] It has been said that a culture of lying is infecting American business.[111]

Why is ethics such a problem today? There is no easy answer, but in addition to our prior discussion, here are a few more reasons.

- A root cause of the problem is that greed tends to overtake ethics, through looking out only for one's own self-interest, often at the expense of others. Many people have the idea that if you are making money, any behavior is acceptable.[112] This notion is supported by reality TV shows set in a cut-throat world where business competition is likened to a struggle for survival on an island. The message people are absorbing from these shows, and the unethical news headlines, is that success means clawing your way to the top of the heap at the expense of your competition—so long as you don't get caught.[113]

• Some people have lost touch with basic ethical values. Being unethical is a more accepted part of doing business today; unfortunately, being ethical is not often rewarded, and being unethical is even rewarded.[114] Some whistle-blowers suffer negative consequences.

• When it comes to ethics, most people are followers, not leaders.[115] More than half the people surveyed said they would be willing to misrepresent financial information if asked to by a superior.[116] A survey found that 19 percent of employees have seen coworkers lie to customers, vendors, or the public, and that 12 percent have seen coworkers steal from customers or the company. And 35 percent admit keeping quiet when they see coworker misconduct.[117] Are you a leader or follower? Refer back to Self-Assessment 6—how many unethical behaviors have you observed? How many have you reported?

Now let's focus on how to be an ethical leader, not necessarily an ethical manager. Most people are followers when it comes to ethics, and to some degree, silence means you are a follower despite your own personal conduct.[118] So you have to lead by example from the postconventional level, be one of the 20 percent, by doing the right thing, even when no one is looking, and you should blow the whistle when appropriate.

Ethical leadership requires *courage*—the ability to do the right thing at the risk of rejection and loss. Courage is difficult in an organization that focuses on getting along and fitting in without rocking the boat in order to get approval, promotions, and raises. It is difficult to say no when most others are saying yes, to go against the status quo and offer new alternatives to the group. Courage doesn't mean that you don't have doubt or fear rejection, ridicule, and loss; it means you do the right thing in spite of fear. You need to take risks to make change by speaking your mind and fighting for what you believe is right. Courage also requires taking responsibility for mistakes and failures, rather than trying to cover them up or blaming others when you do take risks.

You need to remember that moral values are important and that business is not just about making money; it's about meeting the needs of all stakeholders. It's not okay to lie. Any lie has hidden costs, not only in teamwork and productivity, but also in your own self-respect. One lie often leads to a trail of lies as you try to cover up the first lie. Once you start to lie, it's easy to continue on to bigger lies.[119] It is okay to blow the whistle.

People tend to make rapid judgments about ethical dilemmas.[120] So slow down your decisions that affect various stakeholders. Seek out mentors who can advise you on ethical dilemmas.[121] If you are a manager, make sure you lead by ethical example and enforce ethical standards. If you are not in power and observe unethical behavior and want to blow the whistle, go to someone higher in the organization who is committed to ethical behavior.[122] If there are no higher-level managers who care about ethics, maybe you should search for another job.

Here are a few ways you can find courage to do the right thing.[123]

• Focus on a higher purpose, such as helping or looking out for the well-being of customers and employees.

- Draw strength from others. People with courage often get it from the support of friends at work and/or a supporting family.
- Take risk without fear of failure. Accept the fact that we all fail at times and that failure leads to success. Thomas Edison had something like a thousand failures before he got the electric light to work. Learn from failure and don't repeat the same mistakes, but focus on the positive successes. Recall that happiness is nothing more than a poor memory for failure. Keep taking reasonable risks.
- Use your frustration and anger for good. When you observe unethical or ineffective wrong behavior, use your emotions to have the courage to take action to stop it and prevent it from happening again.

Here are a couple of examples of ethical leadership. When Warren Buffett took over Salomon Brothers it was full of scandals for unethical behavior. Buffett called a meeting with employees saying the unethical behavior had to stop. He was the compliance officer; he gave his home phone number and told employees to call him if anyone observed any unethical behavior.[124] FBI staff attorney Colleen Rowley, in Minneapolis, blew the whistle by sending a letter calling attention to the FBI shortcoming that may have contributed to the September 11, 2001 terrorist tragedy.

Go to the Internet (academic.cengage.com/management/lussier) where you will find a broad array of resources to help maximize your learning.

- Review the vocabulary
- Try a quiz
- View chapter videos

WorkApplication11

Give examples of times when you or others you know had the courage to do what was right.

_____

_____

_____

_____

_____

Chapter Summary

The chapter summary is organized to answer the 10 learning outcomes for Chapter 2.

1. List the benefits of classifying personality traits.
Classifying personality traits helps to explain and predict behavior and job performance.

2. Describe the Big Five personality dimensions.
The _surgency_ personality dimension includes leadership and extraversion traits. The _agreeableness_ personality dimension includes traits related to getting along with people. The _adjustment_ personality dimension includes traits related to emotional stability. The _conscientiousness_ personality dimension includes traits related to achievement. The _openness-to-experience_ personality dimension includes traits related to being willing to change and try new things.

3. Explain the universality of traits of effective leaders.
Traits are universal in the sense that there are certain traits that most effective leaders have. However, traits are not universal in the sense that there is no one list of traits that is clearly accepted by all researchers, and not all effective leaders have all the traits.

4. Discuss why the trait of dominance is so important for managers to have.
Because the dominance trait is based on desire to be a leader, this trait affects the other traits in a positive or negative way based on that desire.

5. State how the Achievement Motivation Theory and the Leader Profile are related and different.
Achievement Motivation and Leader Profile theories are related because both are based on the need for achievement,

power, and affiliation. They are different because the Achievement Motivation Theory is a general motive profile for explaining and predicting behavior and performance, while the LMP is the one profile that specifically explains and predicts leadership success.

6. Identify similarities and differences among Theory X and Theory Y, the Pygmalion effect, and self-concept.

The concept of Theory X and Theory Y is similar to the Pygmalion effect, because both theories focus on the leader's attitude about the followers. The Pygmalion effect extends Theory X and Theory Y attitudes by including the leader's expectations and how he or she treats the followers, using this information to explain and predict followers' behavior and performance. In contrast, Theory X and Theory Y focus on the leader's behavior and performance. Both approaches are different from self-concept because they examine the leader's attitudes about others, whereas self-concept relates to the leader's attitude about themselves. Self-concept is also different because it focuses on how the leader's attitude about themselves affects his or her behavior and performance.

7. Describe how attitudes are used to develop four leadership styles.

The leader's attitude about others includes Theory Y (positive) and Theory X (negative) attitudes. The leader's attitude about themselves includes a positive self-concept or a negative self-concept. Combinations of these variables are used to identify four leadership styles: Theory Y positive self-concept, Theory Y negative self-concept, Theory X positive self-concept, and Theory X negative self-concept.

8. Compare the three levels of moral development.

At the lowest level of moral development, preconventional, behavior is motivated by self-interest, seeking rewards, and avoiding punishment. At the second level, conventional, behavior is motivated by meeting the group's expectations to fit in by copying others' behavior. At the highest level, postconventional, behavior is motivated to do the right thing, at the risk of alienating the group. The higher the level of moral development, the more ethical is the behavior.

9. Explain the stakeholder approach to ethics.

Under the stakeholder approach to ethics, the leader (or follower) creates a win-win situation for relevant parties affected by the decision. If you are proud to tell relevant stakeholders your decision, it is probably ethical. If you are not proud to tell others your decision, or you keep justifying it, the decision may not be ethical.

10. Define the following key terms (in order of appearance in the chapter).

Select one or more methods: (1) fill in the missing key terms from memory, (2) match the key terms from the following list with their definitions below, (3) copy the key terms in order from the list at the beginning of the chapter.

_____ are distinguishing personal characteristics.

_____ is a combination of traits that classifies an individual's behavior.

_____ categorizes traits into dimensions of surgency, agreeableness, adjustment, conscientiousness, and openness to experience.

_____ includes leadership and extraversion traits.

_____ includes traits related to getting along with people.

_____ includes traits related to emotional stability.

_____ includes traits related to achievement.

_____ includes traits related to being willing to change and try new things.

_____ identify individual stronger and weaker traits.

_____ relates to being conscious of your emotions and how they affect your personal and professional life.

_____ relates to the ability to understand others.

_____ relates to the ability to control disruptive emotions.

_____ relates to the ability to work well with others.

_____ attempts to explain and predict behavior and performance based on a person's need for achievement, power, and affiliation.

_____ attempts to explain and predict leadership success based on a person's need for achievement, power, and affiliation.

_____ includes a high need for power, which is socialized; that is, greater than the need for affiliation and with a moderate need for achievement.

_____ are positive or negative feelings about people, things, and issues.

_____ attempt to explain and predict leadership behavior and performance based on the leader's attitude about followers.

_____ proposes that leaders' attitudes toward and expectations of followers, and their treatment of them, explain and predict followers' behavior and performance.

_____ refers to the positive or negative attitudes people have about themselves.

_____ are the standards of right and wrong that influence behavior.

_____ is the process of reinterpreting immoral behavior in terms of a higher purpose.

_____ is the process of blaming one's unethical behavior on others.

_____ is the process of the group using the unethical behavior with no one person being held responsible.

_____ is the process of comparing oneself to others who are worse.

_____ is the process of minimizing the harm caused by the unethical behavior.

_____ is the process of claiming the unethical behavior was caused by someone else's behavior.

_____ is the process of using "cosmetic" words to make the behavior sound acceptable.

_____ creates a win-win situation for relevant parties affected by the decision.

Key Terms

Achievement Motivation Theory, 42

adjustment personality dimension, 33

advantageous comparison, 59

agreeableness personality dimension, 33

attitudes, 47

attribution of blame, 59

Big Five Model of Personality, 32

conscientiousness personality dimension, 33

diffusion of responsibility, 59

displacement of responsibility, 59

disregard or distortion of consequences, 59

ethics, 55

euphemistic labeling, 59

Leader Motive Profile (LMP), 43

Leader Motive Profile Theory, 43

moral justification, 59

openness-to-experience personality dimension, 33

personality, 31

personality profiles, 34

Pygmalion effect, 50

relationship management, 40

self-awareness, 39

self-concept, 51

self-management, 40

social awareness, 40

stakeholder approach to ethics, 61

surgency personality dimension, 33

Theory X and Theory Y, 49

traits, 31

Review and Discussion Questions

1. Would you predict that a person with a very strong agreeableness personality dimension would be a successful computer programmer? Why or why not?
2. What is the primary use of personality profiles?
3. What are some of the traits that describe the high-energy trait?
4. Is locus of control important to leaders? Why?
5. What does intelligence have to do with leadership?
6. Does sensitivity to others mean that the leader does what the followers want to do?
7. Does McClelland believe that power is good or bad? Why?
8. Should a leader have a dominant need for achievement to be successful? Why or why not?
9. McGregor published Theory X and Theory Y over 30 years ago. Do we still have Theory X managers? Why?
10. In text examples related to the Pygmalion effect, Lou Holtz calls for setting a higher standard. Have the standards in school, society, and work increased or decreased over the last five years?
11. Do you believe that if you use ethical behavior it will pay off in the long run?
12. Can ethics be taught and learned?
13. Which personality traits are more closely related to ethical and unethical behavior?
14. Do people change their level of moral development based on the situation?
15. Why do people justify their unethical behavior?
16. Which justification do you think is used most often?
17. As related to the simple guide to ethical behavior, how do you want to be led?

Case

BILL GATES—MICROSOFT

William (Bill) H. Gates III was born in 1955 and began programming mainframe computers at age 13. While attending Harvard University, Gates developed a version of the programming language BASIC for the first microcomputer—the MITS Altair. In 1975, Gates and his childhood friend Paul Allen founded Microsoft as a partnership, and it was incorporated in 1981. Today, Microsoft is the worldwide leader in software, services, and Internet technologies for personal and business computing. Gates is consistently ranked as the richest man in the world. Depending on how the stock market is doing, his stock ownership has been valued at over $70 billion.

Gates was a true visionary leader of his time, and he still is. When the mainframe computers were still the focus of computing, with the personal computer (PC) in its infancy, Gates envisioned the future of today with a computer on every office desktop and in every home. Unlike IBM, the developer and clear leader in early business PC sales, Microsoft stayed away from hardware and focused on software. IBM did not envision the value of software. Only in his 20s, Gates, from small Microsoft, convinced giant IBM to put his operating system on its PCs. As hardware sales became very competitive with low profit margins, IBM lost its dominance in PC sales. After IBM realized it missed the future, it developed its own operating system and some software, with poor results. IBM purchased Lotus to acquire its software, but the move was too little too late. With PC sales lagging behind Dell, HP, and Gateway, IBM sold its PC business. In 2004, Microsoft was the world's third-largest public company, ahead of IBM in fifteenth place.[125]

Gates gave his CEO position to Steve Ballmer. He still runs Microsoft with his current title of chairman and chief software architect. Gates still provides strong leadership but now focuses more on software development, with Ballmer focusing on managing Microsoft. Gates actively participates in and coordinates business units, and holds Microsoft together, but he delegates authority to managers to run their independent departments.

Today, Microsoft's mission is to help people and businesses throughout the world realize their full potential. To this end, it has seven core business units: Windows Clients, Information Worker, Microsoft Business Solutions, Server and Tools, Mobile and Embedded Devices, MSN, and Home and Entertainment.[126] Bill Gates's current vision is for Microsoft to play a leading role in entertainment by combining products and services from its core businesses.

With the explosion of digital music, movies, and images, Microsoft has lined up partners to deliver such products and services in a more integrated way than any competitors. The plan is to bring the PC into the living room experience through its "Media Center PC," which runs a version of Windows designed to be navigated by a remote control and viewed from 10 feet or so away; it will also popularize Portable Media Centers that play music, videos, and other content.

Gates's vision is total access to your digital media, with every screen in the house being a portable device. You can pick up a single remote control to get a rich, simple user interface that works for photos, music, video, instant messaging, and all the things you want to do. Yes, cable and satellite providers, Apple, Yahoo, and Google are doing pieces of this, but Microsoft will be the first one to put it all together.[127]

Gates is known as a demanding boss who encourages creativity and recognizes employee achievements. Several of his early employees are now millionaires. Gates uses teams to improve existing software and to develop new products. Employees are expected to be well informed, logical, vocal, and thick-skinned. Teams must present their ideas at "Bill" meetings. During the meetings, Gates often interrupts presentations to question facts and assumptions. He shouts criticisms and challenges team members. Team members are expected to stand up to Gates, giving good logical answers to his questions.

Bill Gates founded the Bill & Melinda Gates Foundation, which has given away millions of dollars to charity causes worldwide. On the other hand, Gates has been accused of trying to monopolize the World Wide Web (Internet) software market and has had legal problems with the Department of Justice. He admitted that Microsoft restricted the ability of its Internet partners to deal with its rivals.[128]

GO TO THE INTERNET: To learn more about Bill Gates and Microsoft, log on to InfoTrac® College Edition at **academic.cengage.com/infotrac** and use the advanced search function.

Support your answers to the following questions with specific information from the case and text or other information you get from the Web or other sources.

1. What do you think Bill Gates's personality traits are for each of the Big Five dimensions?
2. Which of the nine traits of effective leaders would you say has had the greatest impact on Bill Gates's success?
3. Which motivation would McClelland say was the major need driving Bill Gates to continue to work so hard despite being worth many billions of dollars?
4. Does Bill Gates have an LMP?
5. What type of self-concept does Bill Gates have, and how does it affect his business success?
6. Is Bill Gates ethical in business? Which level of moral development is he on?

Cumulative Case Question

7. Which leadership managerial role(s) played by Bill Gates had an important part in the success of Microsoft? (Chapter 1)

Case Exercise and Role-Play

Preparation. Think of a business that you would like to start some day and answer these questions that will help you develop your plan. (1) What would be your company's name? (2) What would be its mission (purpose or reason for being)? (3) What would your major products and/or services be? (4) Who would be your major competitors? (5) What would be your competitive advantage? (What makes you different from your competitors? Why would anyone buy your product or service rather than the competition's?) Your instructor may elect to let you break into groups to develop a group business idea. If you do a group business, select one leader with thick skin who can handle a "Bill" meeting to present the proposal to the entire class. An alternative is to have a student(s) who has an actual business idea/project/proposal of any type present it for feedback.

Role-Play "Bill" Meeting. One person (representing oneself or a group) may give the business proposal idea to the entire class, or break into groups of 5 to 6 and, one at a time, deliver proposals. The members of the class that listen play the role of Bill Gates during the "Bill" meeting, or they challenge presenters and offer suggestions for improvement.

Video Case

The Timberland Company: Ethics and Social Responsibility

Timberland is a global retailer that designs premium-quality footwear, apparel, and accessories for consumers who value the outdoors. Timberland's dedication to making quality products is matched by the company's commitment to "doing well and doing good"—forging powerful partnerships among employees, consumers, and service partners to carry out various social responsibility initiatives. In addition to making quality products, Timberland strongly believes that it has a responsibility to help effect positive change in local communities.

View the Video (10 minutes)

View the video on Timberland in class or at **academic. cengage.com/management/lussier.**

Read the Case

Timberland considers a broad range of stakeholders in its business dealings. The company first recognizes the responsibility to be profitable for investors. In addition to bottom-line considerations, Timberland seeks to serve its employee stakeholders—

the company is committed to diversity in its workforce and employs a high percentage of non-Caucasian minorities and women. Timberland also believes in bettering communities through a variety of service projects. Employees for the apparel maker have contributed literally hundreds of thousands of hours to company-sponsored community service events. Finally, Timberland considers the impact that its activities may have on the environment. The company's Environmental Affairs department has a specific mission to minimize harmful effects on the ecosystem and to support environmental causes.

While the true value of Timberland's social responsibility efforts is difficult to measure using traditional bottom-line metrics, the company believes its community efforts increase sales, build marketing relationships, and enhance research and development, resulting in increased value for all stakeholders.

Answer the Questions

1. Identify one of the community-service programs sponsored by Timberland, and explain why company leaders consider it important.
2. How do Timberland's social responsibility efforts and high ethical standards benefit the company?

Skill-Development Exercise 1

IMPROVING ATTITUDES AND PERSONALITY TRAITS

Preparing for Skill-Development Exercise 1

You should have read and now understand attitudes and personality traits. Effective leaders know themselves and work to maximize their strengths and minimize their weaknesses. As the name of this exercise implies, you can improve your attitudes and personality traits through this exercise by following these steps.

1. **Identify strengths and weaknesses.** Review the six self-assessment exercises in this chapter. List your three major strengths and areas that can be improved:

Strengths:
1. _____
2. _____
3. _____

Areas to Improve:
1. _____
2. _____
3. _____

We don't always see ourselves as others do. Research has shown that many people are not accurate in describing their own personalities, and that others can describe them more objectively. Before going on with this exercise, you may want to ask someone you know well to complete your personality profile (Self-Assessment 1), rate your attitude as positive or negative, and list your strengths and areas for improvement.

2. **Develop a plan for improving.** Start with your number-one area to improve on. Write down specific things that you can do to improve. List specific times, dates, and places that you will implement your plans. You may want to review the 12 tips for developing a more positive attitude and self-concept for ideas. Use additional paper if you need more space.

_____
_____
_____
_____

3. **Work on other areas for improvement.** After you see improvement in your first area, develop a new plan for your second area, and proceed through the steps again.

Optional. If you have a negative attitude toward yourself or others—or you would like to improve your behavior with others (family, coworkers), things, or issues (disliking school or work)—try following the internationally known motivational speaker and trainer Zig Ziglar's system.[129] Thousands of people have used this system successfully. This system can also be used for changing personality traits as well.

Here are the steps to follow, with an example plan for a person who has a negative self-concept and also wants to be more sensitive to others. Use this example as a guide for developing your own plan.

1. *Self-concept.* Write down everything you like about yourself. List all your strengths. Then go on and list all your weaknesses. Get a good friend to help you.
2. *Make a clean new list, and using positive affirmations, write all your strengths.* Example: "I am sensitive to others' needs."
3. *On another sheet of paper, again using positive affirmations, list all your weaknesses.* For example, don't write "I need to lose weight." Write, "I am a slim (whatever you realistically can weigh in 30 days) pounds." Don't write, "I have to stop criticizing myself." Write, "I positively praise myself often, every day." Write "I have good communications skills," not "I am a weak communicator." The following list gives example affirmations for improving sensitivity to others. Note the repetition; you can use a thesaurus to help.

   I am sensitive to others.
   My behavior with others conveys my warmth for them.
   I convey my concern for others.
   My behavior conveys kindness toward others.
   My behavior helps others build their self-esteem.
   People find me easy to talk to.
   I give others my full attention.
   I patiently listen to others talk.
   I answer others slowly and in a polite manner.
   I answer questions and make comments with useful information.
   My comments to others help them feel good about themselves.
   I compliment others regularly.

4. *Practice.* Every morning and night for at least the next 30 days, look at yourself in the mirror and read your list of positive affirmations. Be sure to look at yourself between each affirmation as you read. Or, record the list on a tape recorder and listen to it while looking at yourself in the mirror. If you are really motivated, you can repeat this step at other times of the day. Start with your areas for improvement. If it takes five minutes or more, don't bother with the list of your strengths. Or stop at five minutes; this exercise is effective in short sessions. Although miracles won't happen overnight, you may become more aware of your behavior in the first week. In the second or third week, you may become aware of yourself using new behavior successfully. You may still see some negatives, but the number will decrease in time as the positive increases.

Psychological research has shown that if a person hears something believable repeated for 30 days, they will tend to believe it. Ziglar says that you cannot consistently perform in a manner that is inconsistent with the way you see yourself. So, as you listen to your positive affirmations, you will believe them, and you will behave in a manner that is consistent with your belief. Put simply, your behavior will change with your thoughts without a lot of hard work. For example, if you listen to the affirmation, "I am an honest person" (not, "I have to stop lying"), in time—without having to work at it—you will tell the truth. At first you may feel uncomfortable reading or listening to positive affirmations that you don't really believe you have. But keep looking at yourself in the mirror and reading or listening, and with time you will feel comfortable and believe it and live it.

Are you thinking you don't need to improve, or that this method will not work? Yes, this system often does work. Zig Ziglar has trained thousands of satisfied people. One of this book's authors tried the system himself, and within two or three weeks, he could see improvement in his behavior. The question isn't will the system work for you, but rather will you work the system to improve?

5. *When you slip, and we all do, don't get down on yourself.* In the sensitivity-to-others example, if you are rude to someone and catch yourself, apologize and change to a positive tone. Effective leaders admit when they are wrong and apologize. If you have a hard time admitting you are wrong and saying you are sorry, at least be obviously nice so that the other person realizes you are saying you are sorry indirectly. Then forget about it and keep trying. Focus on your successes, not your slips. Don't let 10 good discussions be ruined by one insensitive comment. If you were a baseball player and got 9 out of 10 hits, you'd be the best in the world.
6. *Set another goal.* After 30 days, select a new topic, such as developing a positive attitude toward work, school, or trying a specific leadership style that you want to develop. You can also include more than one area to work on.

Doing Skill-Development Exercise 1 in Class

Objective

To develop your skill at improving your attitudes and personality traits. As a leader, you can also use this skill to help your followers improve.

Preparation

You should have identified at least one area for improvement and developed a plan to improve.

Procedure 1 (1–2 minutes)

Break into groups of two or preferably three; be sure the others in your group are people you feel comfortable sharing with.

Procedure 2 (4–6 minutes)

Have one of the group members volunteer to go first. The first volunteer states the attitude or personality trait they want to work on and describes the plan. The other group members give feedback on how to improve the plan. Try to give other plan ideas that can be helpful, and/or provide some specific help. You can also make an agreement to ask each other how you are progressing at set class intervals. Don't change roles until you're asked to do so.

Procedure 3 (4–6 minutes)

A second group member volunteers to go next. Follow the same procedure as above.

Procedure 4 (4–6 minutes)

The third group member goes last. Follow the same procedure as above.

Conclusion

The instructor may lead a class discussion and/or make concluding remarks.

Apply It (2–4 minutes)

What did I learn from this exercise? Will I really try to improve my attitude and personality by implementing my plan?

_____

_____

_____

Sharing

In the group, or to the entire class, volunteers may give their answers to the "Apply It" questions.

Skill-Development Exercise 2

PERSONALITY PERCEPTIONS

Preparing for Skill-Development Exercise 2

Read the section on "Personality Traits and Leadership," and complete Self-Assessment 1. From that exercise, rank yourself below from the highest score (1) to lowest (5) for each of the Big Five traits. Do not tell anyone your ranking until asked to do so.

_____ surgency   _____ agreeableness
_____ adjustment   _____ conscientiousness
_____ openness to experience

Doing Skill-Development Exercise 2 in Class

Objective

To develop your skill at perceiving personality traits of other people. With this skill, you can better understand and predict people's behavior, which is helpful to leaders in influencing followers.

Procedure 1 (2–4 minutes)

Break into groups of three, with people you know the best in the class. You may need some groups of two. If you don't know people in the class, and you did Skill-Development Exercise 1 in Chapter 1, "Getting to Know You by Name," get in a group with those people.

Procedure 2 (4–6 minutes)

Each person in the group writes down their perception of each of the other two group members. Simply rank which trait you believe to be the highest and lowest (put the Big Five dimension name on the line) for each person. Write a short reason for your perception, including some behavior you observed that leads you to your perception.

Name _____ Highest personality score _____ Lowest score _____

Reason for ranking _____

_____

Name _____ Highest personality score
_____ Lowest score _____
Reason for ranking _____
_____

Procedure 3 (4–6 minutes)

One of the group members volunteers to go first to hear the other group members' perceptions.

1. One person tells the volunteer which Big Five dimension he or she selected as the person's highest and lowest score, and why these dimensions were selected. Do not discuss this information yet.
2. The other person also tells the volunteer the same information.
3. The volunteer gives the two others his or her actual highest and lowest scores. The three group members discuss the accuracy of the perceptions.

Procedure 4 (4–6 minutes)

A second group member volunteers to go next to receive perceptions. Follow the same procedure as above.

Procedure 5 (4–6 minutes)

The third group member goes last. Follow the same procedure as above.

Conclusion

The instructor may lead a class discussion and/or make concluding remarks.

Apply It (2–4 minutes)

What did I learn from this exercise? How will I use this knowledge in the future?

_____
_____
_____

Sharing

In the group, or to the entire class, volunteers may give their answers to the "Apply It" questions.

Skill-Development Exercise 3

ETHICS AND WHISTLE-BLOWING

Preparing for Skill-Development Exercise 3

Now that you have completed Self-Assessment 6 regarding ethical behavior, answer the discussion questions based on that assessment.

Discussion Questions

1. For the "College" section, items 1–3, who is harmed and who benefits from these unethical behaviors?
2. For the "Workplace" section, items 1–17, select the three items (circle their numbers) you consider the most severely unethical behavior. Who is harmed and who benefits by these unethical behaviors?
3. If you observed unethical behavior but didn't report it, why didn't you report the behavior? If you did blow the whistle, why did you report the unethical behavior? What was the result?
4. As a manager, it is your responsibility to uphold ethical behavior. If you know employees are using any of these unethical behaviors, will you take action to enforce compliance with ethical standards?

Doing Skill-Development Exercise 3 in Class

Objective

To better understand ethics and whistle-blowing, and decide what you will do about unethical behavior.

Preparation

You should have completed the preparation for this exercise.

Experience

You will share your answers to the preparation questions, but are not requested to share your ethics score.

Procedure 1 (5–10 minutes)

The instructor writes the numbers 1–20 on the board. For each statement, students first raise their hands if they have observed this behavior, then if they have reported the behavior. The instructor writes the numbers on the board. (Note: Procedure 1 and procedure 2A can be combined.)

Procedure 2 (10–20 minutes)

Option A: As the instructor takes a count of the students who have observed and reported unethical behavior, he or she leads a discussion on the statements.

Option B: Break into groups of four to six, and share your answers to the four discussion questions at the end of the preparation part of this exercise. The groups may be asked to report the general consensus of the group to the entire class. If so, select a spokesperson before the discussion begins.

Option C: The instructor leads a class discussion on the four discussion questions at the end of the preparation part of this exercise.

Conclusion

The instructor may make concluding remarks.

Apply It (2–4 minutes)

What did I learn from this exercise? How will I use this knowledge in the future to be ethical? When will I use a simple guide to ethics?

_____

_____

_____

Sharing

Volunteers may give their answers to the "Apply It" questions.

Leadership Behavior and Motivation

LEARNING OUTCOMES

After studying this chapter, you should be able to:

1. List the University of Iowa leadership styles. p. 75

2. Describe similarities and differences between the University of Michigan and Ohio State University leadership models. p. 76

3. Discuss similarities and differences between the Ohio State University Leadership Model and the Leadership Grid. p. 80

4. Discuss similarities and differences among the three content motivation theories. p. 85

5. Discuss the major similarities and differences among the three process motivation theories. p. 93

6. Explain the four types of reinforcement. p. 100

7. State the major differences among content, process, and reinforcement theories. p. 106

8. Define the following **key terms** (in order of appearance in the chapter):

leadership style

University of Michigan Leadership
  Model

Ohio State University Leadership
  Model

Leadership Grid

motivation

motivation process

content motivation theories

hierarchy of needs theory

two-factor theory

acquired needs theory

process motivation theories

equity theory

expectancy theory

goal-setting theory

writing objectives model

reinforcement theory

giving praise model

Opening Case Application

J. R. Ridinger founded Market America in April of 1992 with a unique franchise business model to sell directly to consumers through UnFranchise® Owners. It markets a wide variety of high quality products and services (including anti-aging, health, nutrition, and personal care) through its Mall Without Walls™ Concept, which are sold through approximately 100,000 Independent Distributors and UnFranchise Owners, with both groups together being called distributors. Market America places the dream of starting your own business to achieve financial independence and freedom of time within the reach of anyone. It offers the benefits of franchising (a proven business plan, management and marketing tools and training) without the risk and high cost (franchise fees, monthly royalties, territorial restrictions) of a traditional franchise. There are minimal startup expenses and most people start part time (8 to 12 hours per week).

Market America is located in Greensboro, North Carolina, with over 300 employees in its sophisticated and state-of-the-art warehouse distribution systems. It also utilizes the e-commerce power of its Distributor Custom Web Portals and innovative Web site **http://www. marketamerica.com**. Market America offers mass customization and the one-to-one marketing and personal service of its distributor network. CEO Ridinger took Market America international in 2002 by expanding to Canada and Australia (**http://www.marketaustralia.com.au.**), with plans for further expansion in 2005.[1]

Opening Case Questions:

1. Which Ohio State University and Leadership Grid leadership style is emphasized at Market America?
2. What does Market America do to motivate its distributors, and how does it affect performance?
3. (a-c). How does Market America meet its distributors' content motivation needs?
4. (a-c). How does Market America meet its distributors' process motivation needs?
5. How does Market America use reinforcement theory to motivate its distributors?

To learn more about Market America, visit the company's Web site at **http://www. marketamerica.com** or log on to InfoTrac® College Edition at **academic.cengage. com/infotrac**, where you can research and read articles on Market America: select the advanced search option and key in record number A76746727 or A64784709 to get started.

L et's begin this chapter by discussing the importance of leadership and motivation. Recall that our definition of leadership stressed the importance of influencing others to achieve organizational objectives through change. High levels of performance occur when leaders establish motivational environments that inspire followers to achieve objectives.[2] Motivating workers produces distinctive firm competencies that give advantages over competitors.[3] Hence, the ability to motivate others, or motivational skills, are critical to leadership success.[4] But how effective are managers at motivating workers? In America, 46 percent of workers say that they are highly motivated but only 18 percent of their colleagues are motivated. Nearly two out of three workers say that their organizations do not do enough to motivate them and their colleagues, and about three out of four workers believe that their organization would benefit from a formal program to increase motivation.[5]

Why do people leave their jobs? Researchers report that people stay if they are satisfied with their jobs and are committed to their organizations and leave if they are not satisfied. Satisfaction with one's boss is an important part of job satisfaction.[6] Poor leaders drive employees to quit. Thus, job dissatisfaction progresses into employee turnover.[7] Unmotivated employees are usually not satisfied with their jobs. Are Americans satisfied with their jobs? A survey found that 77 percent of workers are not satisfied with their jobs.[8] Many employees do enough work to get by, but they are not satisfied with their jobs and they don't try to excel at their jobs.[9] So how can you, as a leader, motivate followers to go beyond mediocrity? That is what this chapter is all about. We will discuss four behavioral leadership models and seven motivation theories.

Leadership Behavior and Styles

Leadership Behavior

By the late 1940s, most of the leadership research had shifted from the trait theory paradigm to the behavioral theory paradigm, which focuses on what the leader says and does.[10] In the continuing quest to find the one best leadership style in all situations, researchers attempted to identify the differences in the behavior of effective leaders versus ineffective leaders. Although the behavioral leadership theory made major contributions to leadership research, which we will discuss more fully later, it never achieved its goal of finding one best style. Unfortunately, no leadership behaviors were found to be consistently associated with leadership effectiveness.[11] The leadership behavior theory paradigm lasted nearly 30 years. Today research continues to seek a better understanding of behavior.[12] And more importantly, to predict behavior.[13]

Leadership Behavior Is Based on Traits

Although the behavioral theorists focus on behavior, it's important to realize that leaders' behavior is based on their traits and skills.[14] A good predictor of employee retention is the relationship between manager and employee.[15] Employees who have a good relationship with their boss are more likely to be motivated than workers with a poor relationship with their manager, who are more likely to quit.[16] The relationship is based on the manager's leadership personality traits and attitudes, which directly affect his or her behavior with the employee.[17] Recall that the Pygmalion effect is based on traits, attitude expectations, and the manager's treatment (behavior) of employees, which in turn determines the followers' behavior and performance.

Leading by example is important to managers. In fact, as Albert Einstein said, "Setting an example is not the main means of influencing another, it is the only means." Leading by example takes place as followers observe the leader's behavior and copy it. And the leader's behavior is based on his or her traits. Thus, traits and behavior go hand-in-hand, or trait leadership theory influences behavioral leadership theory. However, behavior is easier to learn and change than traits.

Learning Outcome 1

List the University of Iowa leadership styles.

Leadership Styles and the University of Iowa Research

Leadership style *is the combination of traits, skills, and behaviors leaders use as they interact with followers.* Although a leadership style is based on traits and skills, the important component is the behavior, because it is a relatively consistent pattern of behavior that characterizes a leader. A precursor to the behavior approach recognized autocratic and democratic leadership styles.

University of Iowa Leadership Styles

In the 1930s, before behavioral theory became popular, Kurt Lewin and associates conducted studies at the University of Iowa that concentrated on the leadership style of the manager.[18] Their studies identified two basic leadership styles:

- *Autocratic leadership style.* The autocratic leader makes the decisions, tells employees what to do, and closely supervises workers.
- *Democratic leadership style.* The democratic leader encourages participation in decisions, works with employees to determine what to do, and does not closely supervise employees.

The autocratic and democratic leadership styles are often placed at opposite ends of a continuum, as shown in Exhibit 3-1; thus a leader's style usually falls somewhere between the two styles.

The Iowa studies contributed to the behavioral movement and led to an era of behavioral rather than trait research. With the shift in paradigm from management to leadership, the leadership style of effective managers is no longer autocratic, but more democratic.

WorkApplication1

Recall a present or past manager. Which of the University of Iowa leadership styles does or did your manager use most often? Describe the behavior of your manager.

_____

_____

_____

_____

_____

Exhibit 3-1 *University of Iowa leadership styles.*

Autocratic------------------------------Democratic

Source: Adapted from K. Lewin, R. Lippett, and R. K. White. 1939. "Patterns of Aggressive Behavior in Experimentally Created Social Climates." *Journal of Social Psychology* 10: 271–301.

University of Michigan and Ohio State University Studies

Leadership research was conducted at Ohio State and the University of Michigan at about the same time during the mid-1940s to mid-1950s. These studies were not based on prior autocratic and democratic leadership styles, but rather sought to determine the behavior of effective leaders. Although these two studies used the term *leadership behavior* rather than *leadership styles*, the behaviors identified are actually more commonly called leadership styles today. In this section we discuss leadership styles identified by these two universities. Before reading about these studies, complete Self-Assessment 1 to determine your leadership style.

─────────── Learning Outcome 2 ───────────

Describe similarities and differences between the University of Michigan and Ohio State University leadership models.

University of Michigan: Job-Centered and Employee-Centered Behavior

The University of Michigan's Survey Research Center, under the principal direction of Rensis Likert, conducted studies to determine leadership effectiveness. Researchers created a questionnaire called the "Survey of Organizations" and conducted interviews to gather data on leadership styles. Their goals were to (1) classify the leaders as effective and ineffective by comparing the behavior of leaders from high-producing units and low-producing units; and (2) determine reasons for effective leadership.[19] The researchers identified two styles of leadership behavior, which they called *job-centered* and *employee-centered*. The U of Michigan model stated that a leader is either more job-centered or more employee-centered. *The* **University of Michigan Leadership Model** *thus identifies two leadership styles: job-centered and employee-centered*. See Exhibit 3-2 for the University of Michigan Leadership Model: a one-dimensional continuum between two leadership styles.

Job-Centered Leadership Style

The job-centered style has scales measuring two job-oriented behaviors of goal emphasis and work facilitation. Job-centered behavior refers to the extent to

---

Exhibit 3-2 *The University of Michigan Leadership Model: Two leadership styles, one dimension.*

Job-Centered
Leadership Style ···|·································· Employee-Centered
Leadership Style

Source: R. Likert, *New Patterns of Management.* (New York: McGraw-Hill: 1961).

| Self-Assessment 1 |

Your Leadership Style

For each of the following statements, select one of the following:

1– "I **would not** tend to do this."

0– "I **would** tend to do this."

as a manager of a work unit. There are no right or wrong answers, so don't try to select correctly.

_____ 1. I (would or would not) let my employees know that they should not be doing things during work hours that are not directly related to getting their job done.

_____ 2. I (would or would not) spend time talking to my employees to get to know them personally during work hours.

_____ 3. I (would or would not) have a clearly written agenda of things to accomplish during department meetings.

_____ 4. I (would or would not) allow employees to come in late or leave early to take care of personal issues.

_____ 5. I (would or would not) set clear goals so employees know what needs to be done.

_____ 6. I (would or would not) get involved with employee conflicts to help resolve them.

_____ 7. I (would or would not) spend much of my time directing employees to ensure that they meet department goals.

_____ 8. I (would or would not) encourage employees to solve problems related to their work without having to get my permission to do so.

_____ 9. I (would or would not) make sure that employees do their work according to the standard method to be sure it is done correctly.

_____ 10. I (would or would not) seek the advice of my employees when making decisions.

_____ 11. I (would or would not) keep good, frequent records of my department's productivity and let employees know how they are doing.

_____ 12. I (would or would not) work to develop trust between my employees and me, and among the department members.

_____ 13. I (would or would not) be quick to take corrective action with employees who are not meeting the standards or goals.

_____ 14. I (would or would not) personally thank employees for doing their job to standard and meeting goals.

_____ 15. I (would or would not) continue to set higher standards and goals and challenge my employees to meet them.

_____ 16. I (would or would not) be open to employees to discuss personal issues during work time.

_____ 17. I (would or would not) schedule my employees' work hours and tasks to be completed.

_____ 18. I (would or would not) encourage my employees to cooperate with rather than compete against each other.

_____ 19. I (would or would not) focus on continually trying to improve the productivity of my department with activities like cutting costs.

_____ 20. I (would or would not) defend good employees of mine if my manager or peers criticized their work, rather than agree or say nothing.

Add up the number of **would do** this for all *odd*-numbered items and place it here _____ and on the continuum below.

High Task 10—9—8—7—6—5—4—3—2—1 *Low Task*
Leadership Style   *Leadership Style*

Add up the number of **would do** this for all *even*-numbered items and place it here _____ and on the continuum below.

High People 10—9—8—7—6—5—4—3—2—1 *Low People*
Leadership Style   *Leadership Style*

The higher your score for task leadership, the stronger is your tendency to focus on getting the job done. The higher your score for people leadership, the stronger is your tendency to focus on meeting people's needs and developing supportive relationships. Read on to better understand these leadership styles.

which the leader takes charge to get the job done. The leader closely directs subordinates with clear roles and goals, while the manager tells them what to do and how to do it as they work toward goal achievement. Review the odd-numbered items in Self-Assessment 1 for examples of job- (task-) oriented leadership behavior.

Employee-Centered Leadership Style

The employee-centered style has scales measuring two employee-oriented behaviors of supportive leadership and interaction facilitation. Employee-centered behavior refers to the extent to which the leader focuses on meeting the human needs of employees while developing relationships. The leader is sensitive to subordinates and communicates to develop trust, support, and respect while looking out for their welfare. Review the even-numbered items in Self-Assessment 1 for examples of employee-oriented (people) leadership behavior.

Based on Self-Assessment 1, is your leadership style more job- (task-) or employee- (people-) centered?

Ohio State University: Initiating Structure and Consideration Behavior

The Personnel Research Board of Ohio State University, under the principal direction of Ralph Stogdill, began a study to determine effective leadership styles. In the attempt to measure leadership styles, these researchers developed an instrument known as the *Leader Behavior Description Questionnaire (LBDQ)*. The LBDQ had 150 examples of definitive leader behaviors, which were narrowed down from 1,800 leadership functions. Respondents to the questionnaire perceived their leader's behavior toward them on two distinct dimensions or leadership types, which they eventually called *initiating structure* and *consideration*.[20]

Applying the Concept 1

University of Michigan Leadership Styles

Identify each of these five behaviors by its leadership style. Write the appropriate letter in the blank before each item.

a. job-centered   b. employee-centered

_____ 1. The manager is influencing the follower to do the job the way the leader wants it done.

_____ 2. The manager just calculated the monthly sales report and is sending it to all the sales representatives so they know if they met their quota.

_____ 3. The leader is saying a warm, friendly good morning to followers as they arrive at work.

_____ 4. The manager is in his or her office developing plans for the department.

_____ 5. The leader is seeking ideas from followers on a decision he or she has to make.

- *Initiating structure behavior.* The initiating structure leadership style is essentially the same as the job-centered leadership style; it focuses on getting the task done.
- *Consideration behavior.* The consideration leadership style is essentially the same as the employee-centered leadership style; it focuses on meeting people's needs and developing relationships.

Because a leader can be high or low on initiating structure and/or consideration, four leadership styles are developed. **The Ohio State University Leadership Model** *identifies four leadership styles: low structure and high consideration, high structure and high consideration, low structure and low consideration, and high structure and low consideration.* Exhibit 3-3 illustrates the four leadership styles and their two dimensions.

Leaders with high structure and low consideration behavior use one-way communications, and decisions are made by the managers, whereas leaders with high consideration and low structure use two-way communications and tend to share decision making. To determine your two-dimensional leadership style from Self-Assessment 1, put your two separate ("task" and "people") scores together and determine which of the four styles in Exhibit 3-3 is the closest match.

Exhibit 3-3 *The Ohio State University Leadership Model: Four leadership styles, two dimensions.*

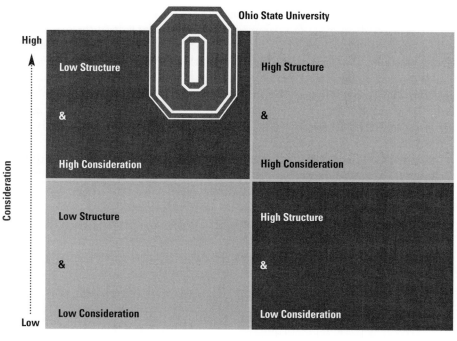

Source: R. Likert, *New Patterns of Management.* (New York: McGraw-Hill: 1961).

WorkApplication2

Recall a present or past manager. Which of the four Ohio State leadership styles does or did your manager use most often? Describe the behavior of your manager.

_____

_____

_____

_____

_____

Differences between Leadership Models— and Their Contributions

The Ohio State and University of Michigan leadership models are different in that the University of Michigan places the two leadership behaviors at opposite ends of the same continuum, making it one-dimensional. The Ohio State University Model considers the two behaviors independent of one another, making it two-dimensional; thus this model has four leadership styles.

The two leadership behaviors on which the models of both universities are based have strong research support. Leadership behaviors were developed, and repeatedly tested, using statistical factor analysis to narrow the dimensions down to structure/job-centered and consideration/employee-centered. The LBDQ and modified versions have been used in hundreds of studies by many different researchers.[21]

Research efforts to determine the one best leadership style have been weak and inconsistent for most criteria of leadership effectiveness. In other words, there is no one best leadership style in all situations; this is the first contribution, because it has helped lead researchers to the next paradigm—that of contingency leadership theory. Thus, the contribution of the behavioral leadership paradigm was to identify two generic dimensions of leadership behavior that continue to have importance in accounting for leader effectiveness today.[22]

Although there is no one best leadership style in all situations, there has been a consistent finding that employees are more satisfied with a leader who is high in consideration.[23] Prior to the two university leadership studies, many organizations had focused on getting the job done with little, if any, concern for meeting employee needs. So, along with other behavioral theory research, there was a shift to place more emphasis on the human side of the organization to increase productivity; this is a second contribution. The saying that a happy worker is a productive worker comes from this period of research.

Another important research finding was that most leadership functions can be carried out by someone besides the designated leader of a group.[24] Thus, due to behavioral leadership research, more organizations began training managers to use participative leadership styles. In fact, Rensis Likert proposed three types of leadership behavior: job-centered behavior, employee-centered behavior, and participative leadership.[25] Thus, as a third contribution of these leadership models, Likert can be credited as being the first to identify the participative leadership style that is commonly used today.

The Leadership Grid

In this section we discuss the Leadership Grid theory, including research and contributions of the high-concern-for-people and high-concern-for-production (team leader) leadership styles.

_____ Learning Outcome 3 _____

Discuss similarities and differences between the Ohio State University Leadership Model and the Leadership Grid.

Leadership Grid Theory

Behavior leadership theory did not end in the mid-1950s with the University of Michigan and Ohio State University studies. Robert Blake and Jane Mouton, from the University of Texas, developed the Managerial Grid® and published it in 1964, updated it in 1978 and 1985, and in 1991 it became the Leadership Grid® with Anne Adams McCanse replacing Mouton, who died in 1987.[26] Blake and Mouton published numerous articles and around 40 books describing their theories.[27] Behavioral leadership is still being researched today. The Leadership Grid was applied to project management by different researchers.[28]

The Leadership Grid builds on the Ohio State and Michigan studies; it is based on the same two leadership dimensions, which Blake and Mouton called *concern for production* and *concern for people*.[29] The concern for both people and production is measured through a questionnaire on a scale from 1 to 9. Therefore, the grid has 81 possible combinations of concern for production and people. However, *the* **Leadership Grid** *identifies five leadership styles: 1,1 impoverished; 9,1 authority compliance; 1,9 country club; 5,5 middle of the road; and 9,9 team leader.* See Exhibit 3-4 for an adaptation of the Leadership Grid.

Following are descriptions of leadership styles in the Leadership Grid:

- The *impoverished leader* (1,1) has low concern for both production and people. The leader does the minimum required to remain employed in the position.
- The *authority-compliance leader* (9,1) has a high concern for production and a low concern for people. The leader focuses on getting the job done as people are treated like machines.
- The *country-club leader* (1,9) has a high concern for people and a low concern for production. The leader strives to maintain a friendly atmosphere without regard for production.
- The *middle-of-the-road leader* (5,5) has balanced, medium concern for both production and people. The leader strives to maintain satisfactory performance and morale.
- The *team leader* (9,9) has a high concern for both production and people. This leader strives for maximum performance and employee satisfaction. According to Blake, Mouton, and McCanse, the team leadership style is generally the most appropriate for use in all situations.

To estimate your Leadership Grid leadership style, using Self-Assessment 1, use your task score as your concern for production and your people score, and plot them on the Leadership Grid in Exhibit 3-4. Then select the closest of the five leadership styles.

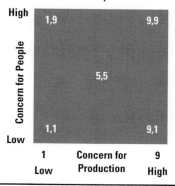

Exhibit 3-4 *Blake, Mouton, and McCanse Leadership Grid.*

Source: Adapted from Robert R. Blake and Jane S. Mouton, *The Managerial Grid III* (Houston: Gulf, 1985); and Robert R. Blake and Anna Adams McCanse, *Leadership Dilemmas—Grid Solutions* (Houston: Gulf, 1991), 29.

WorkApplication3

Recall a present or past manager. Which of the five Leadership Grid styles does or did your manager use most often? Describe the behavior of your manager.

_____

_____

_____

_____

_____

1. Which Ohio State University and Leadership Grid Leadership Style Is Emphasized at Market America?

Market America emphasizes the Ohio State University high structure and high consideration style, which is called the team leader's high concern for people and high concern for production (9,9) leadership style. Distributors make money by bringing in new distributors and selling more products, so they have a high concern for sales. But at the same time, UnFranchise Owners must develop good relationships with distributors who sell for them, so they have a high concern for people as well. Many sales also take place in distributors' homes through presentations, which is a social setting.

OPENING CASE APPLICATION

The Leadership Grid

Identify the five statements by their leader's style. Write the appropriate letter in the blank before each item.

a. 1,1 (impoverished) c. 9,1 (authority compliance) e. 9,9 (team)
b. 1,9 (country club) d. 5,5 (middle of the road)

_____ 6. The group has very high morale; members enjoy their work. Productivity in the department is one of the lowest in the company. The manager is one of the best liked in the company.

_____ 7. The group has adequate morale; the employees are satisfied with their manager. They have an average productivity level compared to the other departments in the company.

_____ 8. The group has one of the lowest levels of morale in the company; most employees do not like the manager. It is one of the top performers compared to other departments.

_____ 9. The group is one of the lowest producers in the company; employees don't seem to care about doing a good job. It has a low level of morale, because the employees generally don't like the manager.

_____ 10. The group is one of the top performers; the manager challenges employees to continue to meet and exceed goals. Employees have high morale because they like the manager.

Leadership Grid and High-High Leader Research and Contributions

The *high-high leader* has concern for both production and people; this is the team leadership style. However, authors of the Leadership Grid were not the only ones to conduct research to determine if the high-high style was the most effective leadership style in all situations. Blake and Mouton did conduct an extensive empirical research study that measured profitability before and after a 10-year period. In the study, one company subsidiary used an extensive Grid Organizational Development program designed to teach managers how to be 9,9 team leaders (experimental group), while another subsidiary did not use the program (control group). The subsidiary using the team leadership style increased its profits four times more than the control subsidiary. Thus, the researchers claimed that team leadership usually results in improved performance, low absenteeism and turnover, and high employee satisfaction.[30] Blake and Mouton support the high-high leader style as a universal theory.

However, another researcher disagreed with these findings, calling high-high leadership a myth.[31] A more objective meta-analysis (a study combining the results of many prior studies) found that although task and relationship behavior tends to correlate positively with subordinate performance, the correlation is usually weak.[32] In conclusion, although there is some support for the universal theory, the high-high leadership style is not accepted as the one best style in all situations.

Critics suggested that different leadership styles are more effective in different situations.[33] Thus, a contribution of behavioral research is that it led to the shift in paradigm to contingency leadership theory. As you will learn in Chapter 5, contingency leadership theory is based on the behavioral theory of production and people leadership styles. Situational leadership models don't agree with using the same leadership style in all situations, but rather prescribe using the existing behavioral leadership style that best meets the situation.

A second contribution of behavioral leadership theory was the recognition that organizations need both production and people leadership. There is a generic set of production-oriented and people-oriented leadership functions that must be performed to ensure effective organizational performance.

A third related contribution of behavioral leadership theory supports coleadership. The manager does not have to perform both production and people functions. Thus, strong production-oriented leaders can be successful if they have coleaders to provide the people-oriented functions for them, and vice versa. So if you tend to be more production- or people-oriented, seek coleaders to complement your weaker area.

Before we go on to motivation, let's tie personality traits from Chapter 2 together with what we've covered so far. Complete Self-Assessment 2 now.

Self-Assessment 2

Your Personality Traits and Leadership Styles

We stated in the first section that *traits affect leadership behavior.* How does this relate to you? For the University of Michigan Leadership Model, generally, if you had a high personality score for the Big Five surgency dimension in Self-Assessment 1 in Chapter 2 (dominance trait, high need for power), you most likely have a high score for the task (job-centered) leadership style. If you had a high score for agreeableness (sensitivity to others trait, high need for affiliation), you most likely have a high score for the people (employee-centered) leadership style. My U of M leadership style is primarily_____

_____.

For the Ohio State University Leadership Model, you need to score your personality for surgency and agreeableness as high or low. Then you combine them, and these personality scores should generally provide the same two-dimensional behaviors corresponding to one of the four leadership styles. My OSU leadership style is primarily_____

_____.

For the Leadership Grid, you need to score your personality for surgency and agreeableness on a scale of 1 to 9. Then you combine them on the grid, and these personality scores should generally provide about the same score as Self-Assessment 1. My Leadership Grid style is primarily_____

_____.

If you scored a Leader Motive Profile, your score for tasks should generally be higher than your score for people, because you have a greater need for power than affiliation. However, your leadership style on the Ohio State model could be high structure and high consideration, because this implies socialized power. You could also have a 9,9 team leader score on the Leadership Grid. My LMP is primarily

_____.

Leadership and Major Motivation Theories

In this section we discuss motivation and leadership, the motivation process (which explains how motivation affects behavior), and three classifications of motivation theories (content, process, and reinforcement. We also briefly describe the need to balance professional and personal needs.

Motivation and Leadership

Motivation *is anything that affects behavior in pursuing a certain outcome.* Recall that we already discussed the importance of motivation in leadership in the introduction to this chapter. Motivating others is difficult and time consuming because you need to motivate each follower on a personal basis.[34] To sum up, if you are going to achieve organizational objectives, you need to motivate yourself and others. Thus, the ability to motivate yourself and others is critical to your success as a leader.[35]

The Motivation Process

Through the **motivation process,** *people go from need to motive to behavior to consequence to satisfaction or dissatisfaction.* For example, you are thirsty (need) and have a drive (motive) to get a drink. You get a drink (behavior) that quenches (consequence and satisfaction) your thirst. However, if you could not get a drink, or a drink of what you really wanted, you would be dissatisfied. Satisfaction is usually short-lived. Getting that drink satisfied you, but sooner or later you will need another drink. For this reason, the motivation process has a feedback loop. See Exhibit 3-5 for an illustration of the motivation process.

Some need or want motivates all behavior. Or, for the most part, we are motivated by self-interest.[36] However, needs and motives are complex: We don't always know what our needs are, or why we do the things we do. Have you ever done something and not known why you did it? Understanding needs will help you to better understand motivation and behavior.[37] You will gain a better understanding of why people do the things they do.

Like traits, motives cannot be observed; but you can observe behavior and infer what the person's motive is (attribution theory). However, it is not easy to know why people behave the way they do, because people do the same things for different reasons.[38] Also, people often attempt to satisfy several needs at once.

Herb Kelleher, founder and chairman of Southwest Airlines, said that superior performance is not achieved through ordinary employee efforts.[39] Leaders need to motivate employees to go above and beyond the call of duty, which is commonly called *organizational citizenship*.[40] Herb Kelleher focused on making work fun to motivate Southwest employees to be organizational citizens, and set many airline industry records, despite the fact that employees were paid less than at traditional airlines. David Neeleman, founder and CEO

Exhibit 3-5 *The motivation process.*

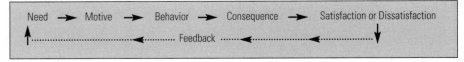

of JetBlue Airways, is described as someone who can inspire employees to organizational citizenship through the sheer force of his personality and the example of his dedication.[41]

2. What Does Market America Do to Motivate Its Distributors, and How Does It Affect Performance?

Market America's primary motivator is self-motivation by making distributors their own boss, which is not successful with people who are not interested in entrepreneurship. Its team approach—with more experienced distributors helping newer distributors, and regular meetings—is key to motivating distributors to succeed. Market America has been successful at finding people who want to be their own boss, and its performance continues to improve. It has consistent sales growth. In 2004, it achieved its goals of having more six-figure earners than any other competitor company in America. The UnFranchise approach motivates utilizing self-interest while helping others to create a win-win situation. The more sales UnFranchisers make, the more money they make. However, by helping other distributors succeed, they also make more money, and without helping customers by selling products they want to buy, UnFranchisers would not have any sales.

An Overview of Three Major Classifications of Motivation Theories

There is no single universally accepted theory of how to motivate people, or how to classify the theories. We will discuss motivation theories and how you can use them to motivate yourself and others. In the following sections, you will learn about content motivation theories, process motivation theories, and reinforcement theory. See Exhibit 3-6 for this classification, which is commonly used,[42] with a listing of major motivation theories you will learn.

After studying all of the theories separately, we put them back together using the unifying motivation process to see the relationship between the theories. You can select one theory to use, or take from several to make your own theory, or apply the theory that best fits the specific situation.

Learning Outcome 4

Discuss similarities and differences among the three content motivation theories.

Content Motivation Theories

Before we present the content motivation theories, let's discuss content motivation theories in general. **Content motivation theories** *focus on explaining and predicting behavior based on people's needs*. The primary reason people do what they do is to meet their needs or wants to be satisfied. People want job satisfaction, and they will leave one organization for another to meet this need.

An employee who has job satisfaction usually has a higher level of motivation and is more productive than a dissatisfied employee.[43] According to content motivation theorists, if you want to have satisfied employees you must meet

Exhibit 3-6 *Major motivation theories.*

CLASSIFICATION OF MOTIVATION THEORIES	SPECIFIC MOTIVATION THEORY
1. *Content motivation theories* focus on explaining and predicting behavior based on employee need motivation.	A. *Hierarchy of needs theory* proposes that employees are motivated through five levels of need—physiological, safety, social, esteem, and self-actualization. B. *Two-factor theory* proposes that employees are motivated by motivators (higher-level needs) rather than maintenance (lower-level needs) factors. C. *Acquired needs theory* proposes that employees are motivated by their need for achievement, power, and affiliation.
2. *Process motivation theories* focus on understanding how employees choose behaviors to fulfill their needs.	A. *Equity theory* proposes that employees will be motivated when their perceived inputs equal outputs. B. *Expectancy theory* proposes that employees are motivated when they believe they can accomplish the task, they will be rewarded, and the rewards for doing so are worth the effort. C. *Goal-setting theory* proposes that achievable but difficult goals motivate employees.
3. *Reinforcement theory* proposes that behavior can be explained, predicted, and controlled through the consequences for behavior.	Types of Reinforcement • Positive • Avoidance • Extinction • Punishment

their needs.[44] When employees are asked to meet objectives, they have the question, although usually not asked, What's in it for me? The key to successful leadership is to meet the needs of employees while achieving organizational objectives,[45] as discussed in the topics of socialized power and ethics (Chapter 2).

Hierarchy of Needs Theory

In the 1940s, Abraham Maslow developed his hierarchy of needs theory,[46] which is based on four major assumptions: (1) Only unmet needs motivate. (2) People's needs are arranged in order of importance (hierarchy) going from basic to complex needs. (3) People will not be motivated to satisfy a higher-level need unless the lower-level need(s) has been at least minimally satisfied. (4) Maslow assumed that people have five classifications of needs, which are presented here in hierarchical order from low to high level of need.

Hierarchy of Needs

The **hierarchy of needs theory** *proposes that people are motivated through five levels of needs—physiological, safety, belongingness, esteem, and self-actualization.*

1. *Physiological needs:* These are people's primary or basic needs: air, food, shelter, sex, and relief or avoidance of pain.

2. *Safety needs:* Once the physiological needs are met, the individual is concerned with safety and security.

3. *Belongingness needs:* After establishing safety, people look for love, friendship, acceptance, and affection. Belongingness is also called *social needs.*

4. *Esteem needs:* After the social needs are met, the individual focuses on ego, status, self-respect, recognition for accomplishments, and a feeling of self-confidence and prestige.

5. *Self-actualization needs:* The highest level of need is to develop one's full potential. To do so, one seeks growth, achievement, and advancement.

Maslow's work was criticized because it did not take into consideration that people can be at different levels of needs based on different aspects of their lives. Nor did he mention that people can revert back to lower-level needs. Today, Maslow and others realize that needs are not on a simple five-step hierarchy. Maslow's assumptions have recently been updated to reflect this insight, and many organizations today are using a variety of the management methods he proposed 30 years ago. Maslow has also been credited with influencing many management authors, including Douglas McGregor, Rensis Likert, and Peter Drucker.[47]

Motivating Employees with Hierarchy of Needs Theory

The major recommendation to leaders is to meet employees' lower-level needs so that they will not dominate the employees' motivational process. You should get to know and understand people's needs and meet them as a means of increasing performance. See Exhibit 3-7 for a list of ways in which managers attempt to meet these five needs.

WorkApplication4

On what level of the hierarchy of needs are you at this time for a specific aspect of your life (professional or personal)? Be sure to specify the level by name, and explain why you are at that level.

3-a. How Does Market America Meet Its Distributors' Content Motivation Needs?

Market America allows people to climb the *hierarchy of needs* as distributors: earn money (*physiological*), with minimum risk (*safety*), through customer contact and meetings (*social*), through the job itself with unlimited growth potential (*esteem*), and being the boss allows control over their job and time (*self-actualization*).

OPENING CASE APPLICATION

Exhibit 3-7 *How organizations motivate with hierarchy of needs theory.*

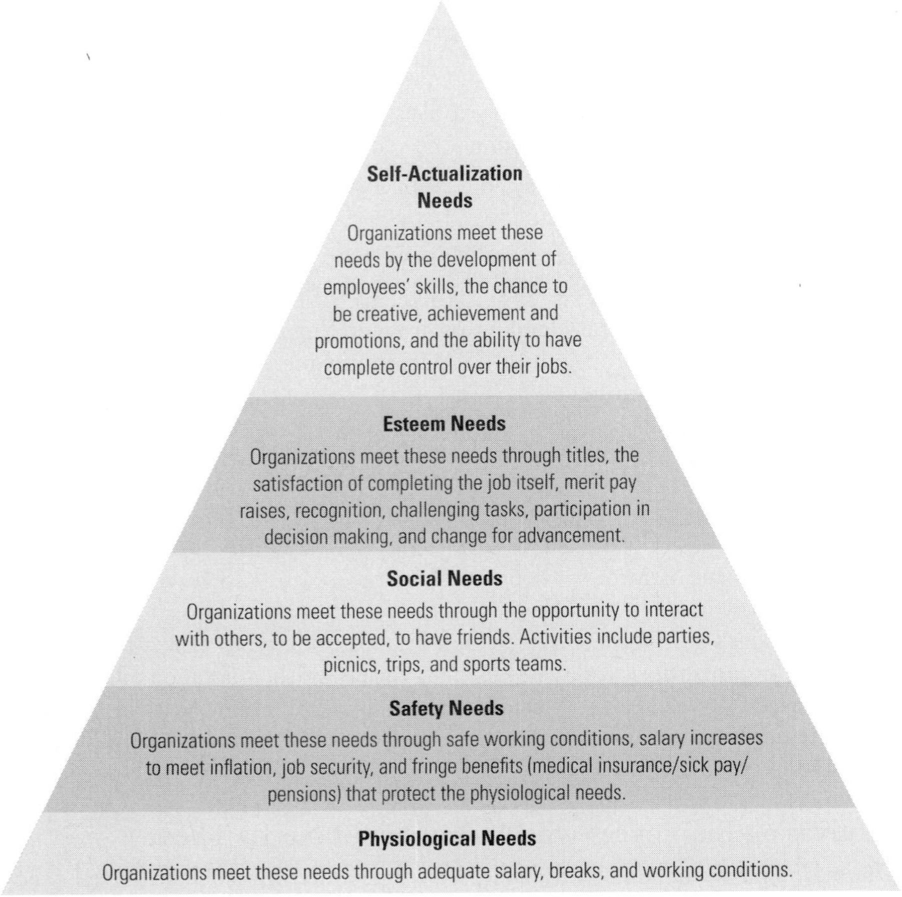

Self-Actualization Needs

Organizations meet these needs by the development of employees' skills, the chance to be creative, achievement and promotions, and the ability to have complete control over their jobs.

Esteem Needs

Organizations meet these needs through titles, the satisfaction of completing the job itself, merit pay raises, recognition, challenging tasks, participation in decision making, and change for advancement.

Social Needs

Organizations meet these needs through the opportunity to interact with others, to be accepted, to have friends. Activities include parties, picnics, trips, and sports teams.

Safety Needs

Organizations meet these needs through safe working conditions, salary increases to meet inflation, job security, and fringe benefits (medical insurance/sick pay/ pensions) that protect the physiological needs.

Physiological Needs

Organizations meet these needs through adequate salary, breaks, and working conditions.

Two-Factor Theory

In the 1960s, Frederick Herzberg published his two-factor theory.[48] Herzberg combined lower-level needs into one classification he called *hygiene* or *maintenance*; and higher-level needs into one classification he called *motivators*. **Two-factor theory** *proposes that people are motivated by motivators rather than maintenance factors*. Before you learn about two-factor theory, complete Self-Assessment 3.

Maintenance—Extrinsic Factors

Maintenance factors are also called *extrinsic motivators* because motivation comes from outside the person and the job itself.[49] Extrinsic motivators include pay, job security, title; working conditions; fringe benefits; and relationships. These factors are related to meeting lower-level needs. Review Self-Assessment 3, the even-numbered questions, for a list of extrinsic job factors.

Motivators—Intrinsic Factors

Motivators are called *intrinsic motivators* because motivation comes from within the person through the work itself.[50] Intrinsic motivators include achievement, recognition, challenge, and advancement. These factors are

Self-Assessment 3

Job Motivators and Maintenance Factors

Here are 12 job factors that contribute to job satisfaction. Rate each according to how important it is to you by placing a number from 1 to 5 on the line before each factor.

Very important		Somewhat important		Not important
5	4	3	2	1

_____ 1. An interesting job I enjoy doing

_____ 2. A good manager who treats people fairly

_____ 3. Getting praise and other recognition and appreciation for the work that I do

_____ 4. A satisfying personal life at the job

_____ 5. The opportunity for advancement

_____ 6. A prestigious or status job

_____ 7. Job responsibility that gives me freedom to do things my way

_____ 8. Good working conditions (safe environment, nice office, cafeteria, etc.)

_____ 9. The opportunity to learn new things

_____ 10. Sensible company rules, regulations, procedures, and policies

_____ 11. A job I can do well and succeed at

_____ 12. Job security and benefits

For each factor, write the number from 1 to 5 that represents your answer. Total each column (should be between 6 and 30 points).

Motivating factors	Maintenance factors
1. _____	2. _____
3. _____	4. _____
5. _____	6. _____
7. _____	8. _____
9. _____	10. _____
11. _____	12. _____
Totals _____	_____

Did you select motivators or maintenance factors as being more important to you? The closer to 30 (6) each score is, the more (less) important it is to you. Continue reading to understand the difference between motivators and maintenance factors.

related to meeting higher-level needs. Doing something we want to do and doing it well can be its own reward. Organizations realize the importance of intrinsic motivation and are making jobs more interesting and challenging,[51] while balancing intrinsic and extrinsic motivation.[52] Review Self-Assessment 3, the odd-numbered questions, for a list of intrinsic job factors.

Herzberg's Two-Factor Motivation Model

Herzberg and associates, based on research, disagreed with the traditional view that satisfaction and dissatisfaction were at opposite ends of one continuum (a one-dimensional model). There are two continuums: not dissatisfied with the environment (maintenance) to dissatisfied, and satisfied with the job itself (motivators) to not satisfied (a two-dimensional model). See Exhibit 3-8 for Herzberg's motivation model. Employees are on a continuum from dissatisfied to not dissatisfied with their environment. Herzberg contends that providing maintenance factors will keep employees from being dissatisfied, but it will not make them satisfied or motivate them. For example, Herzberg believes that if employees are dissatisfied with their pay and they get a raise, they will no longer be dissatisfied. However, before long people get accustomed to the new standard of living and will become dissatisfied again. Employees will need another raise to not be dissatisfied again. The vicious cycle goes on. So Herzberg says you have to focus on motivators—the job itself.

Exhibit 3-8 *Two-factor motivation theory.*

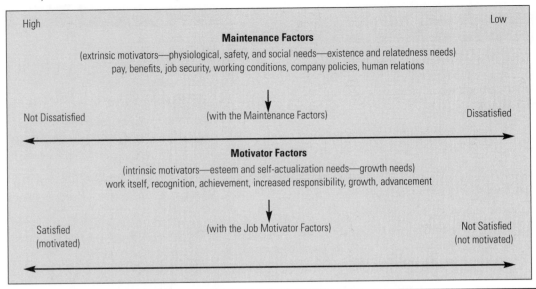

Source: Adapted from F. Herzberg. "The Motivation-Hygiene Concept and Problems of Manpower." *Personnel Administrator*: 3–7 (1964); and F. Herzberg. "One More Time: How Do You Motivate Employees?" *Harvard Business Review* (January–February 1967): 53.

Money as a Motivator

The current view of money as a motivator is that money matters more to some people than others, and that it may motivate some employees. However, money does not necessarily motivate employees to work harder.[53] Money also is limited in its ability to motivate. For example, many commissioned workers get to a comfortable point and don't push to make extra money; and some employees get to the point where they don't want overtime work, even though they are paid two or three times their normal wage.

But money is important. As Jack Welch says, you can't just reward employees with trophies; you need to reward them in the wallet too. Employees often leave one organization for another to make more money. High compensation (pay and benefits) based on performance is a practice of successful organizations.[54] If you got a pay raise, would you be motivated and more productive?

Motivating Employees with Two-Factor Theory

Under the old management paradigm, money (and other extrinsic motivators) was considered the best motivator. Under the new leadership paradigm, pay is important, but it is not the best motivator; intrinsic motivators are. Herzberg's theory has been criticized for having limited research support. However, it continues to be tested: Recently one study supported it, and another only partially supported it.[55] Herzberg fits the new paradigm: He says that managers must first ensure that the employees' level of pay and other maintenance factors are adequate. Once employees are not dissatisfied with their pay (and other maintenance factors), they can be motivated through their jobs. Herzberg also developed *job enrichment,* the process of building motivators into the job itself

WorkApplication5

Recall a present or past job; are you or were you dissatisfied or not dissatisfied with the maintenance factors? Are or were you satisfied or not satisfied with the motivators? Be sure to identify and explain your satisfaction with the specific maintenance and motivator factors.

_____
_____
_____
_____
_____

by making it more interesting and challenging. Job enrichment has been used successfully to motivate employees to higher levels of performance at many organizations, including AT&T, GM, IBM, Maytag, Monsanto, Motorola, Polaroid, and the Traveler's Life Insurance Company.

3-b. How Does Market America Meet Its Distributors' Content Motivation Needs?

Market America allows people to operate their own business. Related to *two-factor theory*, the focus is on *motivators* so that distributors can grow and meet their high-level needs of esteem and self-actualization. So the focus is on motivators not *maintenance* factors, although they are also met through the UnFranchise model.

OPENING CASE APPLICATION

Acquired Needs Theory

Acquired needs theory *proposes that people are motivated by their need for achievement, power, and affiliation.* This is essentially the same definition given for achievement motivation theory in Chapter 2. It is now called *acquired needs theory* because David McClelland was not the first to study these needs, and because other management writers call McClelland's theory *acquired needs theory.* A general needs theory was developed by Henry Murray, then adapted by John Atkinson[56] and David McClelland. You have already learned about McClelland's work, so we will be brief here. It's important to realize how closely linked traits, behavior, and motivation are. Acquired need is also widely classified as both a trait and a motivation, since McClelland and others believe that needs are based on personality traits. McClelland's affiliation need is essentially the same as Maslow's belongingness need; and power and achievement are related to esteem, self-actualization, and growth. McClelland's motivation theory does not include lower-level needs for safety and physiological needs. This theory is still being researched; a recent study used it with nurse managers. The conclusion was that both need for achievement and power motives of nurse managers influenced patient and staff outcomes in health care in the 1990s.[57]

Acquired needs theory says that all people have the need for achievement, power, and affiliation, but to varying degrees. Here are some ideas for motivating employees based on their dominant needs:

- *Motivating employees with a high n Ach.* Give them nonroutine, challenging tasks with clear, attainable objectives. Give them fast and frequent feedback on their performance. Continually give them increased responsibility for doing new things. Keep out of their way.
- *Motivating employees with a high n Pow.* Let them plan and control their jobs as much as possible. Try to include them in decision making, especially when they are affected by the decision. They tend to perform

WorkApplication6

Explain how your need for achievement, power, and/or affiliation has affected your behavior, or that of someone you work with or have worked with. What were the consequences of the behavior, and was the need satisfied?

_____

_____

_____

_____

_____

OPENING CASE APPLICATION

best alone rather than as team members. Try to assign them to a whole task rather than just part of a task.

- *Motivating employees with high n Aff.* Be sure to let them work as part of a team. They derive satisfaction from the people they work with rather than the task itself. Give them lots of praise and recognition. Delegate responsibility for orienting and training new employees to them. They make great buddies and mentors.

3-c. How Does Market America Meet Its Distributors' Content Motivation Needs?

Market America does help distributors meet all three *acquired needs*. It provides support so that they can *achieve* their goal of successfully running their own business, they have the *power* to be in control, and they can develop an *affiliation* with customers and other distributors and owners.

Before we discuss the need to balance professional and personal needs, see Exhibit 3-9 for a comparison of the three content theories of motivation.

The Need to Balance Professional and Personal Needs

You need a healthy balance between your life and your work.[58] The need to balance is currently a hot topic,[59] with the ascent of matrixed organizations working around the clock due to a global marketplace—and with the reengineered, downsizing, right-sizing world that focuses on how to get more done with fewer people.[60] Successful leaders use socialized power and strive to meet the needs of people and the organization to create a win-win situation for all stakeholders. Two major things organizations are doing to help employees meet their personal needs are providing on-site day care centers—or giving

---

Exhibit 3-9 *A comparison of content motivation theories.*

HIERARCHY OF NEEDS THEORY (MASLOW)	TWO-FACTOR THEORY (HERZBERG)	ACQUIRED NEEDS THEORY (MCCLELLAND)
Self-Actualization →	Motivators →	Achievement and Power
Esteem →	Motivators →	Achievement and Power
Belongingness →	Maintenance →	Affiliation
Safety →	Maintenance →	Not classified
Physiological →	Maintenance →	Not classified
Needs must be met in a hierarchical order.	Maintenance factors will not motivate employees.	Employees must be motivated differently based on their acquired needs.

employees information to help them find good day care—and offering flextime. Some leaders are also telling employees to go home and "get a life" before it is too late. Jack Welch says work-life balance is a personal decision, so choose what you want to do and be good at it and live with the consequences.[61]

———————————————— Learning Outcome 5 ————————————————

Discuss the major similarities and differences among the three process motivation theories.

Process Motivation Theories

Process motivation theories *focus on understanding how people choose behavior to fulfill their needs.* Process motivation theories are more complex than content motivation theories. Content motivation theories simply focus on identifying and understanding people's needs. Process motivation theories go a step further, attempting to understand why people have different needs, why their needs change, how and why people choose to try to satisfy needs in different ways, the mental process people go through as they understand situations, and how they evaluate their need satisfaction.[62] In this section you will learn about three process motivation theories: equity theory, expectancy theory, and goal-setting theory.[63]

Equity Theory

If employees perceive organizational decisions and managerial actions to be unfair or unjust, they are likely to experience feelings of anger, outrage, and resentment.[64] Equity theory is primarily J. Stacy Adams' motivation theory, in which people are said to be motivated to seek social equity in the rewards they receive (output) for their performance (input).[65] **Equity theory** *proposes that people are motivated when their perceived inputs equal outputs.*

Rewarding People Equitably

Through the equity theory process, people compare their inputs (effort, experience, seniority, status, intelligence, and so forth) and outputs (praise, recognition, pay, benefits, promotions, increased status, supervisor's approval, etc.) to that of relevant others. A relevant other could be a coworker or group of employees from the same or different organizations, or even from a hypothetical situation. Notice that our definition says *perceived* and not *actual* inputs to outputs. Others may perceive that equity actually exists, and that the person complaining about inequity is wrong.[66]

Equitable distribution of pay is crucial to organizations.[67] Unfortunately, many employees tend to inflate their own efforts or performance when comparing themselves to others. Employees also tend to overestimate what others earn. Employees may be very satisfied and motivated until they find out that a relevant other is earning more for the same job, or earning the same for doing less work. A comparison with relevant others leads to three conclusions: The employee is underrewarded, overrewarded, or equitably rewarded. When inequity is perceived, employees attempt to reduce it by reducing input or increasing output.

Motivating with Equity Theory

Research supporting equity theory is mixed, because people who believe they are overrewarded usually don't change their behavior. Instead, they often rationalize that they deserve the outputs. A recent study used equity theory, and the results did support it.[68] One view of equity is that it is like Herzberg's maintenance factors. When employees are not dissatisfied, they are not actively motivated; but maintenance factors do demotivate when employees are dissatisfied. According to equity theory, when employees believe they are equitably rewarded they are not actively motivated. However, when employees believe they are underrewarded, they are demotivated.

Using equity theory in practice can be difficult, because you don't always know who the employee's reference group is, nor their view of inputs and outcomes. However, this theory does offer some useful general recommendations:

1. Managers should be aware that equity is based on perception, which may not be correct. It is possible for the manager to create equity or inequity. Some managers have favorite subordinates who get special treatment; others don't. So don't play favorites, while treating employees equally but in unique ways.[69]

2. Rewards should be equitable. When employees perceive that they are not treated fairly, morale and performance problems occur. Employees producing at the same level should be given equal rewards. Those producing less should get less.

3. High performance should be rewarded, but employees must understand the inputs needed to attain certain outputs. When incentive pay is used, there should be clear standards specifying the exact requirements to achieve the incentive. A manager should be able to objectively tell others why one person got a higher merit raise than another did.

WorkApplication7

Give an example of how equity theory has affected your motivation, or that of someone else you work with or have worked with. Be sure to specify if you were underrewarded, overrewarded, or equitably rewarded.

_____

_____

_____

_____

_____

OPENING CASE APPLICATION

4-a. How Does Market America Meet Its Distributors' Process Motivation Needs?

Market America's UnFranchise business model treats all distributors with *equity*. Owners have unlimited potential, as the more time and effort (*inputs*) they put into their business, the more potential rewards (*outputs*) are available. However, not everyone is cut out for sales and some people who start as independent distributors drop out or stay at this level, rather than advance to become UnFranchise Owners.

Expectancy Theory

Expectancy theory is based on Victor Vroom's formula: motivation = expectancy × instrumentality × valence.[70] **Expectancy theory** *proposes that people are motivated when they believe they can accomplish the task, they will get the reward, and the rewards for doing so are worth the effort.* The theory is based on the following assumptions: Both internal (needs) and external (environment) factors affect behavior; behavior is the individual's decision; people have different needs, desires, and goals; people make behavior decisions based on their perception of the outcome. Expectancy theory continues to be popular in the motivation literature today.[71]

Three Variables

All three variable conditions must be met in Vroom's formula for motivation to take place.

- *Expectancy* refers to the person's perception of his or her ability (probability) to accomplish an objective. Generally, the higher one's expectancy, the better the chance for motivation.[72] When employees do not believe that they can accomplish objectives, they will not be motivated to try.
- *Instrumentality* refers to belief that the performance will result in getting the reward. Generally, the higher one's instrumentality, the greater the chance for motivation. If employees are certain to get the reward, they probably will be motivated.[73] When not sure, employees may not be motivated. For example, Dan believes he would be a good manager and wants to get promoted. However, Dan has an external locus of control and believes that working hard will not result in a promotion anyway. Therefore, he will not be motivated to work for the promotion.
- *Valence* refers to the value a person places on the outcome or reward. Generally, the higher the value[74] (importance) of the outcome or reward, the better the chance of motivation. For example, the supervisor, Jean, wants an employee, Sim, to work harder. Jean talks to Sim and tells him that working hard will result in a promotion. If Sim wants a promotion, he will probably be motivated. However, if a promotion is not of importance to Sim, it will not motivate him.

Motivating with Expectancy Theory

One study found that expectancy theory can accurately predict a person's work effort, satisfaction level, and performance—but only if the correct values are plugged into the formula. A meta-analysis (a study using the data of 77 other prior studies) had inconsistent findings with some positive correlations. A more recent study found that expectancy theory can be used to determine if leaders can be trained to use ethical considerations in decision making.[75]

Therefore, this theory works in certain contexts but not in others. Expectancy theory also works best with employees who have an internal locus of control, because if they believe they control their destiny, their efforts will result in success. The following conditions should be implemented to make the theory result in motivation:

1. Clearly define objectives and the performance necessary to achieve them.[76]
2. Tie performance to rewards. High performance should be rewarded. When one employee works harder to produce more than other employees and is not rewarded, he or she may slow down productivity.
3. Be sure rewards are of value to the employee. Managers should get to know employees as individuals. Develop good human relations as a people developer.[77]

WorkApplication8

Give an example of how expectancy theory has affected your motivation, or that of someone else you work with or have worked with. Be sure to specify the expectancy and valence.

_____

_____

_____

_____

_____

4. Make sure your employees believe you will do what you say you will do. For example, employees must believe you will give them a merit raise if they do work hard. So that employees will believe you, follow through and show them you do what you say you'll do.

5. Use the Pygmalion effect (Chapter 2) to increase expectations. Your high expectation can result in follower self-fulfilling prophecy.[78] As the level of expectation increases, so will performance.

OPENING CASE APPLICATION

4-b. How Does Market America Meet Its Distributors' Process Motivation Needs?

Market America focuses on attracting people who have the *expectancy* that they can be successful at running their own business, and it provides the business model to help them succeed. The *valence* does vary, but most UnFranchise Owners are seeking their own business, to achieve financial independence, and freedom of time.

Goal-Setting Theory

The research conducted by E. A. Locke and others has revealed that setting objectives has a positive effect on motivation and performance.[79] High-achievement, motivated individuals consistently engage in goal setting.[80] **Goal-setting theory** *proposes that specific, difficult goals motivate people.* Our behavior has a purpose, which is usually to fulfill a need. Goals give us a sense of purpose as to why we are working to accomplish a given task.[81]

Writing Objectives

To help you to write effective objectives that meet the criteria you will learn next, use the model. The parts of the **writing objectives model** *are (1) To + (2) action verb + (3) singular, specific, and measurable result to be achieved + (4) target date.* The model is shown in Model 3-1, which is adapted from Max E. Douglas's model.

Criteria for Objectives

For an objective to be effective, it should include the four criteria listed in steps 3 and 4 of the writing objectives model:

• *Singular result.* To avoid confusion, each objective should contain only one end result. When multiple objectives are listed together, one may be met but the other(s) may not.

Model 3-1 *Writing effective objectives model.*

Four parts of the model with examples						
(1) To	+	(2) action verb	+	(3) singular, specific, and measurable result to be achieved	+	(4) target date.
Comcast To	+	offer	+	phone service to 40 million households	+	by year end 2006.[82]
Burger King To	+	achieve	+	average annual unit revenue of $1.3 million	+	by year end 2005.[83]
Toyota To	+	expand	+	annual sales to 8.5 million vehicles	+	by year end 2006.[84]

- *Specific.* The objective should state the exact level of performance expected.[85]
- *Measurable.* If people are to achieve objectives, they must be able to observe and measure their progress regularly to monitor progress and to determine if the objective has been met.[86]
- *Target date.* A specific date should be set for accomplishing the objective. When people have a deadline, they usually try harder to get the task done on time.[87] If people are simply told to do it when they can, they don't tend to get around to it until they have to. It is also more effective to set a specific date, such as October 29, rather than a set time, such as in two weeks, because you can forget when the time began and should end. Some objectives are ongoing and do not require a stated date. The target date is indefinite until it is changed.

In addition to the four criteria from the model, there are three other criteria that do not always fit within the model:

- *Difficult but achievable.* A number of studies show that individuals perform better with difficult objectives rather than (1) easy objectives, (2) objectives that are too difficult, or (3) simply told "do your best."[88] Be realistic about what you can achieve. Don't over-promise or try to do too much.[89] Jack Welch incorporated "stretch goals" in the early 1990s that led to dramatic improvements in productivity, efficiency, and profitability. Welch got everyone to focus on doing things quicker, better, and cheaper. Steven Kerr developed training programs to teach employees how to set stretch goals.[90]
- *Participatively set.* Teams that participate in setting their objectives generally outperform groups with assigned objectives.[91]
- *Commitment.* For objectives to be met, employees must accept them. If employees are not committed to striving for the objective, even if you meet

WorkApplication9

1. Using the writing objectives model, write one or more objectives for an organization you work for or have worked for that meet the criteria for objectives.

2. Give an example of how a goal(s) affected your motivation and performance, or those of someone else you work with or have worked with.

_____

_____

_____

_____

_____

the other criteria, they may not meet the objective.[92] Using participation helps get employees to accept objectives.

Ethical Dilemma 1

Academic Standards

Lou Holtz, former very successful Notre Dame football coach, said that the power of goal setting is an incredible motivator for high performance; to be successful we need to set a higher goal. Have colleges followed his advice? Have academic standards dropped, maintained, or increased over the years?

The academic credit-hour system was set many years ago so that there would be some standardization across colleges throughout the country, so that academics and employers had the same expectations of the work load that a college student carried to earn a degree. This also allowed students to transfer credit from one university to another, assuming the same standards were met.

The credit-hour system was set at students doing two hours of preparation for each hour of in-class time. So a student taking five classes should spend 15 hours in class and 30 hours preparing for class, or a total of 40+ hours per week—which is a full-time schedule.

1. How many hours outside of class, on average, do you and other students prepare for class each week?
2. Are college professors throughout the country assigning students two hours of preparation for every hour in class today? If not, why have they dropped the standard?
3. Are students who are putting in part-time hours (20–30 hours) during college being well prepared for a career after graduation (40–60 hours)?
4. Is it ethical and socially responsible for professors to drop standards and for colleges to award degrees for doing less work today than 5, 10, or 20 years ago?

Microsoft has a long tradition of having individuals set goals as part of its high performance–based culture. All employees are trained to set "SMART" (Specific, Measurable, Achievable, Results-based, and Time-specific) written goals. Managers are trained to assist in the goal-setting process, including how to provide relevant performance feedback during the review process.[93]

Using Goal Setting to Motivate Employees

Goal setting might be the most effective management tool available.[94] Organizational behavior scholars rated goal-setting theory as number one in importance among 73 management theories.[95] Need we say any more about it?

OPENING CASE APPLICATION

4-c. How Does Market America Meet Its Distributors' Process Motivation Needs?

Market America relies heavily on *goal-setting* theory. Two of its goals are to establish itself as a leader in the Direct Sales Industry and to become a Fortune 500 Company. Goal Setting is the second step in the five basic steps for success at Market America. Attitude & Knowledge, Retailing, Prospecting & Recruiting, and Follow Up & Duplication are the other four. Distributors are taught to set business and personal long-term goals and to break them down for the next year by month, week, and day. Goals are to be read twice a day for motivation.

Reinforcement Theory

B. F. Skinner, reinforcement motivation theorist, contends that to motivate employees it is not necessary to identify and understand needs (content motivation theories), nor to understand how employees choose behaviors to fulfill them (process motivation theories).[96] All the manager needs to do is understand the relationship between behaviors and their consequences, and then arrange contingencies that reinforce desirable behaviors and discourage undesirable behaviors.[97] **Reinforcement theory** proposes *that through the consequences for behavior, people will be motivated to behave in predetermined ways.* Reinforcement theory uses behavior modification (apply reinforcement theory to get employees to do what you want them to do) and operant conditioning (types and schedules of reinforcement).[98] Skinner states that behavior is learned through experiences of positive and negative consequences. The three components of Skinner's framework are found in Exhibit 3-10, with an example.[99]

The other motivation theories do not fundamentally change the motivational structure,[100] as reinforcement theory does. A recent meta-analysis of empirical research over the past 20 years found that reinforcement theory increased performance by 17 percent.[101] Thus, reinforcement theory can be a consistent predictor of job behavior.[102]

As illustrated in the example in Exhibit 3-10, behavior is a function of its consequences.[103] Employees learn what is, and is not, desired behavior as a result of the consequences for specific behavior. The two important concepts

Exhibit 3-10 *Components of reinforcement theory.*

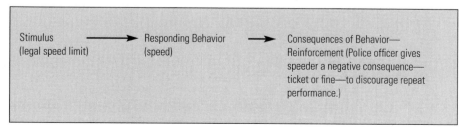

Stimulus (legal speed limit) → Responding Behavior (speed) → Consequences of Behavior—Reinforcement (Police officer gives speeder a negative consequence—ticket or fine—to discourage repeat performance.)

used to modify behavior are the types of reinforcement and the schedules of reinforcement.

Learning Outcome 6

Explain the four types of reinforcement.

Types of Reinforcement

The four types of reinforcement are positive, avoidance, extinction, and punishment.

Positive Reinforcement

A method of encouraging continued behavior is to offer attractive consequences (rewards) for desirable performance.[104] For example, an employee is on time for a meeting and is rewarded by the manager thanking him or her. The praise is used to reinforce punctuality. Other reinforcements are pay, promotions, time off, increased status, and so forth. Author Ken Blanchard says that positive reinforcement results in positive results, and it is the best motivator for increasing productivity.[105]

Avoidance Reinforcement

Avoidance is also called *negative reinforcement*. As with positive reinforcement, you are encouraging continued desirable behavior. The employee avoids the negative consequence. For example, an employee is punctual for a meeting to avoid the negative reinforcement, such as a reprimand. *Rules* are designed to get employees to avoid certain behavior. However, rules in and of themselves are not a punishment. Punishment is given only if the rule is broken.

Extinction

Rather than encourage desirable behavior, extinction (and punishment) attempts to reduce or eliminate undesirable behavior by withholding reinforcement when the behavior occurs. For example, an employee who is late for a meeting is not rewarded with praise. Or the manager may withhold a reward of value, such as a pay raise, until the employee performs to set standards.

From another perspective, managers who do not reward good performance can cause its extinction.[106] In other words, if you ignore good employee performance, good performance may stop because employees think, "Why should I do a good job if I'm not rewarded in some way?"

Punishment

Punishment is used to provide an undesirable consequence for undesirable behavior.[107] For example, an employee who is late for a meeting is reprimanded. Notice that with avoidance there is no actual punishment; it's the threat of the punishment that controls behavior. Other methods of punishment include harassing, taking away privileges, probation, fining, demoting, firing, and so forth. Using punishment may reduce the undesirable behavior; but it may cause other undesirable behaviors, such as poor morale, lower productivity, and acts of theft or sabotage. Punishment is the most controversial and the

Exhibit 3-11 *Types of reinforcement.*

As a manager, you have a secretary who makes many errors when completing correspondence. Your objective, which you discussed with the secretary, is to decrease the error rate by 50 percent by Friday June 2, 2006. Based on the secretary's performance at that time, you have four types of reinforcement that you can use with him or her when you next review the work.

EMPLOYEE BEHAVIOR		TYPE OF REINFORCEMENT		MANAGER ACTION (CONSEQUENCE)		EMPLOYEE BEHAVIOR MODIFICATION (FUTURE)
Improved performance	→	Positive	→	Praise improvements	→	Repeat quality work*
Improved performance	→	Avoidance	→	Do not give any reprimand	→	Repeat quality work
Performance not improved	→	Extinction	→	Withhold praise/raise	→	Do not repeat poor work
Performance not improved	→	Punishment	→	Discipline action, such as a written warning	→	Do not repeat poor work

*Assuming the employee improved performance, positive reinforcement is the best motivator.

least effective method in motivating employees. Exhibit 3-11 illustrates the four types of reinforcement.

Schedules of Reinforcement

The second reinforcement consideration in controlling behavior is determining when to reinforce performance. The two major classifications are continuous and intermittent.

Continuous Reinforcement

With a continuous method, each and every desired behavior is reinforced. Examples of this method would be a machine with an automatic counter that lets the employee know, at any given moment, exactly how many units have been produced, a piece rate of $1 for each unit produced, or a manager who comments on every customer report.

Intermittent Reinforcement

With intermittent reinforcement, the reward is given based on the passage of time or output. When the reward is based on the passage of time, it is called an *interval* schedule. When it is based on output, it is called a *ratio* schedule. When electing to use intermittent reinforcement, you have four alternatives:

- *Fixed interval schedule.* Giving a salary paycheck every week, breaks and meals at the same time every day.
- *Variable interval schedule.* Giving praise only now and then, a surprise inspection, or a pop quiz.
- *Fixed ratio schedule.* Giving a piece rate or bonus after producing a standard rate.
- *Variable ratio schedule.* Giving praise for excellent work, or a lottery for employees who have not been absent for a set time.

Ratios are generally better motivators than intervals. The variable ratio tends to be the most powerful schedule for sustaining behavior.

WorkApplication10

Give one or more examples of the types of reinforcement, and the schedules used, on a present or past job.

_____

_____

_____

_____

_____

Ethical Dilemma 2

Airlines

An airline often charges higher fares for one-way tickets than round-trip tickets, and for direct flight tickets to its hub than for flight connections from its hub to another destination. So some travelers buy round-trip tickets and only go one way, and some end their travel at the hub instead of taking the connection (a "hidden city" itinerary), to save money. The airlines call this breach of contract: they have *punished* travel agencies for tickets that aren't properly used, they sometimes demand higher fares from travelers caught, and they have seized some travelers' frequent-flier miles, saying they were fraudulently obtained.

1. Not using the full travel of a ticket breaks airline rules but not the law, so it's not illegal, unless travelers lie about what they are doing. But is it ethical and socially responsible behavior of travelers?
2. Is it ethical and socially responsible for airlines to charge more for less travel?
3. Is it ethical and socially responsible to punish people who break the ticket rules?
4. Is reinforcement theory effective (does it motivate you and others) in today's global economy?
5. Is reinforcement theory ethical and socially responsible, or manipulative?

You Get What You Reinforce

You get what you reinforce, not necessarily what you reward. Recall that there are four types of reinforcement, and reward is only one of them; it doesn't always motivate the desired behavior. One of the important things you should learn in this course is that people will do what they are reinforced for doing. People seek information concerning what activities are reinforced, and then seek to do (or at least pretend to do) those things, often to the exclusion of activities not reinforced. The extent to which this occurs, of course, depends on the attractiveness of the rewards offered and the penalties for the behavior.[108]

For example, if a professor gives a class a reading list of several sources, but tells students (or they realize without being told) that they will not discuss them in class, nor be tested on them, how many students will read them? Or, if the professor says, "ABC from this chapter are important and I'll test you on them, but XYZ will not be on the test," will students spend equal time studying both groups of material?

In the business setting, if the manager repeatedly says quality is important, but the standard of evaluation includes only quantity and meeting scheduled shipments, how many employees will ship poor-quality products to meet the scheduled shipment? How many will miss the scheduled shipment, take a reprimand for missing the scheduled shipment, and get a poor performance review in order to do a quality job? An incomplete standard measuring only quantitative output that is highly visible and easy to measure is a common problem.[109]

Exhibit 3-12 *Common management reward follies.*

MANAGERS HOPE FOR:	BUT MANAGERS FREQUENTLY REWARD:
Long-term growth and environmental social responsibility	Quarterly earnings
Innovative thinking and risk taking	Proven methods and not making mistakes
Teamwork and collaboration	The best competitive individual performers
Employee involvement and empowerment	Tight control over operations and resources
High achievement	Another year's effort
Candor such as telling of bad news early	Reporting good news, whether it is true or not, and agreeing with the boss, whether the boss is right or wrong

Source: Adapted from S. Kerr. "On the Folly of Rewarding A, While Hoping for B." *Academy of Management Executive* 9 (February 1995): 32–40.

The Folly of Rewarding A, while Hoping for B

Reward systems are often fouled up in that the types of behavior being rewarded are those that the manager is trying to discourage, while the desired behavior is not being rewarded at all. This problem is called the folly of rewarding A, while hoping for B.[110] Exhibit 3-12 presents a couple of examples.

Motivating with Reinforcement

Several organizations, including 3M, Frito-Lay, and B. F. Goodrich, have used reinforcement to increase productivity; Michigan Bell had a 50 percent improvement in attendance and above-standard productivity and efficiency level; and Emery Air Freight went from 30 percent of employees meeting the standard to 90 percent after using reinforcement. Emery estimates that its reinforcement program has resulted in a $650,000 yearly savings.

Generally, positive reinforcement is the best motivator. Continuous reinforcement is better at sustaining desired behavior; however, it is not always possible or practical. Here are some general guidelines for using positive reinforcement:

1. Make sure employees know exactly what is expected of them. Set clear objectives.[111]
2. Select appropriate rewards.[112] A reward to one person could be considered a punishment by another. Know your employees' needs.
3. Select the appropriate reinforcement schedule.
4. Do not reward mediocre or poor performance.
5. Look for the positive and give praise, rather than focus on the negative and criticize. Make people feel good about themselves (Pygmalion effect).
6. Never go a day without giving sincere praise.
7. Do things for your employees, instead of to them, and you will see productivity increases.

As a manager, try the positive first. Positive reinforcement is a true motivator because it creates a win-win situation by meeting the needs of the employee as well as the manager and organization. From the employees' perspective, avoidance and punishment create a lose-win situation. The organization or manager wins by forcing them to do something they really don't want to do.

Giving Praise

Pay can increase performance. But it is not the only, nor necessarily the best, reinforcer for performance. Empirical research studies have found that feedback and social reinforcers (praise) may have as strong an impact on performance as pay.[113] In the 1940s, a survey revealed that what employees want most from a job is full appreciation for work done. Similar studies have been performed over the years with little change in results. Jack Welch says to find ways to celebrate achievements.[114]

Although research has shown praise to be an effective motivator, and giving praise costs nothing and takes only a minute, few employees are getting a pat on the back these days. When was the last time your manager thanked you or gave you some praise for a job well done? When was the last time your manager complained about your work? If you are a manager, when was the last time you praised or criticized your employees? What is the ratio of praise to criticism?

Giving praise develops a positive self-concept in employees and leads to better performance—the Pygmalion effect and self-fulfilling prophecy. Praise is a motivator (not maintenance) because it meets employees' needs for esteem and self-actualization, growth, and achievement. Giving praise creates a win-win situation. It is probably the most powerful, simplest, least costly, and yet most underused motivational technique there is.

Ken Blanchard and Spencer Johnson popularized giving praise through their best-selling book, *The One-Minute Manager.*[115] They developed a technique that involves giving one-minute feedback of praise. Model 3-2, Giving Praise, is an adaptation. *The steps in the* **giving praise model** *are (1) Tell the employee exactly what was done correctly. (2) Tell the employee why the behavior is important. (3) Stop for a moment of silence. (4) Encourage repeat performance.* Blanchard calls it one-minute praise because it should not take more than one minute to give the praise. It is not necessary for the employee to say anything. The four steps are described below and illustrated in Model 3-2.

step 1.   **Tell the employee exactly what was done correctly.** When giving praise, look the person in the eye. Eye contact shows sincerity and concern. It is important to be very specific and descriptive. General

Model 3-2 *Giving praise.*

STEP 1	STEP 2	STEP 3	STEP 4
Tell the employee exactly what was done correctly.	Tell the employee why the behavior is important.	Stop for a moment of silence.	Encourage repeat performance.

statements, like "you're a good worker," are not as effective. On the other hand, don't talk for too long, or the praise loses its effectiveness.

step 2. **Tell the employee why the behavior is important.** Briefly state how the organization and/or person benefits from the action. It is also helpful to tell the employee how you feel about the behavior. Be specific and descriptive.

step 3. **Stop for a moment of silence.** Being silent is tough for many managers. The rationale for the silence is to give the employee the chance to "feel" the impact of the praise. It's like "the pause that refreshes." When you are thirsty and take the first sip or gulp of a refreshing drink, it's not until you stop, and maybe say, "Ah," that you feel your thirst quenched.

step 4. **Encourage repeat performance.** This is the reinforcement that motivates the employee to continue the desired behavior. Blanchard recommends touching the employee. Touching has a powerful impact. However, he recommends it only if both parties feel comfortable. Others say don't touch employees; it could lead to a sexual harassment charge.

As you can see, giving praise is easy, and it doesn't cost a penny. Managers trained to give praise say it works wonders. It's a much better motivator than giving a raise or other monetary reward. One manager stated that an employee was taking his time stacking cans on a display. He gave the employee praise for stacking the cans so straight. The employee was so pleased with the praise that the display went up with about a 100 percent increase in productivity. Note that the manager looked for the positive, and used positive reinforcement rather than punishment. The manager could have given a reprimand comment such as, "Quit goofing off and get the display up faster." That statement would not have motivated the employee to increase productivity. All it would have done was hurt human relations, and could have ended in an argument. The cans were straight. The employee was not praised for the slow work pace. However, if the praise had not worked, the manager should have used another reinforcement method.[116]

---

5. How Does Market America Use Reinforcement Theory to Motivate Its Distributors?

Market America uses *positive reinforcement* with a *continuous reinforcement schedule* as each and every sale results in compensation. It has a standardized meetings system throughout all of the areas. However, the frequency of meetings is based on a *variable ratio schedule* depending on the area and the amount of activity in the area. There are business briefings, showing the business to others, trainings, teaching new and existing distributors, seminars, district rallies and a national convention. *Praise* and other recognition for accomplishments are given during meetings. Distributors share successes stories, testimonials, voice mail tips, tapes and books.

OPENING CASE APPLICATION

Exhibit 3-13 *The motivation process with the motivation theories.*

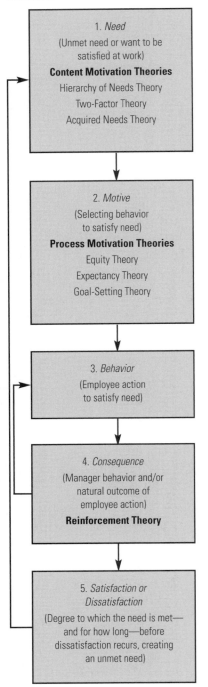

1. *Need*
(Unmet need or want to be satisfied at work)
Content Motivation Theories
Hierarchy of Needs Theory
Two-Factor Theory
Acquired Needs Theory

2. *Motive*
(Selecting behavior to satisfy need)
Process Motivation Theories
Equity Theory
Expectancy Theory
Goal-Setting Theory

3. *Behavior*
(Employee action to satisfy need)

4. *Consequence*
(Manager behavior and/or natural outcome of employee action)
Reinforcement Theory

5. *Satisfaction or Dissatisfaction*
(Degree to which the need is met—and for how long—before dissatisfaction recurs, creating an unmet need)

———— Learning Outcome 7 ————

State the major differences among content, process, and reinforcement theories.

Putting the Motivation Theories Together within the Motivation Process

Goal-setting theory gurus Edwin Locke and Gary Latham recently stated that there is an urgent need to tie motivational theories and processes together into an overall model, insofar as it is possible.[117] That is exactly what we do in this last section of the chapter.

Motivation is important because it helps to explain why employees behave the way they do. At this point you may be wondering: How do these theories fit together? Is one the best? Should I try to pick the correct theory for a given situation? The groups of theories are complementary; each group of theories refers to a different stage in the motivation process. Each group of theories answers a different question. Content motivation theories answer the question: What needs do employees have that should be met on the job? Process motivation theories answer the question: How do employees choose behavior to fulfill their needs? Reinforcement theory answers the question: What can managers do to get employees to behave in ways that meet the organizational objectives?

In this chapter you learned that the motivation process went from need to motive to behavior to consequence to satisfaction or dissatisfaction. Now let's make the motivation process a little more complex by incorporating the motivation theories, or answers to the preceding questions, into the process. See Exhibit 3-13 for an illustration. Note that step 4 loops back to step 3 because, according to reinforcement theory, behavior is learned through consequences. Step 4 does not loop back to steps 1 or 2 because reinforcement theory is not concerned about needs, motives, or satisfaction; it focuses on getting employees to behave in predetermined ways, through consequences provided by managers. Also note that step 5 loops back to step 1 because meeting needs is ongoing; meeting our needs is a never-ending process. Finally, be aware that according to two-factor theory, step 5 (satisfaction or dissatisfaction) is not on one continuum but on two separate continuums (satisfied to not satisfied or dissatisfied to not dissatisfied), based on the level of need being met (motivator or maintenance).

Go to the Internet (academic.cengage.com/management/lussier) where you will find a broad array of resources to help maximize your learning.

• Review the vocabulary

• Try a quiz

• View chapter videos

Motivation Theories

Identify each supervisor's statement of how to motivate employees by the theory behind the statement. Write the appropriate letter in the blank before each item.

a. hierarchy of needs   d. equity   f. expectancy
b. two-factor   e. goal-setting   g. reinforcement
c. acquired needs

_____ 11. I motivate employees by making their jobs interesting and challenging.

_____ 12. I make sure I treat everyone fairly to motivate them.

_____ 13. I know Kate likes people, so I give her jobs in which she works with other employees.

_____ 14. Carl would often yell in the halls because he knew it bothered me. So I decided to ignore his yelling, and he stopped.

_____ 15. I got to know all of my employees' values. Now I can offer rewards that will motivate them when they achieve attainable task performance.

_____ 16. Our company now offers good working conditions, salaries, and benefits, so we are working at developing the third need for socialization.

_____ 17. When my employees do a good job, I thank them using a four-step model.

_____ 18. I used to try to improve working conditions to motivate employees. But I stopped and now focus on giving employees more responsibility so they can grow and develop new skills.

_____ 19. I tell employees exactly what I want them to do, with a tough deadline that they can achieve.

_____ 20. I now realize that I tend to be an autocratic manager because it helps fill my needs. I will work at giving some of my employees more autonomy on how they do their jobs.

Applying the Concept 3

Chapter Summary

The chapter summary is organized to answer the eight learning outcomes for Chapter 3.

1. List the University of Iowa leadership styles.
The University of Iowa leadership styles are autocratic and democratic.

2. Describe similarities and differences between the University of Michigan and Ohio State University leadership models.
The University of Michigan and Ohio State University Leadership Models are similar because they are both based on the same two distinct leadership behaviors, although the models use different names for the two behaviors. The models are different because the University of Michigan model identifies two leadership styles based on either job- or employee-centered behavior. The Ohio State University model states that a leader uses high or low structure and consideration, resulting in four leadership style combinations of these two behaviors.

3. Discuss similarities and differences between the Ohio State University Leadership Model and the Leadership Grid.
Both theories are based on the same two leadership behaviors; but use different names for the two dimensions. The theories

are different because the Leadership Grid identifies five leadership styles, with one being middle of the road, while the Ohio State Model identifies four leadership styles. The Leadership Grid also gives each combination of the two-dimensional behaviors one leadership style name. Authors of the Leadership Grid were strong supporters of the high-high team leadership style as the best.

4. Discuss similarities and differences among the three content motivation theories.

Similarities among the content motivation theories include their focus on identifying and understanding employee needs. The theories identify similar needs, but are different in the way they classify the needs. Hierarchy of needs theory includes physiological, safety, belongingness, esteem, and self-actualization needs. Two-factor theory includes motivators and maintenance factors. Acquired needs theory includes achievement, power, and affiliation needs and includes no lower level needs, as the other two theories do.

5. Discuss the major similarities and differences among the three process motivation theories.

The similarity among the three process motivation theories includes their focus on understanding how employees choose behaviors to fulfill their needs. However, they are very different in their perceptions of how employees are motivated. Equity theory proposes that employees are motivated when their perceived inputs equal outputs. Goal-setting theory proposes that achievable, difficult goals motivate employees. Expectancy theory proposes that employees are motivated when they believe they can accomplish the task and the rewards for doing so are worth the effort.

6. Explain the four types of reinforcement.

(1) Positive reinforcement provides the employee with a reward consequence for performing the desired behavior. (2) Avoidance reinforcement encourages employees to perform the desired behavior in order to avoid a negative consequence. (3) Extinction reinforcement withholds a positive consequence to get the employee to stop performing undesirable behavior. (4) Punishment reinforcement gives the employee a negative consequence to get the employee to stop performing undesirable behavior.

7. State the major differences among content, process, and reinforcement theories.

Content motivation theories focus on identifying and understanding employees' needs. Process motivation goes a step further to understand how employees choose behavior to fulfill their needs. Reinforcement theory is not as concerned about employee needs; it focuses on getting employees to do what managers want them to do through the consequences provided by managers for their behavior. The use of rewards is the means of motivating employees.

8. Define the following key terms (in order of appearance in the chapter).

Select one or more methods: (1) fill in the missing key terms from memory, (2) match the key terms from the following list with their definitions below, (3) copy the key terms in order from the list at the beginning of the chapter.

_____ is the combination of traits, skills, and behaviors leaders use as they interact with followers.

_____ identifies two leadership styles: job-centered and employee-centered.

_____ identifies four leadership styles: low structure and high consideration, high structure and high consideration, low structure and low consideration, and high structure and low consideration.

_____ identifies five leadership styles: 1,1 impoverished; 9,1 authority-compliance; 1,9 country club; 5,5 middle of the road; and 9,9 team leader.

_____ is anything that affects behavior in pursuing a certain outcome.

_____ is when people go from need to motive to behavior to consequence to satisfaction or dissatisfaction.

_____ focus on explaining and predicting behavior based on people's needs.

_____ proposes that people are motivated through five levels of needs—physiological, safety, belongingness, esteem, and self-actualization.

_____ proposes that people are motivated by motivators rather than maintenance factors.

_____ proposes that people are motivated by their need for achievement, power, and affiliation.

_____ focus on understanding how people choose behavior to fulfill their needs.

_____ proposes that people are motivated when their perceived inputs equal outputs.

_____ proposes that people are motivated when they believe they can accomplish the task, they will get the reward, and the rewards for doing so are worth the effort.

_____ proposes that specific, difficult goals motivate people.

_____ includes (1) To + (2) action verb + (3) singular, specific, and measurable result to be achieved + (4) target date.

_____ proposes that through the consequences for behavior, people will be motivated to behave in predetermined ways.

_____ includes four steps—(1) Tell the employee exactly what was done correctly. (2) Tell the employee why the behavior is important. (3) Stop for a moment of silence. (4) Encourage repeat performance.

Key Terms

acquired needs theory, 91

content motivation theories, 85

equity theory, 93

expectancy theory, 94

giving praise model, 104

goal-setting theory, 96

hierarchy of needs theory, 87

Leadership Grid, 81

leadership style, 75

motivation, 84

motivation process, 84

Ohio State University Leadership Model, 79

process motivation theories, 93

reinforcement theory, 99

two-factor theory, 88

University of Michigan Leadership Model, 76

writing objectives model, 96

Review and Discussion Questions

1. How is leadership behavior based on traits?
2. Do you agree with the University of Michigan model (with two leadership styles) or with the Ohio State model (with four leadership styles)?
3. What are three important contributions of the University of Michigan and Ohio State University studies?
4. What are three important contributions of the Leadership Grid and high-high research?
5. What is motivation, and why is it important to know how to motivate employees?
6. Which of the four content motivation theories do you prefer? Why?
7. Which of the three process motivation theories do you prefer? Why?
8. Reinforcement theory is unethical because it is used to manipulate employees. Do you agree with this statement? Explain your answer.
9. Which motivation theory do you feel is the best? Explain why.
10. What is your motivation theory? What major methods, techniques, and so on, do you plan to use on the job as a manager to increase motivation and performance?

Case

ART FRIEDMAN—FRIEDMANS MICROWAVE OVENS

Friedmans Microwave Ovens began in 1976 in Oakland, California, with the goal of being the absolute best place to buy a microwave oven and its accessories. For 30 years, Friedmans has been accomplishing its goal by providing superior service, good prices, unconditional satisfaction guarantees, and cooking classes to educate customers on how to get the most from their microwave. Friedmans also offers installation and repair services. Friedmans has sold more than two million microwaves, and it currently has seven stores in California, and one in Tennessee.

Its most recent strategic expansion has been to the Internet. Friedmans sells a wide range of famous brands of microwave ovens and accessories indirectly through its website at **http://www.friedmansmicrowave.com**. Unlike competitors, at the website, you will not find pictures and descriptions of all the microwaves Friedmans sells with instructions for buying directly over the Internet. You are asked to call or e-mail to discuss what you are looking for, or to ask any questions.

Thus, using the Internet, Friedmans continues to focus on superior customer service.

Going to the Net was Friedmans' third major strategic move. Friedmans actually started in 1970 as Friedmans Appliances, selling all types of major appliances, so it changed its name and focus to microwaves only. Friedmans second strategic move was to franchise its microwave business, using Art Friedman's motivational technique of making everyone a boss. The original appliance store employed 15 people in Oakland, California. Friedman believed that his employees were not motivated, so he implemented the following changes to motivate his employees, and he still uses these techniques today. The following conversation took place between Bob Lussier and founder Art Friedman.

Bob: What is the reason for your success in business?
Art: My business technique.
Bob: What is it? How did you implement it?

Art: I called my 15 employees together and told them, "From now on I want you to feel as though the company is ours, not mine. We are all bosses. From now on you decide what you're worth and tell the accountant to put it in your pay envelope. You decide which days and hours you work and when to take time off. We will have an open petty cash system that will allow anyone to go into the box and borrow money when they need it."

Bob: You're kidding, right?

Art: No, it's true. I really do these things.

Bob: Did anyone ask for a raise?

Art: Yes, several people did. Charlie asked for and received a $100-a-week raise.

Bob: Did he and the others increase their productivity to earn their raises?

Art: Yes, they all did.

Bob: How could you run an appliance store with employees coming and going as they pleased?

Art: The employees made up schedules that were satisfactory to everyone. We had no problems of under- or overstaffing.

Bob: Did anyone steal from the petty cash box?

Art: No.

Bob: Would this technique work in any business?

Art: It did work, it still works, and it will always work!

GO TO THE INTERNET: To learn more about Friedmans Microwave Ovens, log on to InfoTrac® College Edition at **academic.cengage.com/infotrac** and use the advanced search function.

Support your answers to the following questions with specific information from the case and text or other information you get from the Web or other sources.

1. Which University of Iowa, Michigan, and Ohio State leadership styles does Art Friedman use?

2. Which specific motivation level, factor, and need (from the content motivation theories) applies to Friedmans Microwave Ovens?

3. Do equity and expectancy theory apply to this case? Explain.

4. Which type of reinforcement does Friedman use?

5. Do you know of any organizations that use any of Friedman's or other unusual techniques? If yes, what is the organization's name? What does it do?

6. Could Friedman's techniques work in all organizations? Explain your answer.

7. In a position of authority, would you use Friedman's techniques? Which ones?

Cumulative Case Questions

8. Which of the Big Five personality dimensions is best illustrated in this case by Art Friedman (Chapter 2)?

9. Does Friedman have a Theory X or Theory Y attitude (Chapter 2)?

Case Exercise and Role-Play

Preparation: From case question 7, which of Friedman's motivational techniques would you use to motivate franchisees? Which techniques of your own or from other organizations would you use? Justify your choice of motivation techniques.

In-Class Groups: Break into groups of 4 to 6 members, and develop a list of motivational techniques group members would use, with justification. Select a spokesperson to record the techniques with justification and present them to the class.

Role-Play: One person (representing themselves or a group) may give the speech to the entire class, stating which new motivational techniques will be used and explaining each technique.

Video Case

Buffalo Zoo: Motivation in Organizations

When Donna Fernandes first arrived at the Buffalo Zoo in upstate New York, she encountered an organization plagued by flagging attendance, low employee morale, and a reputation for being poorly managed and operated. The autocratic leadership style and heavy-handed policies of former management had created an unpleasant work environment, and the well-trained and educated keepers and staff were not granted the freedom necessary to provide expert animal care.

View the Video (12 minutes)
View the video on Buffalo Zoo in class or at **academic. cengage.com/management/lussier**.

Read the Case
Under the direction of Ms. Fernandes, the Buffalo Zoo has enjoyed a turnaround of mammoth proportions. Fernandes' participatory management style and natural enthusiasm for the job have made her mission to restore greatness to the Buffalo Zoo a dream shared by all. The Zoo's fresh new initiatives and successes have been largely employee-driven, and many observers have noted that the CEO's efforts to empower staff have given new life to the entire organization.

Today, the atmosphere at the Buffalo Zoo is upbeat and optimistic. Employees report being happier in their jobs, and they are given authority to make decisions and act on new ideas. With encouragement from Ms. Fernandes, the staff has created many exciting activities and exhibits to educate and entertain the Zoo's 340,000 annual visitors. Guests at the new and improved Buffalo Zoo can now buy unusual paintings made by elephants and other wild animals. They can feed the giraffes, take a starlight safari, tour the conservation station, or see the vanishing animals exhibit—all within renovated buildings, naturalized habitats, and clean grounds that have replaced the Zoo's old worn exterior.

How Donna Fernandes got everyone to transform a run-down, sparsely visited Zoo in the space of just a few years is a testimony to her motivational abilities. By understanding the underlying needs of her employees, Ms. Fernandes was able to foster a motivated staff committed to the dream of making the Buffalo Zoo an educational and entertaining attraction for individuals and families throughout the region.

Answer the Questions

1. Based on the personal testimonies given in the video, which needs in Maslow's hierarchy do you think are most important to the employees at the Buffalo Zoo? What actions has Donna Fernandes taken to help meet those needs?
2. How does Ms. Fernandes use positive reinforcement to motivate her employees? Give specific examples.

Skill-Development Exercise 1

WRITING OBJECTIVES

Preparing for Skill-Development Exercise 1

For this exercise, you will first work at improving objectives that do not meet the criteria for objectives. Then you will write nine objectives for yourself.

Part 1. For each objective below, identify the missing criteria and rewrite the objective so that it meets all essential criteria. When writing objectives, use the model:

To + action verb + singular, specific, and measurable result + target date

1. To improve our company image by year-end 2007.
Criteria missing: _____
Improved objective: _____

_____

2. To increase the number of customers by 10 percent.
Criteria missing: _____
Improved objective: _____

_____

3. To increase profits during 2006.
Criteria missing: _____
Improved objective: _____

_____

4. To sell 5 percent more hot dogs and soda at the baseball game on Sunday, June 13, 2006.
Criteria missing: _____
Improved objective: _____

_____

Part 2. Write three educational, personal, and career objectives you want to accomplish. Your objectives can be as short term

as something you want to accomplish today, or as long term as 20 years from now. Be sure your objectives meet the criteria for effective objectives.

Educational objectives:
1. _____
2. _____
3. _____

Personal objectives:
1. _____
2. _____
3. _____

Career objectives:
1. _____
2. _____
3. _____

Doing Skill-Development Exercise 1 in Class

Objective
To develop your skill at writing objectives.

Preparation
You should have corrected and have written objectives during the preparation before class.

Experience
You will get feedback on how well you corrected the four objectives and share your written objectives with others.

Options (8–20 minutes)
A. The instructor goes over suggested corrections for the four objectives in part 1 of the preparation, and then

calls on class members to share their written objectives with the class in part 2.

B. The instructor goes over suggested corrections for the four objectives in part 1 of the preparation, and then the class breaks into groups of four to six to share their written objectives.

C. Break into groups of four to six and go over the corrections for the four objectives in part 1. Tell the instructor when your group is done, but go on to part 2, sharing your written objectives, until all groups are finished with the four corrections. The instructor goes over the corrections and may allow more time for sharing objectives. Give each other feedback for improving your written objectives during part 2.

Conclusion

The instructor may lead a class discussion and/or make concluding remarks.

Apply It (2–4 minutes)

What did I learn from this experience? How will I use the knowledge in the future?

_____

_____

_____

Sharing

In the group, or to the entire class, volunteers may give their answers to the "Apply It" questions.

Behavior Model Skills Training 1

Session 1

This training for leadership behavior modeling skills has four parts, as follows.

1. First, read how to use the model.
2. Then, view the behavior model video that illustrates how to give praise, following the four steps in the model.
3. Develop the skill in class by doing Skill-Development Exercise 2.

4. Further develop this skill by using the model in your personal and professional life.

Giving Praise Model

Review Model 3-2, "Giving Praise," in the text.

Behavior Model Video 1

GIVING PRAISE

Objective

To assist you in giving praise that motivates others to high levels of performance.

Video (4½ minutes) Overview

You will watch a bank branch manager give praise to an employee for two different jobs well done.

Skill-Development Exercise 2

GIVING PRAISE

Preparing for Skill-Development Exercise 2

Think of a job situation in which you did something well-deserving of praise and recognition. For example, you may have saved the company some money, you may have turned a dissatisfied customer into a happy one, and so forth. If you have never worked or done something well, interview someone

who has. Put yourself in a management position and write out the praise you would give to an employee for doing what you did. Briefly describe the situation:

_____

_____

_____

Step 1. Tell the employee exactly what was done correctly.

_____

_____

_____

Step 2. Tell the employee why the behavior is important.

_____

_____

_____

Step 3. Stop for a moment of silence. (Count to five silently to yourself.)

Step 4. Encourage repeat performance.

_____

_____

_____

Doing Skill-Development Exercise 2 in Class

Objective
To develop your skill at giving praise.

Preparation
You will need your prepared praise.

Experience
You will give and receive praise.

Procedure (10–15 minutes)
Break into groups of four to six. One at a time, give the praise you prepared.

1. Explain the situation.
2. Select a group member to receive the praise.

3. Give the praise. (Talk; don't read it off the paper.) Try to select the position you would use if you were actually giving the praise on the job. (Both standing, both sitting, etc.)
4. Integration. The group gives the praise-giver feedback on how he or she did:

Step 1. Was the praise very specific and descriptive? Did the giver look the employee in the eye?

Step 2. Was the importance of the behavior clearly stated?

Step 3. Did the giver stop for a moment of silence?

Step 4. Did the giver encourage repeat performance? Did the giver of praise touch the receiver (optional)?

Did the praise take less than one minute? Was the praise sincere?

Conclusion
The instructor leads a class discussion and/or makes concluding remarks.

Apply It (2–4 minutes)
What did I learn from this experience? How will I use this knowledge in the future? When will I practice?

_____

_____

_____

Sharing
In the group, or to the entire class, volunteers may give their answers to the "Apply It" questions.

Influencing: Power, Politics, Networking, and Negotiation

4

LEARNING OUTCOMES

After studying this chapter, you should be able to:

1. Explain the differences between position power and personal power. p. 116
2. Discuss the differences among legitimate, reward, coercive, and referent power. p. 117
3. Discuss how power and politics are related. p. 129
4. Describe how money and politics have a similar use. p. 129
5. List and explain the steps in the networking process. p. 137
6. List the steps in the negotiation process. p. 143
7. Explain the relationships among negotiation and conflict, influencing tactics, power, and politics. p. 143
8. Define the following **key terms** (in order of appearance in the chapter):

influencing	information power
power	connection power
legitimate power	politics
reward power	networking
coercive power	reciprocity
referent power	one-minute self-sell
expert power	negotiating

Opening Case Application

Robert L. Johnson is the founder (1980) of Black Entertainment Television (BET), the leading African-American owned and operated media and entertainment company in America, which is a subsidiary of Viacom. BET offers 24-hour programming targeted at African-Americans in more than 65 million U.S. households, which reaches 90 percent of all black cable homes. Johnson served as chairman and CEO of BET until he retired in January 2006.

Johnson did not start at the top. He spent time climbing the corporate ladder at the Corporation for Public Broadcasting and the Washington Urban League, and was press secretary for a congressman. Prior to founding BET, he was the vice president of government relations for the National Cable & Telecommunications Association (NCTA), which is the trade association representing more than 1,500 cable television companies. Through the years, he has served on several boards of profit and not-for-profit organizations.

Johnson is also the first African-American to be a majority owner of a professional sports franchise in the United States. Johnson is the majority owner of the National Basketball Association (NBA) Charlotte Bobcats and the Charlotte Sting of the Women's National Basketball Association (WNBA).[1]

Opening Case Questions:

1. How did Robert Johnson use power to overcome discrimination in his career?
2. What types of power does Johnson have? How does he use his power?
3. How did Johnson effectively use organizational politics at BET?
4. How did Johnson use networking to advance his career?
5. What types of negotiating and collaborating did Johnson do?

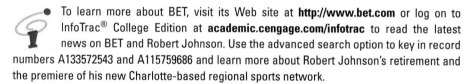 To learn more about BET, visit its Web site at **http://www.bet.com** or log on to InfoTrac® College Edition at **academic.cengage.com/infotrac** to read the latest news on BET and Robert Johnson. Use the advanced search option to key in record numbers A133572543 and A115759686 and learn more about Robert Johnson's retirement and the premiere of his new Charlotte-based regional sports network.

Besides excellent work, what does it take to get ahead in an organization? To climb the corporate ladder, you will have to influence people—to gain power, play organizational politics, network, and negotiate to get what you want. These related concepts are the topics of this chapter. Recall from our definition of leadership (Chapter 1) that leadership is the "influencing" process of leaders and followers to achieve organizational objectives through change. Leaders and followers influence each other, because we are all potential leaders.[2] Influencing is so important that it is called the essence of leadership. Influence has a direct effect on organizational performance.[3] Power, politics, and negotiation are all ways of influencing others. In essence, this chapter is a continuation of Chapter 3 as it focuses on leadership behavior by explaining how leaders influence others at the individual level of analysis. Let's begin with power.

Power

Power may be the single most important concept in all of social science. Scholars have emphasized the need to conceptualize leadership as a power phenomenon.[4] However, there is more confusion about influence and power than any other leadership concept. We defined *influencing,* and power is about influencing others. However, **power** *is the leader's potential influence over followers.* Because power is the *potential* to influence, you do not actually have to use power to influence others.[5] Often it is the perception of power, rather than the actual use of power, that influences others. In this section we discuss sources of power, types of power, influencing tactics, ways to increase your power, and how power is acquired and lost.

―――――――――――――― Learning Outcome 1 ――――――――――――――
Explain the differences between position power and personal power.

Sources of Power

There are two sources of power: position power and personal power.

Position Power

Position power is derived from top management, and it is delegated down the chain of command. Thus, a person who is in a management position has more potential influence (power) than an employee who is not a manager.[6] Power is used to get people to do something they otherwise would not have done. Some people view power as the ability to make people do what they want them to do or the ability to do something to people or for people. These definitions may be true, but they tend to give power a manipulative, negative connotation,[7] as does the old saying by Lord Acton, "Power corrupts. Absolute power corrupts absolutely."

Within an organization, power should be viewed in a positive sense. Without power, managers could not achieve organizational objectives.[8] Leadership and power go hand in hand. Employees are not influenced without a reason, and the reason is often the power a manager has over them. Managers rely on position power to get the job done.[9]

Personal Power

Personal power is derived from the follower based on the leader's behavior. Charismatic leaders have personal power. Again, followers do have some power over leaders. Followers must consent to the governing influence of managers for the organization to be successful. Unions are often the result of follower dissatisfaction with management behavior and the desire to balance power. Followers in units or departments also have personal power to influence their manager's evaluation.[10] Followers can restrict performance, sabotage operations, initiate grievances, hold demonstrations, make complaints to higher managers, and hurt the leader's reputation. Friendship also gives personal power, and personal power can be gained or lost—we will discuss how later.

The two sources of power are relatively independent, yet they have some overlap. For example, a manager can have only position power or both position and personal power, but a nonmanager can have only personal power. The trend is for managers to give more power (empowerment) to employees.[11] Today's effective leaders are relying less on position power and more on personal power to influence others,[12] and they are open to being influenced by followers with personal power.[13] Therefore, as a manager, it is best to have both position power and personal power.

---

1. How Did Robert Johnson Use Power to Overcome Discrimination in His Career?

Robert Johnson overcame prejudice and discrimination because he realized that it was part of the landscape or part of the game. He knew he was going to get hit with it, but he didn't let it stop him from achieving his goals. Johnson looked for commonalities of interest, using his personal power and continuing to gain position power, as he climbed the corporate ladder at different organizations. Johnson proved that he was competent and overcame negative perceptions and attitudes to break the glass ceiling. Johnson believes in himself and knows there are very few things that can stop him from achieving his goals.

OPENING CASE APPLICATION

Learning Outcome 2

Discuss the differences among legitimate, reward, coercive, and referent power.

Types of Power and Influencing Tactics, and Ways to Increase Your Power

Seven types of power are illustrated, along with their source of power and influencing tactics, in Exhibit 4-1. In the late 1950s, French and Raven

Exhibit 4-1 *Sources and types of power with influencing tactics.*

Source	Position Power ————————————————————➤			◄———————————— Personal Power			
Types	Legitimate	Reward	Coercive	Connection	Information	Expert	Referent
Tactics	Legitimization Consultation Rational persuasion Ingratiation	Exchange	Pressure	Coalitions	Rational persuasion	Rational persuasion	Inspirational appeal Personal appeal

Source: Adapted from J. French and B. H. Raven. 1959. "The Bases of Social Power." In *Studies of Social Power*. D. Cartwright, ed. Ann Arbor, MI: Institute for Social Research.

distinguished five types of power (reward, coercive, legitimate, expert, and referent),[14] and they are still being used in research. Connection (politics) and information power have been added to update the important types of power. We will discuss these seven types of power, and explore ways to increase each type with *influencing tactics.* You can acquire power, and you do not have to take power away from others to increase your power. Generally, power is given to those who get results and have good human relations skills.[15]

Legitimate Power

Legitimate power *is based on the user's position power, given by the organization.* It is also called the *legitimization influencing tactic.* Managers assign work, coaches decide who plays, and teachers award grades. These three positions have formal authority from the organization. Without this authority, they could not influence followers in the same way. Employees tend to feel that they ought to do what their manager says within the scope of the job.

Appropriate Use of Legitimate Power

Employees agree to comply with management authority in return for the benefits of membership. The use of legitimate power is appropriate when asking people to do something that is within the scope of their job. Most day-to-day manager-employee interactions are based on legitimate power.

When using legitimate power, it is also helpful to use the *consultation influencing tactic.* With consultation, you seek others' input about achieving an objective and are open to developing a plan together to achieve the objective. This process is also known as *participative management* and *empowering employees.* We will talk more about participative management throughout the book.

Legitimate Use of Rational Persuasion. As a manager meeting objectives through your employees, or in dealing with higher-level managers and people over whom you have no authority, it is often helpful to use the *rational persuasion influencing tactic.* Rational persuasion includes logical arguments with factual evidence to persuade others to implement your recommended action.

When you use rational persuasion, you need to develop a persuasive case based on the other party's needs. What seems logical and reasonable to you may not be to others. With multiple parties, a different logical argument may be made to meet individual needs. Logical arguments generally work well with people whose behavior is more influenced by thinking than emotions. It works well when the leader and follower share the same objective.

When trying to persuade others to do something for you, it is helpful to ask when they are in a good mood. To get people in a good mood, the *ingratiation influencing tactic* may be used by being friendly and praising others before you ask them for what you want. The initial compliment must be sincere (use the giving praise model in Chapter 3), and it helps determine if the other party is in a good mood or not. If not, it is generally a good idea to wait to ask no matter how rational your request.

Using Rational Persuasion

When you develop a rational persuasion, follow these guidelines.

1. Explain the reason why the objective needs to be met. Managers cannot simply give orders, since employees want to know the rationale for decisions.[16] Even if you disagree with higher-level managers' decisions, as a manager it is your job to give employees the rationale for their decisions.[17]

2. Explain how the other party will benefit by meeting the objective. Try to think of the other party's often-unasked question—what's in it for me? Sell the benefits to others, rather than focus on how you and the organization benefit by achieving the objective.

3. Provide evidence that the objective can be met. Remember the importance of expectancy motivation theory (Chapter 3). When possible, demonstrate how to do a task—seeing is believing. Give examples of how others have met the objective. Offer a detailed step-by-step plan. Be supportive and encouraging, showing your confidence in the followers to meet the objective.

4. Explain how potential problems and concerns will be handled. Know the potential problems and concerns and deal with them in the rational persuasion. If others bring problems up that you have not anticipated, which is likely, be sure to address them. Do not ignore people's concerns or make simple statements like, "That will not happen, we don't have to worry about that." Get the followers' input on how to resolve any possible problems as they come up. This will help gain their commitment.

5. If there are competing plans to meet the objective, explain why your proposal is better than the competing ones. Do your homework. You need to be well versed about the competition. To simply say "my idea is better than theirs" won't cut it. Be sure to state how your plan is superior to the others and the weaknesses and problems with the other plans.

Increasing Legitimate Power

To increase your legitimate power, follow these guidelines.

1. To have legitimate power, you need management experience, which could also be a part of your job—for example, being in charge of a team project with your peers. Work at gaining people's perception that you do have power. Remember that people's perception that you have power gives you power.[18]

2. Exercise your authority regularly. Follow up to make sure that policies, procedures, and rules are implemented and that your objectives are achieved.

3. Follow the guidelines for using rational persuasion, especially if your authority is questioned.

4. Back up your authority with *rewards* and *punishment*, our next two types of power, which are primarily based on having legitimate power.

Reward Power

Reward power *is based on the user's ability to influence others with something of value to them.* Reward power affects performance expectations and achievement. In a management position, use positive reinforcements to influence behavior, with incentives such as praise, recognition (with pins, badges, hats, or jackets), special assignments or desirable activities, pay raises, bonuses, and promotions. Many organizations, including Kentucky Fried Chicken (KFC), have employee-of-the-month awards. Tupperware holds rallies for its salespeople, and almost everyone gets something—ranging from pins to lucrative prizes for top performers. A leader's power is strong or weak based on his or her ability to punish and reward followers. The more power, the more favorable the situation for the leader.

An important part of reward power is having control over resources, such as allocating expense and budget funds. This is especially true for scarce resources. Upper- and middle-level managers usually have more discretion in giving rewards (including scarce resources) than do lower-level managers.

Appropriate Use of Reward Power

When employees do a good job, they should be rewarded, as discussed with reinforcement motivation theory (Chapter 3). Catching people doing things right and rewarding them is a great motivator to continue the behavior. When dealing with higher-level managers and people over whom you have no authority, you can use the *exchange influencing tactic* by offering some type of reward for helping you meet your objective. The incentive for exchange can be anything of value, such as scarce resources, information, advice or assistance on another task, or career and political support. Exchange is common in reciprocity (you do something for me and I'll do something for you—or you owe me one, for a later reward), which we will discuss with organizational politics. For example, when Professor Jones is recruiting a student aide, he tells candidates that if they are selected and do a good job, he will recommend them for an MBA fellowship at Suffolk University, where he has connection power. As a result he gets good, qualified help, at minimum wages, while helping both his student aide and his alma mater.

Increasing Reward Power

To increase your reward power, follow these guidelines.

1. Gain and maintain control over evaluating your employees' performance and determining their raises, promotions, and other rewards.

2. Find out what others value, and try to reward people in that way. Using praise can help increase your power. Employees who feel they are appreciated rather than used will give the manager more power.

3. Let people know you control rewards, and state your criteria for giving rewards. However, don't promise more than you can deliver. Reward as promised, and don't use rewards to manipulate or for personal benefit.

Coercive Power

The use of **coercive power** *involves punishment and withholding of rewards to influence compliance.* It is also called the *pressure influencing tactic*. From fear of reprimands, probation, suspension, or dismissal, employees often do as their manager requests. The fear of lost valued outcomes or rewards—such as receiving poor performance evaluations, losing raises and benefits, being assigned to less-desirable jobs, and hurting a relationship—causes employees to do as requested. Other examples of coercive power include verbal abuse, humiliation, and ostracism. Group members also use coercive power to enforce norms.

Appropriate Use of Coercive Power

Coercive power is appropriate to use in maintaining discipline and enforcing rules. When employees are not willing to do as requested, coercive power may be the only way to gain compliance. In fact, without it, employees may not take you seriously and ignore your requests. Coercion is effective when applied to a small percentage of followers under conditions considered legitimate by most of them. When leaders use coercion on a large scale against followers, it undermines their authority and creates a hostile opposition that may seek to restrict their power or to remove them from office. Employees tend to resent managers' use of coercive power. There has been a general decline in use of coercion by all types of leaders. So keep your use of coercive power to a minimum by using it only as a last resort.

Increasing Coercive Power

To increase your coercive power, follow these guidelines.

1. Gain authority to use punishment and withhold rewards. However, make sure employees know the rules and penalties, give prior warnings, understand the situation, remain calm and helpful, encourage improvement, use legitimate punishments (withhold rewards) that fit the infraction, and administer punishment in private.

2. Don't make rash threats; do not use coercion to manipulate others or to gain personal benefits.

3. Be persistent. If you request that followers do something and you don't follow up to make sure it is done, followers will take advantage of the situation and ignore your request. Set specific deadlines for task completion and frequently check progress. Put the deadline and progress checks on your calendar to make sure you persistently follow up.

When former President Okuda replaced about one-third of Toyota's highest-ranking managers, he was using coercive punishment for poor performers. When managers were promoted to replace them, they were rewarded for doing a good job.

WorkApplication1

Select a present or past manager who has or had coercive power. Give a specific example of how he or she uses or used reward and punishment to achieve an objective. Overall, how effective is (or was) this manager at using rewards and punishment?

_____

_____

_____

_____

_____

Ethical Dilemma 1

Following Orders

The armed forces are hierarchical by rank, based on power. Officers tend to give orders to troops using legitimate power. When orders are followed, reward power is common. When orders are not followed, coercive power is commonly used to get the troops to implement the order. The conditioning of the military is to respect the power of authority and to follow orders, usually without questioning authority. As you know, some people in the military throughout the world have intentionally tortured and killed innocent people, including women and children.

1. Is it ethical and socially responsible to teach people to follow orders without questioning authority in the military or any other organization?
2. What would you do if your boss asked you to follow orders that you thought may be unethical? (Some options include: just do it; don't say anything but don't do it; question the motives; look closely at what you are asked to do; go to your boss's boss to make sure its okay to do it; tell the boss you will not do it; ask the boss to do it him or herself; blow the whistle to an outside source like the government or media; and so on.)
3. Is following orders a good justification for unethical practices?

Referent Power

Referent power *is based on the user's personal relationships with others.* It is also called the *personal appeals influencing tactic* based on loyalty and friendship. Power stems primarily from friendship, or the employee's attractiveness to the person using power. The personal feelings of "liking" or the desire to be liked by the leaders also gives referent power. Today's successful leaders are relying more on relationships than position power to get the job done.[19]

Leaders can also use the *inspirational appeals influencing tactic*. The leader appeals to the follower's values, ideals, and aspirations, or increases self-confidence by displaying their feelings to appeal to the follower's emotions and enthusiasm. So rational persuasion uses logic, whereas inspirational persuasion appeals to emotions and enthusiasm. Thus, inspirational appeals generally work well with people whose behavior is more influenced by emotions than logical thinking. Great sports coaches, such as Vince Lombardi, are well respected for their inspirational appeals to get the team to win the game. Have you heard the "win one for the Gipper" saying from Notre Dame?

To be inspirational, you need to understand the values, hopes, fears, and goals of followers. You need to be positive and optimistic and create a vision of how things will be when the objective is achieved. Use nonverbal communication to bring emotions to the verbal message, such as raising and lowering voice tone and pausing to intensify key points, showing moist eyes or a few tears, and maintaining eye contact. Facial expressions, body movement, and gestures like pounding a table effectively reinforce verbal messages. You can also include the ingratiation influencing tactic within your inspirational appeal.

Appropriate Use of Referent Power

The use of referent power is particularly appropriate for people with weak, or no, position power, such as with peers. Referent power is needed in self-managed teams because leadership should be shared.

Increasing Referent Power

To increase your referent power, follow these guidelines.

1. Develop your people skills, which are covered in all preceding chapters. Remember that you don't have to be a manager to have referent power. The better you get along with (good working relationships) more people, the more referent power you will have.

2. Work at your relationship with your manager and peers. Your relationship with your manager will have a direct effect on your job satisfaction. Gain your manager's confidence in order to get more power. Remember that the success of your manager and peers depends to some extent on you and your performance.

Expert Power

Expert power *is based on the user's skill and knowledge.* Being an expert makes other people dependent on you. Employees with expert power have personal power and are often promoted to management positions. People often respect an expert, and the fewer the people who possess an expertise, the more power the individual has. For example, because so few people have the ability to become top athletes like basketball star Shaquille O'Neal, such athletes can command multimillion-dollar contracts. The more people come to you for advice, the greater is your expert power. In the changing global economy, expert power is becoming more important. It's wise to be sure that your expertise does not become unimportant or obsolete. Jack Welch says to go to work thirsty for knowledge. "Being the smartest person in the world doesn't mean anything. You've got to be thirsty to learn."[20] Experts commonly use the *rational persuasion influencing tactic* because people believe they know what they are saying and that it is correct.

Appropriate Use of Expert Power

Managers, particularly at lower levels, are often—but not always—experts within their departments. New managers frequently depend on employees who have expertise in how the organization runs and know how to get things done politically. Thus, followers can have considerable influence over the leader. Expert power is essential to employees who are working with people from other departments and organizations. Because such employees have no direct position power to use, being seen as an expert gives them credibility and power.

Increasing Expert Power

To increase your expert power, follow these guidelines.

1. To become an expert, take all the training and educational programs your organization provides.

2. Attend meetings of your trade or professional associations, and read their publications (magazines and journals) to keep up with current trends in your field. Write articles to be published. Become an officer in the organization.

3. Keep up with the latest technology. Volunteer to be the first to learn something new.

4. Project a positive self-concept (Chapter 2), and let people know about your expertise by developing a reputation for having expertise. You have no expert power unless others perceive that you have an expertise and come to you for advice. You may want to display diplomas, licenses, publications, and awards.

Information Power

Information power *is based on the user's data desired by others.* Information power involves access to vital information and control over its distribution to others. Managers often have access to information that is not available to peers and subordinates. Thus, they have the opportunity to distort information to influence others to meet their objective.[21] Distortion of information includes selective editing to promote only your position, giving a biased interpretation of data and even presenting false information. Managers also rely on employees for information, so followers sometimes have the opportunity to distort information that influences management decisions. Distortion of information is an ethical issue. Some secretaries have more information and are more helpful in answering questions than the managers they work for.

Appropriate Use of Information Power

An important part of the manager's job is to convey information. Employees often come to managers for information on what to do and how to do it. Leaders use information power when making *rational persuasion* and often with *inspirational appeals*. Personal computers give organizational members information power, as information flows freely through informal channels.[22]

Increasing Information Power

To increase your information power, follow these guidelines.

1. Have information flow through you. For example, if customer leads come in to the company and all sales representatives have direct access to them, the sales manager has weak information power. However, if all sales leads go directly to the manager, who then assigns the leads to sales representatives, the manager has strong information power. Having control of information makes it easier to cover up failures and mistakes, and to let others know of your accomplishments, which can also increase expertise.

2. Know what is going on in the organization.[23] Provide service and information to other departments. Serve on committees, because it gives you both information and a chance to increase connection power.

WorkApplication2

Select a past or present job. Who did (or do) you usually go to for expertise and information? Give examples of when you went to someone for expertise and when you went to someone for information.

3. Develop a network of information sources, and gather information from them.[24]

Connection Power

Connection power *is based on the user's relationships with influential people.* Connection power is also a form of politics, the topic of our next major section, but first we discuss how power is acquired and lost. You rely on the use of contacts or friends who can influence the person you are dealing with. The right connections can give power, or at least the perception of having power. If people know you are friendly with people in power, they are more apt to do as you request.[25] For example, if the owner's son has no position power but wants something done, he may gain compliance by making a comment about speaking to his father or mother about the lack of cooperation.

Sometimes it is difficult to influence others all alone. With a *coalition influencing tactic* you use influential people to help persuade others to meet your objective. There is power and safety in numbers. The more people you can get on your side, the more influence you can have on others. Superiors, peers, subordinates, and outsiders can help you influence others. You can tell others who support your idea, have the supporters with you when you make a request, have supporters follow up, or ask a higher authority to get what you need done for you. Coalitions are also a political strategy, a tactic that will be discussed again later in this chapter.

Appropriate Use of Connection Power
When you are looking for a job or promotions, connections can help. There is a lot of truth in the statement, "It's not what you know, it's who you know."[26] Connection power can also help you to get resources you need and increased business.[27]

Increasing Connection Power
To increase connection power, follow these guidelines.

1. Expand your network of contacts with important managers who have power.

2. Join the "in crowd" and the "right" associations and clubs. Participating in sports like golf may help you meet influential people.

3. Follow the guidelines for using the coalition influencing tactic. When you want something, identify the people who can help you attain it, make coalitions, and win them over to your side.

4. Get people to know your name. Get all the publicity you can. Have your accomplishments known by the people in power; send them notices.

Now that you have read about nine influencing tactics within seven types of power, see Exhibit 4-1 for a review, and test your ability to apply them in Applying the Concept 1 and 2. Then, complete Self-Assessment 1 to better understand how your personality traits relate to how you use power and influencing tactics to get what you want.

WorkApplication3

1. Think of a present or past manager. Which type of power does (or did) the manager use most often? Explain.
2. Which one or two suggestions for increasing your power base are the most relevant to you? Explain.

_____

_____

_____

_____

_____

WorkApplication4

Give three different influencing tactics you or someone else used to achieve an objective in an organization you have worked for.

_____

_____

_____

_____

_____

Applying the Concept 1

Influencing Tactics

Select the most approptiate individual tactic for each situation. Write the appropriate letter in the blank before each item.

a. rational persuasion
b. inspirational appeals
c. consultation

d. ingratiation
e. personal appeals
f. exchange

g. coalition
h. legitimization
i. pressure

_____ 1. You are in sales and want some information about a new product that has not yet been produced, nor has it been announced inside or outside the company. You know a person in the production department who has been working on the new product, so you decide to contact that person.

_____ 2. Two of your five crew workers did not come in to work today. You have a large order that should be shipped out at the end of the day. It will be tough for the small crew to meet the deadline.

_____ 3. Although the crew members in situation 2 have agreed to push to meet the deadline, you would like to give them some help. You have an employee whose job is to perform routine maintenance and cleaning. He is not one of your five crew workers. However, you realize that he could be of some help filling in for the two missing workers. You decide to talk to this nonunion employee about working with the crew for two hours today.

_____ 4. The nonunion employee in situation 3 is resisting helping the other workers. He is basically asking, "What's in it for me?"

_____ 5. You have an employee who is very moody at times. You want this employee, who has a big ego, to complete an assignment before the established due date.

_____ 6. You believe you deserve a pay raise, so you decide to talk to your manager about it.

_____ 7. You serve on a committee, and next week the committee members will elect officers. Nominations and elections will be done at the same time. You are interested in being the president, but don't want to nominate yourself and lose.

_____ 8. You have an employee who regularly passes in assignments late. The assignment you are giving the person now is very important to have done on time.

_____ 9. You have an idea about how to increase performance of your department. You are not too sure if it will work, or if the employees will like the idea.

_____ 10. The production person from situation 1 has given you the information you were looking for. She calls a week later to ask you for some information.

2. What Types of Power Does Johnson Have? How Does He Use His Power?

As founder and former chairman and CEO of BET, Robert Johnson clearly has position power. However, he is also well respected and has personal power as well. He also has position power as a member of the board of directors of US Airways, Hilton Hotels, General Mills, United Negro College Fund, National Cable Television Association, and the American Film Institute, and on the board of governors for the Rock and Roll Hall of Fame and the Brookings Institute, because of his management expertise power and connection power. Because of his expert power, Johnson has won several awards, including being named one of the twenty most influential people in the cable industry.

Johnson primarily used referent power by developing and communicating the vision of BET to be the preeminent African-American entertainment media company in the world. He used his power to get the resources necessary to achieve BET's vision. Johnson empowered his employees to pursue the vision, but he was available with expertise and information to help them. Employees were motivated to pursue the vision, not coerced, and those who advanced BET to achieve its vision were well rewarded.

OPENING CASE APPLICATION

Using Power

Identify the relevant type of power to use in each situation. Write the appropriate letter in the blank before each item.

a. coercive   c. reward or legitimate   e. information or expert
b. connection   d. referent

_____ 11. One of your best workers needs little direction from you. However, recently her performance has slumped. You're quite sure that a personal problem is affecting her work.

_____ 12. You want a new personal computer to help you do a better job. PCs are allocated by a committee, which is very political in nature.

_____ 13. One of your best workers wants a promotion. He has talked to you about getting ahead and has asked you to help prepare him for when the opportunity comes.

_____ 14. One of your worst employees has ignored one of your directives again.

_____ 15. An employee who needs some direction and encouragement from you to maintain production is not working to standard today. As occasionally happens, she claims that she does not feel well but cannot afford to take time off. You have to get an important customer order shipped today.

Applying the Concept 2

Review the nine influencing tactics. Which ones do you tend to use most often to help you get what you want? Also review your personality profile self-assessment exercises in Chapter 2.

Surgency/High Need for Power

If you have n Pow, you are apt to try to influence others, and you enjoy it. You tend to hate to lose, and when you don't get what you want, it bothers you. Thus, you are more likely to use harder methods of influence and power, such as pressure, exchange, coalitions, and legitimization than other personality types. You probably also like to use rational persuasion and don't understand why people don't think or see things the way you do. Be careful to use socialized rather than personalized power to influence others.

Agreeableness/High Need for Affiliation

If you have a high n Aff, you are apt to be less concerned about influencing others and gaining power than getting along with them. Thus, you are more likely to use softer methods of influence, such as personal and inspirational appeals and ingratiation, as well as rational appeals. You may tend not to seek power, and even avoid it.

Conscientiousness/High Need for Achievement

If you have a high n Ach, you tend to be between the other two approaches to influencing others. You tend to have clear goals and work hard to get what you want, which often requires influencing others to help you. So you don't want power for its own sake, only to get what you want. But you like to play by the rules and may tend to use rational persuasion frequently.

Based on the preceding information, briefly describe how your personality affects the ways you attempt to influence others.

_____

_____

_____

_____

Acquiring and Losing Power

Power can change over time. Personal power is more easily gained and lost than position power. Having strong power can lead to temptation to act in ways that misuse power and may eventually lead to failure.[28] Although President Clinton was impeached, he did keep his job; but he lost personal power because his integrity was damaged for many people.

Social exchange theory explains how power is gained and lost as reciprocal influence processes occur over time between leaders and followers in small groups. Social interaction is an exchange of benefits or favors. Friendship is a social exchange, and some people place a higher value on the friendships they have at work than on the work itself. Group members especially watch managers, because they each have expectations of the leader. If the leader meets follower expectations, power is acquired and maintained. If not, the leader loses status and expert power with followers, and they may undermine the leader's legitimate authority as well.

Organizational Politics

Political skills are critical to achieving one's goals. Many people with position and personal power and with admirable goals that would benefit the organization have failed because of political ineptness.[29] Thus, to have a successful career, career advisors suggest developing your organizational political skills.[30]

There is a relationship between power and organizational politics.[31] Just as the nine influencing tactics (Exhibit 4-1) are used within the seven types of power, these tactics are also used in organizational politics. For example, to develop a successful rational persuasion, you need to base it within organizational politics. Social skills, such as the ability to read others accurately, make favorable first impressions, adapt to a wide range of social situations, and be persuasive also affect organizational political skills.[32]

In this section, we discuss the nature of organizational politics, political behavior, and guidelines for developing political skills. But first, determine your own use of political behavior by completing Self-Assessment 2.

Learning Outcome 3

Discuss how power and politics are related.

The Nature of Organizational Politics

Because political skills are a part of power, you need to understand politics in terms of power. Managers use their existing position power and politics to increase their power.[33] **Politics** *is the process of gaining and using power.* Politics is a reality of organizational life. The amount and importance of politics varies from organization to organization. However, larger organizations tend to be more political; and the higher the level of management, the more important politics becomes.[34]

Learning Outcome 4

Describe how money and politics have a similar use.

Politics Is a Medium of Exchange

Like power, politics often has a negative connotation due to people who abuse political power. A positive way to view politics is to realize that it is simply a medium of exchange. Like money, politics in and of itself is inherently neither good nor bad. Politics is simply a system of getting what we want.[35] In our economy, money is the medium of exchange (tangible currency); in an organization, politics is the medium of exchange (political behavior). Leaders in organizations use political behavior, our next topic.

Political Behavior

How well you play politics directly affects your success.[36] Networking, reciprocity, and coalitions are common organizational political behaviors.

Networking

Networking *is the process of developing relationships for the purpose of socializing and politicking.* The activities managers engage in and the time spent on each area have been studied. The activities have been categorized into four areas: traditional management, communication, human resource management,

Self-Assessment 2

Use of Political Behavior

Select the response that best describes your actual or planned use of the following behavior on the job. Place a number from 1 to 5 on the line before each statement.

1 — 2 — 3 — 4 — 5
Rarely   *Occasionally*   *Usually*

_____ 1. I use my personal contacts to get a job and promotions.

_____ 2. I try to find out what is going on in all the organizational departments.

_____ 3. I dress the same way as the people in power and take on the same interests (watch or play sports, join the same clubs, and so forth).

_____ 4. I purposely seek contacts and network with higher-level managers.

_____ 5. If upper management offered me a raise and promotion requiring me to move to a new location, I'd say yes even if I did not want to move.

_____ 6. I get along with everyone, even those considered to be difficult to get along with.

_____ 7. I try to make people feel important by complimenting them.

_____ 8. I do favors for others and use their favors in return, and I thank people and send them thank-you notes.

_____ 9. I work at developing a good working relationship with my manager.

_____ 10. I ask my manager and other people for their advice.

_____ 11. When a person opposes me, I still work to maintain a positive working relationship with that person.

_____ 12. I'm courteous, pleasant, and positive with others.

_____ 13. When my manager makes a mistake, I never publicly point out the error.

_____ 14. I am more cooperative (I compromise) than competitive (I seek to get my own way).

_____ 15. I tell the truth.

_____ 16. I avoid saying negative things about my manager and others behind their back.

_____ 17. I work at getting people to know me by name and face by continually introducing myself.

_____ 18. I ask some satisfied customers and people who know my work to let my manager know how good a job I'm doing.

_____ 19. I try to win contests and get prizes, pins, and other awards.

_____ 20. I send notices of my accomplishments to higher-level managers and company newsletters.

To determine your overall political behavior, add the 20 numbers you selected as your answers. The number will range from 20 to 100. The higher your score, the more political behavior you use. Place your score here _____ and on the continuum below.

20 — 30 — 40 — 50 — 60 — 70 — 80 — 90 — 100
Nonpolitical   *Political*

To determine your use of political behavior in four areas, add the numbers for the following questions and divide by the number of questions to get the average score in each area.

A. *Learning the organizational culture and power players*
Questions 1–5 total: _____ divided by 5 = _____

B. *Developing good working relationships, especially with your boss*
Questions 6–12 total: _____ divided by 7 = _____

C. *Being a loyal, honest team player*
Questions 13–16 total: _____ divided by 4 = _____

D. *Gaining recognition*
Questions 17–20 total: _____ divided by 4 = _____

The higher the average score of items A–D, the more you use this type of political behavior. Do you tend to use them all equally, or do you use some more than others?

and networking. Of these four activities, networking has the highest relative contribution to successful management advancement. Successful managers spend around twice as much time networking as average managers, so reach out to establish an ongoing network of contacts.[37] Because networking is so important to career success, we are going to discuss it as our next major section, after we finish our other political skills discussions.

Reciprocity

Using **reciprocity** *involves creating obligations and developing alliances, and using them to accomplish objectives.* Notice that the exchange influencing tactic is used with reciprocity. When people do something for you, you incur an obligation that they may expect to be repaid. When you do something for people, you create a debt that you may be able to collect at a later date when you need a favor.[38] You should work at developing a network of alliances that you can call on for help in meeting your objectives.[39]

Coalitions

Using coalitions as an influencing tactic is political behavior. Each party helps the others get what they want.[40] Reciprocity and networking are used to achieve ongoing objectives, whereas coalitions are developed for achieving a specific objective. A political tactic when developing coalitions is to use co-optation. *Co-optation* is the process of getting a person whose support you need to join your coalition rather than compete.[41] Management has been known to make strong union leaders managers. Presidential candidates have taken competitors as their vice presidential running mates.

Except for networking, we have not listed appropriate use of political behavior and how to increase your political skills with each type of political behavior, because all three may be used at the same time. As you'll see, our upcoming guidelines can be used with any of the three political behaviors. Before considering how to develop political skills, review Exhibit 4-2 for a list of political behaviors and guidelines.

WorkApplication5

Give a job example of how networking, reciprocity, or a coalition was used to achieve an organizational objective.

_____

_____

_____

_____

_____

Exhibit 4-2 *Political behavior and guidelines for developing political skills.*

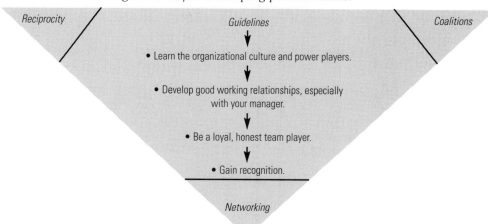

Reciprocity — Guidelines — Coalitions

• Learn the organizational culture and power players.

• Develop good working relationships, especially with your manager.

• Be a loyal, honest team player.

• Gain recognition.

Networking

Ethical Dilemma 2

Dick Grasso, NYSE

Dick Grasso, the former New York Stock Exchange (NYSE) chief, is known to be a powerful man who uses politics to get what he wants. Grasso used coercive power to stop firms from taking trading away from the NYSE by moving it in-house electronically, holding back the computer age.[42]

He was investigated for playing an inappropriate role in setting his own compensation. When Grasso left the NYSE, his retirement and severance package was $197.2 million, and he received $139.5 million.[43]

Here is an example of how Grasso used his power and politics. Michael LaBranche agreed to merge his company with a smaller rival to create the largest specialist firm working on the NYSE. Grasso needed to okay the merger deal. Grasso "strongly" recommended that his longtime friend Robert Murphy, CEO of the smaller company in the merger (who served on the NYSE board and voted to approve his payout of $139.5 million), be named chief executive of the new LaBranche & Company main operating unit after the merger. Murphy had to stay at the top of a specialist firm to continue serving on the NYSE board, where Grasso wanted to, and did, keep him.[44]

1. Did Dick Grasso use the political behaviors (a) networking, (b) reciprocity, and (c) coalitions while running the NYSE?
2. Was Dick Grasso's use of power and politics ethical and socially responsible?

Guidelines for Developing Political Skills

If you want to climb the corporate ladder, or at least avoid getting thrown off it, you should develop your political skills. Successfully implementing the behavior guidelines presented here can result in increased political skills. However, if you don't agree with any political behavior, don't use it. You do not have to use all of the political behaviors to be successful. Learn what it takes in the organization where you work as you follow the guidelines.

Learn the Organizational Culture and Power Players

Develop your connection power through politicking. It is natural, especially for young people, to take a purely rational approach to a job without considering politics. But many business decisions are not very rational; they are based on power and politics.[45] For example, a common reason for choosing the location of a new business facility is simply because it's convenient to where the person in power wants to live.

Learn the cultural (Chapter 10) shared values and beliefs and how business and politics operate where you work. Learn to read between the lines. For example, a manager asked a new employee to select one of two project teams to work on. The employee selected one and told the manager his selection. The manager asked him to rethink the decision. In talking to others, the new employee found out that the manager of the team he wanted to join was disliked by the new CEO. No matter how good the project or how well the team did, the team was doomed to fail.

In all organizations, there are some powerful key players. Your manager is a key player to you. Don't just find out who the managers are; gain an understanding of what makes each of them tick. By understanding them, you can tailor the presentation of your ideas and style to fit each person's needs. For example, some managers want to see detailed financial numbers and statistics, while others don't. Some managers expect you to continually follow up with them, while others will think you are bugging them.

Review Self-Assessment 2, questions 1–5; you can use these tactics to increase your political skills. Network with power players. Try to do favors for power players. When developing coalitions, get key players on your side. When selecting a mentor, try to get one who is good at organizational politics. Your mentor can help you learn how to play politics. Also try to observe people who are good at politics, and copy their behavior.

Develop Good Working Relationships, Especially with Your Manager

The ability to work well with others is critical to your career success, and it's an important foundation of politics.[46] The more people like and respect you, the more power you will gain. Good human relations give you personal power and a basis for using the influencing tactic of personal appeal. You've already learned about relationships with higher-level managers and with peers who have influence and power, so let's focus on the relationship with your boss.

If you want to get ahead, you need to have a good working relationship with your manager. Your boss usually gives you the formal performance appraisals, which are the primary bases for raises and promotions. Fair or not, many evaluations are influenced by the manager's relationship with the employee.[47] If your manager likes you, you have a better chance of getting a good review, raises, and promotions.

Supervisors also give higher ratings to employees who share their goals (goal congruence) and priorities than they give to those who don't. Thus, get to know what your manager expects from you, and do it. Beat or at least meet deadlines, and don't miss them. It's common to put off telling the manager bad news. But if you are having a job problem, don't put off letting your manager know about it. Most managers, and peers, like to be asked for advice. If you are behind schedule to meet an important deadline and your manager finds out about it from others, it is embarrassing, especially if your manager finds out from his or her manager. Also avoid showing up your manager in public, such as during a meeting. If you do, don't be surprised if the next time you open your mouth at a meeting, your manager embarrasses you.

If you cannot get along with your manager and are in conflict, avoid going to his or her manager to resolve the conflict. There are two dangers with going over the manager's head. First, chances are your manager has a good working relationship with his or her manager, who will side with your manager. Even if the higher-level manager agrees with you, you will most likely hurt your relationship with your manager. He or she may consciously or unconsciously take some form of retaliation, such as giving you a lower performance review, which can hurt you in the long run. You need all the friends and allies you can get, so try to resolve important conflicts;[48] use the conflict model (Chapter 6) with everyone you work with.

Review Self-Assessment 2, questions 6–12; you can use these tactics to increase your political skills. Include your manager in your network, try to do favors for your manager, and include your manager in your coalitions. Use the ingratiation tactic with everyone. When was the last time you gave anyone, including your manager, a compliment? When was the last time you sent a thank-you or congratulations note?

Be a Loyal, Honest Team Player

Ethical behavior is important in organizational politics. The Indian leader Mohandas K. Gandhi called business without morality and politics without principle a sin. Some backstabbing gossips may get short-term benefits from such behavior, but in the long run they are generally unsuccessful because others gun them down in return. In any organization, you must earn others' respect, confidence, and trust. Once you are caught in a lie, it's difficult to regain trust. There are very few, if any, jobs in which organizational objectives can be achieved without the support of a group or team of individuals. Even lone-wolf salespeople are subject to the systems effect, and they need the help of production to make the product, transportation to deliver it, and service to maintain it. The trend is toward teamwork, so if you're not a team player, work at it.[49]

Review Self-Assessment 2, questions 13–16; you can use these tactics to increase your political skills. Be a loyal, honest team player in your network, in your reciprocity, and with your coalition members.

Gain Recognition

Doing a great job does not help you to get ahead in an organization if no one knows about it, or knows who you are. Recognition and knowing the power players go hand in hand; you want the power players to know who you are and what you can do. You want people higher in the organization to know your expertise and the contributions you are making to the organization.[50]

Review Self-Assessment 2, questions 17–20; you can use these tactics to increase your political skills. Let people in your network and coalitions, and people you reciprocate with, know of your accomplishments. You can also serve on committees and try to become an officer, which gives you name recognition. A committee job many people tend to avoid is that of secretary. But when the meeting minutes are sent to higher management and throughout the organization with your name on it as secretary, you increase your name recognition.

WorkApplication6

Which one or two suggestions for developing political skills are the most relevant to you? Explan.

_____

_____

_____

_____

_____

OPENING CASE APPLICATION

3. How Did Johnson Effectively Use Organizational Politics at BET?

As founder and former chairman and CEO of BET, Robert Johnson did use organizational politics, but in a positive way. Through networking, Johnson started and expanded BET. He did favors for others, who also did favors for him (reciprocity). He focused on having honest team players. Johnson communicated the BET vision and effectively built consensus with broad-based coalitions among the people who would achieve the vision. Through good working relationships based on consensus, conflict was resolved effectively. He built a company with a culture based on integrity and on mutual respect. Johnson realized that when unethical politics takes place, employees don't feel like they are part of the vision, and they don't contribute to the performance to achieve the vision. So he trusted

Political Behavior

Identify the behavior in each situation as effective or ineffective political behavior. Write the appropriate letter in the blank before each item.

a. effective   b. ineffective

_____ 16. Julio is taking golf lessons so he can join the Saturday golf group, which includes some higher-level managers.

_____ 17. Paul tells his manager's manager about mistakes his manager makes.

_____ 18. Sally avoids spending time socializing, so that she can be more productive on the job.

_____ 19. John sent a very positive performance report to three higher-level managers to whom he does not report. They did not request copies.

_____ 20. Carlos has to drop off a daily report by noon. He delivers the report at around 10:00 A.M. on Tuesday and Thursday, so that he can run into some higher-level managers who meet at that time near the office where the report goes. On the other days, Carlos drops the report off at around noon on his way to lunch.

Applying the Concept 3

employees to be the best they can be, and Johnson gave them recognition for their contributions. By giving others trust and support, that is what he got in return.

Networking

As stated with organizational politics, networking is important to your career.[51] Technical knowledge and skills will help you gain entry into lower management, but networks and social skills gain advancement to higher-level management.[52] It is especially difficult for women to get into the right networks, which contributes to the glass ceiling.[53] When you need any type of help, do you have a network of people ready to turn to or know how to develop a network to assist you? Networking sounds easy and we tend to think it should come naturally. However, the reality is that networking is a learned skill that just about everyone struggles with at sometime or another.[54] Of the many ways to secure a job, networking is by far the most successful way to discover employment opportunities.[55] According to the U.S. Department of Labor, two-thirds of all jobs are located by word of mouth, informal referrals, relatives, friends, and acquaintances. Networking results in more jobs than all of the other job search methods combined.

Steve Case used networking to help him advance in his career to become cofounder of America Online (AOL), and he recommends that you develop your networking skills.[56] In support of his advice, researchers have concluded that successful managers spend more of their time networking than average managers, and that networking may be the most important contributor to their success.[57] Assess your networking skill now in Self-Assessment 3.

Self-Assessment 3

Networking

Identify each of the 16 statements according to how accurately it describes your behavior. Place a number from 1–5 on the line before each statement.

5 — 4 — 3 — 2 — 1
Describes me   Does not describe me

____ 1. When I start something (a new project, career move, a major purchase), I seek help from people I know and seek new contacts for help.

____ 2. I view networking as a way to create win-win situations.

____ 3. I like to meet new people; I can easily strike up a conversation with people I don't know.

____ 4. I can quickly state two or three of my most important accomplishments.

____ 5. When I contact business people who can help me (such as with career information), I have goals for the communication.

____ 6. When I contact business people who can help me, I have a planned short opening statement.

____ 7. When I contact business people who can help me, I praise their accomplishments.

____ 8. When I contact people who can help me, I have a set of questions to ask.

____ 9. I know contact information for at least 100 people who can potentially help me.

____ 10. I have a file/database with contact information of people who can help me in my career, and I keep it updated and continue to add new names.

____ 11. During communications with people who can help me, I ask them for names of others I can contact for more information.

____ 12. When seeking help from others, I ask them how I might help them.

____ 13. When people help me, I thank them at the time and for big favors with a follow-up thanks.

____ 14. I keep in touch with people who have helped or can potentially help me in my career at least once a year, and I update them on my career progress.

____ 15. I have regular communications with people in my industry that work for different organizations, such as members of trade/professional organizations.

____ 16. I attend trade/professional/career types of meetings to maintain relationships and to make new contacts.

Add up your score and place it here _____ and on the continuum below.

80 — 70 — 60 — 50 — 40 — 30 — 16
Effective Networking   Ineffective Networking

If you are a full-time student, you may not score high on networking effectiveness, but that's okay as you can develop networking skills by following the steps and guidelines in this chapter.

Networking is not about asking everyone you know for a job (or whatever you need assistance with, such as feedback on your resume and career preparation, or information on hiring patterns and growth potential in your field; information about your current organization and its culture and power players; support and recognition from a colleague, or a mentor). How would you react if someone directly said, "I sell cars, and I have a good deal for you. Can you give me a job?" Networking is about building professional relationships and friendships,[58] through effective communications. Although the same networking process applies to broad career development,[59] we focus more on the job search. Whenever you start something—a new project, a career move, buying a car or house—use your network.

This section provides a how-to network process that will enhance your career development.[60] The process is summarized in Exhibit 4-3.

——————————— Learning Outcome 5 ———————————

List and explain the steps in the networking process.

Perform a Self-Assessment and Set Goals

The task of self-assessment can help to clarify your skills, competencies and knowledge. Self-assessment can also give you insight into your transferable skills and the criteria that are important to you in a new job.[61] Listing the major criteria that are most important to you in the new job and prioritizing these can help to clarify your ideal next position.[62] Factors to consider are: industry, company size and growth, location, travel and commuting requirements, compensation package/benefits, job requirements, and promotion potential. Other factors to assess are the style of management, culture, and work style of the organization. Critical to career satisfaction are the ability to use your talents, grow in your field, and do what you do best in your job. Although many tools exist to assess skills and preferences, a simple list with priorities can suffice to clarify your talents and the characteristics of an ideal new career or job.

Accomplishments

After completing a self-assessment, you are ready to translate your talents into accomplishments. The results you achieved in your jobs and/or college are the best evidence of your skills. Your future employer knows that your past behavior predicts your future behavior and that if you achieved results in the past, you will likely produce similar results again. Accomplishments are what set you apart and provide evidence of your skills and abilities. To be an effective networker, you must articulate what you have accomplished in your past in a way that is clear, concise, and compelling. Write down your accomplishments (at least two or three) and include them in your resume. Whether you are looking for a job or not, you should always have an updated resume handy.

Tying Your Accomplishments to the Job Interview

You want to be sure to state your accomplishments that are based on your skill during the job interview. Many interviews begin with a broad question such as, "tell me about yourself." Oftentimes candidates do not reveal anything compelling. The second step after listing key results you have achieved is to elaborate on a problem that was solved or an opportunity taken and how you

Exhibit 4-3 *The networking process.*

1. Perform a self-assessment and set goals.
2. Create your one-minute self-sell.
3. Develop your network.
4. Conduct networking interviews.
5. Maintain your network.

achieved it using your skills. These simple result statements should be transferred from your resume as critical results achieved. Thus, if you are asked a broad general question, such as "tell me about yourself," you have accomplishment statements as your answer.

Set Networking Goals

After your self-assessment, focusing on your accomplishments, you need to clearly state your goal. For example: to get a mentor; to determine the expertise, skills, and requirements needed for XYZ position; to get feedback on my resume and job and/or career preparation for a career move into XYZ; or to attain a job as XYZ.

Create Your One-Minute Self-Sell

Based on your goal, your next step is to create a one-minute sell to help you accomplish your goal. *The* **one-minute self-sell** *is an opening statement used in networking that quickly summarizes your history and career plan and asks a question.* To take 60 seconds or less, your message must be concise, but it also needs to be clear and compelling. It gives the listener a sense of your background, identifies your career field and a key result you've achieved, plus provides the direction of your next job. It tells the listener what you plan to do next and why. It also stimulates conversation by asking your network for help in the area of support, coaching, contacts, or knowledge of the industry.

Part 1. History: Start with a career summary, the highlights of your career to date. Include your most recent career or school history and a description of the type of work/internship or courses you have taken. Also include the industry and type of organization.

Part 2. Plans: Next, state the target career you are seeking, the industry you prefer, and a specific function or role. You can also mention names of organizations you are targeting as well as let the acquaintance know why you are looking for work.

Part 3. Question: Last, ask a question to encourage two-way communication. The question will vary depending on the person and your goal or the reason you are using the one-minute self-sell. For example,

- In what areas might there be opportunities for a person with my experience?
- In what other fields can I use these skills or this degree?
- In what other positions in your organization could my skills be used?
- How does my targeted future career sound to you? Is it a match with my education and skills?
- Do you know of any job openings in my field?

Write and Practice Your One-Minute Self-Sell

Write out your one-minute self-sell. Be sure to clearly separate your history, plans, and question, and customize your question based on the contact with whom you are talking. For example, *Hello, my name is Will Smith. I am a junior at Springfield College majoring in marketing, and I have completed an internship in the marketing department at the Big Y supermarket. I am seeking a job in sales in the food industry. Can you give me some ideas on the types of sales positions available in the food industry?* Practice delivering it with family

---

WorkApplication7

Write a networking goal.

_____

_____

_____

_____

WorkApplication8

Write a one-minute self-sell to achieve your networking goal from Work Application 7.

_____

_____

_____

_____

and friends and get feedback to improve it. The more opportunities you find to use this brief introduction, the easier it becomes.

Develop Your Network

Begin with who you know. Everyone can create a written network list of about 200 people consisting of professional and personal contacts. Address books and rolodexes are written network lists, but you need to continually develop them.[63] Professional contacts include colleagues (past and present), professional organizations, alumni associations, vendors, suppliers, managers, mentors, and many other professional acquaintances. On a personal level, your network includes family, neighbors, friends, religious groups, and other personal service providers (doctor, dentist, insurance agent, stock broker, accountant, hairstylist, politician). Compose a list of your network using the above categories and continually update and add to your list with referrals from others. You will discover that your network grows exponentially and can get you closer to the decision makers in a hiring position. In today's job market, it's critical to engage in a "passive job hunt" using your network and having your resume ready. You should have a written network, and there is computer software available that can help you.

Now expand your list to people you don't know. Where should you go to develop your network? Anywhere people gather. To be more specific, get more involved with professional associations. Many have special student memberships and some even have college chapters. If you really want to develop your career reputation, become a leader in your associations and not just a member. Volunteer to be on committees and boards, to give presentations, and so on. Other opportunities to network with people you don't know include the Chamber of Commerce, college alumni clubs/reunions, civic organizations (Rotary, Lions, Kiwanis, Elks, Moose, and so on), courses of any type, trade shows and career fairs, charities, community groups, religious groups (Goodwill, American Cancer Society, your local church), social clubs (exercise, boating, golf, tennis). More and more, online networking is leading to employment.[64]

Another important point is to work at developing your ability to remember people by name. If you want to impress people you have never met or hardly know, call them by their name. Ask others who they are, then go up and call them by name and introduce yourself with your one-minute self-sell. When you are introduced to people, call them by name during the conversation two or three times. If you think the person can help you, don't stop with casual conversation; make an appointment at a later time for a phone conversation, personal meeting, coffee, or lunch. Get their business cards to add to your network list, and give your business card and/or resume when appropriate.

Conduct Networking Interviews

Based on your goal, use your network list of people to set up a networking interview to meet your goal.[65] It may take many interviews to meet a goal, such as to get a job. An informational interview is a phone call or preferably a meeting that you initiate to meet a goal, such as to gain information from a contact with hands-on experience in your field of interest. You are the interviewer (in contrast to a job interview) and need to be prepared with specific questions to ask the contact regarding your targeted career or industry based on your self-assessment and goal. Ask for a 20-minute meeting, and, as a result, many people will talk to you.

These meetings can be most helpful when you have accessed someone who is within an organization you'd like to join, or has a contact in an industry you are targeting. A face-to-face meeting of 20 minutes can have many benefits. Your contact will remember you after a personal meeting, and the likelihood of getting a job lead increases. Keeping them posted on your job search progress as well as a thank-you note after the meeting also solidifies the relationship. The interviewing steps are:

step 1. **Establish Rapport:** Provide a brief introduction and thank the contacts for their time. Clearly state the purpose of the meeting; be clear that you are not asking for a job. Don't start selling yourself; project an interest in the other person. Do some research and impress the person by stating an accomplishment, such as I enjoyed your presentation at the CLMA meeting on. . . .

step 2. **Deliver Your One-Minute Self-Sell:** Even if the person has already heard it, say it again. This enables you to quickly summarize your background and career direction.

step 3. **Ask Prepared Questions:** As stated above, do your homework before the meeting and compose a series of questions to ask during the interview. Your questions should vary depending on your goal, the contact, and how they may help you with your job search. Sample questions include:

- What do you think of my qualifications for this field?
- With your knowledge of the industry, what career opportunities do you see in the future?
- What advice do you have for me as I begin/advance in my career?
- If you were exploring this field, who else would you talk with?

During the interview, if the interviewee mentions anything that could hinder your search, ask how such obstacles could be overcome.

step 4. **Get Additional Contacts for Your Network:** As mentioned previously, always ask who else you should speak with.[66] Most people can give you three names, so if only offered one, ask for others. Add the new contacts to your network list. When contacting new people, be sure to use your network person's name. Be sure not to linger beyond the time you have been offered, unless invited to stay. Leave a business card and/or resume so the person can contact you in case something comes up.

step 5. **Ask Your Contacts How You Might Help Them:** Offer a copy of a recent journal article or any additional information that came up in your conversation. Remember, it's all about building relationships.[67]

step 6. **Follow Up with a Thank-You Note and Status Report:** By sending a thank-you note, along with another business card/resume, and following up with your progress, you are continuing the networking relationship and maintaining a contact for the future.

Be sure to assess the effectiveness of your networking meetings using the five steps as your criteria. Did you establish rapport and were you clear about the intent of the meeting? Did you deliver your one-minute self-sell, including a question? Did you follow with additional prepared questions? Did you get additional names to contact? And finally, did you send a follow-up thank-you note? It is always helpful to create a log of calls, meetings, and contacts in order to maintain your network as it expands.

Maintain Your Network

It is important to keep your network informed of your career progress. Get a mentor in your current or new role that can help you to focus on results that matter to your employer and guide your assimilation process. If an individual was helpful in finding your new job, be sure to let them know the outcome. Saying thank you to those who helped in your transition will encourage the business relationship; providing this information will increase the likelihood of getting help in the future.[68] It is also a good idea to notify everyone in your network that you are in a new position and provide contact information. Networking doesn't stop once you've made a career change. Make a personal commitment to continue networking in order to be in charge of your career development. Go to trade shows and conventions, make business friends, and continue to update, correct, and add to your network list. Always thank others for their time.

Networking is also about helping others, especially your network. As you have been helped, you should help others. You will be amazed at how helping others comes back to you. Jack Gherty, president and CEO of Land O'Lakes, said that he got ahead by helping other people win.[69] Try to contact everyone on your network list at least once a year (calls, e-mail, and cards are good), and find out what you can do for them. Send congratulations on recent achievements.

After you have read this section on networking, you have at least two choices. One is to do nothing with it. The other choice is to begin developing your networking skills, or schedule the time to sit down and do one or all of the steps in the networking process: do a self-assessment and set a goal(s), create your one-minute self-sell to meet your goal, develop your network to meet the goal, set up and conduct network interviews, and maintain your network. What's it going to be? Skill-Development Exercise 3 can help get you started.

---

4. How Did Johnson Use Networking to Advance His Career?

Robert Johnson realized the value of networking early in his career. He readily admits that he had the help of others during his career in multiple organizations and positions. Starting BET required several different types of resources, and Johnson called on his long list of networking relationships to get the necessary resources to start and build BET. Although Johnson founded and was CEO of BET, it is a subsidiary of Viacom, which requires ongoing networking with Viacom executives. BET also has BET Interactive (BET.com), which provides a combination of online content information and community tailored to the unique interests, preferences, and issues of African-Americans. BET Interactive is owned in partnership by BET, Microsoft, Liberty Digital Media, News Corporation, and USA Networks. Thus, Johnson constantly worked with this network of organizations. Although Johnson was extremely busy, he did take time to help others on their way up.

OPENING CASE APPLICATION

Negotiation

In this section, we focus on getting what you want through negotiation. Influence tactics, power, and politics can all be used during the negotiation process. **Negotiating** *is a process in which two or more parties are in conflict and attempt to come to an agreement.*

Are negotiation skills really important? Here are some answers. No one goes through life without negotiating; the sooner you get over it, the better. Deal-making is the ultimate people skill. It's not just about getting more of what you want in business; it's about getting more out of life. Good negotiators are more confident, influential, and prosperous.[70] Negotiating is a core competency in life—particularly in the business world. Your negotiating ability directly affects your income, relationships, and station in life.[71] Whether

---

Self-Assessment 4

Negotiating

Identify each of the 16 statements according to how accurately it describes your behavior. Place a number from 1–5 on the line before each statement.

5 — 4 — 3 — 2 — 1
Describes me   Does not describe me

____ 1. Before I negotiate, if possible, I find out about the person I will negotiate with to determine what they want and will be willing to give up.

____ 2. Before I negotiate, I set objectives.

____ 3. When planning my negotiating presentation, I focus on how the other party will benefit.

____ 4. Before I negotiate, I have a target price I want to pay, a lowest price I will pay, and an opening offer.

____ 5. Before I negotiate, I think through options and tradeoffs in case I don't get my target price.

____ 6. Before I negotiate, I think of the questions and objections the other party might have, and I prepare answers.

____ 7. At the beginning of negotiations, I develop rapport and read the person.

____ 8. I let the other party make the first offer.

____ 9. I listen to what the other parties are saying and focus on helping them get what they want, rather than focus on what I want.

____ 10. I don't give in too quickly to others' offers.

____ 11. When I compromise and give up something, I ask for something in return.

____ 12. If the other party tries to postpone the negotiation, I try to create urgency and tell them what they might lose.

____ 13. If I want to postpone negotiation, I don't let the other party pressure me into making a decision.

____ 14. When I make a deal, I don't second-guess, wonder whether I got the best price, and check prices.

____ 15. If I can't make an agreement, I ask for advice to help me with future negotiations.

____ 16. During the entire business negotiating process, I'm trying to develop a relationship, not just a one-time deal.

Add up your score and place it here _____ and on the continuum below.

80 — 70 — 60 — 50 — 40 — 30 — 16
Effective Negotiating   Ineffective Negotiating

If you did not score high on negotiating effectiveness, that's okay, as you can develop negotiating skills by following the steps and guidelines in this chapter.

you realize it or not, and whether you like it or not, we are all negotiators. Negotiating is a key skill for successful managers.[72] Before we get into the details of negotiating, complete Self-Assessment 4.

Negotiating

At certain times, negotiations are appropriate, such as when conducting management-union collective bargaining, buying and selling goods and services, accepting a new job compensation offer, or getting a raise—all situations without a fixed price or deal. If there's a set, take-it-or-leave-it deal, there is no negotiation. For example, in almost all U.S. retail stores, you must buy the product for the price listed; you don't negotiate price. Some car dealers have also stopped negotiating, in favor of a set sticker price.

All Parties Should Believe They Got a Good Deal

Negotiation is often a zero-sum game in which one party's gain is the other party's loss. For example, every dollar less that you pay for a car is your gain and the seller's loss. Therefore, you don't have a true collaboration (win-win situation). Negotiating is about getting what you want, but at the same time it is about developing ongoing relationships. To get what you want, you have to sell your ideas and convince the other party to give you what you want. However, negotiation should be viewed by all parties as an opportunity for everyone to win some, rather than as a win-lose situation.[73] In other words, all parties should believe they got a good deal.[74] If union employees believe they lost and management won, employees may experience job dissatisfaction, resulting in lower performance in the long run. If customers believe they got a bad deal, they may not give repeat business.

Negotiation Skills Can Be Developed

Not everyone is born a great negotiator. In fact, most people don't have a clue about how to get what they want, other than making demands and digging in their heels. Taking the time to learn how to negotiate before entering a deal is the best way to arrive at a successful conclusion.[75] Following the steps in the negotiation process can help you develop your negotiation skills.

--------- Learning Outcomes 6 and 7 ---------

List the steps in the negotiation process.

Explain the relationships among negotiation and conflict, influencing tactics, power, and politics.

The Negotiation Process

The negotiation process has three, and possibly four, steps: plan, negotiations, possibly a postponement, and an agreement or no agreement.[76] These steps are summarized in Model 4-1 and discussed in this section. Like the other models in this book, Model 4-1 is meant to give you step-by-step guidelines. However, in making it apply to varying types of negotiation, you may have to make slight adjustments.

Model 4-1 *The negotiation process.*

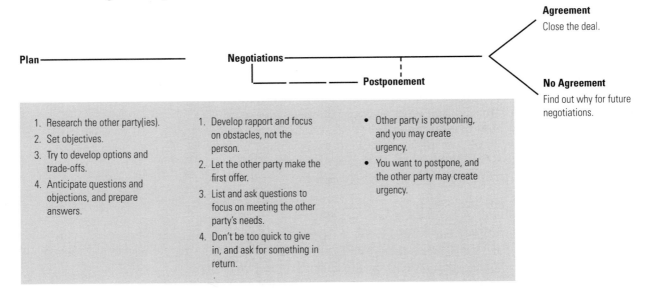

Plan

Success or failure in negotiating is often based on preparation.[77] Be clear about what it is you are negotiating over.[78] Is it price, options, delivery time, sales quantity, or all four? Planning has four steps:

step 1. **Research the other party(ies).** As discussed, know the key power players. Try to find out what the other parties want, and what they will and will not be willing to give up, before you negotiate.[79] Find out their personality traits and negotiation style by networking with people who have negotiated with the other party before. The more you know about the other party, the better your chances of getting an agreement.[80] If possible, establish a personal relationship before the negotiation. If you have experience working with the other party (for example, your manager or a potential customer), what worked and did not work in the past? How can you use that experience in your negotiations (in getting a raise or making a sale)?

step 2. **Set objectives.** Based on your research, what can you expect? You have to identify the one thing you must come away with.[81] Set a lower limit, a target objective, and an opening objective.[82] In many negotiations the objective will be a price, but it could be working conditions, longer vacation, job security, and so on. (a) Set a specific lower limit and be willing to walk away; do not come to an agreement unless you get it.[83] You need to be willing to walk away from a bad deal.[84] (b) Set a target objective of what you believe is a fair deal. (c) Set an opening objective offer that is higher than you expect; you might get it.[85] Remember that the other party is probably also setting three objectives. So don't view their opening offer as final. The key to successful negotiations is for all parties to get between their minimum and target objective. This creates a win-win situation.

step 3. **Try to develop options and trade-offs.** In purchasing something as well as in looking for a job, if you have multiple sellers and job offers, you are in a stronger power position to get your target price. It is common practice to quote other offers and to ask if the other party can beat them.

Try to invent options so that both parties get what they want.[86] Instead of fighting over the pie, think of ways to expand the pie.[87]

If you have to give up something, or cannot get exactly what you want, be prepared to ask for something else in return. If you cannot get the size raise you want, maybe you can get more days off, more in your retirement account, a nicer office, an assistant, and so on. When an airline was having financial difficulty, it asked employees to take a pay cut. Rather than simply accept a cut, they asked for a trade-off and got company stock. Based on your research, what trade-offs do you expect from the other party?

step 4. **Anticipate questions and objections, and prepare answers.** The other party may want to know why you are selling something, looking for a job, how the product or service works, or what are the features and benefits. You need to be prepared to answer the unasked question, "What's in it for me?" Don't focus on what you want, but on how your deal will benefit the other party.[88] Talk in *you* and *we* not *I* terms, unless you are telling others what you will do for them.

There is a good chance that you will face some objection—reasons why the negotiations will not result in agreement or sale. When a union asks for a raise, management typically says the organization can't afford it. However, the union has done its research and quotes the specific profits for a set period of time to overcome the objection. Unfortunately for you, not everyone comes out and tells you their real objections. So you need to listen and ask questions to find out what is preventing the agreement.[89]

You need to fully understand your product or deal, and project positive self-esteem, enthusiasm, and confidence. If the other party does not trust you, and believes the deal is not a good one, you will not reach an agreement.[90] To use our examples, during the selection process, you must convince the manager that you can do the job, or that your product will benefit the customer. When you are in sales, you should have some closing-the-sale statements prepared, such as, "Will you take the white one or the blue one?"

Negotiations

After you have planned, you are now ready to negotiate the deal. Face-to-face negotiations are generally preferred because you can see the other person's nonverbal behavior and better understand objections. However, telephone and written negotiations work too. Again, know the other party's preference.

step 1. **Develop rapport and focus on obstacles, not the person.** Smile and call the other party by name as you greet them. A smile tells people you like them, are interested in them, and enjoy them. Open with some small talk, like the weather. Deciding on how much time to wait until you get down to business depends on the other party's style.[91] Some people like to get right down to business; others, like the Japanese, want to get to know you first. However, you want the other party to make the first offer, so don't wait too long or you may lose your chance.

"Focus on the obstacle, not the person" means never to attack the other's personality[92] or put others down with negative statements like, "You are being unfair to ask for such a price cut." If you do so, the other party will become defensive, you may end up arguing, and it will be harder to reach an agreement. So even if the other person starts it, refuse to fight on a name-calling level. Make statements like, "You think my price is too high?" Not saying negative things about others includes your competitors; just state your competitive advantage in a positive way. People look for four things: inclusion, control, safety, and respect. Most people, if they perceive that you are trying to push them into something, threaten them in some way, or belittle them, will not trust you and make an agreement.

step 2.   **Let the other party make the first offer.** This gives you the advantage, because if the other party offers you more than your target objective, you can close the agreement. For example, if you are expecting to be paid $35,000 a year (your target objective) and the other party offers you $40,000, are you going to reject it? On the other hand, if you are offered $30,000 you can realize that it may be low and work at increasing the compensation. Ask questions like, "What is the salary range?" or "What do you expect to pay for a such a fine product?"

Try to avoid negotiating simply on price. When others pressure you to make the first offer with a common question like, "Give us your best price, and we'll tell you whether we'll take it," try asking them a question such as, "What do you expect to pay?" or "What is a reasonable price?" When this does not work, say something like, "Our usual (or list) price is *xxx*. However, if you make me a proposal, I'll see what I can do for you."

If things go well during steps 1 and 2, you may skip to closing the agreement. If you are not ready to agree, proceed to the next step or two.

step 3.   **Listen and ask questions to focus on meeting the other party's needs.** Create opportunity for the other party to disclose reservations and objections. When you speak you give out information, but when you ask questions and listen, you receive information that will help you to overcome the other party's objections.[93] If you go on and on about the features you have to offer, without finding out what features the other party is really interested in, you may be killing the deal. Ask questions[94] such as, "Is the price out of the ballpark?" or "Is it fast enough for you?" or "Is any feature you wanted missing?" If the objection is a "want" criteria, such as two years of work experience and you have only one, play up the features you know they want and that you do have, and you may reach an agreement. If the objection is something you cannot meet, at least you found out and don't waste time chasing a deal that will not happen. However, be sure the objection is really a "must" criteria: What if the employer gets no applicants with two year's experience and you apply? He or she may offer you the job.

step 4.   **Don't be too quick to give in, and ask for something in return.** Those who ask for more get more. Don't give up whatever it takes to get the agreement.[95] If your competitive advantage is service, and during negotiation you quickly give in for a lower price, you lose all the value in a minute. You want to satisfy the other party without giving up too much during the negotiation.[96] Remember not to go below your minimum objective. If it is realistic, be prepared to walk away. When you are not getting what you want, having other planned options can help give you bargaining power. If you do walk away, you may be called back; and if not, you may be able to come back for the same low price—but not always. If other parties know you are desperate, or just weak and will accept a low agreement, they will likely take advantage of you. Have you ever seen a sign on a product saying, "must sell—need cash?" What type of price do you think that seller gets? You also need to avoid being intimidated by comments such as this said in a loud voice: "Are you kidding me, that's too much." Many people will quickly drop the price, but you don't have to let it happen.

However, when you are dealing with a complex deal, such as a management-union contract negotiation with trade-offs, be willing to be the first to make a concession. The other party tends to feel obligated, and then you can come back with a counter trade-off that is larger than the one you gave up.

Avoid giving unilateral concessions. Recall your planned trade-offs. If the other party asks for a lower price,[97] ask for a concession such as a large-volume sale to get it, or a longer delivery time, a less popular color, and so on. You need to send the message that you don't just give things away.

Postponement

When there doesn't seem to be any progress, it may be wise to postpone the negotiations.[98]

Other Party Is Postponing, and You May Create Urgency

The other party says, "I'll get back to you." When you are not getting what you want, you may try to create urgency. For example, "This product is on sale, and the sale ends today." However, honesty is the best policy. The primary reason people will negotiate with you is that they trust and respect you. Establishing a relationship of trust is the necessary first step in closing a deal. Honesty and integrity are the most important assets a negotiator can possess.[99] If you do have other options, you can use them to create urgency, such as saying, "I have another job offer pending; when will you let me know if you want to offer me the job?"

But what if urgency does not apply—or does not work—and the other party says, "I'll think about it?" You might say, "That's a good idea." Then at least review the major features the other party liked about your proposed deal and ask if it meets their needs. The other party may decide to come to an agreement or sale. If not, and they don't tell you when they will get back to you, ask, for example, "When can I expect to hear if I got the job?" Try to pin the other party down for a specific time; tell the person that if you don't hear from them by then, you will call them. If you are really interested, follow up with a letter (mail, e-mail, or fax) of thanks for their time, and again highlight the features you think they liked. If you forgot to include any specific points during the negotiation, add them in the letter.

One thing to remember when the other party becomes resistant to making the agreement is that the hard sell will not work. Take off the pressure. Ask something like, "Where do you want to go from here?" (to a client). If you press for an answer, it may be no agreement; however, if you wait you may have a better chance. To your manager, you might say, "Why don't we think about it and discuss it some more later?" (then pick an advantageous time to meet with your manager).

You also need to learn to read between the lines, especially when working with people from different cultures. Some people will not come right out and tell you there is no deal. For example, it is common for the Japanese to say something like, "It will be difficult to do business." Americans tend to think this means they can keep trying to close the deal; however, the Japanese businessperson actually means stop trying, but will not say so directly because it is impolite.

You Want to Postpone, and the Other Party May Create Urgency

If you are not satisfied with the deal, or want to shop around, tell the other party you want to think about it. You may also need to check with your manager, or someone else, which simply may be for advice, before you can finalize the deal.[100] If the other party is creating urgency, be sure it really is urgent. In many cases, you can get the same deal at a later date; don't be pressured into making a deal you are not satisfied with or may regret later.[101] If you do want to postpone, give the other party a specific time that you will get back to them, and do so with more prepared negotiations or simply to tell them you cannot make an agreement.

Agreement

Once the agreement has been made, restate it and/or put it in writing when appropriate. It is common to follow up an agreement with a letter of thanks, restating the agreement to ensure the other parties have not changed their mind about what they agreed to. Also, after the deal is made, stop selling it. Change the subject to a personal one and/or leave, depending on the other person's preferred negotiations. If they want a personal relationship, stick around; if not, leave.

No Agreement

Rejection, refusal, and failure happen to us all, even the superstars. The difference between the also-rans and the superstars lies in how they respond to the failure. The successful people keep trying, learn from their mistakes, and continue to work hard; failures usually don't persevere. If you cannot come to an agreement, analyze the situation and try to determine where you went wrong, so that you can improve in the future.[102] You may also ask the other party for advice, such as, "I realize I did not get the job; thanks for your time. Can you offer me any suggestions for improving my resume and interview skills, or other ideas to help me to get a job in this field?"

In general, the Japanese are considered very good negotiators. Toyota is the world's third largest automaker, and it has suppliers from all over the world. Being a large global business gives Toyota the power to negotiate deals worth millions of dollars. With such buying power, Toyota gets great prices. However, Toyota is also known for its quality automobiles, thus, suppliers must also deliver quality parts to Toyota.

5. What Types of Negotiating and Collaborating Did Johnson Do?
As founder of BET, Robert Johnson had to negotiate to get the resources to start, expand, and continue to operate BET. He negotiated with potential employees to come work for BET, and he negotiated with its many suppliers and advertisers. Johnson also negotiated with Viacom to become a subsidiary, and he negotiated a joint venture partnership with Microsoft, Liberty Digital Media, News Corporation, and USA Networks to operate BET Interactive (BET.com).

OPENING CASE APPLICATION

Ethics and Influencing

Recall that *influencing* is the process of affecting others' attitudes and behavior in order to achieve an objective, which is usually to get what you want. Power, politics, networking, and negotiating are all forms of influencing. When influencing, recall that it pays to be ethical (Chapter 2). Power is neither good nor bad; it's what you do with it. Power is unethical (personalized power) when used to promote your self-interest at the expense of others. It is ethical when it is used to help meet organizational objectives and those of its members, as well as to get what you want (socialized power).

When playing organizational politics, it can be tempting to be unethical, but don't. Even if others are using unethical behavior, don't stoop to their level. Talking negatively about people behind their back or stabbing them in the back is usually destructive in the long run. Confront others if you believe they are playing unethical politics and try to resolve the issues. If you cannot, or if the behavior does not directly affect you, going to higher-level managers to inform them of the unethical behavior may be a necessary option.

Recall that networking is about building relationships. Thus, being open and honest during networking is the best policy. You should also try to give to your network, as well as take, and be open to helping others who want to include you in their network. In general, truly successful people take the time to help others. If you haven't learned it already, you will be surprised at how helping others comes back to you.

Ethics of telling the truth, or not lying to the other party or being lied to, is an issue you will face in negotiation.[103] There is a difference between not giving information that is not asked for and lying to the other party. To be a successful negotiator, people have to trust you to do business with you. In most positions, repeat customers are critical to long-term success. Lying to one customer and losing that person's business can cost you greatly in the long term. Also, the person who caught you lying may tell others, and you can lose more business.[104]

So when you are influencing others, try to use the stakeholders' approach to ethics by creating a win-win situation for relevant parties affected by the decision.

Go to the Internet (academic.cengage.com/management/lussier) where you will find a broad array of resources to help maximize your learning.

- Review the vocabulary
- Try a quiz
- View chapter videos

Chapter Summary

The chapter summary is organized to answer the eight learning outcomes for Chapter 4.

1. Explain the differences between position power and personal power.

Position power is derived from top management and is delegated down the chain of command. Thus, people at the top of the organization have more power than those at the bottom of the organization. Personal power is derived from the followers based on the leader's behavior. All managers have position power, but they may or may not have personal power. Nonmanagers do not have position power, but they may have personal power.

2. Discuss the differences among legitimate, reward, coercive, and referent power.

Legitimate, reward, and coercive power are all related. A leader with position power usually has the power to reward and punish (coercive). However, a person with referent power may or may not have position power to reward and punish, and the leader influences followers based on relationships.

3. Discuss how power and politics are related.

Power is the ability to influence others' behavior. Politics is the process of gaining and using power. Therefore, political skills are a part of power.

4. Describe how money and politics have a similar use.

Money and politics have a similar use, because they are mediums of exchange. In our economy, money is the medium of exchange. In an organization, politics is the medium of exchange.

5. List and explain the steps in the networking process.

The first step in the networking process is to perform a self-assessment to determine accomplishments and to set goals. Second, create a one-minute self-sell that quickly summarizes history and career plans and asks a question. Third, develop a written network list. Fourth, conduct networking interviews

to meet your goals. Finally, maintain your network for meeting future goals.

6. List the steps in the negotiation process.

The first step in the negotiation process is to plan for the negotiation. The second step is to conduct the actual negotiation, which can be postponed, and results in an agreement or no agreement.

7. Explain the relationships among negotiation and conflict, influencing tactics, power, and politics.

Negotiations take place when there is a conflict, and influencing tactics, power, and politics can be used during the negotiation process.

8. Define the following key terms (in order of appearance in the chapter).

Select one or more methods: (1) fill in the missing key terms from memory; (2) match the key terms from the following list with their definitions below; (3) copy the key terms in order from the list at the beginning of the chapter.

_____ is the process of affecting others' attitudes and behavior to achieve an objective.

_____ is the leader's potential influence over followers.

_____ is based on the user's position power, given by the organization.

_____ is based on the user's ability to influence others with something of value to them.

_____ involves punishment and withholding of rewards to influence compliance.

_____ is based on the user's personal relationship with others.

_____ is based on the user's skill and knowledge.

_____ is based on the user's data that is desired by others.

_____ is based on the user's relationship with influential people.

_____ is the process of gaining and using power.

_____ is the process of developing relationships for the purpose of socializing and politicking.

_____ involves creating obligations and developing alliances, and using them to accomplish objectives.

_____ is an opening statement used in networking that quickly summarizes your history and career plan and asks a question.

_____ is a process in which two or more parties are in conflict and attempt to come to an agreement.

Key Terms

coercive power, 121

connection power, 125

expert power, 123

information power, 124

legitimate power, 118

negotiating, 142

networking, 129

one-minute self-sell, 138

politics, 129

power, 116

reciprocity, 131

referent power, 122

reward power, 120

Review and Discussion Questions

1. What are the nine influencing tactics?
2. What are the seven types of power?
3. What are the three political behaviors and four guidelines for developing political skills?
4. Can management order the end of power and politics in their organizations?
5. Should people be judged based on their social skills?
6. Do you believe that networking is really all that important?
7. Do people really need a written networking list?
8. How many interview questions should you bring to a networking interview?
9. What type of situation is the goal of negotiation?
10. What are the steps in planning a negotiation?
11. What are the steps in negotiations?

Case

CARLTON PETERSBURG—DEPARTMENT OF LEADERSHIP

Carlton Petersburg is a tenured professor of leadership at a small teaching college in the Midwest.[105] The Department of Leadership (DL) has nine faculty members; it is one of 10 departments in the School of Arts and Sciences (SAS). The leadership department chair is Tina Joel, who is in her first year as chair. Six faculty members, including Carlton, have been in the department longer than Tina. Tina likes to have policies in place, so that faculty members have guides for their behavior. On the collegewide level, however, there is no policy about the job of graduate assistant. Tina has asked the dean of the SAS about the policy. After a discussion with the vice president for academic affairs, the dean told Tina that there is no policy. The vice president and dean suggested letting the individual departments develop their own policy regarding what graduate assistants can and cannot do in their position. So Tina has

made developing a policy for graduate assistants an agenda item for the department meeting.

During the DL meeting, Tina asks for members' views on what graduate assistants should and should not be allowed to do. She is hoping that the department can come to a consensus on a policy. It turns out that Carlton Petersburg is the only faculty member using graduate assistants to grade exams. All but one of the other faculty members speaks out against having graduate assistants grade exams. Other faculty members believe it is the professor's job to grade exams. Carlton makes a few statements in hopes of not having to correct his own exams. Because his exams are objective, requiring a correct answer, Carlton believes it's not necessary for him to personally correct the exams. He also points out that across the campus, and across the country, other faculty members are using graduate assistants to teach entire courses and to correct subjective papers and exams. Carlton states that he does not think it fair to tell him that he cannot use graduate assistants to grade objective exams when others are doing so. He also states that the department does not need to have a policy, and requests that the department not set a policy. However, Tina states that she wants a policy. Carlton holds a single, minority view during the meeting. But, after the meeting, one other member, Fred Robinson, who said nothing during the meeting, tells Carlton he agrees that it is not fair to deny him this use of a graduate assistant.

There was no department consensus, as Tina hoped there would be. Tina says that she will draft a department policy, which will be discussed at a future DL meeting. The next day, Carlton sends a memo to department members asking if it is ethical and legal to deny him the same resources as others are using across the campus. He also states that if the department sets a policy stating that he can no longer use graduate assistants to correct objective exams, he will appeal the policy decision to the dean, vice president, and president.

Support your answers to the following questions with specific information from the case and text, or with information you get from other sources.

1. (a) What source of power does Tina have, and (b) what type of power is she using? (c) Which influencing tactic is Tina using during the meeting? (d) Is negotiation and/or the (e) exchange tactic appropriate in this situation?

2. (a) What source of power does Carlton have, and (b) what type of power is he using during the meeting? (c) Which two influencing tactics is Carlton primarily using during the meeting? (d) Which influencing tactic is Carlton using with the memo? (e) Is the memo a wise political move for Carlton? What might he gain and lose by sending it?

3. What would you do if you were Tina? (a) Would you talk to the dean, letting him know that Carlton said he would appeal the policy decision? (b) Which influencing tactic would this discussion involve? (c) Which political behavior would the discussion represent? (d) Would you draft a policy directly stating that graduate assistants cannot be used to grade objective exams? (e) Would your answer to (d) be influenced by your answer to (a)?

4. (a) If you were Carlton, knowing you had no verbal supporters during the meeting, would you have continued to defend your position or agreed to stop using a graduate assistant? (b) What do you think of Carlton sending the memo? (c) As a tenured full professor, Carlton is secure in his job. Would your answer change if you (as Carlton) had not received tenure or promotion to the top rank?

5. (a) If you were Carlton, and Tina drafted a policy and department members agreed with it, what would you do? Would you appeal the decision to the dean?
(b) Again, would your answer change if you had not received tenure or promotion to the top rank?

6. If you were the dean of SAS, knowing that the vice president does not want to set a collegewide policy, and Carlton appealed to you, what would you do? Would you develop a schoolwide policy for SAS?

7. At what level (collegewide, by schools, or by departments within each school) should a graduate assistants policy be set?

8. (a) Should Fred Robinson have spoken up in defense of Carlton during the meeting? (b) If you were Fred, would you have taken Carlton's side against the other seven members? (c) Would your answer change if you were and were not friends with Carlton, and if you were and were not a tenured full professor?

Cumulative Case Questions

9. Which level(s) of analysis of leadership theory (Chapter 1) is (are) presented in this case?

10. Is it ethical (Chapter 2) for graduate students to correct undergraduate exams?

11. Which of the four Ohio State University leadership styles (Chapter 3) did Tina use during the department meeting?

Case Exercise and Role-Play

Preparation: Read the case and think about whether you agree or disagree with using graduate assistants to correct objective exams. If you do this exercise, we recommend that you complete it before discussing the questions and answers to the case.

In-Class DL Meeting: A person who strongly agrees with Carlton's position volunteers to play his or her role (women can use the name Carly) during a leadership department DL meeting. A second person who also agrees with the use of graduate assistants correcting exams plays the role of Fred (or Freddie). However, recall that Fred/Freddie cannot say anything during the meeting to support Carlton/Carly. One person who strongly disagrees with Carlton—who doesn't want graduate assistants to correct exams, and who also feels strongly that there should be a policy stating what graduate assistants can and cannot do—volunteers to play the role of the department chair (Tina or Tim) who runs the DL meeting. Six others who strongly disagree with graduate assistants grading exams play the role of other department members.

The 10 role players sit in a circle in the center of the room, with the other class members sitting around the outside of the circle. Observers just quietly watch and listen to the meeting discussion.

Role-Play (about 15 minutes): Tina/Tim opens the meeting by simply stating that the agenda item is to set a graduate assistants policy stating what they can and cannot do, and that he or she hopes the department can come to a consensus on a policy. Tina/Tim states his or her position on why graduate students should not be allowed to correct exams, and then asks for other views. Carlton/Carly and the others, except Fred/Freddie, jump in anytime with their opinions.

Discussion: After the role-play is over, or when time runs out, the person playing the role of Carlton/Carly expresses to the class how it felt to have everyone against him or her. Other department members state how they felt about the discussion, followed by observers' statements as time permits. A discussion of the case questions and answers may follow.

Video Case

Buffalo Zoo: Leadership in Organizations

After years of overreaching leadership, flagging attendance, and sinking employee morale, the Buffalo Zoo struggled to update its vision and find its place in the world. Part of finding that place was the selection of Donna Fernandes as the zoo's new president.

View the Video (13 minutes)
View the video on Buffalo Zoo in class or at **academic. cengage.com/management/lussier.**

Read the Case
At first, senior staff were cynical about the arrival of Ms. Fernandes. The Buffalo Zoo's former executives had been unable to follow through on creating and executing a master plan or working effectively with the board to raise money for the organization. The staff soon learned that Ms. Fernandes was a charismatic leader capable of using her power to set realistic goals and establish plans that were both actionable and empowering to employees.

Good leadership requires vision, charisma, and the ability to use power effectively, and Donna Fernandes possesses the right qualities to lead the Buffalo Zoo. Ms. Fernandes has been described as "energetic," "smart," and "willing to get in the trenches"—traits that endear her to her colleagues. One staff member praised the empathetic leadership style of the zoo's new chief, commenting that she feels as though she works *with* Fernandes not *for* her.

Donna Fernandes possesses the hallmarks of good leadership, and the case of the Buffalo Zoo demonstrates how an inspired and inspiring leader can directly effect change in an organization. Ms. Fernandes's ability to build relationships with her staff and the board has prepared the zoo for a bright and promising future.

Answer the Questions
1. In what ways does Ms. Fernandes utilize expert power at the Buffalo Zoo, and how does such power help her lead the organization?
2. Which of the other seven types of power does Donna Fernandes use? Give examples. How do employees at the zoo respond to her use of power?

Skill-Development Exercise 1

INFLUENCING TACTICS

Preparing for Skill-Development Exercise 1

Below are three situations. For each situation, select the most appropriate influencing tactic(s) to use. Write the tactic(s) on the lines following the situation. At this time, don't write out how you would behave (what you would say and do).

1. You are doing a college internship, which is going well. You would like to become a full-time employee in a few weeks, after you graduate.
   Which influencing tactic(s) would you use? _____
   Who would you try to influence? _____
   How would you do so (behavior)? _____

2. You have been working at your job for six months and you are approaching the elevator. You see a powerful person who could potentially help you advance in your career waiting for the elevator. You have never met her, but you do know that her committee has recently completed a new five-year strategic plan for the company and that she plays tennis and is active at the same religious organization (church, synagogue, mosque) as you. Although you only have a couple of minutes, you decide to try to develop a connection.
   Which influencing tactic(s) would you use? _____

How would you strike up a conversation? What topic(s) do you raise?_____

3. You are the manager of the production department. Some of the sales staff has been scheduling deliveries for your product that your department can't meet. Customers are blaming you for late delivery. This is not good for the company, so you decide to talk to the sales staff manager about it over lunch.

Which influencing tactic(s) would you use? _____

How would you handle the situation (behavior)?_____

Now select one of the three situations that seems real to you—you can imagine yourself in the situation. Or briefly write in a real-life situation that you can quickly explain to a small group. Now, briefly write out the behavior (what you would do and say) that you would use in the situation to influence the person to do what you want.

Situation # _____ Or, my situation: _____

_____

Influencing tactic(s) to use _____
Behavior: _____

_____

_____

Doing Skill-Development Exercise 1 In-Class

Objective
To develop your persuasion skills by using influencing tactics.

Experience
You will discuss which influencing tactics are most appropriate for the preparation situations. You may also be given the opportunity to role-play how you would handle the one situation you selected; you will also play the role of the person to be influenced, and observer.

Procedure 1 (10–20 minutes)
Break up into groups of three, with one or two groups of two if needed. Try not to have two members in a group who selected the same situation; use people who selected their own situation. First, try to quickly agree on which influencing tactics are most appropriate in each situation. Select a spokesperson to give group answers to the class. In preparation to role-play, have each person state the behavior selected to handle the situation. The others give feedback for improvement: suggestions to delete, change, and/or add to the behavior (for example, I would not say . . . ., I'd say it this way . . . ., I'd add . . . . to what you have now).

Procedure 2 (5–10 minutes)
One situation at a time, each group spokesperson tells the class which influencing styles it would use, followed by brief remarks from the professor. The professor may also ask people who selected their own situation to tell the class the situation.

Conclusion
The instructor may lead a class discussion and/or make concluding remarks.

Apply It (2–4 minutes)
What did I learn from this exercise? How will I use this knowledge in the future?

_____

_____

_____

Sharing
In the group, or to the entire class, volunteers may give their answers to the "Apply It" questions.

Skill-Development Exercise 2

INFLUENCING, POWER, AND POLITICS

Preparing for Skill-Development Exercise 2

Your instructor will tell you to select one, two, or all three of the following topics (influencing, power, and/or politics) for this preparation.

To get what you want, you need to develop your ability to influence others and gain power through politics. It is helpful to read about these topics and how to improve your skills, but unless you apply the concepts in your personal and professional lives, you will not develop these skills.

This preparation covers three skills, each with two activities. The first activity is to develop a general guide to daily actions you can take to increase your influence, power, and/or understanding of politics. The second is to think of a specific situation in the future, and develop a plan to get what you want. Use additional paper if you need more space to write your plan.

Influencing
Write down the influencing tactic that you are the strongest at using: _____. The weakest: _____.
The one you would like to improve on: _____ (it does not have to be your weakest). Review the ideas for

using this tactic, and write down a few ways in which you will work at developing your skill.

_____
_____
_____
_____

Think of a specific situation in the near future in which you can use this tactic to help you get what you want. Briefly describe the situation, and explain how you will use this tactic—what you will say and do, and so on.

_____
_____
_____
_____

Power

Write down the one type of your power you would like to improve on: _____. Review the ideas for increasing this type of power, and write down a few ways in which you will work at developing your power.

_____
_____
_____
_____

Think of a specific situation in the near future in which you can use this type of power to help you get what you want. Briefly describe the situation, and explain how you will use this tactic—what you will say and do, and so on.

_____
_____
_____
_____

Politics

Write down the one area of politics you would like to improve on: _____. Review the ideas for using this type of politics, and write down a few ways in which you will work at developing your skill.

_____
_____
_____
_____

Think of a specific situation in the near future in which you can use this type of politicking to help you get what you want. Briefly describe the situation, and explain how you will use this tactic—what you will say and do, and so on.

_____
_____
_____
_____

Doing Skill-Development Exercise 2 in Class

Objective
To develop your ability to influence others and gain power through politics.

Experience
You will develop a general guide to daily actions you can take to increase your influence, power, and/or understanding of politics. You'll also develop a plan to get what you want.

Preparation
You should have completed the preparation for this exercise, unless told not to do so by your instructor.

Procedure 1 (10–20 minutes)
Break into groups of three, with some groups of two if necessary. If group members developed plans for more than one skill area, select only one to start with. One group member volunteers to share first and states their preparation for influencing, power, or politics. The other members give input into how effective they think the plan is and offer ideas on how to improve the plan. After the first member shares, the other two have their turn, changing roles with each round. If there is time remaining after all have shared, go on to another skill area until the time is up.

Procedure 2 (2–3 minutes)
Each member commits to implementing their plan by a set time, and to telling the others how well the influence, power, or politics went by a specific date—before or after the class ends.

Name _____
Date of implementation _____
Date to report results _____

Name _____
Date of implementation _____
Date to report results _____

Name _____
Date of implementation _____
Date to report results _____

Conclusion
The instructor may make concluding remarks.

Apply It (2–4 minutes)
What did I learn from this experience? How will I use this knowledge in the future?

_____
_____

Sharing
In the group, or to the entire class, volunteers may give their answers to the "Apply It" questions.

Skill-Development Exercise 3

NETWORKING SKILLS*

Preparing for Skill-Development Exercise 3

Based on the section "Networking" and the subsection on the networking process, complete the following steps.

1. Perform a self-assessment and set goals. List two or three of your accomplishments and set a goal. The goal can be to learn more about career opportunities in your major; to get an internship, part-time, summer, or full-time job; and so on.

_____

_____

_____

_____

2. Create your one-minute self-sell. Write it out. See page 138 for a written example.

History:_____

Plan:_____

Question:_____

3. Develop your network. List at least five people to be included in your network, preferably people who can help you achieve your goal.

_____

_____

_____

4. Conduct networking interviews. To help meet your goal, select one person for a personal 20-minute interview or to interview by phone if it is difficult to meet in person. List the person and write questions to ask during the interview. This person can be a person in your college career center or a professor in your major.

_____

_____

_____

_____

_____

_____

_____

*Source: This exercise was developed by Andra Gumbus, assistant professor, College of Business, Sacred Heart University. (c) Andra Gumbus, 2002. It is used with Dr. Gumbus's permission.

Doing Skill-Development Exercise 3 in Class

Objective

To develop networking skills by implementing the steps in the networking process.

Experience

You will deliver your one-minute self-sell from the preparation and get feedback for improvement. You will also share your network list and interview questions and get feedback for improvement.

Procedure 1 (7–10 minutes)

A. Break into groups of two. Show each other your written one-minute self-sell. Is the history, plan, and question clear (do you understand it), concise (60 seconds or less to say), and compelling (does it promote interest to help)? Offer suggestions for improvement.

B. After perfected, each person states (no reading) the one-minute self-sell. Was it stated clearly, concisely, and with confidence? Offer improvements. State it a second and third time, or until told to go on to the next procedure.

Procedure 2 (7–10 minutes)

Break into groups of three with people you did not work with during procedure 1. Follow procedures A and B above in your triad. Repeating your self-sell should improve your delivery and confidence.

Procedure 3 (10–20 minutes)

Break into groups of four with people you did not work with during procedures 1 and 2, if possible. Share your answers from steps 3 (your network list) and 4 (your interview questions). Offer each other improvements to the questions and new questions. You should also get ideas for writing new questions for your own interview.

Applications (done outside of class)

Expand your written network list to at least 25 names. Conduct the networking interview using the questions developed through this exercise.

Conclusion

The instructor may make concluding remarks, including requiring the network lists and/or networking interview in the "Applications" section. Written network lists and/or interview questions and answers (following the name, title, and organization of interviewee; date, time, and type of interview—phone or in person) may be passed in.

Sharing

In groups, or to the entire class, volunteers may share what they have learned about networking.

Skill-Development Exercise 4

CAR DEALER NEGOTIATION

Preparing for Skill-Development Exercise 4

You should have read and should understand the negotiation process.

Doing Skill-Development Exercise 4 in Class

Objective
To develop your negotiation skills.

Experience
You will be the buyer or seller of a used car.

Procedure 1 (1–2 minutes)
Break up into groups of two and sit facing each other, so that you cannot read each other's confidential sheet. Each group should be as far away from other groups as possible, to avoid overhearing each other's conversations. If there is an odd number of students in the class, one student will be an observer or work with the instructor. Select who will be the buyer and who will be the seller of the used car.

Procedure 2 (1–2 minutes)
The instructor goes to each group and gives each buyer and seller their confidential sheet.

Procedure 3 (5–6 minutes)
Buyers and sellers read their confidential sheets and write down some plans (what will be your basic approach, what will you say) for the lunch meeting.

Procedure 4 (3–7 minutes)
Negotiate the sale of the car. Try not to overhear your classmates' conversations. You do not have to buy or sell the car. After you make the sale, or agree not to sell, read the confidential sheet of your partner in this exercise and discuss the experience.

Integration (3–7 minutes)
Answer the following questions:

1. Which of the nine influencing tactics (Exhibit 4-1) did you use during the negotiations?
2. Which of the seven types of power (Exhibit 4-1) did you use during the negotiations? Did both parties believe that they got a good deal?
3. During your planning, did you (1) research the other party, (2) set an objective (price to pay or accept), (3) develop options and trade-offs, and (4) anticipate questions and objections and prepare answers?
4. During the negotiations, did you (1) develop a rapport and focus on obstacles, not the person; (2) let the other party make the first offer; (3) listen and ask questions to focus on meeting the other party's needs; and (4) were you too quick to give in and did you ask for something in return?
5. Did you reach an agreement to sell/buy the car? If yes, did you get exactly, more than, or less than your target price?
6. When negotiating, is it a good practice to ask for more than you expect to receive, or to offer less than you expect to pay?
7. When negotiating, is it better to be the one to give or receive the initial offer?
8. When negotiating, is it better to appear to be dealing with strong or weak power? In other words, should you try to portray that you have other options and don't really need to make a deal with this person? Or, should you appear to be in need of the deal?
9. Can having the power to intimidate others be helpful in negotiations?

Conclusion
The instructor leads a class discussion, or simply gives the answers to the "Integration" questions, and makes concluding remarks.

Apply It (2–4 minutes)
What did I learn from this experience? How will I use this knowledge in the future? What will I do differently?

_____

_____

_____

Sharing
In the group, or to the entire class, volunteers may give their answers to the "Apply It" questions.

Note: The car dealer negotiation confidential information is from Arch G. Woodside, Wallace Carroll School of Management, Boston College. The Car Dealer Game is part of a paper, "Bargaining Behavior in Personal Selling and Buying Exchanges," that was presented at the 1980 *Eighth Annual Conference of the Association for Business Simulation and Experiential Learning (ABSEL)*. It is used with Dr. Woodside's permission.

Contingency Leadership Theories

5

LEARNING OUTCOMES

After studying this chapter, you should be able to:

1. State the major difference between behavioral and contingency leadership theories, and explain the behavioral contribution to contingency theories. p. 160

2. Describe the contingency leadership theory variables. p. 160

3. Identify the contingency leadership model styles and variables. p. 162

4. State the leadership continuum model major styles and variables. p. 168

5. Identify the path-goal leadership model styles and variables. p. 170

6. State the normative leadership model styles and the number of variables. p. 175

7. Discuss the major similarities and differences between the behavioral and contingency leadership theories. p. 181

8. Compare and contrast four major differences among the four contingency leadership models. p. 181

9. List which leadership models are prescriptive and descriptive, and explain why they are classified as such. p. 183

10. Explain substitutes and neutralizers of leadership. p. 183

11. Define the following **key terms** (in order of appearance in the chapter):

leadership model	normative leadership model
contingency leadership model	prescriptive leadership models
leadership continuum model	descriptive leadership models
path-goal leadership model	substitutes for leadership

Opening Case Application

After Hewlett-Packard (HP) had nine consecutive quarters of poor performance during the largest tech boom in history, HP hired Carleton (Carly) Fiorina as CEO to lead its adaptation to the Internet era in 1999. She was the first outsider to run HP and the first women to lead one of the nation's largest public firms. Carly Fiorina has been called the most powerful woman in the corporate world.[1] Fiorina quickly took strong control of HP, implementing the largest-ever reorganization of HP by reducing the number of business units from 83 down to just 4, consolidating executive authority through her office. Fiorina also made the strategic move to acquire Compaq Computer Corporation, despite opposition, in May 2002.

In 2005, to help HP more quickly meet customer demands and respond to competition, the HP board decided to take some of Fiorina's power away by giving some key day-to-day responsibilities to other executives.[2] Fiorina really did not want to give up complete control. After $5^1/_2$ years the HP board asked CEO Fiorina to step down. Board Chairwoman Patricia Dunn praised Fiorina for doing an "outstanding" job in positioning HP for success, but stated that a new set of capabilities is called for.[3] Mark Hurd left his CEO position of NCR Corporation to replace Fiorina. Hurd stated that HP was not in trouble, having had a 6 percent operating profit margin and significant cash flow in 2004. Hurd plans to run HP differently than Fiorina with his view of management as a team sport.[4]

Opening Case Questions:

1. What does Carly Fiorina losing her job as CEO of HP have to do with contingency leadership theory?
2. Which contingency leadership situation was Carly Fiorina in, and what leadership style was appropriate?
3. Which continuum leadership style did Fiorina tend to use and what style is Mark Hurd using at HP?
4. Which path-goal leadership style did Carly Fiorina tend to use and what style is Mark Hurd using at HP?
5. Which normative leadership style did Carly Fiorina tend to use at HP?

To learn more about HP, visit the company's Web site at **http://www.hp.com** or log on to InfoTrac® College Edition at **academic.cengage.com/infotrac**, where you can research and read articles on HP and the latest developments in technology markets. For in-depth articles on new CEO Mark Hurd and HP's merger with Compaq, select the advanced search option and key in record number A133296095 and A105870432.

As you read this chapter, you will learn more about leadership style as it relates to four contingency leadership theories. We begin with an overview of contingency leadership theories. Next we present four contingency leadership models: contingency leadership, leadership continuum, path-goal, and normative leadership. These are listed in historical sequence by the date each model was published. Then we put the behavioral (Chapter 3) and contingency leadership theories together. We end by discussing leadership theory substitutes.

Learning Outcome 1

State the major difference between behavioral and contingency leadership theories, and explain the behavioral contribution to contingency theories.

Contingency Leadership Theories and Models

Both the trait and behavioral leadership theories were attempts to find the one best leadership style in all situations. In the late 1960s, it became apparent that there is no one best leadership style in all situations.[5] Managers need to adapt different leadership styles to different situations.[6] Thus, contingency leadership theory became the third major leadership paradigm (Chapter 1), and the leadership styles used in its models are based on the behavioral leadership theories.

In this section, we discuss theories versus models, the contingency theory factors, and the need for global contingency leadership.

Leadership Theories versus Leadership Models

As defined in Chapter 1, a *leadership theory* is an explanation of some aspect of leadership; theories have practical value because they are used to better understand, predict, and control successful leadership. *A* **leadership model** *is an example for emulation or use in a given situation.* In earlier chapters we talked about leading by example, which is emulation or the hope that followers will imitate the leader's behavior. In this chapter we discuss using models in a given situation to improve performance of leaders, followers, or both.

All of the contingency leadership theories in this chapter have leadership models. The leadership theory is the longer text that explains the variables and leadership styles to be used in a given contingency situation. The leadership model is the short (one page or less) summary of the theory to be used when selecting the appropriate leadership style for a given situation.

Learning Outcome 2

Describe the contingency leadership theory variables.

Contingency Theory and Model Variables

Contingency means "it depends." One thing depends on other things, and for a leader to be effective there must be an appropriate fit between the leader's behavior and style and the followers and the situation.[7] Recall from Chapter 1 that *contingency leadership theories* attempt to explain the appropriate leadership style based on the leader, followers, and situation.

Exhibit 5-1 *Framework for contingency leadership variables.*

FOLLOWERS	LEADER	SITUATION
Capability	Personality traits	Task
Motivation	Behavior	Structure
	Experience	Environment

Different groups also prefer different leadship styles.[8] Leaders display a range of behavior in different situations, because leadership is largely shaped by contextual factors that not only set the boundaries within which leaders and followers interact but also determine the demands and constraints confronting the leader.[9]

See Exhibit 5-1 for a list of general contingency leadership variables that can be used as a framework in which to place all the contingency leadership model variables for analyzing leadership. Throughout this chapter, each contingency leadership model's variables are described in terms of this framework. For each model, the *leader* variable also includes the leadership styles of each model.

1. What Does Carly Fiorina Losing Her Job As CEO of HP Have to Do with Contingency Leadership Theory?

Contingency theory is about using the right style in the right situation to succeed. Fiorina did turn HP around, back to profits and ready for the future. But as HP Chairwoman Dunn said, the future calls for a new set of capabilities. The HP board believed Fiorina was not longer the right person for the situation, Hurd is.[10] During an interview in February 2005, Carly Fiorina was asked how long she would stay at HP. She stated that she could not put a time frame on how long she would stay. However, Fiorina did say that she knows that every leader has a season and there would come a time when her season was over.[11]

OPENING CASE APPLICATION

Global Contingency Leadership

Before we get into all the theories, let's take a minute to quickly help you realize how important contingency leadership is in the global economy of today. Global companies like McDonald's, with restaurants all over the world, realize that successful leadership styles can vary greatly from place to place. In Europe and other parts of the world, managers have more cultural than technical variables to deal with as they encounter diverse value systems and religious backgrounds among employees. More companies are now looking for graduates with an international openness and flexibility who can master the complexity of the global economy.

Back in the 1970s, Japan was increasing its rate of productivity at a faster pace than that of the United States. William Ouchi found that Japanese firms were managed and led differently than U.S. organizations. He identified seven major differences between the two countries. The Japanese had: (1) longer periods of employment, (2) more collective decision making, (3) more collective responsibility, (4) slower process of evaluating and promoting employees, (5) more implicit mechanisms of control, (6) more unspecialized career paths, and (7) more holistic concern for employees.[12] Ouchi combined practices of U.S. and Japanese companies in what he called *Theory Z*. Over the years, many American companies have adopted more collective decision making and shared leadership responsibilities. On the other side of the ocean, the Japanese have also been influenced by American management practices. Toyota is now using American techniques of shorter employment and faster promotions.

Ethical Dilemma 1

Leadership Gender

Should gender be a contingency variable in leadership? Are there differences in the leadership of men and women? Some researchers say that women tend to be more participative, relationship-oriented leaders and men are more task oriented.[13] However, others say that men and women leaders are more alike than different because they do the same things, so they are equally effective leaders.[14]

1. Do you think that men and women lead the same or differently?
2. Are men or women more ethical and socially responsible leaders?
3. Would you prefer to have a man or woman for a boss?
4. Is it ethical and socially responsible to say that one gender makes better leaders?
5. Should global companies appoint women as managers in countries that believe in equal rights for women, but not allow women to be managers in countries that don't have these beliefs?

Learning Outcome 3

Identify the contingency leadership model styles and variables.

Contingency Leadership Theory and Model

In 1951, Fred E. Fiedler began to develop the first situational leadership theory.[15] It was the first theory to specify how situational variables interact with leader personality and behavior. He called the theory "Contingency Theory of Leader Effectiveness."[16] Fiedler believed that leadership style is a reflection of personality (trait theory–oriented) and behavior (behavioral theory–oriented), and that leadership styles are basically constant. Leaders do not change styles, they change the situation. *The* **contingency leadership model** *is used to determine if a person's leadership style is task- or relationship-oriented, and if the situation (leader-member relationship, task structure, and position power) matches the leader's style to maximize performance.* In this section we discuss Fiedler's leadership styles, situational favorableness, determining the

Exhibit 5-2 *Contingency leadership model variables within the contingency leadership framework.*

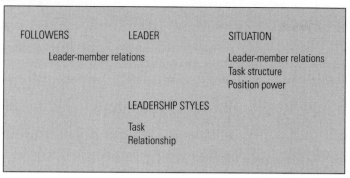

appropriate leadership style for the situation, and research by Fiedler and others. See Exhibit 5-2 to see how Fiedler's model fits into the framework of contingency leadership variables.

Leadership Style and the LPC

Although you may be able to change your behavior with different followers, you also have a dominant leadership style. The first major factor in using Fiedler's model is to determine whether your dominant leadership style is task-motivated or relationship-motivated. People primarily gain satisfaction from task accomplishment or from forming and maintaining relationships with followers. To determine leadership style, using Fiedler's model, you must complete the least preferred coworker (LPC) scales. The LPC essentially answers the question, "Are you more task-oriented or relationship-oriented?" The two leadership styles are (1) *task* and (2) *relationship*. Approximately 200 tests revealed that people who completed the LPC scales did in fact use the preferred leadership style in simulated situations and actual job situations.[17]

Note that Fiedler developed two leadership styles, which is a one-dimensional model. The leadership styles part of Fiedler's model is similar to the University of Michigan Leadership Model, in that it is based on only two leadership styles: one focusing on the task (job-centered leadership) and the other focusing on relationship (employee-centered). To determine your Fiedler leadership style, complete Self-Assessment 1.

Situational Favorableness

After determining your leadership style, determine the situational favorableness. *Situation favorableness* refers to the degree to which a situation enables the leader to exert influence over the followers. The more control the leader has over the followers, the more favorable the situation is for the leader. The three variables, in order of importance, are

1. *Leader-member relations.* This is the most powerful determinant of overall situational favorableness. Is the relationship good (cooperative and friendly) or poor (antagonistic and difficult)? Do the followers trust, respect, accept, and have confidence in the leader (good)? Is there much tension (poor)? Leaders with good relations have more influence. The better the relations, the more favorable the situation.

Your Fiedler LPC Leadership Style

Return to Chapter 3, Self-Assessment Exercise 1, and place your score for tasks on the following Task line and your score for people on the Relationship line.

10 — 9 — 8 — 7 — 6 — 5 — 4 — 3 — 2 — 1
High Task Leadership Style

10 — 9 — 8 — 7 — 6 — 5 — 4 — 3 — 2 — 1
High Relationship Leadership Style

According to Fiedler, you are primarily either a task- or relationship-oriented leader. Your highest score is your primary leadership style. Neither leadership style is the one best style. The one appropriate leadership style to use is based on the situation, our next topic.

2. *Task structure.* This is second in potency; is the task structured or unstructured? Do employees perform repetitive routine, unambiguous, standard tasks that are easily understood? Leaders in a structured situation have more influence. The more structured the jobs are, the more favorable the situation.

3. *Position power.* This is the weakest factor; is position power strong or weak? Does the leader have the power to assign work, reward and punish, hire and fire, give raises and promotions? The leader with position power has more influence. The more power, the more favorable the situation.

The relative weights of these three factors together create a continuum of situational favorableness of the leader. Fiedler developed eight levels of favorableness, going from 1 (highly favorable) to 8 (very unfavorable). See Exhibit 5-3 for an adapted model.[18]

Ethical Dilemma 2

Drug Research

Several drug companies, including Glaxo-SmithKline (Paxil antidepressant drug for children)[19] and Merck (Vioxx arthritis pain medication),[20] have been accused of situationally favorable research reporting. When results support the use of the drug, they are reported; when they don't, results are not reported. Although all medications have side effects, some drug users have died because of medication. As a result, the Food and Drug Administration (FDA) has been criticized for its process of getting drugs approved and monitoring of the safety of drugs.[21]

(Continued)

Ethical Dilemma 2

(*Continued*)

1. Is it ethical and socially responsible to report only the results that help gain FDA approval of drugs?
2. If you worked for a drug company and knew that the results of a study showed negative effects, but were not included in a report, what would you do?
3. If you worked for a drug company and your boss asked you to change negative results into positive results, or to make results even better, what would you do?
4. What would you do if you gave your boss a negative report on a drug and found out the results were changed to positive results?
5. Is the FDA doing a good job of monitoring the safety of drugs? If not, what else should it do?

Exhibit 5-3 *Fiedler contingency leadership model.*

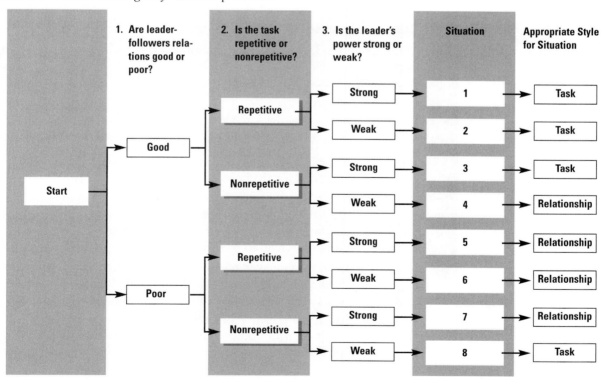

If the managers' LPC leadership style matches the situation, the manager does nothing. If the LPC leadership style does not match the situation, the manager changes the situation to match his or her LPC leadership style.

Source: Adapted from Fred E. Fiedler, *A Theory of Leadership Effectiveness* (New York: McGraw-Hill, 1967).

Determining the Appropriate Leadership Style

To determine whether task or relationship leadership is appropriate, the user answers the three questions pertaining to situational favorableness, using the Fiedler contingency theory model (Exhibit 5-3). The user starts with question 1 and follows the decision tree to Good or Poor depending on the relations. The user then answers question 2 and follows the decision tree to Repetitive or Nonrepetitive. When answering question 3, the user ends up in one of eight possible situations. If the LPC leadership style matches, the user does nothing, since they may be successful in that situation.

Changing the Situation

However, if the leadership style does not match the situation, the leader may be ineffective. One option is to change to a job that matches the leadership style. Fiedler recommends (and trains people to) change the situation, rather than their leadership styles. Here are a few general examples of how to change the situation variables to make a more favorable match for the leader's style.

- The leader generally would not want to change the *relationship* from good to poor, but rather the task structure or position power. If relations are poor, the leader can work to improve them by showing interest in followers, listening to them, and spending more time getting to know them personally.

Applying the Concept 1

Contingency Leadership Theory

Using Exhibit 5-3, determine the situation number with its corresponding appropriate leadership style. Select two answers, writing the appropriate letters in the blanks before each item.

a. 1   b. 2   c. 3   d. 4   e. 5   f. 6   g. 7   h. 8
A. task-oriented   B. relationship-oriented

___ ___ 1. Saul, the manager, oversees the assembly of mass-produced containers. He has the power to reward and punish. Saul is viewed as a hard-nosed manager.

___ ___ 2. Karen, the manager, is from the corporate planning staff. She helps the other departments plan. Karen is viewed as being a dreamer; she doesn't understand the various departments. Employees tend to be rude in their dealings with Karen.

___ ___ 3. Juan, the manager, oversees the processing of canceled checks for the bank. He is well liked by the employees. Juan's manager enjoys hiring and evaluating his employees' performance.

___ ___ 4. Sonia, the principal of a school, assigns teachers to classes and has various other duties. She hires and decides on tenure appointments. The school atmosphere is tense.

___ ___ 5. Louis, the chairperson of the committee, is highly regarded by its volunteer members from a variety of departments. The committee members are charged with recommending ways to increase organizational performance.

- The *task* can be more or less structured by stating more or less specific standards and procedures for completing the task, and giving or not giving clear deadlines.
- A leader with strong *position power* does not have to use it; downplay it. Leaders with weak power can try to get more power from their manager and play up the power by being more autocratic.

---

2. Which Contingency Leadership Situation Was Carly Fiorina in and What Leadership Style Was Appropriate?

Being autocratic, Carly Fiorina had fairly *poor* relations with followers at HP. The task of the top level managers is *unstructured* or *nonrepetitive,* and Fiorina's position power as CEO was *strong.* This is situation 7, in which the appropriate leadership style is *relationship.* If Fiorina's LPC style were *task,* which we believe it is, based on her leadership behavior, Fiedler would say that she needs to change the situation to be task. However, if her LPC style is *relationship,* Fiedler would suggest that she do nothing; it is the right style. Maybe part of the reason Fiorina was asked to step down as CEO is because she was using the wrong leadership style for the situation.

OPENING CASE APPLICATION

Research

Despite its groundbreaking start to contingency theory, Fiedler's work was criticized in the 1970s for conceptual reasons, and because of inconsistent empirical finding and inability to account for substantial variance in group performance.[22] Fiedler disagreed with some of the criticism and published rejoinders to both studies.[23] Over the past 20 years, numerous studies have tested the model. Two meta-analyses concluded that the research tends to support the model, although not for every situation and not as strongly for field studies as for laboratory studies.[24] Thus, the debate continues over the validity of the model.

One criticism is of Fiedler's view that the leader should not change his or her style, rather the situation should be changed. The other situational writers in this chapter suggest changing leadership styles, not the situation. Fiedler has helped contribute to the other contingency theories. Based on the contingency leadership model, Fiedler teamed up with J. E. Garcia to develop cognitive resources theory (CRT).[25]

CRT is a person-by-situation interaction theory in which the person variables are leader intelligence and experience, and the situational variable is stress, experienced by leaders and followers. CRT has important implications for leader selection and for situational management. Fiedler recommends a two-step process for effective utilization of leaders: (1) recruiting and selecting individuals with required intellectual abilities, experience, and job-relevant knowledge, and (2) enabling leaders to work under conditions that allow them to make effective use of the cognitive resources for which they were hired.[26] Fiedler has empirical support for his new CRT, but again, it is not without critics.[27]

WorkApplication1

Select a present or past manager. Which LPC leadership style is or was dominant for that manager? Using the Fiedler model (Exhibit 5-3), which situation number is the manager in? What is the appropriate leadership style for the manager in this situation? Does it match his or her style? How successful a leader is your manager? Do you think there is a relationship between the manager's leadership style and the situation?

If you are a manager, you may want to repeat this work application, using yourself as the manager.

_____

_____

_____

_____

Despite the critics, Fiedler's contingency leadership model and cognitive resources theory are considered the most validated of all leadership theories by some scholars.[28] However, if there were only one accepted valid motivation theory (Chapter 3) and only one leadership theory, this book would not be presenting several of them.

─────── Learning Outcome 4 ───────

State the leadership continuum model major styles and variables.

Leadership Continuum Theory and Model

Robert Tannenbaum and Warren Schmidt also developed a contingency theory in the 1950s.[29] They stated that leadership behavior is on a continuum from boss-centered to subordinate-centered leadership. Their model focuses on who makes the decisions. They noted that a leader's choice of a leadership pattern should be based on forces in the boss, forces in the subordinates, and forces in the situation. Look at Exhibit 5-4 to see how Tannenbaum and Schmidt's variables fit within the framework of contingency leadership variables.

Tannenbaum and Schmidt identify seven major styles the leader can choose from. Exhibit 5-5 is an adaptation of their model, which lists the seven styles.[30] *The **leadership continuum model** is used to determine which one of seven styles to select, based on the use of boss-centered versus subordinate-centered leadership, to meet the situation (boss, subordinates, situation/time) in order to maximize performance.*

Before selecting one of the seven leadership styles, the leader must consider the following three forces or variables:

- *Boss.* The leader's personality and behavioral preferred style—based on experience, expectation, values, background, knowledge, feeling of security, and confidence in the subordinates—is considered in selecting a leadership style. Based on personality and behavior, some leaders tend to be more autocratic and others more participative.
- *Subordinates.* The followers' preferred style for the leader is based on personality and behavior, as with the leader. Generally, the more willing and

---

Exhibit 5-4 *Leadership continuum model variables within the contingency leadership framework.*

FOLLOWERS	LEADER	SITUATION
Subordinates	Boss	Situation (time)
	LEADERSHIP STYLES Boss-centered to subordinate-centered leadership with seven leadership styles along the continuum in Exhibit 5-5	

Exhibit 5-5 *Tannenbaum and Schmidt's leadership continuum model.*

Autocratic Style

Participative Style

1.	2.	3.	4.	5.	6.	7.
Leader makes decision and announces it to followers individually or in a group without discussion (it could also be in writing).	Leader makes decision and sells it to followers through a presentation of why it's a good idea (it could also be in writing).	Leader presents ideas and invites follower questions.	Leader presents tentative decision subject to change.	Leader presents problem, gets suggested solutions, and makes the decision.	Leader defines limits and asks the followers to make a decision.	Leader permits followers to make ongoing decisions within defined limits.

Source: Adapted and reprinted by permission of *Harvard Business Review*. From "How to Choose a Leadership Pattern" by Robert Tannenbaum and Warren H. Schmidt, May–June 1973. Copyright © 1973 by the Harvard Business School Publishing Corporation, all rights reserved.

able the followers are to participate, the more freedom of participation should be used, and vice versa.

- *Situation (time).* The environmental considerations, such as the organization's size, structure, climate, goals, and technology, are considered in selecting a leadership style. Upper-level managers also influence leadership styles.[31] For example, if a middle manager uses an autocratic leadership style, the leader may tend to use it too.

The *time* available is another consideration. It takes more time to make participative decisions. Thus, when there is no time to include followers in decision making, the leader uses an autocratic leadership style.

In a 1986 follow-up by Tannenbaum and Schmidt to their original 1958 and 1973 articles, they recommended that (1) the leader become a group member when allowing the group to make decisions; (2) the leader clearly state the style (follower's authority) being used; (3) the leader not try to trick the followers into thinking they made a decision that was actually made by the leader; and (4) it's not the number of decisions the followers make, but their significance that counts.[32]

Note that Tannenbaum and Schmidt developed two major leadership styles, with seven continuum styles, which is a one-dimensional model. The leadership styles part of their model is similar to the University of Michigan Leadership Model, in that it is based on two major leadership styles: one focusing on boss-centered behavior (job-centered leadership) and the other focusing on subordinate-centered behavior (employee-centered).

Although the leadership continuum model was very popular, it did not undergo research testing like the contingency leadership model. One major

WorkApplication2

Using the leadership continuum model (Exhibit 5-5), identify your manager's most commonly used leadership style by number and description. Would you say this is the most appropriate leadership style based on the leader, the followers, and the situation? Explain.

_____

_____

_____

_____

Applying the Concept 2

Leadership Continuum

Using Exhibit 5-5, identify these five statements by their style. Write the appropriate letter in the blank before each item.

    a. 1   b. 2   c. 3   d. 4   e. 5   f. 6   g. 7

_____ 6. "Chuck, I selected you to be transferred to the new department, but you don't have to go if you don't want to."

_____ 7. "Sam, go clean off the tables right away."

_____ 8. "From now on, this is the way it will be done. Does anyone have any questions about the procedure?"

_____ 9. "These are the two weeks we can go on vacation. You select one."

_____ 10. "I'd like your ideas on how to stop the bottleneck on the production line. But I have the final say on the solution we implement."

criticism of this model is that the three factors to consider when selecting a leadership style are very subjective. In other words, determining which style to use, and when, is not clear in the model. The normative leadership model thus took over in popularity, most likely because it clearly identified which leadership style to use in a given, clearly defined situation.

You will determine your major leadership continuum style later, in Self-Assessment 4, which puts together three of the contingency leadership styles (continuum, path-goal, and normative).

OPENING CASE APPLICATION

3. Which Continuum Leadership Style Did Fiorina Tend to Use and What Style Is Mark Hurd Using at HP?

Carly Fiorina tended to like being in control, thus she used the more autocratic styles. For example, she was autocratic when she reorganized HP from 83 to 4 business units, and when she acquired Compaq Computer. Mark Hurd planned to use a more participative style as he views management as a team sport.

———————— Learning Outcome 5 ————————

Identify the path-goal leadership model styles and variables.

Path-Goal Leadership Theory and Model

The path-goal leadership theory was developed by Robert House, based on an early version of the theory by M. G. Evans, and published in 1971.[33] House formulated a more elaborate version of Evans's theory, one that included situational variables. House intended to reconcile prior conflicting findings concerning task- and relationship-oriented leader behavior. His theory specified a number of situational moderators of relationships between task- and person-oriented leadership and their effects.[34] House attempted to explain how the behavior of a leader influences the performance and satisfaction of the followers (subordinates). Look at Exhibit 5-6 to see how House's model fits into the framework of contingency leadership variables. Note that unlike the earlier contingency leadership models, House's model does not have a leader trait and behavior variable. The leader is supposed to use the appropriate leadership style (one of four), regardless of preferred traits and behavior.

The **path-goal leadership model** *is used to select the leadership style (directive, supportive, participative, or achievement-oriented) appropriate to the situation (subordinate and environment) to maximize both performance and job satisfaction.* Note that path-goal leadership theory is based on motivation theories of goal setting and expectancy theory.[35] The leader is responsible for increasing followers' motivation to attain personal and organizational goals. Motivation is increased by (1) clarifying the follower's path to the rewards that are available, or (2) increasing the rewards that the follower values and desires. *Path clarification* means that the leader works with followers to help them identify and learn the behaviors that will lead to successful task accomplishment and organizational rewards.

The path-goal model is used to determine employee objectives and to clarify how to achieve them using one of four leadership styles. It focuses on how leaders influence employees' perceptions of their goals and the paths they follow toward goal attainment. As shown in Exhibit 5-7 (an adaptation of the model), the situational factors are used to determine the leadership style that affects goal achievement through performance and satisfaction.

Exhibit 5-6 *Path-goal leadership model variables within the contingency leadership framework.*

FOLLOWERS	LEADER	SITUATION
Subordinates (authoritarianism, locus of control, ability)	None	Environment (task structure, formal authority, and work group)

LEADERSHIP STYLES
Directive
Supportive
Participative
Achievement-oriented

Exhibit 5-7 *House path-goal leadership model.*

Source: Adapted from R. J. House, "A Path-Goal Theory of Leader Effectiveness," *Administrative Science Quarterly* 16 (2), 1971: 321–329.

Situational Factors

Subordinate

Subordinate situational characteristics include:

1. *Authoritarianism* is the degree to which employees defer to others, and want to be told what to do and how to do the job.
2. *Locus of control* (Chapter 2) is the extent to which employees believe they control goal achievement (internal) or if goal achievement is controlled by others (external).
3. *Ability* is the extent of the employees' ability to perform tasks to achieve goals.

Environment

Environment situational factors include:

1. *Task structure* is the extent of repetitiveness of the job.
2. *Formal authority* is the extent of the leader's position power. Note that task structure and formal authority are essentially the same as Fiedler's.
3. *Work group* is the extent to which coworkers contribute to job satisfaction or the relationship between followers. Note that House identifies work group as a situational variable. However, under the contingency framework, it would be considered a follower variable.

Leadership Styles

Based on the situational factors in the path-goal model, the leader can select the most appropriate leadership style by using the following general guidelines for each style. The original model included only the directive (based on initiating structure, job-centered style) and supportive (based on consideration and employee style) leadership styles (from the Ohio State and University of Michigan behavioral leadership studies). The participative and achievement-oriented leadership styles were added in a 1974 publication by House and Mitchell.[36]

Directive

The leader provides high structure. Directive leadership is appropriate when the followers want authority leadership, have external locus of control, and the follower ability is low. Directive leadership is also appropriate when the environmental task is complex or ambiguous, formal authority is strong, and the work group provides job satisfaction.

Supportive

The leader provides high consideration. Supportive leadership is appropriate when the followers do not want autocratic leadership, have internal locus of control, and follower ability is high. Supportive leadership is also appropriate when the environmental tasks are simple, formal authority is weak, and the work group does not provide job satisfaction.

Participative

The leader includes employee input into decision making. Participative leadership is appropriate when followers want to be involved, have internal locus of control, and follower ability is high; when the environmental task is complex, authority is either strong or weak, and job satisfaction from coworkers is either high or low.

Achievement-Oriented

The leader sets difficult but achievable goals, expects followers to perform at their highest level, and rewards them for doing so. In essence, the leader provides both high directive (structure) and high supportive (consideration) behavior. Achievement-oriented leadership is appropriate when followers are open to autocratic leadership, have external locus of control, and follower ability is high; when the environmental task is simple, authority is strong, and job satisfaction from coworkers is either high or low.

Research

A meta-analysis based on 120 studies examined directive and supportive behavior and showed that support for path-goal theory was significantly greater than chance, but results were quite mixed. An extensive review of the research on moderator variables in leaders also had inconclusive findings.[37] Recent reviews of the history of path-goal theory have concluded that it has not been adequately tested, possibly because it is such a complex model. It continues to be tested; a recent study used a survey of 1,000 respondents from a governmental and public auditing sample.[38]

Although path-goal theory is more complex and specific than leadership continuum, it is also criticized by managers because it is difficult to know which style to use when. As you can see, there are many situations in which not

Applying the Concept 3

Path-Goal Leadership

Using Exhibit 5-7, and text descriptions, identify the appropriate leadership style for the five situations. Write the appropriate letter in the blank before each item.

a. directive   c. participative
b. supportive   d. achievement

_____ 11. The manager has a new, complex task for her department, and she is not sure how it should be done. Her employees are experienced and like to be involved in decision making.

_____ 12. The manager is putting together a new task force that will have an ambiguous task to complete. The members all know each other and get along well.

_____ 13. The manager has decided to delegate a new task to an employee who has been doing a good job. The employee, however, tends to be insecure and may feel threatened by taking on a new task, even though it is fairly easy and the manager is confident that the employee can do the job easily.

_____ 14. The department members just finished the production quarter and easily met the quota. The manager has strong position power and has decided to increase the quota to make the job more challenging.

_____ 15. The manager has an employee who has been coming in late for work, with no apparent good reason. The manager has decided to take some corrective action to get the employee to come in on time.

all six situational factors are exactly as presented in the guidelines for when to use the style. Judgment calls are required to select the appropriate style as necessary.

Despite its limitations, the path-goal model has already made an important contribution to the study of leadership by providing a conceptual framework to guide researchers in identifying potentially relevant situational variables. It also provides a useful way for leaders to think about motivating followers.

Charismatic Leadership and Value-Based Leadership Theory

Path-goal leadership theory led to the development of the theory of charismatic leadership in 1976. You will learn about charismatic leadership in Chapter 9. Path-goal theory was considerably broadened in scope, and in 1996 House referred to it as value-based leadership theory.[39] Because value-based leadership theory is new and relatively untested, we do not present it here. However, see note 39 for House's further-developed theory.

You will determine your path-goal leadership style in Self-Assessment 4, which puts together the contingency leadership styles.

WorkApplication3

Identify your manager's most commonly used path-goal leadership style. Would you say this is the most appropriate leadership style based on the situational factors? Explain.

_____

_____

_____

_____

_____

4. Which Path-Goal Leadership Style Did Carly Fiorina Tend to Use and What Style Is Mark Hurd Using at HP?

At HP, Carly Fiorina tended to use the directive style, as she liked to be in control. She may have been over-directing her top-level managers. In some situations, over-controlling bosses can be inefficient.[40] The new HP CEO Mark Hurd planned to use the participative style.

Learning Outcome 6

State the normative leadership model styles and the number of variables.

Normative Leadership Theory and Models

An important leadership question today is, "When should the manager take charge and when should the manager let the group make the decision?" In 1973, Victor Vroom and Philip Yetton published a decision-making model to answer this question while improving decision-making effectiveness. Vroom and Arthur Jago refined the model and expanded it to four models in 1988.[41] The four models are based on two factors: individual or group decisions and time-driven or development-driven decisions.

In 2000, Victor Vroom published a revised version entitled "Leadership and the Decision-Making Process." The current model is based on the research of Vroom and colleagues at Yale University on leadership and decision-making processes, with more than 100,000 managers making decisions.[42] We present the latest version with a focus on time and development-driven decisions.

The **normative leadership model** *has a time-driven and development-driven decision tree that enables the user to select one of five leadership styles (decide, consult individually, consult group, facilitate, and delegate) appropriate for the situation (seven questions/variables) to maximize decisions.* See Exhibit 5-8 to see how the normative leadership models fit into the contingency leadership framework variables. It is called a *normative model* because it provides a sequential set of questions that are rules (norms) to follow to determine the best leadership style for the given situation.

To use the normative model, you must have a specific decision to make, have the authority to make the decision, and have specific potential followers to participate in the decision.

Leadership Participation Styles

Vroom identified five leadership styles based on the level of participation in the decision by the followers. Vroom adapted them from Tannenbaum and

Exhibit 5-8 *Normative leadership model variables within the contingency leadership framework.*

FOLLOWERS	LEADER	SITUATION
Development-Driven Decision Model	3. Leader expertise	*Time-Driven Decision Model*
2. Importance of commitment	LEADERSHIP STYLES	1. Decision significance
4. Likelihood of commitment	Decide	
5. Group support for objectives	Consult individually	
6. Group expertise	Consult group	
7. Team competence	Facilitate	
	Delegate	

Schmidt's leadership continuum model (Exhibit 5-5), ranging from autocratic to participative styles; Vroom's five leadership styles follow.

Decide

The leader makes the decision alone and announces it, or sells it, to the followers. The leader may get information from others outside the group and within the group without specifying the problem.

Consult Individually

The leader tells followers individually about the problem, gets information and suggestions, and then makes the decision.

Consult Group

The leader holds a group meeting and tells followers the problem, gets information and suggestions, and then makes the decision.

Facilitate

The leader holds a group meeting and acts as a facilitator to define the problem and the limits within which a decision must be made. The leader seeks participation and concurrence on the decision without pushing his or her ideas.

Delegate

The leader lets the group diagnose the problem and make the decision within stated limits. The role of the leader is to answer questions and provide encouragement and resources.

Model Questions to Determine the Appropriate Leadership Style

To determine which of the five leadership styles is the most appropriate for a given situation, answer a series of diagnostic questions based on seven variables. The seven variables presented in Exhibit 5-8 are repeated in

Exhibit 5-9 *Normative leadership time-driven model.*

Instructions: The model is a decision tree that works like a funnel. Define the problem statement, then answer the questions from left to right as high (H) or low (L), skipping questions when not appropriate to the situation and avoiding crossing any horizontal lines. The last column you come to contains the appropriate leadership participation decision-making style for the situation.

Problem Statement	1. Decide Significance?	2. Importance of Commitment?	3. Leader Expertise?	4. Likelihood of Commitment?	5. Group Supports?	6. Group Expertise?	7. Team Competence?	Leadership Style
	H	H	H	H	−	−	−	Decide
	H	H	H	L	H	H	H	Delegate
	H	H	H	L	H	H	L	Consult (Group)
	H	H	H	L	H	L	−	Consult (Group)
	H	H	H	L	L	−	−	Consult (Group)
	H	H	L	H	H	H	H	Facilitate
	H	H	L	H	H	H	L	Consult (Individually)
	H	H	L	H	H	L	−	Consult (Individually)
	H	H	L	H	L	−	−	Consult (Individually)
	H	H	L	L	H	H	H	Facilitate
	H	H	L	L	H	H	L	Consult (Group)
	H	H	L	L	H	L	−	Consult (Group)
	H	H	L	L	L	−	−	Consult (Group)
	H	L	H	−	−	−	−	Decide
	H	L	L	−	H	H	H	Facilitate
	H	L	L	−	H	H	L	Consult (Individually)
	H	L	L	−	H	L	−	Consult (Individually)
	H	L	L	−	L	−	−	Consult (Individually)
	L	H	−	H	−	−	−	Decide
	L	H	−	L	−	−	H	Delegate
	L	H	−	L	−	−	L	Facilitate
	L	L	−	−	−	−	−	Decide

Source: Adapted from *Organizational Dynamics* 28, Victor H. Vroom, "Leadership and the Decision-Making Process," p. 87, Copyright © 2000 with the permission from Elsevier.

Exhibits 5-9 and 5-10. We now explain how to answer the questions, based on the variables, when using the two models.

1. *Decision Significance.* How important is the decision to the success of the project or organization? Is the decision of high importance (H) or low (L) importance to the success? When making highly important decisions, leaders need to be involved.

Exhibit 5-10 *Normative leadership development-driven model.*

Instructions: The model is a decision tree that works like a funnel. Define the problem statement, then answer the questions from left to right as high (H) or low (L), skipping questions when not appropriate to the situation and avoiding crossing any horizontal lines. The last column you come to contains the appropriate leadership participation decision-making style for the situation.

Problem Statement	1. Decide Significance?	2. Importance of Commitment?	3. Leader Expertise?	4. Likelihood of Commitment?	5. Group Supports?	6. Group Expertise?	7. Team Competence?	Leadership Style
	H	H	—	H	H	H	H	Delegate
							L	Facilitate
						L	—	Consult (Group)
					L	—	—	Consult (Group)
				L	H	H	H	Delegate
							L	Facilitate
						L	—	Facilitate
					L	—	—	Consult (Group)
		L	—	—	H	H	H	Delegate
							L	Facilitate
						L	—	Consult (Group)
					L	—	—	Consult (Group)
	L	H	—	H	—	—	—	Decide
				L	—	—	—	Delegate
		L	—	—	—	—	—	Decide

Source: Adapted from *Organizational Dynamics* 28, Victor H. Vroom, "Leadership and the Decision-Making Process," p. 88, Copyright © 2000 with the permission from Elsevier.

2. *Importance of Commitment.* How important is follower commitment to implement the decision? If acceptance of the decision is critical to effective implementation, importance is high (H). If commitment is not important, it's low (L). When making highly important commitment decisions that followers may not like and may not implement, followers generally need to be involved in making the decision.

3. *Leader Expertise.* How much knowledge and expertise does the leader have with this specific decision? Is expertise high (H) or low (L)? The more expertise the leader has, the less need there is for follower participation.

4. *Likelihood of Commitment.* If the leader were to make the decision alone, is the certainty that the followers would be committed to the decision high (H) or low (L)? When making decisions that followers will like and want to implement, there is less need to involve them in the decision.

5. *Group Support for Objectives.* Do followers have high (H) or low (L) support for the team or organizational goals to be attained in solving the problem? Higher levels of participation are acceptable with high levels of support.

6. *Group Expertise.* How much knowledge and expertise do the individual followers have with this specific decision? Is expertise high (H) or low (L)? The more expertise the followers have, the greater the individual or group participation can be.

7. *Team Competence.* Is the ability of the individuals to work together as a team to solve the problem high (H) or low (L)? With high team competence, more participation can be used.

Not all seven variables/questions are relevant to all decisions. All seven or as few as two questions are needed to select the most appropriate leadership style in a given situation. Tying questions 1, 3, and 6 together, when making important decisions it is critical to include the leader and/or followers with the expertise to solve the problem. Then, the issue of commitment (questions 2 and 4) becomes relevant. Tying questions 5, 6, and 7 together in decision making, the leader should not delegate decisions to groups with low support for objectives, low group expertise, and low team competence. The great thing about the models is that they tie the relevant variables together as you answer the questions to determine the most appropriate leadership style for the given situation.

Selecting the Time-Driven or Development-Driven Model for the Situation

The first step is actually to select one of the two models, based on whether the situation is driven by the importance of time or development of followers. The characteristics of the decision are focus, value, and orientation.

The Time-Driven Model

See Exhibit 5-9. Its three characteristics are:

- *Focus.* The model is concerned with making effective decisions with minimum cost. Time is costly, as it takes longer for groups to make decisions than the leader alone.
- *Value.* Value is placed on time, and no value is placed on follower development.
- *Orientation.* The model has a short-term horizon.

The Development-Driven Model

See Exhibit 5-10. Its three characteristics are:

- *Focus.* The model is concerned with making effective decisions with maximum development of followers. Follower development is worth the cost.
- *Value.* Value is placed on follower development, and no value is placed on time.
- *Orientation.* The model has a long-term horizon, as development takes time.

Computerized Normative Model

Vroom has developed a computerized CD-ROM model that is more complex and more precise, yet easier to use. It combines the time-driven and development-driven models into one model, includes 11 variables/questions (rather than seven), and has five variable measures (rather than H or L). It guides the user through the process of analyzing the situation with definitions, examples, and other forms of help as they progress through the use of the model. The computerized model is beyond the scope of this course, but you will learn how to use the time-driven and development-driven models below and in Skill-Development Exercise 2.

Determining the Appropriate Leadership Style

To determine the appropriate style for a specific situation, use the best model (time-driven or development-driven) for the situation and answer the questions, some of which may be skipped based on the model used and prior questions. The questions are sequential and are presented in a decision-tree format similar to the Fiedler model, in which you end up with the appropriate style to use. Using both models for the same situations, for some decisions the appropriate style will be the same, and it will be different for others.

Research

Numerous studies have tested the normative leadership model.[43] In general, the results found in the empirical research have supported the model. Vroom and Jago conducted research concluding that managers using the style recommended in the model have a 62 percent probability of a successful decision, while not using the recommended style allows only a 37 percent probability of a successful decision.[44] However, the model is not without its critics.[45]

In summary of prior research based on six separate studies conducted in three different countries—contrary to Fiedler—managers do change their style to meet the situation. Managers using the decision style recommended by the normative model were almost twice as likely to be successful as were managers using decisions not recommended by the model. Higher-level managers use more participation in decision making. Women managers tend to use more participation than men. Almost all managers view themselves as using a higher level of participation than do their followers. Over the 25 years of research, there has been a move toward higher levels of participation, greater empowerment, and use of teams.[46]

The Vroom and Vroom Yetton/Jago model tends to be popular in the academic community because it is based on research. However, it is not as popular with managers because they find it cumbersome to select models and to pull out the model and follow a seven-question decision tree every time they have to make a decision. In his defense, Vroom states that his models are not tools to be slavishly embraced and used in all decisions.[47] Besides, once you learn how to use the model, you can better mentally judge the most appropriate style for the situation without the model. Thus, Vroom agrees with other researchers who state that leadership styles evolve,[48] and that leaders can develop their leadership skill[49] by using his normative leadership models.

You will determine your major normative leadership style in Self-Assessment 3.

WorkApplication4

Recall a specific decision you or your boss has or had to make. Is or was the decision time-driven or development-driven? Using Exhibit 5-9 or 5-10, select the appropriate participation style for the situation. Be sure to state the questions you answered and how (H or L) you answered each.

OPENING CASE APPLICATION

5. Which Normative Leadership Style Did Carly Fiorina Tend to Use at HP?

At HP, Carly Fiorina tended to use the decide and consult styles, as she liked to be in control. The decide and consult styles were used to acquire Compaq and reorganize HP. However, part of the reason why she reorganized from 83 business units down to only 4 was to get the business units to use more teamwork, through participating in more integrated products and services.

Learning Outcomes 7 and 8

Discuss the major similarities and differences between the behavioral and contingency leadership theories.

Compare and contrast four major differences among the four contingency leadership models.

Putting the Behavioral and Contingency Leadership Theories Together

Exhibit 5-11 is a review of different words that are used to describe the same two leadership behavior concepts. It includes the number of leadership styles based on the two behavior concepts and the different names given to the leadership styles. You should realize that all the leadership styles are based on the same two behavior concepts. We developed Exhibits 5-11 and 5-12 to put all

WorkApplication5

1. Identify the one contingency leadership model you prefer to use on the job, and state why.
2. Describe the type of leader that you want to be on the job. Identify specific behavior you plan to use as a leader. You may also want to identify behavior you will not use.

_____

_____

_____

_____

_____

Exhibit 5-11 *Names given to the same two leadership behavior concepts.*

	LEADERSHIP & BEHAVIOR/STYLE		NUMBER OF LEADERSHIP STYLES BASED ON BEHAVIOR CONCEPTS
Behavioral Theories			
University of Iowa	Autocratic	Democratic	2
University of Michigan	Job-centered	Employee-centered	2
Ohio State University	Structure	Consideration	4
Leadership Grid®	Concern for production	Concern for people	5
Contingency Theories			
Contingency model	Task	Relationship	2
Leadership continuum	Boss-centered	Subordinate-centered	7
Path-goal model	Directive	Supportive	4
Normative model	Autocratic	Group	5

Exhibit 5-12 *Putting the behavioral and contingency leadership theories together.*

BEHAVIORAL THEORIES / CONTINGENCY THEORIES	LEADERSHIP STYLES				CONTINGENCY VARIABLES	CONTINGENCY CHANGE	DESIRED OUTCOME
	Job-Centered		Employee-Centered				
	High Structure/ Low Consideration	High Structure/ High Consideration	Low Structure/ High Consideration	Low Structure/ Low Consideration			
U of Michigan	Job-Centered		Employee-Centered				
Ohio State U	High Structure/ Low Consideration	High Structure/ High Consideration	Low Structure/ High Consideration	Low Structure/ Low Consideration			
CONTINGENCY THEORIES							
Contingency Leadership Model	Task		Relationship		Leader/Follower Relations, Task Structure, Position Power	Situation	Performance
Leadership Continuum Model	1	2 & 3	4 & 5	6 & 7	Manager, Subordinates, Situation/time	Leadership Style	Performance
Path-Goal Model	Directive	Achievement	Supportive	Participative	Subordinate (authoritarianism, locus of control, ability), Enviroment (task structure, formal authority, work group)	Leadership Style	Performance, Job Satisfaction
Normative Leadership Model	Decide	Consult Individual or Group	Facilitate	Delegate	Development-Driven or Time-Driven Models: (1) Decision significance (2) Importance of commitment (3) Leader expertise (4) Likelihood of commitment (5) Group support for objectives (6) Group expertise (7) Team competence	Leadership Style	Decisions

these contingency leadership theories together with behavioral leadership styles. These exhibits should help you to better understand the similarities and differences between these theories.

As we put the leadership theories together, we acknowledge the brilliant synthesizer Russell Ackoff, founder of systems theory, and present his advice on leadership. Ackoff warns against the continued reliance by management on fads, and he advocates systems leadership. Systems leadership requires an ability to bring the will of followers into agreement with that of the leader so they follow him or her voluntarily, with enthusiasm and dedication.[50]

Learning Outcome 9

List which leadership models are prescriptive and descriptive, and explain why they are classified as such.

Prescriptive and Descriptive Models

One last difference between models, not shown in any figures, is the difference between prescriptive and descriptive models. The contingency leadership model and the normative leadership model are prescriptive models. **Prescriptive leadership models** *tell the user exactly which style to use in a given situation*. However, the continuum and path-goal leadership models are descriptive models. **Descriptive leadership models** *identify contingency variables and leadership styles without specifying which style to use in a given situation*. In other words, users of the descriptive model select the appropriate style based more on their own judgment. Look at all the leadership models and you will see what we mean.

Many managers prefer prescriptive models; this is a reason why the normative leadership model is more commonly used in organizational leadership training programs than the descriptive leadership models. On the other hand, many academic researchers scoff at prescriptive models, especially simple ones, and prefer the more complex descriptive models based on solid theoretical foundations.[51]

Learning Outcome 10

Explain substitutes and neutralizers of leadership.

Leadership Substitutes Theory

The four leadership theories presented assume that some leadership style will be effective in each situation. However, in keeping with contingency theory, there are factors outside the leader's control that have a larger impact on outcomes than do leadership actions.[52] Contingency factors provide guidance and incentives to perform, making the leader's role unnecessary in some situations.[53] Steven Kerr and John Jermier argued that certain situational variables prevent leaders from affecting subordinates' (followers') attitudes and behaviors.[54] **Substitutes for leadership** *include characteristics of the subordinate, task, and organization that replace the need for a leader or neutralize the leader's behavior*.

Exhibit 5-13 *Substitutes for leadership variables within the contingency leadership framework.*

FOLLOWERS	LEADER	SITUATION
Subordinates	None	Task
		Organization

Substitutes and Neutralizers

Thus, *substitutes* for leadership make a leadership style unnecessary or redundant. For example, highly skilled workers do not need a leader's task behavior to tell them how to do their job. *Neutralizers* reduce or limit the effectiveness of a leader's behavior. For example, managers who are not near an employee cannot readily give task-directive behavior. See Exhibit 5-13 to see how the substitutes for leadership fit into the framework of contingency leadership variables. Then, read a description of each substitute.

The following variables may substitute or neutralize leadership by providing task-oriented direction and/or people-oriented support rather than a leader:

1. *Characteristics of followers.* Ability, knowledge, experience, training. Need for independence. Professional orientation. Indifference toward organizational rewards.

2. *Characteristics of the task.* Clarity and routine. Invariant methodology. Provision of own feedback concerning accomplishment. Intrinsic satisfaction. This characteristic is similar to Fiedler's and others' task behavior.

3. *Characteristics of the organization.* Formalization (explicit plans, goals, and areas of responsibility). Inflexibility (rigid, unbending rules and procedures). Highly specified and active advisory and staff functions. Closely knit, cohesive work groups. Organizational rewards not within the leader's control. Spatial distance between leader and followers.

Leadership Style

Leaders can analyze their situation and better understand how these three characteristics substitute or neutralize their leadership style and thus can provide the leadership and followership most appropriate for the situation. The leader role is to provide the direction and support not already being provided by the task, group, or organization. The leader fills the gaps in leadership.

Changing the Situation

Like Fiedler suggested, leaders can change the situation rather than their leadership style. Thus, substitutes for leadership can be designed in organizations in ways to complement existing leadership, to act in leadership absence, and to otherwise provide more comprehensive leadership alternatives. After all, organizations have cut middle-management numbers, and something has to provide the leadership in their absence. One approach is to make the situation more favorable for the leader by removing neutralizers. Another way is to make leadership less important by increasing substitutes such as job enrichment, self-managing teams, and automation.[55]

Research

A study of nursing work indicated that the staff nurses' education, the cohesion of the nurses, and work technology substituted for the head nurse's leadership behavior in determining the staff nurses' performance. Another study found that situational variables directly affect subordinate satisfaction or motivation; however, it also found little support for moderating effects of situational variables on the relationship between leader behavior and subordinate motivation. Another study found that need for supervision moderates the relationship between task-oriented leadership and work stress, but not between task-oriented leadership and job satisfaction; however, a robust relationship between human-oriented leadership and job satisfaction was found.[56]

A meta-analysis was conducted to estimate more accurately the bivariate relationships among leadership behaviors, substitutes for leadership, followers' attitudes, and role perceptions and performance; and to examine the relative strengths of the relationships among these variables. It was based on 435 relationships obtained from 22 studies containing 36 independent samples. Overall, the theory was supported. In summary, as with the other theories, results are mixed. Research has found support for some aspects of the theory, but other aspects have not been tested or supported. Therefore, it is premature to assess the validity and utility of leadership substitutes theory.[57] To close this chapter, complete Self-Assessment 2 to determine how your personality influences your use of contingency leadership theory.

WorkApplication6

Identify your present or past manager. Can the characteristics of followers, task, and/or the organization substitute for this leader? In other words, is his or her leadership necessary? Explain.

_____

_____

_____

_____

_____

Self-Assessment 2

Your Personality and Contingency Leadership Theories

In Self-Assessment 1, were you more task or relationship oriented? Your being more task or relationship oriented is based very much on your personality. Based on surgency, if you have a high need for power, you may tend to be more task oriented. Based on agreeableness, if you are a real people person with a high need for affiliation, you may tend to be more relationship oriented. Based on conscientiousness, if you have a high need for achievement, you may tend to be more task oriented to make sure the job gets done, and done your way.

Based on your personality profile, does it match Fiedler's contingency leadership theory, as presented in Self-Assessment 1? If you have a higher need for power, do you tend to use the autocratic (1–3) leadership continuum styles, the directive and achievement path-goal leadership styles, and the decide and consult normative leadership styles?

If you have a higher need for affiliation, do you tend to use more participative leadership continuum styles, the supportive and participative path-goal styles, and the facilitate and delegate normative leadership styles?

You will better be able to understand which leadership style you do tend to use when you complete Self-Assessment 3, "Determining Your Preferred Normative Leadership Style." The leadership continuum and path-goal styles are explored in Self-Assessment 4. It is important to realize that your personality does affect your leadership style. However, you can use the leadership style that is most appropriate for the situation. You will learn how in Skill Development Exercises 1 and 2.

Go to the Internet (academic.cengage.com/management/lussier) where you will find a broad array of resources to help maximize your learning.

- Review the vocabulary
- Try a quiz
- View chapter videos

Chapter Summary

The chapter summary is organized to answer the 11 learning outcomes for Chapter 5.

1. State the major difference between behavioral and contingency leadership theories, and explain the behavioral contribution to contingency theories.

Behavioral theories attempt to determine the one best leadership style for all situations. Contingency leadership theories contend that there is no one best leadership style for all situations. Behavioral theories contributed to contingency theories because their basic leadership styles are used in contingency leadership models.

2. Describe the contingency leadership theory variables.

The contingency leadership variables used to explain the appropriate leadership style are the leader, followers, and situation. The leader factor is based on personality traits, behavior, and experience. The followers factor is based on capability and motivation. The situational factor is based on task, structure, and environment.

3. Identify the contingency leadership model styles and variables.

The contingency leadership model styles are task and relationship. The variables include (1) the leader-follower relationship, (2) the leadership styles—task or relationship, and (3) the situation—task structure and position power.

4. State the leadership continuum model major styles and variables.

The two major continuum leadership model styles are boss-centered and subordinate-centered. The variables include (1) the boss, (2) the subordinates, and (3) the situation (time).

5. Identify the path-goal leadership model styles and variables.

The path-goal leadership model styles include directive, supportive, participative, and achievement-oriented. Variables used to determine the leadership style are the subordinate and the environment.

6. State the normative leadership model styles and the number of variables.

The five normative leadership model styles are decide, consult individually, consult group, facilitate, and delegate. The model has seven variables.

7. Discuss the major similarities and differences between the behavioral and contingency leadership theories.

The primary similarity between these theories is that their leadership styles are all based on the same two leadership concepts, although they have different names. The major difference is that the contingency leadership models identify contingency variables on which to select the most appropriate behavioral leadership style for a given situation.

8. Compare and contrast four major differences among the four contingency leadership models.

Using Exhibit 5-12, the first difference is in the number of leadership styles used in the four models, which ranges from 2 (contingency) to 7 (continuum). The second difference is in the number of contingency variables used to select the appropriate leadership style, which ranges from 2 (path-goal) to 7 (normative). The third difference is what is changed when using the model. When using the contingency model, the leader changes the situation; with the other three models, the leader changes behavior (leadership style). The last difference is the desired outcome. Contingency and continuum leadership models focus on performance, and the path-goal model adds job satisfaction. The normative model focuses on decisions.

9. List which leadership models are prescriptive and descriptive, and explain why they are classified as such.

The contingency and normative leadership models are prescriptive models, because they specify exactly which leadership style to use in a given situation. The continuum and path-goal leadership models are descriptive models, because users select the appropriate leadership style for a given situation based on their own judgment.

10. Explain substitutes and neutralizers of leadership.

Substitutes for leadership include characteristics of the subordinate, task, and organization that make leadership behavior unnecessary or redundant; neutralizers reduce or limit the effectiveness of a leader's behavior.

11. Define the following key terms (in order of appearance in the chapter).

Select one or more methods: (1) fill in the missing key terms from memory, (2) match the key terms from the following list with their definitions below, (3) copy the key terms in order from the list at the beginning of the chapter.

_____ is an example for emulation or use in a given situation.

_____ determines if a person's leadership style is task- or relationship-oriented, and if the situation (leader-member relationship, task structure, and position power) matches the leader's style to maximize performance.

_____ determines which of seven styles to select, based on the use of boss-centered versus subordinate-centered leadership, to meet the situation (boss, subordinates, situation/time) in order to maximize performance.

_____ determines the leadership style (directive, supportive, participative, or achievement-oriented) appropriate to the situation (subordinate and environment) to maximize both performance and job satisfaction.

_____ has a time-driven and development-driven decision tree that enables the user to select one of five leadership styles (decide, consult individually, consult group, facilitate, and delegate) appropriate for the situation.

_____ tell the user exactly which style to use in a given situation.

_____ identify contingency variables and leadership styles without specifying which style to use in a given situation.

_____ include characteristics of the subordinate, task, and organization that replace the need for a leader or neutralize the leader's behavior.

Key Terms

contingency leadership model, 162

descriptive leadership models, 183

leadership continuum model, 168

leadership model, 160

normative leadership model, 175

path-goal leadership model, 171

prescriptive leadership models, 183

substitutes for leadership, 183

Review and Discussion Questions

1. What contingency leadership variables are common to all of the theories?
2. Do the three situational favorableness factors of the contingency leadership model (Exhibit 5-3) fit in only one of the three variables (follower, leader, situation) of all contingency leadership variables (Exhibit 5-1)? Explain.
3. Do you agree with Fiedler's belief that people have one dominant leadership style and cannot change styles? Explain.
4. Do you believe that managers today are using more boss- or subordinate-centered leadership styles?
5. Do you agree that time is an important situational factor to consider in selecting a leadership style for the situation? Explain.
6. What is the difference in the outcomes of the contingency leadership and the continuum leadership models and that of the path-goal model?
7. What are the three subordinate and environment situational factors of the path-goal model?
8. The normative leadership model is the most complex. Do more variables improve the model?
9. One group of authors believes that Fiedler's contingency leadership model is the model best supported by research. However, a different author believes that it is the normative leadership model. Which model do you believe is best supported by research? Why?
10. What is the primary difference between the contingency leadership model and the other leadership models (leadership, continuum, path-goal, and normative leadership)?
11. What are the three substitutes for leadership?

Case

HANK THOMSON—MOCON

Modern Controls (MoCon) started in 1996. In 1999, it changed its name to MOCON, Inc. Today it is a public corporation headquartered in Minneapolis, MN. In short, MOCON is an analytical instrument specialist manufacturer with a focus on providing products and services that help other manufacturers assess materials and processes, to help *their* customers make and test their products, and it also provides products to service firms as well. MOCON is a leading global provider of technical systems and services in permeation, leak detection, headspace analysis, shelf life determination, heat sealers, and other areas.

MOCON globally markets products and services used in research laboratories, production environments, and quality control applications in a variety of industries. MOCON has customers in the life sciences, pharmaceutical, food, beverage, plastics, packaging, medical device, electronics, oil and gas, paints, and coatings industries. Its analytical instrument products help these companies determine shelf life and permeation of oxygen and other molecules. Its heat sealers are setting new packaging standards all over the world. MOCON also provides testing, consulting and development services for companies who develop and manufacture a variety of products. You may not realize it, but you have bought products that are tested and packaged with MOCON technology and products.[58]

Hank Thomson worked his way up to become the manager in a department making small parts.[59] Thomson's job was to supervise the production of one part that is used as a component in other products. Running the machines to make the standard parts is not complicated and his employees generally find the job to be boring with low pay. Thomson closely supervised the employees to make sure they kept production on schedule. Thomson believed that if he did not watch the employees closely and keep them informed of their output, they would slack off and miss production goals. Thomson's employees viewed him as an okay boss to work for, as he did take a personal interest in them, and employees were productive. Thomson did discipline employees who did not meet standard productivity, and he ended up firing some workers.

Carl, the manager of a larger department that designs instruments to customer specifications, retired and Thomson was given a promotion to manage this department because he did a good job running his old department. Thomson never did any design work himself nor supervised it. The designers are all engineers that are paid well, who were doing a good job according to their prior supervisor Carl. As Thomson observed workers in his usual manner, he realized that all of the designers did their work differently. So he closely observed their work and looked for good ideas that all his employees could follow. It wasn't long before Thomson was telling employees how to do a better job of designing the custom specifications. Things were not going too well, however, as employees told Thomson that he did not know what he was talking about. Thomson tried to rely on his authority, which worked while he was watching employees. However, once Thomson left one employee to observe another, the workers went back to doing things their own way. Thomson's employees were complaining about his being a poor manager behind his back.

The complaints about Thomson being a poor manager got to his boss, Jose Goizueta. Goizueta also realizes that performance in the design department has gone down since Thomson took over as manager. Goizueta decided to call Thomson into his office to discuss how things are going.

GO TO THE INTERNET: To learn more about MOCON log on to InfoTrac® College Edition at **academic.cengage. com/infotrac** and use the advanced search function.

Support your answer to the following questions with specific information from the case and text, or other information you get from the Web or other sources.

1. Which leadership style would Fiedler say Hank Thomson uses?
2. Using Exhibit 5-3, Fiedler's contingency leadership model, what situation and leadership style are appropriate for the production department and for the custom design department?
3. Why isn't Thomson doing an effective job in the design department?
4. What would Fiedler and Kerr and Jermier recommend that Thomson do to improve performance?
5. Which of the two basic continuum leadership styles would Tannenbaum and Schmidt recommend for the manager of the design department?
6. Which path-goal leadership style would House recommend for the manager of the design department?

Cumulative Case Questions

7. Describe Thomson's personality based on the Big Five model of personality (Chapter 2). How does Thomson's personality influence his leadership style?
8. How is Thomson's leadership style and behavior affecting employee needs and motivation (Chapter 3)?
9. Which source and type of power does Thomson use? Is Thomson using the appropriate power? If not, which power should Thomson use (Chapter 4)?

Case Exercise and Role-Play

Preparation: Put yourself in the role of Jose. Which normative leadership style would you use with Thomson during the meeting? How would you handle the meeting with Thomson? What will you say to him?

In-Class Groups: Break into groups of four to six members, and discuss the two preparation questions.

Role-Play: One person (representing themselves or a group) meets with Thomson to role-play the meeting for the class to observe. The person does not identify which normative leadership style they are using. You can discuss the role-play, as discussed next. More than one role-play may also take place.

Observer Role: As the rest of the class members watch the role-play, they should: (1) Identify the leadership style used by the person playing the role of Goizueta. (2) State if it is the appropriate leadership style for this situation. (3) Look for things that Goizueta does well, and not so well. For your suggested improvements, be sure to have alternative behaviors that are coaching.

Discussion: After the first role-play, the class (1) votes for the leadership style used by the person role-playing Goizueta, (2) determines the appropriate leadership style, and (3) discusses good behavior and better behavior that could be used. If additional role-plays are used, skip step 2.

Video Case

The Vermont Teddy Bear Company: Liz Robert—CEO

The Vermont Teddy Bear Company is a direct marketer in the gift delivery industry and the only major American manufacturer of premium teddy bears. Founded in 1981 by entrepreneur John Sortino, the company achieved quick prominence with its popular Bear-Gram specialty gift products, and has twice been named one of the fastest growing privately held companies in the United States by *Inc. Magazine*.

View the Video (11 minutes)

View the video on the Vermont Teddy Bear Company in class or at **academic.cengage.com/management/lussier.**

Read the Case

During its early years, the Shelburne, Vermont–based company was experiencing double-digit growth, mostly due to John Sortino's popular Bear-Gram concept. The best-selling Bear-Gram gift included a customized Vermont Teddy Bear with a personal greeting card and gourmet candy treat, delivered in a colorful gift box. In the mid-1990s, however, increasing competition from candy, flowers, and cigar gift manufacturers cut into profits at the Vermont Teddy Bear Company and forced the firm to think more strategically about its future prospects.

Faced with increasing competition and the reality that its market was smaller than first believed, the Vermont Teddy Bear Company decided it needed new leadership that could inspire confidence, empower workers, and carry out a vision for future growth. After conducting an extensive search, the company promoted CFO Liz Robert to the position of president and CEO, where her leadership has won the admiration of many followers. Whereas the company's former CEOs relied heavily on intuition as a core leadership competency, Robert is known for taking a more scientific approach to understanding the company's market and customers, relying upon market research and other data to help make key decisions.

Liz Robert's leadership style and careful attention to detail are proving to be the right qualities at the right time for the Vermont Teddy Bear Company. Under the strong direction of its respected CEO, the specialty gift maker has been able to refocus its vision and return to the success of its core business.

Answer the Questions

1. Is Liz Robert a task-oriented leader or a relationship-oriented leader? Support your answer.
2. Which path-goal leadership style does Robert use most? Explain your choice.
3. How might Liz Robert's leadership style influence the culture of the Vermont Teddy Bear Company?

Self-Assessment 3

Determining Your Preferred Normative Leadership Style

Following are 12 situations. Select the one alternative that most closely describes what you would do in each situation. Don't be concerned with trying to pick the right answer; select the alternative you would really use. Circle a, b, c, or d. Ignore the S _____ part, which will be explained later in Skill-Development Exercise 1.

1. Your rookie crew seems to be developing well. Their need for direction and close supervision is diminishing. What do you do?

   a. Stop directing and overseeing performance unless there is a problem. S _____
   b. Spend time getting to know them personally, but make sure they maintain performance levels. S _____
   c. Make sure things keep going well; continue to direct and oversee closely. S _____
   d. Begin to discuss new tasks of interest to them. S _____

2. You assigned Jill a task, specifying exactly how you wanted it done. Jill deliberately ignored your directions and did it her way. The job will not meet the customer's standards. This is not the first problem you've had with Jill. What do you decide to do?

   a. Listen to Jill's side, but be sure the job gets done right. S _____
   b. Tell Jill to do it again the right way, and closely supervise the job. S _____
   c. Tell her the customer will not accept the job, and let Jill handle it her way. S _____
   d. Discuss the problem and possible solutions to it. S _____

3. Your employees work well together; the department is a real team. It's the top performer in the organization. Because of traffic problems, the president okayed staggered hours for departments.

As a result, you can change your department's hours. Several of your workers have suggested changing. You take what action?

a. Allow the group to decide its hours. S _____

b. Decide on new hours, explain why you chose them, and invite questions. S _____

c. Conduct a meeting to get the group members' ideas. Select new hours together, with your approval. S _____

d. Send around a memo stating the hours you want. S _____

4. You hired Bill, a new employee. He is not performing at the level expected after one month's training. Bill is trying, but he seems to be a slow learner. What do you decide to do?

a. Clearly explain what needs to be done and oversee his work. Discuss why the procedures are important; support and encourage him. S _____

b. Tell Bill that his training is over and it's time to pull his own weight. S _____

c. Review task procedures and supervise Bill's work closely. S _____

d. Inform Bill that his training is over, and tell him to feel free to come to you if he has any problems. S _____

5. Helen has had an excellent performance record for the last five years. Recently you have noticed a drop in the quality and quantity of her work. She has a family problem. What do you do?

a. Tell Helen to get back on track and closely supervise her. S _____

b. Discuss the problem with Helen. Help her realize that her personal problem is affecting her work. Discuss ways to improve the situation. Be supportive and encourage her. S _____

c. Tell Helen you're aware of her productivity slip, and that you're sure she'll work it out soon. S _____

d. Discuss the problem and solution with Helen, and supervise her closely. S _____

6. Your organization does not allow smoking in certain areas. You just walked by a restricted area and saw Joan smoking. She has been with the organization for 10 years and is a very productive worker. Joan has never been caught smoking before. What action do you take?

a. Ask her to put it out, and then leave. S _____

b. Discuss why she is smoking, and ask what she intends to do about it. S _____

c. Give her a lecture about not smoking, and check up on her in the future. S _____

d. Tell her to put it out, watch her do it, and tell her you will check on her in the future. S _____

7. Your department usually works well together with little direction. Recently a conflict between Sue and Tom has caused problems. As a result, you take what action?

a. Call Sue and Tom together and make them realize how this conflict is affecting the department. Discuss how to resolve it and how you will check to make sure the problem is solved. S _____

b. Let the group resolve the conflict. S _____

c. Have Sue and Tom sit down and discuss their conflict and how to resolve it. Support their efforts to implement a solution. S _____

d. Tell Sue and Tom how to resolve their conflict and closely supervise them. S _____

8. Jim usually does his share of the work with some encouragement and direction. However, he has migraine headaches occasionally and doesn't pull his weight when this happens. The others resent doing Jim's work. What do you decide to do?

a. Discuss his problem and help him come up with ideas for maintaining his work; be supportive. S _____

b. Tell Jim to do his share of the work and closely watch his output. S _____

c. Inform Jim that he is creating a hardship for the others and should resolve the problem by himself. S _____

d. Be supportive, but set minimum performance levels and ensure compliance. S _____

9. Barbara, your most experienced and productive worker, came to you with a detailed idea that could increase your department's productivity at a very low cost. She can do her present job and this new assignment. You think it's an excellent idea; what do you do?

a. Set some goals together. Encourage and support her efforts. S _____

b. Set up goals for Barbara. Be sure she agrees with them and sees you as being supportive of her efforts. S _____

c. Tell Barbara to keep you informed and to come to you if she needs any help. S _____

d. Have Barbara check in with you frequently, so that you can direct and supervise her activities. S _____

10. Your boss asked you for a special report. Frank, a very capable worker who usually needs no direction or support, has all the necessary skills to do the job. However, Frank is reluctant because he has never done a report. What do you do?

a. Tell Frank he has to do it. Give him direction and supervise him closely. S _____

b. Describe the project to Frank and let him do it his own way. S _____

c. Describe the benefits to Frank. Get his ideas on how to do it and check his progress. S _____

d. Discuss possible ways of doing the job. Be supportive; encourage Frank. S _____

11. Jean is the top producer in your department. However, her monthly reports are constantly late and contain errors. You are puzzled because she does everything else with no direction or support. What do you decide to do?

a. Go over past reports with Jean, explaining exactly what is expected of her. Schedule a meeting so that you can review the next report with her. S _____

b. Discuss the problem with Jean, and ask her what can be done about it; be supportive. S _____

c. Explain the importance of the report. Ask her what the problem is. Tell her that you expect the next report to be on time and error free. S _____

d. Remind Jean to get the next report in on time without errors. S _____

12. Your workers are very effective and like to participate in decision making. A consultant was hired to develop a new method for your department using the latest technology in the field. What do you do?

a. Explain the consultant's method and let the group decide how to implement it. S _____

b. Teach them the new method and closely supervise them. S _____

c. Explain the new method and the reasons that it is important. Teach them the method and make sure the procedure is followed. Answer questions. S _____

d. Explain the new method and get the group's input on ways to improve and implement it. S _____

To determine your preferred normative leadership style, follow these steps:

1. In this chart, circle the letter you selected for each situation.

The column headings (S1 through S4) represent the style you selected.

S1 = Decide, S2 = Consult (Individually or Group), S3 = Facilitate, S4 = Delegate

	S1 D	S2 C	S3 F	S4 DL
1	c	b	d	a
2	b	a	d	c
3	d	b	c	a
4	c	a	d	b
5	a	d	b	c
6	d	c	b	a
7	d	a	c	b
8	b	d	a	c
9	d	b	a	c
10	a	c	d	b
11	a	c	b	d
12	b	c	d	a
Totals	___	___	___	___

2. Add up the number of circled items per column. The column with the highest total is your preferred leadership style. There is no correct or best normative leadership style. Below is an explanation about each style.

S1 Decide Leadership Style. The decide style includes making the decision alone. As a decider, you autocratically tell people how to implement your decision and follow up to make sure performance is maintained, or you tell people what to do and make sure they continue to do it.

S2 Consult (Individually or Group) Leadership Style. As they are both consult styles, we combine individual and group styles for this exercise. The consult style includes talking to individuals or groups for input in a supportive way before you make the decision. As a consulter, after making the decision, you also tell people how to implement your decision and follow up to make sure performance is maintained, while you support and encourage them as they implement your decision.

S3 Facilitate Leadership Style. The facilitate style includes having a group meeting to get input from members as you attempt to support the group to agree on a decision within boundaries set by you; in other words, you still have the final say on the decision. As a facilitator, you are supportive and encouraging to the group members to both make the decision and implement the decision.

S4 Delegate Leadership Style. The delegate style includes letting the group make the decision within limits. As a delegater, you don't tell the group what to do or facilitate the group during the decision making and its implementation.

To determine your flexibility to change styles, do the following. Look at your total score for each column leadership style. The more evenly distributed the totals (for example 4, 4, 4, 4), the more flexible you appear to be at changing your leadership style. Having high numbers in some columns and low in others indicates a strong preference to use or avoid using one or more leadership styles.

Note: There is no right, correct, or best normative leadership style. What this self-assessment exercise does is allow you to know your preferred leadership style and your flexibility at changing styles. In Skill-Development Exercise 1, you will develop your skill to identify the normative leadership styles. In Skill-Development Exercise 2, you will learn to use the normative leadership models to select the most appropriate leadership style for a given situation.

Skill-Development Exercise 1

IDENTIFYING NORMATIVE LEADERSHIP STYLES

Preparing for Skill-Development Exercise 1

Return to the 12 situations in Self-Assessment 3. This time, instead of selecting one of the four options, a–d, identify the normative leadership style used in each option, with the aid of the leadership style definitions in Self-Assessment 3 above. Let's do the following example.

Example:

Your rookie crew seems to be developing well. Their need for direction and close supervision is diminishing. What do you do?

a. Stop directing and overseeing performance unless there is a problem. S __DL__

b. Spend time getting to know them personally; but make sure they maintain performance levels. S __C__

c. Make sure things keep going well; continue to direct and oversee closely. S __D__

d. Begin to discuss new tasks of interest to them. S __F__

Answers:

a. As indicated on the S __DL__ line, this is the *delegate* leadership style. As in the definition of *delegate,* you are leaving the group alone—unless there is a problem (limits)—to make and implement its own decisions about work.

b. As indicated on the S __C__ line, this is the *consult* leadership style. As in the definition of *consult,* you are being supportive by getting to know them, yet you are still following up to make sure they get the job done.

c. As indicated on the S __D__ line, this is the *decide* leadership style. As in the definition of *decide,* you are following up to make sure performance is maintained.

d. As indicated on the S __F__ line, this is the *facilitate* leadership style. As in the definition of *facilitate,* you are facilitating a group decision on possible new tasks for the group to perform.

Now, complete situation numbers 2–12 by determining the leadership style and placing the letters D, C, F, and DL on each of the a–d S ___ lines as illustrated above. All four alternative behaviors do represent a different normative leadership style.

Doing Skill-Development Exercise 1 in Class

Objective

To develop the skill of identifying normative leadership styles.

Procedure (5–30 minutes)

Select an option:

A. The instructor goes over the answers.

B. The instructor calls on students and goes over the answers.

C. Break into groups of three and come up with group answers for the 11 situations. This is followed by the instructor going over the answers.

Skill-Development Exercise 2

USING THE NORMATIVE LEADERSHIP MODELS

Preparing for Skill-Development Exercise 2

You should have studied the normative leadership model text material. Using Exhibits 5-9 and 5-10, determine the appropriate leadership style for the given problem statements below. Follow these steps:

1. Determine which normative leadership model to use for the given situation.
2. Answer the variable questions (between 2 to 7) for the problem.
3. Select the appropriate leadership style from the model.

1. Production department manager. You are the manager of a mass-produced manufactured product. You have two major machines in your department with ten people working on each. You have an important order that needs to be shipped first thing tomorrow morning. Your boss has made it very clear that you must meet this deadline. It's 2:00 and you are right on schedule to meet the order deadline. At 2:15 an employee comes to tell you that one of the machines is smoking a little and making a noise. If you keep running the machine, it may make it until the end of the day and you will deliver the important shipment on time. If you shut down the machine, the manufacturer will not be able to check the machine until tomorrow and you will miss the deadline. You call your boss and there is no answer, and you don't know how else to contact the boss or how long it will be before the boss gets back to you if you leave a message. There are no higher-level managers than you or anyone with more knowledge of the machine than you. Which leadership style should you use?

Step 1. Which model should you use? (____ time-driven _____ development-driven)

Step 2. Which questions did you answer and how? (H = high, L = low, NA = not answered/skipped)

1. H L or NA 3. H L or NA 5. H L or NA 7. H L or NA
2. H L or NA 4. H L or NA 6. H L or NA

Step 3. Which leadership style is the most appropriate?
_____ decide _____ consult individually _____ consult group _____ facilitate _____ delegate

2. Religious leader. You are the top religious leader of your church with 125 families and 200 members. You have a Doctor of Religious Studies degree with just two years' experience as the head of a church, and no business courses. The church has one paid secretary, three part-time program directors for religious instruction, music, and social activities, plus many volunteers. Your paid staff serve on your advisory board with 10 other church members who are primarily top-level

business leaders in the community. You make a yearly budget with the board's approval. The church source of income is weekly member donations. The board doesn't want to operate in the red, and the church has very modest surplus funds. Your volunteer accountant (CPA), who is a board member, asked to meet with you. During the meeting, she informed you that weekly collections are 20 percent below budget and the cost of utilities has increased 25 percent over the yearly budget figure. You are running a large deficit, and at this rate your surplus will be gone in two months. Which leadership style will you use in this crisis?

Step 1. Which model should you use? (____ time-driven _____ development-driven)

Step 2. Which questions did you answer and how? (H = high, L = low, NA = not answered/skipped)

1. H L or NA 3. H L or NA 5. H L or NA 7. H L or NA
2. H L or NA 4. H L or NA 6. H L or NA

Step 3. Which leadership style is the most appropriate?
_____ decide _____ consult individually _____ consult group _____ facilitate _____ delegate

3. School of business dean. You are the new dean of the school of business at a small private university. Your faculty includes around 20 professors, only two of whom are non-tenured, and the average length of employment at the school is 12 years. Upon taking the job, you expect to leave for a larger school in three years. Your primary goal is to start a business school faculty advisory board to improve community relations and school alumni relations, and to raise money for financial aid scholarships. You have already done this in your last job as dean. However, you are new to the area and have no business contacts. You need help to develop a network of alumni and other community leaders fairly quickly if you are to show achieved results on your resume in $2^{1}/2$ years. Your faculty gets along well and is talkative, but when you approach small groups of them they tend to become quiet and disperse. Which primary leadership style would you use to achieve your objective?

Step 1. Which model should you use? (____ time-driven _____ development-driven)

Step 2. Which questions did you answer and how? (H = high, L = low, NA = not answered/skipped)

1. H L or NA 3. H L or NA 5. H L or NA 7. H L or NA
2. H L or NA 4. H L or NA 6. H L or NA

Step 3. Which leadership style is the most appropriate?
_____ decide _____ consult individually _____ consult group _____ facilitate _____ delegate

4. Dot.com president. You are the president of a dot.com company that has been having financial problems for a few years. As a result, your top two managers left for other jobs. One left four months ago and the other two months ago. With your networking contacts you replaced both managers within a month; thus, they don't have a lot of time on the job and haven't worked together for very long. Plus, they currently do their own thing to get their jobs done. However, they are both very bright, hard-working, and dedicated to your vision of what the company can be. You know how to turn the company around and so do your two key managers. To turn the company around, you and your two managers will have to work together, with the help of all your employees. Virtually all the employees are high-tech specialists who want to be included in decision making. Your business partners have no more money to invest. If you cannot turn a profit in four to five months, you will most likely go bankrupt. Which primary leadership style would you use to achieve your objective?

Step 1. Which model should you use? (_____ time-driven _____ development-driven)

Step 2. Which questions did you answer and how? (H = high, L = low, NA = not answered/skipped)

1. H L or NA 3. H L or NA 5. H L or NA 7. H L or NA
2. H L or NA 4. H L or NA 6. H L or NA

Step 3. Which leadership style is the most appropriate?
_____ decide _____ consult individually _____ consult group
_____ facilitate _____ delegate

Doing Skill-Development Exercise 2 in Class

Objective
To develop your skill at determining the appropriate leadership style to use in a given situation using the normative leadership models, Exhibits 5-9 and 5-10.

Experience
You will use the normative leadership models in four given problem situations.

Procedure 1 (10–15 minutes)
The instructor goes over the normative leadership models and uses the models to illustrate how to select the appropriate leadership style for problem situation 1.

Procedure 2 (10–20 minutes)
Break into groups of two or three and use the models to determine the appropriate leadership style for situations 2–4 in the preparation above. This is followed by the instructor going over or just stating the answers to situations 2–4.

Conclusion
The instructor may lead a class discussion and/or make concluding remarks.

Apply It (2–4 minutes)
What did I learn from this experience? How will I apply normative leadership in the future?

_____

_____

_____

Self-Assessment 4

Your Leadership Continuum and Path-Goal Leadership Styles

You have already determined your preferred LPC contingency leadership style (Self-Assessment 1) and your preferred normative leadership style (Self-Assessment 3). Using Self-Assessment 4, you can determine your other preferred styles by checking your preferred normative leadership style in the first column. In the same row, the columns to the right show your continuum and path-goal preferred leadership styles. Does your preferred leadership style match your personality for Self-Assessment 2?

NORMATIVE LEADERSHIP STYLE	LEADERSHIP CONTINUUM STYLE	PATH-GOAL LEADERSHIP STYLE
Decide	1 Boss-centered	Directive
Consult (individually or group)	2 or 3	Achievement
Facilitate	4 or 5	Supportive
Delegate	6 or 7 Subordinate-centered	Participative

PART 2

Team Leadership

Communication, Coaching, and Conflict Skills

6

After studying this chapter, you should be able to:

1. List the steps in the oral message-sending process. p. 199
2. List and explain the three parts of the message-receiving process. p. 202
3. Describe paraphrasing and state why it is used. p. 206
4. Identify two common approaches to getting feedback, and explain why they don't work. p. 208
5. Describe the difference between criticism and coaching feedback. p. 217
6. Discuss the relationship between the performance formula and the coaching model. p. 217
7. Define the five conflict management styles. p. 221
8. List the steps in the initiating conflict resolution model. p. 227
9. Define the following **key terms** (in order of appearance in the chapter):

communication
oral message-sending process
message-receiving process
feedback
paraphrasing
360-degree feedback
coaching
job instructional training
coaching feedback

attribution theory
performance formula
mentoring
conflict
initiating conflict resolution model
BCF model
mediator
arbitrator

Opening Case Application

The Ranch Golf Club, where every player is a special guest for the day, opened in 2001 in Southwick, Massachusetts. Prior to being a golf club, it was a dairy farm owned by the Hall family. The Hall family wanted to turn the farm into a golf club, with the help of Rowland Bates as project coordinator. The Halls were to provide the land, and investors would provide the capital.

Peter and Korby Clark were part owners of nearly 50 Jiffy Lubes, selling most to Pennzoil in 1991. At age 37, Peter Clark stopped working at Jiffy Lube full-time to assist his managing partner at 6 Jiffy Lubes and develop three more in the Worcester, Massachusetts area, which they are selling to a third partner. Peter Clark spent more time coaching, relaxing with his family, and doing community service for the Jimmy Fund. Through the 1990s, the Clarks had a variety of opportunities to invest in new and ongoing businesses. Nothing interested the Clarks until the late 1990s. Unlike other businesses looking simply for investors, Bates offered Clark the opportunity to create and help manage a new golf club. Although Clark played golf, it was not so much the golf but the challenge of creating a new course and also playing an ongoing part in its management that interested him. Bates found two more investors, Bernard Chiu and Ronald Izen, to provide the additional funding, creating a one-third ownership by the Halls, one-third by the Clarks, and one-third by other investors.

The Clarks were happy to have the professional golf management team of Willowbend (working for a flat fee plus bonus compensation package) for four reasons. First, they realized that they could not create and run a successful golf club business without expertise. Neither of them ever worked for a golf club and they only played recreational golf. Secondly, they would not have to manage The Ranch full-time. Peter is currently the head baseball coach and assistant football coach for Agawam High School (he was also an assistant football coach for Trinity College), and he wants to continue to coach, and Peter and Korby both want to spend time with their family and perform community service. Third, Peter and Korby are involved in all the important strategic decisions and have input into day-to-day operations, but Willowbend makes the day-to-day decisions. Fourth, the employees work for Willowbend, which offers a good benefits package.

The Ranch's competitive advantage is its upscale public course (peak season green fees are around $100) with links, woods, and a variety of elevations with unsurpassed service in New England. The Ranch is striving to be the best golf club in New England. In less than a year, The Ranch earned a 4 star course rating, one of only four in New England. In the January 2003 issue of *Golf Digest*, The Ranch was rated number 3 in the country in the new upscale public golf course category.[1]

Opening Case Questions:

1. Why is communication important to the management of The Ranch?
2. How do they use feedback at The Ranch?
3. Is there a difference in managing an oil change business, a golf course, and a sports team, and how does Peter Clark use coaching at The Ranch?
4. Which conflict management style does Peter Clark tend to use at The Ranch?
5. What types of conflict resolutions do the Clarks deal with at The Ranch?

To learn more about The Ranch Golf Club, visit their Web site at **http://www. theranchgolfclub.com** or log on to InfoTrac® College Edition at **academic.cengage. com/infotrac**, and select the advanced search option and key in record number A94908255 or A93531784 to get started.

The focus of this chapter is on three related topics. We begin with sending and receiving communications, because it is the foundation for coaching and managing conflict. Next we discuss feedback as it relates to both communication and coaching. Based on this foundation, you will learn how to coach followers, and then how to manage conflicts.

Communication

Communication *is the process of conveying information and meaning.* True communication takes place only when all parties understand the message (information) from the same perspective (meaning). At all organizational levels, it has been estimated that at least 75 percent of each workday is consumed in communication. Thus, every successful person is in the communication business.[2] Your ability to speak, read, and write will have a direct impact on your career success:[3] Organizations recruit people with good communication skills, and organizations offer communication training programs.[4] In this section we discuss the importance of communication in leadership and examine the communication process of sending and receiving messages.

Communication and Leadership

Communication is a major competency for leaders, because effective communication is part of leadership.[5] Empirical research supports the statement that effective leaders are also effective communicators; there is a positive relationship between communication competency and leadership performance.[6]

Good communication skills drive effective leadership.[7] For example, from Chapter 1, our definition of leadership is based on communication: Leaders play informational roles, and the shift in paradigm from management to leadership includes differences in communication skills. From Chapter 2, personality affects the type of communication used: Ethical leaders with integrity will use open and honest communications; the Pygmalion effect requires communication of attitudes. From Chapters 3 through 5, communication varies with leadership style: The autocratic leader uses one-way communication to tell employees what to do, while the democratic leader uses two-way communication as the team decides what to do and how to do it. Leaders use communication to motivate followers.[8]

Organizations with effective communication systems are more likely to be successful. One important part of organizational communications is to convey the mission, vision, and values so that all employees understand the big picture of what is trying to be accomplished.[9] However, research based on 10,000 firms indicates that leaders are not doing an effective job in this area. You will learn more about strategic leadership in Part III, Chapters 9 through 11. Lee Iacocca, former top executive credited with saving Chrysler from bankruptcy, said, "The most important thing I learned in school was how to communicate."[10] Two important parts of leadership communication are sending and receiving messages.

Sending Messages and Giving Instructions

Managers use the communication process of sending a variety of messages in person, on the phone, and in writing. An important part of a manager's job is to give instructions, which is sending a message. Have you ever heard a manager say, "This isn't what I asked for"? When this happens, it is usually the manager's fault. Managers often make incorrect assumptions and do not take 100 percent of the responsibility for ensuring their message is transmitted with mutual understanding. As a manager, how well you give instructions directly affects your ability to motivate your employees, as well as their satisfaction with your supervisory leadership.[11] Before sending a message, you should carefully plan the message. Then, give the message orally using the message-sending process, or send the message in writing.

Planning the Message

Before sending a message, you should plan it, answering these questions:

- *What is the goal of the message?* Is it to influence, to inform, to express feeling, or all of these things? What do you want as the end result of the communication? Set an objective. After considering the other planning dimensions, determine exactly what you want to say to meet your objective.[12] In today's diverse global economy, you also need to be culturally sensitive in deciding what to say in a message.[13]
- *Who should receive the message?* Have you included everyone who needs to receive your message?
- *How will you send the message?* With the receivers in mind, plan how you will convey the message so that it will be understood. Select the appropriate method (see Applying the Concept 1 for a list) for the audience and situation. As a general guide, use rich oral channels for sending difficult and unusual messages, less rich written channels for transmitting simple and routine messages to several people, and combined channels for important messages that employees need to attend to and understand. You should also avoid giving too much detail.[14]
- *When will the message be transmitted?* Timing is important. For example, if it is going to take 15 minutes to transmit a message, don't approach an employee 5 minutes before quitting time. Wait until the next day. Make an appointment when appropriate.
- *Where will the message be transmitted?* Decide on the best setting—your office, the receiver's workplace, and so forth. Remember to keep distractions to a minimum.

Learning Outcome 1

List the steps in the oral message-sending process.

The Oral Message-Sending Process

Be careful not to talk too fast when sending oral messages over the phone or in person. It is helpful to follow the steps in the **oral message-sending process:** (1) *develop rapport;* (2) *state your communication objective;* (3) *transmit your message;* (4) *check the receiver's understanding;* and (5) *get a commitment and follow up.* Model 6-1 lists these steps.

step 1.   **Develop rapport.** Put the receiver at ease. It is usually appropriate to begin communications with small talk correlated to the message. It helps prepare the person to receive the message.[15]

Model 6-1 *The oral message-sending process.*

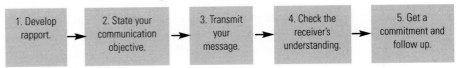

| 1. Develop rapport. | 2. State your communication objective. | 3. Transmit your message. | 4. Check the receiver's understanding. | 5. Get a commitment and follow up. |

step 2. **State your communication objective.** The common business communication objectives are to influence, inform, and express feelings. With the goal of influencing, it is helpful for the receiver to know the desired end result of the communication before covering all the details.

Applying the Concept 1

Methods of Sending Messages

For each of these 10 communication situations, select the most appropriate channel for transmitting the message. Write the appropriate letter in the blank before each item.

Oral communication

a. face-to-face
b. meeting
c. presentation
d. telephone

Written communication (includes e-mail and traditional methods)

e. memo   h. bulletin board
f. letter   i. poster
g. report   j. newsletter

_____ 1. You are waiting for an important letter to arrive by FedEx, and you want to know if it is in the mail room yet.

_____ 2. Employees have been leaving the lights on in the stock room when no one is in it. You want them to shut the lights off.

_____ 3. José, Jamal, and Sam will be working on a new project as a team. You need to explain the project to them.

_____ 4. John has come in late for work again, and you want this practice to stop.

_____ 5. You have exceeded your departmental goals. You want your manager to know about it, because it should have a positive influence on your upcoming performance appraisal.

_____ 6. Your spouse sells Avon products and wants you to help her advertise where you work. However, you don't want to ask anyone directly to buy Avon.

_____ 7. People in another department sent a message asking for some numbers relating to your work.

_____ 8. You have been asked to be the speaker for a local nonprofit organization.

_____ 9. You enjoy writing, and you want to become better known by more people throughout your firm.

_____10. You have been given a written complaint from a customer and asked to take care of it.

step 3. **Transmit your message.** If the communication objective is to influence, tell the people what you want them to do, give instructions, and so forth. Be sure to set deadlines for completing tasks. If the objective is to inform, tell the people the information. If the objective is to express feeling, do so.

step 4. **Check the receiver's understanding.** When influencing and giving information, you should ask direct questions,[16] and/or use paraphrasing. To simply ask, "Do you have any questions?" does not check understanding. In the next section of this chapter, you will learn how to check understanding by using feedback.

step 5. **Get a commitment and follow up.** When the goal of communication is to inform or express feelings, a commitment is not needed. However, when the goal of communication is to influence, it is important to get a commitment to the action. The leader needs to make sure that followers can do the task and have it done by a certain time or date. For situations in which the follower does not intend to get the task done, it is better to know this when sending the message, rather than to wait until the deadline before finding out. When followers are reluctant to commit to the necessary action, leaders can use persuasive power within their authority. When communicating to influence, follow up to ensure that the necessary action has been taken.

Written Communication and Writing Tips

With information technology and the Internet, you can communicate with anyone in the world—in real time.[17] Because the use of e-mail will continue to increase, your written communication skills are more important than ever. So we have included some simple but important writing tips that can help you to improve your writing.

- Lack of organization is a major writing problem. Before you begin writing, set an objective for your communication. Keep the audience in mind. What do you want them to do? Make an outline, using letters and/or numbers, of the major points you want to get across. Now put the outline into written form. The first paragraph states the purpose of the communication. The middle paragraphs support the purpose of the communication: facts, figures, and so forth. The last paragraph summarizes the major points and clearly states the action, if any, to be taken by you and other people.
- Write to communicate, not to impress. Keep the message short and simple. Limit each paragraph to a single topic and an average of five sentences. Sentences should average 15 words. Vary paragraph and sentence length. Write in the active voice (I recommend . . .) rather than the passive voice (it is recommended . . .).
- Edit your work and rewrite where necessary. To improve sentences and paragraphs, add to them to convey full meaning, cut out unnecessary words and phrases, and/or rearrange the words. Check your work with the computer spelling and grammar checkers. Have others edit your work as well.

Ethical Dilemma 1

Advertising

Companies use oral, nonverbal, and written communications to advertise their products in order to increase sales. Selecting the best words to sell a product or service is important. However, some of the terms used in ads are misleading and even deceptive, though in some of those cases the words are legal. For example, some companies use the word "natural" on foods that are highly processed, such as products including white sugar. So some question the use of the term "natural": Bags of chips are advertised as being "all natural," which leads people to think they are healthy, when in fact others classify them as junk food. Because obesity has become such a major health problem, the Food and Drug Administration (FDA) obesity task force is trying to crack down on misleading labels and ads, and is calling for warnings and fines for violators.[18]

1. Is it ethical and socially responsible for food companies to use terms (like "natural") that can be misleading, to increase sales and profits?
2. Should companies use terms that are considered misleading by some but are not illegal?
3. How would you define "natural"?
4. How should the FDA define "natural" so that it is not used to mislead people to buy food thinking that it is healthy, when in fact it is not?

Receiving Messages

The second communication process that leaders are involved in is receiving messages. With oral communications, the key to successfully understanding the message is listening.[19] In fact, failure to listen is one of the top five reasons leaders fail,[20] and Warren Bennis said it is the most common reason CEOs fail.[21] Thus, you need to be patient and listen to others.[22] Complete Self-Assessment 1 to determine how good a listener you are, then read the tips for improving listening skills in the message-receiving process.

When asked, "Are you a good listener?" most people say yes. In reality, 75 percent of what people hear, they hear imprecisely—and 75 percent of what they hear accurately, they forget within three weeks. In other words, most people are really not good listeners. One of the skills we need to develop most is listening.[23] Listening's greatest value is that it gives the speaker a sense of worth.[24] People have a passionate desire to be heard.

—————— Learning Outcome 2 ——————

List and explain the three parts of the message-receiving process.

The Message-Receiving Process

The **message-receiving process** *includes listening, analyzing, and checking understanding.* To improve your listening skills, spend one week focusing your

Self-Assessment 1

Listening Skills

Select the response that best describes the frequency of your actual behavior. Write the letter A, U, F, O, or S on the line before each of the 15 statements.

A—almost always   U—usually   F—frequently
O—occasionally   S—seldom

_____ 1. I like to listen to people talk. I encourage others to talk by showing interest, smiling, nodding, and so forth.

_____ 2. I pay closer attention to people who are more similar to me than I do to people who are different from me.

_____ 3. I evaluate people's words and nonverbal communication ability as they talk.

_____ 4. I avoid distractions; if it's noisy, I suggest moving to a quiet spot.

_____ 5. When people come to me and interrupt me when I'm doing something, I put what I was doing out of my mind and give them my complete attention.

_____ 6. When people are talking, I allow them time to finish. I do not interrupt, anticipate what they are going to say, or jump to conclusions.

_____ 7. I tune people out who do not agree with my views.

_____ 8. While the other person is talking, or professors are lecturing, my mind wanders to personal topics.

_____ 9. While the other person is talking, I pay close attention to the nonverbal communications to help me fully understand what they are trying to communicate.

_____ 10. I tune out and pretend I understand when the topic is difficult for me to understand.

_____ 11. When the other person is talking, I think about and prepare what I am going to say in reply.

_____ 12. When I think there is something missing or contradictory, I ask direct questions to get the person to explain the idea more fully.

_____ 13. When I don't understand something, I let the other person know I don't understand.

_____ 14. When listening to other people, I try to put myself in their position and see things from their perspective.

_____ 15. During conversations I repeat back to the other person what has been said in my own words to be sure I correctly understand what has been said.

If people you talk to regularly were to answer these questions about you, would they have the same responses that you selected? To find out, have friends fill out the questions with you in mind rather than themselves. Then compare answers.

To determine your score, give yourself 5 points for each A, 4 for each U, 3 for each F, 2 for each O, and 1 for each S for statements 1, 4, 5, 6, 9, 12, 13, 14, and 15. Place the numbers on the line next to your response letter. For items 2, 3, 7, 8, 10, and 11 the score reverses: 5 points for each S, 4 for each O, 3 for each F, 2 for each U, and 1 for each A. Place these score numbers on the lines next to the response letters. Now add your total number of points. Your score should be between 15 and 75. Place your score on the continuum below. Generally, the higher your score, the better your listening skills.

15–20–25–30–35–40–45–50–55–60–65–70–75
Poor listener   *Good listener*

attention on listening, by concentrating on what other people say and the nonverbal communications they send when they speak. Notice if their verbal and nonverbal communication are consistent. Do the nonverbal messages reinforce the speaker's words or detract from them? Talk only when necessary, so that you can listen and "see" what others are saying.[25] If you apply the following tips, you will improve your listening skills. The tips are presented in the

Exhibit 6-1 *The message-receiving process.*

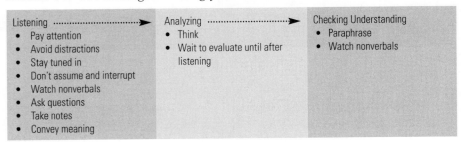

depiction of the message-receiving process (Exhibit 6-1): We should listen, analyze, and then check understanding.

Listening

Listening is the process of giving the speaker your undivided attention. As the speaker sends the message, you should listen by:

- *Paying attention.* When people interrupt you to talk, stop what you are doing and give them your complete attention immediately. Quickly relax and clear your mind, so that you are receptive to the speaker. This will get you started correctly. If you miss the first few words, you may miss the message.
- *Avoiding distractions.* Keep your eye on the speaker. Do not fiddle with pens, papers, or other distractions. For important messages, put your phone on "take a message." If you are in a noisy or distracting place, suggest moving to a quiet spot.
- *Staying tuned in.* While the other person is talking or the professor is lecturing, do not let your mind wander to personal topics. If it does wander, gently bring it back. Do not tune out the speaker because you do not like something about the person or because you disagree with what is being said. If the topic is difficult, do not tune out; ask questions. Do not think about what you are going to say in reply, just listen.
- *Not assuming and interrupting.* Do not assume you know what the speaker is going to say, or listen to the beginning and jump to conclusions. Most listening mistakes are made when people hear the first few words of a sentence, finish it in their own minds, and miss the second half. Listen to the entire message without interrupting the speaker.[26]
- *Watching nonverbal cues.* Understand both the feelings and the content of the message. People sometimes say one thing and mean something else. So watch as you listen to be sure that the speaker's eyes, body, and face are sending the same message as the verbal message. If something seems out of sync, get it cleared up by asking questions.
- *Asking questions.* When you feel there is something missing, contradictory, or you just do not understand, ask direct questions to get the person to explain the idea more fully.
- *Taking notes.* Part of listening is writing important things down so you can remember them later, and document them when necessary. This is especially true when you're listening to instructions. You should always have

something to take notes with, such as a pen and a notebook or some index cards.

- *Conveying meaning.* The way to let the speaker know you are listening to the message is to use verbal clues, such as, "you feel . . . ," "uh huh," "I see," and "I understand." You should also use nonverbal communication such as eye contact, appropriate facial expressions, nodding of the head, or leaning slightly forward in your chair to indicate you are interested and listening.

Analyzing

Analyzing is the process of thinking about, decoding, and evaluating the message. Poor listening occurs in part because people speak at an average rate of 120 words per minute, while they are capable of listening at a rate of over 500 words per minute. The ability to comprehend words more than four times faster than the speaker can talk often results in minds wandering. As the speaker sends the message, you should analyze by:

- *Thinking.* To help overcome the discrepancy in the speed between your ability to listen and people's rate of speaking, use the speed of your brain positively. Listen actively by organizing, summarizing, reviewing, interpreting, and critiquing often. These activities will help you to do an effective job of decoding the message.
- *Waiting to evaluate until after listening.* When people try to listen and evaluate what is said at the same time, they tend to miss part or all of the message. You should just listen to the entire message, then come to your conclusions.[27] When you evaluate the decision, base your conclusion on the facts present rather than on stereotypes and generalities.

Checking Understanding

Checking understanding is the process of giving feedback. After you have listened to the message—or during the message if it's a long one—check your understanding of the message by:

- *Paraphrasing.* Begin speaking by giving feedback, using paraphrasing to repeat the message to the sender. When you can paraphrase the message correctly, you convey that you have listened and understood the other person. Now you are ready to offer your ideas, advice, solution, decision, or whatever the sender of the message is talking to you about.
- *Watching nonverbal cues.* As you speak, watch the other person's nonverbal cues. If the person does not seem to understand what you are talking about, clarify the message before finishing the conversation.

Do you talk more than you listen? To be sure your perception is correct, ask your manager, coworkers, and friends who will give you an honest answer. If you spend more time talking than listening, you are probably failing in your communications,[28] and boring people too. Regardless of how much you listen, if you follow these guidelines, you will improve your conversation and become a person that people want to talk to, instead of a person they feel they have to listen to. To become an active listener, take the responsibility for ensuring mutual understanding.

WorkApplication3

Refer to Self-Assessment 1 and the listening tips. What is your weakest listening skill area on the job? How will you improve your listening ability?

_____

_____

_____

_____

_____

Work to change your behavior to become a better listener. Review the 15 statements in Self-Assessment 1. To improve your listening skills, practice doing items 1, 4, 5, 6, 9, 12, 13, 14, and 15; and avoid doing items 2, 3, 7, 8, 10, and 11. Effective listening requires responding to the message to ensure mutual understanding takes place.

OPENING CASE APPLICATION

1. Why Is Communication Important to the Management of The Ranch?

The key to success at The Ranch is comanaging between the Clarks and Willowbend with clear open communications of expectations. Peter Clark has to continually communicate with his partners and managers at Willowbend, and nothing takes the place of sitting down face-to-face during regular weekly meetings and listening to each other to continually improve operations. Meetings of department managers with employees continually focus on the importance of communicating the philosophy of unsurpassed professional service. To communicate professionalism, all employees wear The Ranch uniforms and are trained with instructions on how to perform high-quality service. Even the words used are chosen to communicate professionalism. For example, The Ranch has player assistance, not rangers; golf cars, not golf carts; and it has a golf shop, not a pro shop.

--- Learning Outcome 3 ---

Describe paraphrasing and state why it is used.

Feedback

In this section, we discuss the importance of feedback, the common approach to getting feedback—and why it doesn't work, and how to get feedback. We end with formal 360-degree feedback. In the next section we discuss how to give feedback as part of coaching.

The Importance of Feedback

Feedback _is the process of verifying messages and determining if objectives are being met._ Determining if objectives are being met has a very broad range. In essence, any time a person is sending or receiving job-related information that affects performance, they are giving or getting feedback.[29]

The Role of Feedback in Verifying Messages

Questioning, paraphrasing, and allowing comments and suggestions are all forms of feedback that check understanding. Recall that checking receiver understanding is the fourth step in the oral message-sending process. Feedback when giving and receiving messages facilitates job performance.[30] Feedback motivates employees to achieve high levels of performance.[31] Organizations train employees to give effective feedback, because it is an essential part of leadership communication.[32]

Mutual understanding of the meaning of the message must exist for communication to take place. The best way to make sure communication has taken place is to get feedback from the receiver of the message through questioning and paraphrasing. **Paraphrasing** is the process of *having the receiver restate the message in his or her own words*. If the receiver of the message can answer the questions or paraphrase the message, communication has taken place.

The Role of Feedback in Meeting Objectives

Feedback is also essential to knowing how the leader and organization are progressing to meet objectives.[33] Recall from Chapter 3 that objectives must be measurable. Feedback is used to measure performance. And giving and receiving feedback must be an ongoing process to be effective. Thus, leaders should set specific measurable objectives and monitor the process through feedback. Although research has clearly shown the importance of feedback in organizational performance, many organizations fail to use effective feedback.[34]

The Need to Be Open to Feedback—Criticism

To improve your performance and get ahead in an organization, you have to be open to feedback—commonly called *criticism*. How willing a person is to accept feedback depends on some of the same personality traits of effective leaders, which you learned about in Chapter 2. Ironically, the employees who could benefit the most from job-related feedback are often the ones who resist feedback and are unwilling to change. People who are defensive and insecure, and those with an external locus of control, tend to ignore feedback about their weaknesses.[35]

To improve, you need to solicit feedback on your performance.[36] If you're asking for personal feedback, remember that you are asking to hear things that may surprise, upset, or insult you, and even hurt your feelings. If you become defensive and emotional, and it is tough not to when you feel attacked, feedback will stop. People do not really enjoy being criticized; even when it is constructive, you should realize that criticism from your manager, peers, or others is painful. Keep the phrase, "no pain, no gain" in mind when it comes to criticism. If you want to improve your performance, and your chances of having a successful career, seek honest feedback about how you can improve your performance.[37] When you get criticism, whether you ask for it or not, view it as an opportunity to improve, stay calm (even when the other person is emotional), and don't get defensive. Use the feedback to improve your performance.

WorkApplication4

Are you really open to feedback—criticism from others at work? How can you improve on accepting criticism?

_____

_____

_____

_____

_____

Ethical Dilemma 2

Academic Grades

Grades are a form of feedback and are often criticism. (Recall Ethical Dilemma "Academic Standards" in Chapter 3.) Successful managers set and maintain high expectations for all their employees, and as Lou Holtz said, we need to set a higher standard. While students are doing less work than in prior years, grades continue to increase, which is called grade inflation. At one time, most colleges had a set grade point average (GPA) to determine honors. But today,

(Continued)

Ethical Dilemma 2

(*Continued*)

most colleges use a ranking system of GPA, because of grade inflation, to limit the number of students graduating with honors.

1. How do you react when you get a grade that is lower than you wanted or expected?
2. Do you use the feedback of correcting and grades to help you improve? Why or why not, and if yes, how?
3. Why are professors giving higher grades today than were given 5, 10, or 20 years ago?
4. Are students who are putting in less time and getting higher grades being well prepared for a career with high standards after graduation?
5. Is it ethical and socially responsible for professors to drop standards and for colleges to award degrees with higher grades today than 5, 10, or 20 years ago?

Learning Outcome 4

Identify two common approaches to getting feedback, and explain why they don't work.

Common Approaches to Getting Feedback on Messages—and Why They Don't Work

One common approach that ignores feedback is to send the entire message and then assume that the message has been conveyed with mutual understanding. A second approach is to give the entire message and then ask "Do you have any questions?" Feedback usually does not follow, because people have a tendency not to ask questions. There are at least four good reasons why people do not ask questions:

1. *Receivers feel ignorant.* To ask a question, especially if no one else does, is often considered an admission of not paying attention or not being bright enough to understand the issue.

2. *Receivers are ignorant.* Sometimes people do not know enough about the message to know whether it is incomplete, incorrect, or subject to interpretation. There are no questions, because what was said sounds right. The receiver does not understand the message or does not know what to ask.

3. *Receivers are reluctant to point out the sender's ignorance.* This is very common when the sender is a manager and the receiver is an employee. Employees often fear that asking a question suggests that the manager has done a poor job of preparing and sending the message. Or it suggests that the manager is wrong. Regardless of the reason, the result is the same: generally, employees don't ask questions when they do not understand.[38]

4. *Receivers have cultural barriers.* For example, in many Asian countries it is considered impolite to disagree with the manager, so the employee

would answer yes when asked by the manager if the message was understood.

After managers send a message and ask if there are questions, they then proceed to make another common error. Managers assume that no questions being asked means communication is complete, that there is mutual understanding of the message. In reality, the message is often misunderstood. When "this isn't what I asked for" happens, the task has to be done all over again. The end result is often wasted time, materials, and effort.

The most common cause of messages not resulting in communication is the lack of getting feedback that ensures mutual understanding. The proper use of questioning and paraphrasing can help you ensure that your messages are communicated.[39]

How to Get Feedback on Messages

Here are four guidelines you should use when getting feedback on messages. They are appropriate for managers and nonmanagers.

- *Be open to feedback.* There are no dumb questions. When someone asks a question, you need to be responsive, and patiently answer questions and explain things clearly. If people sense that you get upset if they ask questions, they will not ask questions.
- *Be aware of nonverbal communication.* Make sure that your nonverbal communications encourage feedback. For example, if you say, "I encourage questions," but when people ask questions you look at them as though they are stupid, or you are impatient, people will learn not to ask questions. You must also be aware of, and read, people's nonverbal communications. For example, if you are explaining a task to Larry and he has a puzzled look on his face, he is probably confused but may not be willing to say so. In such a case, you should stop and clarify things before going on.
- *Ask questions.* When you send messages, it is better to know whether the messages are understood before action is taken, so that the action will not have to be changed or repeated. Communicating is the responsibility of both the message sender and receiver. So you should ask questions to check understanding, rather than simply asking, "Do you have any questions?" Direct questions dealing with the specific information you have given will indicate if the receiver has been listening, and whether he or she understands enough to give a direct reply. If the response is not accurate, try repeating, giving more examples, or elaborating further on the message. You can also ask indirect questions to attain feedback. You can ask "how do you feel?" questions about the message. You can also ask "if you were me" questions, such as, "If you were me, how would you explain how to do it?" Or you can ask third-party questions, such as, "How will employees feel about this?" The response to indirect questions will often tell you other people's attitudes.
- *Use paraphrasing.* The most accurate indicator of understanding is paraphrasing. How you ask the receiver to paraphrase will affect his or her attitude. For example, if you say "Joan, tell me what I just said so that I can be sure you will not make a mistake as usual," would probably result in

defensive behavior on Joan's part. Joan would probably make a mistake. Here are two examples of proper requests for paraphrasing:

> *"Now tell me what you are going to do, so we will be sure that we are in agreement."*
> *"Would you tell me what you are going to do, so that I can be sure that I explained myself clearly?"*

Notice that the second statement takes the pressure off the employee. The sender is asking for a check on his or her ability, not that of the employee. These types of requests for paraphrasing should result in a positive attitude toward the message and the sender. They show concern for the employee and for communicating effectively.

360-Degree Multirater Feedback

So far, we have discussed the informal methods of getting feedback. We now turn to a formal evaluation process using 360-degree multirater feedback. The use of feedback from multiple sources has become popular as a means of improving performance.[40] Almost all of the Fortune 500 companies are using some type of multirater feedback instrument to evaluate their managers and key individual contributors.[41]

As the name implies, **360-degree feedback** *is based on receiving performance evaluations from many people.* Most 360-degree evaluation forms are completed by the person being evaluated, his or her manager, peers, and subordinates when applicable. Customers, suppliers, and other outside people are also used when applicable. See Exhibit 6-2 for an illustration of the 360-degree feedback process.

When the employee's final evaluation is based on multiple sources, it may be more objective than one completed only by the manager.[42] However, the manager may be the one who gives the final evaluation, or their evaluation may be given the most weight. If you are serious about getting ahead, it is critical for you to focus on the feedback from your manager and do what it takes to receive a good evaluation. Employees usually receive the results of their 360-degree evaluation from someone in the human resources department or from an external consultant, who often helps the person develop an action plan for improving performance. The manager also has input into the plan for improvement and works with the employee during the next evaluation period.

WorkApplication5

Recall a past or present manager. Did or does your manager use the common approach to getting feedback on messages regularly? Was or is he or she open to feedback and aware of nonverbal communication on a regular basis? Did the manager regularly ask questions and ask you to paraphrase?

_____

_____

_____

_____

_____

Exhibit 6-2 *360-degree feedback sources.*

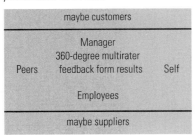

maybe customers		
	Manager	
	360-degree multirater	
Peers	feedback form results	Self
	Employees	
maybe suppliers		

---

2. How Do They Use Feedback at The Ranch?

OPENING CASE APPLICATION

Feedback is critical to success at The Ranch, as it is how the Clarks and the Willowbend managers know if the players are getting quality service and learn how to improve service. The Clarks, Willowbend managers, and employees are open to player criticism because they realize that the only way to improve is to listen and make changes to improve performance. In fact, Peter and Korby Clark spend much of their time at The Ranch talking to players about their experience, with the focus on listening for improvements. The Clarks and Willowbend managers set clear objectives and have regular meetings with employees to get and give feedback on how The Ranch is progressing toward meeting its objectives. Being a small business, The Ranch does not have a formal 360-degree feedback system. However, managers who evaluate employee performance do interact regularly with each employee, employee peers, the players, and other managers at The Ranch, and they use the feedback from others in their performance appraisals.

Coaching

Coaching is one of the most written- and talked-about leadership skills.[43] Coaching is based on feedback and communications: It involves giving feedback, which requires communication.[44] In this section we discuss coaching and leadership, how to give coaching feedback, and what criticism is—and why it doesn't work. We then present a coaching model you can use on the job, and end by briefly discussing mentoring, which may be considered a form of coaching.

Coaching and Leadership

Coaching *is the process of giving motivational feedback to maintain and improve performance.* Coaching is designed to maximize employee strengths and minimize weaknesses.[45] Coaching helps leaders concentrate on goals, develop resiliency, and build interpersonal savvy. One of its goals is to make life better for employees and the organization.[46] Managers from the management paradigm didn't see coaching in their job description. However, leaders from the leadership paradigm view developing effective followers as a key part of a leader's job.[47] As a means of improving performance, organizations are training their managers to be coaches, and this trend is expected to continue. Coaching boosts performance.[48]

Developing your coaching skills is an important part of your leadership development.[49] Whether you are a manager or not, you can be a leader and coach others, including your manager. Coaching is especially important when an employee is new to the job and organization.

How to Give Coaching Feedback

When people hear the word *coaching,* they often think of athletes, but managers should also be looking for steady performance and continual improvement. Athlete-coaching skills are being used successfully in the business world. If you have ever had a good coach, think about the behavior he or she used that helped to maintain and improve your performance and that of other team members. The next time you watch a sporting event, keep an eye on the coaches and learn some ways to coach employees.

We next discuss some guidelines that will help you to be an effective coach; the guidelines are also shown in Exhibit 6-3. The guidelines are designed primarily for use with employees who are doing a good job. As in the definition of coaching, the focus is on maintaining and continually improving performance. In the next section we present more specific guidelines and a coaching model for leading employees who are not performing as expected.

Develop a Supportive Working Relationship

Research has shown that the most important contributor to employee success and retention is their relationship with their manager. The relationship will be

Exhibit 6-3 *Coaching guidelines.*

1. Develop a supportive working relationship.
2. Give praise and recognition.
3. Avoid blame and embarrassment.
4. Focus on the behavior, not the person.
5. Have employees assess their own performance.
6. Give specific and descriptive feedback.
7. Give coaching feedback.
8. Provide modeling and training.
9. Make feedback timely, but flexible.
10. Don't criticize.

based on personality styles, and the manager and employee do not have to be friends and socialize together. People who are very different and don't really like each other personally can still have a good working relationship. Your relationship with followers needs to convey your concern for them as an individual and your commitment to coach them to success. A supportive working relationship can build enthusiasm and commitment to continual performance improvement.[50]

You should periodically ask employees if there is anything you could do to help them do a better job. Take the time to listen to them. There will seldom be big problems. Problems are often caused by petty annoyances that an employee believes are too trivial to bother the manager with. Your job as a manager is to run interference, to remove the stumbling blocks for the employees to improve their performance and that of the business unit.

Give Praise and Recognition

Why should you give recognition to employees for doing their job? The reason is simple: It motivates employees to maintain and increase performance. In Chapter 3 you learned the importance of giving praise, and how to use the giving praise model. We cannot overemphasize the importance of giving praise and recognition, and you cannot give too much of it. Recognition includes praise, awards, and recognition ceremonies. Awards include certificates of achievement, a letter of commendation, a pin, a plaque, a trophy, a medal, a ribbon, clothing, cash, trips, meals, employee of the month, and so on. Awards are symbolic acts of thanks for contributions to the success of the organization. Recognition ceremonies ensure that individual, team, and work-unit achievements are acknowledged by others in the organization. Most highly successful organizations celebrate their success in some way. Mary Kay owes much of the success of its cosmetics business to its elaborate recognition systems, with the ultimate award of the pink Cadillac. True leaders are always quick to give recognition to their followers.

Avoid Blame and Embarrassment

The objective of coaching is to develop employees' knowledge, abilities, and skills. Thus, any leadership behavior that focuses on making the person feel bad does not help to develop the employee.[51] Some things are best not said. For example, if an employee makes a mistake and realizes it, verbalizing it is not needed; doing so only makes them feel bad. Statements like, "I'm surprised that you did XYZ," or "I'm disappointed in you" should also be avoided. Besides, effective leaders treat mistakes as learning experiences.

Focus on the Behavior, not the Person

The purpose of coaching is to achieve desirable behavior, not to belittle the person. Let's use examples to illustrate the difference between coaching by focusing on changing behavior rather than by focusing on the person. Notice that the statements focusing on the person would be placing blame and embarrassment—or belittling the person.

- *Situation 1.* The employee is dominating the discussion at a meeting.
  Focus on person—You talk too much; give others a chance.

Focus on behavior—I'd like to hear what some of the other group members have to say.

- *Situation 2.* The employee is late for a meeting again.
  Focus on person—You are always late for meetings; why can't you be on time like the rest of us?
  Focus on behavior—This is the second time in a row that you arrived late for our meeting. The group needs your input right from the start of the meeting.

Have Employees Assess Their Own Performance

Here are some examples of criticism and self-evaluation coaching feedback to help explain the difference.[52]

- *Situation 3.* The employee has been making more errors lately.
  Criticism—You haven't been working up to par lately; get on the ball.
  Self-evaluation—How would you assess the amount of errors you have been making this week?
- *Situation 4.* The employee is working on a few reports, and one is due in two days. The manager believes the employee may not meet the deadline.
  Criticism—Are you going to meet the deadline for the report?
  Self-evaluation—How are you progressing on the cost-cutting report that's due this Thursday? Is there something I can do to help?

Can the criticism statements result in defensive behavior, not listening, feeling bad about oneself, and disliking the task and the manager? Do the self-evaluation statements create different feelings and behavior?

Give Specific and Descriptive Feedback

Specific feedback is needed to avoid confusion over which particular behavior needs to be improved.[53] Compare the preceding criticism statements, which are not specific, to the self-evaluation statements, which are specific. Can you understand how the person being criticized may not understand specifically what the manager is talking about, so may be unable to change even if they are willing to do so?

Descriptive feedback can be based on *facts* or *inferences*. Facts can be observed and proven; inferences cannot. In situation 3, the manager can observe and prove that the employee made more errors this week than in prior weeks. However, the manager cannot observe or prove why. The manager may infer many reasons for the changed behavior, such as laziness, illness, a personal problem, and so on. In situation 4, the manager cannot prove that the report will be late; the manager is inferring that it will be and attempting to coach the employee to make sure it is completed on time. Give factual rather than inferential feedback, because factual tends to be positive, while inferential tends to be more negative criticism.

Give Coaching Feedback

Self-assessment can work well, especially when performance needs to be maintained rather than improved.[54] However, it is not always appropriate; if overused, it can have limited success. There are often times when you will want to

WorkApplication6

Recall the best and worst manager you ever had. With which manager did you have the best working relationship? Which one gave you the most encouragement, praise, and recognition for a job well done? Which one gave you the most negative criticism? Was your performance at a higher level for your best or worst manager?

_____

_____

_____

_____

_____

offer coaching feedback without self-assessment. It is important to respond positively to negative behavior and outcomes, and the way to do this is not by pointing out mistakes but by selling the benefits of positive behavior.[55] Here are some examples of how to coach versus criticize.

- *Situation 5.* The manager just saw an employee, who knows how it should be done, incorrectly pick up a fairly heavy box.
  Criticism—You just picked up the box wrong. Don't let me catch you again.
  Coaching feedback—If you don't want to injure your back, use your legs—not your back.
- *Situation 6.* A student sees a fellow student going to the Yahoo! website by typing in the entire address, **http://www.yahoo.com.**
  Criticism—You just wasted time typing in the entire Yahoo! website address. Don't use the entire address, or make it a favorite address.
  Coaching feedback—Would you like me to show you a faster way to get to the Yahoo! home page?
- *Situation 7.* A worker is completing a task by following an inefficient, step-by-step procedure.
  Criticism—You're not doing that the best way. Do X, Y, then Z from now on.
  Coaching feedback—Have you given any thought to changing the sequence of steps for completing that task to X, Y, then Z?

Provide Modeling and Training

A good manager leads by example. If employees see the manager doing things in an effective manner, they will tend to copy the manager. As illustrated in situations 4 and 5, coaching often requires some training. Failing to train and coach new employees is failing to lead. The job instructional training method is widely used (see Model 6-2). *The* **job instructional training** (JIT) *steps include* (1) *trainee receives preparation;* (2) *trainer presents the task;* (3) *trainee performs the task; and* (4) *trainer follows up.* Remember that tasks we know well seem very simple, but they are usually difficult for the new trainee. You can also use coleadership and have others do the training, especially if they are better at training than you are.

step 1. **Trainee receives preparation.** Put the trainee at ease as you create interest in the job and encourage questions. Explain the quantity and quality requirements and why they are important.

step 2. **Trainer presents the task.** Perform the task yourself at a slow pace, explaining each step several times. Once the trainee seems to have the steps memorized, have the trainee explain each step as you

Model 6-2 *Job instructional training steps.*

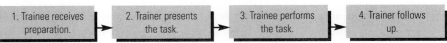

| 1. Trainee receives preparation. | 2. Trainer presents the task. | 3. Trainee performs the task. | 4. Trainer follows up. |

slowly perform the task again. For complex tasks with multiple steps, it is helpful to write them out and to give a copy to the trainee.

step 3. **Trainee performs task.** Have the trainee perform the task at a slow pace, while explaining each step to the trainer. Correct any errors and be patiently willing to help the trainee perform any difficult steps. Continue until the trainee is proficient at performing the task.

step 4. **Trainer follows up.** Tell the trainee who to ask for help with any questions or problems. Gradually leave the trainee alone. Begin by checking quality and quantity frequently, and decrease checks based on the trainee's skill level. Observe the trainee performing the task, and be sure to correct any errors or faulty work procedures before they become a habit. As you follow up, be sure to be patient and encouraging. Praise a good effort, at first, and good performance as skills develop.

Make Feedback Timely, but Flexible

Feedback should be given *as soon as possible* after the behavior has been observed. For example, in situation 5 you would want to give the coaching feedback as soon as you saw the employee lift the box incorrectly. To tell the employee about it a few days later would have less impact on changing the behavior, and the employee could be injured by then. The *flexibility* part comes into play (1) when you don't have the time to do the full coaching job, and (2) when emotions are high. For example, if you were late for an important meeting and wanted to sit down with the employee to fully discuss the problem of lifting incorrectly, a later date could be set. If you were really angry and yelled at the employee and the employee yelled back, it is usually a good idea to make an appointment to discuss it later when emotions have calmed, to rationally discuss the matter using coaching feedback. Besides, yelling rarely works; it is a form of criticism. Even if you yelled in anger while following every other coaching guideline, it would be criticism.

Remember that everyone can be a coach. Coaches can be effective by following simple guidelines, presented here. So don't criticize, start coaching—today. These general guidelines apply to any leadership situation, such as being a parent or guardian. Next we focus on how to coach the employee who is performing below expected standards.

Don't Criticize

Jack Falvey, management consultant and author, takes the positive versus negative feedback to the point of recommending only positive feedback:

> *Criticism is to be avoided at all costs (there is no such thing as constructive criticism; all criticism is destructive). If you must correct someone, never do it after the fact. Bite your tongue and hold off until the person is about to do the same thing again and then challenge the person to make a more positive contribution.*[56]

What Is Criticism and Why Doesn't It Work?

Falvey's statement may seem a bit extreme, but it is true. Placing blame and embarrassment and focusing on the person are types of criticism. Criticism is

WorkApplication7

Recall a present or past manager. Which of the 10 guidelines does or did the manager use most frequently and least frequently?

_____

_____

_____

_____

_____

rarely effective. Criticism involves a judgment, which is that either the person is right or wrong. Criticism is also the process of pointing out mistakes, which places blame and is embarrassing.[57] Once you tell a person they are wrong or made a mistake, directly or indirectly, four things usually happen: (1) They become defensive and justify their behavior, or they blame it on someone or something. (2) They don't really listen to so-called constructive feedback. (3) They are embarrassed and feel bad about themselves, or they view themselves as losers. (4) They begin to dislike the task or job, as well as the critic. The more criticism employees receive, the more defensive they become. They listen less, they are in conflict as their self-concept is threatened or diminishes, they eventually hate the task or job and usually the critic, and they often quit the job, get a transfer, or are fired. Giving praise has an opposite, positive effect on employees, their behavior, and their performance.

The Sandwich Approach to Criticism, and Why It Doesn't Work

The sandwich approach offers both praise and criticism at the same time, to help offset the negative. But, if your manager tells you five good things about how you are doing and one bad thing, which do you remember? What we remember depends on what we believe, and employees rely on misinformation even when shown to be wrong.[58]

Demotivating

Employees with overly critical managers tend to develop the attitude of, "My manager doesn't care about me or appreciate my work, so why should I work hard to do a good job?" They play it safe by doing the minimum, taking no

---

Applying the Concept 2

Criticism or Coaching Feedback

Identify each of these five statements as criticism or coaching feedback. For each criticism only, write a coaching feedback statement to replace it.

a. criticism   b. coaching feedback

____11. You just dropped it on the floor.

_____

____12. This is still dirty. You are going to have to clean it again.

_____

____13. I couldn't help overhearing your conflict with Jack. Would you like me to tell you how you can minimize this problem in the future?

_____

____14. You are a poor speller. Make sure you don't forget to use the spell check before you pass in your work.

_____

____15. *In a loud, angry voice:* Let me help you with that.

_____

risk, focusing on not making errors, and covering up any errors so they aren't criticized.[59] They avoid contact with the manager and they feel stress just seeing the manager approach them. They think, "What did I do this time?"[60]

--- **Learning** Outcome 5 ---

Describe the difference between criticism and coaching feedback.

The Difference between Criticism and Coaching Feedback

By now you probably agree that criticism usually does not work; in fact, it often makes the behavior worse.[61] But you may be thinking that you can't always catch an employee in the act and challenge them to perform better. What do you do? The major difference between criticism and coaching feedback is that **coaching feedback** *is based on a good, supportive relationship; it is specific and descriptive; and it is not judgmental criticism.* And coaching is often based on the employee doing a self-assessment of performance. Criticism makes employees feel like losers; praise and coaching feedback makes them feel like winners. And nothing breeds success like good coaches. Before getting into how to give coaching feedback, with examples of criticism and coaching praise, we discuss its components.

--- **Learning** Outcome 6 ---

Discuss the relationship between the performance formula and the coaching model.

The Coaching Model for Employees
Who Are Performing Below Standard

When managers are giving feedback to employees who are performing below standard, all 10 of the coaching guidelines are important. However, most managers are more apt to use embarrassment, to focus on the person, and to criticize the person who is performing below standard than the person who is doing a good job. Avoid this temptation, because it doesn't really work. Don't exclude poor performers and develop negative relationships with them. They need your one-on-one coaching, at its best. Be patient but persistent; don't give up on them. Before getting into the coaching model, let's discuss attribution theory and the performance formula because they affect the coaching model.

Attribution Theory

Attribution theory *is used to explain the process managers go through in determining the reasons for effective or ineffective performance and deciding what to do about it.* The reaction of a manager to poor performance has two stages. First, the manager tries to determine the cause of the poor performance, and then he or she selects an appropriate corrective action. To help you determine the cause of poor performance, we provide you with the performance formula; and to take corrective action, the coaching model.

Managers tend to attribute the cause of poor performance by certain employees to internal reasons (ability and/or motivation) within their control, and poor performance by other employees to external reasons (resources) beyond their control. Managers are less critical of those employees whose poor performance is attributed to external reasons beyond their control. Effective leaders try to avoid this problem. (Chapter 7 examines these "in-group" and "out-group" relationships in depth.)

Determining the Cause of Poor Performance and Corrective Coaching Action

The **performance formula** *explains performance as a function of ability, motivation, and resources.* Model 6-3 is a simple model that can help you determine the cause of poor performance and the corrective action to take based on the cause. When ability, motivation, or resources are low, performance will be lower.

When the employee's *ability* is the reason for keeping performance from being optimal, the corrective coaching action is training (JIT). When *motivation* is lacking, motivational techniques (discussed in Chapter 3) such as giving praise might help. Coach the employee, and work together to develop a plan to improve performance. When *resources* (tools, material, equipment, information, others did not do their part, bad luck or timing, and so on) are the problem, you need to get the resources. When obstacles are getting in the way of performance, you need to overcome them.

Improving Performance with the Coaching Model

The steps in the coaching model are (1) describe current performance; (2) describe desired performance; (3) get a commitment to the change; and (4) follow up. Again, use all 10 guidelines to coaching within the framework of the coaching model.

step 1. **Describe current performance.** In detail, using specific examples, describe the current behavior that needs to be changed.[51]

For example, for an ability or motivation problem, say something like, "There is a way to lift boxes that will decrease your chances of getting injured."

step 2. **Describe desired performance.** Tell the employee exactly what the desired performance is, in detail. If *ability* is the reason for poor performance, modeling and training the employee with JIT are very appropriate. If the employee knows the proper way, the reason for poor performance is *motivational*. Demonstration is not needed; just describe desired performance as you ask the employee to state why the performance is important.

For example, *Ability*—"If you squat down and pick up the box using your legs instead of your back, it is easier and there is less chance of injuring yourself. Let me demonstrate for you." *Motivation*—"Why should you squat and use your legs rather than your back to pick up boxes?"

step 3. **Get a commitment to the change.** When dealing with an *ability* performance issue, it is not necessary to get employees to verbally commit to the change if they seem willing to make it. However, if employees defend their way, and you're sure it's not as effective, explain why your

---

Model 6-3 *The performance formula.*

Performance (f)*
Ability, Motivation, and Resources

*(f) = is a function of

proposed way is better. If you cannot get the employee to understand and agree based on rational persuasion, get a verbal commitment through coercive power, such as a threat of discipline. Also, for *motivation* performance issues, this is important because, if the employee is not willing to commit to the change, he or she will most likely not make the change.

For example, *Ability*—the employee will most likely be willing to do it correctly, so skip the step. *Motivation*—"Will you squat rather than use your back from now on?"

step 4. **Follow up.** Remember, some employees do what managers inspect, not what they expect. You should follow up to ensure that the employee is behaving as desired.

When you are dealing with an *ability* performance issue, and the person was receptive and you skipped step 3, say nothing. But watch to be sure the task is done correctly in the future. Coach again, if necessary. For a *motivation* problem, make a statement that you will follow up, and describe possible consequences for repeat performance.

For example, *Ability*—say nothing, but observe. *Motivation*—"Picking up boxes with your back is dangerous; if I catch you doing it again, I will take disciplinary action." See Model 6-4 for a review of the steps in the coaching model.

Mentoring

Mentoring *is a form of coaching in which a more-experienced manager helps a less-experienced protégé.* Thus, the 10 tips for coaching apply to mentoring. However, mentoring includes more than coaching, and it is more involved and personal than coaching. The formal mentor is usually at a higher level of management and is not the protégé's immediate manager. Family, friends, and peers can also be mentors. The primary responsibility is to coach the protégé by providing good, sound career advice and to help develop leadership skills necessary for a successful management career.[62] However, the protégé should not try to become just like the mentor; we all need to learn from others yet we need to be ourselves to be effective.[63]

Research studies have found that mentoring results in more career advancement and job satisfaction for the protégé.[64] Based on success of mentoring, many organizations—including the IRS, Hewlett-Packard, and IBM—have formal mentoring programs, while others have informal mentoring.

We all need mentors, so don't wait for someone to ask you. Seek out a mentor.[65] If your organization has a formal mentoring program, try to sign up for it. If it is informal, ask around about getting a mentor, and remember that a mentor can be from another organization. Whenever you have job- or career-related questions and would like advice, contact your mentor.

WorkApplication8

Recall a person who is or was a mentor to you. Briefly describe the relationship and type of advice you got from your mentor.

_____

_____

_____

_____

_____

Model 6-4 *Coaching model.*

| 1. Describe current performance. | 2. Describe desired performance. | 3. Get a commitment to the change. | 4. Follow up. |

3. Is There a Difference in Managing an Oil Change Business, a Golf Course, and a Sports Team, and How Does Peter Clark Use Coaching at The Ranch?

Peter Clark says there are more similarities than differences in running a Jiffy Lube business and a golf club and coaching sports. The focus is the same—high-quality service. You have to treat the customer or player right. Clark uses the same 3 I's coaching philosophy for all three: You need Intensity to be prepared to do the job right, Integrity to do the right thing when no one is watching, and Intimacy to be a team player. If one person does not do the job right, everyone is negatively affected. In business and sports, you need to strive to be the best. You need to set and meet challenging goals.

Clark strongly believes in being positive and the need to develop a supportive working relationship, which includes sitting down to talk and really listen to the other person. He also strongly believes in the need for good training. Employees at The Ranch give high-quality service because they are thoroughly trained to do so, and they are continually coached to maintain and improve performance. Although The Ranch does not have a formal mentoring program, Clark clearly sees mentoring as an important role he plays at The Ranch.

Managing Conflict

There is no problem more central to human relations than conflict,[66] and conflict is increasing in organizations.[67] A **conflict** *exists whenever people are in disagreement and opposition.* In the workplace, conflict is inevitable because people don't see things exactly the same way, nor should they.[68] An organization's success is based on how well it deals with conflicts.[69] In this section we discuss the psychological contract, conflict and leadership, and present five conflict management styles you can use to resolve conflicts.

The Psychological Contract

All human relations rely on the psychological contract.[70] The *psychological contract* is the unwritten implicit expectations of each party in a relationship. At work, you have a set of expectations of what you will contribute to the organization (effort, time, skills) and what it will provide to you (compensation, job satisfaction, etc.). We are often not aware of our expectations until they have not been met (for example, how you are treated by your manager).[71]

Conflict Arises by Breaking the Psychological Contract

The psychological contract is broken for two primary reasons: (1) We fail to make explicit our own expectations and fail to inquire into the expectations of the other parties. (2) We further assume that the other party(ies) has the same expectations that we hold. So as long as people meet our expectations, everything is fine, but when they don't meet our expectations, we are in conflict. Thus, it is important to share information and negotiate expectations assertively.[72] After all, how can you expect others to meet your expectations when they don't know what they are?

Conflict and Leadership

Many leaders are constantly exposed to conflict.[73] Research suggest that managers devote approximately one-fifth of their time to handling conflict. Thus, handling conflict constructively is an important leadership skill.[74] Your ability to resolve conflicts will have a direct effect on your leadership success. With the trend toward teamwork, conflict skills are increasingly important to team decision making.[75] In the global economy, you need to be sensitive to cultural differences so that you don't create additional conflicts based on diversity.[76]

Conflict Can Be Dysfunctional or Functional

Conflict is an inherent part of organizational activity. People often think of conflict as fighting and view it as disruptive. When conflict is not resolved effectively, negative consequences occur.[77] When conflict prevents the achievement of organizational objectives, it is negative or *dysfunctional conflict*. However, it can be positive. *Functional conflict* exists when disagreement and opposition supports the achievement of organizational objectives. Functional conflict increases the quality of group decisions and leads to innovative changes. The question today is not whether conflict is negative or positive, but how to manage conflict to benefit the organization.

Conflict Can Be Problem- or Relationship-Oriented

The appropriate action to resolve a conflict depends on the type of conflict. Problem-oriented conflict resolution focuses on finding a mutually satisfactory solution to the conflict problem. Relationship-oriented conflict resolution focuses on reducing hostility and distrust. However, as discussed with coaching, you need to focus on the behavior, not the person; and you need good communication skills and feedback to resolve conflicts effectively.

--- Learning Outcome 7 ---

Define the five conflict management styles.

Conflict Management Styles

Conflict management skills can be developed with appropriate training. In this discussion, we focus more on resolving conflicts in your own personal and professional lives and less on mediating conflicts between others.

When you are in conflict, you have five conflict management styles to choose from. The five styles are based on two dimensions of concern: concern for others' needs and concern for your own needs. These concerns result in three types of behavior:

- A low concern for your own needs and a high concern for others' needs results in passive behavior.
- A high concern for your own needs and a low concern for others' needs results in aggressive behavior.
- A moderate or high concern for your own needs and others' needs results in assertive behavior.

Exhibit 6-4 *Conflict management styles.*

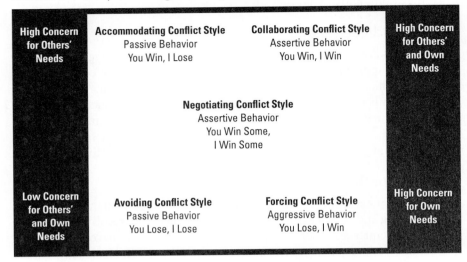

Each conflict style behavior results in a different combination of win-lose situations. The five styles, along with concern for needs and win-lose combinations, are presented in Exhibit 6-4 and discussed here in order of passive, aggressive, and assertive behavior. The conflict style that you tend to use the most is based on your personality and leadership style. There is no one best conflict management style for all situations; in this section you will learn the advantages and disadvantages and the appropriate use of each conflict management style.

Avoiding Conflict Style

The *avoiding conflict style* user attempts to passively ignore the conflict rather than resolve it.[78] When you avoid a conflict, you are being unassertive and uncooperative. People avoid conflict by refusing to take a stance, or escape conflict by mentally withdrawing and physically leaving.[79] A lose-lose situation is created because the conflict is not resolved.

Advantages and Disadvantages of the Avoiding Conflict Style
The advantage of the avoiding style is that it may maintain relationships that would be hurt through conflict resolution. The disadvantage of this style is that conflicts do not get resolved.[80] An overuse of this style leads to conflict within the individual. People tend to walk all over the avoider. Some managers allow employees to break rules without confronting them. Avoiding problems usually does not make them go away; the problems usually get worse. And the longer you wait to confront others, the more difficult the confrontation usually is.[81]

Appropriate Use of the Avoiding Conflict Style
The avoiding style is appropriate to use when: (1) the conflict is trivial; (2) your stake in the issue is not high; (3) confrontation will damage an important relationship; (4) you don't have time to resolve the conflict; or (5) emotions are high. When you don't have time to resolve the conflict or people are emotional, you should confront the person(s) later. However, it is inappropriate to repeatedly avoid confrontation until you get so upset that you end up yelling at the

other person(s). This passive-aggressive behavior tends to make the situation worse by hurting human relations. Often people do not realize they are doing something that bothers you (that you are in conflict), and when approached properly, they are willing to change.

Accommodating Conflict Style

The *accommodating conflict style* user attempts to resolve the conflict by passively giving in to the other party. When you use the accommodating style, you are being unassertive but cooperative. You attempt to satisfy the other party, neglecting your own needs by letting others get their own way. A win-lose situation is created, as you try to please everyone.[82]

Differences between the Avoiding and Accommodating Styles

A common difference between the avoiding and accommodating styles is based on behavior. With the avoiding style, you don't have to do anything you really did not want to do; with the accommodating style, you do. For example, if you are talking to someone who makes a statement that you disagree with, to avoid a conflict you can say nothing, change the subject, or stop the conversation. However, suppose you have to put up a display with someone who says, "Let's put up the display this way." If you don't want to do it the other person's way, but say nothing and put it up the other person's way, you have done something you really did not want to do.

Advantages and Disadvantages of the Accommodating Conflict Style

The advantage of the accommodating style is that relationships are maintained by doing things the other person's way. The disadvantage is that giving in may be counterproductive. The accommodating person may have a better solution, such as a better way to put up a display. An overuse of this style tends to lead to people taking advantage of the accommodator, and the type of relationship the accommodator tries to maintain is usually lost.

Appropriate Use of the Accommodating Conflict Style

The accommodating style is appropriate when (1) the person enjoys being a follower; (2) maintaining the relationship outweighs all other considerations; (3) the changes agreed to are not important to the accommodator, but are to the other party; or (4) the time to resolve the conflict is limited. This is often the only style that can be used with an autocratic manager who uses the forcing style.

Forcing Conflict Style

The *forcing conflict style* user attempts to resolve the conflict by using aggressive behavior to get their own way.[83] When you use the forcing style, you are uncooperative and aggressive, doing whatever it takes to satisfy your own needs—at the expense of others, if necessary. Forcers use authority, threaten, intimidate, and call for majority rule when they know they will win. Forcers commonly enjoy dealing with avoiders and accommodators. If you try to get others to change without being willing to change yourself, regardless of the means, then you use the forcing style. A win-lose situation is created.

Advantages and Disadvantages of the Forcing Style

The advantage of the forcing style is that better organizational decisions will be made, when the forcer is correct, rather than less-effective compromised decisions. The disadvantage is that overuse of this style leads to hostility and resentment toward its user. Forcers tend to have poor human relations.

Appropriate Use of the Forcing Style

Some managers commonly use their position power to force others to do what they want them to do. The forcing style is appropriate to use when (1) unpopular action must be taken on important issues; (2) commitment by others to proposed action is not crucial to its implementation—in other words, people will not resist doing what you want them to do; (3) maintaining relationships is not critical; or (4) the conflict resolution is urgent.

Negotiating Conflict Style

The *negotiating conflict style* user attempts to resolve the conflict through assertive, give-and-take concessions. This is also called the *compromising style*. When you use the compromising approach, you are moderate in assertiveness and cooperation. An "I win some, you win some" situation is created through compromise. As discussed in Chapter 4, negotiation skills are important to both your personal and your professional life.[84]

Advantages and Disadvantages of the Negotiating Conflict Style

The advantage of the compromise style is that the conflict is resolved relatively quickly, and working relationships are maintained. The disadvantage is that the compromise often leads to counterproductive results, such as suboptimum decisions. An overuse of this style leads to people playing games such as asking for twice as much as they need in order to get what they want. It is commonly used during management and labor collective bargaining.

Appropriate Use of the Negotiating Conflict Style

The compromise style is appropriate to use when (1) the issues are complex and critical, and there is no simple and clear solution; (2) parties have about equal power and are interested in different solutions; (3) a solution will be only temporary; or (4) time is short.

Collaborating Conflict Style

The *collaborating conflict style* user assertively attempts to jointly resolve the conflict with the best solution agreeable to all parties. It is also called the *problem-solving style*. When you use the collaborating approach, you are being assertive and cooperative. Although avoiders and accommodators are concerned about others' needs, and forcers are concerned about their own needs, the collaborator is concerned about finding the best solution to the problem that is satisfactory to all parties. Alan Greenspan said, "I have found no greater satisfaction than achieving success through honest dealing and strict adherence to the view that, for you to gain, those you deal with should gain as well."[85] Unlike the forcer, the collaborator is willing to change if a better solution is presented. While negotiating is often based on secret information, collaboration is based on open and honest communication.[86] This is the only style that creates a true win-win situation.

Differences between the Negotiating and Collaborating Styles

A common difference between negotiating and collaborating is the solution. Let's continue with the example of putting up a display. With negotiation, the two people may trade off by putting up one display one person's way and the next display the other person's way. This way they each win and lose. With collaboration, the two people work together to develop one display method that they both like. It may be a combination of both, or simply one person's if after an explanation, the other person really agrees that the method is better. The key to collaboration is agreeing that the solution is the best possible one.

Advantages and Disadvantages of the Collaborating Style

The advantage of the collaborating style is that it tends to lead to the best solution to the conflict, using assertive behavior. The disadvantage is that the skill, effort, and time it takes to resolve the conflict are usually greater and longer than the other styles. There are situations, mentioned under "Negotiating Conflict Style," when collaboration is difficult, and when a forcer prevents its use. The collaborating style offers the most benefit to the individual, group, and organization.

WorkApplication9

1. Select a present or past manager. Which conflict management style did that manager use most often? Explain by giving a typical example.
2. Which one of the five conflict management styles do you tend to use most often? Explain your answer.

_____

_____

_____

_____

_____

Selecting Conflict Management Styles

For each of these five conflict situations, identify the most appropriate conflict management style. Write the appropriate letter in the blank before each item.

a. avoiding b. accommodating c. forcing d. negotiating e. collaborating

_____ 16. You have joined a committee in order to meet people. Your interest in what the committee does is low. While serving on the committee, you make a recommendation that is opposed by another member. You realize that you have the better idea. The other party is using a forcing style.

_____ 17. You are on a task force that has to select a new computer. The four alternatives will all do the job. It's the brand, price, and service that people disagree on.

_____ 18. You are a sales manager. Beth, one of your competent salespeople, is trying to close a big sale. The two of you are discussing the next sales call she will make. You disagree on the strategy to use to close the sale.

_____ 19. You're late and on your way to an important meeting. As you leave your office, at the other end of the work area you see Chris, one of your employees, goofing off instead of working.

_____ 20. You're over budget for labor this month. It's slow, so you ask Kent, a part-time employee, to leave work early. Kent tells you he doesn't want to go because he needs the money.

Applying the Concept 3

Appropriate Use of the Collaborating Conflict Style

The collaborating style is appropriate when (1) you are dealing with an important issue that requires an optimal solution, and compromise would result in suboptimizing; (2) people are willing to place the group goal before self-interest, and members will truly collaborate; (3) maintaining relationships is important; (4) time is available; and (5) it is a peer conflict. Remember, there is no one right way to do anything; be innovative.[87]

Of the five styles, the most difficult to implement successfully, due to the complexity and level of skill needed, is the collaborative style. It is most likely to be underutilized when it would have been appropriate. Organizations around the globe are training employees to resolve conflicts using collaboration. Therefore, in order to develop your conflict skills, the collaborative style is the only one that we cover in detail, in the next section. You learned how to negotiate in Chapter 4.

OPENING CASE APPLICATION

4. Which Conflict Management Style Does Peter Clark Tend to Use at The Ranch?

At The Ranch, with three partners and a management company, conflict is inevitable. Peter Clark prefers to use the collaborating conflict style, which goes back to the importance he places on open communications and a good supportive working relationship, to sit down and work through problem issues together and agree on solutions. He believes that when you have a conflict problem, ignoring it using the avoiding conflict style usually does not solve the problem. When Clark is in conflict with the Willowbend managers, he does not like to simply accommodate when he does not agree with what they want to do, but he has accommodated, such as in the case of building a waterfall on the course. Clark does not like to use the forcing conflict style, but there are times when he says no to Willowbend managers, such as operating an expensive waterfall on the course—he stopped it based on his guiding question: Will spending the money clearly improve player satisfaction enough to pay for itself? Having a waterfall is attractive, but it will not be a deciding factor in playing golf at The Ranch. Clark also has to negotiate the management contract with Willowbend.

Collaborating Conflict Management Style Models

Effective leaders encourage conflict resolution and build collaboration throughout the organization.[88] They challenge all of us to learn to get along with each other. Although you can help prevent conflict, you will not eliminate it completely—nor should you try to, because it can be functional.[89] You will develop your skill to assertively confront (or be confronted by) people you are in conflict with, in a manner that resolves the conflict without damaging interpersonal relationships. The model of conflict management can be used to develop conflict skills. We provide a model with the steps you can follow when initiating, responding to, and mediating a conflict resolution. The same steps for resolving conflict effectively are applicable to coworkers, people we live with, and international political situations.

———————————— Learning Outcome 8 ————————————

List the steps in the initiating conflict resolution model.

Initiating Conflict Resolution

An initiator is the person who confronts the other person(s) to resolve the conflict. Confronting others you are in conflict with is usually the better solution to conflict, rather than avoiding or accommodating.[90] When initiating a conflict resolution using the collaborating style, use the following model: *The* **initiating conflict resolution model** *steps are (1) plan a BCF statement that maintains ownership of the problem; (2) present your BCF statement and agree on the conflict; (3) ask for, and/or give, alternative conflict resolutions; and (4) make an agreement for change.* This model is part of behavior modeling, which is an effective training method to develop your conflict resolution leadership skills.

| step 1. | **Plan a BCF statement that maintains ownership of the problem.** Planning is the starting management function and the starting point of initiating a conflict resolution. Let's begin by stating what *maintains ownership of the problem* means. Assume you don't smoke, and someone |

visits you while smoking. Is it you or the smoker who has a problem? The smoke bothers you, not the smoker. It's your problem. Open the confrontation with a request for the respondent to help you solve your problem. This approach reduces defensiveness and establishes an atmosphere of problem solving that will maintain the relationship.

The **BCF model** *describes a conflict in terms of behavior, consequences, and feelings.* When you do B (behavior), C (consequences) happens, and I feel F (feelings). For example, when you smoke in my room (behavior), I have trouble breathing and become nauseous (consequence), and I feel uncomfortable and irritated (feeling). You can vary the sequence by starting with a feeling or consequence to fit the situation and to provide variety. For example, I fear (feeling) that the advertisement is not going to work (behavior), and that we will lose money (consequences).

When developing your opening BCF statement, as shown in the examples just given, be descriptive, not evaluative. Keep the opening statement short. The longer the statement, the longer it will take to resolve the conflict. People get defensive when kept waiting for their turn to talk. Avoid trying to determine who is to blame for something or who is right and wrong. Both parties are usually partly to blame or correct. Fixing blame or correctness only gets people defensive, which is counterproductive to conflict resolution. Timing is also important. If others are busy, see them later to discuss the conflict. In addition, don't confront a person on several unrelated issues at once.

After planning your BCF statement, you should practice saying it before confronting the other party. In addition, think of some possible alternatives you can offer to resolve the conflict. However, be sure your ideas show high concern for others rather than just for yourself; create a win-win situation. Try to put yourself in the other person's position. If you were the other person, would you like the ideas presented by the confronter?

| step 2. | **Present your BCF statement and agree on the conflict.** After making your short, planned BCF statement, let the other party respond. If the other party does not understand or avoids acknowledgment of |

the problem, persist. You cannot resolve a conflict if the other party will not even acknowledge its existence. Repeat your planned statement several times by explaining it in different terms until you get an acknowledgment or realize it's hopeless. But don't give up too easily. If you cannot agree on a conflict, you may have to change your approach and use one of the other four conflict management styles.

step 3.   **Ask for, and/or give, alternative conflict resolutions.** Begin by asking the other party what can be done to resolve the conflict. If you agree, great; if not, offer your resolution. However, remember that you are collaborating, not simply trying to change others. When the other party acknowledges the problem, but is not responsive to resolving it, appeal to common goals. Make the other party realize the benefits to him or her and the organization as well.

step 4.   **Make an agreement for change.** Try to come to an agreement on specific action you will both take to resolve the conflict. Clearly state— or better yet for complex change, write down—the specific behavior changes necessary by all parties to resolve the conflict. Again, remember that you are collaborating, not forcing. The steps are also listed in Model 6-5.

Responding to Conflict Resolution

As the responder, an initiator has confronted you.[91] Here's how to handle the role of the responder to a conflict. Most initiators do not follow the model. Therefore, the responder must take responsibility for successful conflict resolution by following the conflict resolution model steps:

1. Listen to and paraphrase the conflict using the BCF model.
2. Agree with some aspect of the complaint.
3. Ask for, and/or give, alternative conflict resolutions.
4. Make an agreement for change.

The steps are also listed in Model 6-5.

Mediating Conflict Resolution

Frequently, conflicting parties cannot resolve their dispute alone. In these cases, a mediator should be used.[92] A **mediator** *is a neutral third party who helps*

WorkApplication10

Use the BCF model to describe a conflict you face or have faced on the job.

_____

_____

_____

_____

_____

Model 6–5 *The collaborating conflict style.*

Initiating Conflict Resolution	Responding to Conflict Resolution	Mediating Conflict Resolution
Step 1. Plan a BCF statement that maintains ownership of the problem.	Step 1. Listen to and paraphrase the conflict using the BCF model.	Step 1. Have each party state his or her complaint using the BCF model.
Step 2. Present your BCF statement and agree on the conflict.	Step 2. Agree with some aspect of the complaint.	Step 2. Agree on the conflict problem(s).
Step 3. Ask for, and/or give, alternative conflict resolutions.	Step 3. Ask for, and/or give, alternative conflict resolutions.	Step 3. Develop alternative conflict resolutions.
Step 4. Make an agreement for change.	Step 4. Make an agreement for change.	Step 4. Make an agreement for change.
		Step 5. Follow up to make sure the conflict is resolved.

resolve a conflict. In nonunionized organizations, managers are commonly the mediators. But some organizations have trained and designated employees as mediators. In unionized organizations, the mediator is usually a professional from outside the organization. However, a conflict resolution should be sought internally first.[93]

Before bringing the conflicting parties together, the mediator should decide whether to start with a joint meeting or conduct individual meetings. If one employee comes to complain, but has not confronted the other party, or if there is a serious discrepancy in employee perceptions, meet one-on-one with each party before bringing them together. On the other hand, when both parties have a similar awareness of the problem and motivation to solve it, you can begin with a joint meeting when all parties are calm. The manager should be a mediator, not a judge. Get the employees to resolve the conflict, if possible. Remain impartial, unless one party is violating company policies. Do a good job of coaching.[94] Avoid blame and embarrassment. Don't make comments such as, "I'm disappointed in you two," or "you're acting like babies."

When bringing conflicting parties together, follow the mediating conflict model steps. These steps are listed in Model 6-5.

If either party blames the other, make a statement such as, "We are here to resolve the conflict; placing blame is not productive." Focus on how the conflict is affecting their work. Discuss the issues by addressing specific behavior, not personalities. If a person says, "We cannot work together because of a personality conflict," ask the parties to state the specific behavior that is bothering them. The discussion should make the parties aware of their behavior and the consequences of their behavior. The mediator may ask questions or make statements to clarify what is being said. The mediator should develop one problem statement that is agreeable to all parties, if possible.[95]

If the conflict has not been resolved, an arbitrator may be used. *An* **arbitrator** *is a neutral third party who makes a binding decision to resolve a conflict*. The arbitrator is like a judge, and their decision must be followed. However, the use of arbitration should be kept to a minimum because it is not a collaborative conflict style. Arbitrators commonly use a negotiating style in which each party wins some and loses some. Mediation and then arbitration tends to be used in management–labor negotiations, when collective bargaining breaks down and the contract deadline is near.[96]

OPENING CASE APPLICATION

5. What Types of Conflict Resolutions Do the Clarks Deal with at The Ranch?

At The Ranch, Peter Clark more often responds to conflict than initiating conflict resolutions since, when problems arise, he is asked for solutions or to approve actions. Clark also has to occasionally mediate a conflict between partners or between partners and Willowbend managers, as well as between his baseball players or his football players.

As we end this chapter, you should understand how important communication, feedback, coaching, and conflict resolution are to leadership effectiveness in all organizations. Self-Assessment 2 will help you to understand how your personality traits affect your communication, feedback, coaching, and conflict management style.

Self–Assessment 2

Your Personality Traits and Communication, Feedback, Coaching, and Conflict Management Style

Let's tie personality traits from Chapter 2 together with what we've covered in this chapter. We are going to present some general statements about how your personality may affect your communication, feedback, coaching, and conflict. For each area, determine how the information relates to you. This will help you better understand your behavior strengths and weaknesses, and identify areas you may want to improve.

Communication. If you have a high *surgency* personality, you most likely are an extravert and have no difficulty initiating and communicating with others. However, you may be dominating during communication and may not listen well and be open to others' ideas. Be careful not to use communications simply as a means of getting what you want; be concerned about others and what they want. If you are low in surgency, you may be quiet and reserved in your communications. You may want to be more vocal.

If you are high in *agreeableness* personality trait, you are most likely a good listener and communicator. Your *adjustment* level affects the emotional tone of your communications. If you tend to get emotional during communications, you may want to work to keep your emotions under control. We cannot control our feelings, but we can control our behavior. If you are high in *conscientiousness*, you tend to have reliable communications. If you are not conscientious, you may want to work at returning messages quickly. People who are open to *new experience* often initiate communication, because communicating is often part of the new experience.

Feedback and Coaching. If you have a high *surgency* personality, you have a need to be in control. Watch the tendency to give feedback, but not listen to it. You may need to work at *not* criticizing. If you have low surgency, you may want to give more feedback and do more coaching. If you have a high *agreeable-*

ness personality, you are a people person and probably enjoy coaching others. However, as a manager, you must also discipline when needed, which may be difficult for you. If you are high on the *adjustment* personality trait, you may tend to give positive coaching; people with low *adjustment* need to watch the negative criticism. If you have a high *conscientiousness* with a high need for achievement, you may tend to be more concerned about your own success. This is also true of people with a high *surgency* personality. Remember that an important part of leadership is coaching others. If you have a low *conscientiousness*, you may need to put forth effort to be a good coach. Your *openness to experience* personality affects whether you are willing to listen to others' feedback and make changes.

Conflict Styles. Generally, the best conflict style is collaboration. If you have a high *surgency* personality, you most likely have no problem confronting others when in conflict. However, be careful not to use the forcing style with others; remember to use social, not personal power. If you have a high *agreeableness* personality, you tend to get along well with others. However, be careful not to use the avoiding and accommodating styles to get out of confronting others; you need to satisfy your needs too. *Adjustment* will affect how to handle a conflict situation. Try not to be low in adjustment and get too emotional. If you are *conscientious*, you may be good at conflict resolution; but again, be careful to meet others' needs too. *Openness to experience* affects conflicts, because their resolution often requires change; be open to new things.

Action Plan. Based on your personality, what specific things will you do to improve your communication, feedback, coaching, and conflict management style?

_____

_____

_____

Go to the Internet (academic.cengage.com/management/lussier) where you will find a broad array of resources to help maximize your learning.

- Review the vocabulary
- Try a quiz
- View chapter videos

Chapter Summary

This chapter summary is organized to answer the nine learning outcomes for Chapter 6.

1. List the steps in the oral message-sending process.

The five steps in the oral message-sending process are (1) develop rapport; (2) state your communication objective; (3) transmit your message; (4) check the receiver's understanding; (5) get a commitment and follow up.

2. List and explain the three parts of the message-receiving process.

The three parts of the message-receiving process are listening, analyzing, and checking understanding. Listening is the process of giving the speaker your undivided attention. Analyzing is the process of thinking about and evaluating the message. Checking understanding is the process of giving feedback.

3. Describe paraphrasing and state why it is used.

Paraphrasing is the process of having the receiver restate the message in his or her own words. Paraphrasing is used to check understanding of the transmitted message. If the receiver can paraphrase the message accurately, communication has taken place. If not, communication is not complete.

4. Identify two common approaches to getting feedback, and explain why they don't work.

The first common approach to getting feedback is to send the entire message and to assume that the message has been conveyed with mutual understanding. The second approach is to give the entire message followed by asking, "Do you have any questions?" Feedback usually does not follow because people have a tendency not to ask questions. There are at least four good reasons why people do not ask questions: receivers feel ignorant, receivers are ignorant, receivers are reluctant to point out the sender's ignorance, and receivers have cultural barriers.

5. Describe the difference between criticism and coaching feedback.

Criticism is feedback that makes a judgment about behavior being wrong. Coaching feedback is based on a supportive relationship and offers specific and descriptive ways to improve performance. Criticism focuses on pointing out mistakes, while coaching feedback focuses on the benefits of positive behavior.

6. Discuss the relationship between the performance formula and the coaching model.

The performance formula is used to determine the reason for poor performance and the corrective action needed. The coaching model is then used to improve performance.

7. Define the five conflict management styles.

(1) The *avoiding conflict style* user attempts to passively ignore the conflict rather than resolve it. (2) The *accommodating conflict style* user attempts to resolve the conflict by passively giving in to the other party. (3) The *forcing conflict style* user attempts to resolve the conflict by using aggressive behavior to get his or her own way. (4) The *negotiating conflict style* user attempts to resolve the conflict through assertive give-and-take concessions. (5) The *collaborating conflict style* user assertively attempts to jointly resolve the conflict with the best solution agreeable to all parties.

8. List the steps in the initiating conflict resolution model.

The initiating conflict resolution model steps are (1) plan a BCF statement that maintains ownership of the problem; (2) present your BCF statement and agree on the conflict; (3) ask for, and/or give, alternative conflict resolutions; and (4) make an agreement for change.

9. Define the following key terms (in order of appearance in the chapter).

Select one or more methods: (1) fill in the missing key terms from memory, (2) match the key terms from the following list with their definitions below, (3) copy the key terms in order from the list at the beginning of the chapter.

_____ is the process of conveying information and meaning.

_____ steps include (1) develop rapport; (2) state your communication objective; (3) transmit your message; (4) check the receiver's understanding; and (5) get a commitment and follow up.

_____ includes listening, analyzing, and checking understanding.

_____ is the process of verifying messages and determining if objectives are being met.

_____ is the process of having the receiver restate the message in his or her own words.

_____ is a formal evaluation process based on receiving performance evaluations from many people.

_____ is the process of giving motivational feedback to maintain and improve performance.

_____ steps include (1) trainee receives preparation; (2) trainer presents the task; (3) trainee performs the task; and (4) trainer follows up.

_____ is (1) based on a good, supportive relationship; (2) specific and descriptive; and (3) not judgmental criticism.

_____ is used to explain the process managers go through in determining the reasons for effective or ineffective performance and deciding what to do about it.

_____ explains performance as a function of ability, motivation, and resources.

_____ is a form of coaching in which a more experienced manager helps a less experienced protégé.

_____ exists whenever people are in disagreement and opposition.

_____ steps are (1) plan a BCF statement that maintains ownership of the problem; (2) present your BCF statement and agree on the conflict; (3) ask for, and/or give, alternative conflict resolutions; (4) make an agreement for change.

_____ describes a conflict in terms of behavior, consequences, and feelings.

_____ is a neutral third party who helps resolve a conflict.

_____ is a neutral third party who makes a binding decision to resolve a conflict.

Key Terms

arbitrator, 229	conflict, 220	message-receiving process, 202
attribution theory, 217	feedback, 206	oral message-sending process, 199
BCF model, 227	initiating conflict resolution model, 227	paraphrasing, 207
coaching, 211	job instructional training, 214	performance formula, 218
coaching feedback, 217	mediator, 228	360-degree feedback, 210
communication, 198	mentoring, 219	

Review and Discussion Questions

1. What should be included in your plan to send a message?
2. What are the three parts of a written outline?
3. As an average, how many words should a sentence have, and how many sentences should there be in a paragraph?
4. Which personality traits are associated with being closed to feedback?
5. What are the four guidelines to getting feedback on messages?
6. What is 360-degree feedback, and are many organizations using it?
7. Should a supportive working relationship be a true friendship?
8. Why doesn't criticism work?
9. Are all managers mentors?
10. How do you know when you are in conflict?
11. What is the difference between functional and dysfunctional conflict, and how does each affect performance?
12. What is meant by *maintaining ownership of the problem?*
13. How is the BCF model used?
14. What is the difference between a mediator and an arbitrator?

Case

LAWRENCE WEINBACH—UNISYS CORPORATION

Unisys Corporation has been in business for more than 130 years. Unisys contributed to the computer revolution with the first commercial large-scale system, its 29,000-pound UNIVAC computer back in 1951. Although Unisys has stayed in the communications business, its focus has changed over the years, which is illustrated in its symbol "Unisys e-@ction" and its slogans "We have a head for e-business" and "Imagine it. Done."

Today, Unisys is a global information technology (IT) services and solutions company focused on helping businesses and governments apply IT to achieve new levels of competitiveness and success. Unisys combines expertise in consulting, systems integration, outsourcing, infrastructure, and server technology. It serves six primary vertical markets: financial services, public sector, communications, transportation, commercial, and media. Unisys has thousands of customers in more than 100 countries.

Unisys not only understands the importance of communications as a line of business, but it also understands the importance of good communications within the organization. In other words, Unisys practices what it preaches—good communication. In fact, former Unisys chairman of the board Lawrence A. Weinbach won the Excellence in Communication Leadership (EXCEL) Award. The EXCEL Award is the highest honor the International Association of Business Communicators (IABC) gives to nonmembers, usually to CEOs of major companies. Weinbach's communications strategy was credited as a principal factor in his outstanding success in boosting employee morale and productivity while at the same time generating a record-breaking financial turnaround.

Here are some of the communications methods Weinbach used to transform Unisys from primarily a computer company to a full-service IT company. A major challenge was to change the culture through communications. Within three or four days after taking over as CEO, Weinbach sent a letter to customers and shareholders introducing himself and telling them that if they had any questions or concerns, to write to him and he would personally respond to them. Weinbach also hired a vice president of corporate communications, who reported directly to him.

Unisys was not doing well when Weinbach took over as CEO. As an outsider, Weinbach realized that the employees had lost some confidence in the company and themselves. To regain their confidence, he went on the road and talked to 12,000 employees, asking them to send him ideas to improve Unisys. Within six weeks, Weinbach received 4,500 e-mails, and he answered about 2,000 of them himself before the task became too difficult for him. He then developed "Ask Larry" on the intranet in order to respond to more generic questions, and he followed this with a monthly newsletter to all employees so that employees could feel like they were a part of what was going on in the company.

Weinbach transformed Unisys from a hierarchical flow of information to a more decentralized flow of authority and communications, in which the person with the information needed could be contacted. Having been in the service business, Weinbach knew that the key to success was getting people first motivated and then willing to follow where he wanted the company to go; that is, follow his vision. Weinbach believed the vision had to be simple. The vision of Unisys is illustrated through its "three-legged stool," which focuses on customers, employees, and reputation. All three values are equally important and each is represented by a leg; if any one is missing, the stool (Unisys) falls. In fact, all employees were given a three-legged-stool pin to remind them of the Unisys vision. Weinbach always wore the pin, and if anyone asked him what his vision for the company was, he just pointed to the pin.

Good communication skills are very important to career success, so here is advice from Weinbach on how you can improve your communication skills and have more effective

working relationships: You have to develop a personal rapport with others to create a level of trust and confidence. Be very direct (whether you have good news or bad news, give it directly); be caring (have concern for others and create a win-win situation for all stakeholders); and be available (put people first and spend time with them, which shows that you care). You also need to be consistent in your message. The manager has to develop the kind of environment where employees want to work and are happy at work; to do this, you have to be a good communicator, and people have to trust you and what you are saying.

GO TO THE INTERNET: To learn more about Larry Weinbach and Unisys Corporation, log on to InfoTrac® College Edition at **academic.cengage.com/infotrac** and use the advanced search function.

Support your answers to the following questions with specific information from the case and text, or information you get from the Web or other sources.

1. Which major topic of this chapter (communications, feedback, coaching, conflict) was Weinbach's primary focus as he took over as CEO of Unisys?

2. Which communication method did CEO Weinbach use within his first few days, with customers and shareholders, and then with employees? Which method of communication did he primarily use with all three groups?

3. Was Weinbach's communication focus on sending or receiving messages?

4. How would you assess Weinbach's use of feedback?

5. Did Weinbach use coaching? If yes, how?

6. Using Exhibit 6-3, "Coaching Guidelines," did Weinbach use each of the ten guidelines as a new CEO at Unisys? Be sure to explain your answers.

7. Did Weinbach use criticism or coaching feedback when he took over as CEO?

8. Which conflict management style did Weinbach use as CEO?

9. Which one of Weinbach's suggestions for communication skills do you believe is most relevant?

10. What additional advice would you give to others to improve their communication skills? To come up with an answer, you may want to think about a person you know who is a very effective communicator. What makes that person successful?

Cumulative Case Questions

11. Which level of analysis and leadership paradigm are presented in this case, and did Weinbach use the management or leadership paradigm (Chapter 1)?

12. What do the Pygmalion effect and job satisfaction have to do with this case? (Chapter 2)?

13. What role did Weinbach's leadership behavior and ability to motivate employees (Chapter 3) play in the Unisys turnaround?
14. Which one of the contingency leadership theories (Chapter 5) do you think Weinbach used as CEO?

Case Exercise and Role-Play

Preparation: An important part of getting ideas for improving Unisys comes from asking customers questions and then listening to them. Your role is an executive at Unisys. List some questions that you would ask customers to get ideas for improvement.

In-Class Groups: Break into groups of four to six members, and develop a list of questions to ask customers to get ideas for improving Unisys. Select a spokesperson to record the questions and then ask them of a customer in front of the class.

Role-Play: One person (representing themselves or a group) asks question of a customer to get ideas for improving Unisys.

Video Case

Le Meridien Hotel: Communicating in Organizations

Le Meridien is a luxury hotel chain famous for offering a unique European experience with a French flair to its more than 100,000 visitors each year. The hotel group operates over 130 hotels in 56 countries around the globe, and its reputation for service has made it one of the leading hotel brands in the world.

View the Video (11 minutes)
View the video on Le Meridien Hotel in class or at **academic. cengage.com/management/lussier**.

Read the Case
For Assistant General Manager Bob van den Oord, communication plays a crucial role in managing Le Meridien's world-class operations. His job involves communicating with department heads, staff, guests, suppliers, and senior management, through both formal and informal channels. The assistant general manager is personable and has become known for his "management by walkabout" style—a daily routine of monitoring operations and staff by conducting a walk-through inspection of the entire hotel.

In addition to his daily walkabout encounters with employees, van den Oord creates a variety of meetings where managers can discuss their duties and schedules while receiving important feedback. Between meetings, employees utilize various communications technologies to coordinate efforts and report back to the assistant general manager. Although van den Oord concedes that technology-based communications like e-mail and text messaging are convenient and have a place in hotel operations, he prefers the channel richness of face-to-face communication and tells his workers that digital communications should never be a substitute for personal interaction.

Bob Van den Oord believes that good communication is the key to good business at Le Meridien. The ability to communicate consistently and clearly is essential for developing a happy staff and serving customers properly. And, as van den Oord notes with a smile, "A happy staff equals happy guests."

Answer the Questions
1. Explain how Bob van den Oord uses the oral message-sending process.
2. How important is nonverbal communication at Le Meridien Hotel? On what types of nonverbal communication does Bob van den Oord rely?
3. How does van den Oord foster effective communication at Le Meridien Hotel?

Skill-Development Exercise 1

GIVING INSTRUCTIONS

Doing Skill-Development Exercise 1 in Class

Objective
To develop your ability to give and receive messages (communication skills).

Preparation
No preparation is necessary except reading and understanding the chapter. The instructor will provide the original drawings that must be drawn.

Experience

You will plan, give, and receive instructions for completing a drawing of three objects.

Procedure 1 (3–7 minutes)

Read all of procedure 1 twice. The task is for the manager to give an employee instructions for completing a drawing of four objects. The objects must be drawn to scale and look like photocopies of the originals. You will have up to 15 minutes to complete the task.

The exercise has four separate parts or steps:

1. The manager plans.
2. The manager gives the instructions.
3. The employee does the drawing.
4. Evaluation of the results takes place.

Rules: The rules are numbered to correlate with the four parts of the exercise.

1. *Planning.* While planning, the manager may write out instructions for the employee, but may not do any drawing of any kind.
2. *Instructions.* While giving instructions, the manager may not show the original drawing to the employee. (The instructor will give it to you.) The instructions may be given orally, and/or in writing, but no nonverbal hand gestures are allowed. The employee may take notes while the instructions are being given, but cannot do any drawing with or without a pen. The manager must give the instructions for all four objects before drawing begins.
3. *Drawing.* Once the employee begins the drawing, the manager should watch but no longer communicate in any way.
4. *Evaluation.* When the employee is finished or the time is up, the manager shows the employee the original drawing. Discuss how you did. Turn to the "Integration" section of this exercise, and answer the questions. The manager writes the answers, not the employee. The employee will write when playing the manager role.

Procedure 2 (2–5 minutes)

Half of the class members will act as the manager first and give instructions. Managers move their seats to one of the four walls (spread out). They should be facing the center of the room with their backs close to the wall.

Employees sit in the middle of the room until called on by a manager. When called on, bring a seat to the manager. Sit facing the manager so that you cannot see any managers' drawing.

Procedure 3 (Up to 15 minutes for drawing and integration)

The instructor gives each manager a copy of the drawing, being careful not to let any employees see it. The manager plans the instructions. When a manager is ready, she or he calls an employee and gives the instructions. It is helpful to use the

message-sending process. Be sure to follow the rules. The employee should do the drawing on an $8^1/_2''$ by $11''$ sheet of paper, not in this book. If you use written instructions, they may be on the reverse side of the page that the employee draws on or on a different sheet of paper. You have up to 15 minutes to complete the drawing and about five minutes for integration (evaluation). When you finish the drawing, turn to the evaluation questions in the "Integration" section.

Procedure 4 (up to 15 minutes)

The employees are now the managers, and they sit in the seats facing the center of the room. New employees go to the center of the room until called for.

Follow procedure 3, with the instructor giving a different drawing. Do not work with the same person; change partners.

Integration

Evaluating Questions: You may select more than one answer. The manager and employee discuss each question; and the manager, not the employee, writes the answers to the questions.

1. The goal of communication was to:
   a. influence   b. inform   c. express feelings

2. The manager transmitted the message through _____ communication channel(s).
   a. oral   b. written
   c. nonverbal   d. combined

3. The manager spent _____ time planning.
   a. too much   b. too little
   c. the right amount of

Questions 4 through 8 relate to the steps in the message-sending process.

4. The manager developed rapport. (Step 1)
   a. true   b. false

5. The manager stated the communication objective. (Step 2)
   a. true   b. false

6. The manager transmitted the message _____. (Step 3)
   a. effectively   b. ineffectively

7. The manager checked understanding by using _____. (Step 4)
   a. direct questions   b. paraphrasing
   c. both   d. neither

   The amount of checking was _____.
   a. too frequent   b. too infrequent
   c. about right

8. The manager got a commitment and followed up. (Step 5)
   a. true   b. false

9. The employee did an _____ job of listening, an _____ job of analyzing, and an _____ job of checking understanding through the receiving message process.
   a. effective   b. ineffective

10. When going over this integration, the manager was _____ and the employee was _____ to criticism that can help improve communication skills.
    a. open   b. closed

11. Were the objects drawn to approximate scale (same size)? If not, why not?

12. Did you follow the rules? If not, why not?

13. If you could do this exercise again, what would you do differently to improve communications?

_____

_____

_____

Conclusion

The instructor leads a class discussion and/or makes concluding remarks.

Apply It (2–4 minutes)

What did I learn from this experience? How will I use this knowledge in the future? When will I practice?

_____

_____

_____

Sharing

Volunteers may give their answers to the "Apply It" questions.

Behavior Model Skills Training 1

Session 1

In this behavior model skills training session, you will perform four activities:

1. Complete Self-Assessment 3 (to determine your preferred communication style).
2. Read "The Situational Communications Model."

3. Watch Behavior Model Video 1, "Situational Communications."
4. Complete Skill-Development Exercise 2 (to apply the model to various situations).

For practice, use the situational communications model in your personal and professional communication.

Self-Assessment 3

Determining Your Preferred Communication Style

To determine your preferred communication style, select the one alternative that most closely describes what you would do in each of the 12 situations described. Do not be concerned with trying to pick the correct answer; select the alternative that best describes what you would actually do. Circle the letter a, b, c, or d.

For now, ignore these three types of lines:

- ____ 1. (before each number)
- ____ time   ____ information
  ____ acceptance   ____ capability
  ____ communication style
- S____ (following each letter)

They are explained later, and will be used during the in-class part of Skill-Development Exercise 2.

____ 1. Wendy, a knowledgeable person from another department, comes to you, the engineering supervisor, and requests that you design a special product to her specifications. You would:

____ time _____ information
____ acceptance _____ capability
____ communication style

a. Control the conversation and tell Wendy what you will do for her. S _____

b. Ask Wendy to describe the product. Once you understand it, you would present your ideas. Let her realize that you are concerned and want to help by offering your ideas. S _____

c. Respond to Wendy's request by conveying understanding and support. Help clarify what is to be done by you. Offer ideas, but do it her way. S _____

d. Find out what you need to know. Let Wendy know you will do it her way. S _____

____ 2. Your department has designed a product that is to be fabricated by Saul's department. Saul has been with the company longer than you have; he knows his department. Saul comes to you to change the product design. You decide to:

_____ time _____ information
_____ acceptance _____ capability
_____ communication style

    a. Listen to the change and why it would be beneficial. If you believe Saul's way is better, change it; if not, explain why the original design is superior. If necessary, insist that it be done your way. S _____

    b. Tell Saul to fabricate it any way he wants to. S _____

    c. You are busy; tell Saul to do it your way. You don't have time to listen and argue with him. S _____

    d. Be supportive; make changes together as a team. S _____

_____ 3. Upper management has a decision to make. They call you to a meeting and tell you they need some information to solve a problem they describe to you. You:

_____ time _____ information
_____ acceptance _____ capability
_____ communication style

    a. Respond in a manner that conveys personal support and offer alternative ways to solve the problem. S _____

    b. Just answer their questions. S _____

    c. Explain how to solve the problem. S _____

    d. Show your concern by explaining how to solve the problem and why it is an effective solution. S _____

_____ 4. You have a routine work order. The work order is to be placed verbally and completed in three days. Sue, the receiver, is very experienced and willing to be of service to you. You decide to:

_____ time _____ information
_____ acceptance _____ capability
_____ communication style

    a. Explain your needs, but let Sue make the order decision. S _____

    b. Tell Sue what you want and why you need it. S _____

    c. Decide together what to order. S _____

    d. Simply give Sue the order. S _____

_____ 5. Work orders from the staff department normally take three days; however, you have an emergency and need the job today. Your

colleague Jim, the department supervisor, is knowledgeable and somewhat cooperative. You decide to:

_____ time _____ information
_____ acceptance _____ capability
_____ communication style

    a. Tell Jim that you need it by three o'clock and will return at that time to pick it up. S _____

    b. Explain the situation and how the organization will benefit by expediting the order. Volunteer to help in any way you can. S _____

    c. Explain the situation and ask Jim when the order will be ready. S _____

    d. Explain the situation and together come to a solution to your problem. S _____

_____ 6. Danielle, a peer with a record of high performance, has recently had a drop in productivity. Her problem is affecting your performance. You know Danielle has a family problem. You:

_____ time _____ information
_____ acceptance _____ capability
_____ communication style

    a. Discuss the problem; help Danielle realize the problem is affecting her work and yours. Supportively discuss ways to improve the situation. S _____

    b. Tell the manager about it and let him decide what to do about it. S _____

    c. Tell Danielle to get back on the job. S _____

    d. Discuss the problem and tell Danielle how to solve the work situation; be supportive. S _____

_____ 7. You are a knowledgeable supervisor. You buy supplies from Peter regularly. He is an excellent salesperson and very knowledgeable about your situation. You are placing your weekly order. You decide to:

_____ time _____ information
_____ acceptance _____ capability
_____ communication style

    a. Explain what you want and why. Develop a supportive relationship. S _____

    b. Explain what you want, and ask Peter to recommend products. S _____

    c. Give Peter the order. S _____

d. Explain your situation and allow Peter to make the order. S _____

____ 8. Jean, a knowledgeable person from another department, has asked you to perform a routine staff function to her specifications. You decide to:

_____ time _____ information
_____ acceptance _____ capability
_____ communication style

a. Perform the task to her specifications without questioning her. S _____
b. Tell her that you will do it the usual way. S _____
c. Explain what you will do and why. S _____
d. Show your willingness to help; offer alternative ways to do it. S _____

____ 9. Tom, a salesperson, has requested an order for your department's services with a short delivery date. As usual, Tom claims it is a take-it-or-leave-it offer. He wants your decision now, or within a few minutes, because he is in the customer's office. Your action is to:

_____ time _____ information
_____ acceptance _____ capability
_____ communication style

a. Convince Tom to work together to come up with a later date. S _____
b. Give Tom a yes or no answer. S _____
c. Explain your situation, and let Tom decide if you should take the order. S _____
d. Offer an alternative delivery date. Work on your relationship; show your support. S _____

____10. As a time-and-motion expert, you have been called regarding a complaint about the standard time it takes to perform a job. As you analyze the entire job, you realize that one element of the job should take longer, but other elements should take less time. The end result is a shorter total standard time for the job. You decide to:

_____ time _____ information
_____ acceptance _____ capability
_____ communication style

a. Tell the operator and foreman that the total time must be decreased and why. S _____

b. Agree with the operator and increase the standard time. S _____
c. Explain your findings. Deal with the operator and/or foreman's concerns, but ensure compliance with your new standard. S _____
d. Together with the operator, develop a standard time. S _____

____ 11. You approve budget allocations for projects. Marie, who is very competent indeveloping budgets, has come to you. You:

_____ time _____ information
_____ acceptance _____ capability
_____ communication style

a. Review the budget, make revisions, and explain them in a supportive way. Deal with concerns, but insist on your changes. S _____
b. Review the proposal and suggest areas where changes may be needed. Make changes together, if needed. S _____
c. Review the proposed budget, make revisions, and explain them. S _____
d. Answer any questions or concerns Marie has and approve the budget as is. S _____

____ 12. You are a sales manager. A customer has offered you a contract for your product, but the contract has a short delivery date: only two days. The contract would be profitable for you and the organization. The cooperation of the production department is essential to meet the deadline. Tim, the production manager, and you do not get along very well because of your repeated request for quick delivery. Your action is to:

_____ time _____ information
_____ acceptance _____ capability
_____ communication style

a. Contact Tim and try to work together to complete the contract. S _____
b. Accept the contract and convince Tim in a supportive way to meet the obligation. S _____
c. Contact Tim and explain the situation. Ask him if you and he should accept the contract, but let him decide. S _____

d. Accept the contract. Contact Tim and tell him to meet the obligation. If he resists, tell him you will go to his manager.
S _____

To determine your preferred communication style: (1) Circle the letter you selected as the alternative you chose in situations 1–12. The column headings indicate the style you selected.

(2) Add up the number of circled items per column. The total for all the columns should not be more than 12. The column with the highest number represents your preferred communication style. There is no one best style in all situations. The more evenly distributed the numbers are between the four styles, the more flexible are your communications. A total of 0 or 1 in any column may indicate a reluctance to use the style(s). You could have problems in situations calling for the use of this style.

	Autocratic (S1A)	Consultative (S2C)	Participative (S3P)	Empowerment (S4E)
1.	a	b	c	d
2.	c	a	d	b
3.	c	d	a	b
4.	d	b	c	a
5.	a	b	d	c
6.	c	d	a	b
7.	c	a	b	d
8.	b	c	d	a
9.	b	d	a	c
10.	a	c	d	b
11.	c	a	b	d
12.	d	b	a	c
Totals				

The Situational Communications Model

The Interactive Process System

Communication has the following five dimensions, which are each on a continuum:[97]

Initiation_____Response

- *Initiation.* The sender starts, or initiates, the communication. The sender may or may not expect a response to the initiated message.
- *Response.* The receiver's reply or action to the sender's message. In responding, the receiver can become an initiator. As two-way communication takes place, the role of initiator (sender) and responder (receiver) may change.

Presentation_____Elicitation

- *Presentation.* The sender's message is structured, directive, or informative. A response may not be needed, although action may be called for. ("We are meeting to develop next year's budget." "Please open the door.")

- *Elicitation.* The sender invites a response to the message. Action may or may not be needed. ("How large a budget do we need?" "Do you think we should leave the door open?")

Closed_____Open

- *Closed.* The sender expects the receiver to follow the message. ("This is a new form to fill out and return with each order.")
- *Open.* The sender is eliciting a response as a means of considering the receiver's input. ("Should we use this new form with each order?")

Rejection_____Acceptance

- *Rejection.* The receiver does not accept the sender's message. ("I will not fill out this new form for each order!")
- *Acceptance.* The receiver agrees with the sender's message. ("I will fill out the new form for each order!")

Strong_____Mild

- *Strong.* The sender will use force or power to have the message acted upon as directed. ("Fill in the form or you're fired.")
- *Mild.* The sender will not use force or power to have the message acted upon as directed. ("Please fill in the form when you can.")

Situational Communication Styles

Following is the interactive process. Acceptance or rejection can come from any of the styles because, to a large extent, it is out of the sender's control.

The Autocratic Communication Style (S1A). This style demonstrates high task/low relationship behavior (HT-LR), initiating a closed presentation. The other party has little, if any, information and is low in capability.

- *Initiation/Response.* You initiate and control the communication with minimal, if any, response.
- *Presentation/Elicitation.* You make a presentation letting the other parties know they are expected to comply with your message; there is little, if any, elicitation.
- *Closed/Open.* You use a closed presentation; you will not consider the receiver's input.

The Consultative Communication Style (S2C). This style demonstrates high task/high relationship behavior (HT-HR), using a closed presentation for the task with an open elicitation for the relationship. The other party has moderate information and capability.

- *Initiation/Response.* You initiate the communication by letting the other party know that you want him or her to buy into your influence. You desire some response.
- *Presentation/Elicitation.* Both are used. You use elicitation to determine the goal of the communication. For example, you may ask questions to determine the situation and follow up with a presentation. When the communication goal is known, little task elicitation is needed. Relationship communication is elicited in order to determine the interest of the other party and acceptance of the message. The open elicitation should show your concern for the other party's point of view and motivate him or her to follow your influence.
- *Closed/Open.* You are closed to having the message accepted (task), but open to the person's feelings (relationship). Be empathetic.

The Participative Communication Style (S3P). This style demonstrates low task/high relationship behavior (LT-HR), responding with open elicitation, some initiation, and little presentation. The other party is high in information and capability.

- *Initiation/Response.* You respond with some initiation. You want to help the other party solve a problem or get him or her to help you solve one. You are helpful and convey personal support.

- *Presentation/Elicitation.* Elicitation can occur with little presentation. Your role is to elicit the other party's ideas on how to reach objectives.
- *Closed/Open.* Open communication is used. If you participate well, the other party will come to a solution you can accept. If not, you may have to reject the other party's message.

The Empowerment Communication Style (S4E). This style demonstrates low task/low relationship behavior (LT-LR), responding with the necessary open presentation. The other party is outstanding in information and capability.

- *Initiation/Response.* You respond to the other party with little, if any, initiation.

- *Presentation/Elicitation.* You present the other party with information, structure, and so forth, which the sender wants.

- *Closed/Open.* Open, you convey that the other party is in charge; you will accept the message.

Situational Variables

When selecting the appropriate communication style, you should consider four variables: time, information, acceptance, and capability. Answering the questions related to each of these variables can help you select the appropriate style for the situation.

Time. Do I have enough time to use two-way communication—yes or no? When there is no time, the other three variables are not considered; the autocratic style is appropriate. When time is available, any of the other styles may be appropriate, depending on the other variables. Time is a relative term; in one situation, a few minutes may be considered a short time—in another situation, a month may be a short time.

Information. Do I have the necessary information to communicate my message, make a decision, or to take action? When you have all the information you need, the autocratic style may be appropriate. When you have some of the information, the consultative style may be appropriate. When you have little information, the participative or empowerment style may be appropriate.

Acceptance. Will the other party accept my message without any input? If the receiver will accept the message, the autocratic style may be appropriate. If the receiver will be reluctant to accept it, the consultative style may be appropriate. If the receiver will reject the message, the participative or empowerment style may be appropriate to gain acceptance. There are situations in which acceptance is critical to success, such as in the area of implementing changes.

Capability. Capability has two parts. *Ability:* Does the other party have the experience or knowledge to participate in two-way communications? Will the receiver put the organization's goals ahead of personal needs or goals? *Motivation:* Does the other party want to participate? When the other party is low in capability, the autocratic style may be appropriate; moderate in capability, the consultative style may be appropriate; high in capability, the participative style may be appropriate; outstanding in capability, the empowerment style may be appropriate. In addition, capability levels can change from one task to another. For example, a professor may have outstanding capability in classroom teaching but be low in capability for advising students.

Selecting Communication Styles

Successful managers rely on different communication styles according to the situation. There are three steps to follow when selecting the appropriate communication style in a given situation. After reading these steps and looking at Model 6-6, you will get to practice this selection process in the section, "Determining the Appropriate Communications Style for Situation 1."

step 1. Diagnose the situation. Answer the questions for each of the four situational variables (time, information, acceptance, and capability). In Self-Assessment 3 at the beginning of this training session, you were asked to select an alternative to 12 situations. You were told to ignore certain lines. When completing the in-class part of Skill-Development Exercise 2, you will place the style letters (S1A, S2C, S3P, S4E) on the lines provided for each of the 12 situations.

step 2. Select the appropriate communication style for the situation. After analyzing the four variables, you select the appropriate communication style for the situation. In some situations, variables may have conflicting styles; you should select the style of the most important variable for the situation. For example, capability may be outstanding (S4E) but you have all the information needed (S1A). If the information is more important, use the autocratic style even though the capability is outstanding. When doing the in-class part of Skill-Development Exercise 2, place the letters (S1A, S2C, S3P, S4E) for the appropriate communication styles on the style lines (S _____).

step 3. Use the appropriate communication style for the situation. During the in-class part of Skill-Development Exercise 2, you will identify one of the four communication styles for each alternative action; place the S1A, S2C, S3P, or S4E on the S ____ lines. Select the alternative (a, b, c, or d) that represents the appropriate communication style for each of the 12 situations, and place it on the line before the number of the situation.

Model 6-6 summarizes the material in this preparation for the exercise. Use it to determine the appropriate communication style in situation 1 and during the in-class part of Skill-Development Exercise 2.

Model 6-6 *Situational communication.*

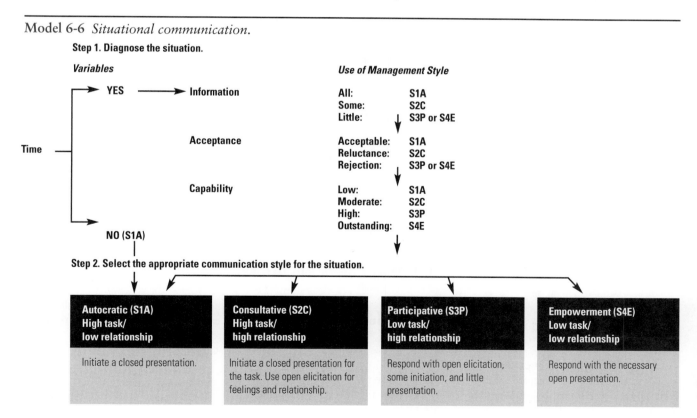

Determining the Appropriate Communication Style for Situation 1

step 1. **Diagnose the situation.** Answer the four variable questions from the model, and place the letters on the four variable lines for situation 1.

___ 1. Wendy, a knowledgeable person from another department, comes to you, the engineering supervisor, and requests that you design a special product to her specifications. You would:

_____ time   _____ information
_____ acceptance   _____ capability
_____ communication style

    a. Control the conversation and tell Wendy what you will do for her. S _____

    b. Ask Wendy to describe the product. Once you understand it, you would present your ideas. Let her realize that you are concerned and want to help by offering your ideas. S _____

    c. Respond to Wendy's request by conveying understanding and support. Help clarify what is to be done by you. Offer ideas, but do it her way. S _____

    d. Find out what you need to know. Let Wendy know you will do it her way. S _____

step 2. **Select the appropriate communication style for the situation.** Review the four variables. If they are all consistent, select one style. If they are conflicting, select the most important variable as the style to use. Place its letters (S1A, S2C, S3P, or S4E) on the style line.

step 3. **Use the appropriate communication style for the situation.** Review the four alternative actions. Identify the communication style for each, placing

its letters on the S _____ line, then place the appropriate match (a, b, c, d) on the line before the number.

Let's See How You Did.

1. *Time:* Time is available (or yes, you have time); it can be any style. *Information:* You have little information, so you need to use a participative or empowerment style to find out what Wendy wants done (S3P or S4E). *Acceptance:* If you try to do it your way rather than Wendy's way, she will most likely reject it. You need to use a participative or empowerment style (S3P or S4E). *Capability:* Wendy is knowledgeable and has a high level of capability (S3P).

2. Reviewing the four variables, you see that there is a mixture of S3P and S4E. Because you are an engineer, it is appropriate to participate with Wendy to give her what she needs. Therefore, the choice is S3P.

3. Alternative (a) is S1A; this is the autocratic style, high task/low relationship. Alternative (b) is S2C; this is the consultative style, high task/high relationship. Alternative (c) is S3P; this is the participative style, low task/high relationship. Alternative (d) is S4E; this is empowerment style, low task/low relationship behavior. If you selected (c) as your action, you chose the most appropriate action for the situation. This was a three-point answer. If you selected (d) as your answer, this is also a good alternative; it scores two points. If you selected (b), you get one point for overdirecting. If you selected (a), you get zero points; this is too much directing and will most likely hurt communications.

The better you match your communication style to the situation, the more effective you will be at communicating. In the in-class part of Skill-Development Exercise 3, you will apply the model to the other 11 situations in Self-Assessment 3 to develop your ability to communicate as a situational communicator.

Behavior Model **Video 1**

SITUATIONAL COMMUNICATIONS

Objectives
To better understand the four situational communication styles and which style to use in a given situation.

Video (12 minutes) Overview
You will first listen to a lecture to understand how to use the situational communications model. Then, you will view two managers, Steve and Darius, meeting to discuss faulty parts. You are asked to identify the communication style Darius uses

in four different scenes. Write the letters of the style on the scene line after each scene. This may be completed as part of Skill-Development Exercise 2.

Scene 1. _____   Autocratic (S1A)
Scene 2. _____   Consultative (S2C)
Scene 3. _____   Participative (S3P)
Scene 4. _____   Empowerment (S4E)

Skill-Development Exercise 2

SITUATIONAL COMMUNICATIONS

Doing Skill-Development Exercise 2 in Class

Objectives

To develop your ability to communicate using the appropriate style for the situation.

Preparation

You should have competed Self-Assessment 3, and finished the reading about situational communications. You may also want to view Behavior Model Video 1.

Experience

You will select the appropriate style for the 12 situations in Self-Assessment 3. On the *time* line, place Y (yes); on the *information*, *acceptance*, and *capability* lines, place the letters S1A, S2C, S3P, or S4E that are appropriate for the situation. Based on your diagnoses, select the one style you would use by placing its letters (S1A, S2C, S3P, or S4E) on the *communication style* line. On the four S lines, write the letters S1A, S2C, S3P, or S4E to identify each style being used. Place the letter a, b, c, or d on the line before the exercise number that represents the most appropriate communication style for the situation.

Procedure 1 (10–20 minutes)

The instructor shows the video and then reviews the situational communications model, explaining how to apply it to determine the appropriate style for situation 2.

Procedure 2 (4–8 minutes)

Students, working alone, complete situation 3 of Self-Assessment 3 using the model. The instructor then goes over the recommended answers.

Procedure 3 (20–50 minutes)

A. Break into groups of two or three. As a team, apply the model to situations 4 through 8. The instructor will go over the appropriate answers when all teams are done, or the time is up.

B. Break into new groups of two or three and do situations 9 through 12. The instructor will go over the appropriate answers.

Conclusion

The instructor leads a class discussion and/or makes concluding remarks.

Apply It (2–4 minutes)

What did I learn from this experience? How will I use this knowledge in the future? When will I practice using the model?

_____

_____

_____

Sharing

In the group, or to the entire class, volunteers may give their answers to the "Apply It" questions.

Behavior Model Skills Training 2

Session 2

In this behavior model skills training session, you will perform three activities:

1. Read "Improving Performance with the Coaching Model" on pages 218–219 (to review how to use the model).

2. Watch Behavior Model Video 2, "Coaching."

3. Complete Skill-Development Exercise 3 (to develop your coaching skills).

   For further practice, use the coaching model in your personal and professional life.

The Coaching Model

In the text, on pages 218–219, read about the coaching model and review Model 6-4.

Behavior Model Video 2

COACHING

Objective
To assist you in coaching to improve performance of employees who are not performing to standard.

Video (3$^1/_2$ minutes) Overview
You will watch a Web development manager coach an employee who has missed deadlines for completing websites.

Skill-Development Exercise 3

COACHING

Preparing for Skill-Development Exercise 3

You should have read and understood the text material on coaching. You may also view Behavior Model Video 2.

Doing Skill-Development Exercise 3 in Class

Objective
To develop your skill at improving performance through coaching.

Experience
You will coach, be coached, and be observed coaching using Model 6-4 from the text.

Procedure 1 (2–4 minutes)
Break into groups of three. Make some groups of two, if necessary. Each member selects one of the following three situations in which to be the manager, and a different one in which to be the employee. In each situation, the employee knows the standing plans, but is not motivated to follow them. You will take turns coaching and being coached.

Three Employee-Coaching Situations

1. *Employee 1 is a clerical worker.* The person uses files, as do the other 10 employees in the department. The employees all know that they are supposed to return the files when they are finished, so that others can find the files when they need them. Employees should have only one file out at a time. The supervisor notices that employee 1 has five files on the desk, and another employee is looking for one of them. The supervisor thinks that employee 1 will complain about the heavy workload as an excuse for having more than one file out at a time.
2. *Employee 2 is a server in an ice cream shop.* The person knows that the tables should be cleaned up quickly after customers leave, so that new customers do not have to sit at dirty tables. It's a busy night. The supervisor finds dirty dishes on two of this employee's occupied tables.

Employee 2 is socializing with some friends at one of the tables. Employees are supposed to be friendly; employee 2 will probably use this as an excuse for the dirty tables.
3. *Employee 3 is an auto technician.* All employees at the garage where this person works know that they are supposed to put a paper mat on the floor of each car, so that the carpets don't get dirty. When the service supervisor got into a car repaired by employee 3, the car did not have a mat and there was grease on the carpet. Employee 3 does excellent work and will probably mention this fact when coached.

Procedure 2 (3–7 minutes)
Prepare for coaching to improve performance. On the following lines, each group member writes an outline of what he or she will say when coaching employee 1, 2, or 3, following the coaching steps listed:

1. Describe current performance. _____
   _____
2. Describe the desired behavior. _____
   _____
3. Get a commitment to the change. _____
   _____
4. Follow up. _____
   _____

Procedure 3 (5–8 minutes)
A. Role-playing. The manager of employee 1, the clerical worker, coaches him or her as planned. (Use the actual name of the group member playing employee 1. Talk— do not read your written plan.) Employee 1, put yourself in the worker's position. You work hard; there is a lot of pressure to work fast. It's easier when you have more than one file. Refer to the workload while being coached. Both the manager and the employee will have to improvise their roles.

The person not playing a role is the observer. He or she takes notes using the observer form. Try to make positive coaching feedback comments for improvement. Give the manager alternative suggestions for what he or she could have said to improve the coaching session.

Observer Form

1. How well did the manager describe current behavior?

   _____

   _____

2. How well did the manager describe desired behavior?

   _____

   _____

3. How successful was the manager at getting a commitment to the change? Do you think the employee would change?

   _____

   _____

4. How well did the manager describe how he or she was going to follow up to ensure that the employee performed the desired behavior?

   _____

   _____

B. Feedback. The observer leads a discussion of how well the manager coached the employee. (This should be a coaching discussion, not a lecture.) Focus on what the manager did well, and on how the manager could improve. The employee should also give feedback on how he or she felt, and what might have been more effective in getting him or her to change.

Do not go on to the next interview until you are told to do so. If you finish early, wait for the others to finish.

Procedure 4 (5–8 minutes)

Same as procedure 3, but change roles so that employee 2, the server, is coached. Employee 2 should make a comment about the importance of talking to customers to make them feel welcome. The job is not much fun if you can't talk to your friends.

Procedure 5 (5–8 minutes)

Same as procedure 3, but change roles so that employee 3, the auto technician, is coached. Employee 3 should comment on the excellent work he or she does.

Conclusion

The instructor leads a class discussion and makes concluding remarks.

Apply It (2–4 minutes)

What did I learn from this experience? How will I use this knowledge in the future? When will I practice?

_____

_____

_____

Sharing

In the group, or to the entire class, volunteers may give their answers to the "Apply It" questions.

Behavior Model Skills Training 3

Session 3

In this behavior model skills training session, you will perform three activities:

1. Read "Initiating Conflict Resolution" on pages 227–228 (to review how to use the model).
2. Watch Behavior Model Video 3, "Initiating Conflict Resolution."

3. Complete Skill-Development Exercise 4 (to develop your conflict resolution skills).

For further practice, use the conflict resolution model in your personal and professional life.

The Initiating Conflict Resolution Model 6-5

In the text, on pages 227–228, read the initiating conflict resolution model and review Model 6-5.

Behavior Model Video 3

INITIATING CONFLICT RESOLUTION

Objective

To assist you in resolving conflicts.

Video (4$^1/_2$ minutes) Overview

You will watch an advertising agency's employees. Alex initiates a conflict resolution with Catherine to resolve a conflict over a client.

Skill-Development Exercise 4

INITIATING CONFLICT RESOLUTION

Preparing for Skill-Development Exercise 4

During class you will be given the opportunity to role-play a conflict you face, or have faced, in order to develop your conflict skills. Students and workers have reported that this exercise helped prepare them for a successful initiation of a conflict resolution with roommates and coworkers. Fill in the following information.

Other party(ies) (You may use fictitious names.)

_____

Describe the conflict situation:

_____
_____
_____

List pertinent information about the other party (i.e., relationship with you, knowledge of the situation, age, background, etc.).

_____
_____
_____

Identify the other party's possible reaction to your confrontation. (How receptive will they be to collaborating? What might they say or do during the discussion to resist change?)

_____
_____
_____

How will you overcome this resistance to change?

_____
_____
_____

Following the initiating conflict resolution model steps, write out your planned opening BCF statement that maintains ownership of the problem.

_____
_____
_____

Doing Skill-Development Exercise 4 in Class

Objective

To experience and develop skills in resolving a conflict.

Preparation

You should have completed the questionnaire in "Preparing for Skill-Development Exercise 4."

Experience

You will initiate, respond to, and observe a conflict role-play, and then evaluate the effectiveness of its resolution.

Procedure 1 (2–3 minutes)

Break into as many groups of three as possible. If there are any people not in a triad, make one or two groups of two. Each member selects the number 1, 2, or 3. Number 1 will be the first to initiate a conflict role-play, then 2, followed by 3.

Procedure 2 (8–15 minutes)

A. Initiator number 1 gives his or her information from the preparation to number 2 (the responder) to read. Once number 2 understands, role-play (see item B). Number 3 is the observer.

B. Role-play the conflict resolution. Number 3, the observer, writes his or her observations on the feedback form at the end of this exercise.

C. Integration. When the role-play is over, the observer leads a discussion on the effectiveness of the conflict resolution. All three should discuss the effectiveness. Number 3 is not a lecturer. Do not go on until told to do so.

Procedure 3 (8–15 minutes)

Same as procedure 2, only number 2 is now the initiator, number 3 is the responder, and number 1 is the observer.

Procedure 4 (8–15 minutes)

Same as procedure 2, only number 3 is the initiator, number 1 is the responder, and number 2 is the observer.

Conclusion

The instructor leads a class discussion and/or makes concluding remarks.

Apply It (2–4 minutes)

What did I learn from this experience? How will I use this knowledge in the future? When will I practice?

_____

_____

_____

Sharing

In the group, or to the entire class, volunteers may give their answers to the "Apply It" questions.

Feedback Form

Try to have positive coaching improvement feedback comments for each step in initiating conflict resolution. Remember to be *specific* and *descriptive*, and for all improvements have an alternative positive behavior (APB). (For example: "If you would have said/done . . . , it would have improved the conflict resolution by . . .")

Initiating Conflict Resolution Model Steps

step 1. Plan a BCF statement that maintains ownership of the problem. (Did the initiator have a well-planned, effective BCF statement?)

_____

_____

_____

step 2. Present your BCF statement and agree on the conflict. (Did the initiator present the BCF statement effectively? Did the two agree on the conflict?)

_____

_____

_____

step 3. Ask for, and/or give, alternative conflict resolutions. (Who suggested alternative solutions? Was it done effectively?)

_____

_____

_____

step 4. Make an agreement for change. (Was there an agreement for change?)

_____

_____

_____

Behavior Model Video 4

MEDIATING CONFLICT RESOLUTION

Objective

To view the process of mediating a conflict resolution between employees.

Video (6½ minutes) Overview

This is a follow-up to the advertising agency conflict (Video 3). The two employees end up in conflict again. Their manager, Peter, brings them together to resolve the conflict by following the steps in "Mediating Conflict Resolution" on pages 228–229 (Model 6-5 in text).

Note: There is no skill-development exercise.

Leader/Follower Relations

LEARNING OUTCOMES

After studying this chapter, you should be able to:

1. List the four stages of development of the dyadic approach. p. 250
2. Define the two kinds of relationships that can occur among leaders and followers under the vertical dyadic linkage model. p. 251
3. Describe the main focus of team-building from a Leader-Follower perspective. p. 255
4. Discuss the focus of the systems and networks approach from a Leader-Follower perspective. p. 256
5. Discuss the key limitation or drawback with LMX application. p. 261
6. Describe three determining factors of high-quality LMX relationships. p. 263
7. Explain the cycle that leads to the Pygmalion effect. p. 264
8. Explain how LMX relationships can lead to unintended bias in HR practices. p. 265
9. Discuss the three follower influencing characteristics. p. 272
10. List five things a leader should delegate. p. 280
11. Define the following **key terms** (in order of appearance in the chapter):

dyadic	followership
dyadic theory	follower
vertical dyadic linkage (VDL) theory	alienated follower
in-group	conformist follower
out-group	passive follower
leader-member exchange (LMX)	effective follower
impressions management	pragmatic follower
ingratiation	locus of control
self-promotion	delegation
	delegation model

Opening Case Application

Kim Wung is a small entrepreneur who specializes in manufacturing custom-made furniture for retail chains like Pier 1, Ikea, and Stein Mart, which target customers with stylish and eclectic taste. Ms. Wung started with a small team of three employees, designing and producing wood furniture, beautifully handcrafted with Asian artistic designs. She attributes the quality of her furniture to the members of her work team and the relationship she has with each of them. Pier 1 Imports, a company known for its creative and unique product lines, searches for suppliers like Kim Wung. Pier 1 wants to feature some of Ms. Wung's furniture lines in its stores. In response, Ms. Wung has hired twelve more employees to produce the needed volume for her new customer. There are three teams (of four members), each headed by a team leader. Ms. Wung has made each of her three original employees (Yeng-Lee, Chang, and Sung-Mee) a team leader.

While all three teams started off well, Ms. Wung has observed some changes in the behavior and output of some of the teams. Yeng-Lee's team is leading the way with the highest quality and quantity. Chang's team is barely meeting quality standards. There is division within the team with two members supporting him and two against him. The same is true with Sung-Mee's crew where the team has fractured into two camps—Sung-Mee and her best crew member against the other three members she describes as lazy and unproductive. These complaints have surfaced in Chang's group as well. According to Ms. Wung, the main issue seems to be the quality of the relationships that the three leaders have with members of their teams. The one-on-one or dyadic relationship that Yeng-Lee has with members of her team seems to be of the highest quality compared to the other two teams. Also, there seems to have developed a closer and friendly relationship between Ms. Wung and Yeng-Lee.

To satisfy Pier 1's quality standards, Ms. Wung will have to revisit leader-member relations both at her level and the supervisors' level. She has called a meeting with her three leaders to discuss and resolve these matters. Under the leadership of its current Chairman and CEO, Marvin Girouard, Pier 1 Imports continues to emphasize that the key to its success is creativity and novelty in its product mix. This is good news to suppliers like Kim Wung.

Opening Case Questions:

1. Explain the dyadic relationship between Chang and each of his followers, and how this affects the way each follower perceives him.
2. Explain the concept of in-groups and out-groups, and the impact they are having on Sung-Mee's team.
3. What leadership qualities distinguish Yeng-Lee from the other two leaders, and to what extent has this affected the level of teamwork in the groups?
4. Describe the quality of the LMX relationship in each of the three groups and how this has affected each group's overall performance.
5. Ms. Wung has called a meeting with her three leaders. How should she conduct this feedback session to insure greater success?

To learn more about Pier 1, visit the company's Web site at **http://www.pier1.com**, or log on to InfoTrac® College Edition at **academic.cengage.com/infotrac,** where you can research and read articles on Pier 1. To learn more about Pier 1's revamped advertising campaign, select the advanced search option and key in record number A128031534 or CJ133996733 to get started.

In this chapter, you will learn more about the intricate nature of dyadic relationships. We will discuss the evolution of dyadic theory, including the vertical dyadic linkage (VDL) theory and leader-member exchange (LMX) theory. Then we will turn our attention to followership, an often ignored but relevant component of effective leadership. The last section of the chapter covers delegation, including a model that can help you develop your delegation skills.

Evolution of the Dyadic Theory

Most of the early theory and research on leadership has focused on leaders and not paid much attention to followers. However, it is evident that good or effective leadership is in part due to good relationships between leaders and followers. Relationship-based approaches to leadership theory have been in development over the past 25 years, and they continue to evolve. Each unique association between a leader and a follower is called a *dyad*. For our purposes, **dyadic** *refers to the individualized relationship between a leader and each follower in a work unit.* Dyadic theorists focus on the development and effects of separate dyadic relationships between leaders and followers. **Dyadic theory** *is an approach to leadership that attempts to explain why leaders vary their behavior with different followers.* The dyadic approach concentrates on the heterogeneity of dyadic relationships, arguing that a single leader will form different relationships with different followers. For instance, if we were to sample the opinions of different followers about one leader, they would reveal different dyadic relationships. One group of followers may characterize their relationship with the leader in positive terms, while another group characterizes their relationship with the same leader in negative terms. A central theme in dyadic leadership is the notion of "support for self-worth" that leaders provide to followers, and the return performance that followers provide to leaders. Support for self-worth is defined as a leader's support for a follower's actions and ideas; building follower's confidence in his/her ability, integrity, and motivation; and paying attention to follower's feelings and needs.

OPENING CASE APPLICATION

1. Explain the Dyadic Relationship between Chang and Each of His Followers, and How This Affects the Way Each Follower Perceives Him.

The nature of the dyadic relationship between Chang and his crew will influence how he treats each member. Each of the two members of his team that he gets along with will definitely characterize their relationship with Chang as positive, while each of the other two members with whom he does not associate will characterize their relationship with him in negative terms. Instead of attempting to identify a single most effective leadership style, dyadic theory concentrates on the examination of unique, independent relationships between followers and the same leader.

Learning Outcome 1

List the four stages of development of the dyadic approach.

Exhibit 7-1 *Dyadic approach: Stages of development.*

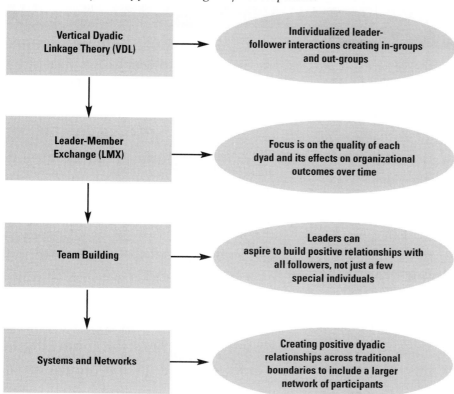

As shown in Exhibit 7-1, the four stages of evolution in the dyadic approach are vertical dyadic linkage theory (VDL), leader-member exchange theory (LMX), team building, and systems and networks theory. The first evolutionary stage (VDL) is the awareness of a relationship between a leader and a follower, rather than between a leader and a group of followers. The second stage (LMX) proposes that the quality of the relationship between a leader and a follower is an important determinant of how each follower will be treated. The third stage (team building) explores the relationship between the leader and the followers as a team concept rather than as a dyad, and the fourth stage (systems and networks) examines relationships at a much broader scale involving multiple levels and structural units within the organization. The four evolutionary stages of dyadic theory are presented separately.

―――――――― Learning Outcome 2 ――――――――

Define the two kinds of relationships that can occur among leaders and followers under the vertical dyadic linkage model.

Vertical Dyadic Linkage (VDL) Theory

Before we begin, determine the dyadic relationship with your manager by completing Self-Assessment 1.

Self-Assessment 1

Dyadic Relationship with Your Manager

Select a present or past manager and answer each question describing your relationship using the following scale:

1 — 2 — 3 — 4 — 5
Is descriptive of   *Is not descriptive*
our relationship   *of our relationship*

1. ____ I have quick, easy access to talk with my manager anytime I want to.

2. ____ I get along well with my manager.

3. ____ I can influence my manager to get things done my way, to get what I want.

4. ____ When I interact with my manager, our conversation is often relationship-oriented (we talk on a personal level), rather than just task-oriented (we talk only about the job).

5. ____ We have a loyal, trusting relationship. We look out for each other's interest.

6. ____ My manager understands my job and the problems that I face; he or she appreciates the work I do.

7. ____ My manager recognizes my potential and gives me opportunities to grow on the job.

8. ____ My manager listens carefully to what I have to say and seeks my advice.

9. ____ My manager gives me good performance evaluations.

10. ____ My manager gives me rewards (raises and other perks) in excess of the minimum.

Add up the numbers on lines 1–10 and place your score here _____ and on the continuum below.

In-group 10 — 20 — 30 — 40 — 50 *Out-group*

The lower your score, the more characteristic your relationship is of the in-group. Read on to better understand the in- and out-group.

The vertical dyad approach is an evolutionary phase from individualized leadership research. Early research on individualized leadership focused on the traditional average leadership style (ALS) approach, in which a leader applies the same style of leadership towards a group as a whole. The perception is that the leader/superior treats everyone the same. However, others describe another approach; whereby the leader treats his/her followers differently. It is called the vertical dyad linkage approach. This is essentially a dyads-within-dyads view of leadership.[1] VDL describes a situation whereby a leader forms dyadic in-group relationships with some followers and dyadic out-group relationships with other followers. Therefore, **vertical dyadic linkage (VDL) theory** *examines how leaders form one-on-one relationships with followers, and how these often create in-groups and out-groups within the leader's work unit.* Central to VDL theory is the notion of "support for self-worth" that one individual provides for another. A leader provides support for feelings of self-worth to a follower.[2] For example, a leader may provide closer attention, guidance, feedback, and consideration to a follower. The follower in turn provides exceptional performance to the leader—for example, a follower performing above standards and always willing to go the extra mile for the leader. Studies have revealed that relationships developed in these dyads may occur at a formal or informal level, whereby some dyads are linked to assigned work group and others are independent of the formal work group. Also, a leader may link (one-on-one) with many individuals, or only a few individuals, and not others.

This selective association or differentiation by leaders among formally as-signed subordinates leads to in-groups and out-groups that tend to remain sta-ble over time. These relationships affect the types of power and influence tac-tics leaders use. *The* **in-group** *includes followers with strong social ties to their leader in a supportive relationship characterized by high mutual trust, respect, loyalty, and influence.* Leaders primarily use expert, referent, and reward power to influence members of the in-group. *The* **out-group** *includes followers with few or no social ties to their leader, in a strictly task-centered relationship characterized by low exchange and top-down influence.* Leaders mostly use reward, as well as legitimate and coercive power, to influence out-group mem-bers (these types of power were discussed in more detail in Chapter 4). To sat-isfy the terms of the exchange relationship, out-group followers need only comply with formal role requirements (such as duties, rules, standard proce-dures, and legitimate direction from the leader). As long as such compliance is forthcoming, the out-group follower receives the standard benefits for the job (such as a salary) and no more.

2. Explain the Concept of In-Groups and Out-Groups, and the Impact They Are Having on Sung-Mee's Team.

In the opening case, Sung-Mee's crew exhibits all the symptoms of a work unit divided into in-groups and out-groups. Sung-Mee gets along with one crew member that she describes as a fast worker, and the two of them don't get along with the rest of the crew. Lead-ers have considerably more influence with in-group followers.

OPENING CASE APPLICATION

Members of the in-group are invited to participate in important decision making, are given added responsibility, and have greater access to the leader. Members of the out-group are managed according to the requirements of the employment contract. They receive little inspiration, encouragement, or recog-nition. In terms of influence and support, in-group members experience greater mutual influence and collaborative effort with the leader, while out-group mem-bers tend not to experience positive relationships and influence. The in-group versus out-group status also reveals an element of reciprocity or exchange in the relationship. The leader grants special favors to in-group members in exchange for their loyalty, commitment, and outstanding performance. This creates mu-tual reinforcement based on common needs and interests. Ultimately, these formations create stronger social ties within the groups as well as intergroup biases between the groups. Thus, individuals will be more likely to share with members of their own group (in-group) than with members of other groups (out-groups).

WorkApplication1

Recall a work unit or organization you worked at that had both in-groups and out-groups. Describe some of the ways in which the manager's behavior and actions toward in-group and out-group members varied.

_____

_____

_____

_____

_____

In-Groups vs. Out-Groups

From each of the following statements from a subordinate, identify which group he or she belongs to. Write the appropriate letter in the blank before each item.

a. in-group   b. out-group

1. ____ My boss and I are similar in a lot of ways.

2. ____ When I am not sure what is going on, I can count on my boss to tell me the truth even if it will hurt my feelings.

3. ____ When I have a major problem at work or in my personal life, my boss would do only that which is required of him or her as my manager without going out of his or her way.

4. ____ As far as my feelings toward my boss go, we relate to each other strictly along professional lines and work.

5. ____ I seldom have any direct contact with my boss unless something is wrong in the way I have done my job.

Leader-Member Exchange (LMX) Theory

The next evolutionary stage in the dyadic approach is the leader-member exchange (LMX) theory. Leader-member interaction plays a critical role in organizational life. Unfortunately, such exchanges can also be a leading cause of employee distress. The underlying assumption of LMX theory is that leaders or superiors have limited amounts of social, personal, and organizational resources (such as energy, time, attention and discretion), and as a result tend to distribute them among followers selectively.[3] Leaders do not interact with all followers equally, which ultimately results in the formation of LMXs that vary in quality. High-quality LMX relationships are often characterized by greater input in decisions, mutual support, informal influence, trust, and greater negotiating latitude. Low-quality LMX relationships are characterized by less support, more formal supervision, little or no involvement in decisions, and less trust and attention from the leader.[4] Therefore, **leader-member exchange (LMX)** *is defined as the quality of the exchange relationship between an employee and his or her superior.*[5]

It is evident that the quality of LMX relationships is a determinant of how each follower will be treated. High-quality exchange relationships (also known as in-groups) reveal a high degree of mutual positive affect, loyalty, respect, and trust, whereas low-quality exchange relationships reveal the opposite (also known as out-groups). Therefore, LMX theory and research offers an alternative way of examining organizational leadership, arguing that the quality of a leader-follower dyadic relationship would be more predictive of positive follower and organizational outcomes than traits or behaviors of superiors.[6] It is evident that the quality of LMX is pivotal in influencing employees' work-related cognitive, affective, and behavioral experiences, roles, and fate in their organizations. We will examine these outcomes later when LMX theory is discussed in greater depth.

Ethical Dilemma 1

LMX at Work

Leader-member exchange (LMX) theory states that in each work group some employees belong to the in-group and others belong to the out-group. Think about your present or past employment. Can you identify members of the in- and out-group? Which group were you in?

1. Is it ethical to exclude employees from the in-group?
2. Do you think people in the in-group tend to think exclusion is ethical and those in the out-group tend to think it is unethical?
3. Is your answer to question 1 based on whether you were a member of the in- or out-group?
4. Is it possible for all employees to be in the in-group?
5. Should managers work to overcome LMX Theory by including all employees in the in-group?

Learning Outcome 3

Describe the main focus of team-building from a Leader-Follower perspective.

Team Building

Given the increasingly complex and uncertain environment in which organizations find themselves, many have responded by adopting teams as their fundamental unit of organizational structure, in an effort to decentralize decision making and respond more effectively to external opportunities and threats. Leadership in the team structure involves a primary concern to motivate a group of individuals to work together to achieve a common objective, while alleviating any conflicts or obstacles that may arise while striving toward that objective.[7] The emphasis is on forming relationships with all group members, not just with a few special individuals. Effective leaders know that while it is not possible to treat all followers in exactly the same way, it is important that each person perceive that he or she is an important and respected member of the team rather than a "second-class citizen." Therefore, the manager must provide all employees access to high-quality leader-member exchanges that are based on mutual trust, supportiveness, respect, and loyalty. For instance, not every employee may desire greater responsibility, but each should feel that there is equal opportunity based on competence rather than on being part of some in-group in the organization. Leader-member exchange relationships can result in greater teamwork, as employees pursue cooperation with other team members as a way to reciprocate to the leader who desires such behavior.[8] Therefore, workplace social exchanges between individual employees, work groups, and managers are critical to team building. The concept of social capital is used to describe group members' social relationships within and outside their groups and how these relationships affect group effectiveness.[9] As a result, some see team building as a multilevel social exchange concept wherein the interface of leadership and team processes is quite evident.

3. What Leadership Qualities Distinguish Yeng-Lee from the Other Two Leaders, and to What Extent Has This Affected the Level of Teamwork in the Groups?

Of the three crew leaders in the opening case, Yeng-Lee's crew best represents a team in the way they work and relate to each other. There is clear evidence of a much closer relationship between Yeng-Lee and her followers.

Studies have shown that when leaders are trained to develop and nurture high-quality relationships with all of their followers, the results on follower performance are dramatic. Followers who feel they have developed a positive one-on-one relationship with the leader tend to exhibit higher productivity and performance gains. As these relationships mature, the entire work group becomes more cohesive, and the payoffs are evident to all participants. In some sense, partnership building enables a leader to meet both the personal and work-related needs of each group member, one at a time. Through the leader's support, encouragement, and training, the followers feel a sense of self-worth, appreciation, and value for their work, and they respond with high performance. The concept of leading teams is covered in detail in Chapter 8.

--- **Learning** Outcome 4 ---

Discuss the focus of the systems and networks approach from a Leader-Follower perspective.

Systems and Networks

Across all sectors of our economy, there is a noticeable trend of organizations seeking and getting involved in a variety of collaborative arrangements (such as partnerships, consortia, alliances, and networks) for the purposes of entering new markets, gaining innovations, or new products. From this perspective, dyadic theory maintains that LMX does not exist in isolation, but rather is embedded within a larger system of networks and work groups. By collaborating, organizations hope to exchange strengths (such as skills, capabilities, knowledge, and resources) with others, which will allow all partners to develop timely, innovative, synergistic solutions to complex problems they could not address on their own.[10] From a network perspective, the focus is on relations among actors, whether they are individuals, work units, or organizations. The actors are embedded within networks of interconnected relationships that provide opportunities and constraints on behavior.[11,12] Effective LMX at this level would determine the extent to which individual participants are able to draw on their group ties and, at the same time, transcend those ties to act collectively. A systems-oriented perspective focuses on how the quality of the LMX relationship affects followers at the interpersonal, group, and organizational levels. For instance, studies have found that the quality of LMX strongly influences subordinates' communication satisfaction at the interpersonal (personal feedback and supervisory communication), group (coworker exchange and organizational integration in the workgroup), and organizational (corporate communications and communications climate) levels.[13,14] Proponents of the systems and networks view contend that leader relationships are not limited to followers, but include peers, customers, suppliers, and other relevant stakeholders in the collectives of workgroups and organization-wide networks. The organization is viewed as a system of interrelated parts. To be effective, groups need to manage "boundary-spanning" relationships with other groups and external members in their organization in order to gain access to information and political resources. Accomplishing this outcome requires effective leadership.

Today, organizations are structured along functional, divisional, product, customer, and geographic lines. Research on group dynamics and culture does reveal that such organizational structures also affect employee cognitive structures. In other words, these structures form departmental boundaries that create stronger social ties within the group as well as intergroup biases between the groups. Individuals and groups are connected to certain people (and not to others), and this pattern of connection creates a network of interdependent social exchanges wherein certain people become trusted exchange partners who can be called upon for resources and support.[15] As a result, individuals will be more inclined to align or associate with members of their own functional group (in-group) than with members of other functional groups (out-groups). Such alliance networks may provide members such benefits as access to knowledge, information, referrals, and career opportunities.[16,17] However, it should also be noted that organizational group boundaries create actual and perceived difficulties in integrating and coordinating organizational activities. A study comparing perceptual sharing to actual sharing between employees revealed that individuals understated the extent of their sharing with out-group members and overstated their sharing with in-group members. Therefore, there is a need for groups to more actively manage their cooperation and coordination with other organizational units.[18]

Leaders must create processes and networks that bring all workers (across functional lines) together to talk to one another, listen to one another's stories, and reflect together. Developing relationships of trust, where people from various backgrounds, disciplines, and hierarchies talk to one another, would no doubt avoid the polarization that dominates organizations characterized by in-groups and out-groups.[19]

Leader-Member Exchange Theory

Leadership is a relationship that is jointly produced by leaders and followers. There is no doubt that the relationships between leaders and their followers are critical to organizational success. LMX theory has enhanced our

Stages of Development of the Dyadic Approach

Which stage is described by the following statements? Write the appropriate letter in the blank before each item.

a. vertical dyadic linkage theory   c. team building
b. leader-member exchange theory   d. systems and networks

6. ____ A dyadic approach that focuses on creating positive dyadic relationships across traditional boundaries to include more participants.

7. ____ A hierarchical relationship in which leader-follower dyads develop, and the emphasis is on the quality of each relationship and its effects on organizational outcomes over time.

8. ____ A dyadic approach that encourages leaders to aspire to having positive relationships with all followers, not just a few special individuals.

9. ____ A relationship in which leader-follower interactions lead to the creation of in-groups and out-groups.

understanding of the interaction process between leaders and followers. The quality of LMX affects employees' work ethic, productivity, satisfaction, and perceptions. Studies that have used leader-member exchange theory to examine the effects of the employee-supervisor relationship on important job-related outcomes have come to the same conclusion: employees who perceive themselves to be in supportive relationships with their supervisors tend to have higher performance, job satisfaction, and organizational commitment.[20] For a better appreciation of the concept, this section will briefly discuss the following related topics: the influence of LMX quality on followers; the ways in which leader-member relationships develop; measurement of LMX variables; behavioral elements that influence the initiation of leader-member relationships, also referred to as antecedents of LMX relationships; and bias in LMX relationships.

The Influence of LMX on Follower Behavior

Those who hold the view that building positive relationships is a key ingredient for leadership development have focused on leader-member exchange theory as the basis for understanding leadership development and its role in creating social capital for organizations.[21] Leader-member exchange theory supporters argue that similarities between a leader and a follower exert a positive influence on the relationship and on outcome variables.[22] Studies examining the characteristics of LMX relationships have explored such factors as communication frequency, turnover, job satisfaction, performance, job climate, and commitment.[23,24] The underlying assumption of LMX is that leaders do not interact with all followers equally, which ultimately results in the formation of leader-member relations that vary in quality. A number of studies have demonstrated that the quality of LMX is central in influencing followers' affective, cognitive, and behavioral experiences; roles; and fate in their organizations. High-quality LMX relationships are characterized by favorable outcomes, such as higher levels of leader support and guidance, higher levels of follower satisfaction and performance, wide latitude of discretion for followers, and lower levels of follower turnover.[25–27] A recent study found that LMX and perceived organizational support (POS) were positively related to follower perceptions of career success and job satisfaction.[28] LMX and POS were found to play compensatory roles in helping employees cope with low work-value congruence. When an employee perceives that there is a gap between his or her values and the organization's values, this can create low work-value congruence, which is more likely to result in less satisfaction. LMX was found to make up for low work-value congruence in that even when an employees' values are not very similar to those of the organization, a high LMX relationship can allow the employee to negotiate with the leader to create organizational experiences that are positive, and in line with his or her values. For example, high-LMX employees may experience lower levels of cognitive dissonance because they have higher negotiating latitude, or freedom to design their own jobs with the leader's support. In essence, compared to employees in low-quality LMXs, high-LMX employees are more likely to report greater communication satisfaction and rapport in their interactions with leaders.[29,30]

Followers with strong social ties to the leader (high LMX) are said to belong to the in-group while those with weak social ties to the leader (low LMX) are said to belong to the out-group. Being a member of the in-group puts you in a very favorable position. For example, in-group followers routinely receive higher performance ratings than out-group followers; out-group followers routinely show higher levels of turnover than in-group followers; and, finally, when asked to evaluate organizational climate, in-group followers give more positive ratings than out-group followers. Overall, studies have found that the quality of the LMX relationship for in-group members is substantially superior to out-group members. The benefits of in-group members to a leader are evident. When a leader has tasks that require considerable initiative and effort on the part of group members to be carried out successfully, the assistance and commitment of followers in the in-group becomes an invaluable asset to the leader.

4. Describe the Quality of the LMX Relationship in Each of the Three Groups and How This Has Affected Each Group's Overall Performance.

In the opening case, Yeng-Lee's crew works together as a team. She has a high-quality relationship with all her crew, and they help each other and get along well. As a result, Yeng-Lee's crew has the highest productivity of the three crews.

OPENING CASE APPLICATION

Self-Assessment 2

In-Group and Out-Group

Based on Self-Assessment 1 and your reading of VDL and LMX theory, place the people who work or have worked for your present or past manager in the in-group or out-group. Be sure to include yourself.

In-Group Members	Out-Group Members
_____	_____
_____	_____
_____	_____

However, the special relationship with in-group followers creates certain obligations and constraints for the leader. To maintain the relationship, the leader must continuously pay attention to in-group members, remain responsive to their needs and feelings, and rely more on time-consuming influence methods such as persuasion and consultation. The leader cannot resort to coercion or heavy-handed use of authority without endangering the quality of the relationship. The followers are therefore said to have developed social capital, defined as the set of resources that inheres in the structure of relations between members of the group, which helps them get ahead.[31,32] The basis for establishing a deeper exchange relationship with in-group members is the leader's control over outcomes that are desirable to the followers. These outcomes include such benefits as helping with a follower's career (for example, recommending advancement), giving special favors (bigger office, better work schedule), allowing participation in decision making, delegating greater responsibility and authority, more sharing of information, assigning in-group members to interesting and desirable tasks, and giving tangible rewards such as a pay increase. In return for these benefits, in-group members have certain obligations and expectations beyond those required of out-group members. In-group members are expected to be loyal to the leader, to be more committed to task objectives, to work harder, and to share some of the leader's administrative duties. To the leader this represents social capital that gives him or her power and influence over followers. Unless this cycle of reciprocal reinforcement of leader and member behavior is interrupted, the relationship is likely to develop to a point where there is a high degree of mutual dependence, support, and loyalty.[33]

Now that you understand LMX, complete Self-Assessment 2.

Strategies for Developing Positive Leader-Member Relations

In a revision of LMX theory, the development of relationships in a leader-member dyad was described as a "life-cycle model" with three possible stages. In the first stage, the leader and follower conduct themselves as strangers, testing each other to identify what kinds of behavior are acceptable. Each relationship is negotiated informally between each follower and the leader. The definition of each group member's role determines what the leader expects the member to do. Here, impressions management by the follower would play a critical role in influencing how the leader perceives him or her. **Impressions management** *is a follower's effort to project a favorable image in order to gain an immediate benefit or improve a long-term relationship with the leader.* Impressions management is most critical during the early stages (stage 1 and 2) of the life-cycle model. It is a valuable tool that, if used well, can enhance the visibility of the follower's strengths and performance. Studies have shown that impressions management tactics such as ingratiation can influence the leader in very positive ways. **Ingratiation** *is the effort to appear supportive, appreciative, and respectful.* Ingratiatory influence tactics include favor rendering, self-promotion, and behavioral conformity. In this instance, followers go beyond the call of duty to render services to the leader and to conform their behavior to the expectations of the leader. **Self-promotion** *is the effort to appear competent and dependable.* Most studies find a positive correlation between ingratiation by a follower and affection (or liking) of the leader for the follower. Affection in turn is positively related to the quality of the exchange relationship and the leader's assessment of the follower's competence, loyalty, commitment, and work ethic. It would appear, therefore, that one's social skills are critical in influencing the leader-member relations. Employees in the in-group may be those who believe in their capabilities to orchestrate performance in the social domain and capture the leader's attention.[34]

In the second stage of the life-cycle model, as the leader and follower become acquainted, they engage in further refining the roles they will play together. Mutual trust, loyalty, and respect begin to develop between leader and follower. There is "open" communication in which followers are afforded greater attention, confidence, influence, inside information, and negotiating latitude without recourse to authority. Followers in this type of relationship are more likely to be very proactive. Relationships that remain at the first stage may deteriorate and remain at the level of an out-group member. Here, there is more of a "closed" communication system in which followers are afforded limited opportunities to influence decisions or interact informally with leaders.

Some exchange relationships advance to a third stage as the roles reach maturity. Here, exchange based on self-interest is transformed into mutual commitment to the mission and objectives of the work unit. It would appear from examining these three stages that the end result of the life cycle model of LMX relationships is the creation of actual and perceived differences between in-group (high-quality LMX) and out-group (low-quality LMX) members. For example, from a communications perspective, one study concluded that subordinates in low-quality LMXs are likely to experience less communications satisfaction with superiors than employees involved in high-quality LMXs.[35,36] Critics point out that these differences could lead to intergroup conflicts and undermine teamwork within the broader work unit. It is only natural that members of low-quality LMXs may feel that they are being unfairly treated and thus resent those in high-quality LMXs. Hostility between the two groups is likely to undermine necessary cooperation and teamwork for the work unit as a whole.

WorkApplication2

Recall an occasion when you had the opportunity to make a positive first impression on your manager. Describe what tactics you employed and their effect on your manager.

_____

_____

_____

_____

_____

--- Learning Outcome 5 ---

Discuss the key limitation or drawback with LMX application.

Limitation of LMX Application

A major limitation of LMX is measurement difficulty. LMX theory deals with attitudes and perceptions of individuals; two issues that are often difficult to quantify and measure. For this reason, recent research efforts on LMX have focused on instrumentation of the theory. The way in which the attributes of high-quality LMX relationships have been defined and measured have varied somewhat from study to study. Most studies have measured LMX with a scale based on a questionnaire filled out by the follower. The LMX-7 scale is the most commonly used instrument for defining and measuring the quality of relationships. Examples of questions featured on the LMX-7 scale included structured questions, such as the following:

- How well does your leader understand your job problems and needs? (Not a bit, a little, a fair amount, quite a bit, and a great deal)
- How well does your leader recognize your potential? (Not at all, a little, moderately, mostly, and fully)
- How would you characterize your working relationship with your leader? (Extremely ineffective, worse than average, average, better than average, and extremely effective)

In studies using this scale, the quality of relationships is usually assumed to involve attributes such as mutual trust, respect, affection, and loyalty. Complete Self-Assessment 3 to determine your LMX relationship with your manager.

Other researchers have recently used more diverse questionnaires in an attempt to identify separate dimensions of LMX relationships and unique attributes.[37] These new measures appear to combine quality of the relationship with determinants of the relationship, such as perceived competence or behavior of the other person. It is not clear yet whether the newest scales offer any advantages over a single scale in identifying and measuring attributes that can be described as more broad-based or universal. Only a few studies have measured LMX from the perception of both the leader and the follower.[38] Contrary to

---

Self-Assessment 3

Your LMX Relationship with Your Manager

Self-Assessment 1 is a form of measuring your LMX relationship with your manager. Note that some of the questions are similar to the LMX-7 questions. The score, ranging from 10 to 50, gives you more than a simple in-group or out-group assessment. Place your score here _____ and on the following continuum.

10 —— 20 —— 30 —— 40 —— 50
High-quality LMXrelationship   *Low-quality LMX relationship*

The lower your score, generally, the better is your relationship with your manager. We say generally, because you could have a manager who does not have a good relationship with any employee. Thus, a good LMX can be a relative measure.

expectations of high correlation on LMX attributes, the correlation between leader-rated LMX and follower-rated LMX is low enough to raise questions about scale validity for one or both sources. It is unclear whether the low correlation reflects instrument reliability or actual differences in the perception of LMX attributes. Characteristics of LMX deemed positive to the exchange relationship may vary among leaders and followers, depending on key influencing factors. Despite recent research support for LMX theory, it is evident from the above discussion that further research on instrumentation is needed.

--- Learning Outcome 6 ---

Describe three determining factors of high-quality LMX relationships.

Factors that Determine LMX Quality

Behavioral and situational factors influence the creation of high- or low-quality leader-member exchange relationships. LMX relationship antecedents include (1) follower attributes, (2) leader and follower perceptions of each other, and (3) situational factors. The difference between contingency theories and LMX is that while the former emphasizes how a good leader facilitates employee job performance, the latter emphasizes how a good employee facilitates leader job performance.[39] The leader-member exchange model suggests that proactive employees possess additional characteristics. Proactive employees show initiative even in areas outside their immediate responsibility, possess a strong sense of commitment to work unit goals, and show a greater sense of responsibility for unit success. These follower attributes influence leaders to show support, delegate, allow discretion, engage in open communication, and encourage mutual influence between themselves and their followers. Most of the research on LMX theory since the initial studies of the 1970s has focused on examining the strength of these exchanges between the leader and the followers.

The leader and follower perceptions of each other will also predict the quality of the LMX relationship. In this case, the leader's first impressions of the follower can influence the leader's behavior toward the follower. Studies examining this proposition found that a favorable relationship is more likely when the follower is perceived to be competent and dependable, and when the follower's values and attitudes are similar to those of the leader.[40] The leader's first impression of a group member's competency plays an important role in defining the quality of the LMX relationship. It can be assumed that group members who make effective use of impressions management tactics such as ingratiation and self-promotion increase their chances of positively influencing the LMX relationship. A favorable exchange relationship is said to correlate with more supportive behavior by the leader toward the follower, less close monitoring, more mentoring, and more involvement and delegation. From the follower's perspective, a more favorable exchange relationship is correlated with more support for the leader, fewer pressure tactics (for example, threats and demands) to influence the leader, and more open communication with the leader. The quality of the relationship is thus dependent on the type of leader and follower behavior.

Situational factors also do play a role in determining the quality of LMX relationships. Follower reaction to "tryouts," described as "role episodes,"[41] will give leaders clues about employees. For example, a manager asks a new

WorkApplication3

Recall two leaders you have worked with over a period of time. Identify specific attributes that would describe the true nature of your relationship with these leaders. Identify one leader with whom you feel you had a high-quality relationship, and one with whom you had a low-quality relationship. What attributes describe the high-quality and the low-quality relationships with these leaders?

_____

_____

_____

_____

WorkApplication4

Recall a work situation in which you were required to do something that was beyond your employment contract. How did you respond to your manager's request, and what consequences did it have on your relationship with him or her?

_____

_____

_____

_____

_____

employee to do something beyond what the formal employment agreement calls for. The new employee's reaction ("sure, glad to help," versus a grumble, or "that's not my job" attitude) indicates potential loyalty, support, and trustworthiness, and leads to more—versus fewer—opportunities for responsibility, personal growth, and other positive experiences. The perception of the leader from this tryout will greatly influence the type of relationship that ensues between the leader and the follower. Followers perceived to be hardworking and willing to go the extra mile for the leader will be in the in-group, while those who are perceived to be lazy or unwilling to go the extra mile will automatically fall in the out-group.

For whatever reasons—ability level, familiarity, liking, loyalty, reputation of followers, or prior performance—selected pairs of leaders and followers develop high-quality LMX relationships. Leaders express positive attitudes such as trust and respect toward these followers. Leaders also express a desire for reciprocity with followers and imply that they expect a high level of mutual support and loyalty in return. Attempts to link loyalty to supervisor and employee performance have been supported through research. One Chinese study found that loyalty to supervisor was strongly associated with both in-role and extra-role employee performance, more so than organizational commitment.[42]

—————————— Learning Outcome 7 ——————————
Explain the cycle that leads to the Pygmalion effect.

WorkApplication5

Identify a particular leader-follower working relationship that you have had with a manager. To what extent did the Pygmalion effect play a role in the quality of this relationship? How did it affect your career development within the organization?

_____

_____

_____

_____

From a leader's perspective, these explicit and implicit exchanges convey expectations of follower loyalty, commitment, mutual obligation, and respect. This information induces a Pygmalion effect, or what others have described as self-fulfilling prophecy and social reciprocation. As mentioned in Chapter 2, the Pygmalion effect occurs when managers reciprocate the friendship and loyalty from some followers with higher performance ratings. Here we apply it to LMX, and consider how it applies to leader performance evaluation. *The Pygmalion effect occurs when selected group members demonstrate loyalty, commitment, dedication, and trust, and as a result, win the liking of leaders who subsequently give them higher performance ratings.* These ratings, which may or may not be tied to actual performance, then influence the member's reputation and often become a matter of record. The ratings may ultimately be used—formally or informally—in future selection, development, and promotion decisions. Consequently, followers with a history of high performance ratings are those who get promoted to higher-level positions. Thus, a positive Pygmalion effect could well result not only in high follower commitment, satisfaction, and performance ratings by leaders, but also in enhanced career development. In examining the factors that contribute to feelings of career success and satisfaction, one study found that two important sources of support are from the supervisor in the form of leader-member exchange (LMX) and from the organization. LMX and perceived organizational support are positively related to job and career satisfaction.[43]

Embedded in LMX theory is the question of bias. To what extent does bias affect the quality of relationships between leaders and followers, and how does it influence their affective, behavioral, and organization-related performance? The next section examines this question.

—————————— Learning Outcome 8 ——————————

Explain how LMX relationships can lead to unintended bias in HR practices.

Bias in LMX: Employee Career Implications

On its face, what we have described would be judged to be a good or effective process of follower growth and promotion—were it not for the possible adverse implications it might have for the development and career advancement of group members who are not similar to, familiar to, and well liked by their leader. The resulting quality of LMX will be high within the in-groups and low in the out-groups. Thus, arbitrary promotions will likely result in disproportional allocation of organizational rewards to in-group members to the exclusion of out-group members.

The preceding scenario describes what seems to be a naturally occurring process. It does not imply intentional favoritism, discrimination, or bias toward selected individuals or minorities. However, it does explain one important process by which unintended bias can occur in organizations. The conclusion to be drawn from this discussion is that leaders, managers, and human resource management specialists need to be made aware of the potential biasing processes associated with high-quality LMX relationships. Procedural checks and balances need to be applied to minimize such biases, if this is indeed possible. Otherwise, the development of high-quality LMX relations could result in organizationally dysfunctional consequences and discrimination against out-group followers. One possible approach to minimizing selective bias that produces favored treatment toward some members consists of training leaders to offer high-quality LMX relationships to all followers, a practice described as partnership or team building. As discussed earlier, the third stage of the evolution of the dyadic approach focuses on this concept of team building. This stage represents an integration of findings from the previous stages to explain team outcomes rather than separate dyadic units.

Followership

Followership *refers to the behavior of followers that results from the leader-follower influence relationship.* Many scholars agree that leadership is a relationship that is jointly produced by leaders and followers, and that to adequately understand it, we must know more about the often-nameless persons who comprise the followers of leaders. However, because leaders are more visible than followers, most leadership research has focused on leaders and ignored the role of followers in explaining organizational successes or failures. Many writers have criticized extant leadership theories for being too "leader-centric." The focus of these theories has been almost exclusively on the impact of leader traits and behaviors on followers' attitudes and behaviors.[44] Much less has been done to advance understanding of the follower component and the psychological processes and mechanisms that connect leaders and followers. As a result, some scholars are pursuing a follower-centric perspective on leadership.[45] There is increasing recognition that leaders are just one part of a duality, because there can be no leaders without followers. Effective leadership requires effective followership, because without followers, there are no leaders. No work unit or organized effort can succeed and be sustained without followers. According to one study's findings, leaders account for as little as 20 percent of a successful venture; with much of the remaining 80 percent coming from followership.[46] Also, to a large extent, societal views about followers have contributed to our limited understanding of followership. From an early age we are taught to focus on becoming a leader, not a follower. Webster defines a follower as "one that follows the opinions or teachings of another." This definition implies that followers are passive partners of the leader-follower dyad until they receive explicit instructions from a leader and then proceed to follow those instructions in an unquestioning manner. Effective followers do more than fulfill the vision laid out by their leader; they are partners in creating the vision. They take responsibility for getting their jobs done, take the initiative in fixing problems, and question leaders when they think they are wrong.[47]

Recall from Chapter 1 that we defined leadership as "the influencing process of leaders and followers to achieve organizational objectives through change." *A **follower** is a person who is being influenced by a leader.* However, there is growing awareness that the influencing process is a two-way street, with followers also influencing leaders. Effective followers can help leaders lead without threatening the leader's position. Good followers who give input that influences managers are vital to the success of any organization. In this section we discuss followership styles, guidelines for effective followership, follower influencing characteristics, effective leader feedback, and the dual roles of being a leader and follower.

The Effective Follower, and Follower Types

Organizational successes and failures are often attributed to effective or ineffective leaders without fully recognizing the contributions of followers. Unfortunately, due to the limited research focusing on the role of followers, there does not appear to be much evidence supporting a strong correlation between effective followership and effective leadership. However, when examining the question of what distinguishes high-performance teams and organizations from average ones, most scholars and practitioners agree that high-performing organizations have good leaders and good followers. Competent, confident, and motivated followers are key to the successful performance of any leader's work group or team. Increasingly, many people are replacing old, negative notions of followers with positive ones. Rather than the conforming and passive role in which followers have been cast, effective followers are described as courageous, responsible, and proactive.[48]

Despite the growing recognition of the importance of followership and the pivotal role followers play in leadership, the most significant attempt to understand followership effectiveness and followership types is still Kelley's conceptualization.[49] Using a combination of two types of behavior—independent critical thinking and active involvement in organizational affairs—Kelley groups followers into five categories based on their specific behavioral mix. The first behavior refers to the follower's ability to examine, analyze, and evaluate matters of significance in the organization's life. Having this ability implies that the follower possesses the requisite knowledge base and is capable of critical thinking. Independent-minded thinkers go beyond standard procedures when rationality calls for independent actions or decisions; they are willing to follow their convictions. They are proactive, creative, innovative, and willing to offer constructive criticism when it's appropriate. Conversely, the opposite of this person is one who is not independent in their thinking. The dependent, noncritical thinker sticks to the procedure or preset instructions with very little deviation—even when circumstances warrant otherwise. He or she accepts the leader's ideas without independent evaluation. The second behavior—active involvement—refers to the follower's willingness to be a visible and active participant. The active individual takes initiative in problem solving and decision making, is highly visible throughout the work unit, and interacts with coworkers at many different levels. He or she is very comfortable sharing ideas with others and generally goes beyond expected behavior when carrying out assignments. The opposite of this person is the passive individual who is barely noticeable within the work unit. With passive followers, their level of involvement or interaction is limited to doing what they are told to do. They avoid responsibility beyond what their job description calls for and need constant supervision. As discussed previously, the response of these followers to leader tryouts will affect the quality of the LMX relationship and automatically place them in the out-group.

According to Kelley, the extent to which a follower is active or passive—and is an independent, critical thinker or a dependent, noncritical thinker—determines whether he or she is an alienated follower, a passive follower, a conformist, a pragmatic follower, or an effective follower (see Exhibit 7-2).[50] *The* **alienated follower** *is a passive yet independent, critical thinker*. The alienated follower is someone who feels cheated, or unappreciated by his or her organization for exemplary work. Often cynical in their behavior, alienated followers

Exhibit 7-2 *Followership types.*

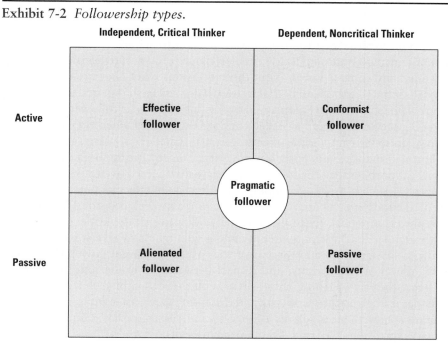

are capable but unwilling to participate in developing solutions to problems. They are just happy to dwell on the negatives and ignore the positives as far as organizational life goes. *The* **conformist follower** *is an active but unassertive, noncritical thinker.* In other words, conformists are the "yes people" of the organization. They carry out all orders without considering the consequences of such orders. A conformist would do anything to avoid conflict. Authoritarian leaders prefer conformist followers. *The* **passive follower** *exhibits neither critical, independent thinking nor active participation.* The passive follower looks to the leader to do all the thinking and does not carry out his or her tasks with enthusiasm. Lacking in initiative and a sense of responsibility, the passive follower requires constant supervision and never goes beyond the job description. They are often described by their leaders as lazy, unmotivated, and incompetent. *The* **effective follower** *is both an independent, critical thinker and a very active member in the group.* The effective follower presents a consistent image of commitment, innovation, creativity, and hard work for achieving organizational goals. Effective followers are not risk averse nor shy of conflict. They have the courage to initiate change and put themselves at risk or in conflict with others, even their leaders, to serve the best interest of the organization. As such, they are often described as proactive. Effective followers tend to function very well in self-managed teams. They are a manager's best asset in that they complement the leader's efforts and can be relied upon to relieve the leader of many tasks. *The* **pragmatic follower** *exhibits a little of all four styles—depending on which style fits the prevailing situation.* Pragmatic followers are "stuck in the middle" most of the time. Because it is difficult to discern just where they stand on issues, they present an ambiguous image, with positive and negative sides. On the positive side, when an organization is going through desperate times, the pragmatic follower knows how to "work the system to get things done." On the negative side, this same behavior can be interpreted as "playing political games," or adjusting to maximize self-interest. Before reading more about how to be an effective follower, and examining some guidelines, complete Self-Assessment 4.

To be effective as a follower, it is important to acquire the skills necessary to combine two opposing follower roles; namely, to execute decisions made by a leader, and to raise issues about those decisions when they are deemed misguided or unethical. In an interview, Ira Chaleff, a consultant and author of the book *The Courageous Follower,* discusses his belief that followers must have the courage to challenge a leader's actions or policies when they are flawed, and to do so in a supportive and effective way. Chaleff goes on to say that if the follower's opposition is based on integrity, concern for the organization, and concern for the leader, the follower may actually succeed in earning the leader's respect.[51] Such a proactive employee is often quite effective precisely because he or she is capable of and willing to question a leader's decisions. Though it is not always practical, followers must be willing to risk the leader's displeasure with such feedback. Moral integrity and a willingness to take stands based on principle are distinguishing characteristics of the effective follower. Developing a high level of mutual trust and respect between the leader and follower can mitigate the risk of falling out of favor with the leader. In such a relationship, a leader is likely to view criticism and dissenting views as an honest effort to facilitate achievement of shared objectives and values, rather than as an intentional expression of personal disagreement or disloyalty.[52]

Self-Assessment 4

Effective Followership

Select a present or past boss and answer each question describing your behavior using the following scale.

$$5 - 4 - 3 - 2 - 1$$
I do this regularly   *I do not do this*

1. ____ I offer my support and encouragement to my boss when things are not going well.

2. ____ I take initiative to do more than my normal job without having to be asked to do things.

3. ____ I counsel and coach my boss when it is appropriate, such as with a new, inexperienced boss, and in a unique situation in which the boss needs help.

4. ____ When the boss has a bad idea, I raise concerns and try to improve the plans, rather than simply implement a poor decision.

5. ____ I seek and encourage the boss to give me honest feedback, rather than avoid it and act defensively when it is offered.

6. ____ I try to clarify my role in tasks by making sure I understand my boss's expectations of me and my performance standards.

7. ____ I show my appreciation to my boss, such as saying thanks when the boss does something in my interest.

8. ____ I keep the boss informed; I don't withhold bad news.

9. ____ I would resist inappropriate influence by the boss; if asked, I would not do anything illegal or unethical.

Add up the numbers on lines 1-9 and place your score here _____ and on the continuum below.

$$9 - 15 - 25 - 35 - 45$$
Ineffective Follower   *Effective Follower*

The higher your score, generally the more effective you are as a follower. However, your boss also has an effect on your followership. A poor boss can affect your followership behavior; however, make sure you do try to be a good follower. Read on to better understand how to be an effective follower.

How followers perceive a leader plays a critical role in their ability to help the leader grow and succeed. Just as leaders make attributions about follower competence, followers make attributions about leader competence and intentions. Followers assess whether the leader's primary motivation is more for his or her personal benefit or career advancement than their own welfare and the organization's well-being. Credibility is increased and follower commitment is enhanced when the leader makes self-sacrifices to gain support for his or her ideas, rather than imposing on followers. Leaders who appear insincere, or motivated only by personal gain, create an atmosphere in which integrating the two opposing follower roles is impossible. Here, followers would play the passive role of conforming to the leader's expectations without offering any constructive criticism, even when it is called for in a leader's decisions and actions.

Guidelines to Becoming an Effective Follower

Research focused on followership has identified certain behaviors that work and others that don't. This has led to a formulation of guidelines on how to become an effective follower. The guidelines, it is argued, distinguish followers on top-performing teams from their counterparts on marginally performing teams. Issues such as how to improve the leader-follower relationship, how to

---

Exhibit 7-3 *Guidelines to becoming an effective follower.*

a. Offer support to leader.
b. Take initiative.
c. Play counseling and coaching roles to leader when appropriate.
d. Raise issues and/or concerns when necessary.
e. Seek and encourage honest feedback from the leader.
f. Clarify your role and expectations.
g. Show appreciation.
h. Keep the leader informed.
i. Resist inappropriate influence of leader.

resist improper influence, and how to challenge flawed plans and actions are dealt with through these guidelines. Also underlying these guidelines are ethical and moral themes, such as maintaining credibility and trust, adhering to your own values and convictions, and taking personal responsibility for team performance and for your own life. Exhibit 7-3 presents nine guidelines for effective followership; note that the nine questions in Self-Assessment 4 are based on these guidelines.

Offer Support to Leader

A good follower looks for ways to express support and encouragement to a leader who is encountering resistance in trying to introduce needed change in his or her organization. Successful organizations are characterized by followers whose work ethic and philosophy are in congruence with those of the leader.

Take Initiative

Effective followers take the initiative to do what is necessary without being told, including working beyond their normally assigned duties. They look for opportunities to make a positive impact on the organization's objectives. When serious problems arise that impede the organization's ability to accomplish its objectives, effective followers take the risk to initiate corrective action by pointing out the problem to the leader, suggesting alternative solutions, or if necessary, resolving the problem outright. While taking the initiative often involves risks, if done carefully and properly, it can make the follower a valuable part of the team and a member of the leader's in-group.[53]

Play Counseling and Coaching Roles to Leader When Appropriate

Contrary to the myth that leaders have all the answers, most people now recognize that followers also have opportunities to coach and counsel leaders, especially when a leader is new and inexperienced. A mutually trusting relationship with a leader facilitates upward coaching and counseling. An effective follower must be alert for opportunities to provide helpful advice, and ask questions, or simply be a good listener when the leader needs someone to confide in. Because some leaders may be reluctant to ask for help, it is the follower's responsibility to recognize such situations and step in when appropriate. For example, a leader whose interpersonal relationship with another follower may be having a different effect than the leader intended could be counseled to see the ineffectiveness of his approach or style by another follower: "I am sure you intended for Bob to see the value of being on time when you said . . ., but that is not how he took it." When coaching and counseling a leader is done with respect, it is most effective. As one author puts it, respect creates symmetry, empathy, and connection in all kinds of relationships, including that between a leader and a follower.[54]

Raise Issues and/or Concerns When Necessary

When there are potential problems or drawbacks with a leader's plans and proposals, a follower's ability to bring these issues or concerns to light is critical. How the follower raises these issues is crucial, because leaders often get defensive in responding to negative feedback. Followers can minimize such defensiveness by acknowledging the leader's superior status and communicating a sincere desire to be of help in accomplishing the organization's goals, rather than personal objectives. When challenging a leader's flawed plans and proposals, it is important for the follower to pinpoint specifics rather than vague generalities, and to avoid personalizing the critique. This guideline corresponds with the emerging view of the proactive employee as a follower who is highly involved and very much an independent thinker with initiative and a well-developed sense of responsibility.[55]

In some cases a leader's refusal to listen to a follower's concerns about a decision or policy that is unethical, illegal, or likely to have significant adverse consequences on the organization may require the follower to use influence tactics, such as threatening to resign or warning of public exposure. However, such drastic steps are appropriate only after other less drastic alternatives (such as rational persuasion or the use of group pressure) have failed to influence the leader. The threat to resign as an influence tactic should not be issued lightly; it should be expressed with the conviction to follow through, or it should not be used at all. Also, the follower must not express such a threat with personal hostility.

Seek and Encourage Honest Feedback from the Leader

Followers can play a constructive role in how their leaders evaluate them. Some leaders are uncomfortable with expressing negative concerns about a follower's performance, so they tend to focus only on the follower's strengths. One way to build mutual trust and respect with the leader is to encourage honest feedback in his or her evaluation of your performance. Encourage the leader to point out the strongest and weakest aspects of your work. To ensure that you have a comprehensive evaluation, consult the leader for his or her input on other things you can do to be more effective, and find out if he or she has concerns about any other aspects of your work performance.

Clarify Your Role and Expectations

Where there is some question of role ambiguity or uncertainty about job expectations, this must be clarified with the leader. As will be revealed in Chapter 8 on leading effective teams, it is the leader's responsibility to clearly communicate role expectations for followers. Nevertheless, many leaders fail to communicate clear job expectations, followers' scope of authority and responsibility, performance targets that must be attained, and appropriate deadlines. Followers must insist on clarification in these areas by their leaders. In some cases the problem is that of role conflict. The leader directs a follower to perform mutually exclusive tasks and expects results on all of them at the same time. Followers should be assertive but diplomatic about resolving role ambiguity and conflict.

Show Appreciation

Everyone, including leaders, loves to be appreciated when they perform a good deed that benefits others. When a leader makes a special effort to help a follower, such as helping to protect the follower's interest, or nurturing and promoting the follower's career, it is appropriate for the follower to show appreciation. Even if the leader's actions don't directly benefit a particular follower but represent a significant accomplishment for the organization (for example, negotiating a difficult joint venture, completing a successful restructuring task, securing a greater share of resources for the group), it is still an appropriate gesture for followers to express their appreciation and admiration for the leader. Recognition and support of this kind only reinforces desirable leadership behavior. Although some may argue that praising a leader is a form of ingratiation easily used to influence the leader, when sincere, it can help to build a productive leader-follower exchange relationship.

Keep the Leader Informed

Leaders rely on their followers to relay important information about their actions and decisions. Accurate and timely information enables a leader to make good decisions and to have a complete picture of where things stand in the organization. Leaders who appear not to know what is going on in their organizations do feel and look incompetent in front of their peers and superiors. It is embarrassing for a leader to hear about events or changes taking place within his or her unit from others. This responsibility of relaying information to the leader includes both positive and negative information. Some followers tend to withhold bad news from their leaders; this is just as detrimental as providing no information at all.

WorkApplication6

Give examples of how you, or someone you worked with, implemented three of the nine guidelines to effective followership.

_____

_____

_____

_____

_____

Resist Inappropriate Influence of Leader

A leader may be tempted to use his or her power to influence the follower in ways that are inappropriate (legally or ethically). Despite the power gap between the leader and follower, the follower is not required to comply with inappropriate influence attempts, or to be exploited by an abusive leader. Effective followers challenge the leader in a firm, tactful, and diplomatic way. Reminding the leader of his or her ethical responsibilities, insisting on your rights, and pointing out the negative consequences of complying are various ways in which a follower can resist inappropriate influence attempts by a leader. It is important to challenge such behavior early, before it becomes habitual, and to do it without personal hostility.

Learning Outcome 9

Discuss the three follower influencing characteristics.

Guidelines to Becoming an Effective Follower

Identify each guideline using the letters a–i from Exhibit 7-3:

_____ 10. We started a new project today, and I did not understand what I was supposed to do. So I went to talk to my boss about what to do.

_____ 11. We have a new boss, and I've been filling her in on how we do things in our department.

_____ 12. My boss and I have short daily meetings.

_____ 13. Employees have not been following safety rules as they should, and the boss hasn't done anything about it. So I went to talk to my boss about it.

_____ 14. We only have performance reviews once a year. But I wanted to know what my boss thinks of my work, so we had a meeting to discuss my performance.

_____ 15. My boss gave me a new assignment that I wanted, so I thanked him.

_____ 16. I showed up early for the meeting and the conference room was messy, so I cleaned up.

_____ 17. My boss hinted about having a sexual relationship, so I reminded her that I was happily married and clearly told her I was not interested and not to talk about it again.

Determinants of Follower Influence

The status of a follower within an organization will affect how he or she treats or is treated by other employees. Some followers seem to have more influence over their peers (and even their leaders) than others. These are the followers that command respect, obedience, and loyalty from their peers and thus are considered of higher status than the rest. The question of what characteristics influence this distinction among followers is the essence of this section. The three influencing characteristics that have been found to play the most part in determining how followers relate to each other and to their leaders are: follower's power position, locus of control, and education and experience (see Exhibit 7-4).

Follower Power Position

It used to be believed that followers in an organization held no power and cared little about long-term issues, but that is no longer the case. In today's workplace, followers can and do command greater degrees of influence, both with other followers and with their leaders. With respect to the position of formal leaders in an organization, the traditional belief was that they were the driving force behind change and were role models for the change process. Leaders need to realize that they are no longer the sole possessors of power and influence in their work units. The new reality is that no matter what position a person holds in the workplace, they are a force for change. Followers are often recognized as innovators, self-managers, or risk-takers. These are terms that were traditionally reserved for describing leaders, not followers. It is now

Exhibit 7-4 *Factors that determine follower influence.*

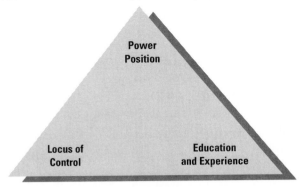

recognized that leaders have to allow themselves room to learn from followers in the modern global economy.

In looking at the leader's in-group and out-group, it is easy to see how followers in a leader's in-group with position power (referent or charismatic) may wield greater influence on the leader than followers in the out-group. Even the employee at the bottom rung of the corporate ladder has personal and position-based sources of power that can be used to boost upward influence, thereby affecting the organization and acquiring an active role in the leadership of the organization.

Position sources of power include information, location, and access. A position that is key to the transmission of information can establish that position, and the follower in it, as critical—thus, influential—to those who seek the information. A central location—such as being a company's office supply clerk or warehouse clerk—provides influence to a follower, because the follower is known to many and contributes to the work of many. Access to people and information in the organization gives the follower in that position a way to establish relationships with others. With a network of relationships resulting from a follower's formal position, there is no doubt that he or she has greater opportunities to influence others at different levels of the organization. In certain situations, followers may even exercise coercive power over leaders. For example, withholding information or not acting promptly on a manager's request may cause delays in the manager's work. To avoid future delays, the manager may adjust his or her behavior toward the follower. How these different bases of follower power and influence affect leader-follower and inter-follower relationships is of importance to leaders and researchers. Leaders cannot afford to ignore followers with significant power and influence, because these followers ultimately can facilitate or hinder the leader's performance.

Follower Locus of Control

As discussed in Chapter 2, **locus of control** *is on a continuum between an external and internal belief over who has control of a person's destiny.* People who believe they are "masters of their own destiny" are said to have an *internal locus of control;* they believe that they can influence people and events in their workplace. Some research suggests that a leader's effectiveness may indeed depend on the match between the leader's style and the followers' personality. Research relating to this proposition found that followers' locus of control did influence their choice of preferred leadership style. Followers with an internal locus of control preferred a participative style, while followers with an external locus of control preferred a directive style. On the leader's locus of control, managers with an internal locus of control were more people-oriented.

Though many personality traits exist, only locus of control has been used consistently as an influencing characteristic in this research area. People who believe they are "pawns of fate" (*external locus of control*) tend to believe they have no influence or control at work. It is also believed that locus of control affects followers' attitude at work. A study of bank tellers found that promoted tellers who had a more internal locus of control maintained improved attitudes over a longer period of time than those who had an external locus of control. Locus of control has also been found to influence a person's belief and value system. One study found that locus of control is related to attitudes about the environment and our role in its preservation. Those with an internal locus of control tend to place much more importance on recycling as a cultural value than those with an external locus of control. It would appear from these studies that followers with an internal locus of control prefer a different type of work environment than those who have an external locus of control. Internal locus of control followers prefer a work environment that facilitates communication with leaders, participation in decision-making, and opportunities to be creative. Also they are more likely to play an activist role in safeguarding the natural environment.

More research needs to be conducted on how other personality traits (such as self-confidence, dominance, tolerance for stress, commitment, and reliability) can affect how followers relate to leaders and other followers. Given the link between a follower's locus of control and preferred leadership style, these characteristics must be taken into account as leaders seek to develop meaningful relationships with their followers.

Follower Education and Experience

Followers with valuable skills and experience may be able to use their expert power to influence other followers and the leader. Popular followers may be able to use their charm or charisma to influence others (see the discussion of different types of power in Chapter 4). To be more effective, leaders will need to understand and appreciate their followers' education, experience, training, and background—and how these factors influence their behavior. This requirement is dictated by the fact that leaders and followers today work in an environment of constant change. Today's workers—most of them followers—are far more educated, mobile, diverse, and younger than the workforce of 20 years ago; yet, the need for continuing education and training on the job will only increase. One reason for this is the increasing pace of technological change at work. To keep up, workers need to regularly update their knowledge and skills to stay ready for new task requirements. Along with technological change is the ongoing flattening of organizational structures. As many organizations reduce middle-management positions, much of the responsibility and authority previously reserved for that level is being delegated to followers. As a result, organizations are increasingly assuming a flat rather than tall structure.

Not all followers have the same level of education or experience. These differences can have a major impact on the relationships among followers, and between leaders and followers. Followers in new job positions with little or no experience tend to need more guidance, coaching, and feedback, whereas followers in long-term employment positions with experience often need only minimal guidance and periodic feedback in order to achieve high levels of performance. To improve their performance, inexperienced employees often seek the assistance of experienced employees.

These facts point in one direction: to succeed in the work environment of the future, it will take a different kind of leadership and a different kind of followership. One implication for leadership is that followers have more options and greater expectations of having input in the design and description of their jobs. One out of every four workers between the ages of 25 and 64 is college educated—twice as many as 20 years ago—and 85 percent have at least a high school education. Coupled with constant updates in their skills and education, workers' job mobility and assertiveness tends to be higher than it was 20 years ago. Another implication for leadership involves a shift away from the top-down directive style of managing that was common when tasks were highly structured and power tended to be centralized in managers' hands, toward a more decentralized, participative style of managing. As workers' education and experience increase, they tend to reject this style of leadership. Leaders who ignore this fact will face higher employee dissatisfaction and turnover. The era of the passive follower, it would appear, is a thing of the past.

A key part of every leader's job is to appraise followers' performance and offer constructive feedback on how the follower can improve. However, few leaders are ever trained in how to perform this task effectively. In the next section we offer some guidelines for effective feedback by leaders.

Effective Leader Feedback

In this section, we continue our discussion of feedback from Chapter 6. Effective followers help the leader get the job done. Followers do more than carry out the directives of the leader; they take responsibility for getting the job done and take the initiative in fixing problems. However, when this does not happen, it is the leader's responsibility to provide appropriate feedback to the followers on their performance.[56] As most leaders will attest, this is an important but difficult managerial responsibility. People in general tend to be defensive about criticism, because it questions their abilities and threatens their self-esteem.

WorkApplication7

Recall a work-related incident when you felt more qualified to do the job than your boss because of your education and experience. Describe how this characteristic enabled you to influence your boss.

_____

_____

_____

_____

_____

Applying the Concept 4

Determinants of Follower Influence

Identify the specific follower influencing characteristic in each of these statements.

a. power position   b. locus of control   c. education and experience

_____ 18. When it comes to selling my points to peers, I easily get them to see things my way rather than the boss's way due to my seniority and popularity in this division.

_____ 19. Many of my peers depend on me for direction because I am the only one in the department who has been trained to work with this new machine successfully.

_____ 20. It's not what you know, it's who you know around here that counts.

Many leaders avoid confronting followers about below-average performance because of the potential for such actions to degenerate into personal conflict that fails to deal with the underlying problem, or does so only at the cost of shattered respect and trust between the leader and follower. While some leaders can use threats to bring about desired behavior, the effective leader is privileged to use the power of trust to effect positive change in followers. Most would agree with the proposition that where trust is present, effective followership would take hold but where it is missing, leaders lose the ability to lead. Correcting a follower's performance deficiencies may be required to help the follower improve, but the way it is done can preserve or strain the leader-follower relationship. Some of the supporting principles of trust that may facilitate effective follower feedback include authentic caring, ethical actions, good leadership, and personal character. The sociological and psychological literature reveals that followers seek, admire, and respect leaders who, through the feedback process, produce within them three emotional responses: a feeling of significance, a sense of belonging, and a sense of excitement. Leaders must recognize the significance of this aspect of their job and take it seriously.

Realizing the delicate nature of this activity and its impact on follower egos and self-perceptions, effective leaders are learning to take a supportive, problem-solving approach when dealing with inappropriate behavior or deficient performance by followers. Leaders must learn to stay calm and professional when followers overreact to corrective feedback. Leaders must avoid a rush to judgment when followers don't perform. The leader must be specific in stating the deficiency, calmly explaining the negative impact of ineffective behavior, involving the follower in identifying the reasons for poor performance, and suggesting remedies for change. At the conclusion of an evaluation session, the follower must come away believing that the leader showed a genuine desire to be of help, and that both parties arrived at a mutual agreement on specific action steps for improvement. The follower's self-confidence should remain intact or be enhanced through feedback, rather than being shattered.[57]

Exhibit 7-5 presents 12 guidelines for effective leader feedback. It should be noted that these 12 guidelines are not in sequential order; however, they have been organized in a three-step process to underscore the importance of careful planning prior to undertaking any feedback activity.

WorkApplication8

Recall the last time you were evaluated on the job by your manager. Describe how you felt at the end of the session. What factors accounted for your feelings? See if some of the factors discussed in this section apply in your particular situation.

_____

_____

_____

_____

_____

5. Ms. Wung Has Called a Meeting With Her Three Leaders. How Should She Conduct This Feedback Session to Insure Greater Success?

In the opening case, Wung clearly saw the need for a review of each crew to determine what the problems were and to follow up with concrete feedback. The case ends with Wung calling a meeting with crew leaders to discuss her observations and to discuss ways of increasing productivity. Using the guidelines to effective feedback in Exhibit 7-5 should significantly increase her chances of success with the process.

OPENING CASE APPLICATION

Exhibit 7-5 *Guidelines for effective leader feedback.*

Pre-Feedback—Leader should:
- remind self to stay calm and professional
- gather accurate facts on follower performance
- remind self to avoid rush to judgment

During Feedback Session—Leader should:
- be specific in stating performance deficiency
- explain negative impact of ineffective behavior
- help follower identify reasons for poor performance
- ask follower to suggest remedies
- arrive at mutual agreement on specific action steps

Post-Feedback Session—Leader should:
- follow up to ensure implementation of action steps
- show desire to be of help to follower
- build follower's self confidence

We conclude this section on followership with a brief discussion of the dual role of being a leader and a follower and the challenges it presents.

Dual Role of Being a Leader and a Follower

As mentioned earlier, leadership is not a one-way street. And as the guidelines for effective followership revealed, good leadership is found in highly effective followers. It is important to recognize that even when someone is identified as a leader, the same person often holds a complementary follower role. It is not at all uncommon to switch between being a leader and being a follower several times over the course of a day's work. For example, within an organization, middle managers answer to vice presidents, who answer to the CEO, who answers to the board of directors; within the school system, teachers answer to the principal, who answers to the school superintendent, who answers to school board members. How to integrate these diverse roles is an interesting question, with valuable lessons for leadership effectiveness.

Research on high-performance teams reveals that organizations are moving more and more toward the use of self-managed teams, in which team members alternate between playing leadership and followership roles. The most successful of these types of teams are those that have a great deal of role switching among the "followers" concerning who is serving a leadership role at any given time. (The duality of playing both leader and follower roles is further examined in Chapter 8 with self-managed teams.) Self-managed teams practice distributed leadership, in which team members take complementary leadership roles in rotation according to their area of expertise or interest. Therefore, they go back and forth as followers and as leaders.

To execute both roles effectively, it is necessary to find a way to integrate them. This is not an easy task, given the high potential for role conflicts and ambiguities. Leaders are held responsible for everything that happens in their work unit and are also required to delegate much responsibility and authority to their followers to empower them in resolving problems on their own. Leaders are also expected to train and develop followers, which may involve training someone who eventually wants the leader's job—even if the leader is not ready to give it up. How to balance these competing and often conflicting demands and perform the dual roles of leader and follower effectively is a subject that deserves much more research focus than it has received.

Delegation

We now focus on developing followers by delegating tasks to them. **Delegation** *is the process of assigning responsibility and authority for accomplishing objectives.* Telling employees to perform the tasks that are part of their job design is issuing orders, not delegating. *Delegating* refers to giving employees new tasks. The new task may become a part of a redesigned job, or it may simply be a one-time task. The true art of delegation lies in a manager's ability to know what cannot be delegated and what should be delegated.[58] Some management experts believe that if there were a top ten list of managerial mistakes, failure to delegate would be one of them.[59] In this section we discuss delegating, delegation decisions, and delegating with a model.

Delegating

Effective delegation requires that a leader should carefully consider several factors relating to the task, time requirement, and follower characteristics before delegating. A leader should delegate work when there is not enough time to attend to priority tasks, when followers desire more challenges and opportunities, and when the tasks match follower skill levels and experiences. Also a leader must find the proper person for the job and provide careful instructions. Effective delegation allows people to prosper in their own uniqueness.

Let's begin by discussing the benefits of delegation, the obstacles to delegation, and signs of delegating too little.

Benefits of Delegation

When managers delegate, they have more time to perform high-priority tasks. Delegation gets tasks accomplished and increases productivity. It enables leaders to mobilize resources and secure better results than they could have gotten alone. Delegation trains employees and improves their self-esteem, as well as easing the stress and burden on managers.[60] By delegating responsibilities, leaders can focus on doing a few tasks well instead of many tasks less effectively.[61] Consequently, they improve their management and leadership potential while training others to succeed them. It is a means of developing followers by enriching their jobs. From the organization's perspective, delegating can result in increased performance and work outcomes. It can also lead to more communication between leaders and followers, thus encouraging followers to voice their opinions on how to improve the work environment.

Obstacles to Delegation

Managers become used to doing things themselves. Managers fear that employees will fail to accomplish tasks. You can delegate responsibility and authority, but not your accountability. Managers believe they can perform tasks more efficiently than others.[62] Some managers don't realize that delegation is an important part of their job, others don't know what to delegate, and some don't know how to delegate. Effective delegation greatly improves a leader's time management, without which efficiency and effectiveness suffer.[63,64] If you let these or other reasons keep you from delegating, you could end up like Dr. Rudenstine, former president of Harvard University, who became ill due to job stress by trying to do too much by himself.

Signs of Delegating Too Little

There are certain behaviors associated with leaders who are reluctant to delegate to their subordinates. These behaviors are signs that a leader is delegating too little. Some of these behaviors include taking work home, performing employee tasks, being behind in work, a continual feeling of pressure and stress, rushing to meet deadlines, and requiring that employees seek approval before acting. Unfortunately, in many of today's cost-cutting environments, you don't always have someone you can delegate some of your tasks to.

─────────────── Learning Outcome 10 ───────────────

List five things a leader should delegate.

Delegation Decisions

As mentioned earlier, an important part of delegation is knowing which tasks to delegate.[65] Successful delegation is often based on selecting what task to delegate and who to delegate it to.[66]

What to Delegate

As a general guide, use your prioritized to-do list and delegate anything that you don't have to be personally involved with because of your unique knowledge or skill. Some possibilities include the following:

- *Paperwork.* Have others prepare reports, memos, letters, and so on.
- *Routine tasks.* Delegate checking inventory, scheduling, ordering, and so on.
- *Technical matters.* Have top employees deal with technical questions and problems.
- *Tasks with developmental potential.* Give employees the opportunity to learn new things. Prepare them for advancement by enriching their job.
- *Employees' problems.* Train employees to solve their own problems; don't solve problems for them, unless their capability is low.

What Not to Delegate

As a general guide, do not delegate anything that you need to be personally involved with because of your unique knowledge or skill. Here are some typical examples:

- *Personnel matters.* Performance appraisals, counseling, disciplining, firing, resolving conflicts, and so on.
- *Confidential activities.* Unless you have permission to do so.
- *Crises.* There is no time to delegate.

WorkApplication9

Describe an obstacle to delegation, or sign of delegating too little, that you have observed on the job.

_____

_____

_____

_____

_____

- *Activities delegated to you personally.* For example, if you are assigned to a committee, do not assign someone else without permission.

Determining to Whom to Delegate

Once you have decided what to delegate, you must select an employee to do the task. When selecting an employee to delegate to, be sure that he or she has the capability to get the job done right by the deadline. Consider your employees' talents and interests when making a selection. You may consult with several employees to determine their interests before making the final choice.

Before you learn how to delegate with the use of a model, complete Self-Assessment 5 to learn how your personality may affect your followership and delegation.

Ethical Dilemma 2

Delegating the Destruction of Documents

Arthur Andersen, a consulting company, and *Global Crossing,* a multimedia communications company, were both taken to court for destroying evidence that could have been used in a court of law to support charges of illegal activities. Arthur Andersen destroyed evidence related to *Enron,* to protect both companies from being found guilty of conducting illegal business practices. Arthur Andersen claimed that it was not trying to destroy incriminating evidence, that it was simply destroying records, which is done periodically. Destroying documents is routine; the question therefore becomes, what is being destroyed and why is it being destroyed?

1. Is it ethically responsible to delegate the task of destroying documents that may potentially be used as evidence of wrongdoing?
2. What would you do if your boss asked you to destroy documents that you thought might be to cover up wrongdoing (evidence) by the firm? (Some options include: just do it, don't say anything but don't do it, question the motives, look closely at what you are asked to destroy, go to your boss's boss to make sure its OK to do it, tell the boss you will not do it, ask the boss to do it him or herself, blow the whistle to an outside source like the government or media, and so on.)
3. If you went to court for destroying evidence, do you believe you would have a good ethical defense by saying "I was only following orders."

Delegating with the Use of a Model

After determining what to delegate and to whom, you must plan for and delegate the tasks. *The* **delegation model** *steps are (1) explain the need for delegating and the reasons for selecting the employee; (2) set objectives that define responsibility, level of authority, and deadline; (3) develop a plan; (4) establish control checkpoints and hold employees accountable.*[67,68] Following these four steps can increase your chances of successfully delegating. As you read on, you

---

Self-Assessment 5

Followership and Personality

Personality Differences

Generally, if you have an agreeableness Big Five personality type, which is a high need for affiliation, you will have a good relationship with your manager, because having a good relationship with everyone helps you to meet your needs. If you have a lower need for power, you prefer to be a follower, rather than a leader. Generally, you will be willing to delegate authority.

If you have a surgency/high need for power, you may have some problems getting along with your manager. You prefer to be in control, or to be a leader rather than a follower. However, if you don't get along well with your manager, you will have difficulty climbing the corporate ladder. You may have some reluctance to delegate authority because you like to be in control—and when you delegate, you lose some control.

If you have a conscientiousness/high need for achievement, you may not be concerned about your relationship with your manager, other than getting what you want to get the job done. However, if you don't get along well with your manager, you will have difficulty getting what you want. You may also be reluctant to delegate tasks that you like to do, because you get satisfaction from doing the job itself, rather than having someone else to do it.

Being well adjusted also helps you to have a good relationship with your manager. Being open to experience, which includes an internal locus of control (Chapter 2), helps you to get along with others since you are willing to try new things.

Gender Differences

Although there are exceptions, generally, women tend to seek relationships that are on a more personal level than men. For example, two women who work together are more apt to talk about their family lives than two men. Men do socialize, but it is more frequently about other interests such as sports. It is not unusual for women who have worked together for months to know more about each other's personal and family lives than men who have worked together for years. Men who do enjoy talking about their personal lives tend to talk more about their families in dyads with women than in those with men. One of the reasons men enjoy working with women is because they often bring a personal-level relationship to the job.

How does your personality affect your dyadic relationships, followership, and delegation?

_____

_____

_____

_____

_____

---

will see how the delegation model is used with the job characteristics model, core job dimensions, and critical psychological states to influence performance and work outcomes.

step 1. **Explain the need for delegating and the reasons for selecting the employee.** It is helpful for the employee to understand why the assignment must be completed. In other words, how will the department or organization benefit? Informing employees helps them realize the importance of the task (experienced meaningfulness of work). Telling the employee why he or she was selected should make him or her feel valued. Don't use the "it's a lousy job, but someone has to do it" approach. Be positive; make employees aware of how they will benefit from the assignment. If step 1 is completed successfully, the employee should be motivated, or at least willing, to do the assignment.

step 2.   **Set objectives that define responsibility, level of authority, and deadline.** The objectives should clearly state the end result the employee is responsible for achieving by a specific deadline. You should also define the level of authority the employee has, as the following choices illustrate:

- Make a list of all supplies on hand, and present it to me each Friday at 2:00 (inform authority).
- Fill out a supply purchase order, and present it to me each Friday at 2:00 (recommend authority).
- Fill out and sign a purchase order for supplies; send it to the purchasing department with a copy put in my in-basket each Friday by 2:00 (report authority).
- Fill out and sign a purchase order for supplies, and send it to the purchasing department each Friday by 2:00, keeping a copy (full authority).

step 3.   **Develop a plan.** Once the objective is set, a plan is needed to achieve it. It is helpful to write out the objective, specifying the level of authority and the plan. When developing a plan, be sure to identify the resources needed to achieve the objectives, and give the employee the authority necessary to obtain the resources. Inform all parties of the employee's authority and with whom the employee must work. For example, if an employee is doing a marketing report, you should contact the marketing department and tell them the employee must have access to the necessary information.

step 4.   **Establish control checkpoints and hold employees accountable.** For simple, short tasks, a deadline without control checkpoints is appropriate. However, it is often advisable to check progress at predetermined times (control checkpoints) for tasks that have multiple steps or will take some time to complete. This builds information flow into the delegation system right from the start. You and the employee should agree on the form (phone call, visit, memo, or detailed report) and time frame (daily, weekly, or after specific steps are completed but before going on to the next step) for information regarding the assignment. When establishing control, consider the employee's capability level. The lower the capability, the more frequent the checks; the higher the capability, the less frequent the checks.

It is helpful to list the control checkpoints in writing on an operational planning sheet, making copies of the finished plan so that the parties involved and you as the delegating manager have a record to refer to. In addition, all parties involved should record the control checkpoints on their calendars. If the employee to whom the task was delegated does not report as scheduled, follow up to find out why the person did not report, and get the information. You should evaluate performance at each control checkpoint, and upon completion provide feedback that develops knowledge of the results of work. Providing praise for progress and completion of the task motivates employees to do a good job. You will recall that Chapter 6 discussed how to give praise.

The four steps of the delegation process are summarized in Model 7-1. In Skill-Development Exercise 2, you will have the opportunity to use the model to delegate a task and to develop your delegation skills.

WorkApplication10

Select a manager you work or have worked for, and analyze how well he or she implements the four steps of delegation. Which steps does the manager typically follow and not follow?

_____

_____

_____

_____

_____

Model 7-1 *Steps in the delegation model.*

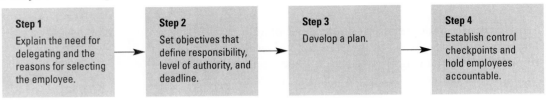

Step 1	Step 2	Step 3	Step 4
Explain the need for delegating and the reasons for selecting the employee.	Set objectives that define responsibility, level of authority, and deadline.	Develop a plan.	Establish control checkpoints and hold employees accountable.

Go to the Internet (academic.cengage.com/management/lussier) where you will find a broad array of resources to help maximize your learning.

- Review the vocabulary
- Try a quiz
- View chapter videos

Chapter Summary

The chapter summary is organized to answer the 11 learning outcomes for Chapter 7.

1. List the four stages of development of the dyadic approach.

The first conception of dyadic theory was the awareness of a relationship between a leader and a follower, rather than between a leader and a group of followers. The second stage of dyadic theory describes specific attributes of exchange between a leader and a follower that lead to high- or low-quality relationships. The third and fourth stages of dyadic theory emphasize team building and systems and networks. Organizations strive for team building between all employees (managers and nonmanagers) and to create valuable systems and networks across traditional boundaries of the organization. Leaders and followers begin to see themselves as part of a larger network rather than as isolated units.

2. Define the two kinds of relationships that can occur among leaders and followers under the vertical dyadic linkage model.

The two types of relationships that can occur among leaders and followers under the VDL model are in-group and out-group members. In-groups include followers with strong social ties to their leader in a people-oriented relationship, characterized by high mutual trust, exchange, loyalty, and influence. Out-groups include followers with little or no social ties to their leader in a strictly task-oriented relationship, characterized by low exchange, lack of trust and loyalty, and top-down influence.

3. Describe the main focus of team-building from a Leader-Follower perspective.

The emphasis of the team-building view is the notion that effective leaders should aspire to establish relationships with all followers, not just with a few special individuals. It is about forging a partnership with each group member without alienating anyone.

4. Discuss the focus of the systems and networks approach from a Leader-Follower perspective.

The systems and networks version of the dyadic approach examines how a dyadic relationship can be created across traditional boundaries to include everyone in the organization. It emphasizes creating relationships that cut across functional, divisional, and even organizational boundaries, rather than including leaders and followers in only a limited section of the organization.

5. Discuss the key limitation or drawback with LMX application.

A major limitation of LMX is measurement difficulty. LMX theory deals with attitudes and perceptions of individuals; two issues that are often difficult to quantify and measure. For this reason, recent research efforts on LMX have focused on instrumentation of the theory. The way in which the attributes of high-quality LMX relationships have been defined and measured have varied somewhat from study to study.

6. Describe three determining factors of high-quality LMX relationships.

High-quality LMX relationships may be influenced by the following three antecedent factors: (1) *Follower attributes*—Attributes such as commitment, trust, respect, and loyalty will influence leaders to show support, delegate more, allow followers more discretion in conducting their work, and engage in open communication with followers. (2) *Situational factors*—Factors such as tryouts or tests of a new employee may be key determinants of a follower's in-group or out-group status. (3) *Leader's perceptions and behavior*—The leader's first impressions of a group member's competency plays an important role in defining the quality of the relationship.

7. Explain the cycle that leads to the Pygmalion effect.

The Pygmalion effect occurs when selected followers demonstrate loyalty, commitment, and trust, as a result winning the favor of leaders who subsequently give those followers higher performance ratings. These ratings, which may or may not be tied to actual performance, then influence the follower's reputation, and often become a matter of record. The ratings may ultimately be used—formally or informally—in future selection, development, and promotion decisions. Consequently, followers with a history of high performance ratings (positive Pygmalion effect) are often promoted to higher-level positions, and those with a history of low performance ratings (negative Pygmalion effect) may never be promoted or, even worse, may be demoted.

8. Explain how LMX relationships can lead to unintended bias in HR practices.

In LMX relationships, leaders develop strong social ties with in-group members. Whether intentionally or unintentionally, this positive relationship has been known to correlate with higher performance ratings for in-group members compared to out-group members. HR decisions regarding promotions, demotions, reassignments, layoffs and salary increases are often based on information accumulated in employee files. An employee's performance evaluation from his/her manager may influence the decision on who gets promoted, demoted or worse, laid off. If the evaluation was based on a manager liking or not liking a follower in the first place, rather than on actual job performance, then it may seem unfair to use it as the basis for any action; and yet it happens everyday.

9. Discuss the three follower influencing characteristics.

The three follower influencing characteristics are: (1) *Power position*—Leaders need to realize that followers also have the power to influence them. (2) *Locus of control*—Followers can have an internal or external locus of control, based on their belief about who is the master of their destiny. Thus, leader-member exchanges should be different based on locus of control. (3) *Education and experience*—Leaders need to realize that followers may have different levels of education and experience, and that they need to supervise them differently.

10. List five things a leader should delegate.

A leader should delegate paperwork, routine tasks, technical matters, tasks with developmental potential, and employee problems.

11. Define the following key terms (in order of appearance in the chapter).

Select one or more methods: (1) fill in the missing key terms from memory, (2) match the key terms from the following list with their definitions below, (3) copy the key terms in order from the list at the beginning of the chapter.

_____ refers to the individualized relationship between a leader and each follower in a work unit.

_____ is an approach to leadership that attempts to explain why leaders vary their behavior with different followers.

_____ examines how leaders form one-on-one relationships with followers, and how these often create in-groups and out-groups within the leader's work unit.

_____ includes followers with strong social ties to their leader in a supportive relationship characterized by high mutual trust, respect, loyalty, and influence.

_____ includes followers with few or no social ties to their leader in a strictly task-centered relationship characterized by low exchange and top-down influence.

_____ is the quality of the exchange relationship between an employee and his or her superior.

_____ is a follower's effort to project a favorable image in order to gain an immediate benefit or improve a long-term relationship with the leader.

_____ is the effort to appear supportive, appreciative, and respectful.

_____ is the effort to appear competent and dependable.

_____ refers to the behavior of followers that results from the leader-follower influence relationship.

_____ is a person who is being influenced by a leader.

_____ is a passive yet independent, critical thinker.

_____ is an active yet dependent, noncritical thinker.

_____ exhibits neither critical, independent thinking nor active participation.

_____ is both an independent, critical thinker and a very active member in the group.

_____ exhibits a little of all four styles—depending on which style fits with the prevailing situation.

_____ is on a continuum between an external and internal belief over who has control over a person's destiny.

_____ is the process of assigning responsibility and authority for accomplishing objectives.

_____ steps are: (1) explain the need for delegating and the reasons for selecting the employee; (2) set objectives that define responsibility, level of authority, and deadline; (3) develop a plan; and (4) establish control checkpoints and hold employees accountable.

Key Terms

alienated follower, 267

conformist follower, 268

delegation, 279

delegation model, 281

dyadic, 250

dyadic theory, 250

effective follower, 268

follower, 266

followership, 265

impressions management, 261

ingratiation, 261

in-group, 253

leader-member exchange (LMX), 254

locus of control, 274

out-group, 253

passive follower, 268

pragmatic follower, 268

self-promotion, 261

vertical dyadic linkage (VDL) theory, 252

Review and Discussion Questions

1. What are the differences between in-groups and out-groups?
2. How do quality leader-member exchange relationships influence follower behavior?
3. How does a leader's first impression and perception of a follower influence the quality of their relationship?
4. What are the three stages of the life-cycle model of LMX theory?
5. How can a follower's perception or attribution of a leader influence their relationship?
6. What is the presence of bias in the LMX relationship? What is its potential impact on out-group and in-group members of the organization?
7. How do education and experience, described as follower influencing characteristics, affect effective followership?
8. What are some of the benefits of delegating?
9. What are some things that a leader should not delegate?

Case

W. L. GORE & ASSOCIATES

Chuck Carroll, President and CEO of W. L. Gore & Associates, is upbeat and optimistic despite the sluggish nature of the economy. His company has much to be proud of. For the eighth consecutive year, W. L. Gore & Associates, Inc., earned a position on *Fortune*'s annual list of the "100 Best Companies to Work For." Gore ranks #2 overall and #1 among mid-sized companies in the magazine's January 24, 2005 issue. For the second year in a row, Gore ranked as #1 among the "100 Best Places to Work in the U.K." (2005). Gore is ranked in the Top 10 in the overall ranking and # 5 in mid-sized companies among the "50 Best Places to Work in Germany" (2005). In 2004, Gore ranked in the Top 20 among the "35 Best Places to Work in Italy." According to CEO Carroll, these rankings reinforce Gore's commitment to key values. "We work hard at maximizing individual potential, maintaining an emphasis on product integrity, and cultivating an environment where creativity can flourish," Carroll said.

Founded in 1958, W. L. Gore & Associates has become a modern-day success story as a uniquely managed, privately owned, family business. Founders Bill and Vieve Gore set out to explore opportunities for fluorocarbon polymers, especially polytetrafluoroethylene (PTFE). Within the first decade, Gore wire and cable landed on the moon, operations began in Scotland and Germany, and a venture partnership was initiated in Japan. Gore is a high-technology company that develops and manufactures, among other products, advanced synthetic fabrics used for aerospace clothing, medical, automotive, chemical, electronic, and other applications. Gore's cash cow continues to be its Gore-Tex high-performance fabric. Despite termination of its Gore-Tex patent, which opened the door for other companies to begin manufacturing Gore-Tex products, W. L. Gore's product development arm has remained healthy. Gore has managed to keep patents for individual Gore-Tex products and manufacturing processes.

How work is conducted at Gore and how employees relate to one another sets Gore apart. To avoid dampening employee creativity, the company has an organizational structure and culture that goes against conventional wisdom. W. L. Gore & Associates have been described as not only unmanaged but also unstructured. Bill Gore (the founder) referred to the company's structure as a "lattice organization." Gore's lattice structure includes the following features:

• Direct lines of communication—person to person—with no intermediary
• No fixed or assigned authority

- Sponsors, not bosses
- Natural leadership as evidenced by the willingness of others to follow
- Objectives set by those who must "make them happen"
- Tasks and functions organized through commitments

The lattice structure as described by the people at Gore encourages hands-on innovation and discourages bureaucratic red tape by involving those closest to a project in decision making. Instead of a pyramid of bosses and managers, Gore has a flat organizational structure. There are no chains of command, no predetermined channels of communication. It sounds very much like a self-managed team at a much broader scale.

Why has Gore achieved such remarkable success? W. L. Gore & Associates prefers to think of the various people who play key roles in the organization as being *leaders, not managers*. While Bill Gore did not believe in smothering the company in thick layers of formal management, he also knew that as the company grew, he had to find ways to assist new people and to follow their progress. Thus, W. L. Gore & Associates came up with its "sponsor" program. The sponsor program is a dyadic relationship between an incumbent, experienced employee and a newly hired inexperienced employee. Before a candidate is hired, an associate has to agree to be his or her sponsor. The sponsor's role is to take a personal interest in the new associate's contributions, problems, and goals, acting as both a coach and an advocate. The sponsor tracks the new associate's progress, offers help and encouragement, points out weaknesses and suggests ways to correct them, and concentrates on how the associate might better exploit his or her strengths. Sponsoring is not a short-term commitment. All associates have sponsors, and many have more than one. When individuals are hired, at first they are likely to have a sponsor in their immediate work area. As associates' commitments change or grow, it's normal for them to acquire additional sponsors. For instance, if they move to a new job in another area of the company, they typically gain a sponsor there. Sponsors help associates chart a course in the organization that will offer personal fulfillment while maximizing their contribution to the enterprise. Leaders emerge naturally by demonstrating special knowledge, skill, or experience that advances a business objective.

An internal memo describes the three kinds of sponsorship and how they might work:

- *Starting sponsor*—a sponsor who helps a new associate get started on his or her first job at Gore, or helps a present associate get started on a new job.
- *Advocate sponsor*—a sponsor who sees to it that the associate being sponsored gets credit and recognition for contributions and accomplishments.
- *Compensation sponsor*—a sponsor who sees to it that the associate being sponsored is fairly paid for contributions to the success of the enterprise.

An associate can perform any one or all three kinds of sponsorship. Quite frequently, a sponsoring associate is a good friend, and it's not uncommon for two associates to sponsor each other as advocates.

Being an associate is a natural commitment to four basic principles articulated by Bill Gore and still a key belief of the company: fairness to each other and everyone we come in contact with; freedom to encourage, help, and allow other associates to grow in knowledge, skill, and scope of responsibility; the ability to make one's own commitments and keep them; and consultation with other associates before undertaking actions that could affect the reputation of the company.

Over the years, W. L. Gore & Associates has faced a number of unionization drives. The company neither tries to dissuade associates from attending organizational meetings nor retaliates against associates who pass out union flyers. However, Bill Gore believes there is no need for third-party representation under the lattice structure. He asks, "Why would associates join a union when they own the company? It seems rather absurd."

Commitment is seen as a two-way street at W. L. Gore & Associates—while associates are expected to commit to making a contribution to the company's success, the company is committed to providing a challenging, opportunity-rich work environment and reasonable job security. The company tries to avoid laying off associates. If a workforce reduction becomes necessary, the company uses a system of temporary transfers within a plant or cluster of plants, and requests voluntary layoffs. Approximately 6,000 associates work at 45 facilities throughout the world. Worldwide sales in the past fiscal year were $1.4 billion.

GO TO THE INTERNET: To learn more about W. L. Gore & Associates, log on to InfoTrac® College Edition at **academic.cengage.com/infotrac** and use the advanced search function.

Support your answers to the following questions with specific information from the case, or information you get from the Web or other sources.

1. What theories from this chapter are revealed through the case?
2. How did Gore's "sponsors" program facilitate the creation of high-quality relationships among leaders, sponsors, and associates?
3. Evaluate followership at W. L. Gore & Associates. What company actions and/or policies account for the quality of followership?

Cumulative Case Questions

4. Would you characterize the leadership style at W. L. Gore and Associates as job-centered or employee-centered (Chapter 3)? Support your answer.

5. Based on the types of power discussed in the text (Chapter 4), what type(s) of power did sponsors have in their relationships with associates?
6. What role, if any, does coaching (Chapter 6) play in W. L. Gore's lattice structure?

Case Exercise and Role-Play

Preparation: You are part of an organization that evaluates its employees at the end of each year. The month of the year when evaluations need to be completed by all leaders and managers is approaching. Your task is to play the role of a leader evaluating your followers, and then play the role of follower being evaluated by your own manager. Based on your understanding of the discussion of guidelines for effective leader feedback and guidelines for effective followership, (1) present a scenario of an effective and an ineffective feedback session, applying at least three of the guidelines discussed in the text, and (2) present a scenario of effective and ineffective followership, applying at least three of the guidelines discussed in the text.

Role-Play: The instructor forms students into leader-follower pairs and has each pair dramatize scenarios 1 and 2 in front of the rest of the class. After each scenario, the class is to contrast the two approaches (effective versus ineffective feedback) by identifying the guidelines that the presenters or actors employed in making their points. Different student teams should try the exercise by employing different guidelines to both scenarios.

Video Case

LaBelle Management: Career Management

In 1948, Norman LaBelle opened his first restaurant in Mt. Pleasant, Michigan. Since then, his two sons Bart and Doug LaBelle have grown their father's business into a very successful company known as LaBelle Management. Today, LaBelle Management is a leader in managing properties for businesses, hotels, and restaurants, operating a variety of business concepts with over 30 locations throughout the Midwest.

View the Video (12 minutes)
View the video on LaBelle Management in class or at **academic.cengage.com/management/lussier**.

Read the Case
LaBelle's owners attribute the company's success to the dedicated managers and employees that operate the business on a day-to-day basis. In today's competitive job market, in which workers change jobs and professions routinely, it can be a challenge to find and retain qualified people. The loyalty and dedication that LaBelle receives from its workers is a result of the firm's focus on career management and development. LaBelle's career management program has two main objectives: to retain qualified employees, and enable workers to achieve personal goals. Executives at LaBelle believe that employees need to be able to see a future at the organization and recognize a clear path for upward mobility if they are to stay. Furthermore, workers must get the message that the company will invest in them and help them achieve their personal goals through training, development, and new opportunities. LaBelle's career management program enables the company to achieve its recruitment and retention objectives, creating a strong foundation for future growth.

The days of working for a single employer for an entire career are long gone. In today's business world, individuals may change jobs and professions many times in the course of a lifetime. Therefore, it is all the more important that managers find ways to keep workers satisfied and create incentives for them to stay with the company. LaBelle's career management program has proven effective in recruiting and maintaining quality workers, providing for the needs of both the company and its employees.

Answer the Questions
1. How might LaBelle Management's organizational needs be met through career management?
2. How does LaBelle motivate its managers to identify and train future leaders?
3. How might LaBelle meet the career needs of its employees?

Skill-Development Exercise 1

IMPROVING DYADIC RELATIONSHIPS—FOLLOWERSHIP

Preparing for Skill-Development Exercise 1

Based on your reading of effective leader-member exchange (LMX) relationships, how can you improve your current or future relationship with your manager?

Be sure to list specific things you plan to do.

_____

_____

_____

Based on Self-Assessment 4, "Effective Followership," how can you improve your followership skills with your present or future manager? Be sure to list specific things you plan to do.

_____

_____

_____

Doing Skill-Development Exercise 1 in Class

Objective
To develop a plan to improve your dyadic relationship with your manager and to improve your followership skills.

Preparation
You should have completed a plan in the preparation part of this exercise.

Experience
You will share your plan in a small group to provide further development.

Procedure 1 (8–12 minutes)
Option A: Break into groups of 3 or 4 and share your plans. Offer each other ideas for improving plans.

Option B: Same as Option A, but add a spokesperson to record some of the best ideas from each group member.

Procedure 2 (10–20 minutes)
Option B, each spokesperson reports to the entire class.

Conclusion
The instructor leads a class discussion and/or makes concluding remarks.

Apply It (2–4 minutes)
What did I learn from this exercise? When will I implement my plan?

_____

_____

_____

Sharing
In the group, or to the entire class, volunteers may give their answers to the "Apply It" questions.

Behavior Model Skills Training

In this behavior model skills training session, you will perform three activities:

1. Read the section, "Delegation," in this chapter (to learn how to use Model 7-1, page 284).
2. Watch Behavior Model Video 1, "Delegating."

3. Complete Skill-Development Exercise 2 (to develop your delegating skills).

For further practice, use the delegation model in your personal and professional life.

The Delegation Model

Step 1
Explain the need for delegating and the reasons for selecting the employee.

Step 2
Set objectives that define responsibility, level of authority, and deadline.

Step 3
Develop a plan.

Step 4
Establish control checkpoints and hold employees accountable.

Behavior Model Video 1

DELEGATING

Objective
To observe a manager delegating a task to an employee.

Video (4½ minutes) Overview
You will watch a production manager, Steve, delegate the completion of a production output form to Dale.

DELEGATING

Preparing for Skill-Development Exercise 2

You should have read and understood the material on delegation.

Doing Skill-Development Exercise 2 in Class

Objective

To experience and develop skills in delegating a task.

Experience

You will delegate, be delegated to, and observe the delegation of a task, and then evaluate the effectiveness of the delegated task. You may also see a video example of how to delegate using the delegation model.

Procedure 1 (4–8 minutes)

Break into as many groups of three as possible with the remainder in groups of two. Each person in the group picks a number 1, 2, or 3. Number 1 will be the first to delegate a task, then 2, and then 3. The level of difficulty of the delegation will increase with the number.

Each person then reads his or her delegation situation below (1, 2, or 3) and plans how he or she will delegate the task. If you prefer, you can use an actual delegation from a past or present job. Just be sure to fully explain the situation to the delegatee. Be sure to follow the four delegation steps in this chapter. An observer sheet is included at the end of this exercise for giving feedback on each delegation.

Delegation Situation 1

Delegator 1, you are a college student with a paper due in three days for your 10:00 a.m. class. It must be typed. You don't type well, so you have decided to hire someone to do it for you. The going rate is $1.50 per page. Think of an actual paper you have written in the past or will write in the future. Plan to delegate. Be sure to include the course name, paper title, special typing instructions, and so on. Assume that you are meeting the typist for the first time. He or she doesn't know you and doesn't expect you.

Delegator 2, assume that you do typing and are willing to do the job if the delegation is acceptable to you.

Delegation Situation 2

Delegator 2, you are the manager of a fast-food restaurant. In the past, you have scheduled the workers. Your policy is to keep changing the workers' schedules. You have decided to delegate the scheduling to your assistant manager. This person has never done any scheduling, but appears to be very willing and confident about taking on new responsibility. Plan your delegation.

Delegator 3, assume that you are interested in doing the scheduling if the manager delegates the task effectively.

Delegation Situation 3

Delegator 3, you own and manage your own business. You have eight employees, one of whom is the organization's secretary. The secretary currently uses an old computer, which needs to be replaced. You have not kept up with the latest technology and don't know what to buy. You can spend $1,200. You try to keep costs down and get the most for your money. Because the secretary will use the new machine, you believe that this employee should be involved or maybe even make the decision. The secretary has never purchased equipment, and you believe he or she will be somewhat insecure about the assignment. Plan your delegation.

Delegator 1, assume that you are able to do the job but are somewhat insecure. Accept the task if the delegator "participates" effectively.

Procedure 2 (7–10 minutes)

A. *Delegation 1*. Delegator 1 delegates the task (role-play) to number 2. Number 3 is the observer. As the delegation takes place, the observer uses the form at the end of this exercise to provide feedback on the effectiveness of the delegator. Answer the questions on the form.

B. *Integration*. The observer (or number 3) leads a discussion of the effectiveness of the delegation, although all team members should participate. Do not continue until you are told to do so.

Procedure 3 (7–10 minutes)

A. *Delegation 2*. Follow procedure 2A, except number 2 is now the delegator, number 3 is the delegatee, and number 1 is the observer.

B. *Integration*. Follow procedure 2B with number 1 as the observer. Do not continue until you are told to do so.

Procedure 4 (7–10 minutes)

A. *Delegation 3*. Follow procedure 2A, except number 3 is now the delegator, number 1 is the delegatee, and number 2 is the observer. If you are in a group of two, be an additional observer for another group.

B. *Integration*. Follow procedure 2B with number 2 as observer.

Conclusion
The instructor may lead a class discussion and make concluding remarks.

Apply It (2–4 minutes)
What did I learn from this experience? When will I delegate using the model?

_____

_____

_____

Sharing
In the group, or to the entire class, volunteers may give their answers to the "Apply It" questions.

Note: Remember that the process does not end with delegating the task; you must control (check progress at control points and help when needed) to ensure that the task is completed as scheduled.

OBSERVER FORM

During the delegation process, the observer checks off the items performed by the delegators. Items not checked were not performed. After the delegation, the delegator and delegatee also check off the items.

This sheet is used for all three situations. Use the appropriate column for each situation.

Delegation items for all situations	Situation 1	2	3

Did the delegator follow these steps?

Step 1. Explain the need for delegating and the reason that the person was selected.

Step 2. Set an objective that defines responsibility and level of authority, and set a deadline.

Step 3. Develop an effective plan.

Step 4. Establish control checkpoints, and hold the employee accountable.

Process
Did the delegate clearly understand what was expected of him or her and know how to follow the plan?

_____

_____

Improvements
How could the delegation be improved if done again?

_____

_____

_____

_____

Team Leadership and Self-Managed Teams

8

After studying this chapter, you should be able to:

1. Discuss the advantages and disadvantages of working in teams. p. 297
2. Briefly describe the seven characteristics of effective teams. p. 301
3. Describe top management's and the team leader's roles in fostering creativity. For each, list activities they should undertake to promote creativity. p. 306
4. Outline the three parts of conducting effective meetings. p. 322
5. Explain the differences between traditional and self-managed teams. p. 326
6. Describe the benefits of using self-managed teams in organizations. p. 329
7. Describe how team member characteristics impact self-managed team effectiveness. p. 332
8. Describe the guidelines for improving self-managed team effectiveness. p. 335
9. Describe the challenges of implementing effective self-managed teams. p. 340
10. Define the following **key terms** (in order of appearance in the chapter):

team	functional team
teamwork	cross-functional team
social loafing	virtual team
groupthink	self-managed teams (SMTs)
team effectiveness	self-managed team champion
team norms	team potency
team cohesion	distributed leadership
team creativity	self-managed team facilitator

Opening Case Application

Jill Lajdziak has come a long way since her first job as a Car Collection Manager at a dealership. Today, Lajdziak is the General Manager of Saturn, admired within General Motors Corporation, and thought to be an up-and-comer. Her most recent move up the ladder of success, in March of 2004, puts this 43-year-old business leader in a position that oversees the overall growth of Saturn and its product lines. Her responsibilities include Saturn brand and product development, marketing/advertising, and ensuring that the brand properly integrates with the field organization to implement programs. Saturn division, once the model for a progressive work structure focused on teamwork, came perilously close to ending up on the scrap heap next to Oldsmobile. Saturn's experiment with teamwork has been so successful that some of the accumulated knowledge, technology, and experience are now being applied to other parts of GM. Despite brand loyalty and manufacturing teamwork breakthroughs, Saturn has never turned a profit for GM. So what happened along the way? According to many, Saturn did not grow its portfolio and the product didn't evolve. The company survived with only one vehicle for 10 straight years. "It's hard to make money when you're starving for product," said Rebecca Lindland, senior analyst at automotive consulting firm Global Insight Inc. "Saturn buyers left the brand because they were forced out, not that they wanted to."

Saturn has a rich and fascinating business story—the rise and fall and rise again of Saturn is a case study worthy of any business textbook. And if there's one thing we love in America, it's a great comeback story—watching the underdog transform and finally succeed, despite overwhelming odds. Lajdziak is determined to make Saturn a great brand again—with great marketing, retail, and product. Lajdziak is very optimistic about the future of Saturn under her leadership. As she put it, ". . . it's an exciting time to be at Saturn—stay tuned as the next chapter of our story unfolds."

Opening Case Questions:

1. Why has Saturn's success with teamwork and customer satisfaction not resulted in financial success so far?
2. What would be the evidence that Saturn is a team of employees and not just a group of workers?
3. Why does Jill Lajdziak believe that she can turn Saturn around?
4. To what extent has Saturn used cross-functional teams in its operations?
5. Describe the nature of self-managed teams at Saturn?
6. To what extent has Saturn's teamwork culture resulted in team decision-making?
7. What has been the impact of self-managed teams on the performance and motivation of Saturn's employees?
8. Describe how top management's commitment and support helped the self-managed team concept and the benefits this has brought Saturn.

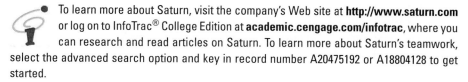

To learn more about Saturn, visit the company's Web site at **http://www.saturn.com** or log on to InfoTrac® College Edition at **academic.cengage.com/infotrac**, where you can research and read articles on Saturn. To learn more about Saturn's teamwork, select the advanced search option and key in record number A20475192 or A18804128 to get started.

The focus of this chapter is on how organizations can develop and use effective teams to achieve organizational goals. We will explore the importance of incorporating teams into the organization's structure and the different types of teams commonly found in organizations. Decision making in teams and leadership skills for conducting effective team meetings is addressed. The chapter concludes with a discussion of self-managed teams.

The Use of Teams in Organizations

Teamwork is a way of life in the postmodern organization.[1] Early discussions of the concept came from post–World War II Japanese management approaches, and led to greater academic scrutiny in the human relations movement before being embraced by major U.S. corporations. Through the years, many studies have documented the importance of teams for achieving organizational success.[2–4] The basic premise of teamwork is that teams offer the best opportunity for better corporate performance in the form of increased productivity and profits. In other words, the synergistic benefits of teamwork are such that members of a team working cooperatively with one another can achieve more than working independently.[5]

Since the early 1990s, various studies have reported greater numbers of U.S. corporations using teams to accomplish organizational tasks.[6,7] The reasons for this trend are obvious. Many companies, large and small, face serious challenges from a dynamic and complex global economy—challenges that have put in question the effectiveness of traditional management methods. Some of these challenges include growing demands from customers for better quality products and services at lower prices, globalization, technological advances, and pressure from competitors and suppliers.[8] More than ever before, teams are now an integral part of the workplace. One recent survey found that companies of all sizes rely on teams to accomplish various business goals. According to some estimates, over 50 percent of all organizations and 80 percent of organizations with more than 100 employees use some form of teams.[9] Many organizations have reengineered their work processes and procedures to accommodate teams. The thinking behind the team approach is that teams form the basic unit of empowerment—large enough for the collective strength and synergy of diverse talents and small enough for effective participation and bonding.[10]

Generally, research has been encouraging, showing that the use of teams has led to desirable performance improvements for many organizations in a variety of industries, although teams have also not worked so well in some cases. Some of the performance indicators include improved productivity, quality, efficiency, employee satisfaction, and customer satisfaction. One study cites several examples of organizational successes using teams:

- A large stamping plant created empowered maintenance teams that took it upon themselves to improve the functionality of specific machines in the operation, for both preventive and rapid response maintenance, resulting in a 28 percent reduction in machine downtime.
- Using self-managed teams, an appliance manufacturing plant increased productivity by 22 percent.

- A large warehousing operation reduced the procurement cycle time by a full day through the creation of an operational improvement team that had the full backing of top management.
- By creating and empowering a new safety team, a mid-sized furniture factory reduced lost time for on-the-job injuries by 30 percent.

1. Why Has Saturn's Success with Teamwork and Customer Satisfaction not Resulted in Financial Success So Far?

Saturn's mission and values statements focus on teamwork, operational excellence, and innovation. Teamwork at Saturn has succeeded in many ways. It has tremendous brand equity in that many of its customers are loyal to the brand. Saturn's conquest rate is 70 percent, which is its ability to attract new buyers to GM—both import intenders and non-GM domestic buyers. Its demographic is terrific: A Saturn owner is most likely a highly educated, affluent, 43-year-old and likely to be a professional. With strong brand loyalty among its customers and more than 2.2 million cars sold, Saturn attributes it success to two basic reasons:putting customers first and working as a team. The problem has been with its parent company, GM. Lack of investment meant the portfolio did not grow and the product didn't evolve. Saturn survived with only one vehicle for 10 straight years. Saturn's 2004 sales dropped 21.8 percent to 212,017 units—the lowest level since 1992—from 2003, according to Autodata Corp. GM blamed the sharp drop on the discontinuation of the midsize L-series last summer. Ultimately, the automaker committed last summer to dig deep into its corporate kitty and make one more big push to turn Saturn into a healthy brand that delivers cars and SUVs to match its sales and service quality. In all, GM plans to spend $3 billion to double Saturn's product line to six models by the end of 2006. Last summer, GM's board of directors approved a $400 million to $500 million investment to upgrade a Spring Hill, Tennessee assembly plant to build new models.

OPENING CASE APPLICATION

However, not all team efforts have resulted in success. The use of teams has resulted in such negative outcomes as increased costs, stress, and lower group cohesion.[11] It is for this reason that some in the field are calling for a "look before you leap" mentality. It is recommended that an organization ask critical questions of itself before embarking on creating teams within its structure, such as whether teams will diffuse important organizational capabilities, how much infrastructure realignment will be required, whether leaders will embrace the team concept and change their styles to suit, whether teams can carry out tasks previously performed by support departments, and how difficult it will be to develop teams' problem-solving capabilities.[12] Also, teams have failed for lack of training. Effective team training has been found to improve collective efficacy and team performance.[13] These issues will be addressed throughout this chapter. This section will define what a team is, distinguish between the concept of a team and a group, and examine the advantages and disadvantages of using teams.

Groups versus Teams: What Is the Difference?

All teams are groups, but not all groups are teams. A manager can put together a group of people and never build a team. *A* **team** *is a unit of two or more people with complementary skills who are committed to a common purpose and set of performance goals and to common expectations, for which they hold themselves accountable.* This definition contains three key points to remember. First, teams are made up of two or more people. Teams can be large, but most tend to be small, with fewer than 15 people. Second, a team is not just a group of individuals brought together at random. A team is made up of individuals with complementary skills. Third, people in a team share common goals for which they are all accountable. The goal could be to build a home, design a network system, or launch a space shuttle. Given this background, it would appear that the terms "team" and "group" are not interchangeable, though some authors have not distinguished between them. A group is simply a collection of people working together. Extensive research in the workplace has confirmed that there do indeed exist some differences between teams and groups. The team concept implies a sense of shared mission and collective responsibility. Whereas groups focus on individual performance and goals, and reliance on individual abilities, teams have a collective mentality that focuses on (1) sharing information, insights, and perspectives; (2) making decisions that support each individual to do his or her own job better; and/or (3) reinforcing each other's individual performance standards. Team members tend to have shared responsibilities, whereas group members sometimes work slightly more independently with greater motivation to achieve personal goals. The leadership style in a group tends to be very hierarchical, while in a team it is more likely to be participative or empowerment-oriented. In a team, performance measures create direct accountability for the team and incentives are team-based; in contrast, a group is characterized by individual self-interest, with a mentality of "what's in it for me." Teams strive for equality between members; in the best teams, there are no stars, and everyone suppresses individual ego for the good of the whole. It is important to bear in mind that these distinctions probably reflect matters of degree. One might consider teams to be highly specialized groups. In this chapter, the two terms will be used interchangeably.

WorkApplication1

Think of a past or present job. Based on your knowledge of the distinction between a group and a team, would you say you were part of a team or a group? Explain.

_____

_____

_____

_____

_____

OPENING CASE APPLICATION

2. What Would Be the Evidence That Saturn Is a Team of Employees and Not Just a Group of Workers?

Saturn's value statement focuses on six core areas: commitment to customer enthusiasm, commitment to excel, teamwork, trust and respect for the individual, and continuous improvement. The teamwork value statement proceeds as follows: "We perform as one team dedicated to and accountable for the success of the Saturn Brand. To generate enthusiasm and effectiveness, we involve team members; engage their talents; consider the effects of our actions on others; and recognize, reward, and celebrate accomplishments. We are able to achieve more through the power of the team." This is clearly consistent with the preceding description of the team concept and not a group.

─────────────── Learning Outcome 1 ───────────────

Discuss the advantages and disadvantages of working in teams.

Advantages and Disadvantages of Teamwork

Teamwork *is an understanding and commitment to group goals on the part of all team members.* The increased acceptance and use of teams suggests that their usage offers many advantages. However, teams also present organizations with many challenges, including the need for effective communication; resolving personality conflicts and egos; establishing unifying goals, direction, and focus; establishing appropriate rewards and incentives; clarity about team structure; effective leadership; and organizing the team's work to ensure timely decisions. Failure to effectively handle these challenges often results in dysfunctional teams, which means there are disadvantages that come with using teams in organizations.[14] This section discusses several of the advantages and disadvantages of teamwork.

Advantages of Teamwork

First, in a team situation it is possible to achieve synergy, whereby the team's total output exceeds the sum of the various members' contributions. Synergy involves the creative cooperation of people working together to achieve something beyond the capacities of individuals working alone. Second, team members often evaluate one another's thinking, so the team is likely to avoid major errors. This tendency of mutual support and peer review of ideas helps teams make better decisions and can provide immunity for an organization against disruptive surprises. Third, teams can and do contribute well to continuous improvement and innovation. For example, a number of companies worldwide have found that self-managed teams create a work environment that encourages people to become self-motivated. Besides speeding up decision making and innovation, team members report greater satisfaction with their jobs.

Group or Team

Based on each statement, identify it as characteristic of a group or a team. Write the appropriate letter in the blank before each item.

a. group   b. team

_____ 1. My boss conducts my performance appraisals, and I get good ratings.

_____ 2. We don't have any departmental goal; we just do the best we can to accomplish the mission.

_____ 3. My compensation is based primarily on my department's performance.

_____ 4. I get the assembled product from Jean; I paint it and send it to Tony for packaging.

_____ 5. There are about 30 people in my department.

Applying the Concept 1

WorkApplication2

Identify a team you were or are a part of and describe the advantages that you derived from being a member of the team.

_____

_____

_____

_____

_____

Job satisfaction is important because it has, in turn, been associated with other positive organizational outcomes. For example, employees who are satisfied with their jobs are less likely to quit, are absent less, and are more likely to display organizational citizenship behavior. Finally, being a member of a team makes it possible to satisfy more needs than if one worked alone; among these are the needs for affiliation, security, self-esteem, and self-fulfillment. Team members develop trust for each other and come to see the team as a social unit that fulfills other needs.[15] Research does provide support for the proposition that people's perceptions of their own interdependence with others (such as in a team) influence both their beliefs about group members' trustworthiness and their attitude toward group members. Thus, interpersonal trust is seen as an important social resource that can facilitate cooperation and enable coordinated social interactions. This adds to team member commitment and motivation. There is ample research support for the position that employees who are more committed are less likely to leave their jobs, less likely to experience stress, and more likely to perform well and behave pro-socially.

OPENING CASE APPLICATION

3. What Benefits Have Saturn Employees Derived from Teamwork Processes?

At Saturn, for example, the team structure has redefined the way work is done. Teams, by their very definition, cross standard job descriptions. A lot of the power of unions stems from the fact that unions regulate jobs. So if you are a machinist class 1, you do a given job. If you are a machinist class 2, you do another job. You do not do both jobs. For proponents of the team concept, it is a welcome replacement for outmoded union bureaucracy. At Saturn, supporters of teamwork say that this kind of production offers a lot more job contentment, while work in the standard assembly line is dull, repetitive, and alienating. At Saturn, at least, teamwork has been a positive experience.

Disadvantages of Teamwork

Teamwork has some potential disadvantages for both organizations and individuals. A common problem may be that members face pressure to conform to group standards of performance and conduct. For example, a team member may be ostracized for being much more productive than his or her coworkers. Also, there are situations in which working in teams is perceived by some individuals to impinge on their autonomy, thus creating resistance to the team effort.[16] Shirking of individual responsibility, also known as _social loafing_, is another problem frequently noted in groups. **Social loafing** _is the conscious or unconscious tendency by some team members to shirk responsibilities by withholding effort towards group goals when they are not individually accountable for their work._ Many students who have worked on team projects (like group term papers) have encountered a social loafer. Social loafing is likely to result when individual effort is not recognized and assessed. Individual performance appraisal helps to discourage social loafing by providing each team member with feedback on the quality of his or her work; however, it goes against the popular view that implementing team-based performance measures is necessary for a strong team identity, and a strong team identity leads to greater coordination.[17] In other words, individual-level performance appraisal helps reduce social loafing, but it risks jeopardizing the interaction and synergy that characterizes excellent team performance.

Another well-known disadvantage associated with highly cohesive groups or teams is groupthink. **Groupthink** *is when members of a cohesive group tend to agree on a decision not on the basis of its merit but because they are less willing to risk rejection for questioning a majority viewpoint or presenting a dissenting opinion.* The group culture values getting along more than getting things done. The group often becomes more concerned with striving for unanimity than with objectively appraising different courses of action. Dissenting views are suppressed in favor of consensus. These problems may explain why some studies have not found consistent support for the strong belief in the effectiveness of teams. Some scholars have argued that our "romance of teams" stems from the psychological benefits members derive rather than the assumed link to high performance.[18] The problem of groupthink can be remedied by training team members to become effective participants in the decision-making process—something that is taken for granted when a team is formed.

Though cohesiveness is a desirable quality of teams, teams that are extremely cohesive can also become, at their worst, a source of conflict with other teams. They may become so cohesive that they resemble cliques with minimal outside interaction or influence, thus creating the potential for significant intergroup conflicts. There is pressure for workers to stand by their teammates and to achieve the team's goals. A production team might devote significant energy to creating problems for the marketing team because the latter requires constant changes in product designs that production finds impossible or difficult to meet. From a leadership standpoint, effective team leaders find ways to maximize the advantages of teams and to minimize the disadvantages of teams. Complete Self-Assessment 1 to evaluate teamwork from your own work experience.

WorkApplication3

Based on Self-Assessment 1, list some things that a team could do to improve its level of teamwork. Use experiences associated with a present or past job.

_____

_____

_____

_____

_____

Ethical Dilemma 1

Team Players

JetBlue Airways is not structured around teams. However, teamwork knowledge, skills, and attitudes are important to the success of JetBlue. In fact, JetBlue gives extensive screening interviews to make sure job candidates are team players. In addition to checking the 6–7 references the job candidate provides, JetBlue recruiters ask the reference people for the names of people that can give insights into the candidate, and they call them as well.[19]

1. Is being a team player really necessary to be a successful employee at JetBlue?

2. Is it ethical and socially responsible of JetBlue to reject job candidates because they are considered not to be good team players?

Self-Assessment 1

Assessing Teamwork in Your Group

Based on experiences you have or have had with teams, indicate whether your team has (or had) the following characteristics by placing a check mark in the appropriate column:

In my team:

	Mostly True	Mostly False
1. There is a common understanding and commitment to group goals on the part of all team members.	___	___
2. Members support and provide constructive feedback to one another's ideas.	___	___
3. Members do not feel the pressure to conform to group standards of performance and conduct.	___	___
4. Dissenting views are accepted and discussed rather than suppressed in favor of consensus.	___	___
5. There is a high level of interpersonal interaction among members.	___	___
6. Much of the responsibility and authority for making important decisions is turned over to the team.	___	___
7. There is an open communication channel for all members to voice their opinions.	___	___

	Mostly True	Mostly False
8. Members are provided with the opportunity for continuous learning and training in appropriate skills.	___	___
9. Every team member is treated equally.	___	___
10. Members are more likely to provide backup and support for one another without the team leader's instruction.	___	___
11. Rewards and recognition are linked to individual as well as team results.	___	___
12. There are clearly established roles and responsibilities for performing various tasks.	___	___

Scoring. Add up the number of mostly true answers and place the total on the continuum below.

12—11—10—9—8—7—6—5—4—3—2—1
Effective teamwork   *Ineffective teamwork*

Interpreting the score. The higher the score, the more effective is the teamwork. Self-assessment exercises like this can be used by groups during team building to improve teamwork. You will learn more about the team leader's role in building effective teams in the next section and about self-managed teams later in the chapter.

Characteristics of Effective Teams

Effective teams are those that meet their performance targets, such as quality, productivity, profitability, worker satisfaction and commitment, and deadlines. Thus, **team effectiveness** *is defined as having three components: (1) task performance—the degree to which the team's output (product or service) meets the needs and expectations of those who use it; (2) group process—the degree to which members interact or relate in ways that allow the team to work increasingly well together over time; and (3) individual satisfaction—the degree* *to which the group experience, on balance, is more satisfying than frustrating to team members.*[20] This definition embodies a number of performance outcomes that others have used as a basis for evaluating team effectiveness. These include innovation/adaptation, efficiency, quality, and employee satisfaction. Innovative or adaptive teams are those with the capability to rapidly respond to environmental needs and changes with creative solutions. Efficient teams enable the organization to attain goals with fewer resources. Quality pertains to the team's ability to achieve superior results with fewer resources, and exceed customer expectations. Satisfaction measures the team's ability to maintain employee commitment to and enthusiasm for the team effort by meeting not just the team's goals but also the personal needs of its members.

Teams vary in terms of their effectiveness. Some are effective and some are not. The obvious question therefore becomes, What makes one team successful and another unsuccessful? Much of the literature portrays team effectiveness as a function of both internal and external factors: task, group, and organization design factors; environmental factors; internal and external processes; and group psychosocial characteristics. Other scholars have focused on internal team processes: self-leadership, interdependence, and team cohesion (also referred to as group potency). One model examined three contextual factors—team design, organizational resources and rewards, and process assistance—as determinants of team effectiveness.[21] We believe organizational context, as well as internal team processes, are contributing factors to determining team effectiveness. Understanding what makes teams effective is of obvious importance to organizational leaders. In this section, the following six factors are described as critical to team effectiveness: team norms, team leadership, team cohesiveness and interdependence, team composition, team structure, and organizational support.[22–24]

Learning Outcome 2

Briefly describe the seven characteristics of effective teams.

Team Norms

Team norms are an important characteristic of effective teams because norms guide team members' behavior. Norms determine what behavior is acceptable and unacceptable. **Team norms** *are acceptable standards of behavior that are shared by team members.* Norms influence how a team's members perceive and interact with one another, approach decisions, and solve problems.[25] An effective team must possess an appropriate set of norms that govern all members' behavior. A team's norms will influence how members perceive and interact with one another, approach decisions, and resolve problems such as conflict. For example, a team norm might specify cooperative over independent behavior; to the outside observer, this may be reflected by the level of importance members place on shared pursuits, objectives, and mutual interests rather than personal interests.

At the early stages of a team's formation, norms begin to develop and often gain acceptance and significance in every team member's work life. Team leaders can play a major role in helping to shape norms that will help the team successfully realize its goals and also keep members satisfied and committed to the team. There are many ways by which team norms get formed; the two most common are critical events and symbols. Norms often emerge out of critical events in the team's history and way(s) in which team members responded. This sets a precedent and becomes the standard for future behavior.

Ethical Dilemma 2

Norms

One or a few employees can break the norms and cause disastrous consequences for not only one organization but also entire industries. On the other hand, one or a few people can blow the whistle to disclose illegal and unethical business practices, which can lead to decreasing unethical behavior,[26] such as at Enron. On the micro team level, employees influence each other's behavior through developing and enforcing norms; we can also call it peer pressure.

1. Should employees be able to do their own thing without the group enforcing norms?
2. Is it ethical and socially responsible for groups to develop and enforce norms? If so, what type of ethical standards should a group have?

Team Leadership

Although an important goal of a team-based organization is for group members to participate in leadership (such as is the case with self-managed teams or semiautonomous work teams), leaders still play an important role in influencing team performance.[27–29] Effective team leaders encourage norms that positively affect the team's goals and alter those that are negative.[30] The need for leadership still exists, because in every work group someone will ultimately be responsible for the outcome. Instead of the leader's job disappearing, leaders will learn to lead in new ways. To be an effective team leader requires a shift in mind-set and behavior for those who are accustomed to working in traditional organizations in which managers make all the decisions.[31] Team-based organizations need leaders who are knowledgeable in the team process and are capable of developing a productive and effective team.[32] If they are to have satisfied, productive, and loyal team members, team leaders must recognize that not everyone knows how to be a team player. Some team members will look to the team leader to put together a game plan and lead the team to success. The team leader must model the behavior that he or she desires. In order to foster the development of team spirit, leaders should observe with a keen eye what's going on in the team, make contributions when necessary, encourage a climate of dialogue, turn obstacles into opportunities, and see themselves and others as part of the team's pool of knowledge, skills, and ideas.[33,34] Therefore, an effective team leader must be adaptive, knowing when to play different roles—manager, facilitator, or coach.[35]

Being an effective team leader means understanding people. This is also referred to as having social skills. According to one study, there are four dimensions that determine whether an individual has high or low social skills:

influence, interpersonal facilitation, relational creativity, and team leadership.[36] Leaders with high social skills tend to have greater influencing abilities and interpersonal skills, and relate well with team members. Without effective leadership, teams can get off course, go too far or not far enough, lose sight of their mission, and become blocked by interpersonal conflict. Therefore, team leaders have an important personal role to play in building effective teams.[37,38] A leader's self-sacrificing behavior and display of self-confidence does influence team members. Self-sacrificing leaders are those who go above and beyond what's expected of them. They don't just issue orders; they get involved in making things happen. The results of a laboratory experiment revealed that productivity levels, effectiveness ratings, and perceived leader group-orientedness and charisma were positively affected by leader self-sacrifice.[39,40]

OPENING CASE APPLICATION

4. Why Does Jill Lajdziak Believe That She Can Turn Saturn Around?

Ms. Lajdziak is convinced that through the years, Saturn employees have worked effectively as a team to create a strong brand and through her leadership, the Saturn team can build on this positive brand equity. "We are determined," she said, "to overcome our odds and make Saturn a great brand again—with great marketing, retail and product." She believes she can achieve this goal by leveraging GM's global resources and continuing the company's culture of teamwork.

The key responsibilities a leader should undertake in order to create an effective team are summarized in Exhibit 8-1.[41]

Team Cohesiveness and Interdependence

Effective teams typically have high levels of cohesion, interdependence, and autonomy.[42] **Team cohesion** *is the extent to which members band together and*

Exhibit 8-1 *The team leader's role in creating effective teams.*

- Emphasize group recognition and rewards.
- Identify and build on the team's strengths.
- Develop trust and a norm of teamwork.
- Develop the team's capabilities to anticipate and deal with change effectively.
- Empower teams to accomplish their work with minimal interference.
- Inspire and motivate teams toward higher levels of performance.
- Recognize individual and team needs and attend to them in a timely fashion.
- Encourage and support team decisions.
- Provide teams with challenging and motivating work.

WorkApplication4

Interview someone you have worked with or know who is a team leader. Ask him or her to provide specific examples for some of the roles outlined in Exhibit 8-1 that he or she employed.

_____

_____

_____

_____

_____

remain committed to achieving team goals. Highly cohesive teams are also described as having high group potency (the collective belief of a group that it can be effective) and a strong self-efficacy (an internal belief held by an individual or group about how well an impending situation can be handled). Studies investigating the relationship between team potency and team effectiveness have found the two to be strongly correlated.[43] Some of the factors that have been found to increase team cohesion include shared purpose and goals, team reputation for success, interteam competition, and personal attraction to the team. Team cohesion is increased when:

- Team members agree on a common purpose and direction.
- There is high praise and recognition by external parties for the team's success.
- The organization encourages and motivates teams to compete with each other for rewards.
- Members find they have common ground and similar attitudes and values and enjoy being on the team.

The presence of all these factors has been shown to have strong correlations with team member satisfaction and commitment. Teams experiencing cohesion are less likely to engage in affective disagreement and more likely to remain together longer and to make more effective decisions.[44]

The degree to which team members depend on each other for information, resources, and other inputs to complete their tasks determines the level of interdependence or mutual influences within the team.[45] In effective teams, interdependence is built into the team's goal, reward, and job structure. Among teams, three types of interdependence have been identified: pooled, sequential, and reciprocal interdependence. Without describing each type in detail, it should be noted that the level of team member interaction and dependency increases successively as one goes from pooled, to sequential, to reciprocal interdependence.

Team Composition

Team composition focuses on the characteristics of team members. Effective teams must have the right mix of complementary skills, knowledge, and ability to perform the team's job.[46] Recognizing the heterogeneous nature of today's workforce, organizational researchers have increasingly focused on teams with multicultural, multifunctional, and multinational characteristics. According to one study, there are three fundamental descriptors of team members— multifunctional knowledge, teamwork skills, and an established good working relationship.[47] To have a good working relationship requires high social skills. According to one study, four dimensions determine an individual's level of social skills—influence, interpersonal facilitation, relational creativity, and team leadership.[48] These factors result in more effective and efficient teams. Also, team diversity in skills, backgrounds, and perspectives increases creativity because members bring diverse points of view to bear on problems. In general, there is a perception that heterogeneous teams outperform homogeneous teams. Another benefit of diversity is the reduced likelihood of groupthink because of greater opportunities for differing points of view. Groupthink, as described earlier, is the tendency for members of cohesive teams to agree on a decision not on the basis of its merit, but because they don't want to disagree with fellow teammates and risk rejection. However, it should be noted that not all diverse teams perform well. Diversity, when not well managed, has produced negative consequences.[49,50] Teams that do not manage diversity well may suffer from intrateam conflicts, lack of communication, an absence of collegiality, and ultimately lack of any team spirit.

Another aspect of team composition is the size of the team. Small teams, typically under 12 people, are generally more effective than larger teams. In small teams, conflicts and differences are more manageable, and the team is able to rally around its mission. Size affects team members' ability to relate closely with other members. In larger teams, it is much more difficult for members to interact and share ideas with each other. Teams made up of more than 12 people have been successful in some cases, but do tend to break into subteams rather than functioning as a single unit. In general, teams that participants perceive as too small or too large relative to the task at hand have been shown to be less effective. In a study conducted at Hewlett-Packard to identity key success factors for cross-functional teams, HP researchers found that successful teams were those with under 25 members. Thus, team size is relative.

Team Structure

Team structure refers to interrelations that determine the allocation of tasks, responsibilities, and authority. In other words, team structure may explain the hierarchical dynamics within the team.[51,52] Also, interdependence and autonomy have been identified as key structural components that influence team effectiveness. Teams that possess high autonomy, broad participation in team decisions, and variety in tasks performed by individual members, are said to have motivational job design characteristics. Team structure will also determine the extent to which team members directly control the actions of each other (horizontal incentive system) or report observations of their peers' efforts to management (vertical incentive system). According to one study, team structures that allow for horizontal incentive systems show higher levels of team identity and coordination than team structures that insist on vertical incentive systems.[53,54] When teams perceive their tasks as motivating, they are generally more effective.

Organizational Support

Effective teams are those that have the strong support of the parent organization, that is, support from the top of the organization. Assessing team effectiveness as it relates to the overall performance of the organization is an important part of top management responsibility.[55] When teams are not achieving expected results, top management must ask itself some key questions. First, do the teams fully understand their mission? Second, are teams getting enough support from top management in the form of training, rewards, information, and material resources that they need? Third, have the appropriate leadership, communication, and task structures been set up for team operations? And, finally, does the organizational culture/environment support teamwork and have reward programs that motivate and reinforce team behavior?[56] These questions address the role of the organization in providing an infrastructure that supports effective teamwork. Exhibit 8-2 summarizes the key responsibilities of an organization in creating an effective team.[57–59]

WorkApplication5

Recall a team you have worked with that you would characterize as effective. What role(s) did your leader and/or organization play in making the team effective?

_____

_____

_____

_____

_____

Exhibit 8-2 *The organization's role in creating effective teams.*

- Top management's unconditional support.
- Adequate information and other resources.
- Flexible task structure.
- Appropriate size and membership mix.
- Clearly defined mission statement and goals.
- Appropriate power sharing structure—shared leadership.
- Competent team leadership.
- Evaluation and solicitation of feedback on team effectiveness.
- Adequate socialization of team members.

──────────────── Learning Outcome 3 ────────────────

Describe top management's and the team leader's roles in fostering creativity. For each, list activities they should undertake to promote creativity.

Creativity Driven

Effective teams are also characterized by higher levels of creativity. **Team creativity** *is the creation of a valuable, useful, and novel product, service, idea, procedure, or process carried out via discovery rather than a predetermined step-by-step procedure, by individuals working together in a complex social system.*[60] Today's economy has been rightly described as a knowledge economy because more companies are gaining competitive advantages based on knowledge rather than physical or financial resources. The companies that will survive and thrive will not be those that have the greatest financial resources, but those that can make use of the creativity of their workforce.[61] Besides the quality of the team itself, research reveals that a number of enabling factors— team autonomy, performance measurement and incentive systems, team bonuses, team continuity, a stable team composition, and sufficient resource endowment—can assist in improving team knowledge management and thus creativity.[62] These are the factors that directly bear on the role that top leaders at the higher levels of the organization must play in designing teams that exemplify creativity. For teams to maximize their creative potential, the organization must rethink its work structures and leadership approaches. Creating an organizational structure and climate that supports and encourages creativity provides the backdrop against which managerial practices can take hold. Without the appropriate organizational support, individual managerial attempts at encouraging and fostering creativity will be ineffective and unsuccessful. The suggestions that follow are ways by which an organization can make known its position on creativity throughout the organization.[63]

- **Provide adequate and quality resources.** To achieve superior quality, teams need not just adequate but also quality resources and state-of-the-art equipment. In allocating scarce resources, top management has to make this a priority if it intends to stay innovative.
- **Provide appropriate recognition and rewards.** Organizations should be aware of the effect various types of incentives or rewards can have on

creativity; certain types of motivation are more conducive to creativity than others. Research has shown that people tend to generate more creative solutions when they are motivated by intrinsic (i.e., sense of accomplishment) as well as (or more than) extrinsic (i.e., pay) rewards.[64] To foster creativity, an organization and its leaders must find the right balance of intrinsic-to-extrinsic rewards for team members because, despite the high intrinsic motivation of creative teams, they also need extrinsic motivation.

- **Provide flexibility and a minimum amount of structure.** Many creative workers (whether in teams or as individuals) regard the tall hierarchical structure as the death knell of creativity. *Structure* for creative teams means rules and regulations, many layers of approval, strict dress codes, fixed office hours, and rigid assignments. The organization must strive to provide greater flexibility and a more decentralized, organic structure for creativity to take place. Some call this *organizational empowerment,* which is the recognition that an untapped potential for creativity exists in your employees and all you need to do is give them the opportunity to realize it. Organizations can facilitate this process by creating a culture of empowerment that replaces hierarchical thinking with self-managed teams.[65]

- **Provide supportive climate and culture.** Employees need to be able to experiment and try out their ideas. The organization can establish a culture in which team leaders can give members free time for activities that are not officially sanctioned. One study of creativity found that in almost every case the essence of the creative act came during the "unofficial" time period.[66] One of the best-known results of this practice is 3M's Post-it Notes, one of the five most popular 3M products and one that resulted from an engineer's free-time experiments with another engineer's "failure"—a not-very-sticky glue. 3M lets employees spend 15 percent of their time (also known as the 15 percent rule) on any projects of their own choosing, without management approval.[67]

It should also be understood that a team leader's actions can support or kill creativity within the team despite the organization's best intentions. Just because senior management establishes supportive policies and practices does not mean that they will automatically be implemented at the team level. That's why it is still important to emphasize team leader responsibilities, which must be carefully executed for creativity to flourish. As mentioned earlier, a distinguishing characteristic of effective teams is the quality and personality of the team leader. With respect to the role of the team leader in fostering creativity, researchers have identified specific actions that can ensure that a creative team spirit is not squashed, including: matching people with the right assignments; giving team members greater autonomy to do the job; ensuring the availability of adequate time, money, and other resources for the team; paying careful attention to the design of teams; emphasizing teamwork; and protecting against "creativity blockers."[68] While this list is not exhaustive, it highlights many of the operational decisions and actions team leaders have to make or take into account to fully realize their team's creative potential.

Self-Assessment 2 should help you assess the climate for creativity in your organization or institution.

WorkApplication6

Think of a work situation in which you were required to do a lot of creative thinking, or in which your job required doing a lot of very creative things. In what ways did the organization and your immediate supervisor or leader facilitate or hinder your effectiveness? Use the discussion of top management and the team leader's roles in facilitating creativity as your guide.

_____

_____

_____

_____

_____

Self-Assessment 2

Assessing the Climate for Creativity

Place a checkmark in the appropriate column for each question.

	Mostly Agree	Mostly Disagree
1. Organizational practices generally encourage creativity.	____	____
2. The reward system has been carefully designed to encourage creativity.	____	____
3. People are not restricted by rules and regulations or many layers of approval when they want to try new ideas.	____	____
4. "Doing things the way they have always been done" is not a slogan that applies in this organization.	____	____
5. People are able to experiment and dream outside their regular functional area on company time.	____	____
6. The organization's culture values and appreciates input from members.	____	____
7. People feel they have been properly matched with tasks that fit their skills, interests, and experiences.	____	____

	Mostly Agree	Mostly Disagree
8. Employees have greater autonomy to think and act freely than they would in another organization.	____	____
9. In looking around, it is certain that the work environment has been carefully designed to encourage creativity.	____	____
10. Managerial practices in this organization would lead to the conclusion that creativity and innovation are highly valued at all levels.	____	____

Scoring. Begin by placing a checkmark in the appropriate column for each question. Add up the number of "mostly agree" checkmarks and place the sum on the continuum below.

10—9—8—7—6—5—4—3—2—1
Supportive climate   Unsupportive climate

Interpreting the Score. The higher the score, the more supportive the organizational climate is of creativity and innovation. Self-assessment exercises like this can be used to encourage students to relate their work environments to the concepts in ways that others can benefit from the experience of their peers.

Types of Teams

Structural metamorphosis seems to be the one constant in organizational life today. Traditional organizational structures, known for their stable designs, are changing in favor of more fluid designs that can respond to external environmental trends. These flexible designs include a flatter and more horizontal structure, a focus on new ways to motivate employees, and the use of teams instead of functional structures. A manufacturing enterprise might, for example, make use of a variety of teams, including quality improvement teams, problem-solving teams, self-managed productive teams, cross-functional teams, technology integration teams, virtual cross-functional teams, and safety teams.

Managing Creative Teams

Identify which strategy for creative teams each statement relates to:

a. quality resources   c. flexibility
b. recognition and rewards   d. free time

_____ 6. They gave me this pin for five years of service to the company.

_____ 7. How does management expect us to make a quality product when they get these cheap parts from our supplier?

_____ 8. There sure are a lot of rules and regulations to know to work here.

_____ 9. I wish I could take my break, and take it on time, regularly.

_____ 10. I don't know why the boss keeps checking to make sure I'm doing my job according to the proper company procedures.

Over the years, increasing competition stemming from the global and technological nature of markets has forced organizations to adopt different team types; going from functional teams to cross-functional teams and then to self-managed teams. We will examine all three types in this section.

Functional Team

A **functional team** *consists of a group of employees belonging to the same functional department, such as marketing, R&D, production, human resources, or information systems, who have a common objective.* One hundred years ago, Frederick Taylor, called the "father of scientific management," espoused a leadership approach whereby managers made themselves functional experts, divided work processes into simple repetitive tasks, and treated workers as interchangeable parts. The functional team was mostly made up of the functional manager and a small group of frontline employees within that department. Over time, the drawbacks of this approach became evident, as workers suffered from boredom due to the repetitive nature of their jobs. The structure of the functional team is generally more hierarchical with the functional leader making all the decisions and expecting his or her followers to implement them. Another drawback of the functional team, though unintended, is the tendency for team members to focus on their local area of specialization and ignore or downplay the overall organizational mission. This can lead to a lack of cooperation between functional groups, resulting in poor quality of decisions and overall organization performance. In fact, rivalry rather than cooperation is what often happens between functional groups that don't interact with each other. A study examining the quality of the relationship between R&D and marketing in a functional organizational structure found that interfunctional rivalry had the following consequences: it severely reduced R&D's use of information supplied by marketing personnel, it lowered the perceived quality of information transferred between the two departments, and it increased political pressures to ignore useful information provided by marketing.

As discussed in Chapter 5, there is no one best leadership style to use in all functional teams. However, in many situations, the size of the team, task description, and membership mix may play a role in determining what leadership style is employed. For instance, functional team leaders in small to medium groups, performing standardized tasks, generally tend to have a more centralized and hierarchical leadership style in place. In one study, the leader of a functional team at an electronics firm describes how he made the transition from a traditional command-and-control organization structure to an empowered workforce structure. Over the lifetime of the project, the leader slowly transformed what started as a rigid functional group of engineers into a team. Along the way, his leadership style also changed to match the situation, following four phases: traditional, direct involvement, team advisor, and observer.

Over the years, the use of functional structure has been in decline. Cross-functional teams became popular in the late 1980s, when companies started to readjust their organizational structures to make them more flexible and competitive.

Cross-Functional Team

Increasingly, organizations are encountering complex and very dynamic external environments requiring flexible and less hierarchical structures. In today's flatter organizations, completing tasks often requires cooperation across boundaries, such as functional areas or divisions. Individuals are continually asked to cross functional boundaries and form teams with individuals of other functional disciplines for the purpose of accomplishing a common objective. The multifunctional team is composed of various members with different backgrounds, knowledge, experience, and expertise, who can solve problems and also help in decision making.[69,70] Another name for this type of team is the cross-functional team. *A* **cross-functional team** *is made up of members from different functional departments of an organization who are brought together to perform unique tasks to create new and nonroutine products or services.*[71] Team member may also include representatives from outside organizations, such as suppliers, clients, and joint-venture partners.

The premise behind the cross-functional team concept is that interaction, cooperation, coordination, information sharing, and cross-fertilization of ideas among people from different functional areas (production, marketing, R&D, etc.) produces better quality products/services with shorter developmental cycles. This is especially true for cross-functional teams charged with developing innovative products/services or new technologies.[72] Here, managing human interactions and coordinating the transfer of knowledge and ideas among individuals and functional groups can be the most challenging aspect of the job. Multifunctional teams are being formed across company lines. In one case, three companies joined forces with the goal of synchronizing activities in software, electronics, and mechanical design, to improve new product introductions and product development processes, better manage outsourcing, and lower manufacturing costs.[73] Communication is the medium through which team members share the information required for successful integration of ideas.[74] Separate cross-functional teams may be formed in an organization for different activities, projects, or customer groups. They may be either temporary or permanent additions to the formal structure of the organization. An example of multifunctional team application is found in concurrent engineering projects, in which team members from different departments of a company simultaneously interact in every phase of project tasks to design products and processes concurrently.[75]

5. To What Extent Has Saturn Used Cross-Functional Teams in Its Operations?

At Saturn, the primary goal of the brand and product development team is keeping people at the center of the vehicle development process. This is accomplished using cross-functional teams. For instance, team members work with many departments to ensure that the voice of the customer is always represented. This includes working with engineers to develop new technologies, features, and new models for the Saturn portfolio, as well as working with design professionals to develop the look and feel of Saturn in terms of color, fabric, design, and so on. Collaboration with the marketing department at Saturn to influence product positioning within the competitive set is also an integral role of the teams.

OPENING CASE APPLICATION

With modern communication technology have come virtual cross-functional teams. In particular, new and advanced technologies are providing the means for work that is dispersed (carried out in different locations) and asynchronous (carried out at different times) to still be performed in team settings.[76–78] This work structure is called the virtual team. *A **virtual team** is one in which members are separated in space and time.*[79] An increasing number of organizations are using virtual teams to provide human resource flexibility, customer service responsiveness, high quality/low-cost solutions to complex organizational problems, and speed in project completion.[80–82] However, organizations face some challenges with virtual teams. Virtual teams create significant communication and leadership challenges.[83–85] Team interaction, information sharing, and knowledge integration are much harder in a virtual team setting. Often, the lack of face-to-face interaction can be challenging because of the absence of facial and other nonverbal signals to help understanding.[86] Recommendations for dealing with these challenges include focusing attention on both technological and human issues, with team leaders staying alert to relational and communication issues.[87–91] Several things must be in place before forming a virtual team, including software programs for electronic communications and the right infrastructure and climate.[92–95] Virtual teams are growing in companies with global operations.[96] In global virtual teams, leaders have to be aware of cultural differences and the various proficiency levels among members. Global virtual team leaders are counseled to employ success strategies, such as building trust-based relationships, encouraging members to show respect for other cultures and languages, and promoting diversity as a team strength and not a weakness.[97–99]

Cross-functional teams typically have a team leader selected by higher management. Team leaders play a crucial role in cross-functional teams. They can affect a team's effort, cohesion, goal selection, and goal attainment. The responsibilities of the cross-functional team leader include ensuring that everyone has the same understanding of the team's objective, defining roles and deliverables up front with each team member, negotiating with team members' managers to establish the amount of time and other resources that members will give to the team, and dealing with all sorts of conflict.[100] It is often difficult to develop trust and cooperation across functional boundaries, because people frequently perceive individuals from other groups or functional areas as potential adversaries with conflicting goals, beliefs, or styles of interacting. There is the possibility that dysfunctional (or even toxic) group and individual dynamics can impede the work of the team. Egos, political infighting, and factionalism on the part of individuals suddenly thrown together to complete a task often keep groups from realizing their full potential and can sometimes sabotage their objectives. Effective cross-functional team leaders understand this dynamic and take proactive steps to develop a climate of trust and understanding within the team. They realize that their role is to act more like coaches or facilitators than managers, share leadership responsibilities, be willing to seek outside help, and empower followers.[101]

As cross-functional team applications continue to grow, the question of what makes one team effective and another ineffective is of significant value to researchers and companies. Research studies attempting to identify key factors responsible for ensuring success have started to emerge. In one study, researchers interviewed 75 current and previous leaders of cross-functional teams in Hewlett-Packard's marketing, R&D, manufacturing, and information systems units. The interviews focused on identifying factors that were critical to the optimal functioning of cross-functional teams.[102] In another study, a survey of frontline managers regarding the barriers and gateways to management cooperation and teamwork revealed a consensus around five keys or gateways proposed by respondents for getting frontline managers to work effectively in cross-functional teams.[103] Combined, these two studies highlight primary success traits of effective cross-functional teams. Exhibit 8-3 summarizes six key success factors for cross-functional team effectiveness.

Cross-functional teams offer many potential benefits to an organization. Bringing together the right people gives the team a rich and diverse base of knowledge and creative potential that far exceeds anything a single functional team could come up with. Coordination is improved and many problems are

Exhibit 8-3 *Key success factors for effective cross-functional teams.*

1. Develop consensus around a common vision or mission as well as goals that focus on organizational outcomes.
2. Implement team-based performance measures, feedback, and reward systems.
3. Ensure effective leadership and top management support.
4. Promote the use of team building, skill development, and team training as common practices.
5. Assemble the right skills.
6. Organize at the right size.

avoided when people from different functions come together to work on a project at the same time, rather than working in separate units. The cross-functional makeup of the team provides the advantages of multiple sources of communication, information, and perspectives; provides contacts outside of one's functional specialty; and provides speed to market, which is critical for success in globally competitive, high-technology markets. The upshot is better new-product quality and shorter development times when cross-functional teams are used. Members can learn new skills that will be carried back to their functional units and to subsequent teams. Finally, the positive synergy that occurs in effective teams can help them achieve a level of performance that exceeds the sum of the individual performances of members. Cross-functional teams are often an organization's first step toward greater employee participation and empowerment. These teams may gradually evolve into self-managed teams, which represent a fundamental change in how work is organized.

The third type of group is called the self-managed team and commonly calls for Vroom's facilitate and delegate leadership styles.

Self-Managed Team (SMT)

The challenges of succeeding in a global economy have reached new levels, as companies strive to develop and sustain competitive advantages with an intensity not seen before, and with the knowledge that the business environment has become ever more turbulent. To meet these challenges and become more competitive, U.S. companies of all types and sizes are acknowledging the need for changes in their internal structures and culture. They will have to create alternatives to hierarchies, change the way decisions are made, redefine jobs, and change assumptions people have about how to structure organizations. To meet these challenges, one structural approach that has been gaining ground is the self-managed work team (SMT).[104] **Self-managed teams (SMTs)** *are relatively autonomous teams whose members share or rotate leadership responsibilities and hold themselves mutually responsible for a set of performance goals assigned by higher management.* Self-managed teams are usually cross-functional in membership makeup, and have wide latitude in decision areas such as managing themselves, planning and scheduling work, and taking action on problems. Within the team, members set task goals for their specific areas of responsibility that support the achievement of overall team goals. There is a general perception that these characteristics make self-managed teams more adaptive and proactive in their behavior than the traditional team.[105]

The amount of delegated authority varies from one organization to another. For example, in some organizations, SMTs may be given the primary responsibility for personnel decisions such as selecting the team leader, hiring and firing team members, and determining compensation rates (within specified limits). In other organizations, such decisions are reserved for higher management. Self-managed teams have been used most often for manufacturing work, but they are finding increasing application in the service sector as well.[106]

Companies are finding out that SMTs create a work environment that stimulates people to become self-motivated. Besides speeding up decision making and innovation, SMTs inspire employees to connect with the company's vision in a very special way: they see the company as the means by which they can affect key issues and develop their leadership skills. Distributed leadership (which will

WorkApplication7

Recall any experience you have had or currently have, working with individuals from disciplines or technical specialties different from yours. How did you get along with these individuals? Describe the positives and negatives of your experience.

_____

_____

_____

_____

_____

Exhibit 8-4 *Evolution of teams and team leadership.*

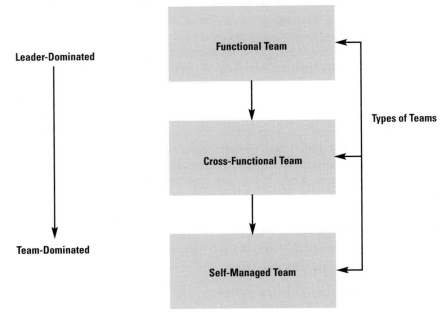

be discussed later) prevails in self-managed team situations. According to this approach, the group as a whole must share the responsibility for leadership functions. The self-managed team concept is discussed later in greater depth. Exhibit 8-4 summarizes our discussion of team types and their evolution.

OPENING CASE APPLICATION

6. Describe the Nature of Self-Managed Teams at Saturn.

Saturn's manufacturing complex is one of the few places in the world where raw iron and aluminum are transformed into parts for a finished car. There's no other place like it. There are no supervisors or time clocks, no "us" and "them." There is only the shared responsibility of getting the job done right and finding new ways to make the cars even better. The educational background of team members includes chemical engineering, electrical engineering, industrial engineering, mechanical engineering, or a degree in a similar technical field.

In summary, the functional team represents grouping individuals by common skills and activities within the traditional hierarchical structure. Leadership is based on command and control. In cross-functional teams, members have more freedom from the hierarchy, but the team typically is still leader-centered and leader-directed. The leader is most often assigned by the organization and is usually a supervisor or manager from one of the departments

Type of Team

Identify each statement as characteristic of the following team types:

a. functional   b. cross-functional   c. self-managed

_____ 11. We are developing a team to speed up processing our orders, and we are including two of our major customers.

_____ 12. Our team has been charged with developing a new product within three months, and we get to come up with it any way we want to.

_____ 13. The boss is conducting a department meeting.

_____ 14. We don't really have a boss in our team.

_____ 15. The manager is setting up a team with three of her employees to come up with ideas to increase productivity.

Applying the Concept 3

represented on the team. Leaders do, however, have to give up some of their control and power in order for the team to function effectively. In the highest stage of evolution, team members work together without the direction of managers, supervisors, or assigned team leaders. Self-directed teams are member- rather than leader-centered and directed. The next section examines creativity in a team context.

Decision Making in Teams

The uncertainty, ambiguity, and ever-changing circumstances of today's environment require that leaders have the courage to make difficult decisions. In this section, we will examine decision making in the context of the team, including the advantages and disadvantages of team decision making relative to decisions made by an individual leader, as well as the determinants of effective team decisions and the leader's role in team decisions.

Team versus Individual Decision Making

When it comes to solving problems and making decisions, organizations have relied on both individuals and teams. Teams are preferred over individuals when relevant information and expertise are scattered among different people, when participation is needed to obtain necessary commitment, when concentrating power in a single individual hurts the group, and when controversial decisions need to be made.[107,108] Using a group to make a decision under these types of circumstances has some definite advantages and disadvantages.

Advantages

Team decisions:

• Can improve decision quality by facilitating the pooling of relevant knowledge, and stimulating creative ideas.

• Can improve decision quality when the problems and issues involve the participation of different functions, subunits, or parties.

WorkApplication8

Recall a present or past job. Describe what type of team you are in or have been in—functional, cross-functional, or self-managed.

_____

_____

_____

_____

_____

- Allow responsibility to be diffused among several people, thereby facilitating support for some types of unpopular decisions (such as budget cutbacks and disciplinary actions).
- Help members understand the nature of the problem and the reasons for the final choice of a solution; this understanding helps members implement the decision effectively.
- Are likely to result in higher commitment by team members to implement decisions as compared to decisions made alone by a manager.

Disadvantages

Team decisions:

- Usually take longer than decisions made alone by a manager, and the cost in terms of participant time is greater.
- Are not necessarily better than those made by a single manager who has all of the relevant information and knowledge needed to make the decision, and in some cases team decisions will be inferior.
- May be self-serving and contrary to the best interests of the organization, if team members have objectives and/or priorities that are different from those of the leader.
- May end up being a poor compromise rather than an optimal solution, when team members cannot agree among themselves about the team's objectives and priorities.
- May symbolize a team's tendency to support each other in defensive avoidance of evidence showing that existing policies are no longer valid or adequate.

OPENING CASE APPLICATION

7. To What Extent Has Saturn's Teamwork Culture Resulted in Team Decision Making?

At Saturn, the word that is heard and used the most is "we," not "I". Employees are highly engaged in decisions involving their jobs and management takes their ideas and suggestions seriously. Saturn is one of the companies best known for its use of self-managed teams, where team decision making is the role, not the exception.

Several factors have been associated with effective team decisions. The contribution of information and ideas by team members—in other words, the degree of team member participation in decision making—has been cited as a key determinant of effective team decisions. The size and composition of the team, as mentioned earlier, also make a difference in the quality of decisions. The clarity of communication coupled with member knowledge and open-mindedness will determine how effectively members share information with each other, and the extent to which group discussion stays focused on the problem. The degree of team cohesiveness, the manner in which disagreement is resolved, and status differentials among members have also been referenced as important factors influencing effective decision making within the team. Finally, and most importantly, the leader's skills, experience, and style in dealing with all these factors cannot be ignored.[109,110]

Research results have revealed that teams with compatible members (similar traits, values, personality) are more productive, especially when joint action is necessary under conditions of time pressure. Members with similar traits and values will more likely have a common frame of reference when making decisions. Personality traits affect team performance. Complete Self-Assessment 3 to better understand how your personality will affect your

Self-Assessment 3

Personality Traits and Teams

Answer the following two questions, and then read how your personality profile can affect your teamwork.

I enjoy being part of a team and working with others more than working alone

7—6—5—4—3—2—1
Strongly agree   *Strongly disagree*

I enjoy achieving team goals more than individual accomplishments

7—6—5—4—3—2—1
Strongly agree   *Strongly disagree*

The stronger you agree with the two statements, the higher the probability that you will be a good team player. However, lower scores do not mean that you are not a good team player. The following is some information on how Big Five personality dimensions and their related motive needs can affect your teamwork.

Surgency—high need for power. If you have a high need for power, whether you are the team leader or not, you have to be careful not to dominate the group. Seek others' input, and know when to lead and when to follow. Even when you have great ideas, be sensitive to others so they don't feel that you are bullying them, and stay calm (adjustment) as you influence them. And be aware of your motives to make sure you use socialized rather than personalized

power. You have the potential to make a positive contribution to the team with your influencing leadership skills. If you have a low need for power, try to be assertive so that others don't take advantage of you, and speak up when you have good ideas.

Agreeableness—high need for affiliation. If you have a high need for affiliation, you tend to be a good team player. However, don't let the fear of hurting relationships get in your way of influencing the team when you have good ideas. Don't be too quick to give in to others, as it doesn't help the performance of the team when you have a better idea that is not implemented. You have the potential to be a valuable asset to the team as you contribute your skills of working well with others and making them feel important. If you have a low need for affiliation, be careful to be sensitive to others.

Conscientiousness—high need for achievement. If you have a high need for achievement, you have to watch your natural tendency to be more individualistic than team-oriented. It's good to have your own goals; but if the team and organization fail, so do you. Remember that there is usually more than one good way to do anything; your way is not always the best. In a related issue, don't be a perfectionist, as you can cause problems with team members. Being conscientious, you have the potential to help the team do a good job and reach its full potential. If you have a low need for achievement, push yourself to be a valuable contributor to the group, or pull your own weight.

teamwork. The characteristics of effective teams discussed earlier will also contribute to effective decision making.

Leader-Centered versus Group-Centered Approaches

The way a manager runs a team meeting greatly affects whether the ideas of team members are expressed. If a team leader takes a power position and uses a top-down directive approach, team member responses will tend to be guarded and cautious. On the other hand, if a team leader uses facilitative skills, such as asking open-ended questions, encouraging cross-discussion, actively listening, "playing back" what he or she hears another person saying, openly accepting the ideas of others, and recognizing how others feel about a proposal, team meetings will be more productive. According to research findings, training managers to act like facilitators differs from traditional training methods in that the former encourages team members to actively question and experiment, creates a dialogue, and makes the team leader or trainer feel responsible for achieving learning outcomes. Over the years, these two opposing perspectives (active-autocratic and passive-democratic styles) have received considerable attention from behavioral scientists. We will refer to these two contrasting leader behavior models as the "leader-centered" and the "group-centered" approach.

Leader-Centered Approach

According to this approach, the leader exercises his or her power to initiate, direct, drive, instruct, and control team members. This focus on the leader points to the following prescriptions for success:

- The leader should focus on the task and ignore personal feelings and relationships whenever possible.
- The leader should seek opinions and try to get agreement but never relinquish the right to make final choices.
- The leader should stay in control of the group discussion at all times and should politely but firmly stop disruptive acts and irrelevant discussion.
- The leader should discourage members from expressing their feelings and should strive to maintain a rational, logical discussion without any emotional outbursts.
- The leader should guard against threats to his or her authority in the group and should fight if necessary to maintain it.[111]

While this kind of leadership role produces some favorable results in certain situations, some behavioral scientists argue that it comes at a price. Meetings are conducted in an orderly fashion and decisions get made, but members become apathetic and resentful, which leads to a decrease in participation and a reduction in quality of decisions. Acceptance of decisions by group members may also be jeopardized if members feel pressured and unable to influence the decisions significantly.

Group-Centered Approach

The group-centered approach empowers group members to make decisions and follow through. Advocates of the group-centered approach argue that empowerment results in a more dedicated, energetic, and creative workforce.[112]

Empowerment is described as recognizing the untapped talents and human potential that lies in the knowledge, experience, and internal motivation of the people in an organization, and releasing that power. One way of releasing this potential is by replacing hierarchical management approaches that are leader-centered with self-managed teams.[113] Empowerment implies the freedom and the ability to make decisions and commitment, not just to be consulted. It is evident that the SMT concept discussed above is a group-centered approach. It is characterized by high involvement from group members. The overriding premise of the group-centered approach is that employees can be trusted to make decisions about their work, that they can be trained to acquire the skills and abilities needed to do so, and that organizational effectiveness is enhanced through this approach. Within the group, members have influence on decisions beyond their own task that affect the team as a whole, have the permission to determine the methods of their own task, and have the freedom to offer ideas.

The group-centered approach offers group leaders the following prescriptions for success:

- The leader should listen attentively and observe nonverbal cues to be aware of member needs, feelings, interactions, and conflict. In doing so, the leader should view the group as a collective entity or social system rather than as merely a collection of individuals. The development and dynamics of the team will greatly affect its effectiveness at problem solving.
- The role of the leader should be to serve as a consultant, advisor, teacher, and facilitator, rather than as a director or manager of the group.
- The leader should model appropriate leadership behaviors and encourage members to learn to perform these behaviors themselves.
- The leader should establish a climate of approval for expression of feelings as well as ideas.
- The leader should encourage the group to deal with any maintenance needs and process problems within the context of the regular group meetings. However, the leader should not try to move too quickly in encouraging group self-evaluation.
- The leader should relinquish control to the group and allow the group to make the final choice in all appropriate kinds of decisions.[114]

There are difficulties with implementing group-centered leadership. Leaders who are accustomed to the leader-centered approach may be afraid to risk sharing control with group members, or fear that if they do, they will appear weak or incompetent. Also, resistance may come from group members who prefer to avoid assuming more responsibility for leadership functions in the group. Despite these difficulties, the group-centered approach to leading teams has received much more attention among scholars than the leader-centered approach. When both approaches have been examined, the group-centered approach has been found to be more effective in some groups, although further research is needed to determine the extent and limits of its usefulness. It is more likely the case that neither approach is inherently good or bad, but rather that it all depends on the situation and circumstances. This is the contingency theory of leadership skills used in meetings discussed in the next section. Such a theory would prescribe more sharing of leadership functions in some situations than in others.

WorkApplication9

Recall a team decision that you were a part of, and describe the team leader's role during the process leading up to the final decision. Would you characterize the leader's role as belonging to the leader-centered or group-centered approach to decision making?

_____

_____

_____

_____

_____

Normative Leadership Model

Recall that in Chapter 5, "Contingency Leadership Theories," we discussed the normative leadership model. Recall that the normative models (Exhibits 5-9 and 5-10) and Chapter 5's Skill-Development Exercise 2 apply to group decision making, because the models are used to determine the level of participation to use in a given decision. Skill-Development Exercise 1 in this chapter presents a contingency leadership decision-making model that is adapted from the normative leadership model. It is a simpler model and uses the same leadership styles as situational communications (Skill-Development Exercise 2 in Chapter 6) to help you determine the appropriate level of participation to use in a given situation.

An important part of a leader's job is conducting team meetings. The next section focuses on strategies for conducting effective meetings.

Leadership Skills for Effective Team Meetings

With a group structure, managers spend a great deal of time in management meetings. Most meetings include employees, and it is common for teams to have daily meetings. With the trend toward teams, meetings are taking up an increasing amount of time. Therefore, the need for meeting management skills is stronger than ever.[115] The success of meetings depends on the leader's skill at managing the group process. The most common complaints about meetings are that there are too many of them, they are too long, and they are unproductive.[116] Meeting leadership skills can lead to more productive meetings. Ford Motor Company spent $500,000 to send 280 employees to a three day training session with three one-day sessions to follow. After the training, fewer employees complained of meetings being too long or unproductive. Managers had gained the necessary meeting leadership skills and were putting this knowledge into practice. Ford's investment had obviously paid off. In this section, we learn how to plan and conduct a meeting and how to handle problem group members.

Planning Meetings

Leader and member preparations for a meeting have a direct effect on the meeting. Unprepared leaders tend to conduct unproductive meetings. There are at least five areas in which planning is needed: objectives, selecting participants and making assignments, the agenda, the time and place for the meeting, and leadership.[117,118] A written copy of the plan should be sent to members prior to the meeting (see Exhibit 8-5).

Objectives

Probably the single greatest mistake made by those who call meetings is that they often have no clear idea and purpose for the meeting. Before calling a meeting, clearly define its purpose and set objectives to be accomplished during the meeting. The only exceptions may be at regularly scheduled information-dissemination or brainstorming meetings.

Participants and Assignments

Before calling the meeting, decide who should attend the meeting. The more members who attend a meeting, the less the chance that any work will get done. Does the full group/team need to attend? Should some nongroup specialist be

Exhibit 8-5 *Meeting plans.*

- **Time.** List date, place (if it changes), and time (both beginning and ending).
- **Objective.** State the objectives and/or purpose of the meeting. The objectives can be listed with agenda items, as shown below, rather than as a separate section. But be sure objectives are specific.
- **Participation and Assignments.** If all members have the same assignment, list it. If different members have different assignments, list their name and assignment. Assignments may be listed as agenda items, as shown below for Ted and Karen.
- **Agenda.** List each item to be covered, in order of priority, with its approximate time limit. Accepting the minutes of the preceding meeting may be an agenda item. Here is an example agenda:

GOLD TEAM MEETING

November 22, 2007, Gold room, 9:00 to 10:00 A.M.

Participation and Assignments

All members will attend and should have read the six computer brochures enclosed before the meeting. Be ready to discuss your preferences.

Agenda

1. Discussion and selection of two PCs to be presented to the team at a later date by PC representatives—45 minutes. (Note that this is the major objective: the actual selection takes place later.)
2. Ted will give the Venus project report—5 minutes.
3. Karen will present an idea for changing the product process slightly, without discussion—5 minutes. Discussion will take place at the next meeting, after members have given the idea some thought.

invited to provide input? On controversial issues, the leader may find it wiser to meet with the key members before the meeting to discuss the issue. Participants should know in advance what is expected of them at the meeting. If any preparation is expected (read material, do some research, make a report, and so forth), they should have adequate advance notice.

Agenda

Before calling the meeting, identify the activities that will take place during the meeting in order to achieve the objective. The agenda tells the members what is expected and how the meeting will progress. Having a set time limit for each agenda item helps keep the group on target; needless discussion and getting off the subject is common at all meetings. However, you need to be flexible and allow more time when really needed. Agenda items may also be submitted from members to include. If you get agenda items that require action, they should have objectives.

Place agenda items in order of priority. That way, if the group does not have time to cover every item, the least important items carry forward. In meetings in which the agenda items are not prioritized, the tendency is for the leader to put all the so-called quick items first. When this happens, the group gets bogged down and either rushes through the important items or puts them off until later.

Date, Time, and Place

To determine which day(s) and time(s) of the week are best for meetings, get members' input. Members tend to be more alert early in the day. When members are close, it is better to have more frequent shorter meetings focusing on one or just a few items. However, when members have to travel, fewer but longer meetings are needed. Be sure to select an appropriate place for the meeting, and plan for the physical comfort of the group. Be sure seating provides eye contact for small discussion groups, and plan enough time so that the members do not have to rush. If reservations are needed for the meeting place, make them far enough in advance to get a proper meeting room.

With advances in technology, telephone conferences are becoming quite common. Videoconferences are also gaining popularity. These techniques have saved travel costs and time and have resulted in better and quicker decisions. Companies using videoconferencing include Aetna, Arco, Boeing, Ford, IBM, TRW, and Xerox. The personal computer has been said to be the most useful tool for running meetings since Robert's Rules of Order. The personal computer can be turned into a large-screen "intelligent chalkboard" that can dramatically change meeting results. Minutes (notes on what took place during the last meeting) can be taken on the personal computer and a hard copy distributed at the end of the meeting.

Leadership

The leader should determine the appropriate leadership style for the meeting. Each agenda item may need to be handled differently. For example, some items may simply call for disseminating information; others require a discussion, vote, or a consensus; while other items require a simple, quick report from a member, and so forth. An effective way to develop group members' ability is to rotate the role of the group moderator/leader for each meeting.

Conducting Meetings

The First Meeting

At the first meeting, the group is in the orientation stage. The leader should use the high-task role. However, the members should be given the opportunity to spend some time getting to know one another. Introductions set the stage for subsequent interactions. A simple technique is to start with introductions, then move on to the group's purpose and objectives, and members' job roles. Sometime during or following this procedure, have a break that enables members to interact informally. If members find that their social needs will not be met, dissatisfaction may occur quickly.

——————————————— Learning Outcome 4 ———————————————

Outline the three parts of conducting effective meetings.

The Three Parts of Meetings

Each meeting should cover the following:

1. *Identifying objectives.* Begin the meetings on time; waiting for late members penalizes the members who are on time and develops a norm for arriving

late. Begin by reviewing progress to date, the group's objectives, and the purpose/objective for the specific meeting. If minutes are recorded, they are usually approved at the beginning of the next meeting. For most meetings it is recommended that a secretary be appointed to take minutes.

2. *Covering agenda items.* Be sure to cover agenda items in priority order. Try to keep to the approximate times, but be flexible. If the discussion is constructive and members need more time, give it to them; however, if the discussion is more of a destructive argument, move ahead.

3. *Summarizing and reviewing assignments.* End the meeting on time. The leader should summarize what took place during the meeting. Were the meeting's objectives achieved? Review all of the assignments given during the meeting. Get a commitment to the task that each member should perform for the next or a specific future meeting. The secretary and/or leader should record all assignments. If there is no accountability and follow-up on assignments, members may not complete them.

Leadership

The team leader needs to focus on group structure, process, and development. As stated, the leadership style needs change with the group's level of development. The leader must be sure to provide the appropriate task and/or maintenance behavior when it is needed.

Handling Problem Members

As members work together, personality types tend to emerge. Certain personality types can cause the group to be less efficient than possible. Some of the problem members you may have in your group are the following: silent, talker, wanderer, bored, and arguer.

Silent

To have a fully effective meeting, all group members should participate. If members are silent, the group does not get the benefit of their input. It is the leader's responsibility to encourage the silent member to participate without being obvious or overdoing it. One technique the leader can use is the rotation method, in which all members take turns giving their input. This method is generally less threatening than directly calling on people. However, the rotation method is not always appropriate. To build up the silent member's confidence, call on them with questions they can easily answer. When you believe they have convictions, ask them to express them. Watch their nonverbal communication as indicators of when to call on them. If you are a silent type, try to participate more often. Know when to stand up for your views and be assertive. Silent types generally do not make good leaders.

Talker

Talkers have something to say about everything. They like to dominate the discussion. However, if they do dominate, the other members do not get to participate. The talker can cause intragroup problems, such as low cohesiveness and conflicts. It is the leader's responsibility to slow talkers down, not to shut them up. Do not let them dominate the group. The rotation technique is also effective with talkers. They have to wait their turn. When not using a rotation method, gently interrupt the talker and present your own ideas or call on other members to present their ideas. Prefacing questions with statements like "let's give those who have not answered yet a chance" can also slow the talker down. If you tend to be a talker, try to slow down. Give others a chance to talk and do things for themselves. Good leaders develop others' abilities in these areas.

Wanderer

Wanderers distract the group from the agenda items, they tend to change the subject, and often like to complain. The leader is responsible for keeping the group on track. If the wanderer wants to socialize, cut it off. Be kind, thank the member for the contribution, then throw a question out to the group to get it back on track. However, if the wanderer has a complaint that is legitimate and solvable, allow the group to discuss it. Group structure issues should be addressed and resolved. However, if an issue is not resolvable, get the group back on track. Griping without resolving anything tends to reduce morale and commitment to task accomplishment. If the wanderer complains about unre-solvable issues, make statements like, "We may be underpaid, but we have no control over our pay. Complaining will not get us a raise; let's get back to the issue at hand." If you tend to be a wanderer, try to be aware of your behavior and stay on the subject at hand.

Bored

Your group may have one or more members who are not interested in the job. The bored person may be preoccupied with other issues and not pay attention or participate in the group meeting. The bored member may also feel superior and wonder why the group is spending so much time on the obvious.

The leader is responsible for keeping members motivated. Assign the bored member a task like recording ideas on the board and recording the minutes. Call on bored members; bring them into the group. If you allow them to sit back, things may get worse and others may decide not to participate either. If you tend to be bored, try to find ways to help motivate yourself. Work at becoming more patient and in control of behavior that can have negative effects on other members.

Arguer

Like the talker, the arguer likes to be the center of attention. This behavior can occur when you use the devil's advocate approach, which is helpful in develop-ing and selecting alternative courses of action. However, arguers enjoy arguing for the sake of arguing, rather than helping the group. They turn things into a win-lose situation, and they cannot stand losing.

The leader should resolve conflict, but not in an argumentative way. Do not get into an argument with arguers; that is exactly what they want to hap-pen. If an argument starts, bring others into the discussion. If it is personal, cut it off. Personal attacks only hurt the group. Keep the discussion moving on tar-get. If you tend to be an arguer, strive to convey your views in an assertive debate format, not as an aggressive argument. Listen to others' views and be willing to change if they have better ideas.

Group Problem People

Identify the problem type as:

a. silent   b. talker   c. wanderer   d. bored   e. arguer

_____ 16. Charlie is always first or second to give his ideas. He is always elaborating on ideas. Because Charlie is so quick to respond, others sometimes make comments to him about it.

_____ 17. One of the usually active group members is sitting back quietly today for the first time. The other members are doing all the discussing and volunteering for assignments.

_____ 18. As the group is discussing a problem, Billy asks the group if they heard about the company owner and the mailroom clerk.

_____ 19. Eunice is usually reluctant to give her ideas. When asked to explain her position, Eunice often changes her answers to agree with others in the group.

_____ 20. Dwayne enjoys challenging members' ideas. He likes getting his own way. When a group member does not agree with Dwayne, he makes wisecracks about the member's prior mistakes.

Working with Group Members

Whenever you work in a group, do not embarrass, intimidate, or argue with any members, no matter how they provoke you. If you do, the result will make a martyr of them and a bully of you to the group. If you have serious problem members who do not respond to the above techniques, confront them individually outside of the group. Get them to agree to work in a cooperative way.

The second half of this chapter will now focus on the concept of self-managed teams, an innovative extension of the team concept.

Self-Managed Teams

Worldwide, companies big and small face serious challenges from a dynamic and complex global economy—challenges that render traditional work methods ineffective.[119] To effectively and efficiently address these challenges, organizations are rethinking the organizing structures upon which their operations are based. Old concepts of hierarchical leadership, centralized decision making, functional specialization, and individualized reward systems are being replaced with new, more flexible and adaptive structures.[120] As discussed earlier in the chapter, management styles have shifted from the "Lone Ranger" model of leadership to participatory management practices, and task structures have gone from functional specialization to group, and now team, formats. The use of teams has become the competitive weapon of choice for many business and nonbusiness organizations, with many of these companies opting for a new form of performing work called the *self-managed team*.[121] In self-managed teams, decision-making authority in many areas of accomplishing the team's assignment is left up to the individual members who make up the team.

WorkApplication10

Recall a meeting you attended. Did you receive an agenda prior to the meeting? How well did the leader conduct the meeting? Give ideas on how the meeting could have been improved. Did the group have any problem members? How well did the leader handle them?

_____

_____

_____

_____

_____

Self-managed teams go by many different names: self-directed, self-maintaining, self-leading, and self-regulating teams, to name a few. The concept itself is not new. It has its roots in sociotechnical systems theory and design, developed by Eric Trist and his colleagues in England in the 1960s.[122] The theory contends that organizations intimately combine people and technology in complex forms to produce outputs. The sociotechnical systems approach worked through sectional design teams, which were usually charged with implementing planned change programs, initiating improvement programs, and encouraging learning. For the concept to work, team members must understand the team's goals and be committed to achieving them. The major contribution of sociotechnical systems theory is the notion that team members involved in formulating tasks are more likely to feel invested in the process and be dedicated to accomplishing the stated goals. This laid the groundwork for self-managed teams, which have become more common as the evolution of total quality management (TQM) has continued.

Some of the potential motivational effects of self-management on a company's employees are evident at Saturn. An immediate result was the change in employee attitudes and motivation. Saturn employees showed a renewed energy and excitement about their work not seen at other GM plants. Instead of team members only worrying about and being responsible for their individual quality, they now took the responsibility for the effect their quality had on the customer.

Because of the increasing use of self-managed teams in organizations, much attention has been devoted to understanding how best to design and launch them, in order to maximize their efficiency and effectiveness. This section examines the unique nature of self-managed teams, their benefits, leadership issues, and the challenges of implementation.

Learning Outcome 5

Explain the differences between traditional and self-managed teams.

The Nature of Self-Managed Teams

In the quest to remain competitive in new product/service development, companies are finding out that effective managing of human interactions and rapid transfer of technology and ideas among individual and functional groups is a prerequisite to success. Studies of the human interaction processes that characterize new product/service development reveal that effective leadership as well as followership, equitable distribution of power, and collaboration among functional groups can make such human interactions more productive, thus enhancing performance and efficiency. This quest to maximize the human potential represents the essence or rationale for the self-managed team concept. The premise of the self-managed team concept is based on these same variables.

Self-managed teams differ from traditional teams in a number of ways. In traditional teams, management provides the team with direction and maintains control over work-related issues. In contrast, self-managed teams have a significant amount of decision-making authority.[123] In self-managed teams, there is much role interchange as members learn to be followers as well as leaders. Rather than being specialized, SMT members develop multiskilled capabilities that make them very flexible in performing various tasks within the team. The nature of self-managed teams is one of group rather than individual empowerment and accountability. Team accountability is a significant responsibility, especially since SMT members determine how they will organize themselves to get the work done, and are responsible not only for their own performance but for that of other team members as well. In teams with high levels of self-management, members perform all the management functions (plan, organize, lead, control, and reward), decide product/service related matters (quantity and quality level), and resolve problems (conflict management). Successful SMTs take on these responsibilities because team members have come to see that what they collectively gain is greater than what they personally sacrifice.

Over the past 15 years, an increasing number of American companies have experimented with self-managed teams. A poll sponsored by Office Team, a national staffing service based in California, revealed that 93 percent of 150 top managers from large companies favored self-managed work teams to achieve their organization's objectives.[124] Self-managed teams give workers, especially nonmanagerial workers, a voice in making decisions about the design of work, as well as greater autonomy and discretion in the structure of their work.[125] Self-managed teams operate without direct managerial supervision—an idea almost unthinkable a generation ago. Part of the popularity of SMTs is based on reports from organizations that suggest that self-managed teams can produce results such as increased performance and innovation, improved product/service quality, and increased employee job satisfaction and commitment.[126] More recently, it has been reported that 68 to 79 percent of Fortune 1000 companies and 81 percent of manufacturing organizations are currently using self-managed work teams.[127,128] It should be noted that back in 1987 a similar survey of Fortune 1000 companies showed that only 28 percent of companies developed such "empowered," "self-managed," or "autonomous" teams. A decade later, in 1996, almost half of all U.S. employers reported that three-quarters or more of their employees were involved in regular meetings to discuss workplace innovations, including the use of self-managed teams.[129] Thus, there has been a steady increase in the popularity and use of self-managed teams. As revealed earlier, SMTs make many structural and operational decisions that previously were made by line managers. Separate tasks that were once completed in different work units or individual settings under the close supervision of a functional manager or operations supervisor are brought together, and a team of workers is given the responsibility of accomplishing these tasks as a collective unit. SMT members often possess a variety of technical skills that enhances their versatility, flexibility, and value to the team.

In a self-managed team, members are charged with duties such as managing themselves, assigning jobs, planning and scheduling work, making production- or service-related decisions, and taking action on problems. Members take responsibility for outlining how they will achieve the team's objectives. Often teams will focus on what some experts have described as the 5Ts: project *targets* (milestones), specific project *tasks*, *team* membership (roles and responsibilities), *time* issues (both team and individual), and *territories* (of personal and collective focus) that would lead to successful planning, design, and completion of specific projects. Self-managed team members share or rotate leadership responsibilities, and hold themselves mutually responsible for a set of performance goals assigned by senior management.

Exhibit 8-6 *Differences between traditional and self-managed teams.*

Characteristics	Self-Managed Teams	Traditional Teams
Leadership	Within the team	Outside the team
Team member role	Interchangeable	Fixed
Accountability	Team	Individual
Work effort	Cohesive	Divided
Task design	Flexible	Fixed
Skills	Multiskilled	Specialized

Depending on the types of decisions, the amount of authority vested in a team varies greatly from one organization to another. For instance, in some organizations, the teams are given the primary responsibility for personnel decisions such as hiring and firing team members, conducting performance appraisals, and determining compensation (within specified limits); while in other organizations, such decisions are left to top management. Teams are usually allowed to make small expenditures for supplies and equipment without prior approval, but in most organizations, any action involving large purchases must be approved by top management. Determining when and at what level a self-managed team should be allowed to make decisions is still an open question. In some cases, SMT ineffectiveness has been blamed as not having enough self-leadership, while in others it has been blamed as just the opposite. In the Saturn case, it has been reported that a misjudgment made early in the company's history was giving too much responsibility too soon to the teams. As such, it has been suggested that the company would have been better served if it had released power and responsibility to the teams as they demonstrated the competence to handle them. Exhibit 8-6 summarizes the key differences between traditional teams and self-managed teams.

WorkApplication11

Using your own experience, or asking someone who has been part of an SMT, describe some of the self-managing activities of the team that made it a truly self-managing team as opposed to a traditional team.

_____

_____

_____

_____

Applying the Concept 5

Types of Teams

Identify each statement below with one of these key terms.

a. group
b. functional team
c. cross-functional team
d. self-managed team

_____ 21. In my department, a couple of us sometimes get together to discuss ways of improving our work processes.

_____ 22. In my organization, I work in a team where leadership roles are rotated and shared, with each of us taking initiative at appropriate times for the good of the group.

_____ 23. At the Appalachian Ice Cream factory, the quality control department headed by a unit supervisor is in charge of testing all incoming ingredients to make sure only the best products go into the company's ice cream.

_____ 24. At Norton Telecom International, a team with members from information technology, finance, customer service, and quality control oversaw an ambitious system—an integration project that spanned operations in the United States and Canada.

Learning Outcome 6

Describe the benefits of using self-managed teams in organizations.

The Benefits of Self-Managed Teams

A primary reason for growth in popularity of the self-managed team concept are the reported benefits by organizations that have adopted it. Self-managed work teams are praised for bringing about results such as increased productivity, accelerated new product development and process improvements, improved worker participation, and decreased hierarchy.[130–132] This has led to increases in job satisfaction and organizational commitment, which in turn have been associated with other positive organizational and employee outcomes, such as lower absenteeism rates, less turnover, more interdependence of objectives, and, ultimately, increased levels of profitability.[133]

---

8. What Has Been the Impact of Self-Managed Teams on the Performance and Motivation of Saturn's Employees?

The Saturn division of General Motors is one of its profitable divisions, and part of this success is attributed to Saturn's total embrace of the self-managed team concept. Since its creation, Saturn has represented itself as an example of what total commitment to partnership and teamwork can achieve. The company has SMTs with no supervisors, inspectors, time clocks, or union stewards. These teams are responsible for their own activities, including quality control, cost management, production scheduling, and people. Management and union leaders play the role of facilitators and also as guardians of the organization's vision and direction.

OPENING CASE APPLICATION

Self-managed teams inspire their members to connect with the company's vision and mission in a very special way. A sense of belonging and ownership in one's work helps to create a linkage between individual goals and aspirations and the company's long-term vision and mission. Employee motivation levels and self-esteem are much higher in SMTs. In the service sector, where there has been some debate as to whether self-managed teams can produce the same positive results as found in manufacturing, there is now strong empirical support that participation in self-managed teams is also associated with significant improvements in service quality.[134] This is significant, as some researchers had predicted a negative or at best weak outcome for SMTs among service establishments because of certain inherent characteristics and qualities of this sector. For instance, in the service sector, technology and organizational structure limit opportunities for self-regulation. The nature of work and technology does not require interdependence, and downsizing has created a pervasive feeling of job insecurity. It was argued that these factors would compromise the effectiveness of self-managed teams in this dominant sector of the economy.[135]

The effectiveness of self-managed teams can be attributed to the fact that this form of work organization has been found to be the best structure to empower individuals to come together and develop and implement continuous improvement, modify and/or correct improvements if necessary, and assess the effects of changes. SMTs bring "a collective seeing and knowing" to the job that surpasses the capability of any individual team member. Any agreed-upon course of action is taken collectively and so has the strong commitment of all team members to make it successful.

In exploring the question of how self-managed teams in high-velocity environments handle unexpected critical incidents, one study found that they responded effectively. Not only did the self-managed team create a context for a shared and emotionally grounded identity, it also allowed for a shared set of guiding principles for action, behavior, and decision making.[136] Besides Saturn, another great example of SMT success is 3M, which has maintained its competitive position by creating self-managed teams that thrive on risk-taking and creativity. The basic corporate message communicated to all SMTs at 3M is that 30 percent of 3M sales must come from products introduced within the previous four years. The SMTs have responded with remarkable success, helping the corporation leverage 100 core technologies into more than 60,000 products so far.

In a study examining the economic benefits of organizing field technicians into self-managed teams, it was found that SMTs absorb the monitoring and coordination tasks of supervisors, substantially reducing indirect labor costs but without adversely affecting objective measures of quality and labor productivity. In another study examining whether self-managed teams increased productivity in automobile service garages, it was found that service garages which used self-managed teams increased productivity compared to service garages that did not use teams.[137] More and more, the service sector is employing self-managed teams in service delivery with great results. A recent Finnish study of home health care workers found that self-designed teams improved productivity and the quality of work life of the agency staff.[138]

Self-managed teams reduce costs because of the reductions in managerial ranks throughout the organization. A study examining the relationship between organizational structural changes and employment changes found that some practices, such as self-managed teams, are associated with greater employment reductions.[139] Also, operating costs are greatly reduced with self-managed teams because they tend to focus on product and process improvement. The focus on a single process, taking time to fully understand it, and collectively identifying opportunities to improve it, is what usually makes SMTs successful at reducing operational costs. It should be noted that self-managed teams do exhibit the same general advantages of teamwork discussed earlier in the chapter. Exhibit 8-7 summarizes the benefits of self-managed teams.

WorkApplication12

If you have been part of an SMT, describe the benefits that you derived from being part of the team. Be specific, matching your description to the list in Exhibit 8-7.

_____

_____

_____

_____

_____

Factors That Influence Self-Managed Team Effectiveness

As discussed, the benefits of self-managed teams have been well documented and should serve as a strong motivator for any organization looking to implement SMTs. Former CEO of Levi Strauss, Robert Haas, captured the strategic value of self-managed teams to his company's future survival this way: "I see us moving into a team-oriented, multiskilled environment in which the self-managed team takes on work that only they as a work unit can accomplish. . . . These teams are a most powerful and proven empowerment strategy that

Exhibit 8-7 *Benefits of self-managed teams.*

- Greater improvements in quality, speed, process, and innovation.
- A sense of belonging and ownership in one's work.
- Greater employee motivation.
- Accelerated new product development.
- Greater employee participation.
- Reduced operational costs because of reductions in managerial ranks and greater efficiencies.
- Greater employee job satisfaction, commitment, and productivity, and lower turnover and absenteeism rates.

accelerates productivity and quality and enhances human competencies and commitment."[140] However, the challenges of implementing SMTs also point to a critical issue: not all SMTs are likely to realize these outcomes that Mr. Haas is alluding to. SMTs that are not effectively managed hardly achieve any meaningful results. There are contradictory findings on the effectiveness of SMTs. Some organizations have managed to effectively implement teams with high levels of self-management, while others have not.[141] The question then becomes: What factors differentiate effective from ineffective SMTs?

Although the self-managed team concept is premised on team members determining how team goals are achieved, self-managed teams can be designed differently (as revealed above in the scope of decisions they are allowed to make), and decisions regarding team designs have implications with respect to team functioning and effectiveness.[142] The effects of team designs that differ with respect to the form of member evaluation (peer versus external evaluation) and team leadership (rotating versus single leadership) have been studied. One study found that relative to teams that relied on external evaluations, teams with peer evaluations had higher levels of workload sharing, voice, cooperation, performance, and member satisfaction. Relative to teams that relied on a single leader emerging, teams that rotated leadership among members (what others have described as distributed leadership) had higher levels of voice, cooperation, and performance.[143–145] Therefore, rather than just focusing inward at team processes or team member characteristics (as discussed earlier) to explain why some self-managed teams are ineffective, attention should also be paid to the organizational context of teams, especially at possible misalignments between team-level and organization-level structural factors.[146] We will re-examine team member characteristics with special emphasis on the SMT concept. Also, unique to the SMTs is the significance of a champion to SMT success. Therefore, the following factors discussed next are significant in influencing SMT effectiveness: organizational support, member characteristics, team norms, and a team champion.

Organizational Support

Moving to self-managed teams requires managers to make significant adjustments. They have the most to lose in the transformation from a hierarchical system to an empowered workplace. Functional departments such as marketing, production, and human resources will lose power as self-managed teams gain more influence over decisions formerly controlled by these departments. Strong support by top management is essential to ensure that managers and other members of the organization support the effort to implement self-managed teams rather than undermine it. Top management must be committed to allocating adequate resources in order for the teams to perform their tasks effectively, creating an organizational culture and structure compatible with the self-management concept, and helping managers go from barking orders to coaching, facilitating, and empowering teams. Only with this kind of support and commitment will initial success of the self-managed team program turn into long-term success.[147]

Scholars have long proposed that a move to a self-managed team structure should be accompanied with a move to a flatter organization structure; however, this has not always been the case. Instead, SMTs often exist as pockets of structural anomaly within hierarchically structured organizations. Such misalignments between team structure (self-management) and organizational structure can be counterproductive. Attempts to implement SMTs in such organizations may cause frustration for both employees and management, when organizational systems and structures do not accommodate self-managing demands.[148] Centralized organizational structures, for example, have low participation in decision making and high authority hierarchy. The structure and climate in such an organization makes it less likely that managers and supervisors will easily relinquish power and control to the team, since managers who are told to empower teams, but experience autocratic leadership from their superiors, are likely to model the behavior of top managers.

OPENING CASE APPLICATION

9. Describe How Top Management's Commitment and Support Helped the Self-Managed Team Concept and the Benefits This Has Brought Saturn.

Top management must help teams create a climate that fosters creativity and risk taking, in which members listen to each other and feel free to contribute ideas without being criticized. Without the unwavering support from Saturn's past presidents, including Jill Lajdziak at the present time, and also without support for Lajdziak from GM's Chairman and CEO, Saturn's experiment with teamwork and self-managed teams will hardly succeed. As the timeline for creating Saturn revealed, there were champions for the SMT concept who went on to sell the idea to the then-CEO of GM, Roger Smith, and when he bought into it, the joint announcement was made creating what was then called the Saturn project.

Learning Outcome 7

Describe how team member characteristics impact self-managed team effectiveness.

Team Member Characteristics

When it comes time to put together a self-managed team, the question of what characteristics successful SMT members possess is of importance to any manager trying to make the shift away from traditional teams to SMTs. It is a critical question that must be carefully dealt with. Rushing to activate an SMT without understanding how to put together a strong, cohesive, experienced, and cross-functional team can be a recipe for failure from the start. A review of the literature on member characteristics that have been identified with effective SMTs does reveal a general consensus on at least seven characteristics. They are listed below and followed by a brief discussion.

- A strong belief in personal accountability
- An internal locus of control coupled with emotional stability
- Openness to new ideas/viewpoints
- Effective communication
- Good problem-solving skills
- Ability to engender trust
- Good conflict resolution skills

The nature of an SMT is such that it is empowered to track its own performance and do self-evaluations. This presumes that individual team members are capable of and will accept responsibility for their own actions. Team members must have a strong belief in personal accountability for this type of team assessment to be effective. The autonomous nature of SMTs also allows for the likelihood that social loafing—a disadvantage of teams discussed earlier—will occur. Therefore, a team member's integrity must be considered. Integrity has been found to be a useful predictor of job performance with self-managed teams, making it a critical factor in team member selection.

A second team member characteristic of effective SMTs is that members have an internal locus of control coupled with emotional stability. As discussed in Chapter 7, an internal locus of control is a belief that you are in control of your destiny. People with this mind-set believe they can influence people and events in the workplace. Effective SMT members are those who have this mind-set, and the emotional stability to work in different situations and with different personalities. Adjusting to a new team environment will come faster for a team member possessing this characteristic.

The third SMT member characteristic is openness to new ideas/viewpoints. The cross-functional diversity of SMTs means that having an open mind is absolutely critical to success. The nature of an SMT is such that members are often uprooted from their specialized areas and thrust into unfamiliar territory with new coworkers, requiring adjusting to new situations and to fellow team members. Closed-minded individuals will find it hard to function in this type of environment, because they are dealing with individuals from other functional areas whose ideas and opinions may not mirror theirs. Being open-minded and able to see the shades of gray inherent in a situation is a critical quality of effective SMT members. They must not be quick to categorize things or people as good or bad, true or false, or black or white.

The fourth characteristic is for the member to possess good problem-solving skills. SMTs are created to solve complex problems, thus this is an important factor to consider in member selection. Members must possess functional skills, teamwork capabilities, and experience at problem solving.[149]

The fifth, sixth, and seventh characteristics speak for themselves. SMT members must be effective communicators, for idea exchange is the soul of SMT work. Quality, honest, and open exchange of ideas is what makes an effective team. SMT members must be capable of understanding one another's ideas and how their decisions might affect others' feelings. Conflict is inevitable in group activities and so being skilled in conflict resolution is essential. The social fabric of the team is affected by the degree to which conflict is either ignored or resolved. Finally, there is trust, described as the "umbrella" that covers all the other effective team member characteristics. Team members must share trust. Trust determines the degree of collegiality between team members and directly affects team performance, regardless of members' knowledge and talents.[150]

Team Norms

An effective SMT must possess an appropriate set of norms that govern all members' behavior. As defined earlier, team norms are socially shared standards against which the appropriateness of behavior can be evaluated. A team's norms will influence how members perceive and interact with one another, approach decisions, and resolve problems. For example, a team might specify cooperative over independent or competitive behavior; to the outside observer, this may be manifested by the level of importance members place on shared pursuits, objectives, and mutual interest rather than personal interests.

A Self-Managed Team Champion

Successful and effective SMTs are those that have a champion to support and defend them from opponents who are threatened by the new concept and what it represents. *A* **self-managed team champion** *is an advocate of the self-managed team concept whose responsibility is to help the team obtain necessary resources, gain political support from top management and other stakeholders of the organization, and defend it from enemy attacks.* This advocacy role is especially critical when the self-managed team concept is being applied on a broader scale throughout the company, and when there is hostility and distrust by other managers who are afraid the self-managed teams will cause major shifts of power and authority in the organization. The SMT champion is therefore constantly engaged in "buying in" and gaining commitment at all levels, while communicating the benefits of the SMT. As mentioned earlier, in highly competitive market environments, the self-managed team structure is often seen as the best approach for pursuing aggressive new product development strategies. Here, success often depends on the self-managed team champion's charisma to bridge the gap between proponents and opponents of this approach. Here are some of the strategic actions a champion undertakes to create a successful self-managed team program.

- Articulates a vision of what self-managed teams can accomplish for the organization
- Communicates clear expectations about the new responsibility of team members for regulating their own behavior
- Makes sure that what self-managed team members do meets the needs and goals of the entire organization
- Coordinates the efforts of different self-managed teams so that their efforts support each other and the organization's mission
- Finds ways to help self-managed teams reach decisions that every employee can support
- Facilitates continuous learning by team members
- Builds and maintains trust between team members and the rest of the organization

WorkApplication13

Based on your own self-assessment, how many of the team member characteristics discussed will apply to you? Explain.

_____

_____

_____

_____

Characteristics of Effective SMTs

Identify the characteristics of effective teams by these statements/questions.

a. norms   c. team member characteristics
b. organizational support   d. champion

_____ 25. At the time of team formation, it is important to determine if team members possess appropriate task skills, sufficient members, and good interpersonal skills to work together cooperatively and to resolve conflicts constructively.

_____ 26. When there is hostility and distrust by other managers who are afraid that SMTs will cause major shifts of power and authority in the organization, it is important to have an advocate whose responsibility is to help the program win the support of top management and other subunits of the organization.

_____ 27. At the formation of an SMT, it is important to address important questions, such as: Is there a strong belief in personal accountability? Is there openness to new ideas and viewpoints? Is there trust between members? and Is there a good conflict-resolution mechanism within the group?

_____ 28. Self-managed team formation must ensure a good start by defining a clear standard of conduct and behavior that is shared by all team members.

Combined, these factors (team member characteristics, team norms, and a strong team champion) contribute to create a very potent team. **Team potency** *is a shared belief that individuals hold about a group.* Effective SMTs are therefore those that possess a strong, positive potency or efficacy. The next section describes the guidelines for improving self-managed team effectiveness.

WorkApplication14

Describe the effectiveness of the SMT or other team you selected for Work Application 11.

_____

_____

_____

_____

—————— Learning Outcome 8 ——————

Describe the guidelines for improving self-managed team effectiveness.

Guidelines for Improving Self-Managed Team Effectiveness

Despite the documented successes and benefits of SMTs, there is still much that needs to be done to improve their effectiveness. Many things can go wrong with self-managed teams, and adjusting to new behavioral expectations can be difficult. Many SMT initiatives are eventually abandoned.[151] For this reason, studies have focused on identifying factors or conditions that are key to building high-performance management teams. As part of a larger survey, managers from various manufacturing industries were asked what they considered to be key factors in getting managers to cooperate with each other and to function as a team. Their responses focused on the significant role that senior management must play to ensure SMT effectiveness and success. At the organizational level, there are important policies, procedures, and practices that can greatly enhance the effectiveness of SMTs.[152,153] In planning the transition to SMTs, management should carry out the following processes:

- Ensure that the whole organization has changed its culture, structure, and climate to support SMTs. This will address questions such as: Does the SMT have sufficient autonomy to perform its task and have access to information? Have conditions been created in which authority can shift between members to appropriately match the demands of their task? Are SMT participants motivated, stimulated, and supported in a fashion that breaks down walls and creates unity of purpose and action?
- Have a well thought-out vision of the way in which SMTs will fit into the scheme of the entire organization.
- Allow time after training for the team members to bond with one another and form team skills. Effective team-building interventions can be used to break down barriers and create opportunities for cooperation.
- Provide adequate training so team member skills and experiences match task requirements. Identify specific areas that need improvement and develop solutions from a team-based perspective.
- Provide objective goals, incentives, and appropriate infrastructure. Self-managed team participants should have a vested interest in clarifying team goals, designing team-based incentive and reward systems, understanding each other's roles, and improving their understanding of processes and systems that will be used.
- Ensure that the organization has the necessary resources to commit to this kind of change in time, money, and people.
- Create a sense of empowerment so SMTs take ownership of what they are doing and how they are going to do it. For example, designating a team leader may help ensure that critical team management functions are accomplished in a timely fashion; however, if leadership responsibilities are rotated among members, a climate of shared leadership may be fostered and this should lead to the team feeling empowered.
- Pay close attention to team design decisions. As mentioned earlier, teams with peer evaluations and rotating leadership among members tend to have higher levels of cooperation, performance, and member satisfaction.
- Develop team-based measurements and corresponding feedback methods that address team performance.
- Recruit and train managers to act as team facilitators or coaches. This will be further elaborated on later in the chapter, as we explore the changing role of leadership in self-managed teams.
- Avoid overreacting at the first sign of crisis. Team-building experts say company leaders should "keep a stiff upper lip" when an SMT starts experiencing problems, because the tendency is to overreact by pulling the plug on the new program or getting too involved. SMTs, they say, fluctuate like stocks—even the blue chips with excellent long-term prospects experience short-term troughs.

The best example to illustrate how the lack of managerial action in these areas can create problems during the implementation of SMT programs is captured in this statement by Asea Brown Boveri's former CEO, Percy Barnevik: "I found myself trying to implement third-generation strategies through second-generation organizations run by first-generation managers."[154] (Asea Brown Boveri is a manufacturer of power transformers and other large, expensive

Applying the Concept 7

Guidelines for Improving SMT Effectiveness

Identify which factor is missing in the scenarios based on the statements below.

a. top management support and commitment
b. unambiguous goals and objectives
c. appropriate compensation structure
d. appropriate task design and measurement system
e. appropriate scope of authority
f. adequate information system
g. strong and experienced facilitator

_____ 29. I get frustrated with this team because no one seems to know what we are doing.

_____ 30. Management expects us to give input into which products we should make. However, they don't give us the numbers we need to make effective decisions.

_____ 31. The thing that bothers me is the fact that we don't have a clear agreement on the quality of the product.

_____ 32. We really need a better manager if we are going to improve our team performance.

_____ 33. The team members are not taking our new self-directed status seriously, because they believe SMTs are just the latest fad, that management will drop it for the next hot topic.

equipment.) Implementing these guidelines will help eliminate mismatches such as this one. The next section examines the impact of self-managed teams on employee creativity.

The Changing Role of Leadership in Self-Managed Teams

It seems contradictory that a self-managed team would need a leader. After all, the concept implies that the team leads itself. However, the concept of a self-managed team does not mean "without management." Rather, it implies self-responsibility and self-accountability. Self-managed teams require a different kind of leadership. Within the broader organizational structure, the self-managed team must still receive direction and instruction from higher levels in the organization. And it must report to that hierarchy through a person who is ultimately held accountable for the team's performance. Many managers find themselves in a conflicting position when called upon to function as external leaders for self-managed teams. Most receive conflicting signals on how to go about it. For example, how involved should they be in their team's decision-making process? How can they get involved without compromising the team's autonomy? Studies have focused on investigating such issues for answers. Contrary to common perceptions, a recent study revealed that the best external leaders were not necessarily the ones who employed a hands-off approach; instead, the external leaders who had contributed most to their team's success excelled at one skill: managing the boundary between the team and the larger organization.[155] Several studies of empowered teams have proposed that managing this boundary is the central focus of the external leader's role. Effective external leaders are able to develop strong relationships both inside the team and across the organizational landscape. External leaders played the role of facilitators, while allowing team members to manage themselves through a process some have described as distributed or shared leadership. The role of the self-managed team facilitator is discussed in greater detail in the next section. *In* **distributed leadership**, *multiple leaders take complementary leadership roles in rotation within the same SMT, according to their area of expertise or interest.*[156] In other words, different members of the SMT assume different leadership roles as circumstances and task requirements warrant. In a study investigating the relationships between structural variables, levels of self-management, and judgments of team effectiveness, the researchers found teams with high levels of self-management may be more effective in organizations in which authority to make decisions about task performance is distributed, and in organizations with fewer explicit rules, policies, and procedures.[157] Teams will vary in how quickly they can transition into distributed leadership practice, based on such factors as their prior experience with teams, the quality of relationships between team members, and their collective orientation and interest. For example, there are some individuals who simply do not like working with others, preferring to work alone on tasks. Other individuals crave attention or compete for power within the team, such as the opportunity to direct and control discussions, or the prerogative to confirm or dispute others' views.

The Self-Managed Team Facilitator

The new role of the external team leader as facilitator can best be described as "out of sight but not out of mind." Instead, the external leader's role is to ensure that SMT projects are on track, that everyone is working with the same information, and that everyone understands the goals of the team and is focused on the team effort.[158] The facilitator remains a member of the SMT, providing knowledge, expertise, and other resources. He or she is available to assist the SMT during troubled times by suggesting new areas for training or new long-term goals for the team to work toward. Therefore, the **self-managed team facilitator** *is the external leader of a self-managed team, whose job is to create optimal working conditions so team members take on responsibilities to work productively and solve complex problems on their own.*[159] Considerable coaching and encouragement from the facilitator are usually necessary to get a new team off to a good start. Coaching helps SMT members learn and grow from their experiences in the team. Some organizations, aware of the high risk of problems arising after an SMT launch, opt to have external facilitators rather than internal managers performing this role. The rationale is that the external facilitator brings objectivity to the process and can be more effective at mediating conflict, compared to an internal manager. Effective facilitators are good at coaching, influencing, and empowering the team.[160]

Effective facilitators are described as being adept at influencing their teams to decisions that best meet the needs of the organization. For example, a self-managed team facilitator collected data from the accounting department to persuade his failing team to think of ways to improve its performance. Using the data, the facilitator, playing the role of external leader, impressed upon his team how much the organization lost in profits every minute because of downtime caused by some workers leaving the manufacturing line. The facilitator told the team, "This is money that we didn't make." He reiterated that someone's decision to cut off the line to eat a sandwich or indulge in a habit was costing everybody. Three months later, the team's performance improved markedly. Remarkably, the team members were going the extra mile without their external leader having to ask (let alone demand) that they do so.[161] The team facilitator had simply influenced their decision by showing them the data from accounting.

Effective facilitators can empower their teams by demonstrating three behaviors: delegating authority, exercising flexibility regarding team decisions, and coaching. Research supports the proposition that effective facilitators tend to empower their teams with more responsibility while the less effective facilitators tend to be fearful of delegating.[162] In exercising flexibility regarding team decisions, effective facilitators tend to keep an open mind even when they are unsure of a decision the team is about to make. When a team is about to be reined in, an effective facilitator will do so very tactfully and only after considering the proposal as open-mindedly as possible. Effective facilitators tend to be active in educating and coaching team members. They focus on strengthening the team's confidence and its ability to manage itself.[163] A self-managed team facilitator must strike a careful balance between too much involvement and not enough. In most cases, external team leaders or facilitators are former hierarchical command-and-control managers who are prone to try to reassert their authority. The desire to take charge or be in control may be too tempting to resist. If SMT leaders don't hand over responsibilities in a timely fashion as the team matures, people will assume that SMTs are a nice concept but do not produce real transformations. On the other hand, if they step back too far from the team process, letting the SMT struggle and make mistakes, such mistakes may develop into crises and lead to the ultimate demise of the team. At this point, echoes of "I told you so" are likely to be heard from former managers who feel displaced by self-managed teams, or employees who are used to protecting their turf and feel as though something has been taken away from them. This is when the role of the facilitator (internal or external) is indispensable. As the team survives and works through its crisis, skeptics who have remained on the sidelines waiting for the opportunity to return to the old ways will start to buy into the SMT concept. This is the moment when the team starts to gel and its members begin to see that their collective gain is greater than the sum of their individual contributions. Allowing teams to manage themselves frees facilitators to focus on team development. A summary of the facilitator's team-building activities is presented in Exhibit 8-8.

These activities should ensure that there is strong identification with the team, especially as pride in the team's accomplishments grows. Also, they will strengthen cohesiveness and the level of mutual cooperation between team members. The type of leadership that is found inside the SMT after an external team leader has successfully steered the team into self-leadership and independence is described as *shared* leadership. As the term implies, all members participate at critical points in the life of the project as leaders. In effect, the goal of external team leaders or facilitators is to constantly guide and develop their teams so that they become increasingly self-managing.

WorkApplication15

Describe which of the facilitator's team-building activities (see Exhibit 8-8) your SMT or other type of team facilitator employed in leading the team.

_____

_____

_____

_____

_____

Exhibit 8-8 *SMT facilitator team-building activities.*

- Opening forums for resolving interpersonal conflicts.
- Creating opportunities for social interaction.
- Increasing mutual acceptance and respect among diverse team members.
- Maintaining an open communication policy.
- Highlighting mutual interest, not differences, of team members.
- Increasing team identification through the use of ceremonies, rituals, and symbols.
- Using team-oriented incentives to foster teamwork.

―――――――――――――――――――― Learning Outcome 9 ――――――――――――――――――――

Describe the challenges of implementing effective self-managed teams.

The Challenges of Implementing Self-Managed Teams

When an organization transforms individually based work units into self-managed work teams, what is the response among the managerial and nonmanagerial ranks of the organization's workers? According to a study examining the differential outcomes of team structures for 1,200 workers, supervisors, and middle managers of a large unionized telecommunications company, participation in self-managed teams was associated with significantly higher levels of perceived discretion, employment security, and satisfaction for workers, and the opposite for supervisors.[164] This supports the perception held by some in the managerial ranks that managers fear their jobs will disappear if work teams become self-directed. As the finding above reveals, this is not an unfounded fear. However, in many organizations where there has been careful planning, former managers become SMT facilitators and are retrained to function differently than they did in their previous role. Many of the drawbacks associated with SMTs stem from the difficulties of transitioning from a traditional command-and-control work environment to self-managed teams. Teambuilding experts contend that managers who have become accustomed to traditional, autocratic management and jaded at management fads that come and go may resist or undermine a team approach.

Even among members of the nonmanagerial ranks, the transition to SMTs has as much potential for frustrations and problems as it does for managers. This is usually due to unfamiliarity with the new structure and new routines, and adjusting to team responsibilities. Team members must learn new behaviors, like putting aside differences in order to make decisions that benefit the team. The need to adapt to a new working environment, in which the definition of teamwork requires a personal, cultural, and behavioral adjustment, may be too much for some members and thus lead to personality and behavior conflicts. Thus, the greatest challenge may lie in setting and enforcing new behavioral expectations, made necessary by the absence of a traditional leader and the presence of new employee rights and responsibilities.

A survey of manufacturing managers who had experienced the shift from hierarchical command-and-control to a self-managed team leadership structure reveals what can go wrong if implementation is not well planned and executed. A sample of manufacturing managers were asked to identify the problems created when managers in a manufacturing operation do not work together as part of a team. Their responses revealed a myriad of potential problems for the team and the organization. When managers do not cooperate with other team members in an SMT environment, coordination suffers and breakdowns in planning increase. This can cause a loss of focus on the teams' objectives. When SMT members are not working together, counterproductive workplace conflict and political activity increase, as do ill will and decrease in morale. Ultimately, when former managers now working as team members in SMTs worry more about their egos and avoid communicating with other members, they set a poor example for the rest of the team; communication breakdowns occur which can lead to a decrease in performance and productivity. Some of the disadvantages of teams in general, discussed earlier in the chapter—such as social loafing and groupthink—are also likely to occur in self-managed teams. The lesson, therefore, is that the decision to use self-managed teams as a tool for re-engineering work in an organization is not always a guaranteed success. It requires a great deal of commitment, effort, and support from all members of the organization. As described earlier, in the long run, the benefits of SMTs to employee morale, efficiency, product quality, economic savings, and overall organizational performance are well worth the growing pains.

As for the future of self-managed teams, there is no doubt that they pose very serious challenges to organizations that experiment with them; however, they probably will continue to ride a growth curve of popularity among employers and new generations of workers because of the productivity gains that they bring.

WorkApplication16

Have you worked in a team in which former managers have been reassigned to function simply as members of the team? What was your experience with the behavior and attitude of these former managers in their new role as team members?

_____

_____

_____

_____

Go to the Internet (academic.cengage.com/management/lussier) where you will find a broad array of resources to help maximize your learning.

- Review the vocabulary
- Try a quiz
- View chapter videos

Chapter Summary

The chapter summary is organized to answer the 10 learning outcomes for Chapter 8.

1. Discuss the advantages and disadvantages of working in teams.

Advantages: In a team situation it is possible to achieve synergy, whereby the team's total output exceeds the sum of individual member contributions. Team members often evaluate and add to one another's thinking, so there are fewer chances of errors and the quality of the decisions is improved. A team atmosphere contributes well towards effective problem solving, continuous improvement, and innovation. Also, being a team member makes it possible for someone to satisfy more needs than working alone; among these are the need for affiliation, security, self-esteem, and self-fulfillment.

Disadvantages: Some teams have the unhealthy practice of pressuring members to conform to lower group standards of performance and conduct. For example, a team member may be ostracized for being more productive than his or her coworkers. Shirking of individual responsibility, or social loafing, is another problem frequently noted in groups. Another well-known problem common in teams is the practice of groupthink, which happens when the team values getting along so much that dissenting views are quickly suppressed in favor of group consensus.

2. Briefly describe the seven characteristics of effective teams.

The seven characteristics of effective teams are: (1) team norms, (2) team leadership, (3) team cohesiveness and interdependence, (4) team composition, (5) team structure, (6) organizational support, and (7) creativity driven. Team norms influence how a team's members perceive and interact with one another, approach decisions, and solve problems; they guide team members' behavior. Teams need effective leaders who will monitor the progress of the team to make sure that the team does not go off track, go too far or not far enough, lose sight of its goal, or become bogged down by conflict. Effective teams have high levels of cohesion and interdependence. Highly cohesive teams are characterized by high group potency and strong self-efficacy. Members of highly effective teams are more interactive and dependent on one another to get tasks done. Effective teams must have the appropriate mix of complementary skills, knowledge, and ability to successfully realize the team's objectives. Effective teams have structures that provide team members with broad participation in decision making. Finally, effective teams have strong support from top management. Management support, both tangible and intangible, is critical for team success. It's management's responsibility to create a work climate that supports and rewards teamwork.

3. Describe top management's and the team leader's roles in fostering creativity. For each, list activities they should undertake to promote creativity.

Top management's role in encouraging creativity is very significant. Creativity does not work in hierarchical command-and-control environments. Top management has the responsibility to create the appropriate setting and support systems that foster and nourish creativity.

Top management activities that can enhance creativity include providing teams with the following: (1) adequate resources, (2) appropriate recognition and rewards, (3) flexibility and a minimum amount of structure, and (4) free time for members to think and experiment with new ideas.

Team leader activities that can help to enhance team creativity include (1) matching members with the right assignments, (2) giving team members greater autonomy to do the job, (3) ensuring the availability of adequate time, money and other resources for the team, (4) paying careful attention to the design of the team, (5) emphasizing teamwork, and (6) protecting against "creativity blockers."

4. Outline the three parts of conducting effective meetings.

The Three Parts of Meetings. Each meeting should cover the following:

1. Identify objectives. Begin the meetings on time. Begin by reviewing progress to date, the group's objectives, and the purpose/objective for the specific meeting. If minutes are recorded, they are usually approved at the beginning of the next meeting.
2. Cover agenda items. Be sure to cover agenda items in priority order. Try to keep to the approximate times, but be flexible. If the discussion is constructive and members need more time, give it to them; however, if the discussion is more of a destructive argument, move ahead.
3. Summarize and review assignments. End the meeting on time. The leader should summarize what took place during the meeting. Were the meeting's objectives achieved? Review all of the assignments given during the meeting. Get a commitment to the task that each member should perform for the next or a specific future meetings. The secretary and/or leader should record all assignments.

5. Explain the differences between traditional and self-managed teams.

Self-managed teams differ from traditional teams in a number of ways. In self-managed teams, there is much role interchange as members learn to be followers as well as leaders. Rather than functioning in their specialized units, SMT members develop multiskilled capabilities that make them very flexible in performing various tasks within the team. The nature of self-managed teams is one of group empowerment and accountability rather than individual empowerment and accountability. Team accountability is a significant responsibility, especially since SMT members determine how they will organize themselves to get the work done and are responsible not only for their own performance but for that of other team members as well.

6. Describe the benefits of using self-managed teams in organizations.

Self-managed teams (1) create a stronger sense of commitment to the work effort among team members, (2) improve quality, speed, and innovation, (3) have more satisfied employees and lower turnover and absenteeism, (4) facilitate faster new-product development, (5) allow cross-trained team members greater flexibility in dealing with personnel shortages due to illness or turnover, and (6) keep operational costs down because of reductions in managerial ranks and increased efficiencies.

7. Describe how team member characteristics impact self-managed team effectiveness.

An SMT is no better than the quality of the members that make up the team. Certain qualities associated with members of effective SMTs have been identified through research. They are (1) a strong belief in personal accountability, (2) an internal locus of control coupled with emotional stability, (3) openness to new ideas/viewpoints, (4) effective communication, (5) good problem-solving skills, (6) ability to engender trust, and (7) good conflict resolution skills. The nature of SMTs is such that they are empowered to plan and schedule their own work, track performance, and do self-evaluations. This presumes that individual team members possess all these qualities in order for the above-mentioned activities to be successfully performed.

8. Describe the guidelines for improving self-managed team effectiveness.

Senior management has the principal responsibility to create the right environment in which self-managed teams can grow and thrive. This involves undertaking activities to ensure that the whole organization has a changed culture, structure, and climate to support SMTs. This requires providing sufficient responses to questions such as whether the SMT has sufficient autonomy to perform its task and has access to information; whether conditions have been created in which authority can shift between members to appropriately match the demands of their task; and whether SMT participants are motivated, stimulated, and supported in a fashion that breaks down walls and creates unity of purpose and action. Management must have a well thought-out vision of the way in which SMTs will fit into the scheme of the entire organization; allow time after training for the team members to bond with one another and form team skills; provide adequate training, so team member skills and experiences match task requirements; provide objective goals, incentives, and appropriate infrastructure; ensure that the organization has the necessary resources to commit to this kind of change (not only in time but also in money and people); and create a sense of empowerment, so SMTs take ownership of what they are doing and how they are going to do it.

9. Describe the challenges of implementing effective self-managed teams.

Many of the challenges of implanting or implementing SMTs stem from the difficulties of transitioning from a traditional command-and-control work environment to self-managed teams. Team-building experts contend that managers who have become accustomed to traditional, autocratic management and jaded at management fads that come and go may resist or undermine a team approach. Even among members of the nonmanagerial ranks, the transition to SMTs has as much potential for frustrations and problems as it does for managers. This is usually due to unfamiliarity with the new structure and new routines, and adjusting to team responsibilities. Team members must learn new behaviors, like putting aside differences in order to make decisions that benefit the team.

The need to adapt to a new working environment in which the definition of teamwork requires a personal, cultural, and behavioral adjustment may be too much for some members and thus lead to personality and behavior conflicts. Thus, the greatest challenge may lie in setting and enforcing new behavioral expectations, made necessary by the absence of a traditional leader and the presence of new employee rights and responsibilities.

10. Define the following key terms (in order of appearance in the chapter):

Select one or more methods: (1) fill in the missing key terms from memory, (2) match the key terms from the end of the review with their definition below, (3) copy the key terms in order from the list at the beginning of the chapter.

_____ is a unit of two or more people with complementary skills who are committed to a common purpose and set of performance goals and to common expectations, for which they hold themselves accountable.

_____ is an understanding and commitment to group goals on the part of all team members.

_____ is the conscious or unconscious tendency by some team members to shirk responsibilities, by withholding effort toward group goals when they are not individually accountable for their work.

_____ happens when members of a cohesive group tend to agree on a decision not on the basis of its merits but because they are less willing to risk rejection for questioning a majority viewpoint or presenting a dissenting opinion.

_____ has three components: (1) task performance—the degree to which the team's output (product or service) meets the needs and expectations of those who use it; (2) group process—the degree to which members interact or relate in ways that allow the team to work increasingly well together over time; and (3) individual satisfaction—the degree to which the group experience, on balance, is more satisfying than frustrating to team members.

_____ are acceptable standards of behavior that are shared by team members.

_____ is the extent to which team members band together and remain committed to achieving team goals.

_____ is the creation of a valuable, useful, and novel product, service, idea, procedure, or process, carried out via discovery rather than by a predetermined step-by-step procedure, by individuals working together in a complex social system.

_____ consists of a group of employees belonging to the same functional department, such as marketing, R&D, production, human resources, or information systems, who have a common objective.

_____ is made up of members from different functional departments of an organization who are brought together to perform unique tasks to create new and nonroutine products or services.

_____ is a cross-functional team in which members are separated in space and time.

_____ are relatively autonomous teams whose members share or rotate leadership responsibilities and hold themselves mutually responsible for a set of performance goals assigned by higher management.

_____ is an advocate of the self-managed team concept, whose responsibility is to help the team obtain necessary resources, gain political support from top management and other stakeholders of the organization, and defend the team from attacks.

_____ is defined as a shared belief that individuals hold about a group.

_____ is the process by which multiple leaders take complementary leadership roles in rotation within the same SMT, according to their area of expertise or interest.

_____ is the external leader of a self-managed team, whose job is to create optimal working conditions so team members take on responsibilities to work productively and solve complex problems on their own.

Key Terms

cross-functional team, 310

distributed leadership, 338

functional team, 309

groupthink, 299

self-managed team champion, 334

self-managed team facilitator, 338

self-managed teams (SMTs), 313

social loafing, 298

team, 296

team cohesion, 303

team creativity, 306

team effectiveness, 300

team norms, 301

team potency, 335

teamwork, 297

virtual team, 311

Review and Discussion Questions

1. Identify and describe any team you have been a member of, or know about otherwise, that has a strong norm of teamwork that all members buy into. What role did the team leader play in making this possible?

2. What is groupthink, and under what conditions is it most likely to occur?

3. Describe the factors that generally contribute high levels of team cohesion.

4. Creativity is usually thought of as a characteristic of individuals, but are some teams more creative than others?

5. What is group-centered leadership, and how does it differ from the leader-centered approach?

6. Describe how a leader can avoid conducting nonproductive meetings.

7. What is the depth of decision-making latitude commonly found in self-managed teams?

8. Briefly discuss some of the potential benefits and drawbacks of using self-managed teams.

9. Why does a self-managed team need a strong and experienced facilitator?

Case

FREDERICK W. SMITH—FEDERAL EXPRESS

Three decades along, Federal Express, also known as FedEx, remains the market leader in an industry it helped create. The name FedEx is synonymous with overnight delivery. To position itself for the 21st century, FedEx is now composed of seven major operating companies: FedEx Express, FedEx Ground, FedEx Freight, FedEx Kinko's Office and Print Services, FedEx Trade Networks, FedEx Supply Chain Services, and FedEx Custom Critical. These companies serve more than 220 countries and territories with operations that include 670 aircraft and more than 70,000 vehicles. More than 250,000 employees and independent contractors worldwide handle more than 6 million shipments each business day. Thirty-four years later, CEO Frederick W. Smith remains the head of FedEx, providing leadership continuity during the company's rapid expansion and change. FedEx has expanded far beyond what Smith started with back in 1971. FedEx has continued to strengthen its industry leadership over the past 34 years, and has been widely acknowledged for its commitment to total quality service. FedEx Express was the first service company to win the Malcolm Baldrige National Quality Award in 1990.

In addition, FedEx has consistently been ranked on *Fortune* Magazine's industry lists, including a #8 ranking in 2005's "World's Most Admired Companies," a #6 ranking in 2005's "America's Most Admired Companies," and a placement in the "100 Best Companies to Work For."

With growth comes difficulties of coordination, maintaining efficiency, meeting customer expectations, and managing employees. Smith realized that a rigid hierarchy of command-and-control groups would only magnify these difficulties. To give his employees the flexibility and freedom they need to move quickly and help FedEx remain the dominant overnight delivery service in the world, Smith decided to restructure FedEx by emphasizing the team approach to getting work done. He directed his leadership team to empower these groups by giving them the authority and the responsibility to make the changes needed to improve productivity and customer satisfaction throughout the FedEx system.

An example of the successful implementation of this new FedEx approach to organizing work can be found in Springfield, Virginia. With strong support from its managers, employees formed the Quality Action Team to overhaul their package-sorting techniques. The improvements they introduced put couriers on the road 12 minutes earlier than before, and halved the number of packages they delivered late. The success of teams at departmental or local levels encouraged Smith and his leadership team to also assign employee teams to companywide projects. Facing growing competition from United Parcel Service, the U.S. Postal Service, and Airborne Express, FedEx organized its 1,000 clerical employees into "superteams" of up to 10 people. These teams operated as self-managed teams with little direct supervision from managers. One team cut service glitches, such as incorrect bills and lost packages, by 13 percent. Another team spotted—and worked until they eventually solved—a billing problem that had been costing the company $2.1 million a year.

FedEx teams have worked so well because Fred Smith sets standards and reinforces them. He spearheaded the concept of the "golden package," the idea that every package FedEx handles is critical and must be delivered on time. Whenever there's a crisis, whether due to competitive pressure or to Mother Nature threatening to ground the company's planes, the team with the golden package takes charge to figure out how to make the delivery on time. Smith reinforces group performance by presenting a monthly Circle of Excellence award to the best FedEx station. He encourages innovative thinking by creating a "job-secure environment." He takes the position that "if you hang people who try to do something that doesn't quite work, you'll get people who don't do anything."

Managers are by no means obsolete at FedEx. Smith has redefined their roles. There has been a shift in mind-set from the traditional leader-centered to the team-centered leadership approach. Managers are expected to formulate clear, attainable goals for their teams, to solicit employee ideas, and to act on the best employee suggestions. FedEx managers perceive their role as facilitators—and sometimes they're players.

During emergencies at the Memphis hub, senior managers hurry down from the executive suite to help load packages onto the conveyer belts that feed the company's planes. They practice team leadership by doing, not by telling.

According to one company executive, "FedEx has built what is the most seamless global air and ground network in its industry, connecting more than 90 percent of the world's economic activity." It is evident that Smith's leadership in pushing for a much more open, flexible, team-based organization has been instrumental in keeping FedEx's lead position in overnight package service. It is also one of the reasons that FedEx has continuously earned high marks as one of the top companies to work for in the United States.

GO TO THE INTERNET: To learn more about Federal Express, log on to InfoTrac® College Edition at **academic. cengage.com/infotrac** and use the advanced search function.

Support your answers to the following questions with specific information from the case and text, or other information you get from the Web or other sources.

1. How do the standards set by Fred Smith for Federal Express teams improve organizational performance?
2. What motivates the members of Federal Express to remain highly engaged in their teams?
3. Describe the role Federal Express managers play in facilitating team effectiveness?
4. What type of teams does FedEx use? Provide evidence from the case to support your answer.
5. Leaders play a critical role in building effective teams. Cite evidence from the case that Federal Express managers performed some of these roles in developing effective teams.

Cumulative Case Questions

6. The Big Five model of personality categorizes traits into dimensions of surgency, agreeableness, adjustment, conscientiousness, and openness to experience (Chapter 2). Which of these dimensions do you think Fred Smith possesses?
7. The normative leadership model (Chapter 5) identifies five leadership styles appropriate for different situations that users can select to maximize decisions. Which of the five leadership styles is practiced by FedEx team leaders?
8. The case reveals that at the Memphis hub, senior managers have been known to hurry down from the executive suite to help load packages during emergencies in order to get the plane off on time. FedEx leaders want to be seen as coaches, not managers. There are specific guidelines that can help a leader become an effective coach (Chapter 6). Which of the guideline(s) does the example above represent?

9. Research on followership describes five types of followership (see Exhibit 7-2, Chapter 7). Which of these types will work best in FedEx's team environment as described in the case, and why?

Case Exercise and Role-Play

Preparation: You are senior vice president for operations at FedEx. FedEx's monthly Circle of Excellence Award is presented to the best FedEx station. This time the best station was one that truly represented the spirit of teamwork in problem solving. The station manager spotted a loading problem that was costing the company millions of dollars a year and decided to leave it up to the station as a group to find ways of solving the problem. After a series of group meetings and key decisions, a solution was found that successfully took care of the loading problem and was adopted by the rest of the company. It has come to Fred Smith's attention that a key reason for the station's success is the leadership role played by the team leader during this process. Mr. Smith has asked that you use the award ceremony as an opportunity to highlight the virtues of the group-centered approach of leadership, particularly with respect to decision making in teams. Develop the key parts of the speech you will give on this occasion.

Your instructor may elect to break the class into groups to share ideas and put together the speech or simply ask each student to prepare an independent speech. If you do a group speech, select one leader to present the speech to the entire class.

Role-Play: One person (representing oneself or a group) may give the speech to the entire class, or break into groups of five to six and deliver speeches one at a time.

Video Case

Cannondale Corporation: Teamwork in Organizations

Cannondale is one of the world's leading manufacturers of high-performance bicycles, providing state-of-the-art racing bikes, technical expertise, and sponsorship support for the competitive riding market.

View the Video (13 minutes)

View the video on Cannondale Corporation in class or at **academic.cengage.com/management/lussier**.

Read the Case

Manufacturing technologically advanced racing bikes that customers can afford requires teamwork, and Cannondale utilizes cross-functional teams both to ensure continuous improvement in quality and to capitalize on the collective strengths of its design and marketing professionals. In the video, the design team for Cannondale's popular Jekyll series works together to meet production objectives set by the entire company. Coordinating efforts with multiple departments, from marketing and sales to manufacturing and testing, is essential in producing world-class bicycles that deliver an enjoyable and durable riding experience for customers.

Cannondale's team members are selected based on particular areas of expertise. Some are materials experts, others skilled at drawing, and still others experienced at proofing designs to ensure that all the pieces fit properly. Once the right people are in place, the research and development group begins designing bicycles on advanced computer systems, developing prototypes of new-model bicycles that eventually gain approval for mass production. If product designs for new bicycles meet company specifications, raw materials are then sent to the factory for manufacturing purposes. Production managers oversee the process from start to finish, ensuring that costs are kept within budget.

Staying on top of the competitive cycling market isn't easy, but the secret of Cannondale's success lies in using effective teamwork to produce high-performance bikes that satisfy the needs of serious cycling enthusiasts.

Answer the Questions

1. Why does Cannondale organize in teams instead of having individuals work alone?
2. What challenges do work teams face at Cannondale? What leadership skills do Cannondale's managers need in order to deal with these challenges?

Behavior Model Skills Training

This behavior model skills training on leadership decision making has four parts, as follows. You should first read how to use the model. Then, you may view the behavior model video that illustrates all four decision making styles for the same decision. Parts three and four are together in Skill-Development

Exercise 1, which gives you the opportunity to develop your ability to select the leadership decision-making style most appropriate for a given situation. Lastly, you further develop this skill by using the model in your personal and professional life.

Leadership Decision-Making Model

(PART I) DECIDING WHICH LEADERSHIP DECISION-MAKING STYLE TO USE

Read the instructions for using the leadership decision-making model, and see Model 8-1 on the next page. You may want to refer to the model as you read.

Managers today realize the trend towards participation in decision making, and managers are open to using participation. It is frustrating for managers to decide when to use participation and when not to, and what level of participation to use. You are about to learn how to use a model that will develop your skill at selecting the appropriate leadership style to meet the needs of the situation. First, let's examine ways in which groups can be used to generate solutions.

Selecting the Appropriate Leadership Decision Style

We have the same four variables as in the Situational Communications Model 6-6—time, information, acceptance, and capability level.

Step 1. Diagnose the situation.

The first step you follow as a leader involves diagnosing the situational variables, including time, information, acceptance, and follower capability.

Time. You must determine whether there is enough time to include followers in decision making. Time is viewed as yes (you have time to use participation) or no (there is no time to use participation). If there is no time, you should use the autocratic style (S1A), regardless of preference. When there is no time to include employees in problem solving and decision making, you ignore the other three variables; they are irrelevant if there is no time. If you say yes there is time, the consultative, participative, or empowerment styles may be appropriate. You use the other three variables to select the style.

Time is a relative term. In one situation, a few minutes may be considered a short time period, but in another a month may be a short period of time. Time is not wasted when the potential advantages of using participation are realized.

Information. You must decide if you have enough information to make a quality decision alone. The more information you have, the less need for participation; the less information you have, the greater the need for participation. If you have all the necessary information, there is no need for follower participation, and the autocratic style (S1A) is appropriate. When you have some information, but need more, which can be obtained by asking questions, the consultative style (S2C) may be appropriate. If you have little information, the appropriate style may be participative (S3P—group discussion) or empowerment (S4E—group makes the decision).

Acceptance. You must decide whether employee acceptance of the decision is critical to implementation of the decision. The more followers will like a decision, the less need there is for participation; the more followers will dislike a decision, the greater the need for participation. If you make the decision alone, will the follower or group willingly implement it? If the follower or group will be accepting, the appropriate style is probably autocratic (S1A). If the follower or group will be reluctant, the appropriate style may be consultative (S2C) or participative (S3P). If they will probably reject the decision, the participative (S3P) or empowerment style (S4E) may be appropriate. When teams make decisions, they are more understanding, accepting, and committed to implementing the decision.

Capability. You must decide whether the follower or group has the ability and motivation to be involved in problem solving and decision making. Does the follower or group have the experience and information needed to be involved? Will followers put the organization's or department's goals ahead of personal goals? Do the followers want to be involved in problem solving and decision making? Followers are more willing to participate when the decisions personally affect them. If the follower or group capability level is low (C1), an autocratic style (S1A) may be appropriate. When capability is moderate (C2), a consultative style (S2C) may be appropriate. If capability level is high (C3), a participative style (S3P) might be adopted. If capability is outstanding (C4), choose the empowerment style (S4E). Remember that an employee or group's capability level can change from situation to situation.

Step 2. Select the appropriate leadership style.

After considering the four variables, you select the appropriate style. In some situations, all variables will indicate that the same style is appropriate, whereas in other cases, the appropriate style is not so clear. For example, you could be in a situation in which you have time to use any style, may have all the information necessary (autocratic), followers may be reluctant (consultative or participative), and their capability may be moderate (consultative). In situations where different styles are indicated for different variables, you must determine which variables should be given more weight. In the above example, assume that acceptance was critical for successful implementation of the decision. Acceptance takes precedence over information. Because the followers involved have moderate capability, the consultative style would be appropriate. Again, Model 8-1 summarizes use of the four situational communication styles in decision making.

Model 8-1 *Leadership decision making.*

Step 1. Diagnose the situation

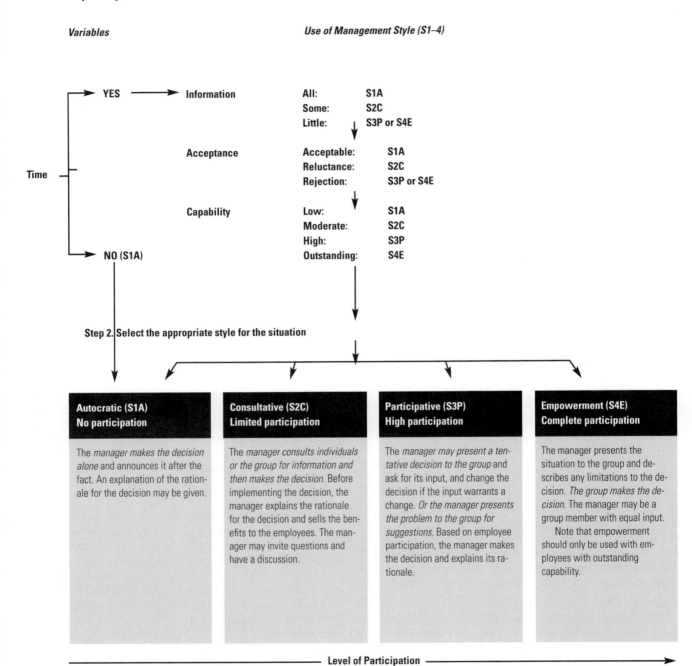

Variables   *Use of Management Style (S1–4)*

YES ───► Information   All: S1A
                          Some: S2C
                          Little: S3P or S4E

                Acceptance   Acceptable: S1A
                              Reluctance: S2C
                              Rejection: S3P or S4E

Time

                Capability   Low: S1A
                              Moderate: S2C
                              High: S3P
NO (S1A)   Outstanding: S4E

Step 2. Select the appropriate style for the situation

Autocratic (S1A) **No participation**	**Consultative (S2C)** **Limited participation**	**Participative (S3P)** **High participation**	**Empowerment (S4E)** **Complete participation**
The *manager makes the decision alone* and announces it after the fact. An explanation of the rationale for the decision may be given.	The *manager consults individuals or the group for information and then makes the decision.* Before implementing the decision, the manager explains the rationale for the decision and sells the benefits to the employees. The manager may invite questions and have a discussion.	The *manager may present a tentative decision to the group* and ask for its input, and change the decision if the input warrants a change. *Or the manager presents the problem to the group for suggestions.* Based on employee participation, the manager makes the decision and explains its rationale.	The manager presents the situation to the group and describes any limitations to the decision. *The group makes the decision.* The manager may be a group member with equal input. Note that empowerment should only be used with employees with outstanding capability.

───────────── **Level of Participation** ─────────────────►

Note that with autocratic, consultative, and participative styles the manager retains the power to make the decision; with empowerment the group makes the decision.

Using the Leadership Decision-Making Model

We will apply the model to the following situation; additional similar situations are presented later with the skill-development exercise.

_____ Manager Ben can give one of his followers a merit pay raise. He has a week to make the decision. Ben knows how well each employee performed over the past year. The followers really have no option but to accept getting or not getting the pay raise, but they can complain to upper management about the selection. The followers' capability levels vary, but as a group they have a high capability level under normal circumstances.

_____ time _____ information _____ acceptance _____ capability

Step 1. Diagnose the situation.

Ben has plenty of time to use any level of participation (place a Y for yes on the "time" line below the situation). He has all the information needed to make the decision (place S1A on the "information" line). Followers have no choice but to accept the decision (place S1A on the "acceptance" line). And the group's capability level is normally high (place S3P on the "capability" line).

Step 2. Select the Appropriate Style for the Situation.

There are conflicting styles to choose from (autocratic and participative): *yes* time; *S1A* information; *S1A* acceptance; *S3P* capability.

The variable that should be given precedence is information. The followers are normally capable, but in a situation like this they may not put the department's goals ahead of their own. In other words, even if followers know who deserves the raise, they may fight for it anyway. Such a conflict could cause future problems. Some ways to make the decision could include the following:

Autocratic (S1A). The manager would select the person to be given the raise without discussing it with any followers. Ben would simply announce the decision after submitting it to the payroll department.

Consultative (S2C). The manager would get information from the followers concerning who should get the raise. Ben would then decide who would get the raise. He would announce the decision and explain the rationale for it. He may invite questions and discussion.

Participative (S3P). The manager could tentatively select the employee who gets the raise, but be open to change if a group member convinces him that someone else should. Or Ben could explain the situation to the group and lead a discussion concerning who should get the raise. After considering their input, Ben would make the decision and explain the rationale for it. Notice that the consultative style does not allow for discussion as the participative style does.

Empowerment (S4E). The manager would explain the situation and allow the group to decide who gets the raise. Ben may be a group member. Notice that this is the only style that allows the group to make the decision.

The autocratic style is appropriate for this situation. The consultative style is also a good approach. However, the participative and empowerment styles use too much participation for the situation. Your skill at selecting the appropriate decision-making leadership style should improve through using the model for the 10 situations in the skill-development exercise. However, the next step is to view the behavior video model.

Behavior Model Video and Video Exercise

(PART II) DECIDING WHICH LEADERSHIP DECISION-MAKING STYLE TO USE

Objectives

To better understand the four leadership decision-making styles, and to select the most appropriate style for a given situation.

Video (13 minutes) Overview

The video begins by telling you how to use the model. Then it shows the human resources director, Richard, meeting with a supervisor, Denise, to discuss training changes. Each of the four styles is shown to illustrate how all four styles can be used in the same situation. Thus, you gain a better understanding of the four styles. During the video you will be asked to identify each of the four styles being used by Richard. The answers will be given by your instructor during or at the end of the video.

In viewing the video, you should also realize that some styles are more appropriate than others for this situation. As a class, you may discuss which style would be the most effective, and at the end of the video, the recommended style is stated.

Preparation

You should have read the "Leadership Decision-Making Model" section of this leadership behavior-modeling skills training.

Procedure 1 (10–20 minutes)

The instructor shows (or you view on your own) the video, "Decision Making." As you view each of the four scenes, identify the four leadership decision-making styles being used by

Richard. Write the letters and number of the style on the line after each scene.

Scene 1. _____   Autocratic (S1A)
Scene 2. _____   Consultative (S2C)
Scene 3. _____   Participative (S3P)
Scene 4. _____   Empowerment (S4E)

Option A: View all four scenes and identify the style used by Richard. Select the one style that you would use in this situation. Are other styles also appropriate? Which style would you not use (not appropriate) for this situation? Next to each style listed above, write the letter "a" for appropriate or "n"

for not appropriate. After everyone is done, the instructor leads a class discussion and/or gives the correct answers.

Option B: After each scene the class discusses the style used by Richard. The instructor states the correct answer after each of the four scenes. Then discuss which style is the most effective for the situation.

Option C: Simply view the entire video without any discussion.

Conclusion

The instructor may lead a class discussion and/or make concluding remarks.

Skill-Development Exercise 1

(PART III & IV) DECIDING WHICH LEADERSHIP DECISION-MAKING STYLE TO USE

Preparation For Skill-Development Exercise 1

Below are 10 situations calling for a decision. Select the appropriate decision-making style for each. Be sure to use Model 8-1 when determining the style to use. First determine the answers to the variables (S1A, S2C, S3P, S4E) and write them on the lines below the situation. Then place the selected style on the "Leadership style" line.

S1A autocratic   S2C consultative

S3P participative   S4E empowerment

1. You have developed a new work procedure that will increase productivity. Your boss likes the idea and wants you to try it in a few weeks. You view your followers as fairly capable, and believe that they will be receptive to the change.

    _____ time ___ information ___ acceptance ___ capability

    Leadership style _____

2. There is new competition in your industry. Your organization's revenues have been dropping. You have been told to lay off 3 of your 15 followers in two weeks. You have been supervisor for over three years. Normally, your followers are very capable.

    _____ time ___ information ___ acceptance ___ capability

    Leadership style _____

3. Your department has been facing a problem for several months. Many solutions have been tried and failed. You've finally thought of a solution, but you're not sure of the possible consequences of the change required, or of acceptance by your highly capable followers.

    _____ time _____information ___ acceptance ___ capability

    Leadership style _____

4. Flextime has become popular in your organization. Some departments let each employee start and end work when they choose. However, because of the cooperation required of your followers, they must all work the same eight hours. You're not sure of the level of interest in changing the hours. Your followers are a very capable group and like to make decisions.

    _____ time ___ information ___ acceptance ___ capability

    Leadership style _____

5. The technology in your industry is changing too fast for the members of your organization to keep up. Top management hired a consultant who has made recommendations. You have two weeks to decide what to do about the recommendations. Your followers are usually capable; they enjoy participating in the decision-making process.

    _____ time ___ information ___ acceptance ___ capability

    Leadership style _____

6. Top management has handed down a change. How you implement it is your decision. The change takes effect in one month. It will affect everyone in your department. Their acceptance is critical to the success of the change. Your followers are usually not interested in making routine decisions.

    _____ time ___ information ___ acceptance ___ capability

    Leadership style _____

7. Your boss called to tell you that someone requested an order for your department's product; the delivery date is very short. She asked you to call her back with a decision about taking the order in 15 minutes. Looking over the work schedule, you realize that it will be very difficult to deliver the order on time. Your followers will have to push hard to make it. They are cooperative, capable, and enjoy being involved in decision making.

_____ time ___ information ___ acceptance ___ capability

Leadership style _____

8. Top management has decided to make a change that will affect all of your followers. You know that they will be upset because it will cause them hardship. One or two may even quit. The change goes into effect in 30 days. Your followers are very capable.

_____ time ___ information ___ acceptance ___ capability

Leadership style _____

9. You believe that productivity in your department could be increased. You have thought of some ways to do it, but you're not sure of them. Your followers are very experienced; almost all of them have been in the department longer than you have.

_____ time ___ information ___ acceptance ___ capability

Leadership style _____

10. A customer offered you a contract for your product with a quick delivery date. The offer is open for two days. To meet the contract deadline, followers would have to work nights and weekends for six weeks. You cannot require them to work overtime. Filling this profitable contract could help get you the raise you want and feel you deserve. However, if you take the contract and don't deliver on time, it will hurt your chances of getting a big raise. Your followers are very capable.

_____ time ___ information ___ acceptance ___ capability

Leadership style _____

Doing Skill-Development Exercise 1 in Class

Objective

To develop your skill at knowing which level of participation to use in a given decision-making situation. You will learn to use the leadership decision-making model.

Experience

You will try to select the appropriate decision-making style for each of 10 situations in preparation for this exercise.

Preparation

You should have completed the preparation for this exercise, unless told not to do so by your instructor. There is an option to do the preparation in class as part of the exercise.

Procedure 1 (8–12 minutes)

The instructor may review the leadership decision-making model (Model 8-1), and will explain how to use it to select the appropriate leadership style for the first situation.

Procedure 2 (4–8 minutes)

Students, working alone, complete situation 2 using the model, followed by the instructor going over the recommend answers. If the instructor will be testing you on leadership decision making, you may be told the details.

Procedure 3 (10–20 minutes)

Break into teams of two or three. Apply the model to situations 3 through 5 as a team. You may decide to change your original answers. The instructor goes over the recommended answers and scoring for situations 3 through 5. Your instructor may tell you not to continue on to situation 6 until he or she goes over the answers to situations 3 through 5.

Procedure 4 (10–20 minutes)

In the same teams, select decision-making styles for situations 6 through 10. The instructor will go over the recommended answers and scoring.

Conclusion

The instructor may lead a class discussion and/or make concluding remarks.

Apply It (2–4 minutes)

What did I learn from this experience? How will I use this knowledge in the future? Identify when you will practice this skill.

_____

_____

_____

Sharing

Volunteers may give their answers to the "Apply It" section.

Skill-Development Exercise 2

INDIVIDUAL VERSUS GROUP DECISION MAKING

Preparation for Skill-Development Exercise 2

To complete this exercise you must answer the questions in Applying the Concept 8-1 to 8-4 in the chapter.

Doing Skill-Development Exercise 2 in Class

Objective

To compare individual and group decision making, to better understand when to use a group to make decisions.

Preparation

As preparation, you should have answered the questions in Applying the Concept 8-1 to 8-4.

Experience

You will work in a group, each member of which will answer the same 20 questions, and then analyze the results to determine if the group or one (or more) of its members had the higher score.

Procedure 1 (1–2 minutes)

Place your answers to the 20 questions in the "Individual Answer" column in the table on page 353.

Procedure 2 (15–20 minutes)

Break into teams of five, with smaller or larger groups as necessary. As a group, come to an agreement on the answers to the 20 questions. Place the group answers in the "Group Answer" column. Try to use consensus rather than voting or majority in arriving at the answers.

Procedure 3 (4–6 minutes)

Scoring

The instructor will give the recommended answers. Determine how many you got right as an individual and as a group. Total your individual and the group's score.

Compute the *average* individual score by adding all the individual scores and dividing by the number of group members. Write it here: _____.

Now calculate the difference between the average individual score and the group score. If the group's score is higher than the average individual score, you have a gain (+) of points; if the group score is lower, you have a loss (–) of points. Write it here, _____ and circle one (+ or –).

Determine the highest individual score. Write it here: _____.

Determine the number of individuals who scored higher than the group's score: _____.

Procedure 4 (5–10 minutes)—Integration

As a group, discuss the advantages or disadvantages of being in a group while making the decisions in this exercise. Go back to the text and review the advantages and disadvantages listed in the "Team versus Individual Decision Making" section, pg. 315 and discuss. Then try to agree on which of the five advantages and disadvantages your group had.

Overall, were the advantages of using a group greater than the disadvantages? If your group were to continue to work together, how could it improve its decision-making ability? Write your answer below.

_____

_____

_____

Conclusion

The instructor may lead a class discussion and/or make concluding remarks.

Apply It (2–4 minutes)

What did I learn from this experience? How will I use this knowledge in the future? Specifically, what will I do the next time I'm in a group to help it make better decisions? When will I have the opportunity?

_____

_____

_____

Sharing

Volunteers may give their answers to the "Apply It" section.

Question Number	Individual Answer	Group Answer	Recommended Answer	Individual Score	Group Score
AC 1: 1					
2					
3					
4					
5					
AC 2: 6					
7					
8					
9					
10					
AC 3: 11					
12					
13					
14					
15					
AC 4: 16					
17					
18					
19					
20					
Total scores					

PART 3

Organizational Leadership

Charismatic and Transformational Leadership

LEARNING OUTCOMES

After studying this chapter, you should be able to:

1. Describe personal meaning and how it influences attributions of charismatic qualities. p. 359
2. Briefly explain Max Weber's conceptualization of charisma. p. 363
3. Explain the locus of charismatic leadership. p. 364
4. Describe the four behavioral components of charisma. p. 365
5. Discuss the effects of charismatic leadership on followers. p. 368
6. Describe the characteristics that distinguish charismatic from noncharismatic leaders. p. 370
7. Discuss how one can acquire charismatic qualities. p. 374
8. Explain the difference between socialized and personalized charismatic leaders. p. 375
9. Distinguish between charismatic and transformational leadership. p. 378
10. Explain the difference between transformational and transactional leadership. p. 382
11. Explain the four phases of the transformation process. p. 384
12. Explain the basis of stewardship and servant leadership. p. 385
13. Define the following **key terms** (in order of appearance in the chapter):

personal meaning	vision
self-belief	socialized charismatic leader(SCL)
legacy	personalized charismatic leader (PCL)
selflessness	transformational leadership
spirituality	transactional leadership
values	stewardship
charisma	servant leadership

Opening Case Application

In 1986, Oprah Winfrey launched Harpo Productions, Inc. Two years later, in October 1988, television history was made when Harpo Productions announced that it was taking over all production responsibilities for the *Oprah Winfrey Show* from Capitol Cities/ABC, making Winfrey the first woman in history to own and produce her own talk show. The *Oprah Winfrey Show* is the highest rated talk show in television history. The show is seen by an estimated 30 million viewers weekly in the United States and airs in 111 countries. She is described by those close to her as confident, brilliant, and personable. She is considered a sister by many of her key employees. She is one of the richest women in America; yet, many say she does not let all of her success go to her head.

In September 1999, Oprah joined Stedman Graham as an adjunct professor at the J. L. Kellogg Graduate School of Management at Northwestern University to coteach "Dynamics of Leadership." The course curriculum, developed by professors Winfrey and Graham, shared insights into how students can cultivate their own leadership skills and develop an approach to management, leadership, and organizational issues suited to their individual circumstances. "Dynamics of Leadership" was offered at Kellogg for a second time in the fall of 2000.

From her humble beginnings in rural Mississippi, Oprah's legacy has established her as one of the most important figures in popular culture. Her contributions can be felt beyond the world of television and into areas such as education, social justice, publishing, music, film, philanthropy, health and fitness, and economic advancement. Through her show, Oprah entertains, enlightens, and empowers millions of viewers around the world.

Opening Case Questions

1. Why is Oprah such a popular and admired figure on TV?
2. Oprah seems to have a very clear sense of her personal meaning or purpose in life. What factors do you think have contributed to her understanding?
3. In your opinion, what is the locus of Oprah's charisma?
4. What effects has Oprah's charisma had on her followers?
5. In your opinion, what qualities of charismatic leadership does Oprah possess?
6. Does Oprah embody the example of a socialized charismatic leader or a personalized charismatic leader?
7. Is Oprah a transformational leader?

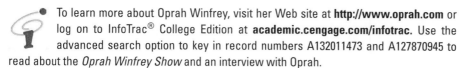 To learn more about Oprah Winfrey, visit her Web site at **http://www.oprah.com** or log on to InfoTrac® College Edition at **academic.cengage.com/infotrac**. Use the advanced search option to key in record numbers A132011473 and A127870945 to read about the *Oprah Winfrey Show* and an interview with Oprah.

The last two decades of the twentieth century have witnessed a renewed interest in and scholarship focus on charismatic and transformational leadership. This growth in interest has coincided with significant geopolitical, social, and economic change. Much higher levels of turbulence, uncertainty, discontinuous change, and global competition characterize today's work environment. The challenge facing many institutions is how to continually cope with new situations in order to survive and prosper. Organizations are faced with the need to adapt or perish. Adaptation requires that organizations learn to do things differently, such as the need to transform internal cultures, empower organizational members, adapt or develop new technologies, restructure personnel and workflow patterns, eliminate concrete and artificial boundaries, pave the path to continuous innovation, and foster a high-involvement and risk-taking organizational climate. The charismatic and transformational leader, according to many scholars and practitioners, represents a new genre of leadership that may be capable of steering organizations through the chaos of the twenty-first century. In the literature, both charismatic and transformational forms of leadership are commonly discussed from two separate but interrelated perspectives: in terms of the effects that leaders have upon followers, and in terms of the relationships that exist between leaders and followers.

Charismatic and transformational theories return our focus to the leader. These theories shine the light on exemplary leaders who have extraordinary effects on their followers and ultimately on entire social, cultural, economic, and political systems. According to this new genre of leadership theories, such leaders transform the needs, aspirations, and values of followers from a focus on self-interest to a focus on collective interest. They practice trust building to create strong commitment to a common mission. They generate emotion, energy, and excitement that cause followers to make significant personal sacrifices in the interest of the mission, and to perform above and beyond the call of duty.

1. Why Is Oprah Such a Popular and Admired Figure on TV?

Oprah possesses the charisma and transformational qualities alluded to above. She has already left an indelible mark on the face of television. She has used her celebrity status to push for social change in our society. She has championed the cause for child abuse, poverty, domestic violence, illiteracy, and much more. Her audience represents a cross-section of the American ethnic landscape. As supervising producer and host of the *Oprah Winfrey Show,* Oprah entertains, enlightens, and empowers millions of viewers not just in the United States, but around the world.

Charismatic and transformational leaders often have a more heightened sense of who they are as human beings than most people do. They seem to have a clearer picture of their personal meaning or purpose in life much sooner, and seek to actualize it through active leadership. To lay the foundation for charisma and charismatic leadership, we will focus the discussion first on the concept of personal meaning. Then we will discuss the unique and complementary qualities of charisma, charismatic leadership, transformational leadership, and servant leadership, focusing on the impact of each on organizational performance.

— Learning Outcome 1 —

Describe personal meaning and how it influences attributions of charismatic qualities.

Personal Meaning

Personal meaning is described in terms of meaningfulness or purpose in life. A more formal definition is *the degree to which people's lives make emotional sense and to which the demands confronted by them are perceived as being worthy of energy and commitment.* Others have described this as the "work-life balance" or the achievement of equilibrium in personal and official life.[1] Thus, personal meaning is that which makes one's life most important, coherent, and worthwhile. The theoretical basis of personal meaning is derived from research on purpose in life (PIL). PIL represents a positive attitude toward possessing a transcendent vision in life. The depth (i.e., strength) and type (i.e., content of meaning associated with a goal) of personal meaning are major determinants of motivation, especially for individuals facing challenges. Given the general recognition of personal meaning as important to explanations of charismatic leadership, the relevant question then becomes how one develops this meaning. The answer to this question lies in looking at the factors that influence personal meaning.

Factors That Influence Personal Meaning

Exhibit 9-1 lists a variety of factors that influence personal meaning, derived from a review of the literature. Each factor is briefly discussed below in terms of its contribution to the personal meaning of leaders.

Exhibit 9-1 *Factors that influence personal meaning.*

> a. Self-belief
> b. Legacy
> c. Selflessness
> d. Cultural heritage and traditions
> e. Activist mind-set
> f. Faith and spirituality
> g. Personal interests
> h. Values

Source: Based on G. T. Reker and P. T. P. Wong (1988), "Meaning and Purpose in Life and Well-Being: A Lifespan Perspective," *Journal of Gerontology* 42 (1992): 44–49.

Self-Belief

Self-belief *is knowing who you are based on your lifespan of experiences, motivation states, and action orientation.* The search for meaning involves finding opportunities to express the aspects of one's self that motivate subsequent behavior. Closely related to self-belief is a trait called positive self-concept. Individuals with a positive self-concept possess emotional stability, believe in their self-worth (high self-esteem), see themselves as generally capable of accomplishing things (high generalized self-efficacy), and feel they are in control of their lives (internal locus of control).[2] In many cases, the charismatic leader is a person who has overcome an inner conflict to realize his or her full potential and, through this process, develop a strong belief in himself or herself. The resolution of this conflict serves as a stimulus and model for followers.

Legacy

The need to leave behind something of enduring value after one's death can be both a powerful motivator and a source of personal meaning. **Legacy** *is that which allows an individual's accomplishments to "live on" in the ideals, actions, and creations of one's followers, long after his or her death.*[3] Charismatic leaders are driven to leave their personal mark on the society they serve. Gandhi advocated passive resistance and passion for truth. His legacy has influenced many subsequent social and political activists and leaders, including Martin Luther King, Jr., and Nelson Mandela. These leaders derived meaning from a realization that their legacy may provide their followers with a framework for self-development, harmony and fellowship, and a more socially desirable future.

Selflessness

Selflessness *is an unselfish regard for or devotion to the welfare of others.* Therefore, a leader with an unselfish attitude derives motivation through concern for others rather than for oneself. Servant leadership is rooted in providing service to followers. For example, helping followers to develop and work toward collective goals may satisfy a charismatic leader's motives and therefore make sacrifices and suffering meaningful. Examples of selfless charismatic leaders include Bishop Desmond Tutu, Mother Teresa, and Princess Diana. They were all driven by a concern for others.

Cultural Heritage and Traditions

Rites and ceremonies may be used as vehicles to transfer charisma to others. Charismatic leaders of religious organizations (e.g., Martin Luther King, Jr.; Rev. Billy Graham) derive personal meaning by leading their churches, while their personal meaning helps define rites, doctrine, and ceremonies. Also, oral and written traditions may make the charismatic leader's vision meaningful over time. For example, Frederick Douglass sought to preserve the traditions and heritage of African people by emphasizing the value of education as a vehicle for self-empowerment and growth. His determination not to live as a slave but to live proudly as a black American is part of the heritage of the African-American culture today and has added meaning to his life.

Activist Mind-Set

Charismatic leaders tend to have a more activist mind-set than noncharismatic leaders. They use political and social causes as opportunities to influence change and provide a better life for their followers. These accomplishments provide charismatic leaders with meaning for their existence and satisfy their motives. Charismatic leaders have a greater sensitivity to political, societal, and organizational situations that are ripe for change. They magnify a climate of dissatisfaction by encouraging activism that heightens followers' willingness to change the status quo. When followers are going through periods of turmoil and collective stress, they may respond to a leader who is able to give meaning to their experiences in terms of a new social or political order. For example, Oprah's commitment to children led her to initiate the National Child Protection Act in 1991, when she testified before the U.S. Senate Judiciary Committee to establish a national database of convicted child abusers. On December 20, 1993, President Clinton signed the national "Oprah Bill" into law.

Faith and Spirituality

Spirituality *concerns an individual's awareness of connections between human and supernatural phenomena, which provide faith explanations of past and present experiences and, for some, predict future experiences.* Supporters believe that religion and spirituality endows individuals' lives with meaning and purpose and gives them hope for a better future. Charismatic leaders face hardship and suffering while leading missions of change. They often rely on their faith for support. Faith and spirituality influence one's meaning and purpose in life, and some argue that without meaning and purpose there would be no reason for charismatic leaders to endure their struggles.[4] In addition, charismatic leaders sustain faith by linking behaviors and goals to a "dream" or utopian ideal vision of a better future. Followers may be driven by such faith because it is internally satisfying. Billy Graham, Martin Luther King, Jr., and Gandhi illustrate charismatic leaders whose purpose in life is or was influenced by their spirituality. In Appendix A, "Spirituality in the Workplace," we provide more details on this topic.

Personal Interests

Personal pursuits may reflect aspects of one's personality. By engaging in meaningful personal pursuits, we may establish and affirm our identity as either extroverts or introverts, high or low risk-takers, and open- or close-minded. Hobbies and other activities of personal interest have been linked to sets of personally salient action that add meaning to individuals' lives and leader behavior.

Values

Values *are stable and enduring beliefs about what an individual considers to be important.* Values provide basis for meaning. Charismatic leadership has been described as values-based leadership. By aligning their values with those of followers, and appealing to followers' subconscious motives, charismatic leaders may derive personal meaning from their actions.

2. Oprah Seems to Have a Very Clear Sense of Her Personal Meaning or Purpose in Life. What Factors Do You Think Have Contributed to Her Understanding?

Much has been published on Oprah in books and on the Internet. It is apparent from reading through these materials that her sense of personal meaning has been influenced by all the factors described above and listed in Exhibit 9-1. The following examples illustrate Oprah's selflessness, values, activist mind-set, and legacy. The Oprah Winfrey Foundation was established to support the inspiration, empowerment, education, and well-being of women, children, and families around the world. Through this private charity, Oprah has directly served the needs of low-opportunity people and has awarded hundreds of grants to organizations that carry out this vision. She has contributed millions of dollars towards providing a better education for underserved students who have merit but no means. She created the "Oprah Winfrey Scholars Program," which gives scholarships to students determined to use their education to give back to their communities in the United States and abroad. The Oprah Winfrey Foundation continues to expand Oprah's global humanitarian efforts in developing countries. In December 2002, Oprah brought a day of joy to tens of thousands of children with "ChristmasKindness South Africa 2002," an initiative that included visits to orphanages and rural schools in South Africa where children received gifts of food, clothing, athletic shoes, school supplies, books, and toys. Sixty-three rural schools received libraries and teacher education, which will continue throughout 2003. In addition, Oprah announced a partnership with South Africa's Ministry of Education to build a model leadership school for girls. The Oprah Winfrey Leadership Academy for Girls—South Africa is scheduled to open in 2006. Oprah speaks openly of her strong faith and spirituality on her show every day.

From this discussion of personal meaning, a framework emerges that links a leader's personal meaning and charismatic leadership. First, a leader's personal meaning influences his or her behavior. In turn, the leader's behavior is reflected in the formulation and articulation of his or her vision. Second, the leader's behavior garners attributions of charisma from followers. Thus a primary aspect of the charismatic leadership process involves the perceptions and evaluations—that is, attributions—made by followers about the behaviors of leaders and their effects.

From a follower perspective, charismatic leaders are viewed as out-of-the-ordinary persons who can satisfy a need for finding meaning in life. The extraordinary quality or image of the charismatic leader is seen not only as a source of influence but also a symbol of the realization of the meaning that is constructed in an appealing and/or evocative vision. Vision is the leader's idealized goal that he or she wants the organization to achieve in the future. Based on this interconnection between a leader's personal meaning, behavior, and attributions of charisma, some scholars have argued that charismatic leaders are "meaning makers" who "interpret reality to offer us images of the future that are irresistible."[5] The next section focuses on this concept of charisma.

Sources of Personal Meaning

Referring to the sources of personal meaning in Exhibit 9-1, match each statement to its source using the letters a–h.

_____ 1. A desire to leave your personal mark on history long after you are dead.

_____ 2. A collection of lifespan experiences, motivation states, and action orientation that serves as a source of personal meaning.

_____ 3. Faith in a higher power that motivates one to endure hardships and struggles and thus serves as a source of personal meaning.

_____ 4. A leader derives personal meaning by being very sensitive to societal, political, and organizational situations that are ripe for change and acting on them.

_____ 5. Rites and ceremonies used as vehicles to transfer charisma to others or to define one's personal meaning.

Charisma

The Greek word *charisma* means "divinely inspired gift." Like the term *leadership* itself, charisma has been defined from various organizational perspectives by researchers studying political leadership, social movements, and religious cults. Nevertheless, there is enough consistency among these definitions to create a unifying theme. This section will focus on the following topics: the definition of charisma beginning with Max Weber's early conceptualization, the locus of charismatic leadership, the role of the leader's personal meaning (also referred to as "purpose in life") in charismatic leadership, the sources of personal meaning, and the behavioral components of charisma.

--- Learning Outcome 2 ---

Briefly explain Max Weber's conceptualization of charisma.

Weber's Conceptualization of Charisma

Of the early theories of charisma, the sociologist Max Weber made what is probably the single most important contribution. Weber used the term "charisma" to explain a form of influence based not on traditional or legal-rational authority systems but rather on follower perceptions that a leader is endowed with the gift of divine inspiration or supernatural qualities. Charisma has been called "a fire that ignites followers' energy and commitment, producing results above and beyond the call of duty." Weber saw in a charismatic leader someone who single-handedly visualizes a transcendent mission or course of action that is not only appealing to potential followers, but compels them to act on it because they believe the leader is extraordinarily gifted. Other attributes of charisma identified in the political and sociological literature include acts of heroism, an ability to inspire and build confidence, espousing of revolutionary ideals, oratorical ability, and a "powerful aura." Combining these attributes with relational dynamics between leaders and followers provides a comprehensive picture of this phenomenon. Therefore, **charisma** *is "a distinct social relationship between the leader and follower, in which the leader presents a revolutionary idea, a transcendent image or ideal which goes beyond the immediate . . . or the reasonable; while the follower accepts this course of action not because of its rational likelihood of success . . . but because of an effective belief in the extraordinary qualities of the leader."*[6]

An issue that has generated much research activity over the years is determining the locus of charismatic leadership. The next section examines this subject.

--------- Learning Outcome 3 ---------

Explain the locus of charismatic leadership.

Locus of Charismatic Leadership

Over the years, scholars from different fields have commented on Weber's conceptualization of charismatic leadership. Perhaps the most controversy concerns the locus of charismatic leadership. Is charisma primarily the result of (1) the situation or social climate facing the leader, (2) the leader's extraordinary qualities, or (3) an interaction of the situation and the leader's qualities? Proponents of the view that charismatic leadership could not take place unless the society was in a crisis argue that before an individual with extraordinary qualities could be perceived as a charismatic leader, the social situation must be such that followers would recognize the need for the leader's qualities. The sociological literature, led by Weber, supports this viewpoint, emphasizing that charismatic leadership is born out of stressful situations. It is argued that under stressful situations, charismatic leaders are able to express sentiments that are different from the established order, and deeply felt by followers. Proponents of this view would argue that neither Martin Luther King, Jr., nor Gandhi would have emerged as charismatic leaders to lead their followers without the prevailing social crisis in their respective countries.

However, others argue that charisma need not be born out of distress but rather that charisma is primarily the result of leader attributes. These attributes include a strong sense of vision, exceptional communication skills, strong conviction, trustworthiness, high self-confidence and intelligence, and high energy and action orientation. Proponents of this view would argue that Martin Luther King, Jr., and Gandhi possessed these qualities, and without them would never have emerged as leaders of their respective followers regardless of the situation.

Finally, there are those who believe that charismatic leadership does not depend on the leader's qualities or the presence of a crisis alone, but rather that it is an interactional concept. There is increasing acceptance of this view. Most theorists now view charisma as the result of follower perceptions and reactions, influenced not only by actual leader characteristics and behavior but also by the context of the situation.

OPENING CASE APPLICATION

3. In Your Opinion, What Is the Locus of Oprah's Charisma?

The locus of Oprah's charisma can be attributed more to her extraordinary qualities than to any external factor in her environment. "Knowledge is power! With knowledge you can soar and reach as high as your dreams can take you," said Oprah. This belief has guided Oprah Winfrey on her brilliant journey from a troubled youth to international fame. Oprah Gail Winfrey was born in Kosciusko, Mississippi. Oprah lived with her grandmother until age six, when she moved to Milwaukee to live with her mother, Vernita Lee. At the age of nine she was sexually abused by a teenage cousin. Over the next five years, she was molested several times by a family friend and once by her uncle. Without a doubt, she became a rebellious child and was reportedly headed towards a juvenile-detention center. Instead, at the age of fourteen, she went to live with her father, Vernon Winfrey, a strict disciplinarian. This, she said, was the turning point in her life. Oprah Winfrey is a success story that the everyday person can relate to. She has worked hard to gain success. Oprah's achievements came after a lot of hard work, determination, and education.

Whether or not leaders can have charismatic effects under nonstressful situations is still an open debate among scholars. However there seems to be a consensus that charisma must be based on the articulation of an ideological goal—a transcendent goal that paints or promises a better future than the present. The question that persists is why a few possess this quality or ability to visualize a future that many other leaders fail to see or grasp.

At the heart of this question lies the concept of personal meaning or self-concept discussed above. Numerous theoretical discussions of charismatic leadership underscore the significance of providing meaning or purpose to followers, especially during a time of crisis. Meaning is important for follower identification with the leader and his or her vision. Charismatic leaders construct meaning for followers based on their own personal meaning. The charismatic leader's meaning or purpose in life is communicated to followers through behavior and actions. The next section discusses the behavioral components of charisma.

WorkApplication1

Think of a leader from your work experience or education who you believe has charisma. Explain why.

_____

_____

_____

_____

—————— Learning Outcome 4 ——————

Describe the four behavioral components of charisma.

Behavioral Components of Charisma

Leader behavior is influenced by the leader's personal meaning or purpose in life. The leader's behavior forms the basis of follower attributions of charisma or charismatic qualities. If the follower's attribution of charisma depends on observed behavior of the leader, the question then becomes: What are the behavioral components responsible for such attributions? Some studies have gone as far as to propose that if these attributions can be identified and operationalized, the knowledge gained can then be used to develop charismatic qualities among organizational leaders.

The attribution of charisma to leaders is believed to depend on four behavior variables:

- The discrepancy gap between the status quo and the vision advocated by the leader
- Vision articulation and role modeling
- Use of unconventional strategies for achieving desired change
- A realistic assessment of resource needs and other constraints for achieving desired change

Discrepancy between Status Quo and Future Vision

The discrepancy between charismatic and noncharismatic leaders is such that the former is very much opposed to the status quo and strives to change it, while the latter essentially agrees with the status quo and strives to maintain it. For the charismatic leader, the more idealized or discrepant the future goal is from the present status quo, the better. And the greater the gap from the status quo, the more likely followers will attribute extraordinary vision to the leader.

Vision Articulation and Role Modeling

Charismatic leaders are thought to differ from mere mortal leaders by their ability to formulate and articulate an inspirational vision.[7] Effective articulation of vision is measured in what is said (content and context) and how it is said (oratorical abilities). In terms of vision content and context, the following four steps are recommended:

- The nature of the status quo
- The nature of the future vision
- The manner through which this future vision, if realized, removes sources of discontent and provides fulfillment of hopes and aspirations of the followers
- Plans of action for realizing the vision

Charismatic leaders articulate the context of their message by highlighting positive images of the future vision and negative images of the present situation. The present situation is often presented as unacceptable, whereas the vision is presented as the most attractive alternative in clear, specific terms. Effective communication skills are an imperative in the successful articulation of a compelling vision and maintenance of a leadership role. Through verbal and nonverbal means, charismatic leaders communicate their self-confidence, convictions, and dedication in order to give credibility to what they advocate. They are often described as great orators who know how to incite passion and action among their followers. Followers tend to model the charismatic leader's high energy and persistence, unconventional and risky behavior, heroic actions, and personal sacrifices.

There is research supporting the position that leaders with charisma tend to model the values and beliefs to which they want their followers to subscribe. That is, the leader "role models" a value system that is congruent with the articulated vision for the followers. Gandhi represents an outstanding example of such systematic and intentional role modeling. He preached self-sacrifice, brotherly love, and nonviolent resistance to British rule. Repeatedly he engaged in self-sacrificing behaviors, such as giving up his lucrative law practice to live the life of a peasant, engaging in civil disobedience, fasting, and refusing to accept the ordinary conveniences offered to him by others.

Charisma and Unconventional Behavior

The noncharismatic leader's expertise lies in using available or conventional means to achieve existing goals, whereas the charismatic leader's expertise lies in using unconventional means to transcend the existing order. Unconventional leader behavior is perceived as novel—that is, original or new. Research linking unconventional leader behavior with subordinate satisfaction and perception of leader effectiveness revealed positive associations between the variables. In other words, unconventional behavior was found to be significantly related to follower satisfaction with the overall experience and perceptions of leader effectiveness.[8]

Admirers of charismatic leaders believe that such individuals possess heroic qualities that enable them to persist in spite of the odds against them. Charismatic leaders are thought to possess heroic characteristics such as courage, determination, and persistence to face and prevail against those who would resist their noble efforts.[9] Follower perceptions of such heroic qualities evoke sentiments of adoration, especially when the leader's activities exemplify acts of heroism involving personal risk and self-sacrificing behavior. Thus, the behavior of the noncharismatic leader is conventional and conforming to existing norms while that of the charismatic leader is unconventional and counter to the norm.

Charisma and Resource Needs Assessment

Charismatic leaders are also very good strategists. They understand the need to perform a realistic assessment of environmental resources and constraints affecting their ability to effect major change within their organization. They are sensitive to both the capabilities and emotional needs of followers, and they understand the resources and constraints of the physical and social environment in which they operate. They are aware of the need to align organizational strategies and capabilities to ensure a successful transformation. This need is low for noncharismatic leaders—fitting with their focus on maintaining the status quo. From the basic concept of charisma, we now turn our attention to the broader concept of charismatic leadership.

Charismatic Leadership

The term *charismatic leadership* has generally been defined in terms of the effects of the leader on followers, or in terms of the relationship between leaders and followers. It is a complex paradigm that has generated a number of theories regarding its nature, causes, and implications for organizational performance. From Weber's early conceptualization of the theory as a distinct style of leadership, contemporary leadership theorists have taken the view that charismatic leadership is a variable—that is, a matter of degree—and have made significant advances in discovering the unique patterns of behavior, psychological motives, and personality traits of leaders that are correlated with varying levels of charismatic effects on followers.[10] Among charismatic leaders of different

WorkApplication2

Think of a leader in our society today who is generally perceived to be a charismatic leader. In your opinion, which of the behavioral components of charisma described in the text can be attributed to him or her?

Charismatic versus Noncharismatic Behavior

Identify which behavior corresponds to either the charismatic or the noncharismatic leader.

a. charismatic behavior   b. noncharismatic behavior

____ 6. Behavior that relies on using unconventional means to transcend the existing order.

____ 7. Accepts the status quo and seeks to maintain it.

____ 8. Modeling the values and beliefs to which you want your followers to subscribe.

____ 9. Behavior that relies on using conventional means to achieve existing goals.

____ 10. Opposes the status quo and seeks to change it.

cultural backgrounds, there are similarities that may be attributable to their intrinsic and universal human desires for autonomy, achievement, and morality.[11] This section will focus on the following topics: the effects of charismatic leadership, characteristics of charismatic leaders, how to develop charismatic qualities in noncharismatic leaders, the notion of charisma as a double-edged sword, and the implications of charismatic leadership on organizational performance.

───────────── Learning Outcome 5 ─────────────

Discuss the effects of charismatic leadership on followers.

The Effects of Charismatic Leadership

An area of interest for many scholars of charisma concerns the uniformity of effects that charismatic leadership achieves across a potentially heterogeneous set of followers. An important distinction of charismatic leadership involves the attributions made by followers about the character of such leaders and their effects. It is argued that such attributions of charisma are either concomitants or early indicators of the onset of other psychological and behavioral outcomes, such as unconditional loyalty, devotion, self-sacrifice, obedience, and commitment to the leader and to the cause the leader represents.[12] The relationship between the charismatic leader and followers is often described as very emotional. This emotional element involves feelings of fulfillment and satisfaction derived from the pursuit of worthwhile activities and goals and from positive beliefs and values about life. Charismatic leaders are seen as generally more positive in their personality than noncharismatic leaders. Research on positiveness as a personality trait has found that people enhance their own feelings of well-being by sharing positive experiences with others and, as a consequence, treat others more positively because they themselves are in a positive mood.[13] Charismatic leaders generally possess this type of positiveness and have the capacity to spread it. When this happens, there is a positive atmosphere that permeates the organization and fuels excitement and energy for the leader's cause. The charismatic leader is seen as an object of identification by followers who try to emulate his or her behavior. Thus, an effect of charismatic leadership is to cause followers to model the leader's behavior, values, self-concept, and cognitions.

Focusing on the effect of charismatic leadership on external support for an organization, some scholars observed that the influence of charismatic appeals and charismatic leadership may indeed make the organization more attractive to outside investors as well as affect the general risk propensities of followers.[14] Followers tend to assume greater risk with charismatic leaders than they would with other types of leaders. They are willing to suffer whatever fate awaits the leader as he or she fights to change the status quo. This was the case with Ghandi and Martin Luther King's followers, as they fought to bring about equality and freedom for all.

Another effect of charismatic leadership on followers is to cause them to set or accept higher goals and have greater confidence in their ability to contribute to the achievement of such goals. By observing the leader display self-confidence, followers develop self-confidence as well.[15] Also, the leader's character has an effect on followers. When the character of the leader is grounded on such core values as integrity, trust, respect, and truth, it influences the leader's vision, ethics, and behavior. The leader is also empowered through his or her character to serve as a mentor. According to some scholars, the effect of the leader's character on followers is more critical than charisma itself. Character, more than charisma, is seen as the basis for leadership excellence.[16]

The relationship between the charismatic leader and the followers is comparable to that of disciples to a master. Though not always the case, followership is not out of fear or monetary inducement, but out of love, passionate devotion, and commitment. Such a strong bond is possible because the charismatic leader is assumed to have the power to effect radical change by virtue of a transcendent vision that is different from the status quo. The strong belief in the vision of the charismatic leader, according to some scholars, is what distinguishes followers of charismatic leaders from those of other types of leaders.[17] Exhibit 9-2 summarizes these effects.

Exhibit 9-2 *Effects of charismatic leadership.*

- Follower trusts in the "rightness" of the leader's vision
- Similarity of follower's beliefs and values to those of the leader
- Heightened sense of self-confidence to contribute to accomplishment of the mission
- Acceptance of higher or challenging goals
- Identification with and emulation of the leader
- Unconditional acceptance of the leader
- Strong affection for the leader
- Emotional involvement of the follower in the mission
- Unquestioning loyalty and obedience to the leader

Source: Based on R. J. House and M. L. Baetx (1979), "Leadership: Some Empirical Generalizations and New Research Directions." In B. M. Staw (ed.), *Research in Organizational Behavior*, vol. 1 (Greenwich, CT: JAI Press, 1979), 399–401.

4. What Effects Has Oprah's Charisma Had on Her Followers?

The effects of charismatic leadership summarized in Exhibit 9-2 are very much applicable to Oprah and her followers. Oprah's followers and supporters seem to have an unquestioning loyalty to her and all that she stands for. There is a strong affection and unconditional acceptance of her, and a willingness to trust in the "rightness" of whatever cause she champions. For example, in a 1997 episode of the *Oprah Winfrey Show,* Oprah encouraged viewers to use their lives to make a difference in the lives of others, which led to the creation of the public charity Oprah's Angel Network in 1998. To date, Oprah's Angel Network has raised nearly $27 million, with 100% of audience donations going to nonprofit organizations across the globe. Oprah's Angel Network has helped establish scholarships and schools, support women's shelters, and build youth centers and homes—changing the future for people all over the world. As John Grace, executive director of Interbrand Group, a New York-based brand consultant, puts it, "Oprah stands for a certain set of very specific American values that very few of her celebrity competitors can claim, like honesty, loyalty, and frankness. It's a value set that is rare in business institutions and celebrities."

Learning Outcome 6

Describe the characteristics that distinguish charismatic from noncharismatic leaders.

Qualities of Charismatic Leaders

A number of studies have identified qualities that differentiate charismatic and noncharismatic leaders, and have described the behaviors that help charismatic leaders achieve remarkable results. These characteristics are attributions by followers based on the behavior of charismatic leaders. These behaviors are not assumed to be present to the same extent in every leader. Attributional theorists have thus used these behaviors as distinguishing characteristics for charismatic and noncharismatic leaders. (Many of these characteristics also apply to transformational leaders because charisma is a key component of transformational leadership, which is the subject of the third major section of this chapter). A study exploring charismatic leadership in the public sector focused on four qualities: (1) energy and determination, (2) vision, (3) challenge and encouragement, and (4) risk taking.[18] Exhibit 9-3 summarizes these qualities, along with other distinguishing characteristics of charismatic leaders, and is followed by an explanation of each. You will realize that many of these characteristics have already been featured throughout the discussion so far. Therefore, the purpose of this section is to bring all the qualities together.

Vision

Charismatic leaders articulate a transcendent vision that becomes the rallying cry of a movement or a cause.[19] Charismatic leaders are future-oriented. They have the ability to articulate an idealized vision of a future that is significantly better than the present. They quickly recognize fundamental discrepancies

Exhibit 9-3 *Qualities of charismatic leaders.*

a. Vision
b. Superb communication skills
c. Self-confidence and moral conviction
d. Ability to inspire trust
e. High risk orientation
f. High energy and action orientation
g. Relational power base
h. Minimum internal conflict
i. Ability to empower others
j. Self-promoting personality

between the status quo and the way things can (or should) be. **Vision** *is the ability to imagine different and better conditions and the ways to achieve them.* A vision uplifts and attracts others. For this to happen, the leader's vision must result from a collaborative effort. Charismatic leaders formulate their vision by synthesizing seemingly disparate issues, values, and problems from many sources of the organization or work unit. They have a compelling picture of the future and are very passionate about it.

Superb Communication Skills

In addition to having a vision, charismatic leaders can communicate complex ideas and goals in clear, compelling ways, so that everyone from the top management level to the bottom level of the organization can understand and identify with their message. Their eloquent, imaginative, and expressive manner heightens followers' emotional levels and inspires them to embrace the leader's vision. Charismatic leaders use their superior rhetorical skills to stir dissatisfaction with the status quo while they build support for their vision of a new future. Fitting examples here include Martin Luther King, Jr.'s "I Have a Dream" speech, Hitler's "Thousand-year Reich," or Gandhi's vision of an India in which Hindus and Muslims live in harmony independent from British rule.

Researchers have identified some of the rhetorical techniques used by charismatic leaders. Charismatic leaders make extensive use of metaphors, analogies, and stories rather than abstract rational discourse to make their points. While metaphors and analogies are inspiring, charismatic leaders are also adept at tailoring their language to particular groups, thereby better engaging them mentally and emotionally. For example, a CEO attempting to inspire vice presidents may use an elevated language style; but that same CEO attempting to inspire first-line employees to keep working hard may speak on a colloquial level. Another significant aspect of the communication style of charismatic leaders is that they make extensive use of anecdotes to get their message across. Communicating through anecdotes tells inspiring stories.

Self-Confidence and Moral Conviction

Charismatic leaders build trust in their followers through unshakable self-confidence, an abiding faith, strong moral conviction, and sacrifice. The importance of self-confidence in everyday interactions is critical, and all the more so for a leader who must convince others to join his or her cause. Studies examining the role and influence of self-confidence on the growth and performance of a leader have found it to be a critical ingredient for success.[20,21] Self-confidence increases one's level of performance. Martin Luther King, Jr.'s "I Have a Dream" speech is an example of how a leader's self-confidence, faith, and strong moral conviction can inspire hope and faith in a better future, and move an entire nation.

Ability to Inspire Trust

Constituents believe so strongly in the integrity of charismatic leaders that they will risk their careers to pursue the leader's visions. Charismatic leaders build support and trust by showing commitment to followers' needs over self-interest, and by being fair. These qualities inspire followers and often result in greater cooperation between a leader and followers.[22] In examining the effects of charisma and procedural fairness on cooperation, one study concluded that both factors engender cooperation because they appeal to relational concerns.[23] Also, a leader's credibility could result from projecting an image of being likable and knowledgeable.

High Risk Orientation

Charismatic leaders earn followers' trust by being willing to incur great personal risk. It is said that charismatic leaders romanticize risk. People admire the courage of those who take high risk. Putting themselves on the line is one way charismatic leaders affirm self-advocacy for their vision and thus gain the admiration and respect of their followers. It has been reported that Martin Luther King, Jr., received death threats against himself and his family almost every day during the civil rights movement. Yet, he persisted with his mission until his assassination. In addition to assuming great risk, charismatic leaders use unconventional strategies to achieve success. Herb Kelleher, former CEO of Southwest Airlines, is a leader who was well known for inspiring employees with his unconventional approach, thus helping to make the airline consistently profitable. Kelleher encouraged employees to break the rules, maintain their individuality, and have fun—a style he called "management by fooling around." It is a style that has made Southwest Airlines' employees the most productive in the industry.

High Energy and Action Orientation

Charismatic leaders are energetic and serve as role models for getting things done on time. They engage their emotions in everyday work life, which makes them energetic, enthusiastic, and attractive to others. Charismatic leaders tend to be emotionally expressive, especially through nonverbal means, such as warm gestures, movement, tone of voice, eye contact, and facial expressions. It is partly through their nonverbal behaviors that charismatic leaders are perceived to have a magnetic personality.

Relational Power Base

A key dimension of charismatic leadership is that it involves a relationship or interaction between the leader and the followers. However, unlike other types of leadership, it is intensely relational and based almost entirely upon referent and expert power (Chapter 4), even when the leader occupies a formal organizational role. Charismatic leadership involves an emotionalized relationship with followers. Followers are often in awe of the leader. There is a powerful identification with and emulation of the leader and an unquestioning acceptance of and affection for the leader.

Minimum Internal Conflict

Typically, charismatic leaders are convinced they are right in their vision and strategies, which explains why they persist and stay the course, even through setbacks. Because of this conviction, they experience less guilt and discomfort in pushing followers to stay the course even when faced with threats.

Ability to Empower Others

Charismatic leaders understand that they cannot make the vision come true alone. They need help and support from their followers. Charismatic leaders empower followers by building their self-efficacy. They do this by assigning followers tasks that lead to successively greater positive experiences and heightened self-confidence, thus persuading followers of their capabilities and creating an environment of positive emotions and heightened excitement. Charismatic leaders also empower followers by role modeling and coaching, providing feedback and encouragement, and persuading followers to take on more responsibilities as their skills and self-confidence grow.

Self-Promoting Personality

Even if no one will take up their cause, charismatic leaders are frequently out promoting themselves and their vision. Richard Branson has relied on self-promotion to help build his empire. Charismatic leaders are not "afraid to blow their own horn."

WorkApplication3

Identify a leader from your past or current employment that you believe is or was a charasmatic leader. Which of the characteristics described in the text did he or she possess? Support your answer.

_____

_____

_____

_____

_____

---

5. In Your Opinion, What Qualities of Charismatic Leadership Does Oprah Possess?

"I am guided by the vision of what I believe this show can be. Originally our goal was to uplift, enlighten, encourage and entertain through the medium of television. Now, our mission statement for 'The Oprah Winfrey Show' is to use television to transform people's lives, to make viewers see themselves differently and to bring happiness and a sense of fulfillment into every home." (Oprah Winfrey).[24] Not only does she have a vision, she is a superb communicator with a strong self-confidence and moral conviction in everything she does. She has inspired and empowered millions of people through her show. She is of high energy and does not shy away from self-promotion. As revealed in the opening case, she is described by those close to her as confident, brilliant, and personable. She is considered a sister by many of her key employees. She is one of the richest women in America; yet, she finds it hard to let all of her success go to her head. Oprah exemplifies all the qualities of charismatic leaders summarized in Exhibit 9-3.

OPENING CASE APPLICATION

Qualities of Charismatic Leaders

Referring to the characteristics listed in Exhibit 9-3, identify each statement by its characteristic using the letters a–j.

_____ 11. We don't need a committee to evaluate the plan. I'm ready to implement it next week. Let's get going before we miss the opportunity.

_____ 12. Last month our department had the highest level of productivity in the organization.

_____ 13. The odds of hitting that high a sales goal are maybe 70 percent. Are you sure you want to set this goal?

_____ 14. Cutting our plant pollution is the right thing to do. I'm sure we can exceed the new EPA standards, not just meet the minimum requirements.

_____ 15. Will you do me a favor and . . . for me, right away?

Applying the Concept 3

─────────────── Learning Outcome 7 ───────────────
Discuss how one can acquire charismatic qualities.

How One Acquires Charismatic Qualities

Given the potential benefits of charismatic leadership, it is reasonable to wonder whether some of the traits, characteristics, and behaviors of charismatic people can be developed or enhanced.

Research Results

While some research supports the possibility of training leaders to be more charismatic, there are those who don't believe that research results are conclusive enough to support such a position. In one laboratory experiment, several actors were coached to display people-oriented, autocratic, or charismatic behaviors as leaders of four-person work groups. In one instance, actors exhibiting charismatic behaviors acted confidently and expressed high confidence in followers, set high performance targets, empowered followers, and empathized with the needs of followers. The results revealed that the four-person work groups of charismatic leaders had higher performance and satisfaction levels than the four-person work groups having an autocratic or task-oriented leader who did not exhibit the same leadership traits. While some researchers have used these findings to argue that it is possible to train leaders to be more charismatic, others think it is still too early to make such a claim. They point out the weaknesses in the study. Since the actors playing leaders in the study were not trained to exhibit both high-task and high-relationship behaviors, it is uncertain whether the followers of charismatic leaders would have higher performance or satisfaction levels than followers of people-oriented or autocratic leaders. However, the very fact that it is possible for actors to exhibit certain charismatic leadership behaviors through training and coaching lends support to the notion that these are trainable behaviors.

Developing Charismatic Qualities

Several of the characteristics of charismatic leaders described in this chapter are capable of enhancement. For example, it is possible through training to enhance communication skills, build self-confidence, and learn techniques to inspire and empower others.[25] Here are suggested strategies for acquiring or enhancing one's charismatic qualities:

- Through practice and self-discipline, you can develop your visionary skills by practicing the act of creating a vision in a college course like this one. This would be a key factor in being perceived as charismatic. The role-play exercise at the end of this chapter is directed at this issue.
- You can practice being candid. Although not insensitive, the charismatic person is typically forthright in giving his or her assessment of a situation, whether the assessment is positive or negative. Charismatic people are direct rather than indirect in their approach, so that there is no ambiguity about their position on issues.
- You can develop a warm, positive, and humanistic attitude toward people rather than a negative, cool, and impersonal attitude. Charisma, as

mentioned earlier, is a relational and emotional concept and ultimately results from the perception of the followers.

- You can develop an enthusiastic, optimistic, and energetic personality. A major behavior pattern of charismatic people is their combination of enthusiasm, optimism, and a high energy level.

—————— Learning Outcome 8 ——————

Explain the difference between socialized and personalized charismatic leaders.

Charisma: A Double-Edged Sword

Most people agree that charisma can be a double-edged sword capable of producing both positive and negative outcomes. It is possible in reading about the personal magnetism, vision, self-confidence, masterful rhetorical skills, and empowering style of charismatic leaders to conclude that they are all good moral leaders that others should emulate. As one observer warns, "it can be foolish, futile and even dangerous to follow leaders just because they are charismatic. Be careful of hero worship.[26] It is important to remind ourselves that not all charismatic leaders are necessarily good leaders. Leaders such as Gandhi, Martin Luther King, Jr., John F. Kennedy, and Winston Churchill exhibited tremendous charisma. So did leaders such as Charles Manson, David Koresh, Adolph Hitler, and the Reverend Jim Jones of the People's Temple. This second group of charismatic leaders represents the dark side of charisma. These leaders and many others like them are prone to extreme narcissism that leads them to promote highly self-serving and grandiose goals.[27,28] Therefore, charisma can cut both ways; it is not always used to benefit others.

One method for differentiating between positive and negative charisma is in terms of the values and personality of the leader. The key question for determining classification is whether the leaders are primarily oriented toward their own needs or the needs of followers and the organization. Valuation theory proposes that two opposing, but complementary basic motives drive an individual's behavior: self-glorification and self-transcendence. The self-glorification motive, based on self-maintenance and self-enhancement, influences one's meaning in life by protecting, maintaining, and aggrandizing one's self-esteem and is consistent with negative or destructive charisma. On the other hand, the self-transcendence motive, based on collective interest, provides meaning through supportive relationships with others and is consistent with altruistic and empowering orientations of positive or constructive charisma.[29]

Based on this notion of positive and negative charisma, two types of charismatic leaders are identified—the socialized or positive charismatic leader and the personalized or negative charismatic leader.[30] *The* socialized charismatic leader (SCL) *is one who possesses an egalitarian, self-transcendent, and empowering personality. The* personalized charismatic leader (PCL) *is one who possesses a dominant, Machiavellian, and narcissistic personality.* Thus, SCLs pursue organization-driven goals and promote feelings of empowerment, personal growth, and equal participation in followers, whereas PCLs pursue leader-driven goals and promote feelings of obedience, dependency, and submission in followers. In the former, rewards are used to reinforce behavior that

WorkApplication4

Identify a leader you have worked with or currently work with who you think has charismatic potential. Describe one trait or characteristic of this individual that, if developed, can transform him or her into an effective charismatic leader.

is consistent with the vision and mission of the organization; in the latter, rewards and punishment are used to manipulate and control followers, and information is restricted and used to preserve the image of leader infallibility or to exaggerate external threats to the organization.[31]

Researchers acknowledge that all charismatic leaders intentionally seek to instill commitment to their ideological goals and, either consciously or unconsciously, seek follower devotion and dependency. Negative charismatic leaders emphasize devotion to themselves more than to ideals. Decisions of these leaders are often self-serving. Group accomplishments are used for self-glorification. In terms of affect, negative charismatic leaders emphasize personal identification rather than internalization. Personal identification is leader-centered while internalization is follower-centered. Ideological appeals are only a ploy to gain power, after which the ideology is ignored or arbitrarily changed to serve the leader's self-interest. In contrast, positive charismatic leaders seek to instill devotion to ideology more than devotion to self. In terms of affect, they emphasize internalization rather than personal identification. Therefore, outcomes of their leadership are more likely to be beneficial to followers and society.

WorkApplication5

Describe a leader in your work experience that mainfested positive or negative charismatic qualities. How did this affect your relationship with the leader?

Ethical Dilemma 1

Obesity and Charismatic Ads

The federal government has reported that obesity might overtake tobacco as the leading cause of death in the United States.[32] Some social activists are blaming part of the obesity problem on marketing junk food to kids,[33] and food makers and ad agencies are defending advertising to children.[34] Some companies use charismatic star performers and athletes to promote their junk food products to get people to eat more. At the same time, American health officials are trying to persuade people to lose weight. The government has taken out public service ads to convince people to get in shape and eat right. Part of the ads' success depends on whether people take personal responsibility for their own health and weight.[35]

1. What is the reason for the increase in obesity in the U.S.? Are junk food ads using charismatic stars to promote their products contributing to the obesity problem?
2. Is it ethical for junk food sellers to use charismatic stars to promote their products?
3. Is it ethical and socially responsible for the government to try to get people to lose weight, through ads and other methods?

Despite the contributions by charismatic theorists to the field of leadership, charisma is not without its limitations. Charismatic leadership theories emphasize the role of an individual leader who takes the initiative for developing and articulating a vision to followers. In this "heroic leadership stereotype," the leader is omnipotent and followers are submissive to the leader's will and demands.[36] However, it is more likely the case that in times of crisis (such as an organization facing significant external challenges or serious internal weaknesses), greater success comes from a shared strategic leadership approach than a lone star individualistic approach. Most of the descriptive literature on effective leaders suggests that charisma in its individualized form may be inadequate to achieve major changes in an organization's performance. In fact, positive organizational change is usually the result of transformational leadership by individuals not perceived as charismatic. Thus, charismatic theories that emphasize "lone star" leadership by extraordinary individuals may be most appropriate for describing a visionary entrepreneur who establishes a new organization. Examples include Richard Branson of the Virgin Group, Stephen Case of America Online, and Jeff Bezos of Amazon.com, and the exceptional "turnaround manager" Al Dunlap, former CEO of Sunbeam Corporation. Lone star leadership is not a panacea for the problems of every organization. The second half of this chapter focuses on transformational leadership.

---

6. Does Oprah Embody the Example of a Socialized Charismatic Leader or a Personalized Charismatic Leader?

Oprah's philanthropic activities and the way she conducts herself would suggest that she is more of a socialized than a personalized charismatic leader. As explained above, the socialized charismatic leader is driven by a self-transcendence motive. The self-transcendence motive focuses on collective interest, provides meaning through supportive relationships with others, and is consistent with altruistic and empowering orientations of positive or constructive charisma. The Oprah Winfrey Foundation was established to support the inspiration, empowerment, education, and well-being of women, children, and families around the world. Through this private charity, Oprah has directly served the needs of low-opportunity people and has awarded hundreds of grants to organizations that carry out this vision. She has contributed millions of dollars towards providing a better education for underserved students who have merit but no means. She created the "Oprah Winfrey Scholars Program," which gives scholarships to students determined to use their education to give back to their communities in the United States and abroad.

OPENING CASE APPLICATION

Transformational Leadership

Transformational leadership focuses on a leader's transforming abilities, rather than on personal characteristics and follower relations. Transformational leaders are known for moving and changing things "in a big way," by communicating to followers a special vision of the future, tapping into followers' higher ideals and motives. They seek to alter the existing structure and influence people to buy into a new vision and new possibilities.[37] As was the case with charismatic leaders, followers trust, admire, and respect the transformational leader. There is a collective "buy in" to the organizational vision put forth by the leader and, as such, followers willingly expend exceptional effort in achieving organizational goals.[38] Therefore, traits associated with transformational leadership include charisma, intellectual stimulation, inspiration, and individual consideration.[39]

As organizations continue to face global challenges, the need for leaders who can successfully craft and implement bold strategies that will transform or align the organization's strengths and weaknesses with emerging opportunities and threats is ever greater. Transformational leadership is about change. It describes a process of positive influence that changes and transforms individuals, organizations, and communities. Transformational leaders influence their constituencies to make the shift from focus on self-interests to a focus on collective interests. They understand the importance of trust building as a means to creating a high commitment to mission-driven outcomes. Effective transformational leaders use their charisma and power to inspire and motivate followers to trust and follow their example. They generate excitement and energy by focusing on the future.[40] Research studies have consistently revealed that transformational leadership is positively related to work outcomes. Transformational leadership has been found to be positively related to organizational commitment and job satisfaction.[41] We will examine the similarities and differences among charismatic, transactional, and transformational leadership, transformational leader behaviors and attributes, and the transformation process.

--- Learning Outcome 9 ---

Distinguish between charismatic and transformational leadership.

Charismatic versus Transformational Leadership

Some authors make no distinction between the charismatic and the transformational leader, preferring to combine them into one theory. They refer to the two theories as charismatic because charisma is a central concept in both of them, either explicitly or implicitly. Others have conceptualized charisma as one of several attributes that may define the transformational leader.[42] The other attributes include honesty, optimism, communication skills, confidence, and consideration.[43] It adds another dimension of behavior traits of the leader. Charisma is seen as just one of a collection of attributes that may explain transformational leadership behavior. Yet, charisma is relational in nature. It is not something found solely in the leader as a psychological phenomenon, nor is it totally situationally determined. Instead, charisma manifests itself in the interplay between the leader (his or her traits and behaviors) and the follower (his or her values, needs, perceptions, and beliefs). There is general agreement that charismatic leaders by nature are transformational, but not all transformational leaders achieve their transforming results through the charismatic effects of their personalities. According to this viewpoint, some transformational leaders lacking in charisma may still be able to influence and inspire others by meeting the emotional needs of their followers through individualized consideration, and/or they may intellectually stimulate their followers through rationalizing the need for change, insight into possible solutions, and the passion to bring about resolution.

From a power and moral leadership perspective, charismatic and transformational leadership support and reinforce each other.[44] A leader like

Nelson Mandela has been described as charismatic and transformational. Mandela is known to live by the tenets of consultation, persuasion, and cohabitation, and shuns coercion and domination.

Transformational leadership *serves to change the status quo by articulating to followers the problems in the current system and a compelling vision of what a new organization could be.* Transformational leaders, therefore, seek to transform or change the basic values, beliefs, and attitudes of followers so that they are willing to perform beyond the minimum levels specified by the organization. Transformational leaders are similar to charismatic leaders in that they can articulate a compelling vision of the future, and influence followers by arousing strong emotions in support of the vision. This vision and the leader-follower relationship must be in line with followers' value systems in order to bridge between the followers' needs and those of the organization.

The transformational leader cultivates follower acceptance of the work group mission. The transformational manager-follower relationship is one of mutual stimulation, and is characterized by four factors: (1) charisma, (2) inspiration, (3) individual consideration, and (4) intellectual stimulation.[45, 46] As discussed earlier, charisma is a fundamental factor in the transformational process. Charismatic leaders possess the ability to develop great symbolic power with which the followers want to identify. Followers idealize such a leader and often develop a strong emotional attachment. A factor very much associated with charisma is inspiration. Transformational leaders tend to be inspirational individuals as well. Inspiration describes how the leader passionately communicates a future idealistic goal or situation that is a much better alternative to the status quo and can be shared. The transformational leader employs visionary explanations to depict what the workgroup can accomplish. Excited followers are then motivated to achieve organizational objectives. Individual consideration is a factor that reveals the mentoring role often assumed by transformational leaders. The leader serves as a mentor to followers. He or she treats followers as individuals and uses a developmental orientation that responds to follower needs and concerns. Finally, intellectual stimulation describes the transformational leader's creative and out-of-the-box thinking style. He or she encourages followers to approach old and familiar problems in new ways. By stimulating novel employee thinking patterns, the leader inspires followers to question their own beliefs and learn to solve problems creatively by themselves.[47]

Transformational leaders can emerge from different levels of the organization. Therefore, an organization may have many transformational leaders. In contrast, charismatic leaders are few in number. Charismatic leaders are most likely to emerge in the throes of a crisis, when an organization is in turmoil because of conflicting value and belief systems. The response by people to a charismatic or transformational leader is often highly polarized, because those with the most to lose by abandoning the old system will put up the most resistance to any change initiative. Additionally, it would appear that the emotional levels of resistance toward charismatic leaders are more extreme than those toward transformational leaders. This may be the underlying cause for the untimely, violent deaths of some charismatic leaders (such as Malcolm X, Martin Luther King, Jr., John F. Kennedy, and Mahatma Gandhi). Both charismatic and transformational leadership always involve conflict and change, and both types of leaders must be willing to embrace conflict, create enemies, make unusual allowances for self-sacrifice, and be extraordinarily focused in order to achieve and institutionalize their vision.

Transformational Leader Behaviors and Attributes

Although much remains to be learned about transformational leadership, there is enough consensus from the many years of research to suggest that there are common behaviors associated with transformational leaders. Like charismatic leaders, effective transformational leadership requires an ability to initiate change and challenge the status quo, recognize opportunities for the organization as well as for others, take risks, and encourage others to do the same. Transformational leadership requires an ability to effectively inspire a shared vision. Such leaders rally others around a common dream and are adept at envisioning the future and enlisting others in seeing and moving toward the vision. They must be able to model the way—that is, set the example of commitment to shared vision and values.[48,49]

Transformational leaders understand that in order to get followers to fully contribute to the transformation process, they have to empower them and offer support in getting things done, encourage creativity, challenge followers to rethink old ways of doing things and to re-examine old assumptions, foster collaboration, motivate, and reinforce positive behavior, (such as recognizing and acknowledging the accomplishments of others, and celebrating small wins).[50] Nelson Mandela led the change that is depolarizing a nation racially polarized for decades. Mandela's transformational leadership humanized apartheid South Africa and led to the emergence of a nation deserving of global recognition. His charismatic effect softened the hardest stances of the haves and have-nots and aligned them in pursuit of a constructive common cause.

Relating the effects of transformational leadership on empowerment and team effectiveness, the findings of one study suggest that transformational leadership contributes to the prediction of subordinates' self-reported empowerment. This outcome led to the study's conclusion that the more a team's members experience team empowerment, the more effective the team will be.[51] From this discussion, we can summarize the key behaviors of transformational leaders, as shown in Exhibit 9-4.

It should be noted that some of these behaviors have received broad conceptual support among researchers while others have only been partially supported. For example, creating and articulating a vision has been identified by virtually every study on the subject as an important component of the transformational leadership process. Also, facilitating acceptance for team goals and modeling appropriate behavior have been identified by a majority of studies as key elements of transformational leadership. From these behaviors, researchers surmise that effective transformational leaders

- See themselves as change agents
- Are visionaries who have a high level of trust for their intuition
- Are risk-takers, but not reckless
- Are capable of articulating a set of core values that tend to guide their own behavior
- Possess exceptional cognitive skills and believe in careful deliberation before taking action
- Believe in people and show sensitivity to their needs
- Are flexible and open to learning from experience

Exhibit 9-4 *Transformational leader behaviors.*

Behavioral Components	Description
Creation and articulation of vision	Leader behavior that is directed at finding new opportunities for the organization; formulating, articulating, and inspiring followers with the vision of a better future.
Role modeling	Setting an example for followers that is consistent with the organizational values and expectations.
Fostering a "buy in" of team goals	Behavior aimed at encouraging and building teamwork among followers and commitment to shared goals.
High performance expectations	Behavior that conveys the leader's expectations for everyday excellence and superior performance on the part of followers.
Personalized leader-member exchange	Behavior that indicates that the leader trusts, respects, and has confidence in each follower, and is concerned about their personal needs, not just organizational needs.
Empowerment	Behavior on the part of the leader that challenges followers to think "outside of the box" and re-examine old ways and methods.

Source: Based on P. M. Podsakoff, S. B. Mackenzie, R. H. Moorman, and R. Fetter, "Transformational Leader Behaviors and Their Effects on Followers' Trust in Leader, Satisfaction, and Organizational Citizenship Behavior," *Leadership Quarterly* 1(2) (1990): 107–142.

7. Is Oprah a Transformational Leader?

A cursory review of the creation and evolution of the *Oprah Winfrey Show* and Harpo Productions is enough to conclude that Oprah is definitely a transformational leader. In 1986, Oprah formed her own production company, Harpo Productions, to bring quality entertainment projects into production. Two years later, television history was made when Harpo Productions announced that it had assumed ownership and all production responsibilities for the *Oprah Winfrey Show* from Capitol Cities/ABC, making Oprah Winfrey the first woman in history to own and produce her own talk show. Today, Harpo is well on its way to becoming a formidable force in film and television production. That growth has meant financial success. Oprah's Harpo Entertainment Group, the corporate umbrella over her film and TV production operations, is privately held and executives do not publicly talk about its finances. However, published reports say Oprah is well on her way to becoming the first African-American billionaire, with an estimated worth of $675 million, according to *Forbes* magazine. Oprah's venture into magazine publishing is another example that she has the ability to start and transform any venture she embarks upon. In April 2000, Oprah and Hearst Magazines introduced O, *The Oprah Magazine,* a monthly magazine that has become one of today's leading women's lifestyle publications. It is credited as being the most successful magazine launch in recent history and currently

OPENING CASE APPLICATION

has an audience of over two million readers each month. O, *The Oprah Magazine,* is another medium through which Oprah connects with her audience and provides possibilities for transforming their lives. In April 2002, Oprah launched the first international edition of O, *The Oprah Magazine,* in South Africa.

Learning Outcome 10

Explain the difference between transformational and transactional leadership.

Transformational versus Transactional Leadership

Begin this section by completing Self-Assessment 1 to determine if you are more of a transactional or transformational leader.

One approach to determining effective leadership is how managers and employees influence one another. It is a well-known fact that managers can and do behave differently in similar organizations and in similar jobs.[52] One explanation for the variance has been found to be the leadership type, whether the leader is transformational or transactional. Leaders rated as transformational were described as influential, inspirational, and charismatic, whereas leaders

---

Self-Assessment 1

Are You More of a Transactional or Transformational Leader?

Complete the following questions based on how you will act (or have acted) in a typical work or school situation. Use the following scale:

$$1 \quad — \quad 2 \quad — \quad 3 \quad — \quad 4 \quad — \quad 5$$
Disagree   *Agree*

____ 1. I enjoy change and see myself as a change agent.

____ 2. I am better at inspiring employees toward a new future than motivating them to perform their current jobs.

____ 3. I have/had a vision of how an organization can change for the better.

____ 4. I see myself as someone who is comfortable encouraging people to express ideas and opinions that differ from my own.

____ 5. I enjoy taking risks, but am not reckless.

____ 6. I enjoy spending time developing new solutions to old problems rather than implementing existing solutions.

____ 7. I deliberate carefully before acting; I'm not impulsive.

____ 8. I like to support change initiatives, even when the idea may not work.

____ 9. I learn from my experience; I don't repeat the same mistakes.

____ 10. I believe the effort to change something for the better should be rewarded, even if the final outcome is disappointing.

Add up the numbers on lines 1–10 and place your total score here _____ and on the continuum below.

$$10 \quad — \quad 20 \quad — \quad 30 \quad — \quad 40 \quad — \quad 50$$
Transactional leader   *Transformational leader*

The higher the score, generally, the more you exhibit transformational leader qualities. However, transformational leaders also perform transactional behaviors. It is also generally easier to be transformational at higher levels of management than at lower levels.

rated as transactional were described as task- and reward-oriented, structured, and passive.[53] James McGregor Burns developed one of the early comparisons of transactional and transformational leadership. Using Weber's seminal work on charismatic leaders as his base, Burns proposed that by engaging followers' higher-level needs, transformational leaders convince followers to substitute self-interest pursuits with societal-interest pursuits for the greater good, and that as they do so, they become leaders themselves. Contrasting such leaders with the transactional types, Burns indicated that the latter influence followers by transactions of exchange in which rewards such as pay, promotions, or status are exchanged for work. Extending this body of knowledge, Bernard Bass argued that contrary to Burns's assertion that transformational and transactional leadership are at opposite ends of a single continuum of leadership, the two approaches are actually independent and complimentary. Bass maintains that transactional leadership revolves around the leader-follower exchange, in which the leader rewards the follower for specific behaviors and performance that meets with the leader's expectations, and punishes or criticizes behavior or performance that does not meet expectations. As such, transactional leadership is also referred to as contingent reward leadership.[54] Such exchanges, according to Bass, cater to the self-interest of followers. Some scholars have referred to transactional leaders as managers.[55–58]

As defined earlier, transformational leadership serves to change the status quo by articulating to followers the problems in the current system and a compelling vision of what a new organization could be. **Transactional leadership** *seeks to maintain stability within an organization through regular economic and social exchanges that achieve specific goals for both the leaders and their followers*. The transactional leader enters into specific contractual arrangements with followers. In exchange for meeting specified objectives or performing certain duties, the leader provides benefits that satisfy followers' needs and desires. An example of transactional leadership occurs when managers give monthly bonuses to salespeople for meeting and exceeding their monthly sales quotas, or to production people for exceeding quality standards. These exchanges involve specific goods that are tangible, not the intangible incentives (such as the mere satisfaction with being part of an inspiring vision, shared values, or emotional bonding) associated with transformational leadership exchanges.

Transactional leadership is conceptually similar to the cultural maintenance form of leadership, which acts to strengthen existing structures, strategies, and culture in an organization. Some scholars have proposed that transactional leadership consist of three dimensions—contingent reward, management by exception, and passive leadership. Depending on a leader's personality traits, each dimension represents an option that can be employed to shape strategies and structures, reward subordinates' efforts and commitment, and take corrective action to address mistakes and deviations from expectations; all efforts aim at achieving established organizational performance goals.[59]

Transactional leadership tends to be transitory, in that once a transaction is completed the relationship between the parties may end or be redefined. Transformational leadership is more enduring, especially when the change process is well designed and implemented. Transactional leaders promote stability, while transformational leaders create significant change in both followers and organizations. Transformational leadership inspires followers to go beyond their own self-interest for the good of the group. Transactional leadership seeks to satisfy followers' individual needs as a reward for completing a given transaction.[60]

Looking at the role of transformational and transactional leadership in creating, sharing, and exploiting organizational knowledge, other writers have argued that managing knowledge effectively can provide firms with sustainable competitive advantages. The process of managing knowledge involves three processes—creating, sharing, and exploiting knowledge. Leaders play a critical role in each of these processes. A study of these relationships concluded that transformational leadership may be more effective in creating and sharing knowledge at the individual and group levels, while transactional leadership is more effective at exploiting knowledge at the organizational level.[61]

In another such test comparing transformational, transactional, and laissez-faire leadership styles between women and men, it was found that female leaders were more transformational than male leaders, and also engaged in more of the contingent reward behaviors that are a component of transactional leadership. Male leaders were generally more likely to manifest the other aspects of transactional leadership (active and passive management by exception) and laissez-faire leadership.[62]

Despite these differences, it is worth mentioning that effective leaders exhibit both transactional and transformational leadership skills in appropriate situations. Along these lines, one study proposed that a manager's perceptions of organizational context and personality variables would influence or constrain his or her utilization of transformational and transactional leadership behaviors.[63,64] A meta-analytic test of the relative validity of transformational and transactional leadership styles revealed that both are valid approaches for achieving organizational objectives,[65] with transformational leadership showing the highest overall relations and transactional or contingent reward leadership a close second.[66]

WorkApplication6

Identify your present or past manager as being more transformational or transactional. Explain why and include examples.

_____

_____

_____

_____

_____

— Learning Outcome 11 —

Explain the four phases of the transformation process.

Applying the Concept 4

Transformational or Transactional Leadership

Identify each statement as being more characteristic of one or the other style:

a. transformational leadership   b. transactional leadership

_____ 16. We don't need a committee to work on a plan. Let's get going on this now.

_____ 17. I'd say we have a 75 percent chance of being successful with the new product. Let's market it.

_____ 18. The present inventory system is working fine. Let's not mess with success.

_____ 19. That is a good idea, but we have no money in the budget to implement it.

_____ 20. We need to monitor the demographics to make sure our products satisfy our customers.

The Transformation Process

Transformational leaders are usually brought into an organization that is experiencing a crisis or approaching total collapse, to institute turnaround strategies that can rescue the organization. This often involves fundamental changes in followers' actions, thoughts, and work ethic to bring about profound and positive outcomes. There is some agreement among scholars and practitioners that certain transformational leadership practices are necessary for successful transformation. Key questions often used to highlight such practices include the transformational leader's ability to (1) challenge the status quo and make a convincing case for change, (2) inspire a shared vision for the future, (3) provide effective leadership during the transition, and (4) make the change a permanent and institutionalized part of the organization. From this discussion, a four-stage process of transformation, focused on these questions, can be developed. Exhibit 9-5 lists these four stages, with suggested activities to ensure effective and efficient execution of each stage.

Learning Outcome 12

Explain the basis of stewardship and servant leadership.

Exhibit 9-5 *The transformation process.*

Stages	Suggested Activities
1. Make a compelling case for change	_ Increase sensitivity to environmental changes and threats.
	_ Initiate change and challenge the status quo.
	_ Search for opportunities and take risks.
2. Inspire a shared vision	_ Encourage everyone to think of a new and brighter future.
	_ Involve others in seeing and moving toward the vision.
	_ Express new vision in ideological, not just economic, terms.
3. Lead the transition	_ Instill in managers a sense of urgency for the change.
	_ Empower, support, foster collaboration, and strengthen followers.
	_ Help followers understand need for change.
	_ Increase followers' self-confidence and optimism.
	_ Avoid the temptation of a "quick fix."
	_ Recognize and deal openly with emotional component of resisting change.
4. Implant the change	_ Enable and strengthen followers with a "greatness attitude." For example, recognize and celebrate accomplishments.
	_ Help followers find self-fulfillment with new vision.
	_ Help followers look beyond self-interests to collective interests.
	_ Change reward systems and appraisal procedures.
	_ Implement team-building interventions and personnel changes.
	_ Appoint a special task force to monitor progress.
	_ Encourage top leaders and managers to model the way.

Source: Based on Carolyn Hines and William Hines Jr., "Seminar on the Essence of Transformational Leadership (Leadership Training Institute)," *Nation's Cities Weekly* 25(9) (March 4, 2002): 8 (1).

Ethical Dilemma 2

Transforming Music and Movies

Transformational leaders at Grokster, StreamCast Networks, and Sharman Networks (Kazaa) have changed the way millions of people globally listen to music and watch movies, through file sharing. The music and movie industries claim copyright law violations and have tried to stop file sharing. Music companies claim that sharing music has led to multiyear declines in global music sales, and they have even taken people to court to collect damages. However, a lower court ruling that was upheld by a federal appeals court, in San Francisco, stated that online trading of movies and music allows creators of Internet file-sharing software to stay in operation, despite piracy by users of their programs. The ruling stated that providing file-sharing software that allows individuals to trade music, movies, and other digital content is not a violation of copyright law. Music and movie companies are fighting the ruling.[67]

1. When music and movies are downloaded, the artists/actors and companies don't get any money. Is it ethical for people to download music and movies without paying for them?
2. Would artists/actors tend to believe it's unethical while others don't?
3. Is it ethical for Grokster and other companies to provide file-sharing software so that people can get free music and movies?

Stewardship and Servant Leadership

Stewardship and servant leadership are related to charismatic and transformational leadership, in that they focus on empowering followers, not leaders, to exercise leadership in accomplishing the organization's goals.[68] Traditional leadership theory emphasized the leader-follower structure in which the follower accepted responsibility from the leader and was accountable to the leader. However, the contemporary view of leadership views the leader as a steward and servant of the people and the organization. Leadership is less about directing or controlling and more about focusing on helping followers do their jobs, rather than having followers help the managers do their jobs. One study suggested that servant leadership leads to a spiritual generative culture while transformational leadership leads to an empowered dynamic culture.[69]

Therefore, stewardship and servant leadership represent a shift in the leadership paradigm toward followers. This shift represents the views of those who believe that leadership has less to do with directing other people and more to do with serving other people. Stewardship and servant leadership are about placing others ahead of oneself, and are viewed as a model for successful leadership in any field or profession. In this section, we discuss the nature and importance of stewardship and servant leadership, and the framework for establishing both.

The Nature of Stewardship and Servant Leadership

Stewardship *is an employee-focused form of leadership that empowers followers to make decisions and have control over their jobs.* **Servant leadership** *is* *leadership that transcends self-interest to serve the needs of others, by helping them grow professionally and personally.* Both leadership styles emphasize patience, kindness, humility, respectfulness, honesty, and commitment. Stewardship and servant leadership describe leaders who lead from positions of authority, not power, and are very follower-centered. Though some may view these two concepts of leadership as synonymous and use the terms interchangeably, there do exist subtle yet significant differences between the two concepts. While both shine the spotlight on those who actually perform the day-to-day tasks of producing goods and services for an organization's customers, servant leadership takes stewardship assumptions about leaders and followers one step further. Servant leadership calls for the highest level of selflessness—a level that some doubt exists in the real world. At the core of servant leadership is self-sacrificing love of others without regard to what one might receive in return. The leader makes a conscious decision to hold followers in high regard. Servant leadership is described as an act of will and intellect, not of the fickleness of fleeting emotions. The leader is driven to serve, not to be served.[70,71] This is similar to qualities of charismatic leaders such as Gandhi. We should not forget, however, that servant leadership is about the leader being a servant, not a slave to others.

Framework for Stewardship

Leadership thinking based on stewardship prescribes a relationship between leaders and followers in which leaders lead without dominating or controlling followers. Leaders who embody the stewardship concept are sincerely concerned about their followers and assist them to grow, develop, and achieve both personal and organizational goals. An effective steward leader creates an environment in which everyone works together as a team to achieve organizational goals.[72] Stewardship is more about facilitating than actively leading. We suggest four key values that describe stewardship; see Exhibit 9-6.

Strong Teamwork Orientation

Stewardship works best in situations where self-managed teams of core employees and the leader work together to formulate goals and strategies for a changing environment and marketplace. Here, the leader's role is less dominant and more supportive of the process. Where a strong team spirit is absent, a leader must play a dominant role to push individuals in the right direction. However, this defeats the purpose of stewardship.

Decentralized Decision Making and Power

Stewardship is realized when authority and decision making are decentralized and brought down to where work gets done and employees interact with

Exhibit 9-6 *Values of stewardship.*

customers. In this environment, stewardship has a great chance to succeed, given the empowered status of employees and the closer relationship between managers and followers. The absence of this principle makes stewardship inoperable.

Equality Assumption

Stewardship works best when there is perceived equality between leaders and followers. It is a partnership of equals rather than a leader-follower command structure. The applicability of stewardship is enhanced as leaders find opportunities to serve rather than manage. Honesty, respect, and mutual trust prevail when there is equality, and these are values that enhance the success of stewardship.

Reward Assumption

Stewardship puts greater responsibility in the hands of employees. Therefore, to realize successful stewardship, the organization must redesign the compensation system to match rewards to actual performance. Employees with more responsibility and authority who are compensated accordingly flourish under stewardship because they are motivated and committed to the organization's mission. Without this value, it is hard to sustain stewardship.

Stewardship leaders are not known for their great deeds but for empowering others to achieve great deeds. Stewardship leaders offer the best chance for organizations to succeed and grow in today's dynamic environment, because these leaders don't just lead, they coach (Chapter 6) followers to do the leading. This focus on people is what encourages followers to be more creative, energetic, and committed to their jobs.[73]

Framework for Servant Leadership

Servant leaders approach leadership from a strong moral standpoint. The servant leader operates from the viewpoint that we all have a moral duty to one another.[74] Servant leadership emphasizes fairness and justice as means for achieving productive organizational citizenship behavior.[75] The servant leader sees leadership as an opportunity to serve at the ground level, not to lead from the top.[76] An individual like Mother Teresa—through her humble and ordinary nature, strong moral values, and dedicated service to the poor and the afflicted—inspired hundreds of followers to join her order and emulate her example. The framework for servant leadership consists of the following basic guidelines,[77-79] as shown in Exhibit 9-7.

Exhibit 9-7 *Guidelines of servant leadership.*

Service to others over self-interest

Earning and keeping others' trust

Servant Leadership

Effective listening

Helping others discover their inner spirit

Source: Based on R. K. Greenleaf, *Servant Leadership: A Journey into the Nature of Legitimate Power and Greatness* (Mahwah, NJ: Paulist Press, 1977), 7.

Helping Others Discover Their Inner Spirit

The servant leader's role is to help followers discover the strength of their inner spirit and their potential to make a difference. This requires servant leaders to be empathetic to the circumstances of others. Servant leaders are not afraid to show their vulnerabilities.

Earning and Keeping Others' Trust

Servant leaders earn followers' trust by being honest and true to their word. They don't have any hidden agendas, and they are willing to give up power, rewards, recognition, and control.

Service Over Self-Interest

The hallmark of servant leadership is the desire to help others, rather than the desire to attain power and control over others. Doing what's right for others takes precedence over protecting one's position. Such leaders make decisions to further the good of the group rather than their own interests.

Effective Listening

Servant leaders do not impose their will on the group; rather, they listen carefully to the problems others are facing and then engage the group to find the best course of action. Servant leaders are more likely to express confidence and commitment in others than other types of leaders.

Leaders like Ghandi, Martin Luther King, Jr., and Nelson Mandela possess both charismatic and servant leader qualities. They have all been described as leaders who put others' interests over self-interests, earned and kept the trust of followers, listened carefully to others' problems and concerns, and inspired followers to belief in their own inner strength and spirit. The discussion in this chapter has emphasized leadership approaches (charismatic, transformational, stewardship, and servant leadership) that operate under the premise that change is inevitable and not every leader is capable of managing it successfully. Thus, we have identified the different leadership theories that equip leaders to deal with change effectively. Self-Assessment 2 provides the opportunity to link these leadership approaches to one personality type.

WorkApplication7

Explain how your present/past leader did, or did not, use stewardship and servant leadership.

_____

_____

_____

_____

_____

Self-Assessment 2

Personality and Charismatic and Transformational Leadership

Charismatic leaders have charisma based on personality and other personal traits that cut across all of the Big Five personality types. Review the 10 qualities of charismatic leaders in Exhibit 9-3. Which traits do you have?

_____

_____

If you have a high surgency Big Five personality style and a high need for power, you need to focus on

using socialized, rather than personalized, charismatic leadership.

Transformational leaders tend to be charismatic as well. In Self-Assessment 1 you determined if you were more transformational or transactional. How does your personality affect your transformational and transactional leadership styles?

_____

_____

Go to the Internet (academic.cengage.com/management/lussier) where you will find a broad array of resources to help maximize your learning.

- Review the vocabulary
- Try a quiz
- View chapter videos

Chapter Summary

This chapter summary is organized to answer the 13 learning outcomes for Chapter 9.

1. Describe personal meaning and how it influences attributions of charismatic qualities.

Personal meaning is defined as the degree to which people's lives make emotional sense and to which the demands confronted by them are perceived as being worthy of energy and commitment. It provides a sense of purpose for one's life. Personal meaning influences attributions of charismatic qualities in that, first, a leader's personal meaning influences his or her behavior. In turn, the leader's behavior is reflected in the formulation and articulation of his or her vision. Second, the leader's behavior garners attributions of charisma from followers.

2. Briefly explain Max Weber's conceptualization of charisma.

Weber used the term *charisma* to explain a form of influence based on follower perceptions that the leader is endowed with the gift of divine inspiration, not a traditional or legal mandate of authority. This gift of divine inspiration is the force behind a charismatic leader's ability to focus society's attention on both the crisis it faces and the leader's vision for a new and better future. According to Weber, charismatic individuals emerge as leaders during times of great social crisis and inspire people to do more than they would under normal circumstances.

3. Explain the locus of charismatic leadership.

The question scholars have entertained since Weber's conception of charisma is whether charisma is a function of the prevailing social climate, the leader's extraordinary qualities, or an interaction between the two. Supporters of the view that charismatic leadership could not take place unless the society were in a tumultuous, unstable situation argue that without a crisis and followers' need for change, a leader's charismatic qualities would be hard to notice or appreciate. Therefore, the locus of charismatic leadership is the status of the society. Opponents argue that charismatic leadership is primarily the result of leader attributes, not the situation. They argue that without strong leader characteristics (such as vision, exceptional communication skills, trustworthiness, self-confidence,

and focus on empowering others), leaders like Martin Luther King, Jr., or Gandhi would never have emerged as leaders of their respective followers, regardless of the situation. Finally, there is an emerging view that charismatic leadership is a convergence of follower perceptions and reactions influenced by leader characteristics and the prevailing social situation.

4. Describe the four behavioral components of charisma.

The attribution of charisma to leaders is believed to depend on four behavior variables:

- *The discrepancy between the status quo and the vision advocated by the leader.* The charismatic leader strives to widen the gap between the status quo and the idealized vision or future he is advocating. The greater the discrepancy between the status quo and the new vision, the more likely that followers will align their interest with that of the charismatic leader.
- *The leader's articulation and role modeling of the vision.* Effective articulation of the vision is measured in terms of what is said (content and context) and how it is said (oratorical skills). Effective communication skills are an imperative in the successful articulation of a compelling vision and maintenance of a leadership role. Through verbal and nonverbal means, charismatic leaders communicate their self-confidence, convictions, and dedication in order to give credibility to what they advocate.
- *The use of unconventional strategies for achieving desired change.* The charismatic leader's expertise lies in using unconventional means to transcend the existing order. Follower perceptions of the leader's revolutionary and unconventional qualities evoke sentiments of adoration, especially when the leader's activities exemplify acts of heroism involving personal risk and self-sacrificing behavior. Thus, the behavior of the noncharismatic leader is conventional and conforming to existing norms while that of the charismatic leader is unconventional and counter to the norm.
- *A realistic assessment of resource needs and other constraints for achieving desired change.* Charismatic

leaders are also very good strategists. They understand the need to perform a realistic assessment of environmental resources and constraints affecting their ability to effect major change within their organization. They are sensitive to the capabilities and emotional needs of followers, and they understand the resources and constraints of the physical and social environment in which they operate. There is a high need to align organizational strategies and capabilities to ensure a successful transformation.

5. Discuss the effects of charismatic leadership on followers.

Charismatic leaders tend to have a strong emotional bond with their followers. The effects of such a bond are that followers are inspired enthusiastically to give unconditional loyalty, devotion, obedience, and commitment to the leader and to the cause the leader represents. There is a sense of fulfillment and satisfaction derived from the pursuit of worthwhile activities and goals and having positive beliefs and values about life as presented by the charismatic leader. Implicitly, the charismatic leader is seen as an object of identification by which a follower emulates his or her behavior; thus, followers model their behavior, values, and cognitions after the leader. For example, followers are more likely to set or accept higher goals and have greater confidence in their ability to contribute to the achievement of such goals. By observing the leader display self-confidence, followers develop self-confidence as well.

6. Describe the characteristics that distinguish charismatic from noncharismatic leaders.

Charismatic leaders have a compelling vision of the future and are very passionate about it, while noncharismatic leaders are satisfied with the status quo and want to maintain it. The charismatic leader is gifted at communicating ideas and goals in very inspiring ways so that everyone can identify with the message. The charismatic leader is self-confident and has a strong moral conviction in his or her cause and the ability to inspire trust among followers and to empower them to achieve organizational goals. The charismatic leader possesses a high risk orientation, high energy and action orientation, minimum internal conflict, and a self-promoting personality. The charismatic leader's power base is intensely relational and based almost entirely on his or her referent and/or expert power.

7. Describe how one can acquire charismatic qualities.

There are suggested strategies for acquiring or enhancing charismatic qualities. Through training and education, people can enhance their communication skills and learn techniques of crafting visionary statements, and how to empower followers. Through practice and self-discipline, an individual can build his or her self-confidence and develop a personality profile that is warm, positive, enthusiastic, and optimistic.

8. Explain the difference between socialized and personalized charismatic leaders.

The charismatic leader seeks to achieve the unconditional commitment and devotion of followers to his or her ideological goals. However, negative charismatic leaders emphasize devotion to themselves more than to ideals, and positive charismatic leaders seek the opposite. It is against this backdrop that negative charismatics are said to have a personalized power orientation and positive charismatics have a socialized power orientation. In the former, ideological appeals are only a ploy to gain power and manipulate and control followers. In the latter, ideological appeals are organization-driven and seek to empower followers to achieve the vision and mission of the organization. Personalized charismatic leaders seek self-glorification, and socialized charismatic leaders seek organizational transformation through empowerment of followers.

9. Distinguish between charismatic and transformational leadership.

Both charismatic and transformational leaders can convey a vision and form strong emotional bonds with followers, but not all charismatic leaders can motivate followers to transcend self-interest for the benefit of a higher ideal or societal need. On the other hand, transformational leaders take charismatic leadership one step further in that they, more often than not, can articulate a compelling vision of the future and also influence followers to transcend self-interest for the benefit of society. The vision and values of transformational leaders are more in line with the values and needs of followers. It is on this basis that some have argued that all transformational leaders are charismatic but not all charismatic leaders are transformational. Also, while charisma is in the eye of the beholder, transformational leaders have a more consistent definition.

10. Explain the difference between transformational and transactional leadership.

Transactional leadership tends to be transitory, in that once a transaction is completed, the relationship between the parties may end or be redefined. Transformational leadership is more enduring, especially when the change process is well designed and implemented. Transactional leaders promote stability, while transformational leaders create significant change in both followers and organizations. Transformational leadership inspires followers to go beyond their own self-interest for the good of the group. Transactional leadership seeks to satisfy followers' individual needs as a reward for completing a given transaction.

11. Explain the four phases of the transformation process.

A transformational leader who is brought into an organization facing a serious crisis or approaching total collapse has to institute a turnaround strategy. Turnaround strategies are often radical transformations that put the organization on a different path for future growth and prosperity. The magnitude of the task and the high risk of failure require that it be approached in a systematic fashion. Thus, the transformation process is a four-phase approach that starts with the recognition of the need for change. This provides the opportunity for the leader to formulate and introduce a new vision for the organization that promises a better and brighter future than the present. Once there is acceptance of the leader's vision, the third phase involves implementing the new vision and effectively managing the transition. Here, instilling in managers a sense of urgency for change, raising followers' self-confidence and optimism, and recognizing and dealing with resistance will greatly increase the chances of a successful transformation. The last phase is institutionalizing the change so that it is not a short-lived transformation. Effective strategies for institutionalizing change are outlined in the text.

12. Explain the basis of stewardship and servant leadership.
The basis of stewardship and servant leadership is serving rather than directing other people. It is leadership based on placing others ahead of oneself. Both shine the spotlight on the employees who actually perform the day-to-day task of meeting organizational goals and objectives. The key to successful stewardship is the presence of four supporting values: equal treatment for all, reward for work, teamwork attitude, and decentralized decision making and authority. The key to successful servant leadership is based on four guiding principles as well: service to others over self-interest, trust, effective listening, and empowering others to discover their inner strength.

13. Define the following key terms (in order of appearance in the chapter):
Select one or more methods: (1) fill in the missing key terms from memory, (2) match the key terms from the following list with their definition below, (3) copy the key terms in order from the list at the beginning of the chapter.
_____ is the degree to which people's lives make emotional sense and to which the demands confronted by them are perceived as being worthy of energy and commitment.
_____ represents knowing who you are based on your lifespan experiences, motivation states, and action orientation.

_____ is that which allows an individual's accomplishments to "live on" in the ideals, actions, and creations of one's followers long after his or her death.
_____ is unselfish regard for, or devotion to, the welfare of others.
_____ concerns an individual's awareness of connections between human and supernatural phenomenon that provides faith explanations of past and present experiences and, for some, predicts future experiences.
_____ are stable and enduring beliefs about what an individual considers to be important.
_____ is a distinct social relationship between the leader and follower, in which the leader presents a revolutionary idea, a transcendent image or ideal that goes beyond the immediate or the reasonable; while the follower accepts the course of action not because of its rational likelihood of success, but because of an effective belief in the extraordinary qualities of the leader.
_____ is the ability to imagine different and better conditions and the ways to achieve them.
_____ is defined as one who possesses an egalitarian, self-transcendent, and empowering personality.
_____ is defined as one who possesses a dominant, Machiavellian, and narcissistic personality.
_____ serves to change the status quo by articulating to followers the problems in the current system and a compelling vision of what the new organization could be.
_____ seeks to maintain stability within an organization through regular economic and social exchanges that achieve specific goals for both the leaders and their followers.
_____ is an employee-focused form of leadership that empowers followers to make decisions and have control over their jobs.
_____ is leadership that transcends self-interest to serve the needs of others, by helping them grow professionally and personally.

Key Terms

charisma, 364

legacy, 360

personal meaning, 359

personalized charismatic leader (PCL), 375

self-belief, 360

selflessness, 360

servant leadership, 386

socialized charismatic leader (SCL), 375

spirituality, 361

stewardship, 386

transactional leadership, 383

transformational leadership, 379

values, 361

vision, 371

Review and Discussion Questions

1. Describe the leading characteristics of charismatic leaders.
2. Martin Luther King, Jr., Gandhi, John F. Kennedy, Adolph Hitler, Nelson Mandela, David Koresh (of the Branch Davidians), Herb Kelleher (of Southwest Airlines), and Richard Branson (of the Virgin Group) are/were charismatic leaders. Can you associate with each name a characteristic (see Exhibit 9-3) of charisma you think best describes the individual? Note: If you are not familiar with these individuals, do library or Internet research on them before attempting an answer.
3. Why is the theory of charisma described as a double-edged sword?
4. Describe the various sources from which one can draw his or her personal meaning.
5. One of the four behavioral variables of charisma is vision articulation and role-modeling behavior of the leader. Describe the four recommended steps to effective vision articulation mentioned in the text.
6. Citing specific examples, explain how charismatic leaders of the past used vision and superb communication skills to make their case.
7. Describe the limitations of charismatic leadership theory.
8. Describe five key behaviors characteristic of transformational leaders.
9. Describe some key attributes of transformational leaders.
10. What is servant leadership?

Case

WILLIAM PEREZ REPLACES PHIL KNIGHT AS CEO OF NIKE, INC.

On December 28, 2004, Nike, Inc., announced the appointment of William D. Perez as President, Chief Executive Officer, and Director of the company. Mr. Perez will succeed Nike cofounder, Chairman, and Chief Executive Officer Philip H. Knight, who will continue as Chairman of the Board of Directors. Mr. Knight, who is 66 years old, cofounded Nike in 1972 with legendary University of Oregon track coach Bill Bowerman. From its fledgling years when Mr. Knight sold track shoes from the trunk of his car, Nike has grown to a $12.3 billion revenue company in fiscal 2004, employing 24,000 people worldwide and selling its products in nearly 200 countries.

Born of Spanish parents in Akron, Ohio, and raised in Colombia, South America, Mr. Perez became the highest Hispanic corporate executive among Fortune 100 companies. A longtime avid runner, Perez has participated in 11 marathons and has worn only Nike shoes for the past 27 years. His acceptance of an offer at the end of last year to become president and CEO of Nike, Inc. seems like a perfect fit.

Speaking on behalf of the board, Mr. Knight said, "This begins an exciting new chapter in Nike's ongoing business evolution. Bill is a highly regarded and deeply talented leader with more than 30 years experience as a builder of global brands and businesses. Bill has a demonstrated commitment to consumers, new product innovation and development, growth, team building and talent development. He also knows how to operate a highly socially responsible global business, all of which make him the right person to lead Nike, Inc." Perez brings organizational skills to the highly creative Nike environment. "This may be a case of: 'How do you bring process to creativity?'" said Scott Bedbury, who ran Nike's worldwide advertising from 1987 to 1994.

Before Nike, Mr. Perez served as president and chief executive officer for SC Johnson & Son, Inc., based in Racine, Wisconsin. He's a 34-year veteran of this privately owned company—whose products include Glade air fresheners, Drano, Pledge, Raid, Windex, and Ziploc. The family-controlled company, like Nike, is also known for social responsibility. "He's got a great success record and comes from a culture that fits with ours," Knight said in a phone interview. "He will fit more easily with this company than any other person I met." During his 34-year career with SC Johnson, Mr. Perez managed country, regional, and worldwide operations and multiple brands of the highly respected, multibillion-dollar global consumer products company. Under his leadership, SC Johnson was recognized for its environmental and community investment leadership and progressive workplace programs.

Reflecting on his appointment, Mr. Perez said, "I am thrilled and honored to run Nike. I was drawn to this company because the Nike brand perpetually stays current, making it one of the best managed on the globe. You can feel the innovative spirit that Phil and his team inspires from product design, to retail to athlete partnerships. And I'm a strong believer in Just Do It. I look forward to working with a terrific team of people and helping build a future that will drive greater value for our shareowners, employees, consumers and communities."

About his personal beliefs and values, Mr. Perez has a firm conviction that governments, school systems, and even parents alone, cannot address the issues faced by today's youth. His sense is that in order for real progress to be made, everybody has to try to make a difference. It was in that spirit that he founded the Racine Youth Leadership Academy, in Racine, Wisconsin, in 1994. The program targets African-American boys between 3rd and 8th grades, offering them after-school tutorials, Saturday leadership development programs, and summer athletics. There are 38 young men in the program today and one of the first graduates is attending Carthage College on a full scholarship that is the ultimate reward for children in the program. His hope is that in his own small way, he has made a difference in the lives of a number of young men and that they will become productive members of society with a true sense of fulfillment.

GO TO THE INTERNET: To learn more about Nike, log on to InfoTrac® College Edition at **academic.cengage.com/ infotrac** and use the advanced search function.

Support your answers to the following questions with specific information from the case, or information you get from the Web or other sources.

1. In your opinion, are Phil Knight and William Perez leaders who exemplify charismatic or transformational leadership qualities?
2. What transformational leadership qualities did Mr. Perez possess that made him an attractive candidate for Nike's top job?
3. A key attribute of servant leadership is that it transcends self-interest to serve the needs of others. Does William Perez fit this bill?
4. Describe Mr. Perez's vision for Nike.
5. Every leader has a sense of their personal meaning, described in the text as the degree to which people's lives make emotional sense and to which the demands confronted by them are perceived as being worthy of energy and commitment. Based on the facts of the case, what are the sources from which William Perez derives his personal meaning?

Cumulative Case Questions

6. According to the leadership continuum model of Tannenbaum and Schmidt (Chapter 5), where would you put William Perez based on the facts of the case?
7. Communication is a major competency for leaders (Chapter 6). Would you agree that this is a quality Mr. Perez possesses, to have been as effective as he has been so far?
8. There are four stages of evolution in the dyadic approach (Chapter 7) to explaining leader-follower relationships. Which of the four stages is attributable to Perez's leadership approach at SC Johnson & Son and now Nike?
9. One of the characteristics of effective teams (Chapter 8) is the presence of a capable and competent team leader. Chapter 8 describes different activities of the team leader in creating an effective team (see Exhibit 8-1), including turning obstacles into opportunities. Would you describe Mr. Perez as an effective team leader?

Case Exercise and Role-Play

Preparation: Assume you are part of the leadership of an organization or organizational unit that is in need of redirection in a changing market environment. Your task is to formulate a new vision and mission statement that would transform your organization.

Role-Play: The instructor forms students into small groups to develop an inspiring vision of no more than 15 words and a mission statement of no more than 100 words. Here are some guidelines:

1. Identify key environmental trends or changes that have influenced your group's vision.
2. Make up a list of core values that your organization holds, or you would want it to have, and incorporate these in your mission statement.
3. Share your vision and mission statement with other members of the class and vote on who has the most inspiring and compelling vision and mission.

Video Case

Le Meridien Hotel: Leadership in the New Workplace

Le Meridien is a chain of over 130 luxury hotels in 56 countries around the globe. The hotel is famous for offering a unique European experience to its more than 100,000 visitors each year, and Le Meridien's reputation for service has made it one of the leading hotel brands in the world.

View the Video (16 minutes)
View the video on Le Meridien Hotel in class or at **academic. cengage.com/management/lussier.**

Read the Case
Le Meridien is part of the new workplace, using a management paradigm that stresses employee empowerment, teamwork, and collaboration. Managers at Le Meridien are responsible

for managing various functional teams and overseeing a multinational staff. The climate of diversity at Le Meridien requires that managers understand the strengths and weaknesses of various personality types, and recognize how different personality characteristics affect behavior within the organization.

Bob van den Oord, assistant general manager at Le Meridien, is a meticulous, detailed, and personable leader, and is famous for his "management by walkabout" style—a daily routine of monitoring all the major hotel operations and staff by literally walking through the entire hotel. In addition to those daily encounters with employees throughout the hotel, van den Oord holds daily and weekly meetings at which managers may discuss their schedule of events and duties while receiving important feedback.

People skills are vitally important in the hotel industry, not only in dealing with staff, but with guests as well. On any given day, Bob van den Oord and his employees may welcome honeymooners, international tourists, business travelers, convention groups, and holiday revelers. Since providing customer service is the backbone of the hotel industry, leadership's effectiveness in dealing with all kinds of people is crucial to Le Meridien's success.

Answer the Questions

1. Choose one of the managers or team leaders spotlighted in the video and identify traits that make that person an effective leader for Le Meridien.
2. Is Bob van den Oord a charismatic leader? Explain your answer.

Skill-Development Exercise 1

IS THE PRESIDENT OF THE UNITED STATES A CHARISMATIC LEADER?

Preparing for Skill-Development Exercise 1

Rate the current president of the United States on each of the 10 characteristics of charismatic leaders. For each characteristic, rate the president as high (H), medium (M), or low (L). Be sure to provide a specific example (what the president did or said) for why you rate the president as H, M, or L for each characteristic.

a. Vision
b. Superb communication skills
c. Self-confidence and moral conviction
d. Ability to inspire trust
e. High risk orientation
f. High energy and action orientation
g. Relational power base
h. Minimum internal conflict
i. Ability to empower others
j. Self-promoting

Based on the text, what specific things do you recommend the president do or say to improve his charismatic leadership?

_____

_____

_____

Doing Skill-Development Exercise 1 in Class

Objective

To develop your ability to assess and advise a leader on charismatic leadership.

Procedure (10–30 minutes)

Option A: As a class, go over the preparation and rate the president as high, medium, or low on each charismatic leadership characteristic, and give an overall rating.

Option B: Break into groups of 4 to 6, go over the preparation, and rate the president as high, medium, or low on each charismatic leadership characteristic, giving an overall rating. Be sure to provide a specific example (what the president did or said) for why your group rated the president as H, M, or L for each characteristic.

Option C: Same as B, but also select a spokesperson to present the group's answers to the entire class.

Conclusion

The instructor may make concluding remarks.

Apply It (2–4 minutes)

What did I learn from this experience? How will I use this knowledge in the future?

_____

_____

_____

Leadership of Culture and Diversity, and the Learning Organization

After studying this chapter, you should be able to:

1. Explain the power of culture in the strategy execution process. p. 399
2. Distinguish between a weak and a strong culture. p. 401
3. Describe the characteristics of low- and high-performance cultures. p. 403
4. Distinguish between symbolic and substantive leadership actions for shaping organizational culture. p. 409
5. Differentiate between the four cultural value types. p. 415
6. Describe the framework for understanding global cultural value differences. p. 423
7. Explain the primary reasons for embracing diversity. p. 430
8. Identify the three areas in which visible and strong leadership action is needed to achieve full diversity. p. 432
9. Explain the leader's role in creating a culture that supports diversity. p. 434
10. Describe the role of leadership in creating a learning organization. p. 443
11. Define the following **key terms** (in order of appearance in the chapter):

culture	high power-distance culture
cooperative culture	low power-distance culture
adaptive culture	masculinity
competitive culture	femininity
bureaucratic culture	demographic diversity
values	diversity
ombudsperson	prejudice
whistle blowing	ethnocentrism
individualism	glass ceiling
collectivism	discontinuous change
high uncertainty avoidance	learning organization
low uncertainty avoidance	organizational knowledge

Opening Case Application

Andrea Jung has been CEO of Avon Company since November 1999. The oldest child of Chinese immigrants, Jung grew up speaking both English and Mandarin Chinese. Ten years ago, Avon, the world's largest direct seller of women's cosmetics, was experiencing some difficulties. Increasing sales in a market saturated with beauty products and savvy consumers was proving to be a daunting task even for a giant of Avon's stature. In 1993, the year before Jung came aboard, the company's U.S. sales dipped by 1% even though sales in all other world markets increased, especially in Asia. Ms. Jung hit the ground running. She gave the company what can only be described as "an extreme makeover," pouring millions into research and development, launching new lines of skin cream, expanding into overseas markets, and developing snazzy ads with celebrities like Salma Hayek. She expanded the number of products offered to longtime customers by introducing a line of lingerie and casual wear. This generated new revenue from an established consumer base. "We were the first to come out with an alpha hydroxide acid product," she says as she explains the need to constantly be on the lookout for new products. These new products have paid off. For the full year 2004, Avon reported that earnings per share increased 27% to US$1.77 per share, versus US$1.39 per share in 2003. Sales rose 13% in 2004 to a record US$7.66 billion, with sales of beauty products growing by 17%, skin care up 20%, fragrance up 13%, color cosmetics up 14%, and personal care up 24%. Avon has also increased its appeal to the younger generation with a new line called "mark," which is expected to bring in $100 million in sales in its first year of business.

Avon embraces diversity in the workforce and continues to be a leader in taking affirmative action to ensure that doors are opened to talented individuals, and that all associates and employees have opportunities for development and advancement. Avon also strives to create a work environment that values and encourages the uniqueness of each individual, and is committed to creating a culture that supports associates as they balance their many, and sometimes competing, work and personal responsibilities. Ms. Jung has definitely transformed Avon and, in the process, some believe she has given herself a career makeover, with her name cropping up on shortlists of candidates to turn around bigger companies.

Opening Case Questions:

1. Is Avon's culture a contributing factor to their success? Explain.
2. The text points out that an organization's culture serves two important functions: (1) it creates internal unity, and (2) it helps the organization adapt to the external environment. Has this been the case at Avon?
3. What role has Andrea Jung played in fostering a climate of strict ethical standards at Avon?
4. What is Avon's stance on diversity, and has it lived up to it so far?
5. The text discusses the distinction between the "traditional" and the "learning" organization. In your opinion, what type of organization is Avon?

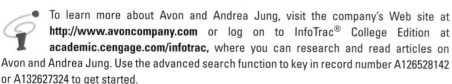 To learn more about Avon and Andrea Jung, visit the company's Web site at **http://www.avoncompany.com** or log on to InfoTrac® College Edition at **academic.cengage.com/infotrac,** where you can research and read articles on Avon and Andrea Jung. Use the advanced search function to key in record number A126528142 or A132627324 to get started.

In this chapter we examine issues of organizational culture, values, and diversity—and the leader's role in shaping them. The final section of the chapter explores elements of organizational design that support efficient operations, comparing them with a new organizational form that emphasizes creativity and innovation. This new organizational form is called the *learning organization.*

Creating a High-Performance Culture

A prevailing belief among researchers is that strong corporate cultures improve performance by facilitating internal behavioral consistency.[1] Regardless of the type of business or the size, the organizations that consistently achieve above-average growth and profits share a common characteristic. High-performance organizations have an unmistakable profile that sets them apart from average performers—a profile that includes distinctive characteristics of the corporate culture, the people, the structure, and the management systems. Increasingly, culture is recognized as a source of competitive advantage.[2] Over the years researchers have proposed a positive relationship between culture strength and performance. Various attempts to test this proposition have found support for the hypothesis.[3] There is a consensus that organizations with rich, healthy cultures perform better than those with less-defined cultures.[4]

Culture *is the aggregate of beliefs, attitudes, values, assumptions, and ways of doing things that is shared by members of an organization and taught to new members.*[5] Every organization has a unique culture, distinguished by its own beliefs and philosophy, and approaches to problems and decision making. An organization's culture is manifested in the values and principles that leaders preach and practice, in its employees' attitudes and behavior, in ethical standards and policies, in the "chemistry" that permeates its work environment, and in the stories people repeat about events in the organization.[6] An organization's position on diversity and multiculturalism can be attributed to its culture, because cultural products include the values and beliefs shared by members of an organization. Within an organization, culture gives meaning to each individual's membership in the workplace and, in so doing, defines the organization's essential being. An organization's culture is fairly enduring and can be described as warm, friendly, aggressive, open, innovative, conservative, liberal, harsh, likable, and so on.[7]

OPENING CASE APPLICATION

1. Is Avon's Culture a Contributing Factor to Their Success? Explain.

It is evident in the opening case that organizational culture at Avon is a significant contributing factor to the company's success. Avon enjoys a proud legacy and commitment to women. By the very nature of its products and customer base, Avon has always had a special connection to women. Through the Avon Foundation, the company has created and significantly funded a number of global initiatives to further women's empowerment. Its philanthropic endeavors and diversity initiatives have received worldwide praise and recognition. The health issues that Avon has chosen to champion are the same issues that many of its customers and direct sales representatives care about, and thus a strong bond has developed between the company and its primary stakeholders. The culture of the organization is encapsulated in what it calls "The Five Values of Avon," which are trust, respect, integrity, belief, and humility. According to the company's management, these five values have served as a continuing source of strength throughout Avon's proud history and will remain at the heart of who they are as a company.

An organization's culture determines the way that it responds to problems of survival in its external and internal environments.[8] The responses to problems in the external environment are reflected in the organization's vision, mission, objectives, core strategies, and ways of measuring success in attaining objectives. The responses to internal problems underscore key aspects of the internal culture, such as revealing how power and status are determined in the organization, the criteria and procedure for allocating resources, the criteria for determining membership, and the guiding principles for interpreting and responding to unpredictable and uncontrollable forces in the external environment. The values and practices that derive from these processes serve as the basis for role expectations that guide behavior, become embedded in how the organization conducts its business, are shared by managers and employees, and then persist as new employees are encouraged to embrace them. As solutions are developed through experience, they become shared values that are passed to new members. Over time, values may become so deeply rooted in a culture that organizational members are no longer consciously aware of them. These basic underlying values (whatever they are) become the essence of the culture. Many components of culture are associated with statements, values, philosophies, or policies articulated by a founder or other pioneering leaders. These principles are often incorporated in the leader's vision, mission statement, and the organization's strategy. An example of this would be Sam Walton's conception of Wal-Mart's culture from its early beginnings. The essence of Wal-Mart's culture is dedication to customer satisfaction, zealous pursuit of low costs, and strong work ethic. In addition to that are the ritualistic Saturday morning executive meetings at headquarters to exchange ideas and review problems, and company executives' commitment to visit stores, talk to customers, and solicit suggestions from employees. Creating a high-performance culture such as Wal-Mart's is critical to organizational success.

In this section, we will examine the power of culture, weak versus strong cultures, characteristics of low- and high-performance cultures, leadership actions for shaping culture, and different types of organizational cultures.

--- Learning Outcome 1 ---

Explain the power of culture in the strategy execution process.

The Power of Culture

When an organization's culture fits the needs of its external environment and strategy, employees usually find it easy to implement the strategy successfully.[9] A culture grounded in values, practices, and behavioral norms that match the requirements for good strategy implementation helps energize people to do their jobs in an effective and efficient manner. One study describes these requirements as happiness, significance, achievement, and legacy; maintaining that performance and business ethics problems can be alleviated by ensuring that an organization's culture addresses these four issues.[10] For example, a strategy of product innovation and technological leadership will thrive in a culture where creativity, innovation, embracing change, risk taking, and challenging the status quo are popular themes. When an organization's culture is not aligned with its strategy, it creates a strategy-culture gap that must be closed by either changing the strategy to fit the culture or changing the culture to fit the strategy. The narrower the strategy-culture gap, the more successful the organization's employees can be in implementing strategy. It is all too common for a company's top leaders to play up the importance of staying innovative and creating new products in order to remain competitive, while in the same organization the culture is very antagonistic towards those who seek to be creative and innovative. Such an organization is filled with unhappy employees who feel confused, frustrated, and unmotivated. There is no satisfaction in the feeling that one is contributing to the organization's overall success and future survival. Therefore, a deeply rooted culture that is well matched to strategy is a strong recipe for successful strategy execution; however, a deeply rooted culture can also become an obstacle to successful strategy execution. In this context, culture serves two important functions in organizations: (1) it creates internal unity, and (2) it helps the organization adapt to the external environment.[11]

Internal Unity

Organizational culture defines a normative order that serves as a source of consistent behavior within the organization. To the extent that culture provides organizational members with a way of making sense of their daily lives and establishes guidelines and rules for how to behave, it is a social control mechanism. A supportive culture provides a system of informal rules and peer pressures, which can be very powerful in determining behavior, thus affecting organizational performance. A strong culture provides a value system in which to operate; and it promotes strong employee identification with the organization's vision, mission, goals, and strategy. Culturally approved behavior thrives and is rewarded, while culturally disapproved behavior is discouraged and even punished. The right culture makes employees feel genuinely better about their jobs, work environment, and the mission of the organization; employees are self-motivated to take on the challenge of realizing the organization's objectives and to work together as a team.[12]

External Adaptation

Culture determines how the organization responds to changes in its external environment. The appropriate cultural values can ensure that an organization responds quickly to rapidly changing customer needs or the offensive actions of a competitor. For example, if the competitive environment requires a strategy of superior customer service, the organizational culture should encourage such principles as listening to customers, empowering employees to make decisions, and rewarding employees for outstanding customer service deeds. The power of culture is in its potential to bring employees together, and create a team rather than a collection of isolated individuals. However, to ensure long-term survival and profitability, the organization's culture should also encourage adaptation to the external environment. In recent years, the airline industry has witnessed increased emphasis on the creation of a culture that fosters the effective implementation of a strong marketing orientation. This heightened interest stems from the knowledge that sound customer-focused marketing practices provide an important source of competitive advantage in the service sector, which is characterized by high levels of interaction between companies and their customers. This move to a marketing culture has strong support from those who maintain that a strong marketing culture leads to customer satisfaction and retention, which, in turn, yields higher profitability.[13]

---

2. The Text Points Out That an Organization's Culture Serves Two Important Functions: (1) It Creates Internal Unity, and (2) It Helps the Organization Adapt to the External Environment. Has This Been the Case at Avon?

Avon's employee-centered culture is what helps to guide and sustain its employees' productive behavior. Its emphasis on social responsibility, participation, and empowerment appeals very well to Avon's employees. Avon strives to create a work environment that values and encourages the uniqueness of each individual, and is committed to creating a culture that supports associates as they balance their many, and sometimes competing, work and personal responsibilities. The culture of Avon is certainly a factor in explaining the strong bond or internal unity that exists among company employees and also between sales representatives and their customers. In terms of the culture facilitating external adaptation, Andrea Jung can be credited with directing the successful transformation of Avon Company by defining its vision as the company for women. She is revitalizing Avon's reputation as the world's foremost direct seller of beauty products while leading the company into exciting new lines of business, launching a series of bold and image-enhancing initiatives, and expanding career opportunities for women around the world. She expanded the number of products offered to long-time customers by introducing a line of lingerie and casual wear, proving that she was not afraid to take risk. This generated new revenue from an established consumer base. "We were the first to come out with an alpha hydroxide acid product," she says, as she explains the need to constantly be on the lookout for new products. There is no doubt that Andrea Jung has created for Avon a culture that encourages internal unity and external adaptation.

OPENING CASE APPLICATION

Despite the importance of culture to strategy execution, not every organization can boast a strong culture. Strong cultures are a contributing factor to attaining a competitive advantage, and a weak culture does the reverse. Therefore, understanding the factors that distinguish between strong and weak cultures is critical to the culture creation process.

Learning Outcome 2

Distinguish between a weak and a strong culture.

Weak versus Strong Culture

There is a growing body of literature that documents the economic benefits of investing in a performance-oriented organizational culture that focuses, to a large extent, on values and leadership.[14] Organizational cultures vary widely in the extent to which they are woven into the fabric of the organization's practices and behavioral norms. The strength of any culture depends on the degree to which a set of norms and values are widely shared and strongly held throughout the organization. A weak culture symbolizes a lack of agreement on key values and norms, and a strong culture symbolizes widespread consensus, with leadership playing a key role in both situations.[15]

Weak Culture

An organization's culture is weak when there is little agreement on the values, beliefs, and norms governing member behavior. In other words, members have not thought deeply enough about what matters to them. This could be because the leader has not articulated a clear vision for the organization, or because members have not bought into the leader's vision for the organization. Without knowledge of what the organization stands for or allegiance to any common vision, weak cultures work against or hinder strategy implementation. Members of the organization typically show no deeply felt sense of identity with the organization's vision, mission, long-term objectives, and strategy. In such organizations, culture has no meaning to the employees and managers. In a weak culture, things like gossiping, manipulation, favoritism, lack of communication, and intense internal competition prevail. Some scholars call this the at-risk culture, and recommend that organizations closely examine their culture to assess its current state and identify areas or segments within it that do not share the same values and norms, in order to reduce the risk.[16] Such a self-assessment and accompanying modifications can help turn a weak culture into a strong culture.

Strong Culture

A strong culture is good for the bottom line of an organization.[17] A research study found that firms identified in 1982 as having strong cultures achieved stock returns nearly double that of the S&P 500 Index between 1982 and 1998. An organization's culture is considered strong and cohesive when it conducts its business according to a clear and explicit set of principles and values. In this culture, management commits considerable time to communicating these principles and values and explaining how they relate to its mission and strategies. Also, these values are shared widely across the organization from top management to rank-and-file employees alike. A strong culture has a bias for action. There is a desire to get things done, and more importantly, do them the right way. The right way involves the core values and principles that everyone adheres to. Managers teach and live the values they espouse. For example, promising autonomy while discouraging such efforts is lip service that is not characteristic of a strong culture. An example is cited of an organization that was so dedicated to its values that it terminated managers "who performed well but who did not live according to the culture—people who tried to get ahead at the expense of others"[18]

In an attempt to quantify and measure culture, one study proposed a model that focused on workplace behaviors and language as manifestations of workplace culture. The model measured four fundamental business culture traits: company mission, involvement, adaptability, and consistency. Results revealed that the best performing companies were strong in all four measured areas.[19] This is consistent with generally accepted precepts for strong-culture organizations—that they typically feature public displays of mission/creeds/values statements that highlight involvement, adaptability, and consistency as the standards for the organization's behavior. Also, employees are urged to use these values and principles as the basis for decision making and other actions taken throughout the organization. In strong cultures, values and behavioral norms are so deeply ingrained that they do not change much even when a new leader takes over.

Factors that contribute significantly to strong cultures include (1) a strong leader or founder who develops principles, practices, and behavioral norms that are aligned with customer needs, strategic requirements, and competitive conditions; (2) total organizational commitment to operating the business according to these established traditions; and (3) unwavering commitment and support from the organization's key stakeholders—employees, customers, and shareholders.[20] A case study describes how a 75-year-old family business achieved powerful results from developing a strong culture. Basing its actions on the principles of trust, respect, employee development, opportunity, and communication, the company set out to develop a strong culture that would enhance the work environment, reduce turnover, improve safety, facilitate union relationships, and provide employees with a wide range of activities and benefits. As a result, staff turnover fell from about 50 percent to only 2 percent.[21] A strong work culture makes for happy employees and helps retention.

A strong culture is a valuable ally when it matches the requirements of a good strategy execution and a formidable enemy when it doesn't. While a shared set of values and beliefs does help in bringing a group of workers together, it could stifle creative impulses and enforce conformist thinking.[22] Therefore, a strong culture by itself is not a guarantee of success unless it also encourages adaptation to a new strategy and the external environment. An example is the extent to which an organization's culture supports or hinders its adaptation to new technology. A strong culture that does not encourage adaptation can be more destructive to an organization than having a weak culture. IBM's strong bureaucratic and mainframe culture clashed with the shift to a PC-dominated world. Apple's culture clash stemmed from strong company sentiment to continue with the internally developed Macintosh technology despite growing preferences for Windows and Intel-compatible equipment and software.

WorkApplication1

Describe the culture where you work or have worked. Is it weak or strong? Explain your answer.

_____

_____

_____

_____

_____

─────────── Learning Outcome 3 ───────────

Describe the characteristics of low- and high-performance cultures.

Characteristics of Low-Performance Cultures

Weak cultures are more likely to be associated with low performance. Low-performance cultures have a number of unhealthy characteristics that can

Strong or Weak Culture

Identify each statement by its culture, writing the appropriate letter in the blank before each item.

a. weak   b. strong

____ 1. I think we spend too much time in meetings hearing about our mission.

____ 2. One thing I like about this place is that I can say and do whatever I want, and no one says anything about my behavior.

____ 3. I think every department in the company has a copy of the mission statement on the wall somewhere.

____ 4. I know that Jean Claude started the company, but he died 10 years ago. Do I have to keep hearing all these stories about him?

____ 5. I find it a bit frustrating because top management seems to change its mind about our priorities whenever it suits them.

undermine an organization's attempt to achieve its objectives. Exhibit 10-1 lists these characteristics.

Insular Thinking

In a low-performance culture, there is a tendency to avoid looking outside the organization for superior practices and approaches. Sometimes a company's past successes and status as an industry leader may lead to complacency. People within these organizations believe they have all the answers. Managerial arrogance and inward thinking often prevents the organization from making the necessary cultural adaptation as external conditions change, thus leading to a decline in company performance. Enron is a company that exemplifies this characteristic. Up until the news media broke open the Enron case, it was a company wowing Wall Street with its growth and steady earnings gains. What many people did not know until it was too late was that the corporate culture at Enron contained the seeds of its demise, a culture of misstated earnings, highly questionable bookkeeping practices, and persistent effort to keep investors and employees in the dark.[23] It was clearly a culture that promoted and supported insular thinking, with senior management being isolated from those at operational levels, individuals pursuing subgoals that were contrary to overall corporate goals, information flow restricted along a narrow linear channel that effectively foreclosed adverse information from getting to senior management, and a corporate culture of intimidation that discouraged open expression of doubt or skepticism.[24]

Exhibit 10-1 *Characteristics of low-performance cultures.*

- Insular thinking
- Resistance to change
- Politicized internal environment
- Unhealthy promotion practices

Resistance to Change

A second characteristic of low-performance cultures is one that can plague companies suddenly confronted with fast-changing domestic and global business conditions: resistance to change. The lack of leadership in encouraging and supporting employees with initiative or new ideas destroys creativity.

Low-performance cultures want to maintain the status quo; as a result, avoiding risk and not making mistakes becomes more important to a person's career advancement than entrepreneurial successes and innovative accomplishments. Companies such as Ford, General Motors, Kmart, Sears, and Xerox enjoyed considerable success in years past. But when their business environments underwent significant change, they were burdened by a stifling bureaucracy and an inward-thinking mentality that rejected change. Today, these companies and many others like them are struggling to reinvent themselves and rediscover what caused them to succeed in the first place.

Politicized Internal Environment

An environment that allows influential managers to operate their units autonomously—like personal kingdoms—is more likely to resist needed change. In a politically charged culture, many issues or problems get resolved along the lines of power. Vocal support or opposition by powerful executives, as well as personal lobbying by key leaders and coalitions among individuals or departments with vested interests in a particular outcome, may stifle important change. Such a culture has low performance because what's best for the organization is secondary to the self-interests of individual players. An example of this is what happened at Enron. Many former Enron employees say that the company's culture became less welcoming with the rise of Jeffrey K. Skilling. Skilling's intense focus on the bottom line and making Enron a success changed the atmosphere at Enron, making it so competitive that employees were afraid to question irregularities for fear of reprisals. It is reported that on Skilling's watch, the Enron that once prided itself on its close team spirit metastasized into a more ruthless, less humane place where employees could be dismissed in an impersonal way.[25] Enron had become a highly politicized environment in which groupthink was the norm.

Unhealthy Promotion Practices

Low-performance cultures tend to promote managers into higher leadership positions without serious consideration of a match between the job demands and the skills and capabilities of the appointee. For the purposes of rewarding a hard-working manager or a longtime employee, an organization may promote a manager who is good at managing day-to-day operations but is lacking in strategic leadership skills such as crafting vision, strategies, and capabilities or inspiring and developing the appropriate culture. This scenario represents a case of promoting a transaction-type manager into a senior executive position requiring transformation skills. While the former is adept at managing day-to-day operations, if he or she ascends to a senior executive position, the organization can find itself without a long-term vision and lack of leadership in forging new strategies, building new competitive capabilities, and creating a new culture—a condition that is ultimately harmful to long-term performance. It is also the case that when top management make icons out of successful unit performers and reward them for their behaviors, they create a powerful disincentive for other managers to aspire to behave as team leaders. The cultural imagery of the unit leader as a hero makes it very difficult for a new model of leader (team leader) to emerge. This is symptomatic of a weak culture.[26]

Ethical Dilemma 1

Buy American

Organizational culture is also based on national culture. People tend to believe their country or company is the best. You most likely have heard the slogan "Buy American." Unions tend to ask Americans to buy products made in the United States to help save their jobs. On the other hand, some Americans ask why they should buy American products, especially if they cost more or they are inferior in quality or style to the foreign-made products. Many (or most) Americans don't know the country of ownership of many products they buy, and some products are made with more than half of the components coming from other countries—so is the product really made in America?

1. Is it ethical and socially responsible to ask people to buy American, or from their home country?
2. Is it ethical and socially responsible to buy foreign products?

Characteristics of High-Performance Cultures

Strong cultures are more likely to be associated with high performance. Much research claims that strong corporate cultures improve firm performance by facilitating internal behavioral consistency. In a high-performance culture, there are a number of healthy cultural characteristics that enhance the organization's performance. High-performance cultures are results oriented, and tend to create an atmosphere in which there is constructive pressure to perform.[27] Exhibit 10-2 lists the key characteristics of high-performance cultures.

Culture Reinforcement Tools

Some of these tools include ceremonies, symbols, stories, language, and policies. High-performance cultures pull together these mechanisms to produce extraordinary results with ordinary people. High-performance organizations have ceremonies that highlight dramatic examples of what the company values. Ceremonies recognize and celebrate high-performing employees and help create an emotional bond among all employees. Also, in high-performance cultures, leaders tell stories to new employees to illustrate the company's primary values and provide a shared understanding among workers. They also use symbols and specialized language (such as slogans) to convey meaning and values. In high-performance cultures, policies on recruitment, selection, and training of new employees are different from those in low-performing cultures. For example, companies with strong, healthy cultures—such as W. L. Gore and Associates, 3M, Southwest Airlines, and Nordstrom—often employ careful and vigorous hiring practices. Chapter 7's end-of-chapter case featured W. L. Gore and Associates. As revealed in the case (p. 286), new employees go through an extensive interviewing process, and when hired, a new employee is assigned a sponsor from within the company. The sponsor, who is usually a veteran of the company, will ensure that the new associate fully understands the company's culture and approach to things. This ensures that the employee and the

Exhibit 10-2 *Characteristics of high-performance cultures.*

- Culture reinforcement tools
- Intensely people oriented
- Results oriented
- Emphasis on achievement and excellence

organization's culture are compatible, something that more companies are now doing. Southwest Airlines looks first and foremost for a sense of humor in the prospective employee; at 3M, creativity and team spirit is critical, and at Nordstrom, "niceness" is an important cultural value.

Intensely People Oriented

Organizations with high-performance cultures reinforce their concern for individual employees in many different ways; they

- Treat employees with dignity and respect
- Grant employees enough autonomy to excel and contribute
- Cultivate a relationship with employees based on mutual respect and interdependency
- Initiate unique one-to-one relationships with top performers
- Give increased responsibility to the best employees
- Implement mentor programs
- Celebrate employee achievements
- Hold managers at every level responsible for the growth and development of the people who report to them
- Use the full range of rewards and punishment to enforce high performance standards
- Encourage employees to use their own initiative and creativity in performing their jobs
- Set reasonable and clear performance standards for all employees.[28]

An organization that treats its employees this way will generally benefit from increased teamwork, higher morale and increased level of job satisfaction, greater employee loyalty, and higher retention rates.[29] There is a reciprocal relationship that develops when organizations are able to attract, retain, motivate, and reward outstanding performers. When this happens, such employees are more likely to behave in ways that help the organization succeed. The cycle of success that results is called a "virtuous spiral," and according to some, is the key to creating and sustaining a high-performance culture.[30] Intensely people-oriented organizations have decentralized management systems and embrace the principles espoused by William Ouchi's "Theory Z." Theory Z opened American corporate doors to participative management, in which employees are considered an integral part of the organization and much emphasis is placed on their involvement in decision making.[31,32] This is in contrast to the task-oriented culture in which decision making is centralized and employees are seen, not heard.

Results Oriented

High-performance cultures invest more time and resources to ensure that employees who excel or achieve performance targets are identified and rewarded. Control systems are developed to collect, analyze, and interpret employee performance data. Quantitative measures of success are used to identify employees who turn in winning performances. To insure accountability, emphasis is placed on individual goal setting, whereby employees draft performance goals and have them approved by their managers. At the end of the year, these goals form the basis of manager-employee performance evaluation and feedback. Corporations with performance-based cultures, such as Microsoft, General Electric, and 3M, follow this approach. At General Electric and 3M, top executives make a point to honor individuals who take it upon themselves to champion a new idea from conception to finished product or service. In these companies, "product champions" are given high visibility and room to push their ideas, with strong backing from managers. In high-performance cultures, every person and every task counts. Companies seek out reasons and opportunities to give out pins, buttons, badges, certificates, and medals to those in ordinary or routine jobs who stand out in their performance. All employees are trained in how to set goals, and managers are trained in the goal-setting process. There is commitment and motivation to achieve goals.[33]

While a discussion of a results-oriented culture tends to emphasize the positive, there are negative reinforcers too. In high-performance cultures, managers whose units consistently perform poorly are quickly replaced or reassigned. In addition, weak-performing employees who reject the cultural emphasis on high performance and results are weeded out. To lessen the use of negative reinforcers, high-performance organizations aim at hiring only motivated, ambitious applicants whose attitudes and work ethic mesh well with a results-oriented work culture.

Emphasis on Achievement and Excellence

High-performance cultures create an atmosphere in which there is constructive pressure to be the best. Achieving excellence requires a corporate culture that holds excellence above all and pursues processes that bring about persistent per-unit cost reductions, zero defects, improved product quality, and extraordinary customer service. Management pursues policies and practices that inspire people to do their best. The thinking is that linking a cultural change, for instance, with improved results, will remind managers of the importance of managing culture and will point to the most efficient way of doing so. When an organization performs consistently at or near peak capability, the outcome is not only more success but also a culture permeated with a spirit of high performance.

WorkApplication2

Describe the culture where you work or have worked as a low- or high-performance culture. Explain your answer.

_____

_____

_____

_____

_____

Applying the Concept 2

Low- or High-Performance Culture

Identify each statement as characteristic of a low- or high-performance culture. Write the appropriate letter in the blank before each item.

a. low   b. high

_____ 6. I wonder how many of the executives here ever climbed so high up the corporate ladder on merit.

_____ 7. I enjoy being treated like a person, not like a number or piece of equipment.

_____ 8. We get together regularly to celebrate one thing or another.

_____ 9. Why do I hear "it's not in the budget" so often around here?

_____ 10. I like the way management just tells us what it wants done. They let us do the job our way, so long as we meet the goals.

——————————— Learning Outcome 4 ———————————

Distinguish between symbolic and substantive leadership actions for shaping organizational culture.

Leaders as Culture Creators

Changing a company's culture and aligning it with strategy are among the most challenging responsibilities of leadership.[34] To build and maintain a strong leadership culture, senior managers must have a clearly defined vision, mission, and culture statements that define the way things will be done. This is the case with the franchise system, in which franchisers must have not only a clearly defined vision, mission, and culture statements, but be willing to share it with franchisees.[35] Senior executives are role models, and the stories they tell, decisions they make, and actions they take build an implicit cultural image of what effective leadership means.[36] There are many options leaders can exercise to create and maintain strong, high-performance cultures that facilitate internal unity as well as enable the organization to adapt to the needs of the external environment. First, the leader must diagnose which aspects of the existing culture are strategy supportive and which are not. Second, the leader must communicate openly and honestly to all employees about those aspects of the culture that have to be changed or about the need for a whole new culture. Third, the leader has to follow swiftly with visible actions to modify the culture or implant a new one. This is the stage when new behaviors and practices reflective of the new culture are implemented. It takes leadership from the top to break the mold of cultural norms in an existing culture and leadership at all levels of the organization to nurture and sustain the new culture.[37] Thus, we cannot ignore the role of middle managers in the transmission and integration of organizational culture.

Mechanisms for effective implementation of a new culture include compensation programs, policies, communications, office design, and perquisites. The selection and use of mechanisms such as these can be embodied in a cultural management plan that is supportive of an organization's goals and objectives. All these mechanisms are present in the case study of how a small frozen Mexican foods processor, Ruiz Foods, employed a strong team culture to raise its game and excel in the competitive food market.[38]

In the process of culture creation, sustenance, and renewal, it is easy to see how the past is often used as an indicator of things to come. In a study analyzing the relationships among the different components of a market-oriented culture, researchers found that artifacts play a crucial role in determining behavior within organizations. Other measured components in the study included the values that support market orientation, norms for market orientation, and market-oriented behaviors.[39] These are all components that define culture and are often the basis for diagnosing a culture for its fit or lack of fit with a new strategy.

To create strong, high-performance cultures, leaders can initiate many different types of organizational processes. Examples of organizational processes that have been studied as tools to embed and reinforce strong, high-performance cultures include the strategy formulation process, the leader's authority and influence, the motivation process, the management control process, the conflict management process, and the customer management process.[40] These processes

Exhibit 10-3 *Leadership actions for shaping culture.*

Symbolic Actions

- Leaders serve as role models
- Ceremonial events for high achievers
- Special appearances by leaders
- Organizational structure

Substantive Actions

- Replacing old-culture members with new members
- Changing dysfunctional policies and operating practices
- Creating a strategy-culture fit
- Realigning rewards/incentives and resource allocation
- Facilities design
- Developing a written values statement

---

represent actions that require significant leadership involvement. Depending on the style or approach used, the outcomes of these processes can significantly influence the culture of the organization. Some of these actions are substantive, while others are primarily symbolic—one scholar used the terms *primary* and *secondary mechanisms* to make the distinction.[41] Symbolic actions are valuable for the signals they send about the kinds of behavior and performance leaders wish to encourage and promote. The meaning is implied in the action taken. One of the first things Sam Palmisano did as IBM Corp.'s new chairman and CEO was to rename IBM's Enterprise Leadership Group to the Enterprise Leadership Team. While some may see this as nothing but a symbolic action, this seemingly minor change sent a clear message that IBM's culture of celebrating individual performers and rewarding hero-leaders was coming to an end, and would be replaced by a strong emphasis on teamwork.[42] Substantive actions are explicit and highly visible and are indicative of management's commitment to new strategic initiatives and the associated cultural changes. These are actions that everyone will understand are intended to establish a new culture more in tune with the organization's strategy. For example, a leader may set as his or her objective to create a culture that supports ethical behavior. Here the leader's actions in serving as a role model (symbolic), and/or developing a written values statement (substantive), may significantly influence the realization of the objective. Exhibit 10-3 summarizes the key managerial actions that offer the greatest potential for shaping organizational culture. These are divided into symbolic and substantive actions.

Leaders Serve as Role Models

Employees learn what is valued most in an organization by watching what attitudes and behaviors leaders pay attention to and reward and whether the leaders' own behavior matches the espoused values.[43] For example, top executives leading a cost-reduction effort by curtailing executive perks, and emphasizing the importance of responding to customers' needs by requiring all managers and executives to spend a portion of each week talking with customers and understanding their needs, sets a good example. The message employees get when a leader institutes a policy or procedure but fails to act in accordance with it is that the policy is really not important or necessary. The new CEO of a conservative midwestern company decided that injecting some fun into the firm's culture could have a positive outcome. She modeled this behavior by being funny herself. By getting people to loosen up and enjoy themselves, she encouraged esprit de corps among her followers and greater camaraderie. Among other benefits, it is reported that this symbolic action started conversations that sparked innovation and increased productivity by reducing stress. As a result of this symbolic cultural change, the company's sales are said to have doubled and its net income and market capitalization nearly tripled.[44] This example supports the notion that something as simple as modeling and promoting fun in a workplace can lead to both a robust corporate culture and improved business performance.

Ceremonial Events for High Achievers

Leaders can schedule ceremonies to celebrate and honor people whose actions and performance exemplify what is called for in the new culture. Ceremonies reinforce specific values and create emotional bonds by allowing employees to share in important moments. This type of culture helps to retain valued employees.[45] A ceremony often includes the presentation of an award. At Mary Kay Cosmetics, for example, awards and prizes ranging from ribbons to pink automobiles are given to beauty consultants who reach various sales targets.

Special Appearances by Leaders

Leaders who are sensitive to their role in creating a high-performance culture make a habit of appearing at ceremonial functions to praise individuals and groups who symbolize the values and practices of the new culture. Effective leaders will also make special appearances at nonceremonial events (such as employee training programs) to stress strategic priorities, values, cultural norms, and ethical principles. They understand the symbolic value of their presence at group gatherings and use the opportunity to reinforce the key aspects of the culture. To organization members, the mere appearance of the executive—and the things he or she chooses to emphasize—clearly communicates management's commitment to the new culture.

Organizational Structure

Organizational structure can symbolize culture. A decentralized structure reflects a belief in individual initiative and shared responsibility, whereas a centralized structure reflects the belief that only the leader knows what is best for the organization.

In addition to symbolic actions that leaders can employ in communicating their organization's culture, substantive actions must also be used to complement the former. Substantive actions have to be credible, highly visible, and indicative of management's commitment to new strategic initiatives and cultural changes. Exhibit 10-3 lists six substantive actions that leaders can initiate to shape culture.

Replace Old-Culture Members with New Members

The strongest sign that management is truly committed to creating a new culture is replacing old-culture members who are unwilling to change with a "new breed" of employees. Beyond immediate actions to replace old-culture employees, leaders can influence culture by establishing new criteria for recruiting, selecting, promoting, and firing employees. These new criteria should be consistent with the new culture of the organization. More and more, organizations are looking for employees who understand their culture and are willing to learn to work within it.

Changing Dysfunctional Policies and Operating Practices

Existing policies and practices that impede the execution of new strategies must be changed. Policies on budgets, planning, reports, and performance reviews can be used to emphasize aspects of the organization's culture. Through these actions, leaders let other members know what is important. Wal-Mart executives have had a long-standing practice of spending two to three days every week visiting Wal-Mart's stores and talking with store managers and employees. Sam Walton, Wal-Mart's founder, was dissatisfied with managerial practices that he observed in competitor's stores. To make sure it did not happen at his stores, he insisted on a different policy and practice. He made sure his managers understood his view on this issue. He believed that to be an effective manager, you had to get out into the store and listen to what the associates have to say, because the best ideas come from clerks and stockpersons. Over the years, this practice has become part of Wal-Mart's culture.

An example of an organization that has had to change its dysfunctional policies and operating practices as part of a cultural transformation is the railroad industry. The railroad industry has never really caught up to its rival transportation modes, despite its long history and pioneer reputation. As other industries have grown, it has experienced decline. Researchers and other interest groups have speculated that part of the problem is the culture. Not too many young people find employment in the railroad industry an attractive option. Many experts in the field believe that the industry must change its culture if it wants to attract and retain new talent. They recommend that for the railroad industry to grow and attract young talent, it must eliminate archaic job titles, outmoded management practices, and abusive management behavior; keep compensation packages competitive; and create effective mentor programs and a career path for young managers.

Creating a Strategy-Culture Fit

It is the leader's responsibility to select a strategy that is compatible with the prevailing culture or to change the culture to fit the chosen strategy. The lack of a fit will hinder or constrain strategy execution. In rapidly changing business environments, the capacity to introduce new strategies is a necessity if a company is to perform well over long periods of time. Strategic agility and fast organizational response to new opportunities requires a culture that quickly accepts and supports company efforts to adapt to environmental change rather than a culture that resists change. A strategy-culture fit allows for easy adaptation, while a strategy-culture mismatch makes for a difficult adaptation. Even during periods of stability and economic growth, it is still critical for the leader to pay attention to the existing culture. The culture of an organization naturally evolves over time, and without strong leadership, it can change in the wrong direction. Key values or practices in a culture may gradually erode if no attention is paid to the culture.[46] For example, incompatible subcultures may develop in various departments of the organization, leading to a culture of isolation rather than teamwork and cooperation.

With mergers and acquisitions dominating global business strategy, the integration of corporate cultures is often the deciding factor in whether a newly merged entity succeeds or fails. It is generally understood that following a merger, a culture assessment needs to be conducted to determine whether the acquired-company's culture will mirror the acquiring-company's culture, or a new culture will be formed from the merger. Senior leaders can improve the likelihood of a merger's success by ensuring that the two organizations' cultures are in sync, or that an attempt is made to develop a common culture that the two sides agree with. The damage that can be caused by cultural incompatibility has been underscored by a series of high-profile mergers and acquisitions that failed to meet expectations. Experts and scholars on mergers and acquisitions seem to favor the creation of a completely new corporate culture for merged organizations. They prefer a complete makeover rather than choosing to leave the cultures separate or permitting one culture to dominate. This was the case with Novartis (formed through the merger of Ciba-Geigy and Sandoz), and the merger of Chrysler and Daimler-Benz. The creation of a new, shared culture in any merged organization may require a careful review of existing practices in the two organizations, the identification and retention of common practices, the introduction of new practices, and the discarding of old, unworkable practices.

Realigning Rewards/Incentives and Resource Allocation

Tying compensation incentives directly to new measures of strategic performance (i.e., strategic goals) is a culture-shaping undertaking, because it gives the leader leverage to reward only those performances that are supportive of the strategy and culture.[47] Shifting resources from old-strategy projects and programs to new-strategy projects and programs will also communicate management's commitment to a new strategy and culture—assuming that there is a strategy-culture fit. Imagine an organization in which top leaders create a reward system to motivate employees to pursue its strategies. When those strategies change, changes to the reward structure often lag behind changes to the strategy. As another example, imagine an organization in which the CEO and his or her top management team have articulated an integration-based strategy that will require middle-level leaders to think and act across boundaries and on behalf of the entire enterprise; however, imagine that the organization's reward system offers leaders incentives for achieving unit success, even when they fail to behave as enterprise leaders.[48] Such reward/incentive misalignments weaken an organization's culture.

Facilities Design

Leaders can design the work environment to reflect the values they want to promote within the organization. For example, having common eating facilities for all employees, no special parking areas, and similar offices is consistent with a value of equality. An open office layout with fewer walls separating employees is consistent with a value for open communication. In designing its new northeast regional headquarters, Nokia wanted to provide open working spaces and an environment that promoted coworker contact and interaction. By providing a clear sense of place and purpose for its employees, Nokia succeeded in communicating an employee-friendly value through its facility, with the uniqueness and comfort of the setting reinforced by the cultural and aesthetic elements in the building.

Developing a Written Values Statement

Many leaders today set forth their organization's values and codes of ethics in written documents. Written statements have the advantage of explicitly stating the company's position on ethical and moral issues, and they serve as benchmarks for judging both company policies and actions and individual conduct. Value statements serve as a building block in the task of culture creation and maintenance, as evident in the opening case. Exhibit 10-4 presents Starbucks' mission statement as it appears on its Web site. It first identifies the mission, the highlights six guiding value statements that symbolize the culture of the company.

Here is an example of a culture transformation employing symbolic and substantive actions: The company is Alberto-Culver North America and the problem was one of declining sales and the toughest competitive environment it had ever faced. After intense analysis and evaluation of solution alternatives, the leadership decided that the best course of action to address these challenges was to change to a new corporate culture that the company did not at the time possess. To change its culture, Alberto-Culver North America went through the following four steps: (1) Culture became a very visible and prominent topic of discussion in all company gatherings, with leaders frequently highlighting desired values and behaviors that already existed in various parts of the firm. (2) A new position category was created to focus on growth development strategies, and growth development leaders (GDLs) were hired to fill these positions. Each GDL was assigned 12 individuals to mentor. (3) To identify areas of improvement in the culture, the firm used an employee survey for input and,

WorkApplication3

Identify and briefly explain which of the 10 leadership actions for shaping culture have been used by a leader where you work or have worked.

_____

_____

_____

_____

_____

Exhibit 10-4 *Starbucks' mission statement.*

Establish Starbucks as the premier purveyor of the finest coffee in the world while maintaining our uncompromising principles while we grow. The following six guiding principles will help us measure the appropriateness of our decisions:

- Provide a great work environment and treat each other with respect and dignity.
- Embrace diversity as an essential component in the way we do business.
- Apply the highest standards of excellence to the purchasing, roasting, and fresh delivery of our coffee.
- Develop enthusiastically satisfied customers all of the time.
- Contribute positively to our communities and our environment.
- Recognize that profitability is essential to our future success.

Source: Used with permission. Copyright © 2005 Starbucks Corporation. http://www.starbucks.com/aboutus/environment.asp.

based on the results, supplied 360-degree feedback to GDLs and top management. (4) Successes were continually celebrated to reinforce positive aspects of the new culture. Alberto-Culver's performance under this new culture has been nothing short of spectacular. Since 1994, the firm has slashed employee turnover by 50 percent, seen sales rise 83 percent, and recorded a pretax profit increase of 336 percent.[49] It is important to note that these four areas of focus are consistent with the systematic process of culture change advocated for leaders at the beginning of this section.

Once values and norms have been formally established, they must be ingrained in the company's policies, practices, and daily operations, as the Alberto-Culver example illustrates. Value statements have no credibility unless all employees at every level of the organization put them into action. Yet, for many organizations, this is where they have failed. Researchers examining this aspect of culture implementation acknowledge that the relationship between culture and implementation of new behaviors and practices has not been adequately investigated, due to the lack of a comprehensive framework for defining and measuring organizational cultures.[50] The next section focuses on culture types, using a construct of two interacting elements.

Learning Outcome 5

Differentiate between the four cultural value types.

Cultural Value Types

Rather than looking at culture as either good or bad, some scholars view it as a construct that varies according to an organization's external environment and its strategic focus. Organizational culture types or styles such as the clan, "adhocracy," hierarchy, and market cultures have been studied for their impact on such employee factors as job satisfaction or retention. The variance associated with different culture types supports the view that organizational culture is not a singular, holistic concept. Rather, it is a multifaceted construct with distinct segments that share similar characteristics. Studies have shown that organizations that operate in similar environments will tend to reveal similar cultural value types. Therefore, an appropriate match of the right cultural value type, organizational strategy, and external environment can enhance organizational performance.[51] For example, in a highly dynamic market environment, a market-oriented culture will be the better choice for meeting changing customer needs and being innovative.[52]

Another framework for classifying culture types suggests that the match between an organization's environment and its strategic focus results in four types of cultures. The makeup of the culture types is based on two dimensions: (1) the degree of environmental turbulence (stable versus dynamic environment) and (2) the organization's leadership focus or orientation (internal versus external focus). The extent to which an organization's external environment is stable or changing will influence its culture. Also, top management's success strategy may be to focus on internal or external requirements as imperatives for achieving organizational objectives; this too will influence the organization's culture. As shown in Exhibit 10-5, the interaction of these two

Exibit 10-5 *Types of organizational culture.*

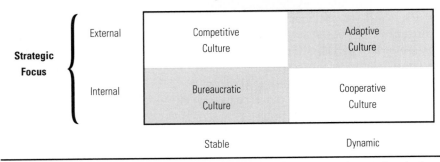

Sources: Based on M. D. Youngblood, "Winning Cultures for the New Economy," *Strategy and Leadership* 28, 6 (Nov./Dec. 2000): 4–9; G. N. Chandler, C. Keller and D. W. Lyon, "Unraveling the Determinants and Consequences of an Innovative-Supportive Organizational Culture," *Entrepreneurship Theory and Practices* 25, 1 (Fall 2000): 59–76; J. R. Fisher Jr., "Envisioning a Culture of Contribution," *Journal of Organizational Excellence* 20, 1 (Winter 2000): 47–52.

constructs—degree of environmental turbulence and management's strategic focus—creates four types of organizational cultures.[53]

The four types of organizational cultures are cooperative, adaptive, competitive, and bureaucratic. These cultural types are not mutually exclusive; an organization may have cultural values that fall into more than one group, or even into all groups. However, high-performance cultures with strong values tend to emphasize or lean more toward one particular culture type. The four cultural value types are discussed below.

Cooperative Culture

In a period of change and uncertainty, cooperative culture is seen by some leaders as the key to superior performance. **Cooperative culture** *represents a leadership belief in strong, mutually reinforcing exchanges and linkages between employees and departments.* In this type of culture, operating policies, procedures, standards, and tasks are all designed with one goal in mind—to encourage cooperation, teamwork, power sharing, and camaraderie among employees. Management thinking is predicated on the belief that organizational success is influenced more by employee relationships inside the organization than by external relationships. It is an internally focused culture. Proponents of cooperative culture argue that in today's dynamic work environment, characterized by constant changes and fluid projects, creating a work environment in which workers feel empowered, support one another, share responsibilities and power, and are part of a team creates synergy and increases productivity. It is a culture where employees are trained to think like owners rather than hired hands.

Adaptive Culture

Adaptive culture *represents a leadership belief in active monitoring of the external environment for emerging opportunities and threats.* This culture is made up of policies, procedures, and practices that support employees' ability to respond quickly to changing environmental conditions. In adaptive cultures, members are encouraged to take risks, experiment, and innovate. Management thinking is based on the belief that organizational success is influenced more by events outside the organization than by internal factors. Therefore, employees are empowered to make decisions and act quickly to take advantage of emerging opportunities or avoid threats. There is greater individual autonomy and tolerance for failure. Responsiveness to customer needs is highly valued and rewarded. There is a spirit of doing what is necessary to ensure both short-term and long-term organizational success, provided core values and business principles are upheld in the process. Adaptive culture is generally known for its flexibility and innovativeness.

The leaders of adaptive cultures are skilled at changing the right things in the right ways, not changing for the sake of change, and not compromising core values or principles. Rewarding employees for experimenting and taking risks is a big factor in gaining their support for change. Leaders consciously seek to train and promote individuals who display initiative, creativity, and risk taking. When 3M's former CEO, James McNerney, Jr., came on board, he was imbued with GE's tough dynamic culture (his former organization), which contrasted with 3M's emphasis on being nice to one another. He instinctively realized that to get the conglomerate's 75,000 employees to implement his strategies, he had to learn to work with the culture. He resisted barking orders and tried to win the hearts and minds of employees. His objective was to boost 3M's growth through cost cutting but preserve the company's hallmark of creativity.[54] A company like 3M, where experimentation and risk taking are a way of life, is a perfect example of adaptive culture at work.

Competitive Culture

Competitive culture *represents a leadership that encourages and values a highly competitive work environment.* Organizational policies, procedures, work practices, rules, and tasks are all designed to foster both internal competition (employee vs. employee, department vs. department, or division vs. division) and external competition (company vs. competitors). An organization with a competitive culture operates in a stable, mature external market environment in which competition for market share is very intense. The organization's strategic focus is external because of the need to keep an eye on competitors who are constantly looking for weaknesses to exploit. The mature and saturated state of the consumer markets these firms operate in makes for very intense competition. Leaders of competitive cultures focus on the achievement of specific targets such as market share, revenue, growth, or profitability. This is a numbers-driven culture that values competitiveness, personal initiative, aggressiveness, achievement, and the willingness to work long and hard for yourself or for the team. The drive to win either against one another internally or against an external competitor is what holds the organization together.

Pepsi-Cola and Coca-Cola are two companies that exemplify competitive culture. Both have the vision to be the best in the world. Each company socializes its members to view the other's employees as enemies and to do whatever is necessary to defeat them in the marketplace. High performance standards and tough reviews are used to weed out the weak and reward the strong. At Pepsi-Cola, for example, former CEO Wayne Calloway was known to set backbreaking standards and then systematically raise them each year. Executives who met his standards were generously rewarded—stock options, bonuses, rapid promotions, and first-class air travel—and those who did not would feel the pressure to produce or risk negative consequences such as demotions, transfers, or job termination. United Parcel Service (UPS) is another company whose competitive strength is directly tied to its unique organizational culture. UPS's competitive culture provides the basis for everything that it does, from technological innovation to skill training. To sustain its culture, UPS relies on recruiting and retraining the right people, motivating competitive behavior, and nurturing a customer-oriented mind-set in all employees.[55]

Facing intense competition in their respective industries, GE, Honeywell, and Ford recently employed Six Sigma to implement a customer-focused, quality-based, competitive culture. Six Sigma, a concept developed by Motorola, focuses on the customer instead of the product. It has helped changed these organizations' cultures, and in the process yielded some impressive results. GE produces annual benefits of over $2.5 billion across the organization from Six Sigma. Honeywell has recorded more than $800 million in savings since its implementation in 1998, and over a three-year period, Ford posted savings of $1 billion from Six Sigma.[56] It can be argued that Six Sigma is a tool, used by these companies to introduce a more aggressive competitive culture that is helping them achieve desired results in response to the dynamic competitive environment of their respective industries. These examples demonstrate how a competitive culture can impact performance if it's properly conceived, developed, and implemented.

Bureaucratic Culture

Bureaucratic culture *represents a leadership that values order, stability, status, and efficiency.* Leaders in bureaucratic cultures perceive their environments as basically stable with an internal strategic focus. Bureaucratic culture emphasizes strict adherence to set rules, policies, and procedures, which ensure an orderly way of doing business. Organizations with bureaucratic cultures are highly structured and efficiency driven. The bureaucratic culture is becoming increasingly difficult to sustain because of the growing level of environmental turbulence facing most organizations. Few organizations operate in a stable environment, forcing their leaders to make the shift away from bureaucratic cultures because of the need for greater flexibility and responsiveness. In 2001, General Motors (GM) hired a new vice chairman for global product development, Robert Lutz. Lutz is credited with transforming GM's bureaucratic culture. Before Lutz's tenure, GM had been criticized for adapting slowly to changing consumer needs and imposing a myriad of restrictions on employees' efforts[57]—issues characteristic of the bureaucratic culture.

Each of the four cultural value types can be successful under different environmental conditions and organizational orientations. The relative emphasis on various cultural values depends on the organization's strategic focus and on the level of environmental turbulence in its industry. It is the responsibility of strategic leaders to create the fit between strategy and culture, by ensuring that organizations do not persist in cultural types that worked in the past but are no

Type of Organizational Culture

Identify each statement as characteristic of one of the types of organizational cultures. Write the appropriate letter in the blank before each item.

a. competitive   b. adaptive   c. bureaucratic   d. cooperative

_____ 11. Things don't change much around here. We just focus on doing our functional tasks to standards.

_____ 12. In the airline industry, we keep a close eye on ticket prices to make sure we are not underpriced.

_____ 13. At Toyota, we focus on teamwork with much input into decision making to satisfy customers.

_____ 14. Being a young Internet company, we go with the flow.

Applying the Concept 3

longer relevant because of changing environmental conditions. The challenge facing many leaders is how to sustain an organization's culture once it has been established or created; especially if it is working well. Several key steps to ensure that a culture is sustained with expansion have been proposed. They include defining a strategic plan for implementing the company culture, using well-trained and experienced employees to train new hires, making sure that employees at all levels know what the culture is and accept it, and instituting a system by which new employees learn the written and unwritten parameters of the culture.[58]

WorkApplication4

Describe which of the four types of organizational cultures (Exhibit 10-5) exist where you work or have worked.

_____

_____

_____

_____

_____

Value-Based Leadership

Values-based leadership examines the influence of an executive's values upon the strategic development of an organization. **Values** *are generalized beliefs or behaviors that are considered by an individual or a group to be important.* Relationships between leaders and members of an organization are based on shared values. How leaders' ethical values influence organizational behavior and performance is the subject of value-based leadership.[59] Employees learn about values by watching leaders. In some cases the values of the organization, espoused by the CEO, violate societal ethical standards. In a recent *New York Times* article titled "Where Have All the Chief Financial Officers Gone?" the writer explored the dilemma that confronts some financial executives: what to do if your values do not reflect those of your organization.[60] Lately, given the high-profile accounting scandals in the news, CFOs have found themselves in the position of being the culture's ethical benchmark in their organizations. In this section we will examine the following topics: the leader's role in advocating and enforcing ethical behavior, a framework for understanding global cultural value differences, and the implications for leadership practice. However, before we begin, complete Self-Assessment 1 to determine your personal values in eight areas.

Self-Assessment 1

Personal Values

Below are 16 items. Rate how important each one is to you on a scale of 0 (not important) to 100 (very important). Write the number 0–100 on the line to the left of each item.

0—10—20—30—40—50—60—70—80—90—100
Not important   Somewhat important   Very important

_____ 1. An enjoyable, satisfying job

_____ 2. A high-paying job

_____ 3. A good marriage

_____ 4. Meeting new people, social events

_____ 5. Involvement in community activities

_____ 6. My relationship with God/my religion

_____ 7. Exercising, playing sports

_____ 8. Intellectual development

_____ 9. A career with challenging opportunities

_____ 10. Nice cars, clothes, home, and so on

_____ 11. Spending time with family

_____ 12. Having several close friends

_____ 13. Volunteer work for not-for-profit organizations like the cancer society

_____ 14. Meditation, quiet time to think, pray, and so on

_____ 15. A healthy, balanced diet

_____ 16. Educational reading, TV, self-improvement programs, and so on

Next, transfer your rating numbers for each of the 16 items to the appropriate columns. Then add the two numbers in each column.

	Professional	Financial	Family	Social
	1. _____	2. _____	3. _____	4. _____
	9. _____	10. _____	11. _____	12. _____
Totals:	_____	_____	_____	_____

	Community	Spiritual	Physical	Intellectual
	5. _____	6. _____	7. _____	8. _____
	13. _____	14. _____	15. _____	16. _____
Totals:	_____	_____	_____	_____

The higher the total in any area, the higher the value you place on that particular area. The closer the numbers are in all eight areas, the better rounded you are.

Think about the time and effort you put forth in your top three values. Is it sufficient to allow you to achieve the level of success you want in each of those areas? If not, what can you do to change? Is there any area in which you feel you should have a higher value total? If yes, which, and what can you do to change?

Advocating Ethical Behavior

There is increasing research revealing the bottom-line benefits of investing in an organizational culture that is centered to a large extent on values and leadership.[61] Studies have found that many successful companies (those with measurable bottom-line revenue and profitability results) are distinguished by their commitment to strong organizational values and a focus on empowering employees. Many values make up an organization's culture but the one that is considered most critical for leaders is ethics. Recall from Chapter 2 that ethics consists of the standards of right and wrong that influence behavior; in Self-Assessment 6 from Chapter 2 you determined how ethical your behavior is. Ethics provides guidelines for judging conduct and decision making. However, for an organization to display consistently high ethical standards, top leadership must model ethical and moral conduct.[62–64] Value-based leaders cultivate a high level of trust and respect from members, based not just on stated values but on their willingness to make personal sacrifices for the sake of upholding values. A leader's ethics reflects the contributions of diverse inputs, including personal beliefs, family, peers, religion, and the broader society. The family and religious upbringing of leaders often influence the principles by which they conduct business.[65,66] A leader's personal beliefs may enable him or her to pursue an ethical choice even if the decision is unpopular.

In organizations that strive hard to make high ethical standards a reality, top management communicates its commitment through formal policies and programs such as codes of ethics, ethics committees, training programs, and disclosure mechanisms. These mechanisms are discussed below.

Code of Ethics

A code of ethics is usually a formal statement of an organization's ethical values. A growing number of organizations have added a code of ethics to their list of formal statements and public pronouncements. According to a study by the Center for Business Ethics, 90 percent of Fortune 500 companies now have a code of ethics.[67,68] The lesson from these companies is that it is never enough to assume that activities are being conducted ethically, nor can it be assumed that employees understand that they are expected to act with integrity. Leaders must consistently communicate to members the value of not only observing ethical codes but also reporting ethical violations. "Gray areas" must be identified and openly discussed with members, and procedures created to offer guidance when issues in these areas arise. It is generally believed that the more an organization's employees are aware of proper conduct, the more likely they are to do the right thing.[69,70] A code of ethics is of no consequence if an ethical corporate culture and top management support are lacking; it is more than just a formal document stipulating company policies and procedures.[71]

Some organizations include ethics as part of their mission. Such mission statements generally define ethical values as well as corporate culture, and contain language about company responsibility, quality of product, and treatment of employees. Developing an effective code of ethics program should incorporate some key components: leaders model expected behaviors, ethics is a core element of the corporate culture, everyone participates in creating the guidelines, ethics is discussed openly, and rules are applied consistently.[72,73] Exhibit 10-4, featuring Starbucks Corporation's mission statement, contains a set of six guiding principles that illustrates how the company's mission and core values translate into ethical business practices.

Ethics Committees

In order to encourage ethical behavior, some organizations are setting up ethics committees charged with overseeing ethical issues. In other organizations the responsibility is given to an ombudsperson. *An ethics* **ombudsperson** *is a single person entrusted with the responsibility of acting as the organization's conscience.* He or she hears and investigates complaints and points out potential ethics failures to top management. In many large corporations, there are ethics departments with full-time staff charged with helping employees deal with day-to-day ethical problems or questions.

Training Programs

Training provides the opportunity for everyone in the organization to be informed and educated on the key aspects of the code of ethics. Training teaches employees how to incorporate ethics into daily behavior. Starbucks Corporation uses new employee training to ingrain values such as embracing diversity, taking personal responsibility, and treating everyone with respect.

Disclosure Mechanism

As part of enforcing ethical conduct, employees are encouraged to report any knowledge of ethical violations. **Whistle blowing** *is employee disclosure of illegal or unethical practices on the part of the organization.* In 2002, the scandals surrounding companies such as Enron and WorldCom left many people wondering why no one blew the whistle on these practices sooner. Later that year, *TIME Magazine* named three women, including Sherron Watkins of Enron Corporation, as People of the Year. Whistle blowing can be risky for those who choose to do it—they have been known to suffer consequences including being ostracized by coworkers, demoted or transferred to less-desirable jobs, and even losing their jobs.[74,75] Policies that protect employees from going through these setbacks will signal management's genuine commitment to enforce ethical behavior.[76] Some organizations have done this by setting up hotlines to give employees a confidential way to report unethical or illegal actions.[77,78] According to a report from nonprofit organization Public Concern at Work, employees are twice as likely to blow the whistle on workplace wrongdoing as they were five years ago.[79]

When faced with difficult decisions, value-based leaders know what they stand for, and they have the courage to act on their principles regardless of external pressures. A manager's values, however, are shaped by differences in national or societal culture. The following section describes a framework for understanding the bases of broad national cultural differences.

WorkApplication5

Discuss which of the four mechanisms for advocating ethical behavior exist where you work or have worked.

_____

_____

_____

_____

OPENING CASE APPLICATION

3. What Role Has Andrea Jung Played in Fostering a Climate of Strict Ethical Standards at Avon?

In September 2004, Andrea Jung delivered the following message to Avon's Associates Worldwide that would seem to address this question. She described Avon's business environment as one that is continually more challenging and complex, particularly for a company such as Avon that conducts business in almost every country in the world. She indicated that only through the highest ethical conduct, and through a corporate culture that recognizes the value of compliance with these standards, can Avon look forward to continued success in the future. Avon's impeccable reputation, she said, is built upon a proud heritage of doing well by doing right. For more than a century, she continued, "We have been setting the very highest example of integrity and ethics in all of our relationships—with our shareholders, associates, and representatives; our suppliers and competitors; governments; and the public. Our values and principles are the bedrock not only of Avon's past—but of its future."[80]

On Avon's company website, the following declaration underscores its commitment to maintaining the highest ethical standards: "At Avon, we strive always to maintain the highest standards of integrity and ethical conduct, consistent with our Company values and in compliance with both the letter and spirit of all applicable laws and regulations. Each Avon Associate is individually responsible for strict compliance with the policies applicable to their work. Information published on this site reflects our commitment to upholding the highest of standards in the area of ethics, corporate governance and compliance." In 2004, Avon's Ethics Education Team created a new Code of Business Conduct and Ethics, as well as a mandatory ethics seminar for Avon's 47,700 associates around the world. Avon continues to enjoy an unmatched reputation for integrity and business conduct. *Business Ethics* magazine has rated Avon one of the 100 Best Corporate Citizens for six consecutive years. In 2001, *TIME Magazine* declared Andrea Jung one of the 25 Most Influential Global Executives, and in January 2003, she was featured in *Business Week* as one of the best managers of the year. She has been ranked among *Fortune* magazine's "50 Most Powerful Women in Business" for the past five years, including being ranked at #3 for 2003 and 2004. In 2004, the *Wall Street Journal* named Ms. Jung one of "50 People to Watch in Business" and *Newsweek* magazine named her one of "10 Prominent People to Watch in 2005." One can safely assume that Andrea Jung's leadership actions are responsible for shaping Avon's culture and ethical climate.

--- Learning Outcome 6 ---

Describe the framework for understanding global cultural value differences.

A Framework of Value Dimensions for Understanding Cultural Differences

Whether organizational or national, culture is a product of values and norms that people use to guide and control their behavior. Relationships between leaders and members of an organization are based on shared values. Values determine what people think are the right, good, or appropriate ways to behave. Values, therefore, specify the norms that prescribe the appropriate behaviors for reaching desired goals. On a national level, a country's values and norms determine what kinds of attitudes and behaviors are acceptable or appropriate. The people of a particular culture are socialized into these values as they grow up, and norms and social guidelines prescribe the way they should behave toward one another. Significant differences between national cultures exist and do indeed make a difference—often substantial—in the way managers and employees behave in organizations.[81]

The growing diversity of the workforce and the increasing globalization of the marketplace create the need for multicultural leaders. Effective managers no longer work solely in the comforts of their home culture, but also must learn to work across cultures. The process of multicultural learning and intercultural adaptation is described as the interaction between person and culture. Multicultural leaders possess competencies (skills and abilities) that enable them to relate effectively to and motivate people across race, gender, age, social strata, and nationality.[82] Each unique culture has overt and subtle differences that influence how its members behave and interact with others. In this section we explore how national cultures differ by examining their values. Five key dimensions of differences in cultural values and the implications for leadership practice are discussed.

Researchers have developed a conceptual framework for analyzing cultural differences. This framework examines seven different value dimensions and how selected nationalities relate to them. Each value dimension represents a continuum. The first five dimensions came from Geert Hofstede's research, spanning almost two decades and featuring people from over sixty countries.[83] Global Leadership and Organizational Behavior Effectiveness (GLOBE) is a research program dedicated to examining the relationship between national culture and attributes of effective leadership in 61 nations. GLOBE examines national cultures in terms of nine dimensions: performance orientation, future orientation, assertiveness, power distance, humane orientation, institutional collectivism, in-group collectivism, uncertainty avoidance, and gender egalitarianism.[84] GLOBE's nine value dimensions incorporate some of Hofstede's dimensions. Our focus will be on Hofstede's value dimensions; Exhibit 10-6 summarizes these values, which are briefly discussed in the following sections.

Individualism–Collectivism

This dimension involves a person's source of identity in society. Some societies value individualism more than collectivism, and vice versa. **Individualism** *is a psychological state in which people see themselves first as individuals and believe their own interest and values are primary.* **Collectivism** (at the other end of the continuum) *is the state of mind wherein the values and goals of the group— whether extended family, ethnic group, or company—are primary.* In a company or business setting, members of a society who value individualism are more concerned with individual accomplishments than with group or team accomplishments. They are highly motivated by individual-based incentives rather than by

Exhibit 10-6 *A framework of value dimensions for understanding cultural differences.*

Individualism	High Uncertainty Avoidance	High Power Distance	Long-term Orientation	Masculinity
↕	↕	↕	↕	↕
Collectivism	Low Uncertainty Avoidance	Low Power Distance	Short-term Orientation	Femininity

Source: Based on G. Hofstede, "Cultural Constraints in Management Theories," *Academy of Management Executive* 7 (1993), pp. 81–94.

group-based incentives. Members of a society who value collectivism, on the other hand, are typically more concerned with the group or organization than with themselves.[85] Also, individualism–collectivism and power distance dimensions have been linked to decision-making theory, with emphasis on participative decision making (PDM). These two cultural dimensions have been used to explain differences in employee behavior during team decision making. Employees from cultures that value individualism tend to prefer a paternalistic approach to participative decision making, whereas those from cultures that value collectivism prefer face-to-face or collective participative decision making.[86] The United States, Great Britain, and Canada have been described as individualistic cultures, while Greece, Japan, and Mexico are said to have collectivistic cultures. Some researchers now believe that a country like Japan is undergoing a gradual shift in its national culture along this dimension because of the long decline in its economy. Tough economic times have Japanese relying on themselves more in the face of corporate downsizing and lower job security. Some experts now believe that because of the changing economic times, Japan may be experiencing a rise in individualism at the expense of collectivism.[87]

High–Low Uncertainty Avoidance

A society with **high uncertainty avoidance** *contains a majority of people who do not tolerate risk, avoid the unknown, and are comfortable when the future is relatively predictable and certain.* In a high uncertainty avoidance country like Japan, managers prefer well-structured and predictable situations. The other end of the continuum is a society where the majority of the people have **low uncertainty avoidance**; *most people in this culture are comfortable with and accepting of the unknown, and tolerate risk and unpredictability.* This dimension is about a person's response to ambiguity. Managers from a low uncertainty avoidance country like the United States are willing to accept risk and uncertainty as part of life. They are more willing to take risks and are less motivated to control the process and outcome of work situations. The United States, Australia, and Canada are associated with low uncertainty avoidance cultures while Argentina, Italy, Japan, and Israel are associated with high uncertainty avoidance cultures.

High–Low Power Distance

This dimension deals with society's orientation to authority. The extent to which people of different status, power, or authority should behave toward each other as equals or unequals is referred to as *power distance. In a* **high power-distance culture,** *leaders and followers rarely interact as equals; while in a* **low power-distance culture,** *leaders and their members interact on several levels as equals.* In an organization with a high power-distance culture, the leader makes many decisions simply because he or she is the leader, and the group members readily comply. On the other end of the continuum, an organization with a low power-distance culture will have employees that do not readily recognize a power hierarchy. Decision making is a group-oriented and participative activity. Members will accept directions from their leaders only when they think the leader is right. High power-distance cultures include Mexico, Japan, Spain, and France. Low power-distance cultures include Germany, the United States, and Ireland.

Long-term–Short-term Orientation

This dimension refers to a society's long- or short-term orientation toward life and work. People from a culture with a long-term orientation have a future-oriented view of life and thus are thrifty (saving) and persistent in achieving goals. They are less inclined to demand immediate returns on their investments. A short-term orientation derives from values that express a concern for maintaining personal stability or happiness and for living for the present. Immediate gratification is a priority. Most Asian countries, known for their long-term orientation, are also known for their high rate of per capita savings, whereas most European countries and the United States tend to spend more, save less, and have a short-term orientation.

Masculinity–Femininity

This value dimension was used by Hofstede to make the distinction between the quest for material assets and the quest for social connections with people. In this context, **masculinity** *describes a culture that emphasizes assertiveness and a competitive drive for money and material objects.* At the other end of the continuum is **femininity,** *which describes a culture that emphasizes developing and nurturing personal relationships and a high quality of life.* Countries with masculine cultures include Japan and Italy; feminine cultures include Sweden and Denmark.

Implications for Leadership Practice

To successfully manage in the global environment, organizations and their leaders have to learn to deal with the different values, norms, and attitudes that characterize different national cultures. Leaders have to recognize, for example, that although organizations in the United States may reward and encourage individual accountability, a different norm applies in industrialized Japan, where the group makes important decisions. In the United States, competition between work-group members for career advancement is desirable. In some other cultures, however, members resist competing with peers for rewards or promotions to avoid disrupting the harmony of the group or appearing self-interested. Value differences can be a source of interpersonal conflict. Often, people on different sides of an issue see only their side as morally justifiable. Nonetheless, in today's global economy, people holding contrasting values need to work together. Dealing with diverse and divergent values will be an increasingly common challenge for leaders. Both leaders and followers will have to learn to minimize the conflict and tension often associated with value differences.

Cross-cultural and international joint venture (IJV) studies often identify cultural differences as the cause of many interpersonal difficulties, including conflict and poor performance. A study examining the effect of dimensions of national and organizational culture differences on international joint venture performance found that presumed negative effects from culture distance on IJV performance originate more from differences in organizational culture than from differences in national culture.[88] However, despite this possibility of conflict, studies of high-performing IJVs and organizations with multinational management teams suggest that cultural diversity does not necessarily lead to

WorkApplication6

Based on the five value dimensions discussed, briefly explain the level of cultural understanding that exists where you work or have worked.

poor performance. Cultural diversity, it is argued, might even confer an advantage by giving managers a broader range of perspectives for managing complex problems and issues.

Finally, it is important to note that people working across cultures are frequently surprised by cultural paradoxes that do not seem to fit the descriptions in Exhibit 10-6. Here are two examples to illustrate this point: (1) Based on Hofstede's value dimensions of uncertainty avoidance, the Japanese have a low tolerance for uncertainty while Americans have a high tolerance. However, Japanese are known to intentionally incorporate ambiguous clauses in their business contracts, which are unusually short, while Americans dot every *i*, cross every *t*, and painstakingly spell out every possible contingency. (2) Americans are described as individualistic and believe very deeply in self-reliance, yet, they have the highest percentage of charitable giving in the world. These examples contradict and confound attempts to neatly categorize cultures. For managerial applications, the way to reconcile these paradoxes or contradictions is through what one study describes as "value trumping." [89] According to this concept, in a specific context, certain cultural values take precedence over others. The authors conclude that culture is embedded in the context and cannot be understood fully without taking context into consideration. Along with other limitations of research on these constructs, some scholars have challenged the validity and measurement of these constructs.[90,91] Strategies for effectively managing multicultural work groups with value differences are discussed in the next section on diversity.

Changing Demographics and Diversity

In the United States and many other societies of the industrialized world, multiculturalism is a fact of life. A number of factors have contributed to make diversity a key leadership issue in the United States. Among these are the Civil Rights Acts, which outlawed most types of employment discrimination; increased immigration, which has resulted in a more racially and ethnically mixed population; and the trend of globalization, which has increased the need for multicultural awareness and understanding.[92] Add to these factors the changing demographic landscape of the United States. **Demographic diversity** *is any characteristic that serves as a basis for social categorization and self-identification.*[93] Some of these characteristics include race, gender, age, ethnicity, physical appearance, language, and dialect. It has been estimated that by the year 2030, less than 50 percent of the U.S. population will be Caucasian. The state of California is already less than 50 percent Caucasian, as are some major cities. According to the 2000 census, Hispanics have surpassed African-Americans as the largest U.S. minority group. Many CEOs of Fortune 500 companies have acknowledged that diversity is a strategic business imperative. **Diversity** *is the inclusion of all groups at all levels in an organization.* With nearly 50 percent of the current U.S. workforce female, and roughly a quarter either African-American or Hispanic (10.9% and 12.2% respectively), managing diversity has become one of the most challenging human resource and organizational issues of the day.[94] There is a greater likelihood that individuals will find themselves leading or under the leadership of someone demographically different from them. Effective diversity management issues and activities such as recruiting, selecting, training, and using diverse human resources are at the forefront of corporate debate. There is now talk of diversity management competency in recruiting and training leaders.[95] There is a growing interest in research on investigating the impact of gender diversity in management and firm performance.[96] Some studies have suggested that racial and ethnic diversity may be positively related with improved cognitive outcomes (such as number and quality of ideas). Others present evidence for the possibility of symbolic consequences of diversity. For example, the presence of women and African-Americans in top management positions may signal access and opportunity to young men and women of this demographic group. In 2001, three African-American men became CEOs of Fortune 500 companies—Kenneth Chenault (American Express), Richard Parsons (Time Warner), and Stanley O'Neal (Merrill Lynch).[97]

The United States has been described as the "melting pot" of cultures. The thinking not long ago was that to make it in this society, one had to blend in with the mainstream culture. Individuals from different cultures responded to this pressure by trying to lose or disguise their identity—adopting new names, changing accents, and abandoning old customs, traditions, and values. The prevailing belief was that to get ahead, one had to assimilate into mainstream culture. Job opportunities favored those who blended in. Now, however, it would appear that the "melting pot" concept has been replaced by the "salad bowl" concept. Rather than assimilation, the emphasis has shifted towards cultural integration without necessarily losing one's identity. Diversity in the workplace, brought on by a multicultural society, is no longer viewed as a liability but an asset. Many organizations have found that tapping into diversity reveals new and innovative ways of viewing traditional problems, and that diversity provides a rich mix of talents for today's globally competitive marketplace. For some, valuing and effectively managing diversity is a competitive imperative. For others, the rationale for valuing and effectively managing diversity is a moral and ethical imperative. They embrace diversity for reasons such as fairness and upholding the dignity of all people—especially those that have been marginalized. Many see diversity as the best approach for optimizing the full breadth of talents and skills of today's workforce.

Researchers have disagreed about the effects of diversity on productivity—there are those who feel that diversity leads to better performance because diverse perspectives add a creative edge to problem solving, and those who feel that diversity impedes performance because diverse teams are less cohesive. In this section, we explore the current state of diversity in the U.S. workforce, reasons for embracing diversity, and strategies organizations are employing to achieve full diversity. These strategies include removing obstacles to achieving diversity, creating a culture that supports diversity, and conducting diversity training and leadership education programs.

Current State of Workforce Diversity

Diversity describes differences resulting from age, gender, race, ethnicity, religion, and sexual orientation. In the last 25 years, attitudes towards diversity have changed for obvious reasons: increasing diversity of the workforce and globalization. There are dramatic changes taking place in the workforce. National demographic changes, as well as greater minority representation in the workforce, have accounted for the most significant increase in workforce diversity. In the United States, the workforce of the next decade will be older and more culturally diverse, with women and minorities in greater proportion than ever before. The population of ethnic minorities, such as African-Americans, Asian-Americans, and Hispanics, is growing at a faster rate than the overall society. The U.S. Census Bureau projects that the number of Hispanics, already the largest minority group, will increase to 15 percent of the population by 2021. This group grew by over 40 percent in the 1990s. The percentage of African-Americans is expected to increase to 14 percent by 2021. Longer term, Caucasians are expected to become a minority by 2050. By the year 2005, African-American and Hispanic employees made up over 25 percent of the workforce, while the percentage of Caucasian males decreased from 51 percent to 44 percent.[98]

In the new work environment, workers must often share work duties and space with coworkers of diverse races, social backgrounds, and cultures. The passage of the Americans with Disabilities Act (ADA) has further broadened the scope of diversity in the workplace. Today, the chances of working with a disabled coworker are much higher than a decade ago.[99] These trends have made it imperative for U.S. companies to pay attention to issues of diversity. Companies that can effectively manage diversity will be able to recruit from a larger pool, train and retain superior performers, and maximize the benefits of this diverse workforce. More organizations are highlighting diversity in their advertising, because they are competing for talent in a tight market, and they recognize that demographic shifts are going to dramatically change their marketplace over the next 20 years. HR recruiters have discovered that focusing on diversity in recruitment advertising helps attract more employees from diverse backgrounds.

The other factor that has led companies to value and manage diversity is globalization. The economies of the world are interconnected, and changes in one economy quickly affect others. Corporations are becoming increasingly global, pursuing merger and acquisition strategies around the world. Globalization has led firms to originate, produce, and market their products and services worldwide. The emergence of a largely borderless economic world has created a new reality for organizations of all shapes and sizes. United States–based companies such as Pepsi-Cola, Coca-Cola, Procter & Gamble, AT&T, Ford, Nike, General Mills, Boeing, McDonald's, and many others have established a significant presence in Europe, Asia, and South America. They face competition from European companies such as Daimler-Chrysler, Nestlé of Switzerland, Canada's Northern Telecom, Siemens of Germany, Sweden's Ericsson, and many others who also have a significant presence in the United States.

Collaboration between companies has become a common way to meet the demands of global competition and to overcome the growing trend of consumer ethnocentrism, which is the tendency to want to purchase products from one's own rather than a foreign country.[100] Global strategic alliances between independent firms for the purpose of achieving common goals and overcoming domestic country bias are becoming quite prevalent.[101] General Mills and Nestlé of Switzerland created Cereal Partners Worldwide for the purpose of fine-tuning Nestlé's European cereal and for marketing and distributing General Mills cereals worldwide.[102] In this global environment, most manufactured

WorkApplication7

Describe diversity where you work or have worked. For example, approximately what percentage are male versus female, Caucasian versus non-Caucasian, older versus younger, and so on?

_____

_____

_____

_____

_____

goods contain components from more than one country. Also, the number of foreign-born managers being appointed to lead U.S. companies is increasing. The list of U.S. companies led by CEOs who emigrated from other countries is growing. In 2000, the Academy of Management Executive selected its Executive of the Year. The honor went to Mr. Hatim Tyabji, born in India but educated in the United States. The academy wanted to showcase a leading CEO who has been successful in creating an innovative and highly profitable company, and who has done so based on a strongly held system of personal values that permeate the organization and everyone in it.[103] Mr. Tyabji fits the bill very impressively. As chairman and CEO of Saraide, an Internet and wireless communications company, he has created a high-performance culture that has helped the company realize the two outcomes of highly effective cultures; that is, the power of culture to create internal unity, and to enhance organizational adaptation to external environmental changes. A cursory review of Mr. Tyabji's background shows that he and many others like him are having a significant impact in the U.S. corporate leadership environment. Almost every employee in the workforce today is dealing with a wider range of cultures than ever before. The challenge for organizational leaders is to recognize that each person can bring value and strengths to the workplace based on his or her own unique background.

Learning Outcome 7

Explain the primary reasons for embracing diversity.

Reasons for Embracing Diversity

From a purely humanistic perspective, some believe that there is an ethical and moral imperative to pursue a policy of inclusion rather than exclusion. Advocates of this position believe that it is a matter of fairness, and that an inclusionary policy signals a company's commitment to uphold the dignity of every person regardless of their circumstance. From a legal perspective, embracing diversity is in compliance with laws that have precedent and historical foundations.[104] From a practical perspective, shifting demographics and increasing globalization have significantly changed the composition of the workforce, forcing corporations to respond or suffer economic loss. Organizations are forced to change their views and their approach to diversity in order to reflect this new reality. There are other pertinent reasons that organizations need to embrace diversity:

- Embracing diversity can offer a company a marketing advantage. There is much support for the view that having a multicultural workforce, supplier network, and customer base is good for business.[105] A diversified workforce may offer insight into understanding and meeting the needs of diverse customers. A representative workforce facilitates selling goods and services, because employees who share similar cultural traits with the customers may be able to develop better, longer-lasting customer relationships. Diversity, therefore, can enable a company to gain access to and legitimacy in diverse markets.

- Embracing diversity can help a company to develop and retain talented people. When an organization has a reputation for valuing diversity, it tends to attract the best job candidates among women and other culturally diverse groups. For example, many HR recruiters have discovered that focusing on diversity in recruitment advertising helps attract more applicants from diverse areas. There is some evidence that minority job seekers tend to look for companies with a proven diversity record.

- Embracing diversity can be cost effective. As organizations become more diversified, some are experiencing higher levels of job dissatisfaction and turnover among minority groups who are finding it hard to fit in with the old, Caucasian-male culture. This has been the case with organizations that have not shown a total commitment and support for diversity. Organizations that wholeheartedly embrace diversity and make everyone feel valued for what they can contribute may increase the job satisfaction of diverse groups, thus decreasing turnover and absenteeism and their associated costs.

- Embracing diversity may provide a broader and deeper base of creative problem solving and decision making. Creative solutions to problems are more likely to be reached in diverse work groups than homogeneous groups. In diverse groups, people bring different perspectives, insights, and skills to problems—resulting in better solutions and greater innovation. In innovative companies, leaders are challenged to create organizational environments that nurture and support creative thinking and the sharing of diverse viewpoints. However, some scholars have cautioned that diversity by itself does not automatically make work groups more productive. Rather, the important factor is how people in diverse teams interrelate. Different experiences and view points without strong working relationships don't make a productive team.[106]

According to the National Minority Business Development Council, the benefits of supplier diversity programs—designed to increase the number of minority business enterprises that supply goods and services to U.S. corporations—include a wider pool of qualified suppliers, better product and service quality resulting from increased competition, enhanced community relations, positive publicity, and increased loyalty among minority consumers.[107] Some examples of companies that have seen the benefits of supplier diversity programs are in the automobile industry. Ford Motor Co., General Motors Corp., and Daimler-Chrysler Corp. are said to be working to diversify their supply bases and develop minority suppliers. In 2000, Ford spent $3.5 billion with minority suppliers, Daimler-Chrysler spent $2.7 billion, and General Motors spent $2.3 billion.[108]

Despite the benefits of diversity just described, it can also bring about negative outcomes if not effectively managed. Increased diversity can also mean increased potential for conflict. This may occur because, in general, people feel more comfortable dealing with others who are like themselves. To some extent, society has played a role in creating the gap that often exists between ethnic groups. In many communities, ethnic groups still do not interact socially, and this carries over into the workplace. Rather than a unified team, competition with, and even distrust toward one another may characterize a diverse work environment. A leader in a diverse work unit may spend more of his or her time and energy dealing with interpersonal issues rather than trying to achieve organizational objectives. Therefore, effective management of a diverse workforce is necessary for an organization to perform at a high level and gain a competitive advantage.

Despite increased levels of diversity training initiatives in many organizations, there is concern that very little is happening in terms of the impact of these initiatives on the hiring practices of many managers and the organizations they represent. One study reports that although financial companies have been trying to hire and promote minorities to executive positions for many years, few companies have actually achieved success in these efforts.[109] Some reasons put forward for this slow progress include the slow rate of college and graduate school graduations for African-Americans and Hispanics, CEO inertia, and racial discrimination. According to the U.S. Department of Justice, federal employment discrimination lawsuits increased by 300 percent from the years 1990 to 2000, with plaintiffs alleging discrimination related to hiring practices, pay, and/or promotions, and harassment.[110]

The results of another study, which focused on the food service and hospitality industry, revealed that only 56 percent of the companies polled have corporate diversity statements—compared with 54 percent in 2000. Furthermore, only 40 percent have supplier/vendor diversity programs or specific programs to recruit, retain, and promote minorities—compared with 68 percent in 2000.[111]

Experts caution that simply responding to legislative mandates does not seem to automatically result in meaningful, substantive change in behaviors and attitudes. Rather, change aimed at valuing diversity has to have top management support and commitment, broad participation through empowerment, involve multiple initiatives, and require constant reinforcement. According to many diversity scholars, diversity management is now considered a new organizational paradigm that has moved beyond a human resource model based solely on meeting legal standards to one that promotes the inherent value of a multicultural workforce. This new model emphasizes that creating a climate of acceptance requires major, systematic, company-wide, planned change efforts, which are typically not part of standard affirmative action plans.[112] The next section focuses on the role of leadership and organizational processes that either enhance or handicap an organization's diversity initiatives.

—————————————— Learning Outcome 8 ——————————————

Identify the three areas in which visible and strong leadership action is needed to achieve full diversity.

Leadership Initiatives for Achieving Full Diversity

For organizations to embrace and value diversity, the concept itself must be embedded in the organizational strategy. When diversity is part and parcel of the organizational strategy, all employees are given equal opportunities to contribute their talents, skills, and expertise toward achieving organizational objectives, independent of their race, gender, ethnic background, or any other definable characteristic. Achieving full diversity requires top management to show its commitment to diversity by (1) removing personal and organizational obstacles to achieving diversity, (2) implanting a diversity-supportive culture, and (3) engaging employees in diversity awareness training and leadership education.[113]

Removing Obstacles to Achieving Diversity

To increase performance, organizations have to unleash and take advantage of the potential of a diverse workforce; however, leaders often face a number of personal and organizational obstacles to realizing the full potential of diverse employees. Removing obstacles to diversity is in effect a transformation from an organizational culture characterized by exclusionary practices to one characterized by inclusionary practices. Exhibit 10-7 lists five obstacles to achieving diversity.[114] Each is then briefly discussed.

Stereotypes and Prejudice

This is perhaps the most prevalent obstacle to achieving diversity in many organizations. **Prejudice** *is the tendency to form an adverse opinion without just cause about people who are different from the mainstream in terms of their gender, race, ethnicity, or any other definable characteristic.* It is an assumption, without evidence, that people who are not part of the mainstream culture (women, African-Americans, and other minorities) are inherently inferior, less competent at their jobs, and less suitable for leadership positions. Leadership commitment toward eradicating stereotypes and prejudice of this kind will pave the way for a diverse workforce to thrive.

Ethnocentrism

Ethnocentrism *is the belief that one's own group or subculture is naturally superior to other groups and cultures.* Ethnocentrism is an obstacle to diversity because it tends to produce a homogeneous culture, a culture where everyone looks and acts the same and shares the same set of values and beliefs. Removing ethnocentrism and replacing it with a belief that all groups, cultures, and subcultures are inherently equal will greatly enhance the achievement of a diverse workforce's full potential.[115,116]

Policies and Practices

A third obstacle to diversity is embedded in organizational policies and practices that work against maintaining a diverse workforce. The leader must perform an audit of the organization to determine if existing policies, rules, procedures, and practices work against minorities; for example, removing barriers to the selection of women and minorities, such as job requirements that may not be valid or relevant to the job. Policies regarding human resource management issues such as hiring, training, promotion, compensation, and retirement or layoffs must be examined to make sure that minorities are not unfairly treated by actions taken in these areas. Xerox Corporation, for example, has undertaken major initiatives to increase diversity by adopting practices that increase the proportion of women and minorities it recruits and promotes. Xerox has also established sophisticated support networks for minority employees (the Xerox Hispanic Professional Association is an example of such a support network). Other companies with pro-diversity policies and practices include Fannie Mae, Cummins Inc., and Medtronic Inc. The corporate diversity

Exhibit 10-7 *Obstacles to achieving diversity.*

- Stereotypes and prejudice
- Ethnocentrism
- Policies and practices
- The glass ceiling
- Unfriendly work environment

efforts of these companies have created true cultures of inclusion and serve as models for others. Human resource practices will be discussed in greater detail in the next section on factors related to diversity success.

The Glass Ceiling

The fourth obstacle to diversity is the presence of the glass ceiling, or what others have described as the "white male" club. The glass ceiling exists between upper-middle management and the executive level. Between these two levels, corporate culture almost always shifts to a culture based on power; and since the power resides in the hands of Caucasian men, women and minorities face an uphill battle getting fair consideration. Caucasian men hold more than 50 percent of all top administrative and managerial positions, while African-American and Hispanic representation is in the single digits. *The* **glass ceiling** *is therefore an invisible barrier that separates women and minorities from top leadership positions.* Evidence of the glass ceiling is seen in the concentration of women and minorities at the lower rungs of the corporate ladder, where the skills and talents of women and minorities are not being fully utilized.[117-120]

Unfriendly Work Environment

The work environment for many minorities is a lonely, unfriendly, and stressful place, particularly in executive-level positions where Caucasian men outnumber women and minorities. Minorities and women may be excluded from social activities in or out of the office, which often leads to feelings of alienation and despair. This in turn often leads to job dissatisfaction and high turnover among minority groups. Removing this obstacle can go a long way toward alleviating the problem of high turnover, and thus preserve diversity initiatives.

WorkApplication8

Identify and briefly explain which of the five obstacles exist and/or have been removed where you work or have worked.

_____

_____

_____

_____

_____

— Learning Outcome 9 —

Explain the leader's role in creating a culture that supports diversity.

Creating a Culture That Supports Diversity

Removing obstacles to diversity creates an environment for diversity initiatives to begin to take root. Management must take the lead in creating an organizational climate that supports diversity. To an individual employee, organizational climate is basically how it feels to work in a certain environment. Research suggests that 50 to 70 percent of an organization's climate can be traced to its leadership or management style. To institutionalize diversity, leaders are encouraged to create a whole new culture of multiculturalism.[121] This involves the development of an institutional readiness for new diversity initiatives and practices. Kmart, for example, has adopted the slogan "Diversity Enriches" as one of five themes for improving its corporate culture. In recruiting staff and serving customers, Kmart intends for its actions to reflect and address the needs of the multiracial neighborhoods in which its stores are located.[122]

A culture of multiculturalism is one that continuously values diversity and as a result has made it a way of life in the organization. An indication that diversity has become a way of life for a company can be found in what happens to diversity programs during an economic downturn. In the past, corporate leaders viewed diversity programs as luxuries, something to be indulged in when times were good but quickly eliminated when the going got tough. More and more, companies are sticking with their diversity programs even during an economic downturn, which indicates the seriousness with which they now take diversity.

To achieve full diversity, leaders are challenged to work to ensure that women, African-Americans, Hispanics, and other minorities have opportunities to move up the corporate ladder into leadership positions. Though slowly changing, it is still the case that top leadership positions in most of corporate America are occupied by white males, despite the growing employee population of minorities. This has led to the underutilization of the talents and skills of minorities. To achieve full diversity, top leaders must actively pursue the objective of changing the organizational culture to one that values diversity at every level of the organization—from the top to the bottom.

Studies have identified factors related to diversity success.[123] Exhibit 10-8 highlights these factors, and is followed by a brief discussion of each.

Corporate Philosophy

For diversity to succeed, there has to be an explicit corporate philosophy that unambiguously supports it. Success is achieved when the organization's diversity philosophy goes beyond simply responding to legislative mandates. Rather, a philosophy that views diversity as a strategic imperative strives to embed diversity into the daily practices and procedures of organizational operations. A corporate philosophy that values diversity will lead to a culture of openness, fairness, inclusion, and empowerment for all.

Top Management Support and Commitment

Achieving diversity success does not happen by chance. Many experts argue that support and commitment from senior management—and, especially, from the CEO—is imperative. A major catalyst behind successful diversity management is the role played by the CEO and his or her management team. The CEO alone has the authority to make diversity part of the organizational mission. The commitment of the CEO and his or her top management team to diversity

Exhibit 10-8 *Factors related to diversity success.*

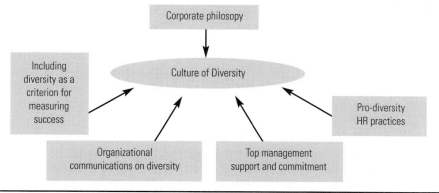

Source: Based on J. A. Gilbert and J. M. Ivancevich, "Valuing Diversity: A Tale of Two Organizations," *Academy of Management Executive* 14(1) (2000): 93–105.

will filter down to individual operating units, thus making diversity an institutionalized concept. Leaders who talk diversity must "walk the talk."

Pro-Diversity Human Resource Practices

In organizations that have achieved diversity success, several types of inclusionary measures are subelements of the HR department. The HR department is the gateway through which all employees pass in order to become members of an organization. HR initiatives can contribute to greater acceptance of diversity. Examples would include an HR initiative that stipulates conducting periodic cultural audits, or one that allows for in-depth assessments of methods of recruitment, compensation, performance appraisal, employee development, and promotion. Other initiatives may include sponsoring diversity workshops and conferences, and establishing policies and practices that aim for outcomes such as full structural integration, a prejudice-free work environment, low levels of inter-group conflict, strong social support networks for minorities, and leadership diversity.[124]

Organizational Communications on Diversity

Organizational efforts to communicate the message of diversity are an important factor for diversity success. Organizational communication in the form of newsletters, posters, calendars, and coffee mugs celebrating diversity achievements, and regular surveys of employee attitudes and opinions, are ways to heighten awareness of diversity. Repeated exposure to diversity themes would help to promote the message that diversity is a normal and accepted part of everyday life in the organization. Also, such in-house communications and newsletters would encourage employee involvement and help transmit the diversity message.

Including Diversity as a Criterion for Measuring Success

A final factor related to a successful diversity program is the extent to which diversity objectives are included among the criteria for measuring managerial performance. An organizational objective to raise awareness of equality may include specific activities, such as writing an article for the company or department newsletter, recruiting more minorities into managerial positions, developing and implementing a discrimination refresher workshop, or addressing diversity concerns in a timely manner. By pursuing this course of action, success is measured not just in financial terms but also in a manager's ability to meet these specific goals. Multiple criteria for success, defined along multiple dimensions, will establish managerial accountability on multiple fronts. With such a system in place, managerial compensation can be easily tied to diversity success by requiring that a certain percentage of a manager's pay be dependent on meeting quantifiable diversity objectives. Not rewarding accomplishment of diversity goals could imply that diversity is not a top management priority.

Diversity Awareness Training and Leadership Education

The benefits of diversity as we have demonstrated are enormous, but without a well-trained workforce that values diversity awareness and leadership commitment, increased cultural diversity may actually lead to decreased productivity and lower financial and strategic performance. As mentioned in the

WorkApplication9

Identify and briefly explain which of the five factors related to diversity success exist or do not exist where you work or have worked.

introduction to this section, the notion that culturally diverse individuals coming into the workforce have to assimilate into the mainstream culture is a thing of the past. The challenge now is for organizations to make the necessary adjustments, such as removing obstacles to achieving diversity, and creating a diversity-supportive culture. As revealed in the preceding discussions, strong leadership commitment is needed to make these adjustments. Many of today's leaders belong to the baby-boom generation; most of them grew up in segregated communities with homogeneous cultures. Some have little experience with managing and leading diverse work groups. For example, some leaders are uncertain how to handle the challenge of communicating with employees whose cultural backgrounds result in assumptions, values, and even language skills that differ from the leaders.' Various racial or ethnic groups may respond differently to the demands of their job responsibilities or to the approaches that leaders are using to manage relationships in the workplace. Similarly, some men still find it difficult to report to or be evaluated by women. Even managers who are sensitive to issues of diversity may not have the skills to deal with other, less obvious forms of discrimination. Diversity awareness training and leadership education will teach employees that even if blatantly sexist, racist, or "ageist" acts do not occur, subtle forms of discrimination, such as exclusion from informal networks, conversations, and social interactions outside of work, will still occur, and, over time, may become standard behavior. These types of exclusionary tactics, if left unchecked, can lead to isolation and reduced opportunities for minorities. Employees of minority groups working in this type of environment often end up leaving, resulting in a loss of valuable human capital for the organization. These are some of the challenges that come with the growing diversity of the workforce and that many leaders are still unprepared to deal with effectively. We will explore the role of diversity training and education in fostering a deeper cultural awareness among leaders and employees, and helping organizations effectively manage diversity.

Diversity Training

Diversity training can facilitate the management of a diverse workforce. The purpose of diversity training is to develop organizations as integrated communities in which every employee feels respected, accepted, and valued regardless of gender, race, ethnicity, or other distinguishing characteristic. Training sessions are aimed at increasing people's awareness of and empathy for people from different cultures and backgrounds. There are many diversity-training programs with many different objectives. Diversity training can include but is not limited to the following:

- Role-playing, in which participants act out appropriate and inappropriate ways to deal with diverse employees
- Self-awareness activities, in which participants discover how their own hidden and overt biases direct their thinking about specific individuals and groups
- Awareness activities, in which participants learn about others who differ from them in race, gender, culture, and so on

Diversity training programs can last hours or days. They can be conducted by outside experts on diversity, or by existing members of an organization with expertise in diversity. Small organizations are more likely to rely on outside assistance; larger organizations often have their own in-house staff. Leaders in these companies understand the value for their future competitiveness of effectively managing diversity. The primary objectives of diversity training programs include one or more of the following:

- Helping employees of varying backgrounds communicate effectively with one another
- Showing members how to deal effectively with diversity-related conflicts and tensions
- Exploring how differences might be viewed as strengths, not weaknesses, in the workplace
- Improving members' understanding of each other and their work relations

Not all diversity-training programs are successful. Diversity training is most likely to be successful when it is not a one-time event, but an ongoing or repeated activity, and when there are follow-up activities to see whether the training objectives were accomplished.

Education

Sometimes effectively managing diversity requires that leaders of an organization receive additional education to make them better able to communicate and work with diverse employees. Through training and education, leaders develop personal characteristics that support diversity. Through education, leaders are taught to see diversity in the larger context of the organization's long-term vision. Managers should have long-term plans to include employees of different cultures at all levels of the organization. They should be educated on the strategic significance of linking diversity to the organization's competitiveness, rather than simply being told to do it.

To develop and implement diversity programs, leaders must first examine and change themselves. Through education, leaders learn how to communicate effectively and encourage feedback from all employees regardless of background, how to accept criticism, and how to adjust their behavior when appropriate. A broad knowledge base on multiculturalism and diversity issues helps.

Also, through education, leaders learn how to mentor and empower employees of diverse cultures. They learn to appreciate their role in creating opportunities for all employees to use their unique abilities.

Without an educated and committed leadership team, the task of creating and managing a diverse workforce is unlikely to yield positive results. Everyone must be involved, including employees and managers at all levels, and top management commitment must be visible, for the benefits of diversity to be realized.

In the last section of this chapter, we describe and explore the emerging concept of the learning organization. The learning organization concept is predicated on the assumption of equality and community, in which people are able to communicate openly and honestly with one another and also maintain their unique differences. The culture of a learning organization is therefore one of accepting the principles and beliefs embedded in multiculturalism and diversity.

WorkApplication10

Does the organization you work or have worked for offer diversity awareness training and education? If you are not sure, contact the human resources department to find out. If it does, briefly describe the program.

_____

_____

_____

_____

_____

4. What Is Avon's Stance on Diversity, and Has It Lived Up to It So Far?

Avon embraces diversity in the workforce, and continues to be a leader in taking affirmative action to ensure that doors are open to talented individuals, and that all associates and employees have opportunities for development and advancement. Avon has more women in management positions than any other Fortune 500 company, and half of its board of directors is women. In the United States and elsewhere, Avon has internal networks of associates including a Parents' Network, a Hispanic Network, a Black Professional Association, an Asian network, and a Gay and Lesbian network. The networks act as liaisons between associates and management, to bring voice to critical issues that impact the workplace and the marketplace. Avon's dedication and commitment to diversity has been honored by several organizations and media. Avon's awards and recognitions include appearance on *Fortune*'s "Most Admired Companies" list for over a decade, selection by *Business Week* as one of the "Top 100 Global Brands," recognition by *Business Ethics* among its "100 Best Corporate Citizens" for six consecutive years, the honor of being one of *Fortune*'s "50 Best Companies for Minorities," and ranking as the #1 company for executive women by the National Association for Female Executives. It is evident that Avon has established and continues to uphold its standards on diversity.

An obvious benefit of the three major diversity programs described above—removing personal and organizational obstacles to achieving diversity, implementing a diversity-supportive culture, and engaging employees in diversity awareness training and leadership education—is in the number of women and minorities occupying top management positions in U.S. corporations today. Andrea Jung, CEO of Avon, is of Asian descent. Kenneth Chanault, CEO of American Express, and Richard Parsons, CEO of Time Warner, are African-Americans, and Hatim Tyabji, CEO of Saraide, is of Indian descent—just to name a few. Diversity and a culture of valuing minority talents and contributions helped launch the career of Oprah Winfrey. Today, Oprah needs no introduction; but back in 1976, she started as a reporter and evening news co-anchor at WJZ-TV in Baltimore. The opportunity led her to co-host WJZ's morning talk show, *People Are Talking,* and later host her own show, *A.M. Chicago,* which later was renamed *The Oprah Winfrey Show.* The rest, as the saying goes, is history.

Ethical Dilemma 2

Sex Discrimination

Wal-Mart, the world's largest retailer, has been hit with a class action lawsuit. Wal-Mart has been accused, but not convicted, of denying women workers equal pay and opportunities for promotion. The suit claims that even if

(Continued)

Ethical Dilemma 2

(Continued)

Wal-Mart policies are not clearly discriminatory, its organizational culture per-petuates gender stereotypes that lead to differences in pay and promotion be-tween men and women. Up to 1.6 million women could join the class action suit. Wal-Mart strongly disagreed with the court decision to proceed with a class action lawsuit, and is appealing. Wal-Mart also faces 30 lawsuits alleging it failed to pay workers overtime pay.[125] CEO Lee Scott rebuts critics of pay scales, but he has initiated workplace-diversity moves to achieve full diversity. Wal-Mart hired a director of diversity and set diversity targets, and executive bonuses are cut if the company doesn't meet the objectives. Wal-Mart now posts management openings on its company-wide computer network.[126]

1. Do you believe that organizational culture can lead to discrimination?
2. Do you believe Wal-Mart is innocent?
3. If Wal-Mart is guilty, do you think that it was intentional discrimination?

The Learning Organization and Its Culture

Published more than a decade ago, *The Fifth Discipline,* by Peter Senge, made a compelling case that an organization's survival was linked to its ability to learn and adapt. He described a true learning organization as one that can develop not only new capabilities, but also a fundamental mind-set transformation.[127] By all accounts, most organizations operate in environments characterized by continuous change, and for some—like the high-tech companies—the level of change is discontinuous. **Discontinuous change** *occurs when anticipated or expected changes bear no resemblance to the present or the past.* The emergence of better and cheaper technologies, rivals' introduction of new or better prod-ucts and services, competition from lower-cost foreign competitors, and demo-graphic shifts represent major threats to the profitability and even survival of many organizations. In this type of environment, changing the way in which employees or teams think and function can be a challenging task for leaders. In promoting such changes, employees are asked to think beyond some of their past successes and current state of knowledge. Leaders must transform their organizations into learning organizations.

In today's business environment, knowledge has been identified as one of the most important resources that contribute to the competitive advantage of an organization. Organizational learning is seen as a fundamental component of the knowledge creation and sharing process.[128] Problems associated with the lack of effective structures for knowledge creation and sharing are often at-tributed to poor leadership and organizational politics.[129,130] To succeed in this dynamic environment, leaders are challenged to transform their organizations into flexible systems capable of continuous learning and greater adaptation.[131] In this section, we examine what a learning organization represents, how a learning organization differs from a traditional organization, and the role of leadership in creating a learning organization.

What Is a Learning Organization?

In a stable environment, change is slow and incremental, and organizations have time to react and still retain their competitive positions. However in rapidly changing environments, change is frequent and discontinuous; and reacting is not the best approach to staying competitive. To succeed, organizations must be proactive or anticipatory, which requires an orientation toward learning and continuous improvement.[132] A **learning organization** *is one that is skilled at creating, acquiring, and transferring knowledge, and at modifying behavior to reflect new knowledge and insights.*[133] There is some agreement among strategy scholars that managing knowledge effectively can provide an organization with sustainable competitive advantages. Leaders are critical to the process of managing knowledge effectively, in part because of the politics involved. Leaders, especially those in top positions, must be able to manage the organizational knowledge base to overcome obstacles and exploit opportunities that are the products of accelerating industry dynamics.[134] **Organizational knowledge** *is the tacit and explicit knowledge that individuals possess about products, services, systems, and processes.*[135] Explicit knowledge is often codified in manuals, databases, and information systems.

Some scholars have focused their research on the politics of organizational learning because, as they put it, "organizations are inherently political."[136,137] These scholars believe that integrating power and politics into research on organizational learning will provide a more effective foundation for understanding why some organizations are better able to learn than others, and why only some of the available useful innovations are embraced by organizations. The following are characteristics of a learning organization:

• Embedded in the organization's culture and included in the reward and appraisal systems are values of experimentation, initiative, innovation, and flexibility.
• There is visible and strong top management support.
• There are mechanisms and structures in place to support and nurture ideas generated by people at all levels in the organization.[138]
• Knowledge and information are disseminated or made accessible to anyone who needs them, and people are encouraged to apply them to their work.[139]
• Resources are committed to fostering learning at all levels (such as at 3M, where employees are allowed to spend 15 percent of the work day experimenting or doing whatever they please—called the 15 percent rule).
• Employees are empowered to resolve problems as they arise and to find better ways of doing work.
• There is equal emphasis on the short- and long-term performance of the organization.
• There is a deep desire throughout the organization to develop and refine knowledge of how things work, how to adapt to the environment, and how to achieve organizational objectives.
• People are not afraid to fail.

In stable environments, organizations focus on being efficient and on achieving this objective by developing highly structured command systems with strong vertical hierarchies and specialized jobs. Today, however, this traditional organizational form is being replaced by the learning organization form.

The Traditional versus the Learning Organization

The traditional organization is based on the bureaucratic model that emphasizes a command and control structure, centralized decision making, highly formalized systems, specialized tasks, competitive strategy, and a rigid, closed culture. The criticism leveled against the traditional organization is that too much emphasis is placed on an "outside-in," macro-organizational perspective of learning, and too little is placed on the "inside-out" perspective, which acknowledges that the main agents of learning and change are people.[140] The learning organization represents a shift in organizational design paradigm to something that is less structured, decentralized, and informal. In the learning organization, strategy formulation is a collaborative process and its culture is more open and adaptable. The learning organization embraces the idea that people will learn if encouraged to face challenges, experiment, fail, and reflect on their experiences. Exhibit 10-9 compares the two organization types, and a brief discussion follows.

As indicated in Exhibit 10-9, the traditional, efficiency-driven organization's structure is vertical (a tall pyramid), starting with the CEO at the top and everyone else functionally organized in layers down below. These vertical structures are effective under stable environmental conditions. The organization's vision, mission, and strategy are formulated at the top and disseminated through the layers of authority and responsibility. There is little or no input from the lower ranks of the organization. Decision making is centralized at the top of the hierarchy, which controls and coordinates all functional units throughout the organization. To ensure reliable and predictable results, tasks are rigidly defined and broken down into specialized jobs. Strict formal rules and procedures for performing each task are enforced. Though repetitive, boring, and unchallenging, it is an efficient way of keeping the production line running smoothly. The culture of the organization is fixed on values, practices, beliefs, and principles that have helped it attain success in the past and the present. The traditional organization often becomes a victim of its own success by aligning with an outdated culture that does not promote adaptability and change. Finally, the traditional organization is characterized by an elaborate formal system of reporting that allows leaders to closely monitor work operations and maintain efficient, steady performance. This formal system is a powerful tool for controlling

Exhibit 10-9 *The traditional versus the learning organization.*

Traditional (efficiency driven)	Learning (learning driven)
• Stable environment	• Changing environment
• Vertical structure	• Flat horizontal structure
• Strategy is formulated from the top and passed down	• Strategy is a collaborative effort within the organization and with other companies
• Centralized decision making	• Decentralized decision making
• Rigidly defined and specialized tasks	• Loose, flexible, and adaptive roles
• Rigid culture that is not responsive to change	• Adaptive culture that encourages continuous improvement and change
• Formal systems of communication tied to the vertical hierarchy with lots of filters	• Personal and group networks of free, open exchanges with no filters

information and often acts as a filter in determining what information leaders decide to pass down to lower-level employees.

By contrast, in learning organizations, the vertical structure is abandoned for a flat, horizontal structure. The horizontal structure is constituted around work flows or processes rather than functional specialties. The learning organization recognizes that work processes and procedures are the means to satisfying customer needs, rather than ends in themselves. The self-managed team concept discussed in Chapter 8 is characteristic of the learning organization, and functions best with less rigid, flexible structures. Flexible structures are appropriate in today's rapidly changing business environment, in which competitive pressures, technological innovations, global market changes, and evolving customer needs require constant adjustments and adaptation. To encourage innovation and creativity in meeting current challenges, learning organizations are designing tasks that are much looser, free flowing, and adaptive. There are few strict rules and procedures prescribing how things should be done. The term *organic* has been used to describe this type of organization. Responsibility and authority are decentralized to lower-level workers, empowering them to think, experiment, create, learn, and solve problems at their level. Teamwork is highly valued, and there are network systems to facilitate open communication and exchange throughout the organization and with other companies. Researchers interested in network relationships have recognized the knowledge dimension of networks, and its link with competitive success. They propose that networks provide firms with access to knowledge, resources, markets, and technologies.[141]

A shared vision, mission, and long-term objectives, and the changes in the internal and external environments are the bases for the emergence of strategy in a learning organization. The input and active participation of employees in strategy formulation is highly valued, because they are at the front line making daily contact with customers, suppliers, competitors, and other stakeholders. Organizational learning is a multilevel process, bringing together individual, group, and organizational levels of analysis. It is dynamic, bridging the levels with specific mechanisms. It involves multiple learning processes (intuition, integrating, interpreting, and institutionalization) that allow learning to feed forward to the organizational level and feed back to the individual.[142] In the end, one of the most important qualities for a learning organization to have is a strong, adaptive culture. An adaptive culture encourages teamwork, openness, equality, relationships, creativity, and innovation.

Examples of learning organizations today include Intel, Microsoft, Starbucks, W. L. Gore and Associates, Lucent Technologies, Motorola, Xerox, 3M, Johnson & Johnson, and many Internet-based companies: America Online, Amazon.com, Yahoo!, and eBay.

WorkApplication11

Using Exhibit 10-9, explain whether where you work or have worked is more a traditional or a learning organization.

_____

_____

_____

_____

_____

———————— Learning Outcome 10 ————————

Describe the role of leadership in creating a learning organization.

The Role of Leaders in Creating a Learning Organization

Leaders in learning organizations face a dual challenge to maintain efficient operations and create an adaptive organization at the same time. Efficient performance often requires incorporation of the characteristics of the traditional vertical organization, which can conflict with the requirements for creating a learning organization. This potential conflict poses a major challenge in creating

Applying the Concept 4

Traditional or Learning Organization

Identify each statement by its type of organization. Write the appropriate letter in the blank before each item.

a. traditional   b. learning

_____ 15. Top-level managers make all the important decisions around here.

_____ 16. There aren't many levels of management in our company.

_____ 17. With a union, we have clearly defined jobs and are not allowed to do other work.

a successful learning organization. Here we identify important leadership initiatives that enhance a learning environment. The following guidelines (see Exhibit 10-10) are ways in which leaders can create conditions conducive to learning and continuous improvement.[143–145]

Encourage Creative Thinking

Although an organization's capacity to become more creative must begin at the individual level, creativity at the organizational level is also essential. At the organizational level, creativity is affected by the type of leadership style, culture, climate, structure, and systems that the organization has in place. Also, the resources and skills that the organization has in place will play a role. These organizational factors are further examined as part of the discussion on guidelines for enhancing organizational learning.

At the individual level, leaders can enhance learning by encouraging members to "think outside the box"—in other words, consider possibilities that do not already exist. Rather than responding to known challenges, employees are encouraged to create the future. This is a culture that encourages innovation by employees. People with maverick ideas or out-of-the-ordinary proposals have

Exhibit 10-10 *Guidelines for enhancing organizational learning.*

- Encourage creative thinking.
- Create a climate in which experimentation is encouraged.
- Provide incentives for learning and innovation.
- Build confidence in followers' capacity to learn and adapt.
- Encourage systems thinking.
- Create a culture conducive to individual and team learning.
- Institute mechanisms for channeling and nurturing creative ideas for innovation.
- Create a shared vision for learning.
- Broaden employees' frame of reference.
- Create an environment in which people can learn from their mistakes.

to be welcomed and given room to operate in a learning organization. People who advocate radical or different ideas must not be looked on as disruptive or troublesome. Another approach to enhance creative thinking is to encourage employees to research and learn from some of the best competitors in the industry. This process, known as *benchmarking,* allows a company to imitate the best practices of others. However, mere imitation does not yield a competitive advantage; it is a follower strategy. An organization must improve upon the best practices of competitors and launch innovations ahead of competitors.

Create a Climate in Which Experimentation Is Encouraged

Learning is more likely to take place in an organization in which experimentation on a small scale is encouraged and permitted. The purpose of an experiment is to learn by trial in a controlled environment. The costs of failure are not as significant as in a real attempt. People who are afraid of failing and risking their reputation or careers may be more likely to try something new or creative on a small scale. Also, the leader must create a culture that nurtures and even celebrates experimentation and innovation.[146] Everybody must be expected to contribute ideas, show initiative, and pursue continuous improvement. One way to do this is to create a sense of urgency in the organization, so that people see change and innovation as a necessity. Another way is to sometimes reward those who fail, because it symbolizes the importance of taking risks.

Provide Incentives for Learning and Innovation

The use of incentives and rewards is a powerful tool that leaders can apply to encourage learning and innovation. Organizations are often criticized for proclaiming themselves as champions of learning but not being able to provide workers with the kind of tangible support needed to motivate them. Rewards for successful ideas and innovations must be large and visible for others to notice. Rewards and incentives reinforce positive learning and innovation in the organization. CEOs must take steps to encourage and support learning and innovation in the workplace.

Build Confidence in Followers' Capacity to Learn and Adapt

The environment of the learning organization is one of rapid change, wherein survival depends on a timely response to threats and opportunities. Providing opportunities for employees to solve problems within the group or unit will increase their confidence and pride in the process. With each celebrated success comes greater confidence in dealing with change. Over time, familiarity with the change process will create an appreciation for flexibility and learning.

Encourage Systems Thinking

To enhance learning, the leader should help members regard the organization as a system in which everybody's work affects the work of everybody else. Therefore, everyone in the organization considers how their actions affect other elements of the organization. The emphasis on the whole system reduces boundaries both within the organization and with other companies, which allows for collaboration and continuous learning. Members begin to see how relationships with other companies can lower costs, increase sales, or bring in new competencies.

Create a Culture Conducive to Individual and Team Learning

Personal development and a lifetime of learning must be strong cultural values in learning organizations. Leaders must create a culture in which each person is valued, and the organization promotes and supports people to develop to their full potential. This type of learning culture encourages self-initiated activity, serendipity, and intra-company communications. In this type of learning culture, there is a flexible workplace, employees take ownership of their work, and managers function more like facilitators than taskmasters. For example, most learning organizations have created self-managed teams made up of employees with different skills who rotate jobs to produce an entire product or service. In self-managed teams, formal leaders are nonexistent; team members have the authority to make decisions about new and creative ways of doing things. This facilitates a learning environment for teams. (The self-managed team concept was covered in Chapter 8.)

Institute Mechanisms for Channeling Knowledge and Creative Ideas for Innovation

Knowledge that is shared can help an employee with a difficult problem or provide an opportunity for employees from different parts of the organization to interact with each other, getting advice and providing support about common problems. Also, ideas generated within an organization may become the source of new products or innovations. Therefore, ensuring that all employees' ideas are properly channeled and evaluated is critical. Most ideas do not pan out, but the individual and the organization learn from a good attempt even when it fails. Leaders should use organizational mechanisms such as venture teams, task forces, information systems networks, seminars, and workshops to diffuse knowledge and to channel creative ideas to the appropriate locations for evaluation.[147] In one organization, to institute a system for channeling ideas and information (especially negative information), every senior manager was assigned a coach from the ranks who regularly sought feedback from everyone about the executive's performance, and the executives learned that they had to face up to the truth about the company's situation. This created an atmosphere in which employees and managers started being honest with one another; managers found that they could look to employees for help in solving problems, and employees who had previously been called passive complainers became active partners in finding solutions. In the process, the company became more powerful, nimble, and tough-minded, able to rapidly respond to internal and external changes.[148]

Create a Shared Vision for Learning

Creating a shared vision enhances learning as organization members develop a common purpose and commitment to make learning an ongoing part of the organization. If employees all believe that the organization is headed toward greatness, they will be motivated to be part of it by learning and contributing their best ideas and solutions.[149]

Broaden Employees' Frame of Reference

People's frame of reference determines how they see the world. The ways we gather, analyze, and interpret information—and how we make decisions based on such information—are affected by our personal frames of reference. A frame of reference determines what implicit assumptions people hold, and those assumptions, consciously or unconsciously, affect how they interpret events. To enhance employees' ability to learn, it is helpful for leaders to broaden the frames employees use to see the organization and its external environment. Learning is constrained when leaders and their followers fail to see the world from a different perspective and therefore are unable to help the organization adapt to a changing environment. Broadening employees' frames of reference or perspective provides for a greater variety of approaches to solving problems and thus facilitates learning and continuous improvement.

Create an Environment in Which People Can Learn from Their Mistakes

Some of the most important inventions or scientific breakthroughs resulted from investigating failed outcomes. Unfortunately, in many organizations, when experiments or full-scale ventures fail, the tendency is to immediately abandon the activity to save face or avoid negative consequences. This is often the wrong approach, because more learning takes place from things that go wrong from than things that go right. After all, when things turn out as expected, it just confirms existing theories or assumptions. New insights are more likely when there is an investigation into why expected outcomes were not realized. Therefore, to encourage learning, leaders must communicate the view that failure is tolerated. Then, they must provide opportunities for people to engage in post-activity reviews regardless of outcome. Creating a culture that rewards those who succeed, as well as occasionally rewarding those who fail, sends a message that the organization encourages risk taking. Creating a strong risk culture and environment is a leadership responsibility that cannot be taken for granted. Organizations with risk-sensitive cultures are noted for high levels of accountability, reinforcement, and communication, with the appropriate risk management and infrastructure resources in place.[150]

Learning is a never-ending exercise. Leaders must communicate the message that learning and continuous improvements are imperative in a highly turbulent environment. Leaders must take the lead in challenging the status quo and creating organizational conditions that are conducive to learning and continuous innovation.

---

5. The Text Discusses the Distinction between the "Traditional" and the "Learning" Organization. In Your Opinion, What Type of Organization Is Avon?

Andrea Jung's vision, mission, and strategies for Avon reveal an organization that fits the description of a learning organization and not the traditional, efficiency-driven type. Her emphasis on participation, empowerment, and creativity are all elements of the learning organization. A learning organization is one that is continuously transforming itself to adapt to the changing environment. Speaking on the subject of transformation and her long-term vision for Avon, Ms. Jung has maintained that over the next three years, she intends to push for further penetration and expansion into rapidly growing economies in which Avon's direct selling model excels. "Our increased scale in the fast-growth and highly profitable developing international markets, combined with a repositioned U.S. business,

OPENING CASE APPLICATION

should enable us to generate continuing growth in sales and earnings as we evolve to the next generation of Avon's transformation," she said. It is evident in the results Avon has achieved so far and the honors Andrea Jung has received that the company's learning culture is yielding big gains.

Now that you have learned about culture, diversity, and learning organizations as described in this chapter, you may find it interesting to see how your own personality traits match up. Complete Self-Assessment 2.

Self-Assessment 2

Personality and Culture, Values, Diversity, and the Learning Organization

Culture and Values

If you scored high on the Big Five personality dimension of conscientiousness (high need for achievement), you tend to be a conformist and will most likely feel comfortable in an organization with a strong culture. If you have a high agreeableness (high need for affiliation) personality, you tend to get along well with people, can fit into a strong culture, and would do well in a cooperative culture that values collectivism, low power distance, and femininity. If you have surgency (high need for power), you like to dominate and may not like to fit into a strong culture that does not reflect the values you have. You would tend to do well in a competitive culture that values individualism, high power distance (if you have it), and masculinity. On the Big Five, if you are open to new experience you will do well in an adaptive culture that values low uncertainty avoidance, whereas if you are closed to new experience, you will tend to do well in a bureaucratic culture that values high uncertainty avoidance. Would you like to work in an organization with a weak or strong culture? What type of culture and values interest you?

_____

_____

Diversity

If you have a Big Five agreeableness personality type (high need for affiliation), are open to experience, and are well adjusted, you will tend to embrace diversity and get along well with people who are different than you. However, if you have a surgency personality type (high need for power), are closed to experience, and are not well adjusted, you will tend to want to have things done your way (melting pot vs. salad bowl) and may have problems with a diverse group of people who don't want to give you the power. If you have a conscientiousness personality type (high need for achievement), are well adjusted, and have openness to experience, you will tend to work with those who share your achievement values regardless of other differences. Do you enjoy working with a diversity of people?

_____

_____

Learning Organization

The key personality trait that differs between the traditional and learning organization is openness to new experience. If you are closed to new experience, you will tend to like a traditional organization in which change is slow and top management makes the decisions. If you are open to new experience, you will tend to enjoy a learning organization in which you are encouraged and valued for implementing change and making many of your own decisions. Would you be more comfortable in a traditional or learning organization?

_____

_____

Go to the Internet (academic.cengage.com/management/lussier) where you will find a broad array of resources to help maximize your learning.

- Review the vocabulary
- Try a quiz
- View chapter videos

Chapter Summary

The chapter summary is organized to answer the 11 learning outcomes for Chapter 10.

1. Explain the power of culture in the strategy execution process.

Strategy execution is a much smoother process when an organization's culture is in sync with its strategy. This strategy-culture match serves two important functions: (1) it creates internal unity, and (2) it helps the organization adapt to the external environment. Culture provides a value system in which to operate, and when all employees buy into such a value system, there is internal unity. Culture determines how the organization responds to changes in its external environment. Appropriate cultural values can ensure that the organization responds quickly or proactively to emerging trends, rather than reacting.

2. Distinguish between a weak and a strong culture.

When there is little or no consensus on the values and norms governing member behavior, the culture of an organization is considered to be weak. The lack of common values and norms means that members of the organization may not show any sense of close identification with the organization's vision, mission, and strategy. On the other hand, a strong culture is one in which values are shared widely across the organization, from top management to rank-and-file employees. In strong cultures, values and behavioral norms are so deeply ingrained that they do not change much even when a new leader takes over.

3. Describe the characteristics of low- and high-performance cultures.

The characteristics of low-performance cultures include insular thinking, resistance to change, a highly politicized internal environment, and poorly conceived promotion or advancement practices for employees. The characteristics of high-performance cultures include a reputation for valuing their employees, being very results oriented, emphasizing everyday outstanding performance and excellence, and using diverse culture reinforcement tools such as ceremonies, symbols, slogans, stories, and language (ceremonies honor and recognize achievement; slogans, symbols, language, and stories

communicate the organization's primary values and provide a shared understanding among members).

4. Distinguish between symbolic and substantive leadership actions for shaping organizational culture.

Symbolic leadership actions are valuable for the signals they send about the kinds of behavior and performance leaders wish to encourage and promote. The meaning is implied in the actions taken. Examples of symbolic leadership actions include leaders serving as appropriate role models for employees; using ceremonies to highlight and honor members whose actions and performance exemplify espoused values; and making special appearances at nonceremonial events such as employee training or orientation programs, using the opportunity to stress strategic priorities, values, and norms.

Substantive leadership actions are highly visible and concrete steps to show management's commitment to new strategic initiatives and cultural changes. The strongest evidence that management is truly committed to creating a new culture is a "shake-up" in both employee and managerial ranks, such as replacing change-resisting, old-culture members with a "new breed" of employees. Another example would be changing dysfunctional operating practices and policies that do not support the new culture.

5. Differentiate between the four cultural value types.

The makeup of the four cultural value types is based on two dimensions: the degree of environmental turbulence (stable versus dynamic) and the organization's strategic focus or orientation (internal versus external). The interaction between these two dimensions creates four different types of cultures that researchers have identified in various organizations.

The cooperative culture is found in organizations that operate in dynamic environments, yet emphasize an internal strategic focus. The belief is that empowering, respecting, rewarding, and trusting employees is the key to capitalizing on external opportunities. The adaptive culture is also found in organizations that operate in dynamic environments; however, the organization's strategic focus is external. Solutions for responding to external opportunities and threats are sought both inside and outside the firm. These organizations pursue outsourcing, strategic alliances, downsizing, and any other options that are available. The adaptive and cooperative cultures are often referred to as cultures of innovation, for their flexibility and creativity in responding to environmental changes. The competitive culture is associated with organizations operating in a stable environment with an external strategic focus. Competitive cultures are common in mature markets in which the emphasis is on the achievement of specific targets (such as market share, revenue growth, and profitability). Last but not least is the bureaucratic culture associated with organizations that operate in stable environments with an internal strategic orientation. The bureaucratic culture emphasizes strict adherence to set rules, procedures, and authority lines. Organizations with bureaucratic cultures are highly structured and efficiency-driven. Change is slow in bureaucratic cultures.

6. Describe the framework for understanding global cultural value differences.

The conceptual framework for understanding global cultural differences proposes that national cultures differ by the values they espouse. Researchers have associated different value dimensions with the cultures of different nationalities and/or regions of the world. Leading this effort is the work of Geert Hofstede, whose research, spanning almost two decades and involving over 160,000 people from over 60 countries, helped identify the first five value dimensions for understanding global cultural differences. Each value dimension represents a continuum, with selected countries and regions located at various points along the continuum. The five value dimensions making up the framework are:

- Individualism–collectivism
- High–low uncertainty avoidance
- High–low power distance
- Long-term–short-term orientation
- Masculinity–femininity

7. Explain the primary reasons for embracing diversity.

The following are primary reasons for embracing diversity:

Changing demographics and increasing globalization have significantly changed the composition of the workforce. With more women and minorities entering the workforce and the growing interdependence between global companies, the need to embrace and value diversity is more critical than ever. The value of diversity is evident in studies that have found, among other things, that a diversified workforce (e.g., sales team) offers an advantage in understanding and meeting the needs of diverse customers; some of the best job candidates are found among women and other culturally diverse groups; embracing and valuing diversity can lower an organization's cost attributed to high turnover and/or absenteeism among minority groups; and diverse work groups are more creative and innovative than homogeneous work groups.

8. Identify the three areas in which visible and strong leadership action is needed to achieve full diversity.

To achieve full diversity, top management must show its commitment to (1) remove all personal and organizational obstacles to achieving diversity, (2) implant a diversity-supportive culture, and (3) engage employees in diversity awareness training and leadership education.

9. Explain the leader's role in creating a culture that supports diversity.

A diversity-supportive culture is one that continuously values diversity and has made it a way of life in the organization. To achieve full diversity, leaders are challenged to create a diversity-supportive culture that ensures women and other minorities have equal opportunities to move up the corporate ladder into leadership positions. The leader's role in creating a diversity-supportive culture is to ensure that the following characteristics are part of the culture: top management support and commitment; pro-diversity human resource practices; a corporate philosophy of diversity; regular organizational communications on diversity; and diversity as a criterion for measuring success.

10. Describe the role of leadership in creating a learning organization.

The learning organization represents a paradigmic shift in the approach organizations take to managing their internal and external relationships. In today's rapidly changing business environment, organizations must transform into active learning organisms or risk becoming extinct. To succeed, organizations must be proactive and anticipatory, which requires continuous improvement. Thus, the traditional organization model that emphasized efficiency and stability is being replaced by a model that is learning-driven and adaptable. Leaders play a critical role in effecting this transformation. Without effective leadership from the top and throughout the organizational structure, it is hard to imagine how the learning organization can succeed. A shared vision and mission are the basis for the emergence of strategy in a learning organization, and this is the responsibility of leadership. Leaders can play a key role in enhancing organizational learning by encouraging creative thinking, creating a climate in which experimentation and risk taking is encouraged, providing incentives for learning and innovation, building confidence in followers' capacity to learn and adapt, encouraging systems thinking, and creating a culture conducive to individual and team learning.

11. Define the following key terms (in order of appearance in the chapter).

Select one or more methods: (1) fill in the missing key terms from memory, (2) match the key terms from the following list with their definitions below, (3) copy the key terms in order from the list at the beginning of the chapter.

_____ is the aggregate of beliefs, attitudes, values, assumptions, and ways of doing things that is shared by members of an organization and taught to new members.

_____ represents a leadership belief in strong, mutually reinforcing exchanges and linkages between employees and departments.

_____ represents a leadership belief in active monitoring of the external environment for emerging opportunities and threats.

_____ represents a leadership that encourages and values a highly competitive work environment.

_____ represents a leadership that values order, stability, status, and efficiency.

_____ are generalized beliefs or behaviors that are considered by an individual or a group to be important.

_____ is a single person entrusted with the responsibility of acting as the organization's conscience.

_____ is employee disclosure of illegal or unethical practices on the part of the organization.

_____ is a psychological state in which people see themselves first as individuals and believe their own interest and values are primary.

_____ is the state of mind wherein the values and goals of the group, whether extended family, ethnic group, or company, are primary.

_____ characterizes people who do not tolerate risk, avoid the unknown, and are comfortable when the future is relatively predictable and certain.

_____ refers to a culture in which most people are comfortable with and accepting of the unknown, and tolerate risk and unpredictability.

_____ is a society in which the leaders and followers rarely interact as equals.

_____ is a society in which leaders and their members interact on several levels as equals.

_____ describes a culture that emphasizes assertiveness and a competitive drive for money and material objects.

_____ describes a culture that emphasizes developing and nurturing personal relationships and a high quality of life.

_____ is any characteristic that serves as a basis for social categorization and self-identification.

_____ is the inclusion of all groups at all levels in an organization.

_____ is the tendency to form an adverse opinion without just cause about people who are different from the mainstream in terms of their gender, race, ethnicity, or any other definable characteristic.

_____ is the belief that one's own group or subculture is naturally superior to other groups and cultures.

_____ is an invisible barrier that separates women and minorities from top leadership positions.

_____ is when anticipated or expected changes bear no resemblance to the present or the past.

_____ is one that is skilled at creating, acquiring, and transferring knowledge; and at modifying behavior to reflect new knowledge and insights.

_____ is the tacit and explicit knowledge that individuals possess about products, services, systems, and processes.

Key Terms

adaptive culture, 416

bureaucratic culture, 418

collectivism, 424

competitive culture, 417

cooperative culture, 416

culture, 398

demographic diversity, 427

discontinuous change, 440

diversity, 427

ethnocentrism, 433

femininity, 426

glass ceiling, 434

high power-distance culture, 425

high uncertainty avoidance, 425

individualism, 424

learning organization, 441

low power-distance culture, 425

low uncertainty avoidance, 425

masculinity, 426

ombudsperson, 421

organizational knowledge, 441

prejudice, 433

values, 419

whistle blowing, 422

Review and Discussion Questions

1. What are the similarities and differences between cooperative culture and adaptive culture?
2. How does a code of ethics help enforce ethical behavior in an organization?
3. How would individualism as a value dimension among followers affect their interaction and relationship with other coworkers who display collectivism?
4. What potential problems could develop in a case in which a leader is from a high power-distance culture, but his followers are from a low power-distance culture?
5. Why has the "melting pot" mentality of multiculturalism been replaced with the "salad bowl" mentality?
6. What are the major obstacles often encountered in trying to achieve diversity?
7. What are the leading characteristics of learning organizations?

Case

ROBERT STEVENS CONTINUES LOCKHEED MARTIN'S DIVERSITY INITIATIVES

Lockheed Martin, a highly diversified, advanced technology multinational corporation with approximately $35.5 billion in annualized sales and approximately 130,000 employees worldwide, has one of the most successful diversity programs in the nation today. Lockheed Martin's varied businesses are organized into five broad strategic business units (SBUs): Aeronautics, Electronic Systems, Integrated Systems & Solutions, Space Systems, and Information & Technology Services. Vance Coffman served as chairman of Lockheed Martin from 1998 to 2004. Coffman was replaced by Robert Stevens in August 2004. Prior to becoming CEO, Stevens served as Lockheed Martin's president and chief operating officer. He has also served as the corporation's chief financial officer, among other key positions. Coffman is most admired for his efforts at creating a work environment that fosters greater awareness and sensitivity to the needs of Lockheed's diverse employee population. These efforts include crafting a "mission success" statement that clearly delineates the corporation's commitment to diversity, and hiring executives with the skills and commitment to implement the corporation's diversity initiatives. Lockheed Martin's core values in its mission statement are ethics, excellence, "can-do," integrity, people, and teamwork. On people, Lockheed maintains that it will "embrace lifelong learning . . . combined with company-sponsored education and development programs." On teamwork, it will "multiply the creativity, talents, and contributions of . . . by focusing on team goals." Teams will "assume collective responsibility for . . . share trust and leadership, embrace diversity, and accept responsibility for prudent risk-taking." It is clear from the speeches and comments of Stevens that he intends to continue right where Coffman left off.

Upon receiving the "Executive of the Year" award from the National Management Association in November 2004, Stevens laid out what Lockheed Martin was looking for in its leaders as follows:

> At Lockheed Martin, we want: . . . highly principled and ethical people who place a high priority on honesty and integrity, both in their personal and professional lives . . . advocates for diversity who actively foster an inclusive environment where individual respect and teamwork matters . . . disciplined hard workers who are fearless in their pursuit of excellence and who demonstrate great pride and loyalty toward their organization . . . "whole-system creative thinkers" who can pursue innovation, get to the root of a challenge, and commit themselves to the process of life-long learning . . . and valued colleagues who possess humor, humility, and common sense.

At Lockheed Martin, the belief is that to attract the best of the best, the corporation must include all segments of the population. In this respect, the corporation's Equal Opportunity Office (EOO) has created a Workforce Diversity Initiative that provides guidelines for implementing diversity programs at the strategic business unit levels. The EOO is set up to provide information to Lockheed Martin's SBUs on how to achieve diversity. Many Lockheed Martin companies have diversity departments charged with ensuring, among other things, that their companies are flexible enough to meet the needs of all employees. A number of Lockheed Martin companies have enhanced their diversity efforts by creating employee councils that serve as the conduits to carry concerns from employees to the councils and from the councils to management. The councils, all of which work on a volunteer basis, carry out the goals and programs suggested by the diversity department and by fellow employees.

Another diversity initiative of Lockheed Martin has been the creation of employee networks. The following affinity groups were established by employees to foster career development and upward mobility through education, training and mentoring programs for employees in minority groups: the African American Mentoring and Information Network; the Gay, Lesbian, or Bisexual at Lockheed Martin (GLOBAL) organization; the Asian American and Pacific-Islander American Lockheed Martin Association (ALMA); Lockheed Martin Employees with Disability; and the Lockheed Martin Latino Mentoring Network. Minority-based social networks such as these are important because they tailor their training and mentoring to the specific issues of a particular subculture.

Lockheed Martin has also actively advocated community outreach, which allows employees of the corporation to work with the community. There are several community programs sponsored by Lockheed. In Baltimore, teachers from around the country explore new, active, collaborative, and project-centered practices that bring math and science to life for kids. In Dallas, a special resource center gives indigent patients the care and guidance they might otherwise never receive; and in classrooms around the globe, students experience the thrill of space through virtual field trips and exciting hands-on activities.

From educational opportunities to career placement to leadership training, Lockheed Martin has made it a priority to reach students from underrepresented groups. Helping to advance minority youth participation in the fields of math, science, and technology is a corporate-wide effort. Lockheed Martin awards scholarships to minority students, and sponsors and participates in local and national conferences, such as the Emerald Honors Conference, the Black Engineer of the Year Awards Conference, the Asian American Engineer of the

Year Awards, the Hispanic Engineer National Achievement Awards, and Women in Aerospace. Lockheed Martin's Math, Engineering, and Science Achievement (MESA) grants are aimed at developing academic and leadership skills, raising educational expectation, and instilling confidence in the nation's African-American, American Indian, Mexican-American, and Latino-American students within the fields of engineering, physical science, and other math-based fields. Its "INROADS" program develops and places talented minority students in business and industry, and prepares them for corporate and community leadership.

Diversity managers and volunteers at companies throughout Lockheed Martin take different approaches to assessing how big a role their diversity initiatives have played in helping current employees feel at home. One of the most quantifiable approaches for self-evaluation is the Diversity Progress Index, which measures improvements in diversity over time. The index, which was first piloted in 1997, evaluates a department's approach to advocacy, assessment, planning, and implementation—as they relate to diversity. The index also allows a department to evaluate the role diversity has played in its business success. Outstanding performers are honored with the prestigious President's Diversity Awards.

Because of strong leadership from Robert Stevens and his executive team and a highly motivated and committed group of managers, Lockheed Martin has received national attention and recognition for its diversity efforts. In 2005 alone, Lockheed Martin received the following recognitions:

- Sustained membership in the "Billion Dollar Roundtable" (BDR). Sponsored by *Minority Business News* and *Women's Enterprise Magazine,* the BDR recognizes companies that achieve annual spending of at least $1 billion with minority and women-owned suppliers
- Voted #1 by readers of *Woman Engineer* magazine as the place they would most like to work or they believe provides the best working environment for women
- Listed as one of the top 10 employers for African-American College Graduates by *The Black Collegian*
- Ranked #2 for the "Top Corporate Supporter of Historically Black Colleges and Universities Engineering Schools"
- Ranked #1 for the "Top Corporate Supporter of the Hispanic Serving Institutions Engineering"
- Listed as one of the "Best Places to Work" by *Baltimore* magazine
- Voted #5 by readers of *Minority Engineering* magazine in "Top 50 Companies"
- Ranked #8 on the Top 100 list by *Training Magazine.* Lockheed is in the top 10 among the national elite of corporate training.

Lockheed Martin is the true embodiment of a company with a high-performance culture and a well-managed diversity program. Diversity at Lockheed Martin is an institutionalized concept, not just a principle on paper.

GO TO THE INTERNET: To learn more about Lockheed Martin, log on to InfoTrac® College Edition at **academic. cengage.com/infotrac** and use the advanced search function.

Support your answers to the following questions with specific information from the case, or information you get from the Web or other sources.

1. Would you say Lockheed Martin Corporation has a low- or high-performance culture? Support your answer with evidence from the case.
2. In what ways has Lockheed Martin taken a proactive approach toward supporting and encouraging diversity?
3. Describe the organizational form (traditional versus learning organization) appropriate for a corporation like Lockheed Martin. Support your answer.
4. Based on the discussion of leadership actions that can help shape culture (Exhibit 10-3), what leadership actions has Lockheed Martin employed in shaping the corporation's culture?

Cumulative Case Questions

5. The self-managed team concept (Chapter 8) deals with the transfer of authority and responsibility to autonomous teams of employees who are responsible for complete, well-defined tasks that relate either to a final product or service or an ongoing process. In your opinion, do you think the self-managed team structure can be used to implement Lockheed Martin's diversity initiatives? Support your answer.
6. Transformational versus transactional leadership (Chapter 9) describes two leadership styles commonly associated with senior leaders of corporations. Which of these types of leadership do you think Robert Stevens represents? Support your answer.

Case Exercise and Role-Play

Preparation

Put yourself in Robert Stevens's position. You have been invited to make a special appearance at a ceremonial event honoring departments that have achieved the highest score on the Diversity Progress Index. Honorees will receive the President's Diversity Award. Develop an inspirational speech highlighting the value of diversity to your corporation and why it is necessary to continue the effort towards greater diversity. Your instructor may elect to form groups to share ideas and develop the speech. Groups should select one leader to present the speech to the entire class.

Role-Play

One student (representing themselves or their group) may give the speech to the entire class. Use information from this chapter on diversity for input.

Video Case

Fannie Mae: Diversity, Corporate Culture

Fannie Mae is a financial services company that works with primary lenders such as banks, credit unions, mortgage companies, and government housing agencies to increase the availability of home ownership for low- and middle-income Americans. With more than 12 million active mortgages issued to its target clientele of women, minorities, and single parents, Fannie Mae is the nation's largest source of financing for homebuyers. The Washington, D.C.–based firm is known for fostering rich diversity among its over 4,000 employees, and each individual at the company contributes to the corporate mission of helping families achieve the American dream of home ownership.

View the Video (13 minutes)

View the video on Fannie Mae in class or at **academic. cengage.com/management/lussier**.

Read the Case

Many companies seek to recruit and develop a truly diverse workforce, but at Fannie Mae diversity is a way of life. More than 47 percent of the company's management group, including officers and directors, are minorities, and nearly 54 percent

of the company's workforce are women. In addition, the company is pledged to equal opportunity for workers with disabilities, older employees, and gay or lesbian workers. Fannie Mae aims to provide equal opportunity for all employees, and its corporate culture communicates the value of diversity throughout the whole company.

For Fannie Mae, diversity simply makes good business sense. By ensuring the fair treatment of all employees in everything from recruitment and hiring to developing internal talent, managers are able to promote accountability and improve relationships with all stakeholders. As the company has demonstrated, organizations that move beyond rules and regulations to embrace diversity as a core value can expect to reap rewards in employee satisfaction and performance.

Answer the Questions

1. What is diversity, and why is it important to Fannie Mae?
2. How can a strong organizational culture help Fannie Mae achieve its objectives?
3. Do you think Fannie Mae's culture and emphasis on diversity would be equally effective for companies in other industries? Why or why not?

Skill-Development Exercise 1

IDENTIFYING AND IMPROVING ORGANIZATIONAL CULTURE

Preparing for Skill-Development Exercise 1

1. Select one organization you work for or have worked for. Identify its culture by answering Work Applications 1 (is it a weak or a strong culture?), 2 (is it a high- or low-performance culture?), 3 (which of the ten leadership actions are used?), 4 (which of the four types of organizational culture does it have?), and 6 (what are the five dimensions of the culture?). Your answers can be between the two poles for Work Applications 1, 2, and 6 (on each of the five dimensions); however, try to identify which end of the spectrum the culture is closest to.
2. What are the mission and values of the organization? Does the culture support the mission and values of the organization? Explain why or why not. If the organization does not have a clearly written mission and values, that would be is a good starting point.
3. Based on the organization's mission and values, how can the culture be improved? Be specific.

Doing Skill-Development Exercise 1 in Class

Objective

To improve your ability to identify and improve an organizational culture in order to support its mission and values.

Preparation

You should have completed the preparation for this exercise.

Procedure (10–45 minutes)

A. The instructor calls on students to give their answers to the preparation, with or without a class discussion.
B. Break into groups of 4 to 6 and share your answers to the preparation.
C. Same as B, but select one group member to present their answer to the entire class.

Conclusion

The instructor may lead a class discussion and/or make concluding remarks.

Apply It (2–4 minutes)

What did I learn from this exercise? When will I implement my plan?

_____

_____

_____

Sharing

Volunteers may give their answers to the "Apply It" questions.

Skill-Development Exercise 2

DIVERSITY TRAINING

Preparing for Skill-Development Exercise 2

In preparation for the in-class exercise, write out the answers to the following questions.

Race and Ethnicity

_____ 1. I am of _____ race and ethnicity(ies).

_____ 2. My name is _____. It is significant because it means _____ and/or I was named after _____.

_____ 3. One positive thing about being this race/ethnicity is _____.

_____ 4. One difficult or challenging thing is _____.

Religion

_____ 1. I am of _____ religion/nonreligious/atheist.

_____ 2. One positive thing about it is _____.

_____ 3. One difficult or challenging thing about it is _____.

Gender

_____ 1. I am of _____ gender.

_____ 2. One positive thing about being this gender is _____.

_____ 3. One difficult or challenging thing is _____.

_____ 4. Men and women are primarily different in _____ because _____.

Age

_____ 1. I am _____ years old.

_____ 2. One positive thing about this age is _____.

_____ 3. One difficult or embarrassing thing about being this age is _____.

Ability

_____ 1. I am of _____ (high, medium, low) ability in college and on the job. I do/don't have a disability.

_____ 2. One positive thing about being of this ability is _____.

_____ 3. One difficult or challenging thing about being of this ability is _____.

Other

_____ 1. The major other way(s) in which I'm different than other people is _____.

_____ 2. One positive thing about being different in this way is _____.

_____ 3. One difficult or challenging thing about being different in this way is _____.

Prejudice, Stereotypes, Discrimination

Identify how you have been prejudged, stereotyped, and discriminated against.

_____

_____

_____

Objectives

To increase your understanding of the value of diversity and being different. The more you value diversity, the more effort you will place on developing good human relations with a diversity of people.

Preparation

You should have answered the preparation questions for this exercise.

Procedure 1 (2–3 minutes)

Break into groups of 4 to 6 with as much diversity as possible. The instructor will check the diversity levels and reassign people to groups to improve diversity, if necessary. Select a spokesperson to give the group's best one or two answers to the "Prejudice, Stereotype, Discrimination" question; it is not necessary to report on any other areas.

Procedure 2 (10–30 minutes)

The instructor sets a time limit and selects the topics in the preparation to be discussed. Start with different areas first, but be sure to allow time (about 5 minutes) to complete the "Prejudice, Stereotype, and Discrimination" question. If you finish the question to be reported before the time is up, go over other areas of difference that were not assigned by the instructor.

Procedure 3 (5–20 minutes)

The spokesperson from each group gives the one or two best examples of prejudice, stereotype, and discrimination.

Conclusion

The instructor may lead a class discussion and/or make concluding remarks.

Apply It (2–4 minutes)

What did I learn from this experience? How will I use this knowledge in the future? More specifically, what will I do differently to personally embrace diversity? How will I encourage others to embrace diversity?

_____

_____

_____

Sharing

Volunteers may give their answers to the "Apply It" questions.

Skill-Development Exercise 3

DEVELOPING AN EFFECTIVE MULTICULTURAL TEAM

Preparing for Skill-Development Exercise 3

Assume you are part of a team and your task is to develop a brand new product called the Mind Reader 2007. It will make it possible for you to tell what someone is thinking by simply focusing the device in their direction. There is currently no product like it on the market—or even substitutes—but time is of the essence and this product has to be on the market within a very short time; otherwise, your other competing groups would beat you to it. You are a multicultural team with members from the following countries: United States, Japan, Argentina, Mexico, and Sweden. As discussed in the text section (p. 423), "A Framework of Value Dimensions for Understanding Cultural Differences," researchers have found key dimensions that explain broad cultural differences among selected nationalities. The following table summarizes the

Country	Masculinity	Femininity	Time Orientation		Individualism	Collectivism	Uncertainty Avoidance		Power Distance	
			Long Term	Short Term			High	Low	High	Low
United States			X		X					
Japan	X			X		X	X			
Argentina								X		
Mexico						X			X	
Sweden		X						X		X

value dimensions of five countries from which team members are to be selected.

Objectives

To learn how to deal with the different values, norms, and attitudes that characterize different cultures. Leaders have to recognize that cultural differences can lead to conflicts in multicultural team settings, and finding common ground where value differences exist is key to effective teamwork.

Preparation

Read and understand the meaning of each value dimension in Exhibit 10-6. Review the table in this exercise for the particular value dimensions of each country.

Procedure 1 (3–5 minutes)

Break up into groups of 4 to 6 with as much diversity as possible. The instructor will check to ensure that each group is well diversified and reassign students to groups needing more diversity, if possible. Select a leader who will present the findings of the group's deliberations.

Procedure 2 (10–20 minutes)

The instructor sets a time limit on the deliberations. If quality, teamwork, and speed are critical to successfully completing this project, what adaptations in behavior would your group have to make, given the different countries your group members are from? Be mindful of the values associated with each country and team member. For example, somebody from an individualistic culture or a high uncertainty avoidance culture

may have difficulty working as part of a team or working with people who are comfortable with and accepting of the unknown, and who tolerate risk and unpredictability. What ideas does the group have to help this individual adapt to the needs of the team to finish the project on time? Other potential areas of conflict exist. Identify them based on the composition of your team, and deliberate on possible solutions, keeping the objective in mind.

Procedure 3 (15–20 minutes)

The leader from each group presents the potential conflicts presented by the differences in the value dimensions of team members, and the team's solutions for dealing with such conflicts in order to achieve the desired objectives.

Conclusion

The instructor may lead a class discussion and/or make concluding remarks.

Apply It (2–4 minutes)

What did I learn from this experience? How will I use this knowledge in the future?

_____

_____

_____

Sharing

Volunteers may give their answers to the "Apply It" questions.

Strategic Leadership and Managing Crises and Change

11

LEARNING OUTCOMES

After studying this chapter, you should be able to:

1. Discuss the role of strategic leadership in the strategic management process. p. 460

2. Describe the relevance of analyzing the internal and external environment to the strategic management process. p. 464

3. Explain the importance of a vision and a mission statement. p. 465

4. Explain the relationship between corporate objectives and strategies. p. 468

5. Explain the importance of strategy evaluation in the strategic management model. p. 472

6. Describe the five-step process for crisis risk assessment. p. 477

7. Describe the three phases of the change process. p. 487

8. Identify the major reasons for resisting change. p. 489

9. Discuss people- and task-oriented techniques for overcoming resistance to change. p. 493

10. Define the following **key terms** (in order of appearance in the chapter):

strategic leadership

strategic management

strategic vision

mission statement

strategy

value

core competence

crisis

press release

press kit

organizational change

survival anxiety

learning anxiety

Opening Case Application

For years Advanced Micro Devices (AMD) played catch-up to its archrival Intel (INTC), the Goliath of the microprocessor industry. Almost overnight, AMD has become a serious threat to Intel. With a strong technology lineup—including its Opteron server chip, AMD Athlon64 PC chip, and MirrorBit flash memory chip—the Sunnyvale, California, company is in the best position to prosper in its 35-year history. For AMD, the Opteron chip marks both a technical and a strategic milestone, and a key step towards the company's mission. Set out almost 35 years ago, the mission statement was: "To build a successful semiconductor company by offering building blocks of ever-increasing complexity to benefit the manufacturers of electronic equipment in the computation, communication, and instrumentation markets."

Jerry Sanders, a former director of worldwide marketing at Fairchild Semiconductor, and seven others founded AMD in 1969. More recently, the company has been run and guided by Hector Ruiz, a semiconductor industry veteran who joined AMD in January 2000 as president and chief operating officer, coming from Motorola, where he had spent 23 years and gone on to head its semiconductor products business. Mr. Ruiz, who was born in Piedras Negras, Mexico, has degrees in electrical engineering and electronics. In April 2002, Mr. Ruiz was named chief executive of AMD and was appointed chairman of the board in April 2004. He says the job has been "far more" hairy than he expected. "When I joined AMD, there was nothing that could stop technology growing, the dot-coms were going strong. But, shortly after, things began to go downhill and we have been in a downturn now for two-and-a-half years." Despite this backdrop, under his leadership AMD has begun to blossom.

Opening Case Questions:

1. Would you agree that strategic leadership is greatly needed at AMD at this time? Why?
2. How effective has Hector Ruiz been in providing the kind of strategic leadership that AMD needs?
3. Strategic leadership is about analyzing and predicting changes in your environment and putting in place responsive strategies. To what extent has Mr. Ruiz demonstrated this skill?
4. How effective has Hector Ruiz been in articulating the financial and strategic objectives of AMD?
5. Describe some of the specific strategies that Hector Ruiz has implemented at AMD, and which have resulted in the success that the company is currently experiencing.
6. Strategic leadership is also about dealing with crisis. What crisis situation has Ruiz had to deal with as CEO of AMD?
7. Why has Hector Ruiz encountered less resistance in bringing about changes at AMD than would have been expected?

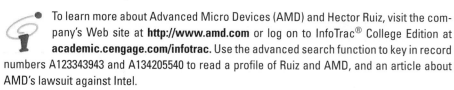 To learn more about Advanced Micro Devices (AMD) and Hector Ruiz, visit the company's Web site at **http://www.amd.com** or log on to InfoTrac® College Edition at **academic.cengage.com/infotrac**. Use the advanced search function to key in record numbers A123343943 and A134205540 to read a profile of Ruiz and AMD, and an article about AMD's lawsuit against Intel.

Organizations are operating in increasingly complex environments, in which an adaptation to environmental changes is an imperative. Strong research evidence shows that the effectiveness of organizations is influenced by the degree of fit between organizations and their environment. This process of adaptation is strongly influenced by the interpretations executives make of the environment. Interpretations of environmental changes play a large part in the future actions that strategic leaders employ to remain competitive.[1] One area in which change is unmistakable is the increasingly global competitive landscape. Virtually every company, large or small, faces competition for critical resources and market opportunities, not just from competitors in the home market but also more and more from distant and often little-understood regions of the world. How successful a company is at exploiting emerging opportunities and dealing with associated threats depends crucially on leadership's ability to cultivate a global mindset among managers and their followers.[2] It's all about reorienting the organization to see change not as a threat but as an opportunity. In some cases, change is triggered by a crisis—an unexpected incident with significant negative consequences. Also imperative for strategists operating in this era of hypercompetition, globalization, and technological revolution, is the need to act fast. Strategists must respond quickly to marketplace demands for immediate action. This is where the need for effective strategic planning comes into play. The pressures of the new competitive landscape are forcing some organizations to push planning aside and simply act faster.[3]

The focus of this chapter is on strategic leadership and the strategic management process, crisis management, and change leadership.

─────────────── Learning Outcome 1 ───────────────

Discuss the role of strategic leadership in the strategic management process.

Strategic Leadership

Achieving organizational success is not a chance occurrence. It is determined largely by the decisions strategic leaders make. It is the responsibility of top managers to monitor the organization's internal and external environments, build company resources and capabilities, track industry and competitive trends, spot emerging market opportunities, identify business threats, and develop a vision for the future that followers can believe in. This series of activities makes up a major part of what is known as strategic leadership. It is hard to overstate the importance of strategic leadership in today's dynamic and uncertain business environment. Although many authors have provided varying definitions of the concept, they all seem to revolve around the same themes: **strategic leadership** *is a person's ability to anticipate, envision, maintain flexibility, think strategically, and work with others to initiate changes that will create a viable future for the organization.*[4] It is a process of providing the direction and inspiration necessary to create and implement a vision, a mission, and strategies to achieve and sustain organizational objectives. Strategic leadership must involve managers at the top, middle, and lower levels of the organization. However, of these three managerial classifications, top-level managers (strategists) are clearly held responsible for the organization's current performance, as well as for creating conditions that will insure the organization's survival in the future. Organizations with effective strategic leadership are more likely to adopt appropriate strategies; have a committed, supportive, and strong management team; identify and focus on target markets; develop and sustain competitive advantages; maintain ethical standards; and have excellent customer and client relationships.

1. Would You Agree That Strategic Leadership Is Greatly Needed at AMD at This Time? Why?

According to the opening case, Hector Ruiz came to AMD at a time when the organization faced some serious external threats. In 2000, when Mr. Ruiz joined AMD, there was nothing that could stop technology growing—the dot-coms were going strong and the economy was in a technology boom. But, shortly after, things began to go downhill. As a result, the company suffered three years of losses. Internally, AMD was undergoing a shift in leadership philosophy and style between Sanders and Ruiz. While Sanders is described as outspoken and flamboyant in his personality, Ruiz is a more soft-spoken and people-oriented leader. Even Ruiz describes his former boss as autocratic and power-centric. Therefore, strategic leadership will be critical in helping the organization adapt to its changing external environment and realign its internal processes (strategy, structure, culture, capabilities, vision, and mission) with this new reality.

OPENING CASE APPLICATION

In today's rapidly changing global world, leaders are bombarded with so much information, often conflicting, making effective decisions becomes a challenge. The complexity of the environment and the uncertainty of the future make the task of the strategic leader more difficult. Effective strategic leaders are said to perform four primary responsibilities: (1) conceptualize the organization's vision, mission, and core values; (2) oversee the formulation of objectives, strategies, policies, and structures that translate vision, mission, and core values into business decisions; (3) create an environment and culture for organizational learning and mutual exchange between individuals and groups; and (4) serve as steward and role model for the rest.[5] Strategists pave the way for ethical behavior in organizations through the influence of leadership. It is evident that all these activities fall under the domain of the strategic management framework. The key question and central issue in strategic management is why some firms perform better than others. Some scholars and practitioners have argued that one solution to this question is the role that strategic leadership plays in the life of the organization. Strategic leadership ensures that the strategic management process is successfully carried out and yields the desired results for the organization. **Strategic management** *is the set of decisions and actions used to formulate and implement specific strategies that will achieve a competitively superior fit between the organization and its environment, so as to achieve organizational goals.*[6] It is important to understand the strategic management model and its application, because success is not always guaranteed.

Strategic decisions often fail due to decision-maker blunders. Blunders occur when decision-makers rush to judgment, use failure-prone practices, engage in or condone unethical conduct, or allocate time and money unwisely.[7] For example, failures have been attributed to the fact that leaders, in the rush to make key decisions, relied too much on intuition to the exclusion of rational analysis. Executive intuition is the instinctive ability to identify weak signals in the environment and respond without the benefit of concrete facts and information. Sometimes, such intuition may fuel imagination, creativity, and innovation, and contribute to corporate success; other times it may result in spectacular blunders. While some see this as too risky, others argue that intuitive decisions are needed in highly volatile, globally competitive business environments in which time is of the essence. Many experts now believe that strategic decision making requires a balancing of intuition and rationality.[8]

While examining the role of ethics in the strategic leadership process, some experts conclude that the ultimate goal of the strategic leader should be to build sustainable integrity programs into the strategic management framework that encourage positive self-regulation of ethical behavior as a matter of routine within the organization.[9] This will not happen unless the leader also demonstrates integrity. Integrity impacts the credibility and reputation of the strategic leader.[10,11] Although Jack Welch, former CEO of General Electric, is often used as a model of successful strategic leadership, some critics have said that Welch's excessive focus on financial business objectives prevented him from leading through a broader and more humane moral horizon. Underscoring the significance of ethics and moral leadership, on July 9, 2002, the President of the United States announced in the wake of a series of business scandals that America's "greatest economic need" was "higher ethical standards to be upheld by responsible business leaders."[12]

OPENING CASE APPLICATION

2. How Effective Has Hector Ruiz Been in Providing the Kind of Strategic Leadership that AMD Needs?

In 2002, AMD lost a stunning $1.3 billion on revenues of $2.7 billion; research expenses that year amounted to an equally stunning 30% of revenues. Ruiz kept hiring the chip architects who he felt were critical to long-term growth—including 70 that were laid off from Sun Microsystems—and acquired two small chip companies full of technical talent. Ruiz has already put his own stamp on the business, instituting a strategic shift that he calls "flipping the company upside down." While AMD had long focused on microprocessors for desktop computers, laptops, and servers, in that order, now it has reversed the list. It also now targets corporate customers. Characteristically, Ruiz refuses to take full credit for the change. Instead, he says, "I recognized the people inside the company who saw that as important and just gave them the encouragement." CFO Rivet explains why the flip was necessary: "As hard as we tried in the past to win the hearts and minds of Chief Information Officers (CIOs), with the desktop as our focus we were going to fail. They made their decisions from the server on down. When Intel had 100% of the x86 server market, it could charge whatever it wanted and use that money to beat us on desktops. We had to be in the profit haven." Ruiz calls the server-led approach "do or die" for AMD: "If we hadn't pulled this off I would have shut the door."[13] It is evident that Mr. Ruiz possesses analytical and cognitive skills that enabled him to see relationships among variables that have led to long-term opportunities for AMD.

This section focuses on the strategic management process shown in Exhibit 11-1. It is often summarized as a three-step process—strategy formulation, implementation, and evaluation. However, much has to happen prior to the first step taking place. Before formulating a strategy, the following elements must be in place: vision, mission, long-term objectives, and the results of the external and internal environmental audit. We will briefly describe each element of the framework, specifying associated decisions, behaviors, and practices that strategic leaders like Hector Ruiz will take at each stage.

As shown in Exhibit 11-1, the strategic management process begins with the strategist's vision. This is a vision statement of where the organization wants and needs to be in the future, given the nature of the environment in which it exists. The vision statement answers the question, "What does the organization want to or aspire to become?" The vision statement lays the foundation for the development of a mission statement which reflects the organization's core values, beliefs, culture, and purpose. The mission statement answers the question, "What is the organization's purpose?" It identifies the scope of an organization's operations in product/service and market terms. Next, long-term or corporate goals define specific outcomes that an organization seeks to achieve in order to realize its mission. The last of the building blocks that lead to the strategy formulation stage is the environmental audit. This is an analysis of the internal and external environment to identify organizational strengths

Exhibit 11-1 *Strategic management framework.*

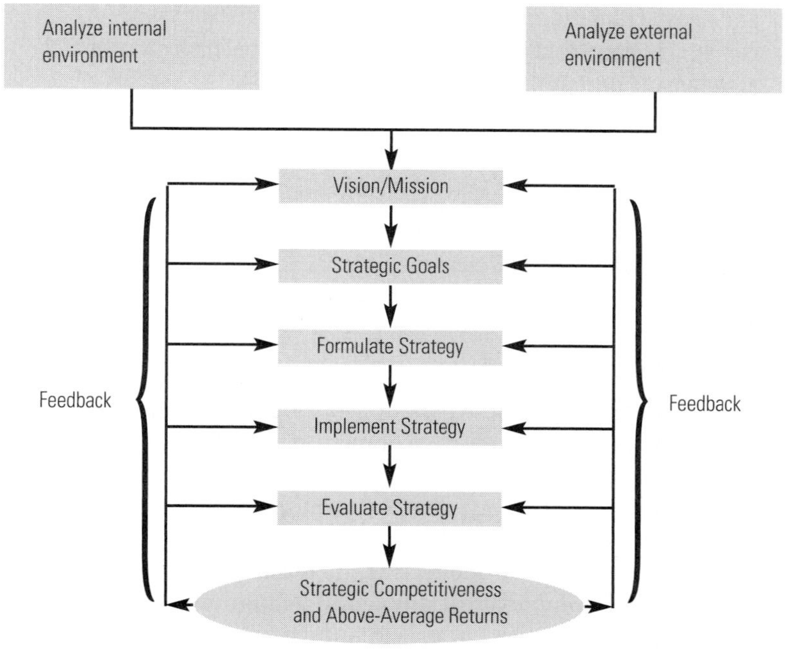

and weaknesses and environmental threats and opportunities. It is performed prior to strategy formulation. The ever more dynamic nature of the external environment demands a periodic reexamination of not just an organization's existing strategies, but also its vision, mission, and long-term objectives. Strategy formulation specifies the strategies for achieving an organization's objectives. Strategies are the means to the ends (objectives). Strategy implementation takes place through the basic organizational architecture (structure, policies, procedures, systems, incentives, and governance) that makes things happen. The final phase, strategy evaluation, involves comparing expected outcomes with actual results after the implementation phase. Each part of this framework is briefly discussed.

Ethical Dilemma 1

Strategic Leadership and Management

An important part of strategic leadership and management is creating the business model of how the business competes. Richard Goldman is a director and an owner of the private high school The University of Miami Online High School (UMOHS), in partnership with The University of Miami. UMOHS is for young athletes and performers (grades 8–12) who are too busy to attend traditional classes; it gives them more time to train, and to travel to compete/perform. It wants to become the establishment school in the sports and performing world. UMOHS also accepts international students who want an American diploma. The tuition charge is $10,750 per year.[14] Some argue that online high school deprives a child of a traditional education and prevents a kid from being a kid and enjoying childhood.

1. How do you feel about high school students enrolling in an online school and missing the experience of attending traditional classes?
2. Is it ethical and socially responsible to offer an online high school for athletes and performers?

Learning Outcome 2

Describe the relevance of analyzing the internal and external environment to the strategic management process.

Analyzing the Environment

One of the most important activities of strategic leadership is understanding the type of industry and general environment in which the organization operates. This involves being able to identify and interpret emerging trends before they become evident to everyone else. As mentioned, organizations operate in highly uncertain and changing environments in which existing strategies quickly become outdated and ineffective. Increasingly, leaders are confronted with environmental complexities, ambiguous situations, and conflicting demands from multiple constituencies. To survive and thrive, strategic leaders must be skilled at managing such environmental complexities and uncertainties.[15] Some describe it as strategic flexibility, which is an organization's capability to identify major changes in the external environment and respond promptly.[16] It is essential to learn and understand the concerns of customers, the availability and bargaining power of suppliers and customers, the actions of competitors, market trends, economic conditions, government policies, and technological advances. From a competitive standpoint, knowing what your competitors are doing and how to respond is clearly important to a firm's survival. It is no surprise that competitive dynamics heavily influence the nature and content of a firm's strategies and its outcomes.[17] The underlying tenet of strategic management, therefore, is that organizations need to formulate strategies to take advantage of external opportunities and to avoid or reduce the negative impact of external threats.

Analyzing the internal environment focuses on assessing the organization's position in the market, financial position, capabilities, core competencies, culture, and structure. This process reveals the organization's strengths and weaknesses. The combined analysis of the external environment (i.e., to identify opportunities and threats) and internal environment (i.e., to identify strengths and weaknesses) is commonly referred to as SWOT (Strengths, Weaknesses, Opportunities, and Threats), or situation, analysis. The effectiveness of an organization's strategies is influenced by the degree of fit or alignment between the organization's internal capabilities/resources and its environmental opportunities.

---

3. Strategic Leadership Is About Analyzing and Predicting Changes in Your Environment and Putting in Place Responsive Strategies. To What Extent Has Mr. Ruiz Demonstrated This Skill?

In a speech describing the state of the IT industry, and the lack of understanding among IT personnel of the changes taking place, Ruiz urged the industry to put the needs of the customers first. He challenged the technology industry to take immediate steps to address the growing level of enterprise customer frustration with expensive, proprietary technologies that do not effectively address their business needs. "Businesses are devoting more and more of their IT budget to integration issues—simply making things work together. That should say to all of us that something is seriously wrong with the current vendor-customer relationship," stated Ruiz. "The IT industry is in the middle of a rather profound sea change. A sea change that should have each and everyone of us re-evaluating who we're buying from, who we are partnering with—indeed—who is going to lead us in another round of innovation." Ruiz went on to discuss how the IT industry can no longer produce new technologies that ignore the current IT landscape and fail to take advantage of the current technologies. Ruiz called on the industry to focus on customer needs when developing new technologies that provide graceful transition paths to next-generation performance.[18] In this piece, Mr. Ruiz is clearly demonstrating his awareness of the transformation that the IT industry is going through, and the apparent gap between the market and the service providers (AMD included).

OPENING CASE APPLICATION

Strategic leadership is about analyzing an organization's changing environment for opportunities and threats and responding with timely strategies.

Accurate interpretation of both types of environments requires considerable analytical and cognitive skills, such as the conceptual skills to think critically, identify and make sense of several complex trends, and streamline available information into a concise plan of action. Accurate and timely interpretation of environmental trends plays a large part in the future actions and the continuing effectiveness of an organization. The importance of speed in recognizing and responding to environmental opportunities and threats has been dramatically accentuated by the highly competitive landscape facing most organizations. As Juergen Schremmpp, former CEO and Chairman of Daimler-Chrysler, puts it, "It's much better to move fast, and make mistakes occasionally, than move too slowly."[19] Because environmental changes are often ambiguous, effective strategic leaders must rely on multiple sources of information for accurate interpretations, and also a balanced application of intuition and rationality. Intuition and rational analysis are viewed as two parallel systems of knowing that allow for high-quality strategic decision making.[20]

Learning Outcome 3

Explain the importance of a vision and a mission statement.

Strategic Vision

According to one expert, organizational leaders too often plunge into a long-term strategic planning process without first deliberating on certain fundamental questions relating to organizational beliefs and values. These questions include: Who are we (core ideology)? Why do we exist (core purpose)? What do we believe in (core values)? What inspires us (envisioned future)? Where we are going (vision statement)? And, finally, What will the future look like when we get there (vivid description)?"[21] These questions embody what a strategic vision and mission represent. A **strategic vision** *is an ambitious view of the future that everyone in the organization can believe in and that is not readily attainable, yet offers a future that is better in important ways than what now exists.*[22] As John Teets, the former chairman of Greyhound, puts it, "a strategist's job is to see the company not as it is . . . but as it can become."[23] According to Warren Bennis, vision is the first basic ingredient of leadership. The leader must have a clear idea of what he or she wants to do and the strength to persist in the face of setbacks and even failures.[24] John F. Kennedy demonstrated vision when he promised that an American would land on the moon during the 1960s, because at the time of his announcement, NASA was in its infancy and the state-of-the-art technology for space exploration was Sputnik. To be motivating, a vision must be expressed in ideological terms, not just in economic terms, to help people develop a personal connection with the organization.

A clear and inspiring vision serves a number of important functions:

• Facilitates decision making, in that it helps people determine what is good or bad, important or trivial

WorkApplication1

Think of your college or university. Prepare a SWOT analysis that identifies one opportunity and one threat facing your institution in the next five years. Also identify a strength and a weakness that you think your institution has.

_____

_____

_____

_____

_____

- Inspires followers by appealing to their fundamental human need to feel important, useful, and to be a part of something great
- Links the present to the past by rationalizing the need for changing old ways of doing work
- Gives meaning to work by explaining not just what people do but why they do it
- Establishes a standard of excellence.[25]

To be widely accepted, vision creation should be a shared exercise. To make a difference, a vision must be based on the input and values of followers and other key stakeholders. A well-crafted vision is one that is the result of teamwork, simple enough to be understood, appealing enough to energize and garner commitment, and credible enough to be accepted as realistic and attainable.[26]

AMD has as its vision: "To build a successful semiconductor company by offering building blocks of ever-increasing complexity to benefit the manufacturers of electronic equipment in the computation, communication and instrumentation markets."[27] Some other examples of companies with simple yet inspiring visions include the following:

- Komatsu: "Encircle Caterpillar"
- Coca-Cola: "A Coke within arm's reach of everyone on the planet"
- Microsoft: "A personal computer on every desk in every home"
- Citibank: "To be the most powerful, the most serviceable, the most far reaching world financial institution that has ever been"
- Nike: "To crush the enemy"
- American Express: "To be the world's most respected service brand"

Mission Statement

A vision statement provides the foundation for developing an organization's mission statement, which describes the general purpose of the organization. There is research support for the proposition that managerial perceptions of mission statement impact their implementation; also, that the mission statement's content and the process of creating it can lead to superior performance.[28] According to a *Business Week* report, firms with well-crafted mission statements have a 30% higher return on certain financial measures than firms that lack such documents. *A **mission statement** is an enduring statement of purpose that distinguishes one organization from other similar enterprises.*[29] It is the organization's core purpose and reason for existence. It answers the question, "What business are we in?" The two components that are often featured in a mission statement are the core values and the core purpose. The core values outline the guiding principles and ethical standards by which the company will conduct business, no matter the circumstance. A well-crafted mission statement can provide many benefits to an organization, including providing direction and focus, forming the basis for objectives and strategies, inspiring positive emotions about the organization, insuring unanimity of purpose, and helping resolve divergent views among managers.[30]

The core purpose doesn't just describe goods and services; it describes the broad needs (immediate and anticipated) of the people served by the organization. For Mary Kay Cosmetics, the mission is "To give unlimited opportunity to women"; for 3M, it is "To solve unsolved problems innovatively"; for Merck, it is "To preserve and improve human life"; for the Army, it is "To be all you can

WorkApplication2

Write an inspiring vision statement for an organization you work or worked for. If the company has one, you may use it or revise it. Explain why you think it has an inspirational appeal.

_____

_____

_____

_____

_____

WorkApplication3

Write an inspiring mission statement for an organization you work or worked for. If it has one, you may use it or revise it. Explain the core values and core purpose of your mission statement.

_____

_____

_____

_____

_____

be"; and for Ford, it is to make "Quality job one." In these and many other examples, there is no mention of the specific products or services these organizations manufacture or serve. Examples abound of organizations that have been adversely affected by poorly crafted mission statements. The railroad industry almost brought about its own demise by defining its mission as being in the railroad business rather than the transportation business. The March of Dimes' original mission was "to cure polio," until a cure was discovered and the organization found itself without a purpose. Today, its mission is to advance human health. Motorola and Zenith were once successful competitors in the manufacture and sale of televisions. Yet, while Zenith has lost ground, Motorola has continued to grow and expand. The difference, according to one source, is that Motorola, unlike Zenith, defined its mission as "applying technology to benefit the public," not as "making television sets."[31] A good mission statement should focus on the needs that the organization's products/services are meeting. The mission should be broad but not so broad that it does not distinguish the organization from its competitors. It should be specific but not so specific that it creates rigidity and resistance to new ideas. Finding an appropriate balance between specificity and generality is difficult, but worth the effort. It is generally believed that mission-driven organizations stand a better chance of succeeding and thus creating long-term shareholder value than those that are not mission-driven.[32]

A vision statement represents a future aspiration, whereas the mission statement represents the enduring character, values, and purpose of the organization in the present. The job of strategic leadership is to ensure that the vision and mission of the organization are realized.

Learning Outcome 4

Explain the relationship between corporate objectives and strategies.

Corporate-Level Objectives

Objectives are the desired outcomes that an organization seeks to achieve for its various stakeholders—employees, customers, suppliers, stockholders, government agencies, activists, and other community groups. Companies develop both financial and strategic objectives. Financial objectives may include measures such as return on investment, sales, profits, earnings per share, or return on equity. Strategic goals may include new customer, market, or product types to pursue. By definition, corporate objectives represent a clear and unambiguous articulation of what needs to be done. According to one study, goal setting has been rated #1 in importance among 73 management theorists. This often leads to difficulties in designing effective incentive/reward systems, because they are not aligned with clear goals and performance measures.[33] Commitment to organizational goals is achieved when there is broad participation in goal setting, and rewards are linked to goal achievement. This is based on the underlying premise that one's conscious goals affect what one achieves. Goal-setting theory asserts that people with specific goals (often called "stretch" goals) perform better than those with vague goals (such as "do your best") or easily attained goals.[34] Stretch goals are difficult yet achievable goals. Stretch goals have been found to improve organizational effectiveness and enhance personal growth and professional development.[35]

Objectives are essential because they help focus everyone in the same direction; they are the target against which actual performance is compared for strategy evaluation (feedback); they create synergy; they are the means by which organizations reveal their priorities; and they are the basis for effective planning, organizing, leading, and controlling activities.[36,37] Organizations must take the time to establish "SMART" objectives (i.e., specific, measurable, achievable, results-based, and time-specific).[38] Refer to Chapter 3 for details on how to write effective objectives (Model 3-1).

---

4. How Effective Has Hector Ruiz Been in Articulating the Financial and Strategic Objectives of AMD?

Though AMD's sales are barely one-tenth of Intel's, Ruiz seems to have proven once and for all that AMD can sustain a challenge against its giant adversary. He has stated that he wants AMD to double its market share throughout the next two or three years. Other AMD executives even expect the company's share in the processor market to rise to 50 percent within ten years. For once, the ever-volatile AMD seems to be showing that it can translate its financial and strategic objectives into the kind of steady numbers that Wall Street looks for. In 2004, revenues topped $5 billion, up more than 40% from 2003. Profits exceeded $150 million, compared with a loss of $274 million the previous year. By employing its own chip-design innovations and exploiting Intel's strategic missteps, AMD has built alliances with the likes of Microsoft, Hewlett-Packard, Sun, Fujitsu, and IBM. Ruiz has also started demanding that the company become obsessed with pleasing customers; he has spent much of his energy building new alliances with the biggest ones. While AMD in the past had periodically sold major PC makers its desktop chips, it had not won a major server maker until last year. Now it counts as its customers not just IBM and Sun but Intel's Itanium partner HP. To foster greater corporate citizenship, Ruiz wants AMD to be the company that helps the world's poor connect to the Internet. It reflects another major change he says he's brought to the company: "I've helped everybody at AMD realize that there's actually a world outside the U.S. that's very important." It is all aimed at a goal Ruiz called "50 × 15," meaning 50 percent of the world's population should be online by 2015. Ruiz agrees with business guru C.K. Prahalad that there are billions of underserved poor consumers. According to Ruiz, "Nobody's worrying about the bottom of the pyramid, and there's an opportunity there."[39] It is evident that having corporate objectives has helped Hector Ruiz move AMD forward.

OPENING CASE APPLICATION

Strategy Formulation

Armed with a vision, mission, corporate objectives, and an assessment of the internal and external environment, a strategist can then select appropriate strategies or plans of action for his or her organization. *A* **strategy** *is an integrated, overarching concept of how an organization will achieve its objectives.*[40]

Strategy represents decisions for exploiting environmental opportunities such as diversification, joint ventures, mergers and acquisitions, new product development, and entering new markets. Selecting among these options is a critical managerial activity, requiring careful consideration of various factors (including the results of SWOT analysis as described above). For example, today's increasing competitive pressures require leaders to continuously seek opportunities for new strategies, to be aware of what reactions such strategies will incite from competitors, and to be prepared to defend their own interests when rivals attack.[41]

A good strategy focuses on exploiting opportunities in the organization's external environment that match the organization's strengths. Also, a good strategy must reflect the core mission and objectives of the organization. To maintain a competitive edge over rivals, effective strategic leaders develop strategies that

- Enhance value to the customers,
- Create synergistic opportunities, and
- Build on the company's core competence.

WorkApplication4

Identify a core competence of an organization you work or worked for. Explain how it differentiates the organization from its competitors.

Delivering value to the customer should be central to any strategy. **Value** *is the ratio of benefits received to the cost incurred by the customer.* A strategy without this quality is sure to fail. Synergy occurs when a chosen strategy (such as in related diversification) calls for organizational units or systems to interact and produce a joint result that is greater than the sum of the parts acting independently—the "2 + 2 = 5" phenomenon. Synergistic benefits include lower cost, greater market power, or superior employee skills and capabilities. Finally, strategies that are based on a company's core competencies have a better chance of improving the company's performance. *A* **core competence** *is a capability that allows an organization to perform extremely well in comparison to competitors.* A strategic leader's job is to identify the organization's unique strengths—what differentiates the organization from its competitors in the industry. Unlike physical resources, which are depleted when used, core competencies increase (in terms of their efficient application) as they are used. They represent the source of a company's competitive advantage over its rivals.

It is important to pause and reiterate that the ultimate purpose of any strategic plan is to identify and satisfy customers' needs with an organization's products/services. This is accomplished through strategic market planning, a subset of the overall strategic management process. However, a strategy is just the means to this end. Many business failures can still be attributed to companies paying too much attention to the means and ignoring the customer. Creating a winning market leadership program is one way of ensuring that this doesn't happen.[42] Concentrating on what actually constitutes "strategy," one study proposed that strategy has five elements that provide answers to five questions. According to these scholars, a good strategy should specify the following:

- Arena: Where will the organization focus its resources?
- Vehicles: How will the organization get there?
- Differentiators: How will the organization stand out in the marketplace?
- Staging: What will be the speed and sequence of moves?
- Economic logic: How will the organization obtain its returns?[43]

5. Describe Some of the Specific Strategies That Hector Ruiz Has Implemented at AMD, and Which Have Resulted in the Success That the Company Is Currently Experiencing.

Hector Ruiz has pursued a number of strategies, including downsizing, divestiture, partnership, new product development, operational efficiency, and new market development. AMD aims to go toe-to-toe with rival Intel by delivering supporting and performance-enhancing technology to its processor lineup. AMD says that 25 of the 100 largest firms on *Fortune*'s Global 500 list now use Opteron servers in some substantial way. The chip really does perform better for many applications: Microsoft adopted Opteron for highly complex risk-management software it uses to manage its $60 billion in cash. The time to run the program dropped from 40 hours on Intel machines to 13 hours with Opteron. AMD has almost exited flash memory business, as it has spun off its Spansion flash business venture in an attempt to maintain its focus on the high-end microprocessor market. AMD is also gaining critical PC-maker converts around the globe, notably in the world's fastest-growing PC market—China. Recently it sold to both the top local server maker—Dawning Information Industry—as well as the #1 desktop computer company—Lenovo. The deal helped Lenovo lower the price of its cheapest PC. Winning this one was a particular coup. Lenovo has been so close to Intel that then-CEO Andy Grove himself traveled to Beijing to be presented with the company's one-millionth PC when it came off the assembly line in 1998. As mentioned earlier, during the downturn in 2000, Mr. Ruiz had to lay off 4,500 employees.

Strategy Implementation

StrategAy implementation has been described as the most important and most difficult part of the strategic management process. Strategy implementation requires galvanizing the organization's employees and managers at all levels to turn formulated strategies into action. It is considered the most difficult stage because it involves dealing with people who come with varying levels of motivation, commitment, and dedication. Successful strategy implementation rests on the shoulders of managers who must be able to motivate employees to perform at high levels—a task that is not always easy to undertake when the right employees are not in place. An excellent strategy that is poorly executed will yield the same poor results as a bad strategy. Strong leadership is considered one of the most important tools for successful strategy implementation. Another factor that makes strategy implementation a difficult process is related to the many components that need to be integrated in order to turn a chosen strategy into action. Leadership decisions on key issues such as appropriate annual goals, structural design, culture, pay or reward systems, budget allocation, and organizational rules, policies, and procedures will determine the success or failure of strategy implementation. Decisions in these areas must match the requirements of the chosen strategy, mission, and objectives of the company.[44] For example, a mismatch, such as a company pursuing a strategy of differentiation through innovation in a bureaucratic, hierarchical structure will result in poor performance and objectives not met. However, a company

Strategic Leadership

Identify in each statement if the view expressed is reflective of a strategic or nonstrategic thinker.

a. strategic thinker   b. nonstrategic thinker

_____ 1. It makes good sense for top management to frequently ask themselves the question, "What will the future of this industry look like?"

_____ 2. I spend my time focusing on solving the day-to-day problems.

_____ 3. We are not concerned about developing skills or capabilities that cannot help us perform the present job.

_____ 4. A company cannot reach its full potential without an inspiring vision.

_____ 5. In our business the environment changes very quickly. Therefore, we generally take things one week at a time.

pursuing a strategy of internal efficiency and stability, aimed at offering customers lower prices than competitors, will succeed with this type of centralized structure. Rewards and other forms of compensation must be aligned with the goals that employees are seeking to accomplish. Also, time is of the essence in strategy implementation. Being careful and rational during strategy formulation is important but not sufficient if managers are slow to initiate actions. For example, managers must avoid becoming trapped in the vicious cycle of rigidity and inaction that prevents them from acting in a timely fashion.[45]

Achieving strategic competitiveness and earning above-average returns for a company is not a matter of luck. It is determined by the decisions and actions of leaders throughout the strategic management process. Determining the outcome of implemented strategies is critical, especially because the basis (i.e., the internal and external environment) upon which the strategies were formulated is constantly changing. Assessing the extent to which stated goals have been achieved or not achieved is strategy evaluation.

Learning Outcome 5

Explain the importance of strategy evaluation in the strategic management model.

Strategy Evaluation

Strategy evaluation is the final stage in the strategic management process; it is the primary means of determining the effectiveness of the strategic choices the organization made during the strategy formulation stage. Effective strategy evaluation involves three fundamental activities: (1) reviewing internal and external factors that are the bases for the current strategies, (2) measuring performance against stated objectives, and (3) taking corrective action.

What this three-step sequence of activities reveals is that strategy evaluation is a tool that leaders use to assess the effectiveness of an organization's strategy towards the accomplishment of its goals, and when discrepancies exist, to support change efforts. It is the task of the strategic leader to encourage meaningful communication and interaction among managers and employees across hierarchical levels, so that feedback from strategy evaluation can be shared throughout the organization and necessary changes implemented. It is the job of strategic leadership to foster and promote a culture of teamwork throughout the organization.

The discussion of strategic leadership, using the strategic management model presented above, offers the lens through which to view the various levels and components of this type of leadership; however, the model does not reveal another key component of strategic leadership, which is dealing with crisis. A crisis can strike any organization without warning. A crisis is characterized by the stress of sudden change that cannot be resolved by routine procedures. As mentioned, a key benefit of performing an environmental analysis is to be able to anticipate or predict changes that may impact the organization negatively if not addressed in a timely manner. However, a crisis by its very nature is an event that could not be predicted or anticipated prior to its occurrence. Therefore, avoidance is rarely possible. Crises are indeed damaging to an organization. In a crisis, stock prices plummet and operating costs escalate, causing both short- and long-term financial losses. A crisis that is mismanaged can also damage an organization's reputation and diminish consumer confidence in the organization's mission, or in some cases lead to its demise altogether. Also, an organization in crisis tends to be defensive and vulnerable to attacks from its competitors. An effective strategist must have the skills necessary to manage a crisis successfully. Therefore, the next section focuses on crisis leadership.

Crisis Leadership

Today, more than ever, there is a great need for leaders from all walks of life to show that they possess the skills and competence to lead during times of crisis. In the wake of the September 11, 2001, World Trade Center attacks, people are looking for leaders who can provide stability, reassurance, confidence, and a sense of control during and after a crisis.[46] In today's volatile global marketplace, many experts believe that organizations (whether for-profit or not-for-profit) should recognize the inevitable—that crises can and will emerge.[47] Many proactive corporations are now putting in place strategic planning and crisis readiness plans. Many organizations are taking appropriate steps to design systems and tools to respond effectively to a crisis before it happens. The key, according to one expert, is to be proactive and build your dream team before disaster hits, "because tough times won't create leaders, . . . they show you what kind of leaders you already have."[48] A **crisis** *is a low-probability, high-impact event that threatens the viability of the organization and is characterized by ambiguity of cause, effect, and means of resolution, as well as by a belief that decisions must be made swiftly.*[49]

Crises come in many forms. There are natural disasters (hurricanes and tsunamis), terrorist attacks (9/11 and the 2005 London bombings), product failures (Firestone and Ford tire problems), human error disasters (Bhopal and *Exxon Valdez* oil spill incidents), unexpected death of the CEO (McDonald's CEO and Chairman, Jim Catalupo), and system failures (Challenger accident and Chernobyl nuclear plant explosion). Also, there are the crises that don't always make the front pages of newspaper or feature in the TV news, such as sexual harassment, executive misconduct, product recalls, and computer hackings. To address the crisis of the sudden demise of the CEO, some scholars recommend that companies develop deep, enduring bench strength by combining succession planning and leadership development to create a long-term process for managing the talent pool.[50] Regardless of the nature of the crises, what they all have in common is the stress and pressure they place on key organizational resources and systems. Any weaknesses that may have been present in the system prior to a crisis are exacerbated at the very time they are needed the most.

Though suffering some loss is almost unavoidable, proper management can reduce the duration of the crisis, enhance or retain a socially responsible corporate image, and secure future profitability. Effective crisis management depends on planning and people. According to experts in the field, an effective crisis management plan is one that is (1) comprehensive, with clear leadership, team, and individual assignments in the form of roles and responsibilities; (2) upgraded frequently and supported by training and periodic drill sessions; and (3) coordinated and controlled across levels and units of the organization.[51]

Building from existing models, a more recent comprehensive model of the crisis management process asserts that readiness to respond appropriately at each stage of the crisis management process is a function of (1) knowing and accepting one's assigned role in the crisis management plan, (2) sufficient training specific to the assigned role to enable one to perform his or her responsibilities competently, and (3) complementary and integrated roles and responsibilities at all levels of the organization, so the crisis management response is controlled and coordinated.[52]

OPENING CASE APPLICATION

6. Strategic Leadership Is Also About Dealing with Crisis. What Crisis Situation Has Ruiz Had to Deal with As CEO of AMD?

As revealed earlier, not long after Mr. Ruiz took over as CEO of AMD, things got rough. As the chip project known as AMD64 progressed, the dot-com bubble burst and the bottom fell out of the technology market. AMD was hurt even more than most technology companies because the downturn coincided with a production problem that prevented it from churning out as many of its then-hot K6 microprocessors as customers wanted. This was clearly a crisis for Ruiz and AMD. He made the rational decision to lay off 4,500 employees, mostly by closing two factories and axing unnecessary internal tasks—in one instance he cut AMD's 15-person travel department and told employees to book trips online instead. However, as evidence of his strategic and leadership astuteness, he kept spending on R&D. Ruiz kept hiring the chip architects he felt were critical to long-term growth—including 70 laid off from Sun—and acquired two small chip companies full of technical talent. Ruiz's effective decision making minimized the negative impact of the crisis and led to positive results a year later.

This section examines the challenges facing leaders and managers attempting to prepare their organizations to engage in effective crisis management. We propose a model of crisis management that includes the following components: pre-crisis planning, risk assessment, crisis management, and crisis communication.

Precrisis Planning

There is increasing awareness that without a strategy that incorporates crisis planning, an organization is at high risk. Many people seldom contemplate the chances that a fire, coworker violence, robbery, or a natural disaster could occur where they work. The tendency is to develop a mentality of detachment from the issue—it happens to other people, not me or our organization.[53] Some leaders rationalize that the present systems are adequate to deal with such crises should they arise, while others find solace in the "positive thinking" (nothing bad will happen) approach. Denial of the occurrence of these low-probability events makes thinking the unthinkable a major leadership challenge. Leaders who are able to overcome these psychological roadblocks and perceive risks realistically can approach crisis management preparedness as a proactive choice closely linked to the strategic management process. They can (1) use the SWOT technique to identify events that could trigger crises in the future, (2) integrate crisis management into the strategic management process so it remains a regular part of the assessment process, and (3) establish a philosophy that recognizes and supports crisis management as an essential component of organizational existence.[54]

There are emerging factors and trends in the current business environment that underscore the importance of having a crisis plan in place before it happens. Technological advances involving the Internet and communication networks allow millions to analyze and critique virtually every aspect of an organization's response to a crisis—such as a violent act on the job, major accident, or product recall. There is a growing trend of class-action lawsuits on behalf of those who have been "hurt" by a company crisis (such as a fire or harmful product). These lawsuits could and have put companies out of business simply because the costs to defend against them are sometimes overwhelming. A company today may have only minutes, not hours, to contain a crisis. In many cases, there is a minute-by-minute real-time analysis of the financial implications of the crisis by investors, customers, and analysts, as Internet and cable television are linked with investment portfolios. Stakeholders may have more information at their fingertips about an ongoing crisis than the company itself. Therefore, proactive leaders are incorporating crisis management into their strategic management models. Not only are they requiring the creation of crisis teams, they are charging these teams to look at crisis management as a strategic challenge.[55] As one expert puts it, "the best crisis is the one prevented!"[56] The problem is detecting the signals that warn of a crisis. Many organizations are presented with early warning signals of an impending crisis but fail to recognize and heed them. It is for this reason that experts recommend precrisis planning for any size business. A study of the perceived importance of crisis planning for small businesses found that interest in crisis planning is motivated more by experiencing crisis events than by management's proactive behavior. In other words, a small business's commitment to crisis planning was not due to the presence of a crisis management team but rather to the past crisis history of the organization.[57,58] This is a dangerous approach because you may not always have a second chance to learn from your mistakes.

There are three components to precrisis planning that every organization (large, small, for-profit, or non-profit) should address: (1) appointing a crisis leader, (2) creating a crisis response team, and (3) assessing risk. We will briefly describe each one of these separately.

Crisis Leader

Given the dynamic environment of business, proactive organizations have found it prudent to designate one or more senior executives with the task of scanning and monitoring the internal and external environments for potential threats on an ongoing basis. The crisis leader initiates the planning process and sets the strategic objectives for the crisis management plan. Along with the crisis management team and other technical experts needed (discussed next), the leader is responsible for keeping the team informed about changes in the strategic plan and/or the organization's internal and external environments that might affect the effectiveness of the plan. In the event of a crisis, the leader must be visible, in control, and overseeing all aspects of the execution of the plan. The crisis leader may report directly to the CEO or to the head of communications or public relations. The duties of the crisis leader may include activities such as the following:

- Requiring individuals or departments to keep logs of complaints or incidents
- Monitoring customer and employee complaints and behavior
- Identifying emerging patterns or trends in the regulatory environment, competitive landscape, and social environment
- Coordinating the activities of the crisis management team to ensure that the members work well together.[59]

The ability of crisis leaders to grasp the impact of events in the early stages of development has helped some organizations avert a crisis and even helped others turn would-be threats into opportunities.

The crisis leader who monitors the radar for the organization must have the power, resources, position, and stature to influence events if a crisis is pending. For example, an organization must empower the crisis leader to be able to make a critical decision such as shutting down a product line if a defect is suspected, or halting operations on an assembly line if multiple injuries or malfunctions have occurred.

Crisis Team

A crisis management team should involve a good mix of representatives from all sectors of the organization. It should draw on critical internal resources (e.g., human resources) and external resources (e.g., trauma counselors). In most medium- to large-sized organizations, the crisis management team is led by a senior-level executive and composed of representatives from Production/Operations, HR, Legal, Security and Maintenance, Marketing, R&D, and Finance/Accounting departments. Diversity in the makeup of the crisis management team is emphasized because crises can affect any number of areas, or the entire organization. In the precrisis planning phase, a leader wants a team that is representative of the population mix of the organization, hardworking, creative, organized, and motivated. Therefore, the personality of the crisis team is as important as the crisis plan itself. During an actual crisis, the team whose members are calm, self-confident, assertive, and dependable is more likely to succeed than a team whose members have the opposite personality traits.[60]

This team approach contrasts with what many organizations practice, which is to divide the duties of crisis management throughout the organization without a central command. Experience reveals that this divided approach often results in conflict—sometimes motivated by varying ideologies, resource allocation, or office politics—over just who will be singularly responsible for managing a crisis. In this situation, it is not uncommon to have the directors of various company departments argue that they and their staff are best equipped to manage a crisis, often to the disapproval of other directors.

An effective team functions as one unit with one voice under a single unit command. Such a team is made up of members who can challenge one another's ideas without resorting to personal attacks, engage in debates without coercion or blame, and unite behind decisions once they are made. Members don't circumvent or undermine each other; instead they work cooperatively, sharing information and encouraging teamwork. This unity and spirit prevents the team from becoming dysfunctional.[61] In the words of one expert, "If a team is dysfunctional before a crisis, that team will have a dysfunctional response during an incident."[62]

Because the warning signals of an impending crisis may be too weak to identify, or accurately interpret, they are often missed or ignored. For this reason, an increasing number of organizations are, in addition to creating a crisis management team, designating a senior manager to monitor the "radar screen" for the company.

Another area of precrisis planning is assessing risk using various tools that include SWOT analysis and "what if" scenario analysis.

Risk Assessment

Anticipating the kinds of crises that an organization can encounter is not an easy task for any manager. An organization's strategic plan allows it to align its internal capabilities (that is, strengths) with external opportunities. The process of strategizing also enables an organization to identify weaknesses in its internal environment and threats in its external environment. The goal of this process is to minimize or eliminate weaknesses and avoid threats or devise strategies to counter their negative impact. Incorporating crisis planning into the strategic management process is becoming a common practice. The reason is obvious: There are literally thousands of incidents that can turn into crises and handicap an organization's attempts to successfully achieve its strategic goals. Therefore, the same degree of care invested in putting together a strategic plan for growth, stability, or renewal must be devoted to crisis planning.

Risk assessment is a common tool used in crisis planning. Borrowing from the field of risk management, crisis teams set out to identify potential incidents that could hit the organization and then determine the degree of preparedness necessary. A crisis will negatively impact an organization's people, its financial condition, or its image. The crisis leader and crisis team members begin the risk assessment process by engaging in "what-if" scenario analysis that focuses on creating realistic incidents under each crisis category. Members may entertain questions such as, "What could happen? Where are we vulnerable? What is the worst-case scenario? What is the short- and long-term outlook?" This series of "what if" scenarios set the stage for a five-step risk assessment plan.

WorkApplication5

Identify someone who has been or is part of a crisis prevention and management team. Ask him or her to describe the makeup and functioning of the team.

_____

_____

_____

_____

_____

Learning Outcome 6

Describe the five-step process for crisis risk assessment.

Exhibit 11-2 *Risk assessment model.*

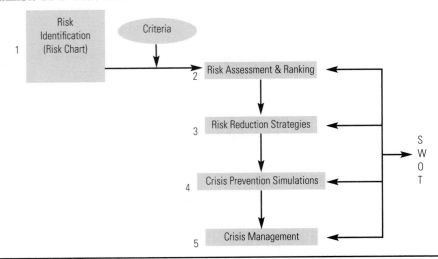

Source: Based on Lawrence Barton, *Crisis in Organizations,* 2nd ed., South-Western/Thomson Learning, 2000, p. 19.

Five-Step Process for Crisis Risk Assessment

Ideally, every organization should follow a five-step process to develop a comprehensive precrisis risk assessment plan. See Exhibit 11-2 for the model depicting these steps.

The five-step process for risk assessment consists of (1) risk identification, (2) risk assessment and ranking, (3) risk reduction strategies, (4) crisis prevention simulations, and (5) crisis management.[63] In step one, crisis team members will begin by first identifying the worst-case incidents that could have severe consequences on people, the organization's financial position, or its image. This process is described as risk identification and results in the creation of a risk chart. Next, these incidents are analyzed and ranked using criteria such as loss of life, injuries, emotional trauma, or minimal inconvenience for each incident's human impact. On the financial and image side, ranking criteria such as extraordinary impact (i.e., will bankrupt the organization), serious but insured (i.e., we are covered), or small impact (i.e., nothing to worry about) may be employed. This information is then used as the basis for launching the third step, which is risk reduction.

During the risk reduction step, the crisis leader shares the risk chart created during risk assessment and ranking with team members or larger audiences, and they begin debating and formulating strategies for countering each crisis or threat. SWOT analysis comes into play as a tool in determining what resources and capabilities are available or needed to better manage each crisis. For instance, say the organization is a chemical plant. An item on the risk chart may indicate the risk of a "poisonous gas leak" as a likely event. A SWOT analysis of this particular risk may progress as follows: the crisis team would identify capabilities the organization has if such an incident should occur (such as poison gas scientists and materials), weaknesses (such as the present lack of a poisonous gas leak response plan), opportunities (such as community support for the plant because of its economic impact on area), and threats (such as environmentalists who are likely to protest and demand that the plant be closed). Based on this analysis, the crisis team may recommend as a risk reduction plan that the organization begin safety awareness programs and conduct joint meetings with local emergency response teams.

The fourth step in the risk assessment process is crisis prevention. Here, tests and simulations are conducted to test employees under pressure. Again, SWOT analysis information is used to fine-tune this step. This step helps to sensitize the organization to the need for crisis planning. After the tests and simulations and the resulting discussions, evaluations, and feedback from managers at all levels of the organization, the crisis team can then rest easy with the assurance that the organization is better ready to handle a crisis. The fifth step of risk assessment is crisis management. A team is assembled and ready to respond in the event of a real crisis.

Ultimately, the best gauge to determine an organization's readiness to respond to a crisis is how it rates according to the following five factors:

- Quality of strategic crisis plan
- Awareness and access to crisis management information
- Readiness for a quick response
- Effective communication plan in place
- Effective crisis leadership

It is a fact of life that in spite of all the crisis prevention planning that organizations undergo, sooner or later, a crisis will emerge and an organization will have to deal with it. The next section focuses on crisis management.

Crisis Management

When a crisis erupts, a rapid response is vital. An effective response in the event of a crisis is relevant to an organization's survival. An organization should make itself accessible as quickly and as openly as possible. It is generally believed that within an hour of becoming aware that a crisis situation may exist, company officials must be prepared to issue an initial statement to the media and other key stakeholder groups—providing facts as they are known and an indication of when additional details will be made available.[64]

The purpose of an immediate response on the part of the affected organization is to fill an information vacuum with facts and perspectives. Experience has shown that the longer companies wait, the more likely the vacuum will be filled with inaccurate statements and outright misinformation that becomes accepted as truth. This underscores the importance of crisis planning and risk assessment as discussed above.

How a company deals with a crisis from a communications standpoint can make or break it. This section focuses on leadership's role in managing a crisis, and the importance of effective communication.

Leadership's Role

An organization's degree of preparedness for a potential crisis depends upon top managers and other responsible personnel. When there is a crisis, employees will seek guidance from company leaders as to how business operations will continue and ways to cope with the situation.[65] Unfortunately, some leaders have been known to retreat behind closed doors when a crisis hits, instead of getting out where the action is.[66] Three key tenets of crisis leadership, according to some experts, are (1) stay engaged and lead from the front, (2) focus on the big picture and communicate the vision, and (3) work with your crisis management team. Organizations with established crisis management teams are able to communicate and effectively respond in the event of a crisis.[67]

An example of how not to lead during a crisis is the leader who digs deeper into his or her foxhole after a crisis hits. Leaders who develop this type of bunker mentality start playing not to lose instead of playing to win. A recent example of a leader who stayed engaged and led from the front lines is former New York Mayor Rudolph Giuliani. In the aftermath of the September 11, 2001, attacks, he took to the streets, modeling visibility and accessibility while he encouraged, consoled, communicated, listened, planned, and executed strategy for rescue and clean up.

In times of crisis, effective leaders try not to lose sight of the big picture. They remain focused on the vision and mission of the organization despite dealing with the reality of the present. There is an unwavering faith that they and their followers will prevail. Guiliani shared in the sadness and loss of the 9/11 tragedy; but, at the same time, he maintained and conveyed uncompromising faith that New Yorkers would triumph and emerge stronger than ever. Effective leaders rely on the values and principles found in their mission statements to guide company decision making during a crisis. Though rare, in some situations, crisis leadership may require reevaluation of a company's values and mission. When a company's values and principles don't seem relevant to the present crisis, effective crisis leadership calls for a new purpose statement—something to the effect of "Principles That Will Guide Our Company During This Time of Crisis." A document such as this will set the tone for everyone in the organization, and build a sense of unity of purpose in handling the crisis.

Effective leaders view crisis management as a team effort. They understand very clearly that it is precisely at this time that a good leader needs a team who can offer wise counsel, debate opposing points of view without coercion, and challenge one another without blame, arriving at a consensus in a timely manner. In a time of crisis, a team with a balance of complementary skills and talents can move quickly and effectively. This is where having gone through crisis planning and risk assessment pays big dividends and often means the difference between survival and extinction. Also, not only should a leader seek wise counsel from his team, he or she should instill a greater feeling of camaraderie among all employees by allowing them to share their emotions and feelings with each other in group settings. In the aftermath of September 11, 2001, a law firm with 1,586 employees in midtown Manhattan held various meetings, including grief-counseling sessions, so employees could share their experiences. Bosses who fail to acknowledge their employees' grief and fears during and after a crisis are likely to end up with an alienated and unproductive staff, according to one executive. In today's Internet age, United Airlines and American Airlines' response to the 9/11 crisis took shape through the use of the Web.[68]

Effective Crisis Communication

Effective crisis communication is very important, because it can make or break a company's reputation.[69] Over the past few years, it is increasingly clear that

WorkApplication7

Think of a leader whom you have observed in a crisis situation, either in person or on TV. Compare your evaluation of this leader's performance to former New York Mayor Guiliani's performance during the September 11, 2001 crisis.

maintaining an effective crisis communication system with primary stakeholders, especially employees, is very critical for survival when a crisis hits. Effective pre-crisis planning should designate who will speak for the organization in the event of a crisis. Without a formal channel of open communication between the executive leadership and all other levels, the risk of a protracted and debilitating crisis is much greater. Much of the literature related to crisis communication focuses on the need for an organization to stay in touch with its external stakeholders—customers, suppliers, local/state/federal agencies, activist groups, and the community at large. In a survey of 107 state governmental agencies to learn about government efforts in situations requiring crisis communications, the results revealed that state agencies have little proactive communication with the media and less than half have a written crisis communication plan.[70]

A well-designed crisis communication system should inform employees at all levels who to call, what procedures to follow, and what they should and should not say to a variety of individuals and agencies. Such procedures should also inform appropriate managers what role(s) they would play in the event of a crisis, and how communication will be handled within and between offices. Investing time and other resources in developing an effective crisis communication system with employees has significant short- and long-term benefits. In the short term, well-informed employees will assist the organization in presenting the facts to the outside world. Invariably, someone from outside is going to ask an employee what happened, or how it happened, or what the organization is doing to remedy the situation. An effective internal crisis communication system that informs the employees of pertinent facts of an incident early, would equip them to respond to such questions. Also, employees, even those at the lower levels of the organization, may have excellent insight on the incident and valuable suggestions on solution alternatives. Their immediate input may provide the pathway to a quick recovery.

From a leadership perspective, it is important to note that during times of crisis, company executives are not the only leaders. Anyone, from an administrative assistant or a salesperson to the head of the human resource department, can be a leader and assist his or her fellow workers in times of need. Through their words and actions, employees at any level can take simple steps to encourage, support, and calm others during a crisis. However, this can happen only if employees are well informed. In the long term, the organization will have won over the confidence, loyalty, and commitment of the employees for being involved and listened to during the crisis. Employees' sense of belonging and self-worth is enhanced and a culture of teamwork and cohesion is created. The postcrisis feeling of "we did it together" can carry over into other areas as the organization moves forward.

Three questions that often emerge after a crisis are: What happened? How did it happen? and What are you going to do to ensure it never happens again? A fourth question to add to the list should be, What are you doing to address this crisis? Also, who is doing the answering does matter. It is generally believed that it makes a difference if the company representative is a senior level manager or someone at a lower level of responsibility. The level of seniority demonstrates to the public the seriousness with which the incident is viewed.

The literature is rich with several "dos" and "don'ts" when it comes to responding to questions such as those posed above. Whether the audience is internal or external stakeholders, these guidelines will apply.

Guidelines for Effective Crisis Communication

It is generally believed that the first 24 hours of a crisis are very crucial because of the media's need to know what happened so they can tell their audiences. There is an information vacuum that, if left unfilled by the organization(s) involved, will be filled for them by others. The longer companies wait, the more likely falsehoods will become accepted as truths.[71] It is for this reason that most consultants in the field recommend telling the truth and telling it quickly. There are a number of avenues for an organization to disseminate its information or tell its side of the story, to weather the storm brought on by a crisis. These include press releases, press kits, news conferences, and one-on-one interviews with the various media. *A* **press release** *is a printed statement that describes how an organization is responding to a crisis and who is in charge. A* **press kit** *is a package of information about a company, including names and pictures of its executives, fact sheet, and key milestones in the company's history.* In the event of a crisis, the last item included in the press kit is a specific press release related to the current incident. This package is ready for distribution to the media when a crisis breaks. Telling the truth up front is the simplest and most effective way of defusing public hostility, no matter how bad the incident. Rather than being preoccupied with protecting itself from liability, a company must demonstrate a strong sense of integrity, responsibility, and commitment.

To ensure that the organization's side of the crisis is heard and that the media coverage is balanced, the media and other key constituencies must be provided with accurate, honest, and timely information about what is happening and what to expect. This will enhance the organization's credibility with the press. Telling what your organization is doing to address a crisis is especially important to family or close relatives of victims. They must be handled with utmost sensitivity. The absence of concern and empathy can lead to a perception of arrogance. It is also important to add to the discussion of what is being done, a plan showing how a similar crisis will be avoided in the future. This is when input from the crisis management team and other technical experts become very valuable to the spokesperson. In addition to providing an overview of the progress being made to address the crisis, the spokesperson should involve technical specialists to provide more expert and detailed background information. This is especially critical during a press conference.

Exhibit 11-3 presents 10 proposed guidelines for effective crisis communication and management based on a study of various crises. Some of the crises cited include the Russian submarine disaster, the Exxon oil spill disaster in Alaska, the French authorities and the Concorde crash, the coal mine cave-in in Pennsylvania, and the September 11, 2001, terrorist attacks.

It is evident from the discussion so far that effective crisis communications rests on the following principles: prepare for crises, respond quickly, act with integrity, and disclose fully. The bottom line, according to one researcher, is to be mindful of the "three A's." *Acknowledge* or admit to the situation, specify what *action* you are taking to contain or repair the damage, and tell the public what you are going to do to *avoid* a repeat in the future.[72]

A postcrisis evaluation plan is a necessity. Most forward-looking organizations now do what the experts have long recommended; in the aftermath of a crisis, top management should launch an evaluation (preferably conducted by an objective third party) of the organization's effectiveness in managing the crisis. This should include effectiveness in communicating with key stakeholder

Exhibit 11-3 *Guidelines to effective crisis communication and management.*

a. Be present.

b. Don't "spin."

c. Communicate plan of action.

d. Be sensitive with affected parties.

e. Avoid conflicting messages.

f. Show a plan for how you will avoid a repeat in the future.

g. Don't make excuses for the leader.

h. Go the extra mile. Go beyond the requirements of the situation.

i. When things are going good, take credit for it without being self-absorbed.

j. The media is your friend and link to the public. Be honest and straightforward with them.

groups.[73] The analysis should focus on questions pertaining to how effectively the crisis team and the crisis management plan performed, how effectively the organization handled victims and family members, and what worked the least in mitigating the problem. These questions are relevant for many reasons, the most important of which are the lessons learned that can help prevent future crises.

If there is one certainty in organizational life today, it is that change will happen. Some have described strategic leadership simply as managing change. More and more organizations are discovering that they operate in highly turbulent environments in which the level of change is discontinuous, rendering past models of successful leadership obsolete for future use. The pressure on

Guidelines to Effective Crisis Communications

Using the letters a through j that accompany the guidelines in Exhibit 11-3, identify which guideline is explained by the statement below.

_____ 6. The CEO of a company is on vacation when a crisis breaks out, but refuses to cancel his vacation and return home to deal with the crisis.

_____ 7. Information is held back or filtered to say only what the leaders or those in charge want you to know about a crisis.

_____ 8. Bringing family or close ones of victims, or those affected, to a central location and providing them with services such as counseling, support, and other facilities that might be needed to help them cope.

_____ 9. Expect and treat victims and/or family members' emotional outbursts with empathy.

_____ 10. After the Concorde crashed, the French authorities along with British Airways immediately grounded all Concorde flights until the designers came up with a fuel tank protection solution.

Applying the Concept 2

leaders to constantly initiate new strategies and approaches for their implementation is enormous. The next section examines the concept of change and how to effectively manage it.

Leading Change

Recall that change is part of our definition of leadership (Chapter 1); leadership is the process of influencing followers to achieve organizational objectives through change. As the discussion of charismatic, transformational, and strategic leadership has revealed, the outcome of each of these three leadership disciplines is change—not stability. Therefore, the focus of this section is on understanding how change processes can be managed in order to improve the effectiveness of individual leaders and ultimately, organizational success. **Organizational change** *consists of the activities associated with planning, designing, implementing, and internalizing tools, procedures, routines, processes, or systems that will require people to perform their jobs differently.*[74] In today's turbulent environment, where change is a fact of life, organizations must constantly cope with unfamiliar events or situations in order to survive and stay competitive. Corporations and government institutions spend millions of dollars on change efforts. Examples of change efforts include process improvement or re-engineering, restructuring, business acquisitions or mergers,

Ethical Dilemma 2

Change through Upgrading

SAP—with 12 million users, 96,400 installations, and more than 1,500 partners—is the world's largest interenterprise software company, and the world's third-largest independent software supplier overall. SAP, headquartered in Germany, employs more than 32,000 people in more than 50 countries.[75]

Fluor Corporation is one of the world's largest publicly owned engineering, procurement, construction, and maintenance services organizations. Fluor has more than 30,000 employees, and it maintains a network of offices in more than 25 countries across 6 continents.[76]

Fluor and other businesses have accused SAP and other software companies of forcing them to upgrade their software. Fluor claims that SAP upgrades are often minor and not needed, yet Fluor is required to purchase the upgrades. In fact, Fluor dropped parts of the products it had licensed from SAP and tried to take over its own software, hiring its own Chief Information Officer (CIO), taking a $13 million charge. However, SAP told Fluor that it would have to install a new version or pay even higher annual fees to get updates, fixes for bugs, and access to SAP's technicians.[77]

1. Do you believe that companies come out with upgrades just to make more money (sometimes called *planned obsolescence*), or do you believe companies are being honestly innovative and customers are just resistant to change?

(Continued)

Ethical Dilemma 2

(*Continued*)

2. As a sales rep, would you push selling an upgrade to a customer who doesn't really need one so that you can make a commission?
3. What would you do if your boss pressured you to sell unneeded upgrades?
4. Is it ethical and socially responsible to "require" updates to continue using a product or service?

business contractions or expansions, new technologies, or a new organizational culture. In essence, organizational change is any transition that requires a change in human performance. In this last section we discuss the need for change, the change process, why people resist change, and guidelines for overcoming resistance to change.

The Need for Change

In the past two decades, institutional theorists have been able to offer more insights into the processes that explain institutional stability than those that explain institutional change.[78] However, rapid environmental changes are causing fundamental transformations that are having a dramatic impact on organizations and presenting new opportunities and threats for leadership.[79] The need to manage change rather than merely reacting to it seems to have become even more crucial in the past decade. Every organization is facing an environment characterized by rapid technological changes, a global economy, changing market requirements, and intense domestic and international competition. These changes have created opportunities such as larger, underserved markets in developing economies and falling trade barriers. Threats in the form of more domestic competition, increased speed in innovations, shortened product life cycles, and global competition are also evident in this type of environment. The opening case revealed AMD as a company clearly in need of change.

To respond to the pace of change, organizations are adopting flatter, more agile structures and more empowering, team-oriented cultures. A central strategic challenge of many managers is managing these changes. Change-oriented leaders are responding by seeking flexibility so that they can quickly adapt to environmental changes, explore new solutions or alternatives, reduce overhead costs, and hopefully keep or gain a competitive advantage over their rivals. For instance, many organizations are responding to these challenges by downsizing; re-engineering business processes; negotiating new partnerships, mergers, and acquisitions; and developing quality products, and new technologies.

The Change Process

Despite the growing consensus that change is imperative if organizations are to grow and thrive in the current and future environment, effecting change, especially major change, is still not an easy undertaking. Many change efforts don't meet the expectations of the organization. The following three statistics tell the story: (1) approximately 75 percent of mergers and acquisitions among European and Americans companies fail to reach their financial targets or expected synergies, (2) fewer than 50 percent of companies undergoing restructuring (such as downscaling or downsizing) realize the anticipated lower costs or higher productivity gains envisioned by the organization, and (3) approximately 30 percent of all mergers and acquisitions fail outright.[80] Efforts to improve success have focused on strategies that leaders can use to effectively manage change rather than simply reacting to it. There is growing interest in understanding how change processes can be managed in order to improve the effectiveness of individual leaders and, consequently, of organizational leadership.[81] These strategies involve focusing on the business environment and examining the fit or lack of fit between the business and its changing environment, challenging conventional wisdom, articulating a compelling vision, forming a coalition of supporters and experts in the field during the early stages of the change, leading the implementation process, staying the course in spite of perceived difficulties, and recognizing and rewarding the contributions of others to the process. Managing change is a complicated and sensitive responsibility.

Ultimately, the role of the leader is to facilitate change that results in better organizational performance; however, the question has always been how to do it effectively and successfully, given the stress, discomfort, and dislocation associated with it. One solution has been to view change as a process, not a product. The change process is the means to transform an organization, a way to realize the new vision for the organization. It requires moving through several stages and executing different tasks, including performing an organizational audit, planning, formulating the change strategy, communicating, persuading others, and consolidating the change. It takes transformational leadership (at the individual, group and organizational levels) to accomplish all these activities.[82] Change process theories describe a typical pattern of events that occur from the identification of a problem to when it is resolved. It is important for leaders to recognize that each stage is critical and requires different actions and commitments from the leader. Ignoring stages or having leaders who lack temporal skills to effectively sequence, time, pace, and combine various interventions at critical phases of the planned change effort can cause the change process to fail.

One of the earliest and most widely used change process theories that incorporates these tasks is the force-field model. This model proposed that the change process is divided into three phases: unfreezing, changing, and refreezing (see Exhibit 11-4). A more recent theory is the eight-stage model of planned organizational change.[83] The two models complement each other; however, the difference between the two models seems to be the expansion of the changing phase of the force-field model. The eight-stage model of planned organizational change covers considerably more ground in describing the necessary steps to implementing phase two of the force-field model. These steps include the need to form a support platform (pro-change coalition), develop a compelling vision, diffuse the vision throughout the organization, train and empower followers to act on the vision, allow for short-term accomplishments and reward performance, and consolidate gains by changing the culture, systems, policies, and structures to align with the new vision. The remaining

Exhibit 11-4 *Stages in the change process: A comparison of the force-field model and eight-stage model.*

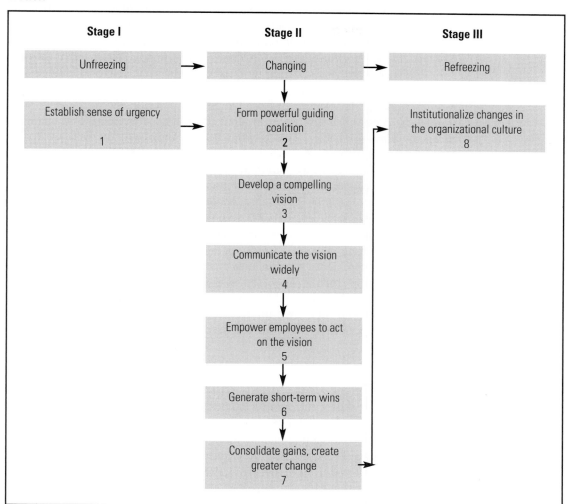

two steps of the eight-stage model are to establish a sense of urgency (step one) and institutionalize the change in the organizational culture (step eight). These two steps match-up with phase I and phase II of the force-field model.

We will focus discussion on the three basic phases of the change process, with an expansion of phase II (changing) to incorporate some of the elements of the eight-stage model of planned organizational change.

Learning Outcome 7

Describe the three phases of the change process.

Unfreezing Phase

Instigated by the actions of a charismatic, strategic, or transformational leader, people in an organization may become aware of the need for change. In other words, a leader may inspire people with a vision of a better future that is sufficiently attractive to convince them that the old ways of doing business are no longer adequate. This recognition may occur as a result of an immediate crisis, may have been proposed earlier as a precursor to charismatic leadership, or it may result from the efforts of a transformational or strategic leader to describe threats and opportunities not yet evident to most people in the organization.

Evidence seems to be tilting more toward the view that real change does not start to happen until the organization is experiencing some real threat or imminent danger of significant loss. The first step, according to the eight-stage model, is to establish a sense of urgency. People need to know that change is needed—now—and why. This is what Edgar Schein—Sloan Fellows Professor of Management Emeritus and senior lecturer at MIT's Sloan School of Management—refers to as "survival anxiety." **Survival anxiety** *is the feeling that unless an organization makes a change, it is going to be out of business or fail to achieve some important goals.* According to Schein, survival anxiety is a necessary but not sufficient stimulus to change. He argues that the reason survival anxiety is not sufficient to stimulate change is because the prospect of learning something new itself produces anxiety, what he calls "learning anxiety"; and this can create resistance to change even with a high survival anxiety.[84] This will be further discussed in the next section on why people resist change. Awareness of the need for change, and a leader's ability to inspire followers to transcend their own immediate interests for the sake of the organization's mission, set the stage for the second phase of the change process to begin.

Changing Phase

This is the stage where the actual change takes place. It is the implementation phase. Here people look for leadership in finding new ways of doing things. Lack of a carefully designed plan of action at this stage will result in an uninspiring outcome. The difference between the force-field model and the eight-stage model occurs during this stage. The eight-stage model prescribes six systematic steps for the leader to follow in implementing change.

The second step, according to the eight-stage model, is for the leader to form a powerful guiding coalition (Chapter 4) by establishing a cross-functional team with enough power to guide the change process and develop a sense of teamwork among the group. According to some experts, a support platform of personalities who can rally followers around the need for change should be the number one consideration. Examples of such personalities include people who are well respected, seen as very credible, and well liked. Another recommendation is that such a pro-change coalition should consist of people who can act in a way that is visionary and inspirational, and who understand the roadblocks, inertia, fears, and political issues that would impede adoption of change initiatives. Next, the leader must develop and articulate a compelling vision that will guide the change effort, and formulate the strategies for achieving that vision. To be committed to the change process, people need to have a vision of a promising future that is significantly better than the present to justify the costs and hardships the transformation will bring. Researchers caution that the context for change needs to be established by the CEO and the executive team. Also, a shared vision must be debated and a consensus hammered out before any attempt is undertaken to communicate the vision more broadly to the entire organization. The fourth step is active communication of the new vision and strategies. The leader's excellent communication skills and ability to mobilize widespread participation in the change process are critical for success. To be effective in communicating the vision requires that the senior leadership of the organization stay in constant contact with members of the organization, and do it in a consistent manner and from a unified front. It is generally believed that the most effective leaders have strong interpersonal skills that blend the instrumental and charismatic qualities of change leadership. The fifth step describes the importance of empowering employees throughout the organization to act on the vision. The leader must empower people with resources, information, and discretion to make decisions. Successful organizational adaptation is increasingly dependent on winning employee support and enthusiasm for proposed changes, rather than merely overcoming resistance. Therefore, empowerment must also include removing obstacles to change, which may include adapting the infrastructure (systems, structure, procedures, policies, and rules) to match the requirements of the change effort. The sixth and seventh steps require the leader to organize the change activities in ways that allow for short-term accomplishments and to celebrate such accomplishments. Major change takes time to complete, and without some visible signs of progress, the transformation effort may lose momentum. Charismatic and transformational leaders understand that actions speak louder than words in creating and sustaining internal momentum for change, even if such actions are merely symbolic. Confidence, enthusiasm, and pride gained via short-term wins will create the drive and motivation to tackle bigger challenges and bring about a faster completion of the change.

Refreezing Phase

In this phase, the change process has been completed. However, this phase also involves institutionalizing the new approach in the organizational culture—the last stage of the eight-stage model. Old habits, values, traditions, attitudes, and mind-sets are permanently replaced. New values and beliefs are instilled in the culture in order to avoid a reversion to the old ways after implementation.

Though stages in the change process generally overlap, each phase is critical for success. An attempt to start implementing change without first unfreezing old attitudes is likely to meet with strong resistance. Not refreezing new attitudes and behaviors may result in the change being reversed soon after implementation. Understanding these phases is important for change-oriented leaders, who must exercise good judgment throughout the process.

Learning Outcome 8

Identify the major reasons for resisting change.

Why People Resist Change

Change disrupts the status quo and often leads to stress, discomfort, and for some even dislocation. These conditions motivate people to resist change. Earlier, we touched on learning anxiety as a factor that can contribute to change resistance. **Learning anxiety** *is the prospect of learning something new* *in itself.* As mentioned above, survival anxiety is a necessary but not a sufficient stimulus for change because the prospect of learning something new itself produces anxiety, which then makes us react defensively by denying the reality or validity of the information that triggered the survival anxiety.[85] This then allows us to rationalize that we do not really need the change after all. Therefore, according to Dr. Schein, learning anxiety is the basis for resistance to change.[86]

This theory supports the view held by some that, for managers and employees, change is often perceived as a win-loss proposition where managers see it as a positive way to strengthen the organization but employees view it as a threat to their status and livelihood.[87] Attempts to implement change are more likely to be successful if leaders understand the reasons behind employees' resistance to change. Resistance is a natural response by employees who want to protect their self-interest in the organization. Change implies learning new ways to do things, and people realize that new learning may make them temporarily incompetent, may expose them to rejection by valued groups, and, in the extreme, may cause them to lose their jobs or positions. For new learning and change to begin, survival anxiety has to be greater than learning anxiety. There are two ways to accomplish this outcome. The wrong way, according to Dr. Schein, is to increase survival anxiety, because that leads to more defensiveness and denial. The right way is to reduce learning anxiety by creating psychological safety for the learner. Effective change agents/leaders create psychological safety by recognizing the existence of learning anxiety and reducing it by providing ample opportunities for training and communication. (This is covered next, as part of the discussion of the most common reasons that people resist change, and also in the section dealing with guidelines for overcoming resistance to change.) Effective leaders do not downplay resistance or perceive it as a discipline problem to be dealt with through punishment or coercion. Rather, leaders view resistance as energy that can be redirected to support change.[88] Exhibit 11-5 summarizes research findings on the most common reasons that people resist change.[89]

Threat to One's Self-Interest

An employee's self-interest in protecting his or her power, position, prestige, pay, and company benefits is a major reason for opposing change. When an organization embarks on a major change, such as pursuing a new strategy, it often results in a shift in the relative power structure and the status of individuals and units within the organization.[90] For example, changes in job design or technology may require knowledge and skills not currently possessed by employees. For these employees, the fear of losing their jobs or status is a major impetus for resisting change, regardless of the benefits to the organization. This is what was referred to as learning anxiety.

Uncertainty

Uncertainty represents a fear of the unknown. Lack of information about a change initiative creates a sense of uncertainty. When employees don't have full knowledge of how a proposed change will affect them, they may worry that replacing skills they have mastered over the years with new ones may prove too

Exhibit 11-5 *Reasons for resisting change.*

a. Threat to one's self-interest
b. Uncertainty
c. Lack of confidence that change will succeed
d. Lack of conviction that change is necessary
e. Distrust of leadership
f. Threat to personal values
g. Fear of being manipulated

difficult to achieve. Therefore, a proposed change may have a better chance of acceptance if it includes a generous provision for helping employees learn new skills required by the change. This is the psychological safety net that was discussed above. The key to creating psychological safety is to try to make the learning process as painless as possible.

Lack of Confidence That Change Will Succeed

A proposed change may require such a radical transformation from the old ways of doing business that employees will question its likelihood of succeeding. In this case, even though there may be a general acknowledgment of problems and the need for change, the lack of confidence that the change will succeed creates resistance. Also, if there have been instances of past failures, this may create cynicism and doubt of future change proposals.

Lack of Conviction That Change Is Necessary

People may resist change if the leader has failed to articulate a real need and urgency for change. This is especially true in cases in which employees believe that the current strategy has been successful, and there is no clear evidence of impending problems in the near future. In other words, survival anxiety is absent or very low; there is no sense that the organization is facing a real threat that could impact its survival or future well-being.

Distrust of Leadership

Trust between parties is the basic requirement for sustaining any relationship. The absence of trust will cause people to resist change, even if there are no obvious threats. Change is resisted if people suspect that there are hidden consequences or motives that management is not revealing. Trust is a valuable currency for leaders to have, because it is the basis upon which the benefits of a proposed change can be sold to employees who may suffer personal losses from such action.

Threat to Personal Values

When a proposed change threatens a person's values, it ignites powerful feelings that fuel resistance to change. Any proposed change must take into account its impact on the values of those who are affected by the change, especially values that are closely aligned with an entrenched organizational culture. If threatened, values that are aligned with an entrenched organizational culture will ignite resistance that is organization-wide rather than isolated.[91]

Fear of Being Manipulated

When people perceive change as an attempt by others to control them, they will resist. However, when people understand and accept the need for change and believe that they have a voice in determining how to implement the change, resistance is lessened.

In the end, leaders who regard resistance as a distraction rather than a real and legitimate concern will find it hard to move beyond the first stage of the change model (Exhibit 11-4). Effective leaders will not only follow the steps in the model but also employ the best implementation techniques or guidelines to overcome employee resistance.

7. Why Has Hector Ruiz Encountered Less Resistance in Bringing About Changes at AMD Than Would Have Been Expected?

For 58-year-old Ruiz, it is more than just taking on Intel and winning. It is also about rebuilding AMD in his image—a tough job at a company that has long been seen as an extension of Sanders' outsized personality. The gold-jewelry-sporting Sanders drove a white Rolls-Royce and commuted from his home in Bel Air, California. AMD executives say that he had an answer for every question, whether or not he knew anything about the subject, and that he managed strategy single-handedly, making all critical decisions. The result was a company that Wall Street viewed as prone to inordinate risks and, too often, to losing its bets. Ruiz took a different path. He worked his way up from a poor border town in Mexico to his current position by relying on his smarts, an almost photographic memory, and the help of others. And he's still inclined to listen where his old boss might have talked. Sanders used to host a regular quarterly meeting with executives called "Breakfast with Jerry." Ruiz maintained the tradition, but he took his name off what's now known as the management committee meeting. Sanders would talk for the entire 45 minutes; Ruiz speaks for 20. "Under Jerry, frankly, the company was very autocratic and power-centric," says the candid and soft-spoken Ruiz. Says CFO Bob Rivet, who worked with both men: "Jerry's style was home run or strikeout, with nothing in between. Either you had a great year or it was a flaming disaster. Hector's more process-driven. Now we worry more about getting men on

WorkApplication9

Give an example of when you were resistant to change. Be sure to identify your resistance by one of the seven reasons in Exhibit 11-5.

_____

_____

_____

_____

_____

Resistance to Change

Using the letters a through g that accompany the reasons listed in Exhibit 11-5, identify which reason for resisting change explains each employee statement.

_____ 11. I'm not too sure about this new program. Is it going to be another fad?

_____ 12. If we get these new machines, we will need fewer operators.

_____ 13. How can management ask us to take a pay cut when they are the ones who are making all the money? We shouldn't let them take advantage of us.

_____ 14. Why should our company get bought out? What do we know about that foreign company anyway?

_____ 15. Why do we have to put in a new system when the current one is only a year old and is working fine?

base."[92] It seems that Ruiz has a way of relating to his followers that increases their commitment to effect needed changes and limits resistance. His personality and leadership style would seem to address some or all of the reasons that followers resist change, and offers support to the guidelines for overcoming resistance to change.

Learning Outcome 9

Discuss people- and task-oriented techniques for overcoming resistance to change.

Guidelines for Overcoming Resistance to Change

There are guidelines that, if followed, can significantly reduce the level of resistance encountered during the change implementation process. These guidelines or actions can be grouped into two separate but overlapping categories—people-oriented actions and task-oriented actions. People-oriented actions acknowledge the human element of change. Change is about people doing things differently.

People-Oriented Actions

These are the various techniques or guidelines that leaders can exercise to keep employees informed, supportive, and motivated about a change. Effective communication before, during, and after the change implementation process will prevent misunderstandings, false rumors, and conflict.[93] It is important that those responsible for implementing change not learn about it from second-hand sources. Also, because major change involves adjustments, disruptions, and even dislocation, training and guidance is needed to help employees acquire skills and capabilities for their role in the implementation process or for their new responsibilities. Through research and case studies, several techniques for overcoming resistance have been identified.[94] They are listed in Exhibit 11-6.

Task-Oriented Actions

These are task-focused activities dealing with power and structural issues of implementing major change. Focusing on key tasks needed to accomplish implementation enables leaders to apply appropriate techniques that can simplify

---

Exhibit 11-6 *Guidelines for overcoming resistance to people-oriented change.*

To reduce or eliminate resistance to change, effective leaders:

- Show relentless support and unquestionable commitment to the change process.
- Communicate the need and the urgency for change to everyone.
- Maintain ongoing communication about the progress of change.
- Avoid micromanaging and empower people to implement the change.
- Ensure that change efforts are adequately staffed and funded.
- Anticipate and prepare people for the necessary adjustments that change will trigger, such as career counseling and/or retraining.

Exhibit 11-7 *Guidelines for overcoming resistance to task-oriented change.*

To reduce or eliminate resistance to change, effective leaders:

- Assemble a coalition of supporters inside and outside the organization.
- Align organizational structure with a new strategy, for consistency.
- Transfer the implementation process to a working team.
- Recruit and fill key positions with competent and committed supporters.
- Know when and how to use ad hoc committees or task forces to shape implementation activities.
- Recognize and reward the contributions of others to the change process.

Self-Assessment 1

Personality, Leadership, and Change

Strategic leadership is less based on personality than charismatic and transformational leadership. Management level also has a lot to do with strategic planning and leadership, as it is primarily a function of top-level managers. Are you a strategic thinker with a focus on long-term planning? Do you have any business or personal plans for three to five years from now, or do you take things as they come without planning for the future?

_____

_____

_____

Change leadership is based on the Big Five personality type openness to experience. Charismatic, transformational, and strategic leadership all require being receptive to change and influencing others to change. Are you open to trying new things and to change, or do you tend to like the status quo and resist change? Do you attempt to influence others to try new things?

_____

_____

_____

and facilitate successful completion of each task. Also, the approach used in designing tasks will affect the level of resistance encountered. Although it is time consuming, getting employees involved in designing change activities pays off by giving people a sense of control. Specific techniques for designing appropriate task and power structures are identified in the literature and summarized in Exhibit 11-7.[95] Now that you have learned about strategic leadership and change leadership, complete Self-Assessment 1 to determine how your personality affects your strategic planning and ability to change.

Go to the Internet (academic.cengage.com/management/lussier) where you will find a broad array of resources to help maximize your learning.

- Review the vocabulary
- Try a quiz
- View chapter videos

Chapter Summary

The chapter summary is organized to answer the 10 learning outcomes for Chapter 11.

1. Discuss the role of strategic leadership in the strategic management process.

Strategic leaders establish organizational direction through vision and strategy. They are responsible for analyzing the organization's environment, considering how it may be different in the future, and setting a direction everyone can believe in and work toward. Strategic leaders must then craft the organization's mission, which includes its core values and purpose for existence. Strategy formulation is the leader's responsibility: He or she must guide the selection among alternative plans and choose the best option for translating goals and objectives into action. The final step is strategy implementation and evaluation. Successful completion of the strategic management process and the attainment of superior organizational performance is not a chance occurrence. It is determined by the decisions and actions strategic leaders take during the process.

2. Describe the relevance of analyzing the internal and external environment to the strategic management process.

The underlying tenet of strategic management is that organizations need to formulate strategies to take advantage of external opportunities and to avoid or reduce the negative impact of external threats. This takes place by monitoring customer behavior, supplier and vendor activities, actions of competitors, market trends, economic conditions, government policies, and technological advances. Analyzing the internal environment focuses on assessing the organization's position in the market, financial position, capabilities, core competencies, culture, and structure. This process reveals the organization's strengths and weaknesses. The combined analysis of the external environment (i.e., to identify opportunities and threats) and internal environment (i.e., to identify strengths and weaknesses) is commonly referred to as SWOT or situation analysis.

3. Explain the importance of a vision and a mission statement.

Many organizations develop both a vision and a mission statement. Whereas the vision statement answers the question, "What do we want to become?" the mission statement answers the question, "What is our business?" Both the vision and mission statements ensure unanimity of purpose within the organization and make important statements about "who the firm is" and "what it wants to become" to outside stakeholders. In other words, reaching agreement on formal mission and vision statements can greatly facilitate the process of reaching agreement on an organization's strategies, objectives, and policies. Organizational success depends on reasonable agreement on these issues.

4. Explain the relationship between corporate objectives and strategies.

Objectives are the desired outcomes that an organization seeks to achieve for its various stakeholders. Strategies are the means by which objectives will be realized. It is for this reason that the mission and objectives of an organization are established before the strategy formulation phase in the strategic management model.

5. Explain the importance of strategy evaluation in the strategic management model.

Note in the strategic management model that feedback is critically important. Changes can occur that impact all strategic management activities. The strategy evaluation stage allows these changes to be identified and adjustments to be made. The feedback that results from the strategy evaluation process promotes the creation of a climate for two-way communication throughout the organization. Strategy evaluation involves three fundamental activities: (1) reviewing internal and external factors that are the bases for the current strategies, (2) measuring performance against stated objectives, and (3) taking corrective action. Corrective action utilizes the feedback that results from the strategy evaluation process.

6. Describe the five-step process for crisis risk assessment.

The five-step process for risk assessment consists of: (1) risk identification, (2) risk assessment and ranking, (3) risk reduction strategies, (4) crisis prevention simulations, and (5) crisis management. In step one, crisis team members begin by first identifying the worst-case incidents that could have severe consequences on people, the organization's financial position, or its image. This process is described as risk identification and results in the creation of a risk chart. Next, these incidents are analyzed and ranked. During the risk reduction step, the crisis leader shares the risk chart created during risk assessment and ranking with team members or larger audiences, and they begin debating and formulating strategies for countering each crisis or threat. The fourth step in the risk assessment process is crisis prevention. Here, tests and simulations are conducted to test employees under pressure. The fifth step of risk assessment is crisis management. A team is assembled and readied to respond in the event of a real crisis.

7. Describe the three phases of the change process.

The force-field model proposes that the change process can be divided into three phases: unfreezing, changing, and refreezing. During the unfreezing phase, the leader establishes the need for change by establishing the problems associated with the current situation and presenting a vision of a better future. Awareness of the need for change and acceptance of a new vision sets the stage for the changing phase. It is during the second phase that the proposed vision is implemented. It is action oriented. The leader must actively and effectively communicate the vision with a tone of urgency. He or she must empower followers to act on the vision by giving them resources, information, and discretion to make decisions. Empowerment must also include removing obstacles to change, which may include adapting the infrastructure to the new strategy or strategies of the organization. Other motivational strategies for achieving success at this stage are described in the text. The third phase, refreezing, involves cementing the new vision in the organizational culture so that the change is not reversed soon after it is implemented. The change must be institutionalized so that old habits, values, traditions, and attitudes are permanently replaced.

8. Identify the major reasons for resisting change.

Change is not a risk-free proposition. Change often brings with it pain and stress. Some people get demoted, reassigned, relocated, or even fired from their jobs. With all of these negative possibilities, the first reaction of most people is to resist any attempts at making a change. Some of the major reasons why people resist change are the threat to one's self-interest, lack of conviction that change is necessary, fear of being manipulated, threat to personal values, lack of confidence that change will succeed, distrust of leadership, and uncertainty. These are further elaborated on in the text.

9. Discuss people- and task-oriented techniques for overcoming resistance to change.

To overcome resistance to change, effective managers must think in terms of people actions and task actions. People actions involve undertaking the following: anticipate change and prepare people for the necessary adjustments that change will trigger, avoid micromanaging and empower people to implement the change, help people deal with the trauma of change, communicate a strong message about the urgency for change, celebrate and maintain ongoing communication about the progress of change, and show a strong commitment to the change process. Task-based actions include assembling a coalition of supporters inside and outside the organization, recruiting and filling key positions with competent and committed supporters, aligning the organizational structure and other infrastructure with the new strategy, and using qualified task forces to shape and support implementation activities.

10. Define the following key terms (in order of appearance in the chapter):

Select one or more methods: (1) fill in the missing key terms from memory, (2) match the key terms from the following list with their definition below, (3) copy the key terms in order from the list at the beginning of the chapter.

_____ a person's ability to anticipate, envision, maintain flexibility, think strategically, and work with others to initiate changes that will create a viable future for the organization.

_____ is the set of decisions and actions used to formulate and implement specific strategies that will achieve a competitively superior fit between the organization and its environment, so as to achieve organizational goals.

_____ is an ambitious view of the future that everyone in the organization can believe in and that is not readily attainable, yet offers a future that is better in important ways than what now exists.

_____ is an enduring statement of purpose that distinguishes one organization from other similar enterprises.

_____ is an integrated, overarching concept of how an organization will achieve its objectives.

_____ is the ratio of benefits received to the cost paid by the customer.

_____ is a capability that allows an organization to perform extremely well in comparison to competitors.

_____ is a low-probability, high-impact event that threatens the viability of the organization and is characterized by ambiguity of cause, effect, and means of resolution, as well as by a belief that decisions must be made swiftly.

_____ is a printed statement that describes how an organization is responding to a crisis and who is in charge.

_____ is a package of information about a company, including names and pictures of its executives, fact sheet, and key milestones in the company's history.

_____ consists of the activities associated with planning, designing, implementing, and internalizing tools, procedures, routines, processes, or systems that will require people to perform their jobs differently.

_____ is the feeling that unless an organization makes a change, it is going to be out of business or fail to achieve some important goals.

_____ is the prospect of learning something new in itself.

Key Terms

core competence, 470

crisis, 473

learning anxiety, 489

mission statement, 467

organizational change, 484

press kit, 482

press release, 482

strategic leadership, 460

strategic management, 461

strategic vision, 466

strategy, 469

survival anxiety, 488

value, 470

Review and Discussion Questions

1. Discuss how an organization's objectives may affect its search for opportunities.
2. What are the key elements of the strategic management process?
3. What is the difference between a strategic vision and a mission statement?
4. The essence of the strategic management process is adapting to change. Discuss.
5. What are the current factors or trends that make precrisis planning an important aspect of strategic leadership?

6. What are the three main components of a precrisis plan?
7. Describe the responsibilities of the crisis leader.
8. What is the appropriate role of an organization's top leadership during a crisis?
9. What are the phases of the eight-stage model of planned change?
10. What is the difference between people- and task-oriented approaches to overcoming resistance to change?

Case

STRATEGIC LEADERSHIP SUCCESS AT EXXONMOBIL

Lee R. Raymond is the former chairman and chief executive officer of ExxonMobil Corporation. He was first appointed chairman and CEO of Exxon Corporation in 1993. He assumed the top leadership position at Exxon by replacing Lawrence Rawl, the prior CEO of Exxon on whose watch the *Exxon Valdez* oil spill occurred in 1989. In March 1989, the oil tanker *Exxon Valdez* crashed in Prince William Sound, off the port of Valdez, Alaska, spilling 260,000 barrels of crude oil. The cleanup effort cost Exxon $2.5 billion alone, and the company was forced to pay out $1.1 billion in various settlements. A 1994 federal jury also fined Exxon an additional $5 billion for its "recklessness."[96] The resulting public relations damage brought on by the crisis threatened Exxon's future.

Raymond came to the helm of Exxon at a time when the company was facing severe external threats. The crisis brought on by the *Valdez* oil spill was still unresolved. The company faced intense competition from companies such as Shell, Texaco, Phillips, and Amoco. Prices were falling as fuel production and costs went up. There was pressure from environmental groups calling for greater government regulation of the industry, including strict limitations on explorations for new oil reserves. Exxon was a company in need of a new strategic leader who could carve out a new roadmap for the future. Change was needed. Lee Raymond was seen as the right person for the job. In 2005, speaking before the Energy Policy Foundation of Norway, Mr. Raymond likened the job of CEO to a batter stepping up to home plate to face the pitcher. He said stepping up to the plate for companies in the energy industry means having the courage and wisdom to face the realities of the energy market, and being willing to tell the public about those realities in a forthright way.

To improve the competitive position of Exxon, Raymond pursued a growth-by-merger strategy. He initiated friendly merger talks with his rival, Mobil. In 1999, Exxon and Mobil signed an agreement to merge and form a new company called ExxonMobil Corporation. At the time of the signing, Raymond and Lou Noto (chairman and CEO of Mobil) said they believed the merger would enhance the new company's ability to be "an effective global competitor in a volatile world economy and in an industry that is more and more competitive."

In order to counter the external threats that ExxonMobil was facing, Raymond developed a strategic plan that focused on a clear vision and long-term objectives. The vision of ExxonMobil, according to former CEO Raymond, was to remain an industry leader in every aspect of the energy and petrochemical business. The primary objective of ExxonMobil, he maintained, was to achieve better shareholder returns than the market. The cornerstone to achieving this outcome was a focus on strict financial controls, reliable operations, and sound safety and environmental performance. Raymond acknowledged and emphasized that ExxonMobil's success in these areas rested on a number of factors—chief among them being the quality, dedication, and professionalism of all ExxonMobil employees. Their work, according to Mr. Raymond, is based on a number of long-held ExxonMobil strategies—maintaining investment discipline and leading-edge operating efficiency. "We have known for many years that a cornerstone to our success is flawless operations—which include strict financial controls, reliable operations, and sound safety and environmental performance."[97]

In the area of safety and the environment, ExxonMobil set as its goal to be the industry leader. To translate this into action, ExxonMobil embarked on a proactive Oil Spill Response Preparedness plan.

2004 was an excellent year for ExxonMobil. The company earned a record $25.3 billion, achieved a return on capital employed of 24%, and earned more than $43 billion from cash flow from operations and asset sales.[98] Raymond emphasized that while these results were significant in and of themselves, they also reflected a more important achievement—completion of the merger and the implementation of the new organization. Mr. Raymond revealed that since the merger was announced in December of 1998, ExxonMobil had generated $120 billion in cash and $47 billion to shareholders. In addition, ExxonMobil had captured $10 billion in synergies and cost efficiencies.[99] In the area of safety and the environment, he reported that the company's goal of being an industry leader had been achieved. In 2000, worldwide employee incidents resulting in time away from work were lower than any of ExxonMobil's international competitors—representing a reduction of nearly 70% from 6 years ago. "We have delivered a significant reduction in the number of spills from our operations, to the point where the total volume of oil spilled by our own marine vessels is less than 2 teaspoons for every million gallons of oil transported," said Raymond. In the area of energy efficiency, ExxonMobil achieved record performance in 2004 across their worldwide refining and chemical businesses, improving by more than 3% over 2000. Since 2000, their refineries have improved at a rate three times greater than the historical industry rate, improving energy efficiency by 5% and, in fact, by nearly 10% since 1990.[100]

It is evident that former CEO Raymond significantly transformed Exxon. First, he successfully merged Exxon with its rival, Mobil, which led to a new name—ExxonMobil. Second, his relentless focus on efficiency, safety, and the environment transformed the culture of ExxonMobil from what it was prior to his arrival. The company's financial position under Raymond was the best it had been in years.

GO TO THE INTERNET: To learn more about ExxonMobil, log on to InfoTrac® College Edition at **academic. cengage.com/infotrac** and use the advanced search function.

Based on the case and the material in this chapter address the following issues:

1. What external and internal pressures did Lee Raymond face when he assumed the leadership of ExxonMobil, and how did he respond to these challenges?
2. Strategic management is about formulating strategies that align an organization's internal capabilities with external opportunities, while avoiding or minimizing threats. How effective was Mr. Raymond as a strategist?
3. Part of strategic management is accomplished via SWOT analysis. What is the evidence that the leadership at ExxonMobil is making use of this tool?
4. What is the significance of having strategic or corporate goals? Relate your response to former Chairman Raymond's strategic goals for ExxonMobil.

5. Part of being a strategic leader is dealing with crisis. One of the worst oil spill crises and the most publicized in recent times was the *Exxon Valdez* oil spill in Alaska. How effective was Chairman Raymond in addressing the crisis and insuring that it does not happen again?
6. Effective crisis management involves precrisis planning. In what ways has ExxonMobil prepared itself for a future crisis through precrisis planning?

Cumulative Case Questions

7. According to the Big Five Model of Personality (Chapter 2), what traits would former Chairman Raymond consider critical for his managers to possess?
8. The interactions among power, politics, networking, and negotiation (Chapter 4) are a common occurrence in organizational life. CEOs have to deal with various stakeholders (shareholders, employees, the board of directors, the customers, suppliers, unions, government and state regulators, etc.). Describe how a CEO like Mr. Raymond would employ power, politics, networking, and negotiation as effective tools of leadership.
9. Communication, coaching, and conflict management (Chapter 6) are said to be skills that have a direct and significant impact on a leader's career success. Given the situation that ExxonMobil was in prior to Mr. Raymond's arrival, how critical were these skills in his efforts to reposition the company and address the problems he inherited?

Case Exercise and Role-Play

Preparation: Assume you are part of the leadership of an organization or organizational unit that is in need of training the management team of its foreign subsidiary to think and act more strategically than they are used to. Your organization has come to the realization that a multidomestic or country-specific strategy is required due to the differences between the two countries' cultures and politics. A multinational corporation like ExxonMobil faces this challenge every day. ExxonMobil has operations in many countries around the world (visit ExxonMobil's Web site at **www.exxonmobil.com** for more information) and has to prepare its managers before sending them out to these countries. Your task is to help this team of leaders develop a vision and mission statement for their organization that is in congruence with the overall vision and mission of the parent corporation.

Role-Play: The instructor forms students into small groups (representing top leadership of the foreign subsidiary) to develop an inspiring vision of no more than 15 words and a mission statement of no more than 100 words. Here are some guidelines:

1. Identify key environmental trends or changes that have influenced your group's vision.

2. Make up a list of core values that your organization now holds or you would want it to have, and incorporate them in your mission statement.

3. Share your mission statement with other members of the class, and vote on who has the most inspiring and compelling mission.

Video Case

Fallon Worldwide: Maintaining Its Strategic Vision

Advertising agency Fallon Worldwide has grown from a Minneapolis-based American firm into an international business with billings of over $800 million and clients all over the globe. From the beginning, the agency's founders emphasized a strategy in global markets, recruiting employees from Europe, South America, and Australia while creating a client base of multinational corporations such as BMW, United Airlines, and L'Oreal.

View the Video (13 minutes)
View the video on Fallon Worldwide in class or at **academic.cengage.com/management/lussier.**

Read the Case
Fallon has gained many advantages through globalization. By going global, the ad agency reaches consumers well beyond the North American region. Expansion into emerging markets like Sao Paulo and Hong Kong allows the firm to develop campaigns that effectively advertise brands across geographic and cultural borders. Additionally, by becoming a global organization, Fallon has been able to benefit from the perspective and experience of marketers from around the world.

Despite its advantages, globalization can also be a source of crisis in organizations. Global expansion has created organizational and technological challenges for Fallon's employees, and many workers have expressed fears about the possibility of losing the creative freedom and inspiring corporate culture that helped make the company great. In addition, the global environment introduces language and cultural barriers that create many challenges for Fallon's managers.

The pressures associated with becoming an international agency are enormous. Yet even with all the difficulties, working globally can be fun. Alliances have to be forged, and managers have to think seriously about guiding a business through different cultures. In the end, it all comes down to planning, strategy, and maintaining the corporate vision and values.

Answer the Questions
1. What strategic factors did Fallon consider when deciding to expand its business globally?
2. Find Fallon's strategic vision statement on its web site. What does the statement say about the company's commitment to a global strategy?
3. What techniques could Fallon's leaders use to help its employees overcome the resistance to going global?

Skill-Development Exercise 1

STRATEGIC PLANNING

Preparing for Skill-Development Exercise 1

Think of a business that you would like to start someday. Develop a simple strategic plan for your proposed business by following steps 1 through 4 below. If you cannot think of a business you would like to start, select an existing business. Do not select a company if you are familiar with their strategic plan. What is the name and location of the business?

1. What would be some of your strengths and weaknesses, opportunities and threats, compared to your competitors? It may be helpful to think about your answer to step 4 below before doing your SWOT analysis.

_____

_____

2. Develop a vision statement for your business.

_____

3. Develop a mission statement for your business.

_____

4. As part of the strategy formulation, identify your core competencies. Be sure they answer the questions, "What will your business do better or different than your competitors? Why should someone do business with you

rather than your competitors?" This stage is related to the SWOT analysis in step 1 above.

_____

_____

Doing Skill-Development Exercise 1 in Class

Objective

To develop a simple strategic plan for a business you would like to start someday.

Procedure (10–30 minutes)

Option A: Break into groups of 3 to 6 and share your strategic plans. Offer each other suggestions for improvements.

Option B: Same as A, but select the best strategy from the group to be presented to the entire class. Each group's selected strategy is presented to the class.

Conclusion

The instructor may make concluding remarks.

Apply It (2–4 minutes)

What did I learn from this exercise? How will I use this knowledge in the future?

_____

_____

_____

Sharing

In the group, or to the entire class, volunteers may give their answers to the "Apply It" questions.

Skill-Development Exercise 2

PLANNING A CHANGE USING THE FORCE-FIELD MODEL

Preparing for Skill-Development Exercise 2

Select a change at work or in your personal life that you would like to make, and develop a plan as follows.

1. *Unfreezing.* Briefly describe the change and why it is needed.

   _____

   _____

2. *Changing.* State the beginning-of-change date _____ and end-of-change date _____.
   Develop a plan for making the change.

   _____

   _____

   _____

   _____

3. *Refreezing.* Identify plans for maintaining the new change.

   _____

   _____

   _____

Doing Skill-Development Exercise 2 in Class

Objective

To develop a plan for change.

Procedure (10–30 minutes)

Option A: Break into groups of 3 to 6 and share your change plans. Offer each other suggestions for improvements.

Option B: Same as A, but select the best plan from the group to be presented to the entire class. Each group's selected plan is presented to the class.

Conclusion

The instructor may make concluding remarks.

Apply It (2–4 minutes)

What did I learn from this experience? How will I use this knowledge in the future? Relist your beginning and ending target dates for the change.

_____

_____

_____

Sharing

In the group, or to the entire class, volunteers may give their answers to the "Apply It" questions.

Appendix

Leadership and Spirituality in the Workplace

Judith A. Neal, Ph.D.*

The purpose of this appendix is threefold: (1) It provides an overview of the concept of spirituality in the workplace. (2) It provides spiritual principles that have been useful to many leaders in their personal and professional development. (3) It provides a list of some of the resources that are available to people who are interested in learning more about the relationship between leadership and spirituality.

Spirituality in the Workplace

Tom Aageson, former Director of Aid to Artisans—a nonprofit organization that helps artists in third world countries—takes an annual retreat in which he contemplates questions about the purpose of his life, and evaluates how well he is living in alignment with his values. Angel Martinez, former CEO of Rockport Shoes, invited all his top executives to a retreat that included exploring the integration of each person's spiritual journey with his or her work journey. At Integrated Project Systems (IPS) in San Francisco, CEO Bill Kern created a document called "The Corporate Stand" that is very explicit about "The Integrity of the Human Spirit." These are key principles that employees live by at IPS. Rodale Press, publisher of such well-known magazines as *Prevention, Men's Health, Runner's World,* and *Organic Gardening,* has a "kiva room" at corporate headquarters where employees may go to meditate, pray, or just spend quiet time when things get too stressful.

Stories like these are becoming more and more common in all kinds of workplaces. Academic and professional conferences are offering an increasing number of sessions that have words such as *Spirituality* or *Soul* in the title. There is a new openness in management education to recognition of our spiritual nature. This recognition can be on a personal level, such as when a person explores his or her own spiritual journey and struggles with what this means for their work. It is also on a conceptual level, as both academics and practitioners explore the role that spirituality might have in bringing meaning, purpose, and increased performance to organizational life. There is a major

*Appendix written by Judith A. Neal, Ph.D., Executive Director, Association for Spirit at Work, http://www.spiritatwork.org. © 2005 by Judith Neal; used by permission of the author.

change going on in the personal and professional lives of leaders, as many of them more deeply integrate their spirituality and their work. And most would agree that this integration is leading to very positive changes in their relationships and their effectiveness.

Defining Spirituality in the Workplace

Spirituality is difficult to define. The Latin origin of the word "spirit" is *spirare*, meaning, "to breathe." At its most basic, then, spirit is what inhabits us when we are alive and breathing, it is the life force. Spirituality has been defined as "that which is traditionally believed to be the vital principle or animating force within living beings; that which constitutes one's unseen intangible being; the real sense or significance of something"[1] A fairly comprehensive definition, part of which is provided here, is as follows:

> *One's spirituality is the essence of who he or she is. It defines the inner self, separate from the body, but including the physical and intellectual self. . . . Spirituality also is the quality of being spiritual, of recognizing the intangible, life-affirming force in self and all human beings. It is a state of intimate relationship with the inner self of higher values and morality. It is a recognition of the truth of the inner nature of people. . . . Spirituality does not apply to particular religions, although the values of some religions may be a part of a person's spiritual focus. Said another way, spirituality is the song we all sing. Each religion has its own singer.*[2]

Perhaps the difficulty people have had in defining spirituality is that they are trying to objectify and categorize an experience and way of being that is at its core very subjective and beyond categorizing. For this reason, some have resorted to poetry as a way of trying to capture the essence of the experience of spirituality. Lee Bolman did this very effectively in his keynote presentation on spirituality in the workplace to the Eastern Academy of Management in May 1995. He quoted the Persian poet Rumi:[3]

> *All day I think about it, then at night I say it*
> *Where did I come from and what am I supposed to be doing?*
> *I have no idea*
> *My soul is elsewhere, I'm sure of that*
> *And I intend to end up there.*

James Autry, a successful Fortune 500 executive, wrote a poem called "Threads." Here is an excerpt from that poem:[4]

> *Listen.*
> *In every office*
> *You hear the threads*
> *of love and joy and fear and guilt,*
> *the cries for celebration and reassurance,*
> *and somehow you know that connecting those threads*
> *is what you are supposed to do*
> *and business takes care of itself.*

Spirituality in the workplace is about people seeing their work as a spiritual path, as an opportunity to grow personally and to contribute to society in a meaningful way. It is about learning to be more caring and compassionate with fellow employees, with bosses, with subordinates and customers. It is about integrity, being true to oneself, and telling the truth to others. Spirituality in the workplace can refer to an individual's attempts to live his or her values more fully in the workplace. Or it can refer to the ways in which organizations structure themselves to support the spiritual growth of employees.

In the final analysis, the understanding of spirit and of spirituality in the workplace is a very individual and personal matter. There are as many expressions of these concepts as there are people who talk or write about them.

Levels of Spirituality Development

In practice, organizations are implementing spirituality in the workplace approaches at one or more of the following four levels:[5]

Level 1: Individual Development

At this level, programs focus on helping the individual employee understand more about his or her values, spiritual principles, and sense of purpose. The organization is committed to helping individuals live in alignment with their spiritual path, and may offer meditation rooms or courses on spiritual practices and/or teachings, and may bring in speakers who talk about spiritual development. There is an understanding that if people can discover and respond to their own "calling" or sense of purpose, they will be more creative, committed, and service-oriented.

Level 2: Leadership and Team Development

Organizations are offering courses to leaders with titles like "Authentic Leadership," "Leading With Soul," and "Spiritual Leadership." Leaders are encouraged to apply spiritual values such as humility, trust, courage, integrity, and faith to their work with teams. They may offer courses such as "Team Spirit" and "Noble Purpose" developed by Barry Heerman.[6] Some organizations are offering lunchtime Spirit at Work discussion groups. Others are offering team building courses that incorporate spiritual values or practices.

Level 3: Total System Development

A growing number of CEOs and organizational leaders have become personally committed to creating organizations that nurture the human spirit of the company's employees, customers, and other stakeholders. Several systemic approaches have been developed to help organizations evolve to a higher level of congruence with spiritual values. These include "Corporate Tools" by Richard Barrett,[7] "Spiral Dynamics" by Don Beck and Chris Cowan,[8] "Appreciative Inquiry," by David Cooperrider and colleagues,[9] "Positive Organizational Scholarship" and "The Abundance Framework" by Kim Cameron,[10] and "Open Space Technology," by Harrison Owen.[11] The key aim in each of these organizational development processes is to help an organization move beyond just a focus on profits and the bottom line to a commitment to human development and a positive contribution to society.

Level 4: Redefining the Role of Business

A new paradigm is emerging among business leaders that redefines the purpose of business as the solution to solving problems in society and around the globe, rather than being a contributor to them. The focus is on using the creative energy and talent of their employees, along with their vast capital resources and international reach, to truly make a positive difference in the world. Willis Harman, cofounder of the Institute of Noetic Sciences and of the World Business Academy, was probably the first person to speak about the important role of business in increasing consciousness in the world.[12] More recently, Case Western Reserve's Wetherhead School of Management has created a Center of Excellence called the *Center of Business As Agent of World Benefit (BAWB)*, which has sponsored an ongoing inquiry research project into the ways business is making a positive difference in the world. People can get involved by going to their website at **http://www.worldinquiry.org**.

Each organization is unique in terms of its values, vision, and readiness for spirituality in the workplace, so there is no one formula that leaders can use to implement spiritual values and practices in their organizations. The best thing to do is to learn as much as possible from organizations that have been successful in this integration. A great place to start is to study the organizations that have received the International Spirit at Work Award for their explicit spiritual practices and commitment to nurturing the human spirit of their employees; for more information, go to **http://www.spiritatwork.org/awards/ willisharman/index.htm**.

Guidelines for Leading from a Spiritual Perspective

Following are five spiritual principles that have been useful to many leaders in their personal and professional development.

Know Thyself

All spiritual growth processes incorporate the principle of self-awareness. Leading provides a great opportunity to become more self-aware. Examine why you respond to situations the way you do. Take a moment in the morning to reflect on the kind of leader you would like to be today. At the end of the day, take quiet time to assess how well you did, and to what extent you were able to live in alignment with your most deeply held core values.

Act with Authenticity and Congruency

Followers learn a lot more from who we are and how we behave than from what we say. Authenticity means being oneself, being fully congruent, and not playing a role. Many managers really get into the role of "leader," and they see managing as a place to assert their superiority and control. They would never want employees to see the more human, softer parts of them. Yet we are finding that managers who are more authentic, humble, and congruent tend to be more effective.[13]

It is a real challenge to be authentic and congruent in the workplace. Most people feel that if they are truly themselves and if they say what they are really thinking, it will be the end of their careers. But I believe that if we don't do this, we sell a little bit of our souls every time we are inauthentic, and that saps our creative energy and our emotional intelligence. It also reduces our sense of commitment to the work we do, and we cannot perform at our highest level.

Experiment with greater authenticity and with showing more of your human-ness. You will be surprised at how positively people will respond.

It is also important to create a climate in which employees are encouraged to behave authentically and congruently. This means that they should be comfortable expressing feelings as well as thoughts and ideas. Contrary to popular opinion, humility accompanied by a strong will does create an enduring organization, and is a much more powerful tool for success than a strong ego.

Respect and Honor the Beliefs of Others

It can be very risky and maybe even inappropriate to talk about your own spirituality in the workplace. Yet if spirituality is a guiding force in your life and your leading, and if you follow the guideline of authenticity and congruency, you cannot hide that part of yourself. It is a fine line to walk.

What seems to work best is to build a climate of trust and openness first, and to model an acceptance of opinions and ideas that are different from yours. Then, if an appropriate opportunity comes up in which you can mention something about your spiritual beliefs, you should emphasize that they are yours alone. Explain that people have different beliefs and that you respect those differences. It is extremely important that employees do not feel that you are imposing your belief system (spiritual, religious, or otherwise) on them. At the same time, it is worthwhile to do anything that you can do to nurture spiritual and ethical development in your employees in a way that allows them to explore their own deepest values and beliefs.

Be as Trusting as You Can Be

This guideline operates on many levels. On the personal level, this guideline of "being as trusting as you can be" applies to trusting oneself, one's inner voice, or one's source of spiritual guidance. This means trusting that there is a Higher Power in your life and that if you ask you will receive guidance on important issues. It also operates on the interpersonal, team, and organizational level. If you truly learn to see yourself as trustworthy, and believe that it is our essential nature as humans to be trustworthy, then you will naturally feel trusting of colleagues and subordinates. And you will also feel more trusting that the processes and events that are happening have a higher purpose to them if you look for it and amplify it.

Maintain a Spiritual Practice

In a research study on people who integrate their spirituality and their work, the most frequently mentioned spiritual practice is spending time in nature. Examples of other practices are meditation, prayer, reading inspirational literature, hatha yoga, shamanistic practices, writing in a journal, and walking a labyrinth. People reported that it is very important for them to consistently commit to whatever individual spiritual practice they have chosen. The regular involvement in a chosen practice appears to be the best way to deepen one's spirituality.[14]

When leaders faithfully commit to a particular spiritual practice they are calmer, more creative, more in tune with employees and customers, and more compassionate.[15]

Categorized Bibliography on Spirituality in the Workplace

The materials listed here were selected for their ability to inform the leader about issues related to spirituality in the workplace. This list is not exhaustive, and suggestions are provided on where to find more in-depth information on resources related to spirituality in the workplace. There are 42 books categorized in eight sections in this review. Due to space limitations, the fact that the book reviews are available online, and because the list continues to grow, there are no book reviews provided in this appendix. However, you can go to the Spirit at Work Website to read reviews of the books listed here, plus many others. We begin by describing the Spirit at Work Web site, followed by an explanation of the eight categories of books with the list of 42 references.

Spirit at Work Website

The Spirit at Work Web site, **http://www.spiritatwork.org,** is the most comprehensive site devoted to spirituality in the workplace. It is designed to be a resource to people interested in integrating their deepest values and their work. It consists of information about the Association for Spirit at Work, a Community section for people who want to connect with others who share their interests—including local chapters throughout the United States and abroad; a Members Center that has case studies, research, inspirational quotes, presentations, exercises, and other change management tools for members of our organization; an Events Calendar that lists conferences and workshops on spirituality in the workplace from around the world; and an Info Center where people can access the Spirit at Work bibliography, research articles, and the Spirit at Work newsletter. In addition, there is an entire section devoted to the International Spirit at Work Awards.

Overview of Spirituality in the Workplace

The books described in this section are edited books that offer a wide array of perspectives on spirituality in the workplace and provide a good overview for someone who is just beginning to explore this field.

1. *The New Paradigm in Business: Emerging Strategies for Leadership and Organizational Change,* edited by Michael Ray and Alan Rinzler. New York: Jeremy Tarcher, 1993.

2. *New Traditions in Business: Spirit and Leadership in the 21st Century,* edited by John Renesch. San Francisco: Berrett-Koehler, 1992.

3. *Work and Spirit: A Reader of New Spiritual Paradigms for Organizations,* edited by Jerry Biberman and Michael D. Whitty. Scranton, PA: University of Scranton Press, 2000.

4. *The Spirit at Work Phenomenon,* by Sue Howard and David Welbourne. London: Azure, 2004.

Leadership from a Spiritual Perspective

Perhaps more has been written about leadership and spirituality than any other topic related to spirituality in the workplace. The books highlighted here are only a small sampling of what is available, but I believe that they are among the best on the topic. The offerings here include two books that are leadership parables, a book that explores what the new sciences have to teach us about leadership, a book of essays, a workbook, and several books that offer leading-edge concepts on leadership that incorporate body, mind, heart and spirit.

5. *Leading with Soul: An Uncommon Journey of Spirit,* by Lee Bolman and Terrence Deal. San Francisco: Jossey-Bass, 1995.

6. *The Corporate Shaman: A Business Fable,* by Richard Whiteley. New York: HarperCollins, 2002.

7. *Leadership and the New Science: Learning About Organizations from an Orderly Universe,* by Margaret Wheatley. San Francisco: Berrett-Koehler, 1992.

8. *Invisible Leadership: Igniting the Soul at Work,* by Robert Rabbin. Lakewood, CO: Acropolis Books, 1998.

9. *Leadership & Spirit: Breathing New Vitality and Energy into Individuals and Organizations,* by Russ Moxley. San Francisco: Jossey-Bass, 2000.

10. *Leadership from the Inside Out: Seven Pathways to Mastery,* by Kevin Cashman. San Francisco: Berrett-Koehler, 1998.

11. *The Highest Goal: The Secret That Sustains You in Every Moment,* by Michael Ray. San Francisco: Berrett-Koehler, 2004.

12. *Learning as a Way of Being: Strategies for Survival in a World of Permanent White Water,* by Peter Vaill. San Francisco, CA: Jossey-Bass, 1996.

13. *Leading Consciously: A Pilgrimage Towards Self-Mastery,* by Debashis Chatterjee. Boston, MA: Butterworth-Heinemann, 1998.

14. *Inspire! What Great Leaders Do,* by Lance Secretan. Hoboken, NJ: Wiley & Sons, 2004; and *Reclaiming Higher Ground: Creating Organizations That Inspire the Soul,* by Lance Secretan. Toronto: McMillan Canada, 1996.

15. *Edgewalkers: The New Global Human,* by Judi Neal. Westport, CT: Praeger, 2006.

Case Studies of Leaders Who Have Applied Spiritual Principles to the Organizations Where They Work

This section lists five books that provide concrete examples of leaders who are integrating spirituality and work. The first book is a collection of interviews with business leaders, and the last three books are written by CEOs who applied spiritual principles and practices to their organizations.

16. *Merchants of Vision: People Bringing New Purpose and Values to Business,* by James E. Liebig. San Francisco: Berrett-Koehler, 1994.

17. *The Soul of a Business: Managing for Profit and the Common Good,* by Tom Chappell. New York: Bantam Books, 1993.

18. *Love and Profit: The Art of Caring Leadership,* by James Autry. New York: Avon Books, 1991.

19. *Spirituality in Business: The Hidden Success Factor,* by Michael Stephen. Scottsdale, AZ: Inspired Productions Press.

20. *The Spirited Business: Success Stories of Soul-Friendly Companies,* by Georgeanne Lamont. London: Hodder & Stoughton, 2002.

Creativity and Spirituality in the Workplace

Poetry, music, and other forms of art are shortcuts to the human soul. Enlightened leaders are beginning to recognize this, and to build artistic approaches into their leadership style and into their organizational transformation processes.

21. *The Heart Aroused: Poetry and Preservation of the Soul in Corporate America,* by David Whyte. New York: Currency Doubleday, 1994.

22. *Small Decencies: Reflections and Meditations on Being Human at Work,* by John Cowan. New York: HarperBusiness, 1992.

23. *The Common Table: Reflections and Mediations on Community and Spirituality in the Workplace,* by John Cowan. New York: HarperBusiness, 1993.

24. *Artful Work: Awakening Joy, Meaning, and Commitment in the Workplace,* by Dick Richards. San Francisco: Berrett-Koehler, 1995.

25. *Creating an Imaginative Life,* by Michael Jones. Berkeley, CA: Conari Press, 1995.

Spiritual Principles for Career Development

The most important management principle of all is "Know Thyself." And it certainly is the most important principle to keep in mind when making career decisions. These three books each take a slightly different approach to self-knowledge, but the goal is the same in each—to choose work that is in alignment with your soul's path.

26. *Do What You Love, the Money Will Follow: Discovering Your Right Livelihood,* by Marsha Sinetar. New York: Dell Publishing, 1987.

27. *Find Your Calling, Love Your Life: Paths to Your Truest Self in Life and Work,* by Martha Finney and Deborah Dasch. New York: Simon & Schuster, 1998.

28. *The Path: Creating Your Mission Statement for Work and for Life,* by Laurie Beth Jones. New York: Hyperion, 1996.

Spirituality at the Team Level

The following two books have been used extensively in corporate programs that implement spirituality at the team level.

29. *Building Team Spirit: Activities for Inspiring and Energizing Teams,* by Barry Heerman. New York: McGraw Hill, 1997.

30. *Chicken Soup for the Soul at Work: 101 Stories of Courage, Compassion & Creativity in the Workplace,* by Jack Canfield, Mark Victor Hansen, Maida Rogerson, Martin Rutte, & Tim Clauss. Deerfield Beach, FL: Health Communications, Inc., 1997.

Systemic Approaches

The concept of spirituality in the workplace can be looked at from the individual level, the team level, the organizational level, and the societal level. At the organizational level the main concern is how to incorporate attention to spirit in organizational transformation approaches. Six books are offered here that have very different but compatible approaches.

31. *Managing with the Wisdom of Love: Uncovering Virtue in People and Organizations,* by Dorothy Marcic. San Francisco: Jossey-Bass, 1997.

32. *The Living Organization: Spirituality in the Workplace,* by William Guillory. Salt Lake City, UT: Innovations International, Inc., 1997.

33. *Liberating the Corporate Soul: Building a Visionary Organization,* by Richard Barrett. Boston, MA: Butterworth-Heinemann, 1998.

34. *Awakening Corporate Soul: Four Paths to Unleash the Power of People at Work,* by Eric Klein and John B. Izzo. Canada: Fairwinds Press, 1999.

35. *The Inner Edge: Effective Spirituality in Your Life and Work,* by Richard A. Wedemeyer and Ronald W. Jue. Chicago, IL: 2002.

36. *The Path for Greatness: Work as Spiritual Service,* by Linda J. Ferguson. Victoria, BC, Canada: Trafford Press, 2000.

The Role of Business in a Changing World

These six books take a very macro view of the issue of spirituality and business. Each of them postulates that we are entering a new era in which it can no longer be "business as usual," and the authors offer their visions of what the world can be like and their prescriptions for how we can get there.

37. *Creative Work: The Constructive Role of Business in Transforming Society,* by Willis Harman and John Hormann. Indianapolis: Knowledge Systems, 1990.

38. *The Global Brain Awakens: Our Next Evolutionary Leap,* by Peter Russell. Palo Alto, CA: Global Brain Inc., 1995.

39. *Conscious Evolution: Awakening the Power of Our Social Potential,* by Barbara Marx Hubbard. Novato, CA: New World Library, 1998.

40. *Building a Win-Win World: Life Beyond Global Economic Warfare,* by Hazel Henderson. San Francisco: Berrett-Koehler, 1996.

41. *The Reinvention of Work: A New Vision of Livelihood for Our Time,* by Matthew Fox. San Francisco: HarperCollins, 1994.

42. *Megatrends for Managers,* by Patricia Aburdene (in press).

Summary

There is a growing trend to talk more openly about spirituality and to want to integrate spiritual principles into all aspects of life—relationships, community, and work. This appendix has presented some resources for leaders who are interested in more fully integrating their spirituality and their leadership. Living more congruently with deeply held spiritual principles is never easy, but it is extremely rewarding and meaningful. I hope that some of the resources provided here will help to make the journey a little easier.

WorkApplication

A-1. Give an example of spirituality in the workplace where you work or worked.
A-2. Have you or anyone you know struggled with spiritual journey and what this means for work? Explain.

_____

_____

_____

_____

_____

Review and Discussion Questions

1. There is no single accepted definition of spirituality in the workplace. What is your definition?
2. Spirituality is about learning to be more caring and compassionate in the workplace. Should we be more caring and compassionate with others at work? Why or why not?
3. Spirituality is about integrity, being true to oneself, and telling the truth to others in the workplace. Should we be honest with others at work? Why or why not?
4. Is knowing oneself important to leading from a spiritual perspective? Why or why not?
5. Should leaders let followers see the more human, softer parts of them (truly be themselves)? What effect would this have on productivity?
6. Are managers who have a spiritual practice more effective leaders than those who do not?
7. Do you have a spiritual practice? If yes, what is it?

Glossary

A

Achievement Motivation Theory attempts to explain and predict behavior and performance based on a person's need for achievement, power, and affiliation.

acquired needs theory proposes that people are motivated by their need for achievement, power, and affiliation.

adaptive culture represents a leadership belief in active monitoring of the external environment for emerging opportunities and threats.

adjustment personality dimension traits related to emotional stability.

advantageous comparison the process of comparing oneself to others who are worse.

agreeableness personality dimension traits related to getting along with people.

alienated follower a passive yet independent, critical thinker.

arbitrator a neutral third party who makes a binding decision to resolve a conflict.

attitudes positive or negative feelings about people, things, and issues.

attribution of blame the process of claiming the unethical behavior was caused by someone else's behavior.

attribution theory used to explain the process managers go through in determining the reasons for effective or ineffective performance and deciding what to do about it.

B

BCF model describes a conflict in terms of behavior, consequences, and feelings.

behavioral leadership theories theories that attempt to explain distinctive styles used by effective leaders or to define the nature of their work.

Big Five Model of Personality categorizes traits into dimensions of surgency, agreeableness, adjustment, conscientiousness, and openness to experience.

bureaucratic culture represents a leadership that values order, stability, status, and efficiency.

C

charisma a distinct social relationship between the leader and follower, in which the leader presents a revolutionary idea, a transcendent image or ideal which goes beyond the immediate . . . or the reasonable; while the follower accepts this course of action not because of its rational likelihood of success . . . but because of an effective belief in the extraordinary qualities of the leader.

coaching the process of giving motivational feedback to maintain and improve performance.

coaching feedback feedback that is (1) based on a good, supportive relationship; (2) specific and descriptive; and (3) not judgmental criticism.

coercive power involves punishment and withholding of rewards to influence compliance.

collectivism the state of mind wherein the values and goals of the group—whether extended family, ethnic group, or company—are primary.

communication the process of conveying information and meaning.

competitive culture represents a leadership that encourages and values a highly competitive work environment.

conflict exists whenever people are in disagreement and opposition.

conformist follower an active but unassertive, noncritical thinker.

connection power based on the user's relationship with influential people.

conscientiousness personality dimension traits related to achievement.

content motivation theories focus on explaining and predicting behavior based on people's needs.

contingency leadership model determines if a person's leadership style is task- or relationship-oriented, and if the situation (leader-member relationship, task structure, and position power) matches the leader's style to maximize performance.

contingency leadership theories theories that attempt to explain the appropriate leadership style based on the leader, followers, and situation.

cooperative culture represents a leadership belief in strong, mutually reinforcing exchanges and linkages between employees and departments.

core competence a capability that allows an organization to perform extremely well in comparison to competitors.

crisis a low-probability, high-impact event that threatens the viability of the organization and is characterized by ambiguity of cause, effect, and means of resolution, as well as by a belief that decisions must be made swiftly.

cross-functional team is made up of members from different functional departments of an organization who are brought together to perform unique tasks to create new and nonroutine products or services.

culture the aggregate of beliefs, attitudes, values, assumptions, and ways of doing things that is shared by members of an organization and taught to new members.

D

decisional leadership roles entrepreneur, disturbance handler, resource allocator, and negotiator.

delegation the process of assigning responsibility and authority for accomplishing objectives.

delegation model steps are (1) explain the need for delegating and the reasons for selecting the employee; (2) set objectives that define responsibility, level of authority, and deadline; (3) develop a plan; (4) establish control checkpoints and hold employees accountable.

demographic diversity any characteristic that serves as a basis for social categorization and self-identification.

descriptive leadership models identify contingency variables and leadership styles without specifying which style to use in a given situation.

diffusion of responsibility the process of the group using the unethical behavior with no one person being held responsible.

discontinuous change when anticipated or expected changes bear no resemblance to the present or the past.

displacement of responsibility the process of blaming one's unethical behavior on others.

disregard or distortion of consequences the process of minimizing the harm caused by the unethical behavior.

distributed leadership multiple leaders take complementary leadership roles in rotation within the same self-managed team, according to their area of expertise or interest.

diversity the inclusion of all groups at all levels in an organization.

dyadic refers to the individualized relationship between a leader and each follower in a work unit.

dyadic theory an approach to leadership that attempts to explain why leaders vary their behavior with different followers.

E

effective follower is both an independent, critical thinker and a very active member in the group.

equity theory proposes that people are motivated when their perceived inputs equal outputs.

ethics the standards of right and wrong that influence behavior.

ethnocentrism the belief that one's own group or subculture is naturally superior to other groups and cultures.

euphemistic labeling the process of using "cosmetic" words to make the behavior sound acceptable.

expectancy theory proposes that people are motivated when they believe they can accomplish the task, they will get the reward, and the rewards for doing so are worth the effort.

expert power based on the user's skill and knowledge.

F

feedback the process of verifying messages and determining if objectives are being met.

femininity describes a culture that emphasizes developing and nurturing personal relationships and a high quality of life.

follower a person who is being influenced by a leader.

followership refers to the behavior of followers that results from the leader-follower influence relationship.

functional team consists of a group of employees belonging to the same functional department, such as marketing, R&D, production, human resources, or information systems, who have a common objective.

G

giving praise model includes four steps—(1) Tell the employee exactly what was done correctly. (2) Tell the employee why the behavior is important. (3) Stop for a moment of silence. (4) Encourage repeat performance.

glass ceiling an invisible barrier that separates women and minorities from top leadership positions.

goal-setting theory proposes that specific, difficult goals motivate people.

groupthink is when members of a cohesive group tend to agree on a decision not on the basis of its merit but because they are less willing to risk rejection for questioning a majority viewpoint or presenting a dissenting opinion.

H

hierarchy of needs theory proposes that people are motivated through five levels of needs: physiological, safety, belongingness, esteem, and self-actualization.

high power-distance culture leaders and followers rarely interact as equals.

high uncertainty avoidance society with a majority of people who do not tolerate risk, avoid the unknown, and are comfortable when the future is relatively predictable and certain.

I

impressions management a follower's effort to project a favorable image in order to gain an immediate benefit or improve long-term relationship with the leader.

individualism a psychological state in which people see themselves first as individuals and believe their own interest and values are primary.

influencing is the process of a leader communicating ideas, gaining acceptance of them, and motivating followers to support and implement the ideas through change.

information power based on the user's data that is desired by others.

informational leadership roles monitor, disseminator, and spokesperson.

ingratiation the effort to appear supportive, appreciative, and respectful.

in-group includes followers with strong social ties to their leader in a supportive relationship characterized by high mutual trust, respect, loyalty, and influence.

initiating conflict resolution model (1) plan a BCF statement that maintains ownership of the problem; (2) present your BCF statement and agree on the conflict; (3) ask for, and/or give, alternative conflict resolutions; and (4) make an agreement for change.

integrative leadership theories theories that attempt to combine the trait, behavioral, and contingency theories to explain successful, influencing leader-follower relationships.

interpersonal leadership roles figurehead, leader, and liaison.

J

job instructional training (1) trainee receives preparation; (2) trainer presents task: (3) trainee performs task; and (4) trainer follows up.

L

Leader Motive Profile (LMP) includes a high need for power, which is socialized; that is, greater than the need for affiliation and with a moderate need for achievement.

Leader Motive Profile Theory attempts to explain and predict leadership success based on a person's need for achievement, power, and affiliation.

leader-member exchange (LMX) the quality of the exchange relationship between an employee and his or her superior.

leadership the process of influencing leaders and followers to achieve organizational objectives through change.

leadership continuum model determines which of seven styles to select, based on the use of boss-centered versus subordinate-centered leadership, to meet the situation (boss, subordinates, situation/time) in order to maximize performance.

Leadership Grid identifies five leadership styles—1,1 impoverished; 9,1 authority compliance; 1,9 country club; 5,5 middle of the road; and 9,9 team leader.

leadership model an example for emulation or use in a given situation.

leadership paradigm a shared mindset that represents a fundamental way of thinking about, perceiving, studying, researching, and understanding leadership.

leadership style the combination of traits, skills, and behaviors leaders use as they interact with followers.

leadership theory an explanation of some aspect of leadership; theories have practical value because they are used to better understand, predict, and control successful leadership.

leadership theory classifications trait, behavioral, contingency, and integrative.

leadership trait theories theories that attempt to explain distinctive characteristics accounting for leadership effectiveness.

learning anxiety the prospect of learning something new in itself.

learning organization one that is skilled at creating, acquiring, and transferring knowledge, and at modifying behavior to reflect new knowledge and insights.

legacy that which allows an individual's accomplishments to "live on" in the ideals, actions, and creations of one's followers, long after his or her death.

legitimate power based on the user's position power, given by the organization.

levels of analysis of leadership theory individual, group, and organizational

locus of control is on a continuum between an external and internal belief over who has control of a person's destiny.

low power-distance culture leaders and their members interact on several levels as equals.

low uncertainty avoidance most people in this culture are comfortable with and accepting of the unknown, and tolerate risk and unpredictability.

M

managerial role categories interpersonal, informational, and decisional.

masculinity describes a culture that emphasizes assertiveness and a competitive drive for money and material objects.

mediator a neutral third party who helps resolve a conflict.

mentoring a form of coaching in which a more experienced manager helps a less experienced protégé.

message-receiving process listening, analyzing, and checking understanding.

mission statement an enduring statement of purpose that distinguishes one organization from other similar enterprises.

moral justification the process of reinterpreting immoral behavior in terms of a higher purpose.

motivation anything that affects behavior in pursuing a certain outcome.

motivation process people go from need to motive to behavior to consequence to satisfaction or dissatisfaction.

N

negotiating a process in which two or more parties are in conflict and attempt to come to an agreement

networking the process of developing relationships for the purpose of socializing and politicking.

normative leadership model a time-driven and developmental-driven decision tree that enables the user to select one of five leadership styles (decide, consult individually, consult group, facilitate, and delegate) appropriate for the situation.

O

Ohio State University Leadership Model identifies four leadership styles: (1) low structure and high consideration, (2) high structure and high consideration, (3) low structure and low consideration, (4) high structure and low consideration.

ombudsperson a single person entrusted with the responsibility of acting as the organization's conscience.

one-minute self-sell an opening statement used in networking that quickly summarizes your history and career plan and asks a question.

openness-to-experience personality dimension traits related to being willing to change and try new things.

oral message-sending process (1) develop rapport; (2) state your communication objective; (3) transmit your message; (4) check the receiver's understanding; (5) get a commitment and follow up.

organizational change the activities associated with planning, designing, implementing, and internalizing tools, procedures, routines, processes, or systems that will require people to perform their jobs differently.

organizational knowledge the tacit and explicit knowledge that individuals possess about products, services, systems, and processes.

out-group includes followers with few or no social ties to their leader, in a strictly task-centered relationship characterized by low exchange and top-down influence.

P

paraphrasing the process of having the receiver restate the message in his or her own words.

passive follower exhibits neither critical, independent thinking nor active participation.

path-goal leadership model determines the leadership style (directive, supportive, participative, or achievement-oriented) appropriate to the situation (subordinate and environment) to maximize both performance and job satisfaction.

performance formula explains performance as a function of ability, motivation, and resources.

personal meaning the degree to which people's lives make emotional sense and to which the demands confronted by them are perceived as being worthy of energy and commitment.

personality a combination of traits that classifies an individual's behavior.

personality profiles identify individual stronger and weaker traits.

personalized charismatic leader (PCL) one who possesses a dominant, Machiavellian, and narcissistic personality.

politics the process of gaining and using power.

power the leader's potential influence over followers.

pragmatic follower exhibits a little of all four styles—depending on which style fits the prevailing situation.

prejudice the tendency to form an adverse opinion without just cause about people who are different from the mainstream in terms of their gender, race, ethnicity, or any other definable characteristic.

prescriptive leadership models tell the user exactly which style to use in a given situation.

press kit a package of information about a company, including names and pictures of its executives, fact sheet, and key milestones in the company's history.

press release a printed statement that describes how an organization is responding to a crisis and who is in charge.

process motivation theories focus on understanding how people choose behavior to fulfill their needs.

Pygmalion effect leaders' attitudes toward and expectations of followers, and their treatment of them, explain and predict followers' behavior and performance.

R

reciprocity creating obligations and developing alliances, and using them to accomplish objectives.

referent power based on the user's personal relationship with others.

reinforcement theory proposes that through the consequences for behavior, people will be motivated to behave in predetermined ways.

relationship management relates to the ability to work well with others.

reward power based on the user's ability to influence others with something of value to them.

S

self-awareness relates to being conscious of your emotions and how they affect your personal and professional life.

self-belief knowing who you are based on your lifespan of experiences, motivation states, and action orientation.

self-concept the positive or negative attitudes people have about themselves.

selflessness an unselfish regard for or devotion to the welfare of others.

self-managed team champion an advocate of the self-managed team concept whose responsibility is to help the team obtain necessary resources, gain political support from top management and other stakeholders of the organization, and defend it from enemy attacks.

self-managed team facilitator the external leader of a self-managed team, whose job is to create optimal working conditions so team members take on responsibilities to work productively and solve complex problems on their own.

self-managed teams (SMTs) relatively autonomous teams whose members share or rotate leadership responsibilities and hold themselves mutually responsible for a set of performance goals assigned by higher management.

self-management relates to the ability to control disruptive emotions.

self-promotion the effort to appear competent and dependable.

servant leadership leadership that transcends self-interest to serve the needs of others, by helping them grow professionally and personally.

social awareness relates to the ability to understand others.

social loafing the conscious or unconscious tendency by some team members to shirk responsibilities by withholding effort towards group goals when they are not individually accountable for their work.

socialized charismatic leader (SCL) one who possesses an egalitarian, self-transcendent, and empowering personality.

spirituality concerns an individual's awareness of connections between human and supernatural phenomena, which provide faith explanations of past and present experiences and, for some, predict future experiences.

stakeholder approach to ethics creates a win-win situation for relevant parties affected by the decision.

stewardship an employee-focused form of leadership that empowers followers to make decisions and have control over their jobs.

strategic leadership a person's ability to anticipate, envision, maintain flexibility, think strategically, and work with others to initiate changes that will create a viable future for the organization.

strategic management the set of decisions and actions used to formulate and implement specific strategies that will achieve a competitively superior fit between the organization and its environment, so as to achieve organizational goals.

strategic vision an ambitious view of the future that everyone in the organization can believe in and that is not readily attainable, yet offers a future that is better in important ways than what now exists.

strategy an integrated, overarching concept of how an organization will achieve its objectives.

substitutes for leadership include characteristics of the subordinate, task, and organization that replace the need for a leader or neutralize the leader's behavior.

surgency personality dimension leadership and extraversion traits.

survival anxiety the feeling that unless an organization makes a change, it is going to be out of business or fail to achieve some important goals.

T

360-degree feedback a formal evaluation process based on receiving performance evaluations from many people.

team a unit of two or more people with complementary skills who are committed to a common purpose and set of performance goals and to common expectations, for which they hold themselves accountable.

team cohesion the extent to which members band together and remain committed to achieving team goals.

team creativity the creation of a valuable, useful, and novel product, service, idea, procedure, or process carried out via discovery rather than a predetermined step-by-step procedure, by individuals working together in a complex social system.

team effectiveness having three components: (1) task performance—the degree to which the team's output (product or service) meets the needs and expectations of those who use it; (2) group process—the degree to which members interact or relate in ways that allow the team to work increasingly well together over time; and (3) individual satisfaction—the degree to which the group experience, on balance, is more satisfying than frustrating to team members.

team norms acceptable standards of behavior that are shared by team members.

team potency a shared belief that individuals hold about a group.

teamwork an understanding and commitment to group goals on the part of all team members.

Theory X and Theory Y attempt to explain and predict leadership behavior and performance based on the leader's attitude about followers.

traits distinguishing personal characteristics.

transactional leadership seeks to maintain stability within an organization through regular economic and social exchanges that achieve specific goals for both the leaders and their followers.

transformational leadership serves to change the status quo by articulating to followers the problems in the current system and a compelling vision of what a new organization could be.

two-factory theory proposes that people are motivated by motivators rather than maintenance factors.

U

University of Michigan Leadership Model identifies two leadership styles: (1) job-centered and (2) employee-centered.

V

value the ratio of benefits received to the cost incurred by the customer.

values generalized beliefs or behaviors that are considered by an individual or a group to be important.

values stable and enduring beliefs about what an individual considers to be important.

vertical dyadic linkage (VDL) theory examines how leaders form one-on-one relationships with followers, and how these often create in-groups and out-groups within the leader's work unit.

virtual team is one in which members are separated in space and time.

vision the ability to imagine different and better conditions and the ways to achieve them.

W

whistle blowing employee disclosure of illegal or unethical practices on the part of the organization.

writing objectives model (1) To + (2) action verb + (3) singular, specific, and measurable result to be achieved + (4) target date.

Endnotes

Preface

1. J. Pfeffer and R. I Sutton, *The Knowing-Doing Gap* (Boston: Harvard Business School Press, 2000).

2. *Journal of Management Education 17* (3), 1993: 399–415.

3. R. N. Lussier, *Human Relations in Organizations: Applications and Skill Building* (Burr Ridge, IL: Irwin/McGraw-Hill, 1999), 4.

Chapter 1

1. "The World's 100 Largest Public Companies," *The Wall Street Journal,* September 27, 2004, R1.

2. Information taken from the GE website: **http://www.ge.com,** March 4, 2005.

3. "GE Expects," *The Wall Street Journal,* March 2, 2005, A1.

4. S. A. Zahra, "An Interview with Peter Drucker," *Academy of Management Executive 17*(3) (2003): 9–12.

5. S. A. Zahra, "The Practice of Management: Reflections on Peter F. Drucker's Landmark Book," *Academy of Management Executive 17*(3) (2003): 16–23.

6. N. M. Ashkanasy, "Leader Development for Transforming Organizations," *Academy of Management Executive 18*(4)(2004): 165.

7. C. Chao Yang Zhang, "China's Leading Internet Guru Charles Zhang, Chairman of SOHU.com Inc., on How the Internet Has Changed the World's Most Populous Nation," *Academy of Management Executive 18*(4)(2004): 143–157.

8. E. White, "To Keep Employees, Domino's Decides It's Not All About Pay," *The Wall Street Journal,* February 17, 2005, p. A1.

9. G. Williams, "Whale Watching," *Entrepreneur* (June 2002): 32.

10. See note 9.

11. M. M. Koerner, "Treat People Right," *Academy of Management Executive 18*(4)(2004): 163–164.

12. See note 6.

13. H. H. Beam, "Why Smart Executives Fail," *Academy of Management Executive 18*(2)(2004): 157–158.

14. R. J. Sternberg, "WICS: A Model of Leadership in Organizations," *Academy of Management Learning and Education 2*(4)(2003): 386–401.

15. M. Murray, "GE's Immelt Frets Over Economy, Not About Filling Welch's Shoes," *The Wall Street Journal,* September 5, 2001, B1.

16. M. Murray, "Jack Welch Isn't All That Retiring," *The Wall Street Journal,* October 3, 2001, C1, C13.

17. T. Stevens, "Follow the Leader: Under CEO Jack Welch, Leadership Development Is Priority No. 1 at GE," *Industry Week* (November 18, 1996): 16–18.

18. M. Murray, "Jack Welch's Next Act: Confidant to CEOs, Corporate Coach, Author," *The Wall Street Journal,* March 30, 2001, B1.

19. G. Williams, "Comic Belief: Is Leadership Really a Crock?" *Entrepreneur* (April 2003): 28.

20. See note 5.

21. See note 14.

22. J. A. Raelin, "Don't Bother Putting Leadership into People," *Academy of Management Executive 18*(3)(2004): 131–135.

23. W. Bennis, "'Owed' to Rosabeth Moss Kanter: Impact on Management Practice," *Academy of Management Executive 18*(2)(2004): 106–107.

24. M. A. McFadyen and A. A. Cannella, "Social Capital and Knowledge Creation: Diminishing Returns of the Number and Strength of Exchange Relationships," *Academy of Management Journal 47*(5)(2004): 735–746.

25. S. M. Puffer, "Changing Organizational Structures: An Interview with Rosabeth Moss Kanter," *Academy of Management Executive 18*(2)(2004): 96–105.

26. M. L. Lengnick-Hall and C. A. Lengnick-Hall, "HR's Role in Building Relationship Networks," *Academy of Management Executive 17*(4)(2003): 53–61.

27. See note 22.

28. M. J. Provitera, "What Management Is: How It Works and Why It's Everyone's Business," *Academy of Management Executive 17*(3)(2003): 152–153.

29. E. A. Locke, "Guest Editor's Introduction: Goal-Setting Theory and Its Applications to the World of Business," *Academy of Management Executive 18*(4)(2004): 124–125.

30. J. Amis, T. Slack, and C. R. Hinings, "The Pace, Sequence, and Linearity of Radical Change," *Academy of Management Journal 47*(1)(2004): 15–39.

31. See note 13.

32. H. Mintzberg, "Leadership and Management Development: An Afterword," *Academy of Management Executive 18*(3)(2004): 140–142.

33. P. S. Goodman and D. M. Rosseau, "Organizational Change That Produces Results: The Linkage Approach," *Academy of Management Executive 18*(3)(2004): 7–19.

34. L. A. Hill, "New Manager Development for the 21st Century," *Academy of Management Executive 18*(3)(2004): 121–126.

35. W. J. Everton, "Manager of Choice: 5 Competencies for Cultivating Top Talent." *Academy of Management Executive 18*(2)(2004): 162–163.

36. G. Gendron, "Practitioners' Perspectives on Entrepreneurship Education,"

Academy of Management Learning and Education 3(3)(2004): 302–314.

37. E. J. Romero, "Are the Great Places to Work Also Great Performers?" *Academy of Management Executive* 18(2)(2004): 150–152.

38. D. Ellerman, "Global Institutions," *Academy of Management Executive* 13(1)(1999): 25–27.

39. See note 15.

40. See note 18.

41. J. A. Conger, "Developing Leadership Capability: What's Inside the Black Box?" *Academy of Management Executive* 18(3)(2004): 136–139.

42. W. E. Rothschild, "Where Are the Leaders?" *Financial Executive* 18(6) (July–August 2002): 26.

43. See note 34.

44. See note 41.

45. C. Wittmeyer, "The Practice of Management: Timeless Views and Principles," *Academy of Management Executive* 17(3)(2003): 13–15.

46. H. Mintzberg, *The Nature of Managerial Work* (New York: Harper & Row, 1973).

47. C. Tourtellotte, "Leadership Roles," *Firehouse Magazine* 30(4) (2005): 10–11.

48. L. Kurke and H. Aldrich, "Mintzberg Was Right! A Replication and Extension of the Nature of Managerial Work," *Management Science* 29(8) (1983): 975–984; C. Pavett and A. Lau, "Managerial Work: The Influence of Hierarchical Level and Functional Specialty," *Academy of Management Journal* 26(1) (1983): 170–177; and C. Hales, "What Do Managers Do? A Critical Review of the Evidence," *Journal of Management Studies* 23 (1986): 88–115.

49. See note 34.

50. See note 5.

51. R. J. House and R. N. Aditya, "The Social Scientific Study of Leadership: Quo Vadis?" *Journal of Management* 23(3) (May–June 1997): 409–474.

52. D. J. Brass, J. Galaskiewicz, H. R. Greve, and W. Tsai, "Taking Stock of Networks and Organizations: A Multilevel Perspective," *Academy of Management Journal* 47(6)(2004): 795–817.

53. S. E. Seibert, S. R. Silver, and W. A. Randolph, "Taking Empowerment to the Next Level: A Multiple-Level Model of Empowerment, Performance, and Satisfaction," *Academy of Management Journal* 47(3)(2004): 332–349.

54. F. J. Flynn, "How Much Should I Give and How Often? The Effects of Generosity and Frequency of Favor Exchange on Social Status and Productivity," *Academy of Management Journal* 46(5)(2003): 539–553.

55. J. G. Combs and M. S. Skill, "Managerialist and Human Capital Explanations for Key Executive Pay Premiums: A Contingency Perspective," *Academy of Management Journal* 46(1)(2003): 63–73.

56. A. Gupta, "The Death of Shame," *Mid-American Journal of Business* 18(2) (2003): 4–8.

57. See note 56.

58. J. B. Miner, "The Rated Importance, Scientific Validity, and Practical Usefulness of Organizational Behavior Theories: A Quantitative Review" *Academy of Management Learning and Education* 2(3) (2003): 250–268.

59. See note 51.

60. See note 51.

61. See note 48.

62. See note 51.

63. E. A. Locke and G. P. Latham, "What Should We Do About Motivation Theory?" *Academy of Management Review* 29(3) (2004): 388–403.

64. See note 51.

65. See note 24.

66. G. M. Pedroza, "Balancing the Books," *Entrepreneur* (March 2003): 25.

67. See note 22.

68. See note 32.

69. C. D. Herring, "Dedicated to a Service Orientation," *MG Alert*, Vol. (March 3, 1999), 1.

70. See note 32.

71. S. Nadkarni, "Instructional Methods and Mental Models of Students: An Empirical Investigation" *Academy of Management Learning and Education* 2(4) (2003): 335–351.

72. L. E. Greiner, A. Bhambri, and T. G. Cummings, "Searching for a Strategy to Teach Strategy," *Academy of Management Learning and Education* 2(4) (2003): 402–420.

73. J. P. Meyer, "Four Territories of Experience: A Developmental Action Inquiry Approach to Outdoor-Adventure Experiential Learning," *Academy of Management Learning and Education* 2(4) (2003): 352–363.

74. S. Kerr, "Executives Ask: How Can Organizations Best Prepare People to Lead and Manage Others?" *Academy of Management Executive* 18(3) (2004): 118–120.

75. See note 72.

76. G. Benson, D. Finegold, and S. A. Mohrman, "You Paid for the Skills, Now Keep Them: Tuition Reimbursement and Voluntary Turnover," *Academy of Management Journal* 47(3) (2004): 315–331.

77. See note 22.

78. S. L. Rynes, C. Q. Trank, A. M. Lawson, and R. Ilies, "Behavioral Coursework in Business Education: Growing Evidence of a Legitimacy Crisis," *Academy of Management Learning and Education* 2(3) (2003): 269–283.

79. See note 35.

80. See note 5.

81. M. Sorcher and A. P. Goldstein, "A Behavior Modeling Approach in Training," *Personnel Administration* 35 (1972): 35–41.

82. E. Sadler-Smith and E. Shefy, "The Intuitive Executive: Understanding and Applying 'Gut Feel' in Decision-Making," *Academy of Management Executive* 18(4) (2004): 76–91.

83. M. Maremont and R. Brooks, "Once-Hot Krispy Kreme Ousts Its CEO Amid Accounting Woes," *The Wall Street Journal*, January 19, 2005, A1, A6; Information also taken from Krispy Kreme's website: **http://www.krispykreme.com**.

Chapter 2

1. Information taken from the Lorraine Monroe Leadership Institute website: **http://www.lorrainemonroe.com**, May 11, 2005.

2. J. M. Howell and B. Shamir, "The Role of Followers in the Charismatic Leadership Process: Relationships and Their

Consequences," *Academy of Management Review* 30(1) (2005): 96–112.

3. U. Raja, G. Johns, and F. Ntalianis, "The Impact of Personality on Psychological Contracts," *Academy of Management Journal* 47(3) (2004): 350–367.

4. K. J. Klein, B. Lim, J. L. Saltz, and D. M. Mayer, "How Do They Get There? An Examination of the Antecedents of Centrality in Team Networks," *Academy of Management Journal* 47(6) (2005): 952–963.

5. T. A. Judge and R. Ilies, "Is Positiveness in Organizations Always Desirable?" *Academy of Management Executive* 18(4) (2004): 151–155.

6. H. H. Tan, M. D. Foo, and M. H. Kwek, "The Effects of Customer Personality Traits on the Display of Positive Emotions," *Academy of Management Journal* 47(2) (2004): 287–296.

7. D. J. Brass, J. Galaskiewicz, H. R. Greve, and W. Tsai, "Taking Stock of Networks and Organizations: A Multilevel Perspective," *Academy of Management Journal* 47(6) (2004): 795–817.

8. H. Liao and A. Chuang, "A Multilevel Investigation of Factors Influencing Employee Service Performance and Customer Outcomes," *Academy of Management Journal* 47(1) (2004): 43–58.

9. See note 5.

10. D. A. Waldman and T. Korbar, "Student Assessment Center Performance in the Prediction of Early Career Success," *Academy of Management Learning and Education* 3(2) (2004): 151–167.

11. See note 4.

12. E. A. Locke and G. P. Latham, "What Should We Do About Motivation Theory? *Academy of Management Review* 29(3) (2004): 388–403.

13. See note 10.

14. See note 10.

15. See note 10.

16. R. E. Ployhart, Beng-Chong Lim, and Kim-Yin Chan, "Exploring Relations between Typical and Maximum Performance Ratings and the Five Factor Model of Personality," *Personnel Psychology* 54 (Winter 2001): 809–844.

17. S. Bates, "Personality Counts: Psychological Tests Can Help Peg the Job

Applicants Best Suited for Certain Jobs," *HR Magazine* 47 (February 2002): 287–294.

18. J. F. Salgado, "The Five-Factor Model of Personality and Job Performance in the European Community," *Journal of Applied Psychology* 82 (1997): 30–43.

19. M. W. Morgan and M. M. Lombardo, *Off the Track: Why and How Successful Executives Get Derailed* (Greensboro, NC: Center for Creative Leadership, January 1988), Technical Report nos. 21 & 34.

20. R. Lubit, "The Long-Term Organizational Impact of Destructively Narcissistic Managers," *Academy of Management Executive* 16 (2002): 127–138.

21. J. Jusko, "Why Leaders Fail (Leadership)," *Industry Week* 25 (March 2002): 15–16.

22. C. Hymowitz, "Parents Gain Insight Into Art of Managing During Family Time," *The Wall Street Journal,* (August 24, 2004), B1.

23. M. G. Seo, L. F. Barrett, and J. M. Bartunek, "The Role of Affective Experience in Work Motivation," *Academy of Management Review* 29(3) (2004): 423–439.

24. J. A. Conger, "Developing Leadership Capability: What's Inside the Black Box?" *Academy of Management Executive* 18(3) (2004): 136–139.

25. C. Hymowitz, "Yes, Ambition is Good, But How You Display It Can Get You Into Trouble," *The Wall Street Journal,* September 14, 2004, B1.

26. See note 24.

27. J. Murphy, "Good as Gold," *Entrepreneur* (August 2003): 60.

28. Human Side, "Effective Leaders . . . Made or Born?" *Leadership for the Front Lines* 2 (June 15, 2002): 3.

29. C. Hymowitz, "Some Tips From CEOs to Help You to Make a Fresh Start in 2005," *The Wall Street Journal,* December 28, 2004, B1.

30. S. Meisel, review of "The Practical Coach," by P. J. Caproni, *Academy of Management Learning and Education* 3(4) (2004): 458–459.

31. See note 24.

32. See note 27.

33. S. E. Seibert, S. R. Silver, and W. A. Randolph, "Taking Empowerment to the Next Level: A Multiple-Level Model of Empowerment, Performance, and Satisfaction", *Academy of Management Journal* 47(3) (2004): 332–349.

34. J. A. Raelin, "Don't Bother Putting Leadership Into People," *Academy of Management Executive* 8(3) (2004): 131–135.

35. R. N. Lussier, "Dealing with Anger and Preventing Workplace Violence," *Clinical Leadership & Management Review* (March/April 2004): 117–120.

36. J. Zaslow, "Why Jerks Get Ahead in the Workplace," *The Wall Street Journal,* March 29, 2004, R6.

37. N. M. Ashkanasy and C. S. Daus, "Emotion in the Workplace: The New Challenge for Managers," *Academy of Management Executive* 16 (2002): 76–86.

38. R. C. Ford, "Darden Restaurants CEO Joe Lee on the Importance of Core Values: Integrity and Fairness," *Academy of Management Executive* 16 (2002): 31–36.

39. P. A. Saparito and C. C. Chen, "The Role of Relational Trust in Bank–Small Firm Relationships," *Academy of Management Journal,* 47(3) (2004): 400–410.

40. C. Wittmyer, "The Practice of Management: Timeless Views and Principles," *Academy of Management Executive* 17(3) (2003): 13–15.

41. S. A. Zahra, "The Practice of Management: Reflections on Peter F. Drucker's Landmark Book," *Academy of Management Executive* 17(3) (2003): 16–23.

42. S. Puffer, "CompUSA's CEO James Halpin on Technology, Rewards, and Commitment," *Academy of Management Executive* 13 (May 1999): 29–36.

43. C. W. Langfred, "Too Much of a Good Thing? Negative Effects of High Trust and Individual Autonomy in Self-Managing Teams," *Academy of Management Journal* 47(3) (2004): 385–389.

44. M. C. Bolino and W. H. Turnley, "Going the Extra Mile: Cultivating and Managing Employee Citizenship Behavior," *Academy of Management Executive* 17(3) (2003): 60–71.

45. W. F. Cascio, "Strategies for Responsible Restructuring," *Academy of Management Executive* 16(3) (2002): 80–81.

46. C. Ansberry, "Laid-Off Factory Workers Find Jobs Are Drying Up for Good," *Wall Street Journal,* July 21, 2003, A1.

47. J. Child and R. G. McGrath, "Organizations Unfettered: Organizational Form in an Information-Intensive Economy," *Academy of Management Journal 44*(6) (2001): 1135–1146.

48. See note 24.

49. L. A. Hill, "New Manager Development for the 21st Century" *Academy of Management Executive 18*(3) (2004): 121–126.

50. See note 23.

51. G. Gendron, "Practitioners' Perspectives on Entrepreneurship Education," *Academy of Management Learning and Education 3*(3) (2004): 302–314.

52. F. Luthans, "Positive Organizational Behavior: Developing and Managing Psychological Strengths," *Academy of Management Executive 16* (2002): 57–72.

53. R. E. Boytzis and D. Goleman, *The Emotional Competence Inventory* (Boston: Hay Group, 2001).

54. See note 30.

55. See note 51.

56. See note 36.

57. D. A. Shepherd, "Educating Entrepreneurship Students About Emotion and Learning From Failure," *Academy of Management Learning and Education 3*(3) (2004): 274–287.

58. See note 12.

59. C. Hymowitz, "Some Tips From CEOs to Help You to Make a Fresh Start in 2005," *The Wall Street Journal,* March 16, 1999, A1.

60. See note 41.

61. L. S. Demorest and D. Grady, "In Search of a Leader," *Women in Business 54* (March–April 2002): 11–12.

62. R. J. House and R. N. Aditya, "The Social Scientific Study of Leadership: Quo Vadis?" *Journal of Management 23* (May–June 1997): 409–474.

63. D. McClleland, *The Achieving Society* (New York: Van Nostrand Reinhold, 1961); and D. McClleland and D. H. Burnham, "Power Is the Great Motivator," *Harvard Business Review* (March–April 1978): 103.

64. See note 25.

65. R. J. House, D. Spangler, and J. Woycke, "Personality and Charisma in the U.S. Presidency: A Psychological Theory of Leadership Effectiveness," *Administrative Science Quarterly 36* (1991): 364–396.

66. N. E. Peterman and J. Kennedy, "Enterprise Education: Influencing Students' Perceptions of Entrepreneurship," *Entrepreneurship Theory and Practice 27* (Winter 2003): 129–162.

67. D. C. McClelland and R. E. Boyatzis, "Leadership Motive Pattern and Long-Term Success in Management," *Journal of Applied Psychology 6* (1982): 737–743.

68. D. C. McClelland, *Human Motivation* (Glenview, IL: Scott Foresman, 1985).

69. See note 12.

70. J. A. Chatman and C. A. O'Reilly, "Asymmetric Reactions to Work Group Sex Diversity Among Men and Women," *Academy of Management Journal 47*(2) (2004): 193–208.

71. See note 27.

72. P. Camilli, "Fish! A Remarkable Way to Boost Morale and Improve Productivity—Review," *Mid-American Journal of Business 18*(2) (2003): 62–63.

73. H. Angelo, "Welch Electrifies UMass Students," *The Republican,* April 12, 2005, A1, A10.

74. B. Farber, "Star Power," *Entrepreneur* (February 2003): 102–103.

75. D. McGregor, *Leadership and Motivation* (Cambridge, MA: MIT Press, 1966).

76. See note 66.

77. See note 2.

78. J. Hall and S. M. Donnell, "Managerial Achievement: The Personal Side of Behavioral Theory," *Human Relations 32* (1979): 77–101.

79. See note 72.

80. J. S. Livingston, "Pygmalion in Management," in *Harvard Business Review on Human Relations* (New York: Harper & Row, 1979), 181; G. Baxter and J. Bower, "Beyond Self-Actualization: The Persuasion of Pygmalion," *Training and Development Journal* (August 1985): 69; and J. Kouzes and B. Posner, *Encouraging the Heart: A Leader's Guide to Rewarding and Recognizing Others* (San Francisco: Jossey-Bass, 1999).

81. G. H. Seijts, G. P. Latham, K. Tasa, and B. W. Latham, "Goal Setting and Goal Orientation: An Integration of Two Different Yet Related Literatures," *Academy of Management Journal 47*(2) (2004): 227–239.

82. G. Chen and R. J. Klimoski, "The Impact of Expectations on Newcomer Performance in Teams as Mediated by Work Characteristics, Social Exchange, and Empowerment," *Academy of Management Journal 46*(5) (2003): 591–607.

83. R. Kanfer and P. L. Ackerman, "Aging Adult Development, and Work Motivation," *Academy of Management Review 29*(3) (2004): 440–458.

84. See note 33.

85. See note 52.

86. See note 5.

87. D. V. Day, A. L. Unckless, D. J. Schleicher, and N. J. Hiller, "Self-Monitoring Personality at Work: A Meta-Analytic Investigation of Construct Validity," *Journal of Applied Psychology 87* (April 2002): 390–401.

88. See note 12.

89. B. Faber, "Get Over It," *Entrepreneur* (October 2003): 88–89.

90. See note 2.

91. C. Reeve, "A Message from Christopher Reeve," *Success 1998 Yearbook* (1998): 77.

92. S. Kerr, "Executives Ask: Is Ethical Management Behavior Good for the Bottom Line? Introduction: Ethical Behavior in Management," *Academy of Management Executive 18*(2) (2004): 112–113.

93. D. Seidman, "The Case for Ethical Leadership," *Academy of Management Executive 18*(2) (2004): 134–138.

94. P. Plitch, "Blowing the Whistle," *The Wall Street Journal,* June 21, 2004, R6.

95. T. Thomas, J. R. Schermerhorn, and J. W. Dienhart, "Strategic Leadership of Ethical Behavior in Business," *Academy of Management Executive 18*(2) (2004): 56–66.

96. S. Begley, "Researchers Seek Roots of Morality in Biology, Without Intriguing Results," *The Wall Street Journal,* June 11, 2004, B1.

97. A. B. Carroll, "Managing Ethically with Global Stakeholders: A Present and

Future Challenge," *Academy of Management Executive 18*(2) (2004): 114–120.

98. J. F. Veiga, "'Special Topic' Ethical Behavior in Management, Bringing Ethics into the Mainstream: An Introduction to the Special Topic," *Academy of Management Executive 18*(2) (2004): 37–38.

99. C. Hymowitz, "Managers Must Respond to Employee Concerns about Honest Business," *The Wall Street Journal,* February 19, 2002, B1.

100. See note 94.

101. J. O'Connor, M. D. Mumford, T. C. Clifton, T. L. Gessner, and M. S. Connelly, "Charismatic Leaders and Destructiveness: A Historiometric Study," *Leadership Quarterly 6* (2002): 529–555.

102. M. E. Schweitzer, L. Ordonez, and B. Douma, "Goal Setting as a Motivator of Unethical Behavior," *Academy of Management Journal 47*(3) (2004): 422–432.

103. R. L. Hughes, R. C. Ginnet, and G. J. Curphy, *Leadership: Enhancing the Lessons of Experience 4/e* (Burr Ridge, IL: McGraw Hill, 2005).

104. J. F. Veiga, T. D. Golden, and K. Dechant, "Why Managers Bend Company Rules," *Academy of Management Executive 18*(2) (2004): 84–90.

105. V. Anand, B. E. Ashforth, and M. Joshi, "Business as Usual: The Acceptance and Perpetuation of Corruption in Organizations," *Academy of Management Executive 18*(2) (2004): 39–53.

106. J. B. Cullen, K. P. Parboteeach, and M. Hoegl, "Cross-National Differences in Managers' Willingness to Justify Ethically Suspect Behaviors: A Test of Institutional Anomie Theory," *Academy of Management Journal 47*(3) (2004): 411–421.

107. A. Spicer, T. W. Dunfee, and W. J. Bailey, "Does National Context Matter in Ethical Decision Making? An Empirical Test of Integrative Social Contracts Theory," *Academy of Management Journal 47*(4) (2004): 610–620.

108. Information taken from the Federal Communications Commission website: **http://www.fcc.gov,** January 3, 2004.

109. S. Warren, "Getting the Letdown on Your Competition Is Just a Few Clicks Away," *The Wall Street Journal,* January 14, 2002, B1.

110. See note 93.

111. J. Jurlantzick, "Liar, Liar," *Entrepreneur* (October 2003): 68–71.

112. See note 111.

113. J. M. Tisch, "From 'Me' Leadership to 'We' Leadership," *The Wall Street Journal,* October 26, 2004, A2.

114. See note 111.

115. See note 98.

116. See note 111.

117. S. Shellenberger, "How and Why We Lie at the Office: From Pilfered Pens to Padded Accounts," *The Wall Street Journal,* March 24, 2005, B1.

118. See note 98.

119. See note 117.

120. See note 96.

121. "Doing What's Right," *Entrepreneur* (March 2003): 52.

122. G. R. Weaver, "Ethics and Employees: Making the Connection," *Academy of Management Executive 18*(2) (2004): 121–125.

123. R. J. Daft, *The Leadership Experience* (Mason, OH: South-Western/Thomson, 2005).

124. See note 121.

125. "The World's 100 Largest Public Companies," *The Wall Street Journal,* September 27, 2004, R10.

126. R. A. Guth, "In Secret Hideaway, Bill Gates Ponders Microsoft's Future," *The Wall Street Journal,* March 28, 2005, A1.

127. Information taken from the Microsoft website: http://www.microsoft.com, March 29, 2005.

128. R. A. Guth, "Bill Gates Entertainer," *The Wall Street Journal,* October 13, 2004, B1, B6.

129. For more information on training materials, contact the Zig Zigler Corporation, 3330 Earhart; Carrollton, TX; 75006; (972) 233–9191; www.zigziglar.com.

Chapter 3

1. Information taken from the Market America Web site: **http://www.marketamerica.com,** May 17, 2005.

2. Y. Fried and L. H. Slowik, "Enriching Goal Setting Theory with Time: An Integrated Approach," *Academy of Management Review 3* (2004): 404–422.

3. M. Osterloh, J. Frost, and B. S. Frey, "The Dynamics of Motivation in New Organizational Forms," *International Journal of the Economics of Business 9*(17) (February 2002): 61.

4. J. M. Howell and B. Shamir, "The Role of Followers in the Charismatic Leadership Process: Relationships and Their Consequences," *Academy of Management Review 30*(1) (2005): 96–112.

5. Newswire Associates Inc., "Motivation Show Survey Finds American Workers Would Benefit from Incentives," *PR Newswire,* September 23, 2002, 1.

6. T. R. Mitchell, B. C. Holtom, T. W. Lee, C. J. Sablynski, and M. Erez, "Why People Stay: Using Job Embeddedness to Predict Voluntary Turnover," *Academy of Management Journal 44* (2001): 1102–1121.

7. P. W. Hom and A. J. Kinicki, "Toward a Greater Understanding of How Dissatisfaction Drives Employee Turnover," *Academy of Management Journal 44* (2001): 975–987.

8. G. Williams, "Whale Watching," *Entrepreneur* (June 2002): 32.

9. J. G. Clawson and M. E. Haskins, "Beating the Career Blues," *Academy of Management Executive 14* (2000): 91–92.

10. J. B. Miner, "The Rated Importance, Scientific Validity, and Practical Usefulness of Organizational Behavior Theories," *Academy of Management Learning and Education 2*(3) (2003): 250–268.

11. E. K. Kelloway, J. Barling, and J. Helleur, "Enhancing Transformational Leadership: The Roles of Training and Feedback," *Leadership & Organizational Development Journal 21*(5) (March 2000): 145.

12. R. M. Steers, R. T. Mowday, and D. L. Shapiro, "The Future of Work Motivation Theory," *Academy of Management Review 29*(3) (2004): 379–387.

13. F. Ferraro, J. Pfeffer, and R. I. Sutton, "Economic Language and Assumptions: How Theories Can Become Self-Fulfilling," *Academy of Management Review 30*(1) (2005): 8–24.

14. A. Hemsley, "Willpower vs. Skill Power: Defeating Self-Doubts and Restoring Self-Confidence are Essential to Achieving Greater Success and Happiness," *Research 24* (November 2001): 26–30.

15. See note 6.

16. See note 8.

17. D. B. Smith and J. E. Ellingson, "Substance versus Style: A New Look at Social Desirability in Motivating Contexts," *Journal of Applied Psychology 87* (April 2002): 211–220.

18. K. Lewin, R. Lippitt, and R. K. White, "Patterns of Aggressive Behavior in Experimentally Created 'Social Climates,'" *Journal of Social Psychology 10* (1939): 271–301.

19. R. Likert, *New Patterns of Management* (New York: McGraw-Hill, 1961).

20. R. M. Stogdill and A. E. Coons, eds., *Leader Behavior: Its Description and Measurement* (Columbus: Ohio State University Bureau of Business Research, 1957).

21. B. M. Bass, *Bass and Stogdill's Handbook of Leadership: A Survey of Theory and Research* (New York: Free Press, 1990).

22. R. J. House and R. N. Aditya, "The Social Scientific Study of Leadership: Quo Vadis?" *Journal of Management 23* (May–June 1997): 409–474.

23. P. J. Jordan, N. M. Ashkanasy, and C. E. J. Hartel, "Emotional Intelligence as a Moderator of Emotional and Behavioral Reactions to Job Insecurity," *Academy of Management Review 27* (2002): 361–372.

24. D. G. Bowers and S. E. Seashore, "Predicting Organizational Effectiveness with a Four-Factor Theory of Leadership," *Administrative Science Quarterly 11* (1966): 238–263.

25. R. Likert, *The Human Organization: Its Management and Value* (New York: McGraw-Hill, 1967).

26. R. Blake and J. Mouton, *The Managerial Grid* (Houston, TX: Gulf Publishing, 1964); R. Blake and J. Mouton, *The New Managerial Grid* (Houston, TX: Gulf Publishing, 1978); R. Blake and J. Mouton, *The Managerial Grid III: The Key to Leadership Excellence* (Houston, TX: Gulf Publishing, 1985); and R. Blake and A. A. McCanse, *Leadership Dilemmas—Grid Solutions* (Houston, TX: Gulf Publishing, 1991).

27. "Robert R. Blake and Jane S. Mouton: The Managerial Grid," *Thinkers* (March 2002).

28. D. J. Jung and B. J. Avolio, "Effects of Leadership Style and Followers' Cultural Orientation on Performance in Group and Individual Task Conditions," *Academy of Management Journal 42* (April 1999): 208–218; L. Pheng and B. Lee, "'Managerial Grid' and Zhuge Liang's 'Art of Management': Integration for Effective Project Management," *Management Decision 35* (May–June 1997): 382–392.

29. R. Blake and J. Mouton, *The Managerial Grid* (Houston, TX: Gulf Publishing, 1964).

30. R. Blake and J. Mouton, *The New Managerial Grid* (Houston, TX: Gulf Publishing, 1978).

31. P. Nystrom, "Managers and the Hi-Hi Leader Myth," *Academy of Management Journal 21* (June 1978): 325–331.

32. B. M. Fisher and J. E. Edwards, "Consideration and Initiating Structure and Their Relationship with Leader Effectiveness: A Meta-Analysis," *Proceeding of the Academy of Management* (August 1988): 201–205.

33. See note 32.

34. N. Ellemers, D. D. Gilder, and S. A. Haslam, "Motivating Individuals and Groups at Work: A Social Identity Perspective on Leadership and Group Performance," *Academy of Management Review 29*(3) (2004): 459–479.

35. D. Matten and A. Crane, "Corporate Citizenship: Toward an Extended Theoretical Conceptualization," *Academy of Management Review 30*(1) (2005): 166–179.

36. R. B. Pickett and M. M. Kennedy, "Understanding and Using Organizational Politics, Part One," *Clinical Leadership & Management Review* (March/April 2004): 120–122.

37. See note 12.

38. M. G. Seo and L. F. Barrett, "The Role of Affective Experience in Work Motivation," *Academy of Management Review 29*(3) (2004): 423–439.

39. M. C. Bolino and W. H. Turnley, "Going the Extra Mile: Cultivating and Managing Employee Citizenship Behavior," *Academy of Management Executive 17*(3) (2003): 60–71.

40. T. W. Lee, T. R. Mitchell, C. J. Sablynski, J. P. Burton, and B. C. Holtom, "The Effects of Job Embeddedness on Organizational Citizenship, Job Performance, Volitional Absences, and Voluntary Turnover," *Academy of Management Journal 47*(5) (2004): 711–722.

41. See note 39.

42. See note 38.

43. See note 34.

44. See note 38.

45. M. M. Koerner, Review of *Treat People Right,* by E. Lawler III, *Academy of Management Executive 18*(4) (2004): 163–164.

46. A. Maslow, "A Theory of Human Motivation," *Psychological Review 50* (1943): 370–396.

47. A. Maslow, *Maslow on Management* (New York: Wiley, 1998); T. Petzinger, "Radical Work by Guru of Leadership Takes 30 Years to Flower," *The Wall Street Journal*, April 25, 1997, 1; and R. Zemke, "Maslow for a New Millennium," *Training* (December 1998): 54–59.

48. F. Herzberg, "The Motivation-Hygiene Concept and Problems of Manpower," *Personnel Administrator* (1964): 3–7; and F. Herzberg, "One More Time: How Do You Motivate Employees?" *Harvard Business Review* (January–February 1968): 53–62.

49. E. A. Locke and G. P. Latham, "What Should We Do About Motivation Theory?" *Academy of Management Review 29*(3) (2004): 388–403.

50. S. E. Seibert, S. R. Silver, and W. A. Randolph, "Taking Empowerment to the Next Level: A Multiple-Level Model of Empowerment, Performance, and Satisfaction," *Academy of Management Journal 47*(3) (2004): 332–349.

51. See note 39.

52. See note 3.

53. A. Kohn, "Challenging Behaviorist Dogma: Myths about Money and Motivation," *Compensation and Benefits Review* (March/April 1998): 27–33.

54. P. Christensen, "Motivational Strategies for Public Managers: The Budgetary Belt-Tightening Precipitated by the Recession Has Placed Renewed Emphasis on the Importance of Employee Motivation," *Government Finance Review 18* (April 2002): 30–36.

55. M. Tietjen and R. Myers, "Motivation and Job Satisfaction," *Management Decisions 36* (May–June 1998): 226–232; and

I. Adigun, "Generalizability of a Theory of Job Attitudes: A Cross-Cultural View," research note, *International Journal of Public Administration* 21 (November 1998): 1629–1637.

56. H. Murray, *Explorations in Personality* (New York: Oxford University Press, 1938); and J. Atkinson, *An Introduction to Motivation* (New York: Van Nostrand Reinhold, 1964).

57. D. McNeese-Smith, "The Relationship between Managerial Motivation, Leadership, Nurse Outcomes, and Patient Satisfaction," *Journal of Organizational Behavior* 20 (March 1999): 243–244.

58. N. L. Torres, "For Sanity's Sake!" *Entrepreneur* (April 2004): 102–103.

59. L. L. Martins, K. A. Eddleston, and J. F. Veiga, "Moderators of the Relationship between Work-Family Conflict and Career Satisfaction," *Academy of Management Journal* 45 (2002): 399–409.

60. J. R. Edwards and N. P. Rothbard, "Mechanisms Linking Work and Family: Clarifying the Relationship between Work and Family Constructs," *Academy of Management Review* 25 (2000): 178–199.

61. H. Angelo, "Welch Electrifies UMass Students," *The Republican,* April 12, 2005, A1, A10.

62. C. P. Maertz and M. A. Campion, "Profiles in Quitting: Integrating Process and Content Turnover Theory," *Academy of Management Journal* 47(4) (2004): 566–582.

63. See note 38.

64. W. R. Boswell and J. B. Olson-Buchanan, "Experiencing Mistreatment at Work: The Role of Grievance Filing, Nature of Mistreatment, and Employee Withdrawal," *Academy of Management Journal* 47(1) (2004): 120–139.

65. J. S. Adams, "Toward an Understanding of Inequity," *Journal of Abnormal and Social Psychology* 67 (1963): 422–436.

66. L. K. Scheer, N. Kumar, and J. E. M. Steenkamp, "Reactions to Perceived Inequity in U.S. and Dutch Interorganizational Relationships," *Academy of Management Journal* 46(3) (2003): 303–316.

67. M. Bloom, "The Performance Effects of Pay Dispersion on Individuals and Organizations," *Academy of Management Journal* 42 (February 1999): 25–40.

68. O. Janssen, "Fairness Perceptions as a Moderator in the Curvilinear Relationships between Job Demands, and Job Performance and Job Satisfaction," *Academy of Management* 44 (2001): 1039–1050.

69. C. Hymowitz, "Parents Gain Insight Into Art of Managing During Family Time," *The Wall Street Journal,* August 24, 2004, B1.

70. V. Vroom, *Work and Motivation* (New York: John Wiley & Sons, 1964).

71. R. Kanfer and P. L. Ackerman, "Aging, Adult Development, and Work Motivation," *Academy of Management Review* 29(3) (2004): 440–458.

72. D. B. McNatt and T. A. Judge, "Boundary Conditions of the Galatea Effect: A Field Experiment and Constructive Replication," *Academy of Management Journal* 47(4) (2004): 550–565.

73. N. E. Peterman and J. Kennedy, "Enterprise Education: Influencing Students' Perceptions of Entrepreneurship," *Entrepreneurship Theory and Practice* 27 (Winter 2003): 129–162.

74. P. F. Hewlin, "And the Award for Best Actor Goes to...: Facades of Conformity in Organizational Settings," *Academy of Management Review* 28(4) (2004): 633–642.

75. D. Ilgen, D. Nebeker, and R. Pritchard, "Expectancy Theory Measures: An Empirical Comparison in an Experimental Simulation," *Organizational Behavior and Human Performance* 28 (1981): 189–223; W. Van Eerde and H. Thierry, "Vroom's Expectancy Models and Work-Related Criteria: A Meta-Analysis," *Journal of Applied Psychology* 81 (October 1996): 548–556; and R. Fudge and J. Schlacter, "Motivating Employees to Act Ethically: An Expectancy Theory Approach," *Journal of Business Ethics* 18 (February 1999): 295–296.

76. E. A. Locke, "Guest Editor's Introduction: Goal-Setting Theory and Its Applications to the World of Business," *Academy of Management Executive* 18(4) (2004): 124–125.

77. R. N. Llewellyn, "The Four Career Concepts: Managers Can Learn How to Better Develop Their People by Learning How They're Motivated," *HR Magazine* 47 (September 2002): 121–125.

78. G. Chen and R. J. Klimoski, "The Impact of Expectations on Newcomer Performance in Teams as Mediated by Work Characteristics, Social Exchanges, and Empowerment," *Academy of Management Journal* 46(5) (2003): 591–607.

79. See note 2.

80. M. J. Provitera, Review of *What Management Is: How It Works and Why It's Everyone's Business,* by J. Magretta and N. Stone, *Academy of Management Executive* 17(3) (2003): 152–153.

81. G. P. Latham, "The Motivational Benefits of Goal-Setting," *Academy of Management Executive* 18(4) (2004): 126–129.

82. "Comcast Said It Plans," *The Wall Street Journal,* May 26, 2004, A1.

83. S. Gray, "Flipping Burger King," *The Wall Street Journal,* April 26, 2005, B1.

84. "Toyota Said," *The Wall Street Journal,* November 2, 2004, A1.

85. P. C. Nutt, "Expanding the Search for Alternatives During Strategic Decision-Making," *Academy of Management Executive* 18(1) (2004): 13–28.

86. K. N. Shaw, "Changing the Goal-Setting Process at Microsoft," *Academy of Management Executive* 18(4) (2004): 139–142.

87. See note 2.

88. M. E. Schweitzer, L. Ordonez, and B. Douma, "Goal Setting as a Motivator of Unethical Behavior," *Academy of Management Journal* 47(3) (2004): 422–432.

89. C. Hymowitz, "Some Tips From CEOs to Help You to Make a Fresh Start in 2005," *The Wall Street Journal,* December 28, 2004, B1.

90. S. Kerr and S. Landauer, "Using Stretch Goals to Promote Organizational Effectiveness and Personal Growth: General Electric and Goldman Sachs," *Academy of Management Executive* 18(4) (2004): 134–138.

91. E. C. Hollensbe and J. P. Guthrie, "Group Pay-for-Performance Plans: The Role of Spontaneous Goal Setting," *Academy of Management Review* 25 (2000): 864–872.

92. B. P. Matherne, "If You Fail to Plan, Do You Plan to Fail?" *Academy of Management Executive* 18(4) (2004): 156–157.

93. See note 86.

94. See note 88.

95. See note 76.

96. See note 34.

97. B. Beersma, J. R. Hollenback, S. E. Humphrey, H. Moon, D. E. Conlon, and D. R. Ilgen, "Cooperation, Competition,

and Team Performance: Toward a Contingency Approach," *Academy of Management Journal* 46(5) (2003): 571–590.

98. See note 49.

99. B. F. Skinner, *Beyond Freedom and Dignity* (New York: Alfred A. Knopf, 1971).

100. C. Hui, S. S. K. Lam, and J. Schaubroeck, "Can Good Citizens Lead the Way in Providing Quality Service? A Field Quasi-Experiment," *Academy of Management Journal* 44(2) (2001): 154–162.

101. A. D. Stajkovic and F. Luthans, "Differential Effects of Incentive Motivators on Work Performance," *Academy of Management Journal* 44(4) (2001): 580–590.

102. A. Erez, and T. A. Judge, "Relationship of Core Self-Evaluations to Goal Setting, Motivation, and Performance," *Journal of Applied Psychology* 86 (December 2001): 56–73.

103. T. A. Judge and R. Ilies, "Is Positiveness in Organizations Always Desirable?" *Academy of Management Executive* 18(4) (2004): 151–155.

104. S. Kerr, "Introduction: Establishing Organizational Goals and Rewards," *Academy of Management Executive* 18(4) (2004): 122–123.

105. See note 8.

106. See note 45.

107. G. R. Weaver, "Ethics and Employees: Making the Connection," *Academy of Management Executive* 18(2) (2004): 121–125.

108. S. Kerr, "On the Folly of Rewarding A, While Hoping for B," *Academy of Management Executive* 9 (February 1995): 32–40.

109. See note 108.

110. See note 108.

111. D. E. Bowen and Cheri Ostroff, "Understanding HRM-Firm Performance Linkages: The Role of the 'Strength' of the HRM System." *Academy of Management Review* 29(2) (2004): 203–221.

112. K. T. Gordon, "Sweet Rewards," *Entrepreneur* (August 2003): 75–76.

113. See note 101.

114. See note 61.

115. K. Blanchard and S. Johnson, *The One-Minute Manager* (New York: Wm. Morrow & Co., 1982).

116. This statement is based on Robert N. Lussier's consulting experience.

117. See note 49.

Chapter 4

1. Lapchick, R. "Robert L. Johnson, Founder (Chairman) CEO of Black Entertainment Television (BET) and Majority Owner of the NBA's Charlotte Bobcats, on Leading Talented People," *Academy of Management Executive* 18(1) (2004): 114–119.

2. D. J. Brass, J. Galaskiewicz, H. R. Greve, and W. Tsai, "Taking Stock of Networks and Organizations: A Multi-level Perspective," *Academy of Management Journal* 47(6) (2004): 795–817.

3. S. Meisel, Review of *The Practical Coach* by P. Caproni, *Academy of Management Learning and Education* 3(4) (2004): 458–459.

4. C. M. Fiol, E. J. O'Connor, and H. Aguinis, "All for One and One for All? The Development and Transfer of Power across Organizational Levels," *Academy of Management Review* 26 (2001): 224–242.

5. S. M. Puffer, "Changing Organizational Structures: An Interview with Rosabeth Moss Kanter," *Academy of Management Executive* 18(2) (2004): 96–105.

6. J. A. Raelin, "Don't Bother Putting Leadership Into People," *Academy of Management Executive* 19(3) (2004): 131–135.

7. C. Hymowitz, "Bosses Create Problems If They're Too Secretive or Divulge Too Much," *The Wall Street Journal*, September 21, 2004, B1.

8. W. Bennis, "'Owed' to Rosabeth Moss Kanter: Impact on Management Practice," *Academy of Management Executive* 18(2) (2004): 106–107.

9. R. D. Ireland and C. C. Miller, "Decision-Making and Firm Success," *Academy of Management Executive* 18(4) (2004): 8–12.

10. T. Welbourne and C. O. Trevor, "The Roles of Departmental and Position Power in Job Evaluation," *Academy of Management Journal* 43 (2000): 761–771.

11. S. E. Seibert, S. R. Silver, and W. A. Randolph, "Taking Empowerment to the Next Level: A Multiple-Level Model of Empowerment, Performance, and Satisfaction," *Academy of Management Journal* 47(3) (2004): 332–349.

12. J. B. Barney, "An Interview with William Ouchi," *Academy of Management Executive* 18(4) (2004): 108–116.

13. "Disney's Future CEO," *The Wall Street Journal*, March 15, 2005, A1.

14. J. R. P. French and B. H. Raven, "The Bases of Social Power" in D. Cartwright, ed., *Studies of Social Power* (Ann Arbor, MI: Institute for Social Research, 1959), 150–167.

15. T. B. Lawrence, M. K. Mauws, B. Dyck, and R. F. Kleysen, "The Politics of Organizational Learning: Integrating Power Into the 4I Framework," *Academy of Management Review* 30(1) (2005): 180–191.

16. C. Hymowitz, "How Managers Can Keep from Being Ambushed by the Boss," *The Wall Street Journal*, April 9, 2002, B1.

17. C. Hymowitz, "When You Disagree with the Boss's Order, Do You Tell Your Staff?" *The Wall Street Journal*, April 16, 2002, B1.

18. See note 4.

19. See note 8.

20. H. Angelo, "Welch Electrifies UMass Students," *The Republican*, April 12, 2005, A1, A10.

21. See note 7.

22. A. C. Inkpen and E. W. K. Tsang, "Social Capital, Networks, and Knowledge Transfer," *Academy of Management Review* 30(1) (2005): 146–165.

23. See note 16.

24. T. G. Pollock, J. F. Porac, and J. B. Wade, "Constructing Deal Networks: Brokers as Network 'Architects' in the U.S. IPO Market and Other Examples," *Academy of Management Review* 29(1) (2004): 50–72.

25. R. B. Pickett and M. M. Kennedy, "Understanding and Using Organizational Politics, Part One," *Clinical Leadership & Management Review* (March/April 2004): 120–122.

26. J. Borzo, "The Job Connection," *The Wall Street Journal*, September 13, 2004, R14.

27. T. M. Begley, W. L. Tan, and H. Schoch, "Politico-Economic Factors Associated with Interest in Starting a Business: A Multi-Country Study," *Entrepreneurship Theory and Practice* (January 2005): 35–42.

28. R. Lubit, "The Long-Term Organizational Impact of Destructively Narcissistic Managers," *Academy of Management Executive 16*(2002): 127–138.

29. L. A. Hill, "New Manager Development for the 21st Century," *Academy of Management Executive 18*(3) (2004): 121–126.

30. P. L. Perrewe, K. Zellars, G. Ferris, A. M. Rossi, C. Kacmar, and D. Ralston, "Neutralizing Job Stressors: Political Skill as an Antidote to the Dysfunctional Consequences of Role Conflict," *Academy of Management Journal 46*(1) (2005): 141–152.

31. See note 15.

32. R. A. Baron and G. D. Markman, "Beyond Social Capital: How Social Skills Can Enhance Entrepreneurs' Success," *Academy of Management Executive 14* (2000): 106–116.

33. M. C. Andrews and K. M. Kacmar, "Discriminating Among Organizational Politics, Justice, and Support," *Journal of Organizational Behavior 22* (June 2001): 34–36.

34. See note 15.

35. N. W. Biggart and R. Delbridge, "Systems of Exchange," *Academy of Management Review 29*(1) (2004): 28–49.

36. See note 25.

37. S. Robbins and D. De Cenzo, *Fundamentals of Management* (Englewood Cliffs, NJ: Prentice Hall, 2004).

38. F. J. Flynn, "How Much Should I Give and How Often? The Effects of Generosity and Frequency of Favor Exchange on Social Status and Productivity," *Academy of Management Journal 46*(5) (2003): 539–553.

39. A. Stewart, "Help One Another, Use One Another: Toward an Anthropology of Family Business," *Entrepreneurship Theory and Practice* (Summer 2003): 383–390.

40. See note 25.

41. J. Gimeno, "Competition Within and between Networks: The Contingent Effect of Competitive Embeddedness on Alliance Formation," *Academy of Management Journal 47*(5) (2004): 620–642.

42. G. Ip, K. Kelly, S. Craig, and I. J. Dugan, "How Grasso's Rule Kept NYSE On Top but Hid Deep Troubles," *The Wall Street Journal*, December 30, 2003, A1, A6.

43. K. Kelly, "Grasso, Spitzer Keep Door Open for a Deal Despite Tough Talk," *The Wall Street Journal*, April 27, 2004, B1.

44. See note 43.

45. See note 9.

46. H. Oh, M.-H. Chung, G. Labianca, "Group Social Capital and Group Effectiveness: The Role of Informal Socializing Ties," *Academy of Management Journal 47*(6) (2004): 660–673.

47. See note 17.

48. See note 16.

49. C. Hymowitz, "Some Tips From CEOs to Help You to Make a Fresh Start in 2005," *The Wall Street Journal*, December 28, 2004, B1.

50. See note 25.

51. A. Hwang, E. H. Kessler, and A. M. Francesco, "Student Networking Behavior, Culture, and Grade Performance: An Empirical Study and Pedagogical Recommendations," *Academy of Management Education and Learning 3*(2) (2004): 139–150.

52. See note 2.

53. P. Tharenou, "Going Up? Do Traits and Informal Social Processes Predict Advancing in Management?" *Academy of Management Journal 44* (2001): 1005–1017.

54. J. Gitomer, "The Best Places for Successful Networking," *Business Record 18*(17) (2002): 23–24.

55. See note 26.

56. G. Gendron, "Practitioners' Perspectives on Entrepreneurship Education," *Academy of Management Learning and Education 3*(3) (2004): 302–314.

57. See note 51.

58. See note 22.

59. L. C. Abrams, R. Cross, E. Lesser, and D. Z. Levin, "Nurturing Interpersonal Trust in Knowledge-Sharing Networks," *Academy of Management Executive 17*(4) (2003): 64–72.

60. This section is adapted from A. Gumbus and R. N. Lussier, "Career Development: Enhancing Your Networking Skill," *Clinical Leadership & Management Review 17*(1) (January–February 2003). Adapted with permission. Also see A. Gumbus, "Networking: A Long-Term Management Strategy," *Clinical Leadership & Management Review 17*(3) (May–June 2003).

61. J. S. Lublin, "Job Seekers, Beware: Inflating Experience Can Deflate Careers," *The Wall Street Journal*, August 3, 2004, B1.

62. See note 2.

63. M. L. Lengnick-Hall and C. A. Lengnick-Hall, "HR's Role in Building Relationship Networks," *Academy of Management Executive 17*(4) (2003): 53–61.

64. See note 26.

65. B. Farber, "Sales Success," *Entrepreneur* (February 2003): 72–73.

66. W. Bennis, "'Owed' to Rosabeth Moss Kanter: Impact on Management Practice," *Academy of Management Executive 18*(2) (2004): 106–107.

67. M. A. McFadyen and A. A. Cannella, "Social Capital and Knowledge Creation: Diminishing Returns to the Number and Strength of Exchange Relationships," *Academy of Management Journal 47*(5) (2004): 735–746.

68. A. Greve and J. W. Salaff, "Social Networks and Entrepreneurship," *Entrepreneurship Theory and Practice* (Fall 2003): 1–14.

69. M. A. Boland and K. P. Katz, "Jack Gherty, President and CEO of Land O'Lakes, on Leading a Branded Food and Farm Supply Cooperative," *Academy of Management Executive 17*(3) (2003): 24–30.

70. M. Diener, "Nothing Personal," *Entrepreneur* (October 2003): 85–86.

71. M. Diener, "Don't Cry Over . . ." *Entrepreneur* (December 2003): 99–100.

72. B. Spector, "An Interview With Roger Fisher and William Ury," *Academy of Management Executive 18*(3) (2004): 101–108.

73. J. Murphy, "Good as Gold," *Entrepreneur* (August 2003): 60.

74. See note 72.

75. K. A. Wade-Benzoni, A. J. Hoffman, L. L. Thompson, D. A. Moore, J. J. Gillespie, and M. H. Bazerman, "Barriers to Resolution in Ideologically Based

Negotiations: The Role of Values and Institutions," *Academy of Management Review* 27 (2002): 41–57.

76. R. N. Lussier, "The Negotiation Process," *Clinical Leadership & Management Review* 14(2) (2000): 55–59.

77. M. Diener, "What's Your Hurry," *Entrepreneur* (April 2004): 81–82.

78. J. Corman, R. Lussier, and L. Pennel, *Small Business Management: A Planning Approach* (Cincinnati, OH: Atomic Dog Publishing, 2005).

79. See note 72.

80. D. Flory, "How to Overcome 15 'Avoidable' Errors When In Negotiation," *SBANC Newsletter* (October 12, 2004): 2–3.

81. S. A. Zahra, "The Practice of Management: Reflections on Peter F. Drucker's Landmark Book," *Academy of Management Executive* 17(3) (2003): 16–23.

82. See note 78.

83. M. Diener, "Deals Unplugged," *Entrepreneur* (August 2003): 69–70.

84. B. Farber, "Back to Basics," *Entrepreneur* (January 2004): 78–79.

85. M. E. Schweitzer, L. Ordonez, and B. Douma, "Goal Setting as a Motivator of Unethical Behavior," *Academy of Management Journal* 47(3) (2004): 422–432.

86. L. Thompson and G. J. Leonardelli, "The Big Bang: The Evolution of Negotiation Research," *Academy of Management Executive* 18(3) (2004): 113–117.

87. See note 80.

88. P. A. Saparito and C. C. Chen, "The Role of Relational Trust in Bank–Small Firm Relationships," *Academy of Management Journal* 47(3) (2004): 400–410.

89. B. Farber, "People Who Need People," *Entrepreneur* (May 2003): 76–77.

90. See note 88.

91. See note 89.

92. See note 80.

93. K. T. Gordon, "No Regrets," *Entrepreneur* (December 2003): 104–105.

94. See note 80.

95. B. Farber, "Star Power," *Entrepreneur* (February 2003): 102–103.

96. M. Diener, "A Tug of War," *Entrepreneur* (September 2003): 81–82.

97. See note 96.

98. See note 70.

99. See note 80.

100. See note 96.

101. See note 77.

102. See note 71.

103. M. Diener, "Fair Enough; Real Deal: To Be a Better Negotiator, Learn to Tell the Difference between a Lie and a Lie," *Entrepreneur* (January 2002): 100–102.

104. See note 80.

105. This is a real-case sample; names have been changed for confidentiality purposes.

Chapter 5

1. C. Hymowitz, "Women to Watch," *The Wall Street Journal,* November 8, 2004, R1.

2. P. W. Tam, "Hewlett-Packard Board Considers a Reorganization," *The Wall Street Journal,* January 24, 2005, A1.

3. P. W. Tam, "Hewlett-Packard Board Ousts Fiorina as CEO," *The Wall Street Journal,* February 10, 2005, A1.

4. P. W. Tam, "Hitting the Ground Running," *The Wall Street Journal,* April 4, 2005, B1.

5. H. Moon, J. R. Hollenbeck, A. Ellis, and C. Porter, "Asymmetric Adaptability: Dynamic Team Structures and One-Way Streets," *Academy of Management Journal* 47(5) (2004): 681–695.

6. E. A. Locke, "Guest Editor's Introduction: Goal-Setting Theory and Its Applications to the World of Business," *Academy of Management Executive* 18(4) (2004): 124–125.

7. W. E. Rothschild, "Where Are the Leaders?" *Financial Executive* 18 (July–August 2002): 26–32.

8. A. J. Magrath, "Leading Without Stripes," *Across the Board* 39 (July–August 2002): 13–15.

9. L. A. Hill, "New Manager Development for the 21st Century," *Academy of Management Executive* 18(3) (2004): 121–126.

10. See note 3.

11. P. W. Tam, "Carly Fiorina's Rough Ride," *The Wall Street Journal,* November 30, 2004, B1.

12. W. Ouchi, *Theory Z: How American Business Can Meet the Japanese Challenge* (Reading, MA: Addison-Wesley, 1981).

13. J. Winter, J. Neal, and K. Waner, "How Male, Female, and Mixed-Gender Groups Regard Interaction and Leadership Differences in the Business Communication Course," *Business Communication Quarterly* (September 2001): 43.

14. R. F. Martell and A. L. DeSmet, "A Diagnostic-Ratio Approach to Measuring Beliefs about the Leadership Abilities of Male and Female Managers," *Journal of Applied Psychology* (December 2001): 1223–1232.

15. R. N. House and R. J. Aditya, "The Social Scientific Study of Leadership: Quo Vadis?" *Journal of Management* 23 (May–June 1997): 409–474.

16. F. E. Fiedler, *A Theory of Leadership Effectiveness* (New York: McGraw-Hill, 1967).

17. F. E. Fiedler, "The Contingency Model and the Dynamics of the Leadership Process," in L. Berkowitz, ed., *Advances in Experimental Social Psychology* (New York: Academic Press, 1978).

18. F. E. Fiedler and M. M. Chemers, *Improving Leadership Effectiveness: The Leader Match Concept,* 2nd ed. (New York: Wiley, 1982).

19. "Antidepressants Debate Intensifies," *The Wall Street Journal,* June 3, 2004, D1.

20. "Merck Records," *The Wall Street Journal,* February 7, 2005, A1.

21. A. W. Matthews, "Vioxx Recall Raises Questions on FDA's Safety Monitoring," *The Wall Street Journal,* October 4, 2004, B1.

22. C. Schriesheim and S. Kerr, "Theories and Measures of Leadership: A Critical Appraisal of Present and Future Directions," in J. G. Hunt and L. L. Larson, eds., *Leadership: The Cutting Edge* (Carbondale, IL: Southern Illinois University Press, 1977), 9–44; and A. S. Ashour, "Further Discussion of Fiedler's Contingency Model of Leadership Effectiveness: An Evaluation," *Organizational Behavior and Human Performance* 9 (1973): 339–355.

23. F. E. Fiedler, "A Rejoinder to Schriesheim and Kerr's Premature

Obituary of the Contingency Model," in J. G. Hunt and L. L. Larson, eds., *Leadership: The Cutting Edge* (Carbondale, IL: Southern Illinois University Press, 1977), 45–50; and F. E. Fiedler, "The Contingency Model: A Reply to Ashour," *Organizational Performance and Human Behavior 9* (1973): 356–368.

24. M. J. Strube and J. E. Garcia, "A Meta-Analytical Investigation of Fiedler's Contingency Model of Leadership Effectiveness," *Psychology Bulletin 90* (1981): 307–321; and L. H. Peters, D. D. Hartke, and J. T. Pohlmann, "Fiedler's Contingency Theory of Leadership: An Application of the Meta-Analysis Procedure of Schmidt and Hunter," *Psychological Bulletin 97* (1985): 274–285.

25. F. E. Fiedler and J. E. Garcia, *New Approaches to Effective Leadership: Cognitive Resources and Organizational Performance* (New York: Wiley, 1987).

26. F. E. Fiedler, "Research on Leadership Selection and Training: One View of the Future," *Administrative Science Quarterly 41* (1996): 241–250; and F. E. Fiedler, "Cognitive Resources and Leadership Performance," *Applied Psychology—An International Review 44* (1995): 5–28.

27. R. P. Vecchio, "A Theoretical and Empirical Examination of Cognitive Resource Theory," *Journal of Applied Psychology 75* (1990): 141–147; and P. J. Bettin and J. K. Kennedy, "Leadership Experience and Leader Performance: Some Empirical Support at Last," *Leadership Quarterly 1* (1990): 219–228.

28. R. L. Hughes, R. C. Ginnett, and G. J. Curphy, *Leadership: Enhancing the Lessons of Experience*, 4th ed. (Burr Ridge, IL: Irwin/McGraw-Hill, 2005).

29. R. Tannenbaum and W. H. Schmidt, "How to Choose a Leadership Pattern," *Harvard Business Review* (March–April 1958): 95–101.

30. R. Tannenbaum and W. H. Schmidt, "How to Choose a Leadership Pattern," *Harvard Business Review* (May–June 1973): 166.

31. J. A. Conger, "Developing Leadership Capability: What's Inside the Black Box?" *Academy of Management Executive 18*(3) (2004): 136–139.

32. R. Tannenbaum and W. H. Schmidt, excerpts from "How to Choose a Leadership Pattern," *Harvard Business Review* (July–August 1986): 129.

33. R. J. House, "A Path-Goal Theory of Leader Effectiveness," *Administrative Science Quarterly 16*(2) (1971): 321–329; and M. G. Evans, "The Effects of Supervisory Behavior on the Path-Goal Relationship," *Organizational Behavior and Human Performance 5* (1970): 277–298.

34. See note 15.

35. A. J. DuBrin, *Leadership: Research Finding, Practice, and Skills* (Boston: Houghton Mifflin, 2004).

36. R. J. House and T. R. Mitchell, "Path-Goal Theory of Leadership," *Contemporary Business* (Fall 1974): 81–98.

37. J. C. Wofford and L. Z. Liska, "Path-Goal Theories of Leadership: A Meta-Analysis," *Journal of Management 19* (1993): 858–876; and P. M. Podsakoff, S. B. MacKenzie, M. Ahearne, and W. H. Bommer, "Searching for a Needle in a Haystack: Trying to Identify the Illusive Moderators of Leadership Behavior," *Journal of Management 21* (1995): 423–470.

38. C. Schriesheim and L. L. Nieder, "Path-Goal Leadership Theory: The Long and Winding Road," *Leadership Quarterly 7*(3) (1996): 317–321; see note 15, House and Aditya; and J. Beeler, "A Survey Report of Job Satisfaction and Job Involvement among Governmental and Public Auditors," *Government Accountants Journal 45* (Winter 1997): 26–32.

39. See note 15, House and Aditya; and see note 33, House, pp. 323–352, for a discussion of how the original path-goal theory led to the development of the 1976 charismatic theory and a description of the 1996 version of path-goal theory.

40. J. Sandberg, "Overcontrolling Bosses Aren't Just Annoying; They're Also Inefficient," *The Wall Street Journal*, March 30, 2005, B1.

41. V. H. Vroom and P. W. Yetton, *Leadership and Decision Making* (Pittsburgh: University of Pittsburgh Press, 1973); and V. H. Vroom and A. G. Jago, *The New Leadership: Managing Participation in Organizations* (Englewood Cliffs, NJ: Prentice-Hall, 1988).

42. V. H. Vroom, "Leadership and the Decision-Making Process," *Organizational Dynamics 28* (Spring 2000): 82–94.

43. R. H. G. Field, P. C. Read, and J. J. Louviere, "The Effect of Situation Attributes on Decision Method Choice in the Vroom-Jago Model of Participation in Decision Making," *Leadership Quarterly 1* (1990): 165–176; and see note 41, Vroom and Jago.

44. See note 41, Vroom and Jago.

45. R. H. G. Field, "A Test of the Vroom-Yetton Normative Model of Leadership," *Journal of Applied Psychology* (October 1982): 523–532; R. H. G. Field, "A Critique of the Vroom-Yetton Contingency Model of Leadership Behavior," *Academy of Management Review 4* (1979): 249–257; and J. B. Miner, "The Uncertain Future of the Leadership Concept: An Overview," in J. G. Hunt and L. L. Larson, eds., *Leadership Frontiers* (Kent, OH: Kent State University, 1975).

46. See note 42.

47. See note 42.

48. "Executive Perspectives: John Sinnot, Chairman & CEO, Marsh Inc.," *Risk Management 49* (September 2002): 20–25.

49. "Effective Leaders . . . Made or Born?" *Leadership for the Front Lines* (June 15, 2002): 3–5.

50. R. L. Ackoff, *Re-Creating the Corporation: A Design of Organizations for the 21st Century* (Oxford: Oxford University Press, 1999).

51. M. H. Bazerman, "Conducting Influential Research: The Need for Prescriptive Implications," *Academy of Management Review 30*(1) (2005): 25–31.

52. C. Markides and C. D. Charitou, "Competing with Dual Business Models: A Contingency Approach," *Academy of Management Executive 18*(3) (2004): 22–36.

53. J. Pfeffer, "The Ambiguity of Leadership," *Academy of Management Review* (April 1977): 104–112; and J. Howell, D. E. Bowen, P. W. Dorfman, S. Kerr, and P. Podsakoff, "Substitutes for Leadership: Effective Alternatives to Ineffective Leadership," *Organizational Dynamics* (Summer 1990): 23.

54. S. Kerr and J. Jermier, "Substitutes for Leadership: Their Meaning and Measurement," *Organizational Behavior and Human Performance 22* (1978): 375–403.

55. P. M. Podsakoff, S. B. MacKenzie, and W. H. Bommer, "Transformational Leader Behaviors and Substitutes for Leadership as Determinants of Employee Satisfaction,

Commitment, Trust, and Organizational Citizenship Behaviors," *Journal of Management* 22(2) (1996): 259–298; and see note 53, Howell et al.

56. J. E. Sheridan, D. J. Vredenburgh, and M. A. Abelson, "Contextual Model of Leadership Influence in Hospital Units," *Academy of Management Journal* 27(1) (1984): 57–78; see note 55, Podsakoff et al.; and R. E. de Vries, R. A. Roe, and T. C. B. Taillieu, "Need for Supervision: Its Impact on Leadership Effectiveness," *Journal of Applied Behavioral Science* 34 (December 1998): 486–487.

57. P. M. Podsakoff, S. B. MacKenzie, and W. H. Bommer, "Meta-Analysis of the Relationships between Kerr and Jermier's Substitutes for Leadership and Employee Job Attitudes, Role Perceptions, and Performance," *Journal of Applied Psychology* 81 (August 1996): 380–400.

58. Information taken from MOCON website: **http://www.mocon.com**, June 3, 2005.

59. MOCON is an existing company. However, Hank Thomson is not the name of an actual manager at MOCON; Thomson is used to illustrate contingency leadership.

Chapter 6

1. Information taken from personal interviews with the Clarks and updated on June 15, 2005.

2. S. A. Zahra, "The Practice of Management: Reflections on Peter F. Drucker's Landmark Book," *Academy of Management Executive* 17(3) (2003): 16–23.

3. J. S. Lublin, "Readers Agree Speech Needs Cleaning Up, and They Provide Tips," *The Wall Street Journal*, October 19, 2004, B1.

4. B. Barry and I. S. Fulmer, "The Medium and the Message: The Adaptive Use of Communication Media in Dyadic Influence," *Academy of Management Review* 29(2) (2004): 272–292.

5. D. J. Brass, J. Galaskiewicz, H. R. Greve, and W. Tsai, "Taking Stock of Networks and Organizations: A Multilevel Perspective," *Academy of Management Journal* 47(6) (2004): 795–817.

6. R. L. Ackoff, speech at the University of New Haven, May 23, 2002.

7. H. H. Beam, review of *Why Smart Executives Fail*, by Sidney Finkelstein *Academy of Management Executives* 18(2) (2004): 157–158.

8. A. Smidts, C. Van Riel, and H. Pruyn, "The Impact of Employee Communication and Perceived External Prestige on Organizational Identification," *Academy of Management Journal* 49 (2001): 1051–1062.

9. See note 7.

10. Lee Iococca, *Iococca: An Autobiography* (New York: Bantam Books, 1985), 15.

11. W. Hutton, "The Problem with Today's Leadership," *Personnel Today* (March 5, 2002): 2.

12. See note 5.

13. See note 4.

14. See note 4.

15. K. T. Gordon, "Words to the Wise," *Entrepreneur* (October 2003): 91–92.

16. See note 15.

17. C. Penttila, "Show of Good Faith," *Entrepreneur* (December 2003): 28–29.

18. "The FDA," *The Wall Street Journal*, March 15, 2004, A1.

19. K. T. Gordon, "No Regrets," *Entrepreneur* (December 2003): 104–105.

20. J. Jusko, "Why Leaders Fail (Leadership)," *Industry Week 25* (March 2002): 15–16.

21. S. Bernhut, "Managing the Dream: Warren Bennis on Leadership," *Ivey Business Journal* 65 (May 2001): 36.

22. S. M. Puffer, "Changing Organizational Structures: An Interview with Rosabeth Moss Kanter," *Academy of Management Executive* 18(2) (2004): 96–105.

23. B. Farber, "All Ears?" *Entrepreneur* (April 2004): 83–88.

24. C. Hymowitz, "Some Tips From CEOs to Help You to Make a Fresh Start in 2005," *The Wall Street Journal*, December 28, 2004, B1.

25. C. Hymowitz, "Like Rumsfeld, CEOs Who Seek Questions May Not Like Them," *The Wall Street Journal*, December 14, 2004, B1.

26. C. Hymowitz, "Parents Gain Insight into Art of Managing During Family

Time," *The Wall Street Journal*, August 24, 2004, B1.

27. See note 26.

28. See note 24.

29. L. C. Abrams, R. Cross, E. Lesser, and D. Z. Levin, "Nurturing Interpersonal Trust in Knowledge-Sharing Networks," *Academy of Management Executive* 17(4) (2003): 64–72.

30. L. A. Hill, "New Manager Development for the 21st Century," *Academy of Management Executive* 18(3) (2004): 121–126.

31. S. E. Moss and J. I. Sanchez, "Are Your Employees Avoiding You? Managerial Strategies for Closing the Feedback Gap," *Academy of Management Executive* 18(3) (2004): 32–44.

32. H. Mintzberg, "Leadership and Management Development: An Afterword," *Academy of Management Executive* 18(3) (2004): 140–142.

33. P. S. Goodman and D. M. Rosseau, "Organizational Change That Produces Results: The Linkage Approach," *Academy of Management Executive* 18(3) (2004): 7–19.

34. See note 31.

35. See note 31.

36. B. Beersma, J. R. Hollenbeck, S. E. Humphrey, H. Moon, D. E. Conlon, and D. R. Ilgen, "Cooperation, Competition, and Team Performance: Toward a Contingency Approach," *Academy of Management Journal* 46(5) (2003): 571–590.

37. M. Diener, "Don't Cry Over . . ." *Entrepreneur* (December 2003): 99–100.

38. S. Shellenbarger, "Work & Family," *The Wall Street Journal*, June 9, 1999, 4.

39. See note 31.

40. J. A. Conger, "Developing Leadership Capability: What's Inside the Black Box?" *Academy of Management Executive* 18(3) (2004): 136–139.

41. J. Ghorpade, "Managing Five Paradoxes of 360-Degree Feedback," *Academy of Management Executive* 14 (2000): 140–150.

42. J. A. Raelin, "Don't Bother Putting Leadership into People," *Academy of Management Executive* 19(3) (2004): 131–135.

43. B. C. Garcia, review of *The Coaching Manager: Developing Top Talent in*

Business, by J. Hunt and J. Weintraub, *Academy of Management Review* 29(2) (2004): 459–460.

44. See note 32.

45. See note 30.

46. See note 43.

47. See note 39.

48. J. M. Hunt and J. Weintraub, "How Coaching Can Enhance Your Brand as a Manager," *Journal of Organizational Excellence* 21 (Spring 2002): 39–44.

49. See note 6.

50. See note 31.

51. R. N. Lussier, "Dealing with Anger and Preventing Workplace Violence," *Clinical Leadership & Management Review* (March/April 2004): 117–120.

52. See note 43.

53. See note 26.

54. See note 43.

55. See note 5.

56. J. Falvey, "To Raise Productivity, Try Saying Thank You," *The Wall Street Journal,* December 6, 1982, B1.

57. C. Hymowitz, "Bosses Create Problems If They're Too Secretive or Divulge Too Much," *The Wall Street Journal,* September 21, 2004, B1.

58. S. Begley, "People Believe a 'Fact' That Fits Their Views Even If It's Clearly False," *The Wall Street Journal,* February 4, 2005, B1.

59. See note 57.

60. See note 31.

61. C. Hymowitz, "Yes, Ambition Is Good, But How You Display It Can Get You into Trouble," *The Wall Street Journal,* September 14, 2004, B1.

62. E. Biech, "Executive Commentary," *Academy of Management Executive* 17(4) (2003): 92–93.

63. M. C. Higgins and K. Kram, "Reconceptualizing Mentoring at Work: A Developmental Network Perspective," *Academy of Management Review* 26 (2001): 149–155.

64. S. C. de Janasz, "Mentor Networks and Career Success: Lessons for Turbulent Times," *Academy of Management Executive* 17(4) (2003): 78–84.

65. R. Wolter, "Success Coach: Follow Your Leader," *Entrepreneur* (April 2004): 124–125.

66. B. Spector, "An Interview with Roger Fisher and William Ury," *Academy of Management Executive* 18(3) (2004): 101–108.

67. C. Bendersky, "Organizational Dispute Resolution Systems: A Complementarities Model," *Academy of Management Review* 28(4) (2003): 643–656.

68. U. Raja, G. Johns, and F. Ntalianis, "The Impact of Personality on Psychological Contracts," *Academy of Management Journal* 47(3) (2004): 350–367.

69. V. T. Ho, "Social Influence on Evaluations of Psychological Contract Fulfillment," *Academy of Management Review* 30(1) (2005): 113–128.

70. J. A. Thompson and J. S. Bunderson, "Violations of Principle: Ideological Currency in the Psychological Contract," *Academy of Management Review* 28(4) (2003): 571–586.

71. See note 68.

72. Adapted from Always Improvement training materials, Bethesda, MD (January 2003).

73. P. L. Perrewe, K. Zellars, G. Ferris, A. M. Rossi, C. Kacmar, and D. Ralson, "Neutralizing Job Stressors: Political Skill as an Antidote to the Dysfunctional Consequences of Role Conflict," *Academy of Management Journal* 46(1) (2005): 141–152.

74. F. Luthans, "Positive Organizational Behavior: Developing and Managing Psychological Strengths," *Academy of Management Executive* 16 (2002): 57–72.

75. See note 66.

76. See note 67.

77. F. J. Flynn, "How Much Should I Give and How Often? The Effects of Generosity and Frequency of Favor Exchange on Social Status and Productivity," *Academy of Management Journal* 46(5) (2003): 539–553.

78. See note 25.

79. See note 31.

80. N. L. Torres, "Animal Instincts," *Entrepreneur* (February 2003): 26–27.

81. K. Shimizu and M. A. Hitt, "Strategic Flexibility: Organizational Preparedness

to Reverse Ineffective Strategic Decisions," *Academy of Management Executive* 18(4) (2004): 44–59; and F. J. Flynn, "How Much Should I Give and How Often? The Effects of Generosity and Frequency of Favor Exchange on Social Status and Productivity," *Academy of Management Journal* 48(5) (2003): 539–553.

82. See note 80.

83. See note 80.

84. G. Gendron, "Practitioners' Perspectives on Entrepreneurship Education," *Academy of Management Learning and Education* 3(3) (2004): 302–314.

85. Quote of Alan Greenspan, SBANC Newsletter (June 14, 2005), 1.

86. See note 80.

87. See note 84.

88. C. Hardy, T. B. Lawrence, and D. Grant, "Discourse and Collaboration: The Role of Conversations and Collective Identity," *Academy of Management Review* 30(1) (2005): 58–77.

89. P. S. Nugent, "Managing Conflict: Third-Party Interventions for Managers," *Academy of Management Executive* 16 (2002): 36–49.

90. See note 80.

91. H. H. Tan, M. D. Foo, and M. H. Kwek, "The Effects of Customer Personality Traits on the Display of Positive Emotions," *Academy of Management Journal* 47(2) (2004): 287–296.

92. See note 89.

93. See note 67.

94. See note 67.

95. M. Diener, "Making Peace," *Entrepreneur* (January 2004): 75–76.

96. See note 67.

97. E. Anderson, "Communication Patterns: A Tool for Memorable Leadership Training," *Training* (January 1984): 55–57.

Chapter 7

1. F. J. Yammarino and F. Dansereau, "Individualized Leadership: A New Multiple-Level Approach," *Journal of Leadership & Organizational Studies* 9 (Summer 2002): 90–100.

2. See note 1.

3. G. B. Graen and M. Uhl-Bien, "Relationships-Based Approach to Leadership: Development of Leader-Member Exchange (LMX) Theory of Leadership over 25 Years: Applying a Multi-Level Multi-Domain Approach," *Leadership Quarterly 6* (1995): 219–247.

4. B. H. Mueller and J. Lee, "Leader-Member Exchange and Organizational Communication Satisfaction in Multiple Contexts," *Journal of Business Communication 39* (April 2002): 220–245.

5. R. M. Dienesch and R. C. Liden. "Leader-Member Exchange Model of Leadership: A Critique and Further Development," *Academy of Management Review 11*: 618–634.

6. B. Erdogan, M. L. Kraimer, and R. C. Liden, "Work Value Congruence and Intrinsic Career Success: The Compensatory Roles of Leader-Member Exchange and Perceived Organizational Support," *Personnel Psychology 57* (Summer 2004): 305–333.

7. R. Nowak, "A License to Lead: Leadership Skills That Make a Difference," *Journal of Banking and Financial Services 118* (April–May 2004): 40–42.

8. S. M. Murphy, S. J. Wayne, R. C. Liden, and B. Erdogan. "Understanding Social Loafing: The Role of Justice Perceptions and Exchange Relationships," *Human Relations 56*: 61–84.

9. H. Oh, M.-H. Chung, and G. Labianca, "Group Social Capital and Group Effectiveness: The Role of Informal Socializing Ties," *Academy of Management Review 47* (2004): 860–875.

10. C. Hardy, T. B. Lawrence, and D. Grant, "Discourse and Collaboration: The Role of Conversations and Collective Identity," *Academy of Management Review 30* (2005): 58–77.

11. D. J. Brass, J. Galaskiewicz, H. R. Greve, and W. Tsai, "Taking Stock of Networks and Organizations: A Multilevel Perspective, *Academy of Management Review 47* (2004): 795–817.

12. See note 9.

13. See note 4.

14. K. S. Campbell, C. D. White, and D. E. Johnson, "Leader-Member Relations as a Function of Rapport Management," *Journal of Business Communication 40* (July 2003): 170–195.

15. See note 11.

16. J. Gimeno, "Competition within and between Networks: The Contingent Effect of Competitive Embeddedness on Alliance Formation," *Academy of Management Review 47* (2004): 820–842.

17. See note 11.

18. N. A. Granitz and J. C. Ward, "Actual and Perceived Sharing of Ethical Reasoning and Moral Intent among In-Group and Out-Group Members," *Journal of Business Ethics 33*(4) (2001): 299–322.

19. A. C. Inkpen and E. W. K. Tsang, "Social Capital, Networks, and Knowledge Transfer," *Academy of Management Review 30* (2005): 146–165.

20. M. A. Gagnon and J. H. Michael, "Outcomes of Perceived Supervisor Support for Wood Production Employees," *Forest Products Journal 54* (December 2004): 172–178.

21. S. E. Murphy and R. E. Riggio. *The Future of Leadership Development*, (Mahwah, NJ: Lawrence Erlbaum Associates, 2003).

22. J. Felfe and B. Schyns, "Is Similarity in Leadership Related to Organizational Outcomes? The Case of Transformational Leadership," *Journal of Leadership & Organizational Studies 10* (Spring 2004): 92–103.

23. See note 20.

24. See note 4.

25. See note 20.

26. See note 4.

27. See note 6.

28. See note 6.

29. See note 4.

30. See note 14.

31. See note 9.

32. See note 19.

33. See note 6.

34. W. A. Hochwarter, C. Kiewitz, M. J. Gundlach, and J. Stoner, "The Impact of Vocational and Social Efficacy on Job Performance and Career Satisfaction," *Journal of Leadership & Organizational Studies 10* (Winter 2004): 27–41.

35. See note 4.

36. See note 14.

37. See note 3.

38. R. J. Deluga and T. J. Perry, "The Role of Subordinate Performance and Ingratiation in Leader-Member Exchanges," *Group and Organization Management 19* (1994): 67–86; R. C. Liden, S. J. Wayne, and D. Stilwell, "A Longitudinal Study on the Early Development of Leader-Member Exchanges," *Journal of Applied Psychology 78* (1993): 662–674; A. S. Philips and A. G. Bedeian, "Leader-Follower Exchange Quality: The Role of Personal and Interpersonal Attributes," *Academy of Management Journal 37* (1994): 990–1001; and R. A. Scandura and C. A. Schriesheim, "Leader-Member Exchange and Supervisor Career Mentoring as Complementary Constructs in Leadership Research," *Academy of Management Journal 37* (1995): 1588–1602.

39. D. J. Campbell, "The Proactive Employee: Managing Workplace Initiative," *Academy of Management Executive 14*(3) (2000): 52–66.

40. See note 1.

41. R. K. House and R. N. Aditya, "The Social Scientific Study of Leadership: Quo Vadis?" *Journal of Management 23* (May–June 1997): 409–474; and V. Singh and S. Vinnicombe, "Impression Management, Commitment and Gender: Managing Others' Good Opinions," *European Management Journal 19*(2) (April 2001): 183–194.

42. Z. X. Chen, A. S. Tsui, and J. Farh, "Loyalty to Supervisor vs. Organizational Commitment: Relationships to Employee Performance in China," *Journal of Occupational and Organizational Psychology 75*(18) (September 2002): 339.

43. See note 6.

44. J. M. Howell and B. Shamir, "The Role of Followers in the Charismatic Leadership Process: Relationships and Their Consequences," *Academy of Management Review 30* (2005): 96–112.

45. R. G. Lord and D. J. Brown, "Leadership Processes and Follower Self-Identity," *Personnel Psychology 57* (Summer 2004): 517–521.

46. P. B. Blackshear, "The Followership Continuum: A Model for Fine Tuning the Workforce," *Public Manager 32* (Summer 2003): 25–30.

47. M. Montesino, "Leadership/Followership Similarities between People in a Developed and a Developing Country: The Case of Dominicans in NYC and

Dominicans on the Island," *Journal of Leadership & Organizational Studies 10* (Summer 2003): 82–93.

48. See note 46.

49. R. E. Kelley, "In Praise of Followers," *Harvard Business Review*, 142–148.

50. See note 49.

51. T. Brown, "Courageous Followers Can Help You Lead," *Management Review 85* (October 1996): 60–61; and I. Chaleff, *The Courageous Follower: Standing Up To and for Our Leaders* (San Francisco: Berret-Koehler Publishers, 1995).

52. See note 39.

53. See note 39.

54. A. J. DeLellis. "Clarifying the Concept of Respect: Implications for Leadership." *Journal of Leadership Studies 7* (Spring 2000): 2–37.

55. D. J. Campbell. "The Proactive Employee: Managing Workplace Initiative. *Academy of Management Executive 14* (August 2000): 3–55.

56. See note 7.

57. See note 14.

58. B. Gunn, "Letting Go to Get Ahead," *Strategic Finance 2* (February 2004): 8.

59. P. M. Buhler, "Managing in the New Millennium: The Top Ten Managerial Mistakes," *Supervision 65* (August 2004): 15–18.

60. D. Orme, "A Corporate Cultivator's Guide to Growing Leaders," *New Zealand Management 51* (September 2004): 41–44.

61. J. Lawton, "Grey Areas," *Commerical Motor* (August 4, 2004): 1.

62. See note 58.

63. A. P. Grimshaw, "Time Management for Busy Managers," *Asia Africa Intelligence Wire* (March 16, 2004).

64. K. Niratpattanasai, "The Art of Time Management by Effective Delegation," *Asia Africa Intelligence Wire* (December 20, 2004).

65. See note 59.

66. M. Ogwo, "Delegation: An Abused Management Tool," *Fire 97* (June 2004): 24–27.

67. T. A. Sykes, "Get Time on Your Side: Accomplish More Using Less Energy," *Black Enterprise 34* (June 2004): 312–313.

68. F. Dalton, "Improving Delegation: When 'Just Do It' Just Won't Do It," *Contract Management 44* (November 2004): 4–7.

Chapter 8

1. T. Doolen, M. E. Hacker, and E. M. Van Aken, "The Impact of Organizational Context on Work Team Effectiveness: A Study of Production Teams," *IEEE Transactions on Engineering Management 50* (August 2003): 285–297.

2. J. Gordon, "Work Teams: How Far Have They Come?" *Training 29* (1992): 59–65.

3. E. E. Lawler, III, S. A. Mohrman, and G. E. Ledford, Jr., *Creating High Performance Organizations: Practices and Results of Employee Involvement and Total Quality Management in Fortune 1000 Companies* (San Francisco, CA: Jossey-Bass Publishers, 1995).

4. T. L. Baker and T. G. Hunt, "An Exploratory Investigation Into the Effects of Team Composition on Moral Orientation," *Journal of Managerial Issues 15* (Spring 2003): 106–120.

5. R. J. Trent, "Becoming an Effective Teaming Organization," *Business Horizons 47* (March–April 2004): 33–41.

6. H. Oh, M.-H. Chung, and G. Labianca, "Group Social Capital and Group Effectiveness: The Role of Informal Socializing Ties," *Academy of Management Review 47* (2004): 860–875.

7. K. L. Towry, "Control in a Teamwork Environment—The Impact of Social Ties on the Effectiveness of Mutual Monitoring Contracts," *Accounting Review 78* (2003): 1069–1096.

8. See note 6.

9. T. C. Brown, "The Effect of Verbal Self-Guidance Training on Collective Efficacy and Team Performance," *Personnel Psychology 56* (Winter 2003): 935–965.

10. See note 5.

11. D. Ancona, H. Bresman, K. Kaeufer, "The Comparative Advantage of X-Teams," *MIT Sloan Management Review 43* (Spring 2002): 33–40.

12. See note 5.

13. See note 9.

14. See note 5.

15. R. Batt, "Who Benefits from Teams? Comparing Workers, Supervisors, and Managers," *Industrial Relations 43* (January 2004): 183–212.

16. D. Knights and D. McCabe, "Governing through Teamwork: Reconstituting Subjectivity in a Call Centre," *Journal of Management Studies 40* (November 2003): 1587–1620.

17. See note 7.

18. N. J. Allen, T. D. Hecht, "The 'Romance of Teams': Toward an Understanding of Its Psychological Underpinnings and Implications," *Journal of Occupational and Organizational Psychology 77* (December 2004): 439–462.

19. JetBlue Web site, http://www.jetblue.com, accessed May 17, 2004.

20. D. E. Warren, "Constructive and Destructive Deviance in Organizations," *Academy of Management Review 28*(4) (2003): 622–632.

21. J. R. Hackman, *Leading Teams: Setting the Stage for Great Performances* (Boston, MA: Harvard Business School Press, 2002).

22. See note 21.

23. P. M. Lencioni, "The Five Dysfunctions of a Team," *HR Magazine 49* (July 2004): S41.

24. G. B. Brumback, review of *Teams that Lead: A Matter of Market Strategy, Leadership Skills, and Executive Strength,*" by T. J. B. Kline, *Personnel Psychology 57* (Summer 2004): 544–549.

25. S. J. Zaccaro and R. Klimoski, "The Interface of Leadership and Team Processes," *Group & Organization Management 27* (March 2002): 4–14.

26. B. Edwards, "Fostering Team Spirit at Work." *Asia Africa Intelligence Wire* (October 5, 2004).

27. J. Z. King, "There's No Substitute for Effective Leadership Training Skills," *Hotel & Motel Management 219* (November 15, 2004): 20–28.

28. N. Gorla and Y. W. Lam, "Who Should Work with Whom? Building Effective Software Project Teams," *Communications of the ACM 47* (August 2004): 79–83.

29. J. A. Raelin, "Growing Group Leadership Skills: Managers Will Get the Most from Workers When They Teach Them to Work in Self-Directed Teams," *Security Management 48* (June 2004): 34–38.

30. See note 26.

31. K. Hawkins and A. Tolzin, "Examining the Team/Leader Interface: Baseball Teams as Exemplars of Postmodern Organizations," *Group & Organization Management* 27(16) (March 2002): 97–113.

32. A. P. Kakabadse, "A Process Perspective on Leadership and Team Development," *Journal of Management Development* 23(1) (January 2004): 7–106.

33. K. T. Jones, "I'm In Charge Now? Understanding Your Role as a Leader Will Benefit Both You and Your Employees," *Journal of Property Management* 69 (July–August 2004): 72.

34. S. Sarin and C. McDermott, "The Effect of Team-Leader Characteristics on Learning, Knowledge Applications, and Performance of Cross-Functional New Product Development Teams," *Decision Sciences* 34 (Fall 2003): 707–740.

35. See note 24.

36. T. Butler and J. Waldroop, "Understanding 'People' People," *Harvard Business Review* 82 (2004): 78–87.

37. L. Hughes, "Do's and Don'ts of Effective Team Leadership," *Women in Business* 56 (January–February 2004): 10.

38. N. Sivasubramaniam, W. D. Murray, B. J. Avolio, and D. I. Jung, "A Longitudinal Model of the Effects of Team Leadership and Group Potency on Group Performance," *Group & Organization Management* 27 (March 2002): 66–97.

39. B. V. Knippenberg and D. V. Knippenberg, "Leader Self-Sacrifice and Leadership Effectiveness: The Moderating Role of Leader Self-Confidence," *Journal of Applied Psychology* 90 (January 2005): 25–38.

40. D. D. Cremer and D. V. Knippenberg, "Leader Self-Sacrifice and Leadership Effectiveness: The Moderating Role of Leader Self-Confidence," *Organizational Behavior & Human Decision Processes* 95 (November 2004): 140–156.

41. See note 27.

42. See note 25.

43. C. L. Pearce, C. A. Gallagher, and M. D. Ensley, "Confidence at the Group Level of Analysis: A Longitudinal Investigation of the Relationship between Potency and Team Effectiveness," *Journal of Occupational and*

Organizational Psychology 75 (March 2002): 115–120.

44. M. D. Ensley, A. W. Pearson, and A. C. Amason, "Understanding the Dynamics of New Venture Top Management Teams: Cohesion, Conflict, and New Venture Performance," *Journal of Business Venturing* 17 (July 2002): 365–387.

45. See note 25.

46. See note 28.

47. S. J. Chen and L. Lin, "Modeling Team Member Characteristics for the Formation of a Multifunctional Team in Concurrent Engineering," *IEEE Transactions on Engineering Management* 51 (May 2004): 111–125.

48. See note 36.

49. B. L. Kirkman, P. E. Tesluk, and B. Rosen, "The Impact of Demographic Heterogeneity and Team Leader–Team Member Demographic Fit on Team Empowerment and Effectiveness," *Group & Organization Management* 29 (June 2004): 334–368.

50. R. Sethi, D. C. Smith, and C. W. Park, "How to Kill a Team's Creativity," *Harvard Business Review* 80 (2002): 16–18.

51. C. Rowe, "The Effect of Accounting Report Structure and Team Structure on Performance in Cross-Functional Teams," *Accounting Review* 79 (2004): 1153–1181.

52. See note 25.

53. G. Hirst and L. Mann, "A Model of R&D Leadership and Team Communication: The Relationship with Project Performance," *R&D Management* 34 (March 2004): 147–161.

54. See note 7.

55. See note 24.

56. M. L. Kraimer and S. J. Wayne, "An Examination of Perceived Organizational Support as a Multidimensional Construct in the Context of an Expatriate Assignment," *Journal of Management* 30 (March–April 2004): 209–238.

57. See note 1.

58. See note 53.

59. B. Erdogan, M. L. Kraimer, and R. C. Liden, "Work Value Congruence and Intrinsic Career Success: The Compensatory Roles of Leader-Member Exchange and Perceived Organizational Support,"

Personnel Psychology 57 (Summer 2004): 305–333.

60. S. Taggar, "Individual Creativity and Group Ability to Utilize Individual Creative Resources: A Multi-Level Model," *Academy of Management Journal* 45(2) (2002): 315–330; and R. W. Woodman, J. E. Sawyer, and R. W. Griffin, "Toward a Theory of Organizational Creativity," *Academy of Management Review* (April 1993): 293.

61. R. L. Firestien and K. F. Kumiega, "Using a Formula for Creativity to Yield Organizational Quality Improvement," *National Productivity Review* 13 (Autumn 1994): 569–585.

62. M. J. Eppler and O. Sukowski, "Managing Team Knowledge: Core Processes, Tools and Enabling Factors," *European Management Journal* 18(3) (June 2000): 334–341.

63. M. J. Eppler and O. Sukowski, "Managing Team Knowledge: Core Processes, Tools and Enabling Factors," *European Management Journal* 18(3) (June 2000): 334–341; and S. Caudron, "Strategies for Managing Creative Workers," *Personnel Journal* (December 1994): 104–113.

64. S. G. Scott and W. O. Einstein, "Strategic Performance Appraisal in Team-Based Organizations: One Size Does Not Fit All," *Academy of Management Executive* 15(2) (2001): 107–116.

65. W. A. Randolph and M. Sashkin, "Can Organizational Empowerment Work In Multinational Settings?" *Academy of Management Executive* 16(1) (2002): 102–115.

66. A. G. Robinson and S. Stern, *Corporate Creativity: How Innovation and Improvements Actually Happen* (San Francisco: Berrett Koehler Publishers Inc., 1998), 14.

67. G. Dutton, "Enhancing Creativity," *Management Review* (November 1996): 44–46.

68. T. M. Amabile, "How to Kill Creativity." *Harvard Business Review* 76(5) (September/October 1998): 76–87.

69. R. R. Patrashkova, S. A. McComb, S. G. Green, and W. D. Compton, "Examining a Curvilinear Relationship between Communication Frequency and Team Performance in Cross-Functional Project Teams," *IEE Transactions on*

Engineering Management 50 (August 2003): 262–270.

70. J. S. Bunderson, "Team Member Functional Background and Involvement in Management Teams: Direct Effects and the Moderating Role of Power Centralization," *Academy pf Management Journal 46* (August 2003): 458–473.

71. See note 70.

72. R. R. Patrashkova and S. A McComb, "Exploring Why More Communication Is Not Better: Insights from a Computational Model of Cross-Functional Teams," *Journal of Engineering and Technology Management 21* (March–June 2004): 84–116.

73. "Triple Team," *Design News 58* (June 2003): 64.

74. See note 69.

75. See note 47.

76. S. B. Knouse, review of *Human Resource Management in Virtual Organizations,* R. L. Heneman, and D. B. Greenberger (eds.), *Personnel Psychology 57* (Summer 2004): 523–527.

77. B. S. Bell and S. W. J. Kozlowski, "A Typology of Virtual Teams: Implications for Effective Leadership," *Group & Organization Management 27* (March 2002): 14–50.

78. D. J. Pauleen, "Leadership in a Global Virtual Team: An Action Learning Approach," *Leadership & Organization Development Journal 24* (March 2003): 153–163.

79. M. Hansen, review of *Virtual Teams That Work: Creating Conditions for Virtual Team Effectiveness,* by C. B. Gibson and S. G. Cohen, *Personnel Psychology 57* (Spring 2004): 243–247.

80. S. A. Furst, M. Reeves, B. Rosen, and R. S. Blackburn, "Managing the Life Cycle of Virtual Teams," *The Academy of Management Executive 18* (May 2004): 6–21.

81. W. Bock, "Some Rules for Virtual Teams," *Journal for Quality and Participation 26* (Fall 2003): 43.

82. J. Tovey, "The Communication Characteristics of Virtual Teams," *Technical Communication 49* (February 2002): 123.

83. See note 76.

84. W. E. Cascio and S. Shurygailo, "E-Leadership and Virtual Teams,"

Organizational Dynamics 31 (Spring 2003): 362–377.

85. I. Zigurs, "Leadership in Virtual Teams: Oxymoron or Opportunity?" *Organizational Dynamics 31* (Spring 2003): 339–352.

86. S. Wilson, "Forming Virtual Teams," *Quality Progress 36* (June 2003): 36–42.

87. N. W. Coppola, S. R. Hiltz, and N. G. Rotter, "Building Trust in Virtual Teams," *IEEE Transactions on Professional Communication 47* (June 2004): 95–105.

88. R. K. Hart and P. L. McLeod, "Rethinking Team Building in Geographically Dispersed Teams: One Message at a Time," *Organizational Dynamics 31* (Spring 2003): 352–362.

89. G. Piccoli and B. Ives, "Trust and the Unintended Effects of Behavior Control in Virtual Teams," *MIS Quarterly 27* (September 2003): 365–396.

90. See note 82.

91. M. Alavi and A. Tiwana, "Knowledge Integration in Virtual Teams: The Potential Role of KMS," *Journal of the American Society for Information Science and Technology 53* (October 2002): 1029–1037.

92. D. M. DeRosa, D. A. Hantula, J. D'Arcy, and N. Kock, "Trust and Leadership in Virtual Teamwork: A Media Naturalness Perspective," *Human Resource Management 43* (Summer–Fall 2004).

93. Y. Y. Shin, "A Person-Environment Fit Model for Virtual Organizations," *Journal of Management 30* (September–October 2004): 725–744.

94. S. L. Jarvenpaa, T. R Shaw, and D. S. Staples, "Toward Contextualized Theories of Trust: The Role of Trust in Global Virtual Teams," *Information Systems Research 15* (September 2004): 250–268.

95. See note 86.

96. D. Davis, "The Tao of Leadership in Virtual Teams," *Organizational Dynamics 33* (February 2004): 47–63.

97. C. Saunders, C. V. Slyke, and D. Vogel, "My Time or Yours? Managing Time Visions In Global Virtual Teams," *The Academy of Management Executive 18* (February 2004): 19–31.

98. V. M. Sharpe, "Global Virtual Teams," *Technical Communication 49* (May 2002): 26.

99. C. U. Grosse, "Managing Communication within Virtual Intercultural Teams," *Business Communication Quarterly 65* (December 2002): 22–39.

100. See note 34.

101. See note 67.

102. C. O. Longenecker, and M. Neubert, "Barriers and Gateways to Management Cooperation and Teamwork," *Business Horizons 43*(5) (September/October 2000): 37–44; and "What Makes a Team?" *HR Focus 79*(4) (April 2002): s3–s4.

103. T. L. Legare, "How Hewlett-Packard Used Cross-Cross-Functional Teams to Deliver Healthcare Industry Solutions," *Journal of Organizational Excellence 20*(4) (Autumn 2001): 29–38.

104. J. Tata and S. Prasad, "Team Self-Management, Organizational Structure, and Judgments of Team Effectiveness," *Journal of Managerial Issues 16* (Summer 2004): 248–268.

105. A. D. Jong and J. C. Ruyter, "Adaptive versus Proactive Behavior in Service Recovery: The Role of Self-Managing Teams," *Decision Sciences 35* (Summer 2004): 457–492.

106. See note 105.

107. R. P. DeShon, S. W. J. Kozlowski, A. M. Schmidt, K. R. Milner, and D. Wiechmann, "A Multiple-Goal, Multilevel Model of Feedback Effects on the Regulation of Individual and Team Performance," *Journal of Applied Psychology 89* (December 2004): 1035–1057.

108. E. McFadzean, "Developing and Supporting Creative Problem-Solving Teams: Part 1, A Conceptual Model," *Management Decision 40* (May–June 2002): 463–475.

109. See note 4.

110. M. J. Waller, J. M. Conte, C. B. Gibson, and M. A. Carpenter, "The Effects of Individual Perceptions of Deadlines on Team Performance," *Academy of Management Review 26*(4) (2001): 586–600.

111. H. Risher, "Tapping Unused Employee Capabilities," *Public Manager 32*(5) (Summer 2003): 34.

112. K. J. Valadares, "The Practicality of Employee Empowerment: Supporting a Psychologically Safe Culture," *The Health Care Manager 23* (July–September 2004): 220–225.

113. See note 112.

114. See note 111.

115. J. E. Ruin, "Conducting Effective Meetings," *Asia Africa Intelligence Wire* (March 27, 2004).

116. See note 115.

117. See note 108.

118. See note 115.

119. R. Donkin, "Lessons from History: Life to Become a Work of Art," *Financial Times* (September 27, 2004), 2.

120. See note 106.

121. W. H. Weiss, "Team Management," *Supervision* 65(3) (November 2004): 19.

122. E. L. Trist, G. Higgins, H. Murray, and A. Pollock, *Organizational Choice* (London: Tavistock, 1963).

123. See note 76.

124. See note 121.

125. S. E. Black, L. M. Lynch, and A. Krivelyova, "How Workers Fare When Employers Innovate," *Industrial Relations* 43 (January 2004): 44–66.

126. S. B. Yang and M. E. Guy, "Self-Managed Work Teams: Who Uses Them? What Makes Them Successful?" *Public Performance and Management Review* 27 (2004): 60–80.

127. See note 104.

128. V. U. Druskat and J. V. Wheeler, "Managing from the Boundary: The Effective Leadership of Self-Managing Work Teams," *Academy of Management Journal* 46 (August 2003): 435–456.

129. See note 125.

130. See note 126.

131. L. Karamally, "Overlooked Keys to Productivity: Automation Gets Too Much Credit," *Workforce Management* 83 (July 1, 2004): 23.

132. L. I. Glassop, "The Organizational Benefits of Teams," *Human Relations* 55 (February 2002): 225–250.

133. See note 15.

134. See note 105.

135. S. C. Kundu and J. A. Vora, "Creating a Talented Workforce for Delivering Service Quality," *Human Resource Planning* 27 (June 2004): 40–52.

136. D. Oliver and J. Roos, "Dealing with the Unexpected: Critical Incidents in the LEGO Mindstorms Team," *Human Relations* 56 (September 2003): 1057–1083.

137. L. D. Fredendall and C. R. Emery, "Productivity Increases Due to the Use of Teams in Service Garages," *Journal of Managerial Issues* 15 (Summer 2003): 221–255.

138. S. Kalliola, "Self-Designed Teams in Improving Public Sector Performance and Quality of Working Life," *Public Performance and Management Review* 27 (2003): 110–123.

139. See note 129.

140. M. Moravec, O. J. Johannessen, and T. A. Hjelmas, "The Well-Managed SMT," *Management Review* 87 (June 1998): 56–58.

141. See note 104.

142. A. Erez, J. A. Lepine, and H. Elms, "Effects of Rotated Leadership and Peer Evaluation on the Functioning and Effectiveness of Self-Managed Teams: A Quasi-Experiment," *Personnel Psychology* 55 (Winter 2002): 929–949.

143. See note 104.

144. See note 29.

145. See note 140.

146. See note 104.

147. See note 104.

148. See note 104.

149. See note 47.

150. See note 47.

151. See note 29.

152. See note 104.

153. See note 140.

154. See note 140.

155. See note 128.

156. See note 29.

157. See note 104.

158. See note 128.

159. See note 128.

160. See note 128.

161. See note 128.

162. See note 128.

163. See note 128.

164. See note 15.

Chapter 9

1. C. Burton, "What Does Work-Life Balance Mean Anyway?" *Journal for Quality and Participation* 27(3) (Fall 2004): 12–14.

2. T. A. Judge and R. Ilies, "Is Positiveness in Organizations Always Desirable?" *Academy of Management Executive* 18(4) (2004): 151–156.

3. J. J. Sosik, "The Role of Personal Meaning in Charismatic Leadership," *The Journal of Leadership Studies* 7(2) (Spring 2000): 60–75.

4. See note 3.

5. J. A. Conger, *The Charismatic Leader: Behind the Mystique of Exceptional Leadership* (San Francisco, CA: Jossey-Bass, 1989).

6. T. E. Dow, Jr., "The Theory of Charisma," *Sociological Quarterly* 10 (1969): 306–318.

7. J. Raelin, "The Myth of Charismatic Leaders: It Can Be Foolish, Futile, and Even Dangerous to Follow Leaders Just Because They're Charismatic," *Training & Development* 57(3) (March 2003): 46–52.

8. K. S. Jaussi and S. D. Dionne, "Unconventional Leader Behavior, Subordinate Satisfaction, Effort and Perception of Leader Effectiveness," *Journal of Leadership & Organizational Studies* 10(3) (Winter 2004): 15–27

9. See note 7.

10. See note 7.

11. M. Javidan and D. E. Carl, "East Meets West: A Cross-Cultural Comparison of Charismatic Leadership Among Canadian and Iranian Executives," *Journal of Management Studies* 41(4) (June 2004): 665.

12. J. M. Howell and B. Shamir, "The Role of Followers in the Charismatic Leadership Process: Relationships and Their Consequences," *Academy of Management Review* 30(1) (January 2005): 96–112.

13. See note 2.

14. F. J. Flynn and B. M. Staw, "Lend Me Your Wallets: The Effect of Charismatic Leadership on External Support for an Organization," *Strategic Management Journal* 25(4) (April 2004): 309–330.

15. A. J. Towler, "Effects of Charismatic Influence Training on Attitudes, Behavior, and Performance," *Personnel Psychology* 56(2) (Summer 2003): 363–382.

16. Y. Sankar, "Character Not Charisma is the Critical Measure of Leadership Excellence," *Journal of Leadership & Organizational Studies* 9(4) (Spring 2003): 45–56.

17. See note 15.

18. M. Javidan and D. A. Waldman, "Exploring Charismatic Leadership in the Public Sector: Measurement and Consequences," *Public Administration Review* 63(2) (March–April 2003): 229–243.

19. M. Frese, S. Biemel, and S. Schoenborn, "Action Training for Charismatic Leadership: Two Evaluations of Studies of a Commercial Training Module on Inspirational Communication of a Vision," *Personnel Psychology* 56(3) (Fall 2003): 671–699.

20. G. P. Hollenbeck and D. T. Hall, "Self-Confidence and Leader Performance," *Organizational Dynamics* 33(3) (August 2004): 254–270.

21. W. Gardner and J. J. Schermerhorn, Jr., "Unleashing Individual Potential: Performance Gains through Positive Organizational Behavior and Authentic Leadership," *Organizational Dynamics* 33(3) (August 2004): 270–282.

22. See note 16.

23. D. De Cremer and D. V. Knippenberg, "How Do Leaders Promote Cooperation? The Effects of Charisma and Procedural Fairness," *Journal of Applied Psychology* 87(5) (October 2002): 858–867.

24. "Oprah Winfrey Biography," *Shwing.com*, February 9, 2004, **http://www.shwing.com/artman/publish/printer_387.shtml.**

25. See note 19.

26. See note 7.

27. See note 16.

28. See note 7.

29. J. A. Fernandez, "The Gentleman's Code of Confucius: Leadership by Values," *Organizational Dynamics* 33(1) (February 2004): 21–32.

30. See note 12.

31. See note 12.

32. B. McKay and S. Vranica, "Government Ads Urge Americans to Shed Pounds," *The Wall Street Journal*, March 10, 2004, B1.

33. B. McKay, "Study Tries to Link Obesity in Children with Food Marketing," *The Wall Street Journal*, January 27, 2005, A1.

34. S. Ellison, "Divided, Companies Fight for Right to Plug Kids' Food," *The Wall Street Journal*, January 26, 2005, A1.

35. See note 32.

36. See note 12.

37. B. A. Tucker and R. Russell, "The Influence of the Transformational Leader," *Journal of Leadership & Organizational Studies* 10(4) (Spring 2004): 103–112.

38. N. Ozaralli, "Effects of Transformational Leadership on Empowerment and Team Effectiveness," *Leadership and Organizational Development Journal* 24(5–6) (May 2003): 335–345.

39. J. H. Humphreys and W. O. Einstein, "Nothing New Under the Sun: Transformational Leadership from a Historical Perspective," *Management Decision* 41(1–2) (January–February 2003): 85–95.

40. See note 37.

41. F. O. Walumbwa, P. Wang, J. J. Lawler, and K. Shi, "The Role of Collective Efficacy in the Relations between Transformational Leadership and Work Outcomes," *Journal of Occupational & Organizational Psychology* 77(4) (December 2004): 515–531.

42. M. Langbert and H. H. Friedman, "Perspectives on Transformational Leadership in the Sanhedrin of Ancient Judaism," *Management Decision* 41(1–2) (January–February 2003): 199–208.

43. See note 42.

44. V. R. Krishnan, "Power and Moral Leadership: Role of Self-Other Agreement," *Leadership and Organizational Development Journal* 24(5–6) (May 2003): 345–352.

45. See note 39.

46. J. E. Bono and T. A. Judge, "Personality and Transformational and Transactional Leadership: A Meta-Analysis," *Journal of Applied Psychology* 89(5) (October 2004): 901–911.

47. See note 39.

48. J. N. Hood, "The Relationship of Leadership Style and CEO Values to Ethical Practices in Organizations," *Journal of Business Ethics* 43(4) (April 2003): 263–274.

49. L. Odom and M. Green, "Law and the Ethics of Transformational Leadership," *Leadership & Organization Development Journal* (January–February 2003): 62–70.

50. See note 37.

51. See note 38.

52. S. L. Shivers-Blackwell, "Using Role Theory to Examine Determinants of Transformational and Transactional Leader Behavior," *Journal of Leadership & Organizational Studies* 10(3) (Winter 2004): 41–51.

53. See note 46.

54. T. Judge and R. Piccolo, "Transformational and Transactional Leadership: A Meta-Analytic Test of Their Relative Validity," *Journal of Applied Psychology* v89 i5 (October 2004): 755 (14).

55. M. Weber, *The Theory of Social and Economic Organizations* (T. Parsons, trans.) (New York: Free Press, 1947). (Original work published in 1924.)

56. J. M. Burns, *Leadership* (New York: Harper & Row, 1978).

57. B. M. Bass, B. J. Avolio, D. I. Jung, and Y. Berson, "Predicting Unit Performance by Assessing Transformational and Transactional Leadership," *Journal of Applied Psychology* 88(2) (April 2003): 207–219.

58. A. Zaleznik, "Managers and Leaders: Are They Different?" in W. W. Rosenbach & R. L. Taylor (eds.), *Contemporary Issues in Leadership* (Oxford: Westview Press, 1993), 36–56.

59. See note 46.

60. See note 46.

61. S. E. Bryant, "The Role of Transformational and Transactional Leadership in Creating, Sharing, and Exploiting Organizational Knowledge," *Journal of Leadership & Organizational Studies* 9(4) (Spring 2003): 23–36.

62. A. H. Eagly, M. C. Johannesen-Schmidt, and M. L. V. Engen. "Transformational, Transactional, and Laissez-Faire Leadership Styles: A Meta-Analysis Comparing Women and Men,"

Psychological Bulletin 129(4) (July 2003): 569–582.

63. See note 52.

64. See note 46.

65. See note 57.

66. See note 54.

67. N. Wingfield and S. McBride, "Green Light for Grokster," *The Wall Street Journal*, August 20, 2004, B1.

68. B. N. Smith. R. V. Montagno, and T. N. Kuzmenko, "Transformational and Servant Leadership: Content and Contextual Comparisons," *Journal of Leadership & Organizational Studies* 10(4) (Spring 2004): 80–92.

59. See note 68.

70. T. A. Williams, "Lead By Love," *Quality* 43(1) (January 2004): 8.

71. R. F. Russell and A. G. Stone, "A Review of Servant Leadership Attributes: Developing a Practical Model," *Leadership & Organization Development Journal* (March–April 2002): 145–158.

72. C. Caldwell, S. J. Bischoff, and R. Karri, "The Four Umpires: A Paradigm for Ethical Leadership," *Journal of Business Ethics* (March 2002): 153–164.

73. T. Keogh and W. Martin, "Managing Unmanageable Physicians: Leadership, Stewardship, and Disruptive Behavior," *Physician Executive* 30(5) (September–October 2004): 18–23.

74. G. F. Cavanagh and M. R. Bandsuch, "Virtue as a Benchmark for Spirituality in Business," *Journal of Business Ethics* (June 2, 2002): 109–118.

75. M. G. Ehrhart, "Leadership and Procedural Justice Climate as Antecedents of Unit-Level Organizational Citizenship Behavior," *Personnel Psychology* 57(1) (Spring 2004): 61–95.

76. R. Blunt, "Leadership in the Crucible: The Paradox of Character and Power," *Public Manager* 32(4) (Winter 2003): 35–40.

77. S. Sendjaya and J. C. Sarros, "Servant Leadership: Its Origin, Development, and Application in Organizations," *Journal of Leadership & Organizational Studies* 9(2) (2002), 57–64.

78. See note 71.

79. See note 68.

Chapter 10

1. J. B. Sorensen, "The Strength of Corporate Culture and the Reliability of Firm Performance," *Administrative Science Quarterly* 47 (March 2002): 70–91.

2. L. M. Chan, M. A. Shaffer, and E. Snape, "In Search of Sustained Competitive Advantage: The Impact of Organizational Culture, Competitive Strategy and Human Resource Management Practices on Firm Performance," *International Journal of Human Resource Management* 15 (February 2004) 17–36; G. Apfelthaler, H. J. Muller, and R. R. Rehder, "Corporate Global Culture as Competitive Advantage: Learning from Germany and Japan in Alabama and Austria," *Journal of World Business* 37(2) (Summer 2002): 108–118.

3. See note 2.

4. E. Beaudan and G. Smith, "Corporate Culture: Asset or Liability?" *Ivey Business Journal* 64(4) (March/April 2000): 29–33.

5. B. Gunn, "Illuminating Culture," *Strategic Finance Magazine* 18(10), (April 2000): 14–16; and R. Connors and T. Smith, "Benchmarking Cultural Transition," *Journal of Business Strategy* 21(3) (May/June 2000): 10–12.

6. V. Vaisnys, "Managing Culture for Strategic Success," *Strategy and Leadership* 28(6) (November/December 2000): 36–38.

7. F. R. David, *Strategic Management: Concept and Cases* (New Jersey: Pearson Prentice Hall, 2005): 118.

8. B. Dobni, "Creating a Strategy Implementation Environment," *Business Horizons* 46 (March–April 2003): 43–46.

9. See note 8.

10. L. Nash and H. Stevenson, "Success That Lasts," *Harvard Business Review* 82 (February 2004): 102–109.

11. E. H. Schein, *Organizational Culture and Leadership*, 2nd ed. (San Francisco, CA: Jossey-Bass, 1992).

12. See note 7.

13. See note 1.

14. M. A. Tannenbaum, "Organizational Values and Leadership," *Public Manager* 32 (Summer 2003): 19–22.

15. See note 1.

16. C. Rossiter, "Risk Culture—Up Close and Personal," *CA Magazine* 134(3) (April 2001): 45–46.

17. See note 1.

18. H. Bruch and S. Ghoshal, *A Bias for Action* (Boston: Harvard Business School Press, 2004): 413.

19. C. J. Fisher, "Like It or Not, Culture Matters—Linking Culture to Bottom Line Business Performance," *Employment Relations Today* 27(2) (Summer 2000): 43–52.

20. See note 14.

21. "How One Company Profits from Its 'Sweeter' Corporate Culture," *HR Focus* 79(8) (August 2002): 5–6.

22. S. Ramachander, "Can One Build a Strong Culture?" *Asia Africa Intelligence Wire,* (December 4, 2003).

23. J. R. Emshwiller and R. Smith, "Corporate Veil—Behind Enron's Fall, a Culture of Operating Outside Public View," *The Wall Street Journal*, December 5, 2001, A1, A10.

24. J. A. Cohan, "'I Didn't Know' and 'I Was Only Doing My Job': Has Corporate Governance Careened Out of Control? A Case Study of Enron's Information Myopia," *Journal of Business Ethics* 40(3) (October 2002): 275–299.

25. J. Schwartz, "As Enron Purged Its Ranks, Dissent Was Swept Away," *The New York Times*, February 4, 2002. C1–C2.

26. D. A. Ready, "Leading at the Enterprise Level," *MIT Sloan Management Review* 45 (Spring 2004): 3–90.

27. See note 18.

28. E. E. Lawler, III, *Treat People Right! How Organizations and Individuals Can Propel Each Other Into a Virtuous Spiral of Success* (San Francisco: John Wiley & Sons, 2003): 416–417.

29. D. B. Lund, "Organizational Culture and Job Satisfaction," *Journal of Business & Industrial Marketing* 18 (February–March 2003): 219–236.

30. See note 28.

31. R. L. Daft, "Theory Z: Opening the Corporate Door for Participative Management," *Academy of Management Executive* 18 (2004): 417–421.

32. B. Barney, "An Interview with William Ouchi," *Academy of Management Executive* 18 (2004): 417–421.

33. K. N. Shaw, "Changing the Goal-Setting Process at Microsoft," *Academy of Management Executive* 18 (2004): 139–142.

34. See note 7.

35. R. Bernstein, "How Franchise Systems Can Build and Maintain a Strong Leadership Culture," *Franchising World* 36 (November–December 2004): 51–61.

36. See note 26.

37. C. L. Valentino, "The Role of Middle Managers in the Transmission and Integration of Organizational Culture," *Journal of Healthcare Management* 49 (November–December 2004): 393–405.

38. B. Garrison, "Team Ruiz: New Products and a Strong Team Culture Help Frozen Mexican Foods Processor Ruiz Foods Raise Its Game and Excel in Competitive Markets," *Refrigerated & Frozen Foods* 15 (September 2004): 9–22.

39. C. Homburg and C. Pflesser, "A Multi-Layer Model of Market-Oriented Organizational Culture: Measurement Issues and Performance Outcomes," *Journal of Marketing Research* 37(4) (November 2000): 449–462.

40. D. W. Young, "The Six Levers for Managing Organizational Culture," *Business Horizons* 43(5) (September/October 2000): 19–28.

41. See note 11.

42. See note 26.

43. See note 26.

44. K. M. Hudson, "Transforming a Conservative Company—One Laugh at a Time," *Harvard Business Review* 79(7) (July/August 2001): 45–53.

45. A. Carmeli, "The Relationship between Organizational Culture and Withdrawal Intentions and Behavior," *International Journal of Manpower* 26 (February 2005): 177–195.

46. See note 8; see note 2, Chan et al.

47. S. Kerr, "Editor's Introduction: Establishing Organizational Goals and Rewards," *Academy of Management Executive* 18 (2004): 122–123.

48. See note 26.

49. C. L. Bernick, "When Your Culture Needs a Makeover," *Harvard Business Review* 79(6) (June 2001): 53–61.

50. J. R. Detert, R. G. Schroeder, and J. J. Mauriel, "A Framework for Linking Culture and Improvement Initiatives in Organizations," *Academy of Management Review* 25(4) (October 2000): 850–863.

51. See note 2, Apfelthaler, et al.

52. R. Deshpande and J. U. Farley, "Organizational Culture, Market Orientation, Innovativeness and Firm Performance: An International Research Odyssey," *International Journal of Research in Marketing* 21 (March 2004) 20–22; and see note 29.

53. J. Kotter and J. Heskett, *Corporate Culture and Performance* (New York: The Free Press, 1992).

54. C. Hymowitz, "How Leader at 3M Got His Employees to Back Big Change," *The Wall Street Journal*, April 23, 2002: B1.

55. L. Soupata, "Managing Culture for Competitive Advantage at United Parcel Service," *Journal of Organizational Excellence* 20(3) (Summer 2001): 19–26.

56. C. Waxer, "Six Sigma Costs and Savings: The Financial Benefits of Implementing Six Sigma at Your Company Can Be Significant," July 29, 2002, **http://www.i6sigma.com/library/content/c020729a.asp**.

57. D. Guilford, "Lutz Shakes Up Staid GM Culture," *Automotive News* 5958 (November 2001): 1, 39.

58. S. Lieberman, "Growth Culture: How to Keep Your Values As You Expand," *Restaurant Hospitality* 81 (i.e. 84)(10) (October 2000): 64.

59. See note 14.

60. See note 14.

61. T. Thomas, J. R. Schermerhorn, and J. W. Dienhart, "Strategic Leadership of Ethical Behavior in Business," *Academy of Management Executive* 18 (May 2004): 56–69.

62. S. Worden, "The Role of Integrity as a Mediator in Strategic Leadership: A Recipe for Reputational Capital," *Journal of Business Ethics* 46 (August 2003): 31–45.

63. R. R. Sims and J. Brinkmann, "Leaders as Moral Role Models: The Case of John Gutfreund at Salomon Brothers," *Journal of Business Ethics* 35 (February 15, 2002): 327–339.

64. See note 62.

65. S. Worden, "The Role of Religious and Nationalist Ethics in Strategic Leadership: The Case of JN Tata," *Journal of Business Ethics* 47 (October 2003): 147–165.

66. E. Schnebel and M. A. Bienert, "Implementing Ethics in Business Organizations," *Journal of Business Ethics* 53 (August 2004): 203–205.

67. G. F. Cavanagh, "Global Business Ethics: Regulation, Code, or Self-Restraint?" *Business Ethics Quarterly* 14(4) (October 2004): 625.

68. M. Messmer, "Does Your Company Have a Code of Ethics?" *Strategic Finance* 84(10) (April 2003): 13.

69. L. B. Chonko, R. R. Wotruba, and T. W. Loe, "Ethics Code Familiarity and Usefulness: Views on Idealist and Relativist Managers under Varying Conditions of Turbulence," *Journal of Personal Selling & Sales Management* 23(3) (Summer 2003): 275.

70. J. Dobson, "Why Ethics Codes Don't Work," *Financial Analysts Journal* 59(6) (November–December 2003): 29.

71. See note 68.

72. See note 63.

73. G. L. Porter, "Whistleblowers: A Rare Breed," *Strategic Finance* (August 2003).

74. N. Folbre, "Blowing the Whistle on Poverty Policy," *Review of Social Economy* 61(4) (December 2003): 479.

75. J. Summers and M. Nowicki, "Whistle-Blowing: Does Anyone Want to Hear?" *Healthcare Financial Management* 57(7) (July 2003): 82.

76. J. P. Near, M. T. Rehg, J. R. Van Scotter, and M. P. Miceli, "Does Type of Wrongdoing Affect the Whistle-Blowing Process?" *Business Ethics Quarterly* 14(2) (April 2004): 219.

77. W. Vandekerckhove and M. S. R. Commers, "Whistle Blowing and Rational Loyalty," *Journal of Business Ethics* 53 (1–2) (August 2004): 225.

78. "Workplace Whistleblowing Doubles," *Public Concern at Work* (October 14, 2003), **http://www.whistleblowing.org.uk/news/press_28.html**.

79. Avon Reaffirms Third Quarter and Full-Year Earning Outlook: **http://www.avoncompany.com/investor/businessnews/index.htm**, July 2, 2005.

80. See note 52, Deshpande and Farley.

81. Y. Yamazaki and D. C. Kayes, "An Experiential Approach to Cross-Cultural Learning: A Review and Integration of Competencies for Successful Expatriate Adaptation," *Academy of Management Learning & Education* 3(4) (2004): 362–379.

82. G. Hofstede, "Cultural Constraints in Management Theories," *Academy of Management Executive* 7(1) (February 1993): 81–94.

83. R. House, M. Javidan, and P. Hanges, "Understanding Cultures and Implicit Leadership Theories across the Globe: An Introduction to Project GLOBE," *Journal of World Business* 37(1) (Spring 2002): 3–10.

84. C. C. Chen, M. W. Peng, and P. A. Saparito, "Individualism, Collectivism, and Opportunism: A Cultural Perspective on Transaction Cost Economics," *Journal of Management* 28(4) (July–August 2002): 567.

85. A. Sagie and Z. Aycan, "A Cross-Cultural Analysis of Participative Decision-Making in Organizations," *Human Relations* 56(4) (April 2003): 453.

86. Y. Ono and B. Spindle, "Japan's Long Decline Makes One Thing Rise: Individualism," *The Wall Street Journal*, December 29, 2000, A1, A4.

87. V. Pothukuchi, F. Damanpour, and J. Choi, "National and Organizational Culture Differences and International Joint Venture Performance," *Journal of International Business Studies* 33(2) (2002): 243–265.

88. J. S. Osland and A. Bird, "Beyond Sophisticated Stereotyping: Cultural Sensemaking in Context," *Academy of Management Executive* 14(1) (2000): 65–79.

89. A. P. Fiske, "Using Individualism and Collectivism to Compare Cultures—A Critique of the Validity and Measurement of the Constructs: Comment on Oyserman et al.," *Psychological Bulletin* 128(1) (January 2002): 78.

90. C. Robert and S. A. Wasti, "Organizational Individualism and Collectivism: Theoretical Development and an Empirical Test of a Measure," *Journal of Management* 28(4) (August 2002): 544.

91. D. R. Avery and K. M. Thomas, "Blending Content and Contact: The Roles of Diversity Curriculum and Campus Heterogeneity in Fostering Diversity Management Competency," *Academy of Management Learning & Education* 3(4) 2004): 380–396.

92. J. A. Clair, J. E. Beatty, and T. L. Maclean, "Out of Sight but Not Out of Mind: Managing Invisible Social Identities in the Workplace," *Academy of Management Review* 30(1) (2005): 433.

93. See note 91.

94. W. J. Mott Jr. "Developing a Culturally Competent Workforce: A Diversity Program in Progress," *Journal of Healthcare Management* 48(5) (September–October 2003): 337.

95. S. Dwyer, O. C. Richard, and K. Chadwick, "Gender Diversity in Management and Firm Performance: The Influence of Growth Orientation and Organizational Culture," *Journal of Business Research* 56 (December 2003) 1009–1020.

96. H. S. Slay, "Spanning Two Worlds: Social Identity and Emergent African-American Leaders," *Journal of Leadership & Organizational Studies* 9(4) (Spring 2003): 56.

97. W. H. Frey, "Micro Melting Pots," *American Demographics* (June 2001): 20–23; "The New America: The New Face of Race," *Newsweek* (September 18, 2000): 38–65; "The New Demographics of Black Americans," *Business Week* (December 4, 2000): 14; W. B. Johnson and A. H. Packer, *Workforce 2000: Work and Workers for the 21st Century* (Indianapolis, IN: Hudson Institute, 1987); and M. Galen and A. T. Palmer, "White, Male and Worried," *Newsweek* (January 31, 1994): 50–55.

98. M. E. McLaughlin, M. P. Bell, and D. Y. Stringer, "Stigma and Acceptance of Persons with Disabilities: Understudied Aspects of Workforce Diversity," *Group & Organization Management* 29(3) (June 2004): 302–333.

99. U. R. Orth and Z. Firbasova, "The Role of Consumer Ethnocentrism in Food Product Evaluation," *Agribusiness* 19(2) (Spring 2003): 137.

100. G. Balabanis and A. Diamantopoulos, "Domestic Country Bias, Country-of-Origin Effects, and Consumer Ethnocentrism: A Multidimensional Unfolding Approach," *Journal of the Academy of Marketing Science* 32(1) (Winter 2004): 80–95.

101. General Mills, Inc., *Annual Report* (1998).

102. D. A. Whetten and A. L. Delbecq, "Saraide's Chairman Hatim Tyabji on Creating and Sustaining a Values-Based Organizational Culture," *Academy of Management Executive* 14(4) (2000): 32–40.

103. J. A. Gilbert and J. M. Ivancevich, "Valuing Diversity: A Tale of Two Organizations," *Academy of Management Executive* 14(1) (2000): 93–105.

104. D. Berta, "Mixing It Up: Diversity Good for Business, Confab Finds," *Nation's Restaurant News* 36(34) (August 26, 2002): 1, 103.

105. L. Yu, "Does Diversity Drive Productivity?" *MIT Sloan Management Review* 43 (Winter 2002): 17.

106. S. T. Brathwaite, "Supplier Diversity: A Hidden Asset," *Franchising World* 34(4) (May/June 2002): 52, 54.

107. D. Hannon, "Big Three Boost Diversity Buy," *Purchasing* 130(15) (Aug. 2001): 31–38.

108. R. Harris, "The Illusion of Inclusion: Why Most Corporate Diversity Efforts Fail," *CFO* 17(6) (May 2001).

109. R. R. Thomas, "Diversity Tension and Other Underlying Factors in Discrimination Suits," *Employment Relations Today* 27(4) (Winter 2001): 31–41.

110. D. Berta, "NRN Study: Industry Diversity Efforts Fall Short," *Nation's Restaurant News* 36(29) (July 2002).

111. See note 103.

112. A. Aguirre, Jr., and R. Martinez, "Leadership Practices and Diversity in Higher Education: Transitional and Transformational Frameworks," *Journal of Leadership Studies* 8(3) (Winter 2002): 53.

113. "Diversity or Diversion?" *Black Enterprise* 32(12) (July 2002): 82–84, 86, 88.

114. See note 100.

115. See note 99.

116. D. E. Arfken, S. L. Bellar, and M. M. Helms, "The Ultimate Glass Ceiling Revisited: The Presence of Women on Corporate Boards," *Journal of Business Ethics* 50(2) (March 15, 2004): 177.

117. D. J. Maume Jr., "Is the Glass Ceiling a Unique Form of Inequality?" *Work and Occupations* 31(2) (May 2004): 250.

118. J. S. Goodman, D. L. Fields, and T. C. Blum, "Cracks in the Glass Ceiling: In What Kinds of Organizations Do Women Make It to the Top?" *Group & Organization Management* 28(4) (December 2003): 475–501.

119. G. F. Dreher, "Breaking the Glass Ceiling: The Effects of Sex Ratios and Work-Life Programs on Female Leadership at the Top," *Human Relations* 56(4) (April 2003): 541.

120. See note 94.

121. D. G. Stankevich, "Diversity Wears Many Faces," *Retail Merchandiser* 41(11) (November 2001): 28.

122. See note 103.

123. See note 94.

124. A. Zimmerman, "Judge Certifies Wal-Mart Suit As Class Action," *The Wall Street Journal,* June 23, 2004, A1, A6.

125. See note 124.

126. J. R. Johnson, "Leading the Learning Organization: Portrait of Four Leaders," *Leadership & Organizational Development Journal,* (May–June 2002): 241 (19).

127. D. A. Bonebright, "Built to Learn: The Inside Story of How Rockwell Collins Became a True Learning Organization," *T&D* 57(8) (August 2003): 67.

128. R. B. Lawrence, M. K. Mauws, and B. Dyck, "The Politics of Organizational Learning: Integrating Power Into the 4I Framework," *Academy of Management Review* 30(1) (2005): 185–191.

129. J. J. Salopek, "Targeting the Learning Organization," *T&D* 58(3) (March 2004): 46.

130. See note 129.

131. See note 129.

132. S. E. Bryant, "The Role of Transformational and Transactional Leadership in Creating, Sharing, and Exploiting Organizational Knowledge," *Journal of Leadership & Organizational Studies* 9(4) (Spring 2003): 32–44.

133. R. D. Ireland and C. C. Miller. "Decision Making and Firm Success," *Academy of Management Executive* 18(4) (2004): 374, 444.

134. See note 132.

135. See note 128.

136. See note 133.

137. A. C. Inkpen and E. W. K. Tsang, "Social Capital, Networks and Knowledge Transfer," *Academy of Management Review* 30 (2005): 146–165.

138. See note 137.

139. R. F. Hurley, "Putting People Back Into Organizational Learning," *Journal of Business and Industrial Marketing* 17(4) (2002): 270–281.

140. See note 137.

141. See note 128.

142. See note 129.

143. D. Vera and M. Crossan, "Strategic Leadership and Organizational Learning," *Academy of Management Review* 29(2) (April 2004): 222.

144. See note 126.

145. See note 129.

146. See note 129.

147. G. L. Graham, "If You Want Honesty, Break Some Rules," *Harvard Business Review* 80(4) (April 2002): 42–47.

148. See note 129.

149. M. Everson, "Creating an Operational Risk-Sensitive Culture," *RMA Journal* 84(6) (March 2002): 56–59.

Chapter 11

1. Chattopadhyay, W. H. Glick, and G. P. Huber, "Organizational Actions in Response to Threats and Opportunities," *Academy of Management Journal* 44(5) (2001): 937–955.

2. A. K. Gupta and V. Govindarajan, "Cultivating a Global Mindset," *Academy of Management Executive* 16(1) (2002): 116–126.

3. B. P. Matherne, "If You Fail to Plan, Do You Plan to Fail?" *Academy of Management Executive* 18 (2004): 156–157.

4. W. P. Barnett, H. R. Greve, and D. Y. Park, "An Evolutionary Model of Organizational Performance," *Strategic Management Journal* 15 (Special Issue 1994): 11–28; and K. D. Miller, "Competitive Strategies of Religious Organizations," *Strategic Management Journal* 23 (2002): 435–456.

5. J. S. Harrison and C. H. St. John, *Foundations in Strategic Management,* 2nd ed. (Cincinnati, OH: South-Western Thomson Learning, 2002).

6. F. R. David, *Strategic Management,* 9th ed. (Upper Saddle River, New Jersey: Prentice Hall, 2003), 5.

7. P. C. Nutt, "Expanding the Search for Alternatives During Strategic Decision-Making," *Academy of Management Executive* 18 (2004): 13–28.

8. E. S. Smith and E. Shefy, "The Intuitive Executive: Understanding and Applying 'Gut Feel' in Decision-Making," *Academy of Management Executive* 18 (2004): 76–91.

9. T. Thomas, J. R. Schermerhorn, and J. W. Dienhart, "Strategic Leadership of Ethical Behavior in Business," *The Academy of Management Executive* 18(2) (May 2004): 56–66.

10. S. Worden, "The Role of Integrity as a Mediator in Strategic Leadership: A Recipe for Reputational Capital," *Journal of Business Ethics* 46 (August 2003): 31–44.

11. S. Worden, "The Role of Religious and Nationalist Ethics in Strategic Leadership: The Case of JN Tata," *Journal of Business Ethics* 47(2) (October 2003): 147–164.

12. P. M. Thompson, "The Stunted Vocation: An Analysis of Jack Welch's Vision of Business Leadership," *Review of Business* 25 (2004): 45–55.

13. D. Kirkpatrick, "Chipping Away at Intel: CEO Hector Ruiz Came from Humble Roots to Propel AMD Into the Big Leagues," *Fortune* 150(9) (November 1, 2004): 107.

14. R. L. Rundle, "Web School Lets Young Athletes Study and Play," *The Wall Street Journal,* March 9, 2004, B1, B8; Information taken from The University of Miami Online High School Web site: **http://www.umohs.org/admissions_ tuition_and_fees.html,** August 19, 2005.

15. M. S. Lane and K. Klenke, "The Ambiguity Tolerance Interface: A Modified Social Cognitive Model for Leading under Uncertainty," *Journal of Leadership & Organizational Studies* 10 (Winter 2004): 69–81.

16. K. Shimizu and M. A. Hitt, "Strategic Flexibility: Organizational Preparedness to Reverse Ineffective Strategic Decisions," *Academy of Management Executive 18* (2004): 44–59.

17. D. J. Ketchen Jr., C. C. Snow, and V. L. Street, "Improving Firm Performance by Matching Strategic Decision-Making Processes to Competitive Dynamics," *Academy of Management Executive 18* (2004): 29–43.

18. "AMD CEO Hector Ruiz's Keynote at TECHXNY Challenges IT Industry to Put the Needs of Customers First," Advanced Micro Devices, September 17, 2003, **http://www.amd.com/us-en/ Corporate/VirtualPressRoom/ 0,51_104_543~74913,00.html,** July 2, 2005.

19. See note 16.

20. See note 8.

21. M. A. Tannenbaum, "Organizational Values and Leadership," *Public Manager 32*(3) (Summer 2003): 19.

22. G. Hamel and C. K. Prahalad, "Competing for the Future," *Harvard Business Review* (July–August 1994): 127–128.

23. See note 1.

24. W. Bennis, *On Becoming a Leader,* 2nd ed. (New York: Perseus Publishing; Upper Saddle River, New Jersey: Harper-Collins Publishing, 2003).

25. See note 6, David, 62.

26. See note 1.

27. P. Taylor, "Stealing a March on Goliath: View from the Top," *Financial Times* (June 4, 2003), 6.

28. J. Sidhu, "Mission Statements: Is It Time to Shelve Them?" *European Management Journal 21*(4) (August 2003): 439–446.

29. F. R. David and F. R. David, "It's Time to Redraft Your Mission Statement," *Journal of Business Strategy 24* (January–February 2003): 11–14.

30. See note 6.

31. W. G. Bennis and B. Nanus, *Leaders: The Strategies for Taking Charge* (New York: Harper & Row, 1985).

32. W. W. George, "Medtronic's Chairman William George on How Mission-Driven Companies Create Long-Term Shareholder Value," *Academy of Management Executive 15*(4) (2001): 39–47.

33. E. A. Locke, "Guest Editor's Introduction: Goal-Setting Theory and Its Applications to the World of Business," *Academy of Management Executive 18* (2004): 124–125.

34. G. P. Latham, "The Motivational Benefits of Goal-Setting," *Academy of Management Executive 18* (2004): 126–129.

35. S. Kerr and S. Landauer, "Using Stretch Goals to Promote Organizational Effectiveness and Personal Growth: General Electric and Goldman Sachs," *Academy of Management Executive 18* (2004): 134–138.

36. See note 35.

37. See note 34.

38. K. N. Shaw, "Changing the Goal-Setting Process at Microsoft," *Academy of Management Executive 18* (2004): 139–142.

39. See note 13.

40. D. C. Hambrick and J. W. Fredrickson, "Are You Sure You Have a Strategy?" *Academy of Management Executive 15*(4) (2001): 48–59.

41. See note 17.

42. A. Ryans, R. Moore, D. Barclay, and T. Deutscher, "Winning Market Leadership: Strategic Market Planning for Technology-Driven Business," *Journal of the Academy of Marketing Science 30*(2) (Winter 2002): 87.

43. See note 40.

44. See note 35.

45. See note 16.

46. R. P. Weiss, "Crisis Leadership," *Training & Development 56* (March 2002): 28–34.

47. F. W. Gluck, "Crisis Management in the Church," *America 189* (December 1, 2003): 7.

48. L. Barton, *Crisis in Organizations,* 2nd ed. (Cincinnati, OH: South-Western Thomson Learning, 2001).

49. C. Pearson and J. A. Clair, "Reframing Crisis Management," *Academy of Management Review 23*(1) (1998): 59–76.

50. R. M. Fulmer and J. A. Conger, "Developing Leaders with 20/20 Vision," *Financial Executive 20* (July–August 2004): 38–41.

51. S. J. Smits and N. E. Ally, "Thinking the Unthinkable—Leadership's Role in Creating Behavioral Readiness for Crisis Management," *Competitiveness Review 13* (2003): 1–23.

52. See note 51.

53. D. J. Middaugh, "Maintaining Management During Disaster. Nursing Management," *MedSurg Nursing 12* (April 2003): 125–127.

54. See note 51.

55. See note 51.

56. See note 48, Barton, 14.

57. J. Spillan and M. Hough, "Crisis Planning in Small Businesses: Importance, Impetus and Indifference," *European Management Journal 21* (June 2003): 398–407.

58. W. T. Coombs, "Impact of Past Crises on Current Crisis Communication: Insights from Situational Crisis Communication Theory," *Journal of Business Communication 41* (July 2004): 265–289.

59. "RI-Based Firms Teach Valuable Lessons on Crisis Management," *Asia Africa Intelligence Wire* (October 2002); and see note 48, Barton, 37.

60. See note 50.

61. See note 50.

62. See note 48, Barton, 18.

63. See note 48, Barton, 19.

64. "Public Communications: Critical Part of Crisis Management," *Asia Africa Intelligence Wire* (October 2002).

65. See note 58.

66. D. Anderson, "Three Keys to Leadership in Times of Crisis," *Leadership for the Front Lines* (June 2002): 2.

67. R. Sherman, "How to Communicate During Times of Crisis," *Business Credit 103*(10) (November/December 2001): 30–31.

68. C. F. Greer and K. D. Moreland, "United Airlines' and American Airlines' Online Crisis Communication Following the September 11 Terrorist Attacks," *Public Relations Review* (2003): 427–441.

69. See note 58.

70. C. Bates, "When in Rome? The Effects of Spokesperson Ethnicity on Audience Evaluation of Crisis

Communication," *Technical Communication 50* (February 2003): 120.

71. See note 58.

72. "Crisis Management or Managing the Crisis," *Africa News Service* (October 21, 2002).

73. See note 70.

74. P. Mourier and M. Smith, *Conquering Organizational Change: How to Succeed Where Most Companies Fail* (Atlanta, Georgia; New York: CEP Press, 2001).

75. Information taken from the SAP Web site, **http://www.sap.com/company/ index.epx**, August 19, 2005.

76. Information taken from the Fluor Web site, **http://www.fluor.com/about/ default.asp**, February 8, 2005.

77. K. J. Delaney and D. Bank, "Large Software Customers Refuse to Get With the Program," *The Wall Street Journal,* January 2, 2004, A1, A6.

78. M. Seo and W. E. D. Creed, "Institutional Contradictions, Praxis, and Institutional Change: A Dialectical Perspective," *Academy of Management Review* 27(2) (2002): 222–247.

79. S. Fox and Y. Amichai-Hamburger, "The Power of Emotional Appeals in Promoting Organizational Change Programs," *Academy of Management Executive* 15(4) (2001): 84–93.

80. See note 74.

81. D. V. Day, S. J. Zaccaro, and S. M. Halpin, "Leader Development for Transforming Organizations: Growing Leaders for Tomorrow," *Academy of Management Executive* 18 (2004): 165.

82. See note 81.

83. J. P. Kotter, *The New Rules: How to Succeed in Today's Post-Corporate World.* Adapted with permission from *U.S. News & World Report* 118(12) (March 27, 1995): 62.

84. J. C. Quick and J. H. Gavin, "The Next Frontier: Edgar Schein on Organizational Therapy," *Academy of Management Executive* 14(1) (2000).

85. M. Pardo del Val and C. M. Fuentes, "Resistance to Change: A Literature Review and Empirical Study," *Management Decisions* 41 (January–February 2003): 148–155.

86. See note 84.

87. S. M. Goltz and A. Hietapelto, "Using the Operant and Strategic Contingencies Models of Power to Understand Resistance to Change," *Journal of Organizational Behavior Management 23* (July 2002): 3–22.

88. J. P. Kotter, *Leading Change* (Boston, MA: Harvard Business School Press, 1996), 20–25; and R. Maurer, *Beyond the Wall of Resistance: Unconventional Strategies That Build Support for Change* (Austin, TX: Bard Books, 1996).

89. S. Oreg, "Resistance to Change: Developing an Individual Differences Measure," *Journal of Applied Psychology 88* (August 2003): 680–693.

90. See note 87.

91. See note 85.

92. See note 13.

93. R. M. Kanter, "The Enduring Skills of Change Leaders," *Ivey Business Journal 64*(5) (May/June 2000): 31–36; and see note 75.

94. See note 85.

95. See note 85.

96. J. Hogue, "Exxon's Oil Spill," **http://iml.jou.ufl.edu/projects/Spring01/ Hogue/exxon.html**, October 18, 2005.

97. "Remarks by Lee R. Raymond— Chairman, Exxon Mobil Corporation. Speech Delivered at the ExxonMobil 119th Annual Meeting, May 30, 2001." **http://www.exxonmobil.com/Corporate/ Newsroom/SpchsIntvws/Corp_NR_ SpchIntrvw_AnnualMeeting_010530.asp,** October 18, 2005.

98. W. Zellner, "ExxonMobil: The Cautious King of the Oil Patch," *Business Week Online*, April 4, 2005, **http://www.businessweek.com/magazine/ content/05_14/b3927408.htm,** October 18, 2005.

99. "Why ExxonMobil 'Makes Bets Early,'" *Business Week Online*, April 5, 2004, **http://www.businessweek.com/ magazine/content/04_14/b3877639_ mz073.htm,** October 18, 2005.

100. ExxonMobil Corporation, "Energy Efficiency," **http://www.exxonmobil.com/ corporate/Campaign/Campaign_ energysaving_conservation.asp,** October 18, 2005.

Appendix

1. K. T. Scott, "Leadership and spirituality: A quest for reconciliation," in J. Conger (ed.), *Discovering the Spirituality in Leadership* (San Francisco: Jossey-Bass, 1994), 63–99.

2. G. Fairholm, *Capturing the heart of leadership: Spirituality and community in the new American workplace.* (Westport, CT: Praeger), 1997.

3. C. Barks, *The Essential Rumi* (San Francisco: Harper, 1996).

4. J. Autry, *Love and profit: The art of caring leadership* (New York: Avon Books, 1991).

5. For details on the four levels of spirituality in the workplace implementation, with case studies, worksheets, and assessments, the *Creating Enlightened Organizations Manual* by J. Neal can be ordered from the Association for Spirit at Work, **http://www.spiritatwork.org.**

6. B. Heermann, *Building team spirit: Activities for inspiring and energizing teams* (New York: McGraw-Hill, 1997). *Noble purpose: Igniting extraordinary passion for life and work* (Fairfax, VA: QSU Publishing, 2004).

7. R. Barrett, *Liberating the corporate soul: Building the visionary organization* (Cambridge, MA: Butterworth-Heinemann, 1998); **http://www. corptools.com.**

8. D. Beck and C. Cowen, *Spiral dynamics: Mastering values, leadership, and change* (Malden, MA: Blackwell Publishing, 1996); **http://www.spiraldynamics. com.**

9. David Cooperrider and Suresh Srivastva first developed the concept of Appreciative Inquiry in 1987, in D. Cooperrider and S. Srivastva, "Appreciative inquiry in organizational life," in R. W. Woodman & W. A. Pasmore (eds.), *Research in organizational change and development.* (Greenwich, CT: JAI Press, 1987). The most recent book in this field is D. Whitney, A. Trosten-Bloom, and D. Cooperrider, *The power of appreciative inquiry: A practical guide to positive change* (San Francisco: Berrett-Koehler, 2003); **http://appreciativeinquiry. cwru.edu/.**

10. Kim Cameron coedited, with Jane Dutton and Robert Quinn, *Positive Organization Scholarship* (San Francisco: Berrett-Koehler, 2003). This book was widely acclaimed by the academic community; however the business community responded that it was too "ivory tower." Cameron has recently written a book for the business community called *The abundance framework* (in press); **http://www.bus.umich.edu/Positive/**.

11. H. Owen, *Open space technology: A user's guide*, 2nd ed. (San Francisco:

Berrett-Koehler, 1997); **http://www.openspaceworld.org/**.

12. W. Harman and J. Hormann, *Creative work: The constructive role of business in transforming society* (Indianapolis: Knowledge Systems, 1990).

13. J. Collins, *Good to great: Why some companies make the leap . . . and others don't* (NY: HarperBusiness, 2001). See Chapter 2 on "Level 5 Leadership," which documents the success of leaders who demonstrate the virtue of humility.

14. J. Neal, B. Lichtenstein, and D. Banner, "Spiritual perspectives on individual, organizational, and societal transformation," *Journal of Organizational Change Management, 12*(3), 175–185.

15. C. Schaefer and J. Darling, "Does spirit matter? A look at contemplative practice in the workplace," *Spirit at Work* newsletter, July 1997.

Index